US Foreign Policy

More praise for *US Foreign Policy*

'This is an exceptional collection of essays written by scholars and policy-makers from around the world with very diverse political perspectives. Yet, all share a commitment to rigorous and critical research and analysis. This is not another collection of essays lamenting the decline of the US or trumpeting its resurgence. Students reading these essays are provided with a framework that will enable them to answer critical questions like: who makes US foreign policy? Why did the US take a particular position? What is the US likely to do in a situation?'

Steven L. Lamy, University of Southern California

'The second edition of Cox and Stokes's *US Foreign Policy* builds on the first, with important new chapters on the Obama foreign policy and a state-of-the-art debate on American decline. This valuable collection provides a clear, comprehensive, and balanced discussion of all aspects of US foreign policy that is invaluable for undergraduate and postgraduate students alike.'

Robert Singh, Birkbeck, University of London

'A terrific and well-chosen collection of works that are must-reads for any student of US foreign policy. The new chapters by Nye, and the debate (Chapter 23) on American primacy are both priceless. Anyone teaching the subject really owes it to their students to make sure this book features prominently on their course reading list.'

John Peterson, University of Edinburgh

'I know of no book on US foreign policy that covers the topic as comprehensively as this one. Cox and Stokes have assembled in one well-structured volume many of the world's leading experts from both inside and outside the United States. The book is indeed wide in scope and pluralist in character.'

Geir Lundestad, Nobel Institute

'Michael Cox and Doug Stokes once again provide us with a broad and provocative treatment of American foreign policy. Treatment of the historical context, American exceptionalism, and the role of domestic institutions is especially useful and enhances understanding of policies and how they are made.'

Robert J. Lieber, Georgetown University

US Foreign Policy

Second edition

Edited by

Michael Cox

Professor of International Relations
London School of Economics and Political Science
London

Doug Stokes

Senior Lecturer in International Relations
University of Kent, Canterbury
Kent

OXFORD

UNIVERSITY PRESS

Great Clarendon Street, Oxford OX2 6DP

Oxford University Press is a department of the University of Oxford.
It furthers the University's objective of excellence in research, scholarship,
and education by publishing worldwide in

Oxford New York

Auckland   Cape Town   Dar es Salaam   Hong Kong   Karachi
Kuala Lumpur   Madrid   Melbourne   Mexico City   Nairobi
New Delhi   Shanghai   Taipei   Toronto

With offices in

Argentina   Austria   Brazil   Chile   Czech Republic   France   Greece
Guatemala   Hungary   Italy   Japan   Poland   Portugal   Singapore
South Korea   Switzerland   Thailand   Turkey   Ukraine   Vietnam

Oxford is a registered trade mark of Oxford University Press in the
UK and in certain other countries

Published in the United States
by Oxford University Press Inc., New York

British Library Cataloguing in Publication Data

Data available

Library of Congress Cataloging in Publication Data

Data available

Typeset by TNQ Books and Journals Pvt. Ltd.
Printed in Great Britain
on acid-free paper by
Ashford Colour Press Ltd, Gosport, Hampshire

ISBN 978-0-19-958581-6

10 9 8 7 6 5 4 3

Acknowledgements

Individually, we would wish to express a debt of gratitude to Fiona, Stephen, Rebecca, Erica, and Lucas Du Rietz for their love and support throughout the completion of this project. We would also like to say a special thank you to all our students, both past and present. Their contributions to this project have been invaluable. We hope this new and updated volume will continue to provide the next generation with the necessary conceptual tools for understanding US foreign policy as we move further into the twenty-first century.

New to this edition

- Includes two new chapters—an assessment of Barack Obama's use of smart power by Joseph Nye, and a debate about whether the US is in a state of decline by William Wohlforth, Stephen Brooks, and Christopher Layne.
- All chapters have been updated with important developments affecting US foreign policy, including the global financial crisis, the ongoing conflict in Afghanistan, and political uprisings in the Middle East.
- Existing chapters have been revised to include more on the practicalities of how foreign policy is made, the relationship between the US and China, and the role played by lobbying and interest groups.
- Maps of the key regions are now included in the text.

Brief contents

Detailed contents

About the editors

Michael Cox lectures at London School of Economics and Political Science. The author of more than 20 volumes—the most recent (in 2010) being *Soft power and US foreign policy* and *The global 1989: continuity and change in world politics*—he has, over a distinguished career, served on the executive committee of the British International Studies Association, the Irish National Committee for the Study of International Affairs, and the United States Discussion Group at Chatham House, London. Between 2006 and 2009 he was chair of the European Consortium for Political Research, and in 2011 was reappointed for the third time as Research Fellow at the Nobel Institute in Oslo. He is currently co-director of IDEAS, a centre of strategy and diplomacy based at the LSE, and editor of the journal *International Politics*.

Doug Stokes is a Senior Lecturer at the University of Kent, Canterbury. His latest book, *Global Energy Security and American Hegemony* (Johns Hopkins, 2010) examines US oil interventions outside of the Middle East. He is currently working on a new book on US grand strategy options in the face of hegemonic transition. He is the editor of the journal *Global Society*.

About the contributors

Stephen G. Brooks is an Associate Professor of Government at Dartmouth College. He is the author of *Producing Security: Multinational Corporations, Globalization, and the Changing Calculus of Conflict* (Princeton University Press, 2005) and *World out of Balance: International Relations and the Challenge of American Primacy* (Princeton University Press, 2008), co-authored with William Wohlforth.

Daniel Deudney is Associate Professor of Political Science at Johns Hopkins University. His most recent book is *Bounding Power: Republican Security Theory from the Polis to the Global Village* (2007).

Toby Dodge is a Reader in International Relations at the London School of Economics and Political Science. Until September 2011 he was a Reader in International Politics in the School of Politics and International Relations, Queen Mary, University of London. He is the author of *Inventing Iraq: The Failure of Nation Building and a History Denied* (2005) and *Iraq's Future: The Aftermath of Regime Change* (2005). He has co-edited *Iraq at the Crossroads: State and Society in the Shadow of Regime Change* (2003) and *Globalisation and the Middle East: Islam, Economics, Culture and Politics* (2002).

Gregory Dubinsky is a graduate of Wesleyan University and Yale Law School.

John Dumbrell is Professor of Government in the School of Government and International Affairs, Durham University. His most recent books are *President Lyndon Johnson and Soviet Communism* (2004), *A Special Relationship: Anglo-American Relations from the Cold War to Iraq* (2006), and *Clinton's Foreign Policy: Between the Bushes* (2009). He is currently working on a new interpretative history of the Vietnam War.

James Dunkerley is Professor of Politics at Queen Mary, University of London, and author of *Americana: The Americas in the World around 1850* (2000).

Robyn Eckersley is Professor in the School of Social and Political Sciences and Director of the Master of International Relations Program at the University of Melbourne. She is the author of *The Green State* (2004), co-editor (with J. Barry) of *The State and the Global Ecological Crisis* (2005) and (with A. Dobson) *Political Theory and the Ecological Challenge* (2006), and co-author (with M. Bukovansky, I. Clark, R. Price, C. Reus-Smit, and N. J. Wheeler) of *Special Responsibilities: Global Problems and American Power* (forthcoming).

Beth A. Fischer is a professor at the Munk School of Global Affairs at the University of Toronto. She is the author of *The Reagan Reversal: Foreign Policy and the End of the Cold War* (1997) and *Triumph?: The End of the Cold War and US Foreign Policy Today* (forthcoming) as well as numerous articles on US foreign policy and international security.

Michael Foley is Head of the Department of International Politics at Aberystwyth University. His most recent book is *American Credo: The Place of Ideas in US Politics* (Oxford University Press 2007). His most recent journal article is 'Bringing realism to American liberalism: Kenneth Waltz and the process of cold war adjustment', published in *International Relations* September 2009. He is currently working on a book entitled *Political Leadership: Contexts, Processes and Paradoxes* as well as engaging in research on projects related to the themes of populist politics, and the position of political leadership within the international dimension.

Peter Gowan (1946–2009) was a Professor of International Relations at London Metropolitan University. He was also the editor of the *New Left Review* from 1990 until his untimely death in 2009.

Caroline Kennedy-Pipe is Professor of War Studies and Director of the Centre for Security Studies at the University of Hull. She is currently running a project on radicalization and IEDs and writing on the shape of wars in the twenty-first century. Her publications include *Russia and the World* (Edward Arnold, 1998) and *The Origins of the Cold War* (Palgrave, 2007).

Walter LaFeber is the Andrew Tisch and James Tisch University Professor Emeritus, and a Weiss Presidential Teaching Fellow at Cornell University. His recent books include *America, Russia, and the Cold War, 1945–2006*, 10th edn (2007), and *Michael Jordan and the New Global Capitalism*, 2nd edn (2002).

Christopher Layne is Professor and Robert M. Gates Chair in National Security at Texas A & M University's George H. W. Bush School of Government and Public Service. He is the author of *The Peace of Illusions: American Grand Strategy from 1940 to the Present* (Cornell University Press, 2006) and (with Bradley A. Thayer) *American Empire: A Debate* (Routledge, 2006). He is currently working on his next book (to be published by Yale University Press), entitled *After the Fall: International Politics, U.S. Grand Strategy, and the End of the Pax Americana*. His articles have appeared in such peer-reviewed journals as *International Security, Security Studies, International History Review, International Politics, Review of International Studies*, and the *Cambridge Review of International Affairs*. He also comments frequently on American foreign policy for such publications as the *National Interest*, the *Atlantic, Foreign Policy, World Policy Journal*, leading newspapers, and the *American Conservative* (of which he is a contributing editor).

Anatol Lieven is chair of international relations and terrorism studies in the War Studies Department at King's College London and a senior fellow of the New America Foundation in Washington DC. He is co-author, with John Hulsman, of *Ethical Realism: A Vision for America's Role in the World* (Pantheon, 2006). His previous book was *America Right or Wrong: An Anatomy of American Nationalism* (HarperCollins, 2004). From 1986 to 1998 he was a British journalist in South Asia, the former Soviet Union, and Eastern Europe. His latest book, *Pakistan: A Hard Country*, was published by Penguin in April 2011.

Jeffrey W. Meiser is an assistant professor in the College of International Security Affairs at the National Defense University in Washington, DC.

Joseph S. Nye, Jr. is University Distinguished Service Professor and former Dean of Harvard's Kennedy School of Government. He has served as Assistant Secretary of Defense, Chair of the National Intelligence Council, and a Deputy Under Secretary of State. His most recent books include *Soft Power, The Powers to Lead*, and *The Future of Power*. In a recent survey of international relations scholars, he was ranked as the most influential scholar on American foreign policy.

Robert G. Patman is a Professor of International Relations at the University of Otago and Director of the postgraduate international studies programme. He is the author or editor of nine books. He is also co-editor for the Praeger Series on *The Ethics of American Foreign Policy*, and an editor for the journal *International Studies Perspectives*. His latest book, a single-authored volume entitled *Strategic Shortfall: The 'Somalia Syndrome' and the March to 9/11* (Praeger), was published in the US in 2010. He is a Fulbright Senior Scholar, a Senior Fellow at the Centre of Strategic Studies, Wellington, and provides regular contributions to the national and international media on global issues and events. His website is www.robertpatman.co.nz.

Piers Robinson is a Senior Lecturer in International Politics at the University of Manchester. He has an international reputation for his research on the relationship between communications and world politics. His most recent book, *Pockets of Resistance: The British Media and the 2003 Invasion of Iraq* (Manchester University Press, 2010), analyses UK media coverage of the 2003 invasion of Iraq. His book *The CNN Effect: the myth of news, foreign policy and intervention* (Routledge, 2002) analyses the relationship between news media, US foreign policy, and humanitarian crises. Other work on media and international politics has been published in leading journals, including *Journal of Communication, Journal of Peace Research, European Journal of Communication, Review of International Studies* and *Media, Culture and Society* amongst others. He is also an editor of the journal *Critical Studies on Terrorism* (Routledge).

Paul Rogers is Professor of Peace Studies at Bradford University and International Security Consultant to the Oxford Research Group. His most recent book is *Losing Control: Global Security in the 21st Century*, 3rd edn (Pluto Press, 2010).

Christina Rowley is Lecturer in American Studies at Swansea University. Her doctoral thesis examined the gendered intertextuality of representations of US identity in Vietnam War films and US presidential rhetoric. She has published on the gendered politics of visual culture and of science fiction, including on the popular TV show 'Firefly' and film 'Serenity'. Her current research project investigates the relationships between US military practices and popular cultural texts and technologies, with a particular focus on soldiers' and veterans' own understandings of these relationships. Her research interests include the Vietnam War and post-Vietnam US foreign policy, feminist and gender theory, militarization, and popular and visual culture.

Peter Rutland is Professor of Government at Wesleyan University. His recent articles include 'Putin's ethnicity policy' and 'The rise and fall of neoliberalism in Russia'.

Richard Saull is Senior Lecturer in International Politics in the Department of Politics, Queen Mary, University of London. He has written two books on the Cold War, *Rethinking Theory and History in the Cold War* (2001) and *The Cold War and After* (2007).

Brian C. Schmidt is Associate Professor of Political Science at Carleton University. He is the author of *The Political Discourse of Anarchy: A Disciplinary History of International Relations* (1998) and *Imperialism and Internationalism in the Discipline of International Relations* (2005), co-edited with David Long.

Michael Smith is Professor of European Politics and Jean Monnet Chair in the Department of Politics, History and International Relations at Loughborough University. Among many other books, articles, and chapters, he is the co-author with Steven McGuire of *The European Union and the United States: Competition and Convergence in the World Arena* (2008), and co-editor, with Christopher Hill, of *International Relations and the European Union*, 2nd edn (2011).

Peter Trubowitz is Professor of Government at the University of Texas at Austin. His most recent book is *Politics and Strategy: Partisan Ambition and American Statecraft* (2011). The winner of the J. David Greenstone Award presented by the American Political Science Association for the best book in politics and history (1999), his writings on world politics and US foreign policy have appeared in leading journals such as *Foreign Affairs*, *International Security*, and *International Studies Quarterly*.

Jutta Weldes is Professor of International Relations at the University of Bristol. Her major research interests are critical international relations theory, US foreign policy, popular culture and international relations, and gender and international relations. She is the author of *Constructing National Interests: The United States and the Cuban Missile Crisis* (University of Minnesota Press, 1999), co-editor of *Cultures of Insecurity: States, Communities, and the Production of Danger* (University of Minnesota Press, 1999), editor of *To Seek Out New Worlds: Science Fiction and World Politics* (Palgrave: 2003), and has published in such journals as *International Studies Quarterly*, the *European Journal of International Relations* and *Millennium*.

William C. Wohlforth is the Daniel Webster Professor at Dartmouth College, where he teaches in the Department of Government. His most recent books are *International Relations Theory and the Consequences of Unipolarity* (2011, co-edited, with G. John Ikenberry and Michael Mastanduno) and *World Out of Balance: International Relations Theory and the Challenge of American Primacy* (2008, co-authored with Stephen Brooks).

Guided tour of textbook features

This book is enriched with a number of learning tools to help you navigate the text and reinforce your knowledge of US foreign policy. This guided tour shows you how to get the most out of your textbook package.

Key quotes boxes

Each chapter contains boxes of key quotes that you can use to gain a wider perspective on the issues being discussed.

KEY QUOTES 2.1: The origins of American exceptionalism

The United States, almost from its start, has had an expanding economic system. The nineteenth-century American economy, as compared to European ones, was characterized by more market freedom, more individual landownership, and a higher wage income structure—all sustained by the national classical liberal ideology. From the Revolution on, it was a laissez-faire country par excellence.

(Lipset 1996: 54)

Hence there was a strong family likeness between all the English colonies as they came to birth. All, from the beginning, seemed destined to let freedom grow, not the aristocratic freedom of their motherland, but a middle-class and democratic freedom of which the world's history had not previously provided a complete example.

(Tocqueville 1988: 34)

I have already sa
zation in its true
continually bear
perfectly distinct
been at war with
somehow possibl
a marvelous com
the spirit of freed

There is therefore
some hidden ter
the general prosp
takes, whereas in
times a secret bi
leads men to

Major debates and their impact boxes

Throughout the book boxes detailing some of the ongoing major debates are provided to show you the most up-to-date state of academic thought in the area.

MAJOR DEBATES AND THEIR IMPACT 1.1: US policies towards

The 'Mars/Venus' debate of the early 2000s

The controversies centring around US and EU responses to the war on terror and the war in Iraq during 2002–4 generated debate not only in policy circles but also in academic analysis. One of the key figures in this debate was the American policy analyst Robert Kagan, who in 2003 published his book *Of Paradise and Power: America and Europe in the New World Order*. Kagan's argument was that there was a deep difference over the interpretation and the uses of power between the United States and Europe, and that this reflected long historical experience as well as current events. To put it simply, the United States had evolved with a strong orientation towards the use of 'hard' military power and a strong position both on sovereignty and national security, as the result of its geopolitical location, its

means of impler
Europe—best rep
by the EU—had
and the building
tional problems.
and cultural exp
of force in Europ
ruling elites that
subjected to rigo
effectively reflect
or individual Eur
the USA in milita
this rationalizatio
was of course cer
a sweeping view
how much can it

Controversies boxes

In each chapter, controversies boxes look at an aspect of foreign policy from a different angle to highlight the complexities of subjectivism in the area.

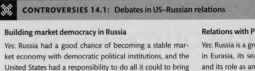

CONTROVERSIES 14.1: Debates in US–Russian relations

Building market democracy in Russia

Yes: Russia had a good chance of becoming a stable market economy with democratic political institutions, and the United States had a responsibility to do all it could to bring that about.

No: American interference in Russia's domestic politics and economics was bound to fail and cause a negative reaction from Russian elites.

NATO enlargement

Relations with P

Yes: Russia is a gre in Eurasia, its sea and its role as an a good working Moscow.

No: Putin is a dict only bring instabi able partner.

Key points

Where necessary, key points boxes appear to give a brief synopsis of the material covered in order to help you consolidate your studies.

or dis-
are not
cannot
wider
impor-
the UK
efforts
rder to
mongst
ce, UK

KEY POINTS

❑ Naturalized power relations can and should be denaturalized.

❑ Claiming that the world is socially constructed does not mean it is false or that the world does not exist.

❑ The social construction of reality means that although the world exists independently of our knowledge of it, we cannot access this knowledge except through discourse(s).

❑ Critiquing discourses is not about political correctness:

Questions

A set of carefully devised questions has been provided to help you assess your comprehension of core themes, and may also be used as the basis of seminar discussion and coursework.

? Questions

1. What motivated US support for the early stage of European integration?

2. What is the importance of John F. Kennedy's 1962 speech on Atlantic par

3. Why were US–EC relations especially difficult in the early 1970s?

4. Why did the 1970s see a new pattern of interaction between political, ec relations?

5. What was the impact of the 'new cold war' during the early 1980s on US

6. What events in the late 1980s created concern in the USA about the futu

7. What role did US policy makers envisage for the EC at the end of the Col

Further reading

To take your learning further, reading lists have been provided as a guide to find out more about the issues raised within each chapter topic and to help you locate the key academic literature in the field.

» Further Reading

Bacevich, A. J. (2004), *American Empire: The Realities and Consequences of US* Cambridge, Mass).

Cohen, W.I. (210), *America's Response to China: A History of Sino-American Rel* University Press, New York).

Holmes, S. (2007), *The Matador's Cape: America's Reckless Response to Terror* (Press)

Hunt, M. H. (1987), *Ideology and US Foreign Policy* (Yale University Press, New

Ikenberry, J. G. (2004), *American Foreign Policy:* Theoretical Essays (Longman,

Guided tour of the Online Resource Centre

US Foreign Policy is also accompanied by an Online Resource Centre that provides students and lecturers with ready-to-use teaching and learning resources. They are free of charge and are designed to maximize the learning experience.

www.oxfordtextbooks.co.uk/orc/cox_stokes2e/

For students

Accessible to all, with no registration or password required, enabling you to get the most from your textbook.

Interactive map

An interactive map containing details of US foreign policy towards a variety of countries and regions provides a visual aid when considering the geographical implications of policy.

Historical timeline

A timeline of the history of US foreign policy gives you a snapshot view of key events, allowing you to put them in geographical and historical context.

speech is thus often seen as a pivotal moment in the onset of what would come to be known as the Cold War, and in shaping US attitudes toward the Soviet Union.

1946: June 14th, Baruch Plan Proposed
The hardening relations and increasing mistrust between the US and the Soviet Union was further exemplified in the proposal and rejection of the Baruch plan of 1946. Hiroshima and Nagasaki had illustrated the catastrophic power of nuclear weapons. Bernard Baruch, the American delegate to the UN Atomic Energy Commission, proposed a plan to oversee the eventual abolition of nuclear weapons under the auspices of an International Atomic Development Authority and promote the global use of nuclear energy for peaceful purposes instead. However, the plan was rejected by the Soviets, who regarded it as a ploy intended to maintain a US monopoly on nuclear weapons, and refused to tolerate inspections on Soviet soil.

1947: March 12th, The Truman Doctrine
On March 12th, 1947, President Truman urged the US Congress to "support free peoples who are resisting attempted subjugations by armed minorities or by outside pressures". The ostensible motive of this appeal was provision of aid to Greece and Turkey which, it

Multiple-choice questions

Multiple-choice questions test and reinforce your understanding of the themes. They are self-marking and allow you to receive immediate feedback on your performance as an aid to direct your studies.

Web links

A comprehensive list of annotated links points you in the direction of important organizations, documents, lectures, and other relevant sources of information.

Question 1

How do Ideational approaches to US foreign policy during the Cold War differ from Realist accounts of the same period?

- a) They place greater emphasis on economic factors
- b) They place greater emphasis on material interests and power
- c) They place greater emphasis on ideology and beliefs
- d) They place greater emphasis on geopolitics

Question 2

What features distinguish Socio-Economic accounts of US Cold War foreign policy?

- a) A focus on class and economic interests
- b) A focus on liberal ideology

---

www.brookings.edu/cuse.aspx
The website for the Brookings Institution's project on the US and Europe. Has a wide range of analytical pieces, working papers etc.

www.eurunion.org/
This is the website of the European Commission Delegation in Washington DC. It contains a wide range of relevant economic and political information, and has links to a large number of other sites dealing with US-EU relations.

www.iie.org/
Website of the institution for International Economics in Washington DC, which has a mass of information and publications dealing with the political economy of US-EU relations among many other issues.

For lecturers

Password protected to ensure only lecturers can access these resources, each registration is personally checked to ensure the security of the site.

Registering is easy: click on 'Lecturer Resources' on the Online Resource Centre, complete a simple registration form which allows you to choose your own username and password, and access will be granted within three working days (subject to verification).

Essay questions and class activities

A suite of questions drawing on themes in each chapter of the text provides an excellent basis for assessing students' understanding of the key points.

Seminar questions and activities

A collection of activities to assist in planning seminars.

Chapter 10

1. Does identity matter in the study of US foreign policy?

2. How does a 'Critical Constructivist Approach' differ from other approaches to US foreign policy?

3. Does the US need an enemy? Answer in relation to the role of identity in US foreign policy.

4. How did the Cold War shape US national identity?

Chapter 16

Class Activities

1. Classroom Debate: 'US policy toward Africa has in general been marked by indifference and neglect.' Discuss.

2. Classroom Debate: Why did the US intervene in Somalia but not in Rwanda during the 1990s?

3. Classroom Debate: 'Africa is the soft underbelly for global terrorism'. Discuss.

4. Presentation: What are the goals of the Millennium Challenge Account (MCA) initiative and how realistic are they?

Weekly Assignments

Assess US policy towards one of the following African states during the Cold War:

1. Angola

2. South Africa

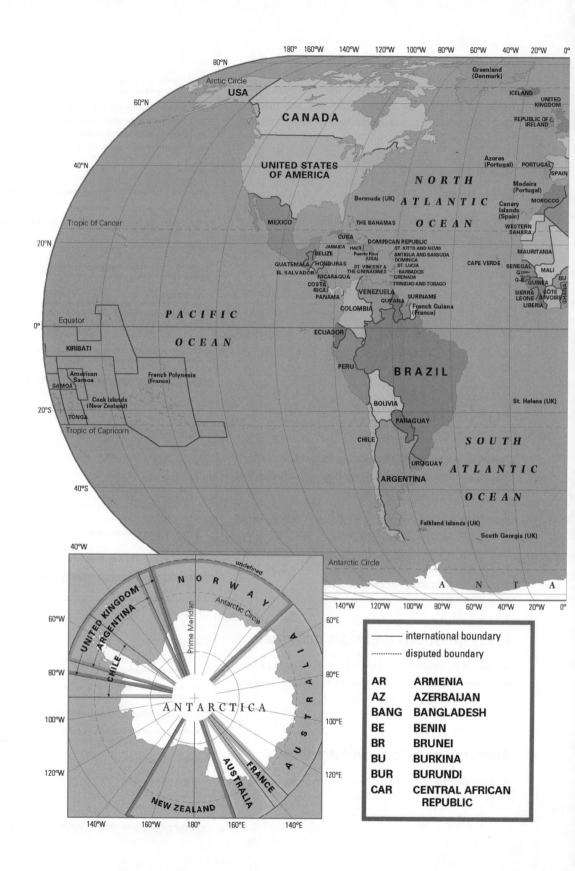

180° 160°W 140°W 120°W 100°W 80°W 60°W 40°W 20°W 0°

80°N

Arctic Circle

60°N

USA

CANADA

Greenland
(Denmark)

ICELAND

UNITED
KINGDOM

REPUBLIC OF
IRELAND

40°N

UNITED STATES
OF AMERICA

N O R T H

A T L A N T I C

O C E A N

Azores
(Portugal)

PORTUGAL

SPAIN

Madeira
(Portugal)

MOROCCO

Bermuda (UK)

Canary
Islands
(Spain)

Tropic of Cancer

MEXICO

THE BAHAMAS

WESTERN
SAHARA

20°N

CUBA

DOMINICAN REPUBLIC

JAMAICA HAITI

BELIZE

Puerto Rico
(USA)

ST. KITTS AND NEVIS

ANTIGUA AND BARBUDA

DOMINICA

ST. LUCIA

MAURITANIA

MALI

CAPE VERDE

SENEGAL

G

G.B

GUINEA

BU

GHANA

GUATEMALA

HONDURAS

EL SALVADOR

NICARAGUA

ST. VINCENT &
THE GRENADINES

BARBADOS

GRENADA

SIERRA
LEONE

CÔTE
D'IVOIRE

COSTA
RICA

TRINIDAD AND TOBAGO

LIBERIA

PANAMA

VENEZUELA

COLOMBIA

GUYANA

SURINAME

French Guiana
(France)

0° Equator

P A C I F I C

ECUADOR

KIRIBATI

O C E A N

PERU

B R A Z I L

American
Samoa

French Polynesia
(France)

St. Helena (UK)

SAMOA

Cook Islands
(New Zealand)

BOLIVIA

20°S

TONGA

PARAGUAY

Tropic of Capricorn

CHILE

URUGUAY

S O U T H

A T L A N T I C

40°S

ARGENTINA

O C E A N

Falkland Islands (UK)

South Georgia (UK)

Antarctic Circle

A   N   T   A

140°W 120°W 100°W 80°W 60°W 40°W 20°W 0°

40°W

60°W

UNITED KINGDOM

ARGENTINA

CHILE

N O R W A Y

undefined

Antarctic Circle

Prime Meridian

60°E

80°W

A U S T R A L I A

80°E

100°W

ANTARCTICA

100°E

120°W

FRANCE

AUSTRALIA

A U S T R A L I A

120°E

NEW ZEALAND

140°W 160°W 180° 160°E 140°E

——— international boundary

--------- disputed boundary

AR	ARMENIA
AZ	AZERBAIJAN
BANG	BANGLADESH
BE	BENIN
BR	BRUNEI
BU	BURKINA
BUR	BURUNDI
CAR	CENTRAL AFRICAN REPUBLIC

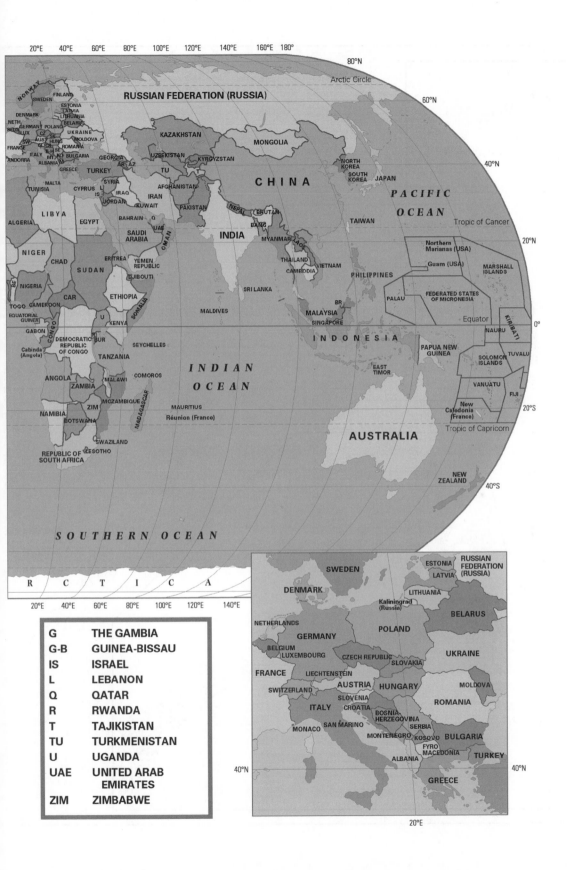

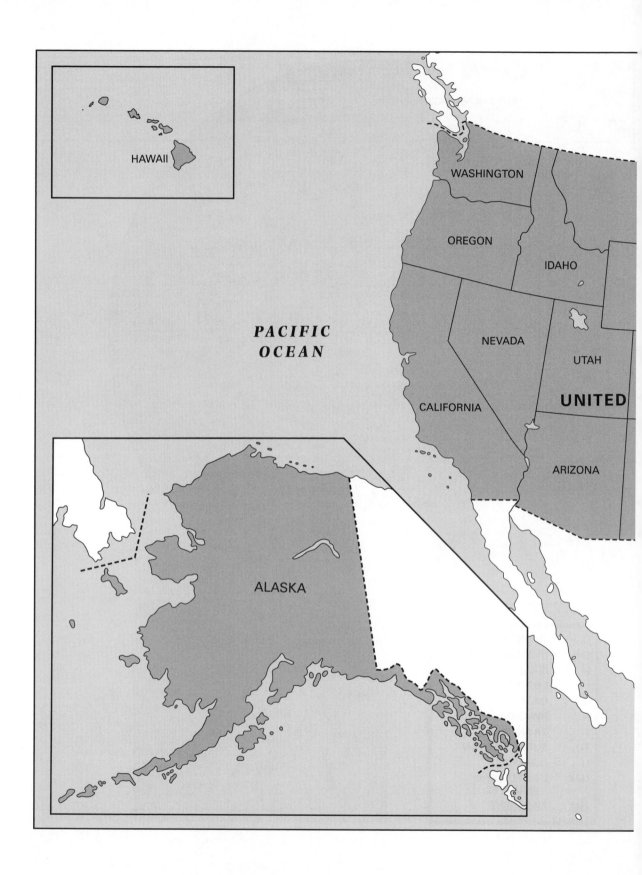

Introduction: US foreign policy—past, present, and future

Michael Cox and Doug Stokes

Over the past few years no single topic has been discussed so frequently—and with so much obvious passion—as how to evaluate the sources of America's conduct, the impact its conduct has had on the wider world, and the extent to which its actions have contributed (or not) to global justice and order. Certainly, it is difficult to recall a moment other than perhaps the years of the early Cold War or the period coinciding with the Vietnam War in the 1960s when the United States and its foreign policy have been the subject of so much intense debate. There are at least three obvious reasons why. First, for better or worse, even for those who regard America's decline as being inevitable, the fact remains that it is still an extraordinarily powerful state. Second, since September 2001 it has also confronted a series of fundamental challenges that range from global terrorism to the economic crisis and to which, although it may appear to have no easy answer, the US continues to remain central to solving. Third, in the short space of eight years it has moved from being led by G. W. Bush, one of the most controversial leaders in modern times to electing to office an African-American with the distinctly 'un-American' name of Barack Hussein Obama. If anything, the transition from Bush from Obama points to quite self-evident truths: namely how difficult it is to characterize America as a polity and America's seemingly endless capacity for at least symbolic renewal. After all, when Bush regained the White House in 2004 critics lamented how deeply conservative the nation had become. However, Obama was swept into office on a platform of profound change with pundits now speaking of the United States as being the last decent beacon of liberal values in a deeply troubled world.

The decade that opened with the fall of the Twin Towers in September 2001 and continued seven years later with the greatest economic crisis to face the United States since the 1930s has indeed been a tumultuous one. Certainly nobody anticipated these twin shocks; and hardly anybody could have foreseen what impact they would have on the United States itself. But the impact has been truly tremendous. Simply compare the US in 2000 with where many now think it is just over a decade on. When the new millennium dawned, Americans in the vast majority truly did feel that they were living in the best, the most prosperous, and the most peaceful of times. This in large part explains why Bill Clinton would have been elected a third time in 2000 if this had been constitutionally possible. What a difference a decade makes. Only a few years later the mood had changed almost completely. Now, as the US moves into the second decade of the new century, poll after poll seems to reveal a new sense of uncertainty about where America now stands in the world, what the future holds for its citizens and whether or not the new century is going to be quite as 'American' as the last one. Deep material insecurity at home, the costs of having fought two very costly wars abroad, and daily headlines informing ordinary Americans that by the year 2020 China will have become the largest economy in the world, told what to many Americans at least must have sounded like a deeply depressing story with only one conclusion to be drawn. The nation's best days were behind it: and worse was likely to follow.

How different it all seemed only twenty years previously as communism as an historic project collapsed around the world to be followed by almost ten years of unalloyed good news for the United States. Who indeed could doubt what the new optimists were saying back then about the 'end of history' and the victory of American values in an international system where the nation faced no serious peer competition and where even old enemies like the former USSR and China acted as if the world was now largely an American-inspired creation underwritten by the most formidable military power known to man, the ever powerful dollar, and of course that most American of idols: the free enterprise system. In 1898 American statesmen might dream of creating a world where no door would remain closed to American influence. But this was merely an aspiration. A hundred years on and it began to look like more than just an aspiration. A new world order beckoned; the final frontier had been conquered.

Victory over fascism followed by victory over communism only confirmed Americans in their already strong belief that the United States was not merely another 'ordinary country' but rather that well-known and much talked about 'City on the Hill'; a true universal model—to be admired, copied, and in certain instances promoted if needs be. Such an outlook, however, has consequences. It was almost certainly this self-confidence born of repeated victories over successive enemies that probably tempted the Bush administration in 2003 to risk turning what many had hitherto seen as an imperfectly conducted but legitimate war against Osama bin Laden and radical Islamism into what many increasingly came to view as an illegitimate and unnecessary war against Iraq in 2003. As we now know, military victory in this particular conflict against a much over-hyped 'rogue state' proved to be remarkably easy—possibly too easy, as the short-term joys of liberation very quickly turned into the brute facts of occupation, leaving the United States standing between a rock and a hard place. Nor did America's woes end there. While Iraq quite literally burned and Iraqis fled and died in their tens of thousands, Afghanistan smouldered and then burst into flames, leaving a region on edge and its next door neighbour—nuclear Pakistan—in a state of deep unrest. What had begun as a short-term exercise to defeat the morally repulsive 'bad guys' with their backward outlook and crude improvised weaponry looked to be turning into the longest war in history. Indeed,

even following the 2011 killing of Osama Bin Laden, it looks very likely that America will continue to be seriously engaged for a very long time to come in the region. There will be no quick fix and no easy exit strategy.

Wars, of course, are appalling things. But one of their more 'positive' consequences from the point of view of the scholar and the student is to increase interest in international affairs, and certainly one of the (unintended) consequences of the so-called 'war on terror' and America's wars in Iraq and Afghanistan (and on a fairly regular basis now in Pakistan too) has been to generate a quite enormous interest in American foreign policy. Much of this has been critical. Indeed, it is difficult to recall a period before when so many commentators have been as sceptical of America's own claims that what it has been doing it has been doing for the sake of world peace and international security rather than for the sake of its economic or political interests. One might even argue that one of the many tasks President Obama set himself when he formally took office in early 2009 was to challenge such cynicism head on by showing to others around the world that the United States could still be a force for good, even in unstable and dangerous times. Abandoning what to many seemed like the imperial policies of his predecessor, Obama and his new team were clear about what had to be done: namely to restore America's political and moral standing in the world and by so doing make the United States, once more, the 'indispensable' nation. Only time will tell whether he has so far—or can ever—regain something which more than a few pundits now insist has been lost for ever.

In this newly revised second edition of our first very successful volume published before the Obama presidency the editors have called upon a range of expert voices representing a spectrum of opinion drawn from at least three continents—in large part because we have been dissatisfied for some time with other volumes on the subject that have generally tended to be written from only one 'national' point of view, invariably American. The book does not pretend to be exhaustive. Nonetheless, it does manage to touch several intellectual bases; many more, we would guess, than the average textbook on the subject. It also has the added virtue from the point of view of the student and teacher of taking the widest possible look at US foreign policy. Thus it treats the 'outside' just as seriously as it does the 'inside', and, within the 'inside', culture as much as it does economics, and public opinion as much as it does the main sites of organized power. It also brings the story right up to date, not only in each of the revised chapters but also in the concluding chapters where we debate America's now rather uncertain future. Based on the research of some of the world's leading experts, but made accessible to the general reader, the volume—wide in scope and pluralist in character—we hope sets new standards for discussing contemporary US foreign policy today.

It would be pointless here to summarize what is in the chapters themselves. They will stand or fall on their own obvious academic merits. That said, there are at least five broad themes that inform the text.

The first is the importance of the past for understanding the present. History, we need to remind ourselves, is not just some distant place that political scientists ought to visit now and again for chunks of interesting, but not necessarily essential, information, but the very source we need to go back to, to understand how a nation like the United States has arrived at the destination it has and with what baggage on board. There is a view (associated with the realist school of thought) which argues that the only thing we need to know about a state is the amount of power it has. Its character as such does not matter. This we believe is not merely too abstract; it ignores the specific way in which the United States rose to power in the first place (a subject dealt with in the chapter by LaFeber), the impact this ascent then had upon the United States as an exceptional kind of nation—an issue discussed in some detail by Deudney—and how that power in turn was translated into policy in the decades after the United States became a superpower in the 1940s. In the process of deploying its mass assets America was also transformed as a nation, most obviously during the Cold War according to Beth Fischer, when in any average year the nation spent nearly spent nearly 10 per cent of its GNP and 30 per cent of its budget waging global conflict against a perceived communist enemy. Modern students may of course wonder why the volume even bothers with an era now so remote as the Cold War. Our reply quite simply is that unless we understand the Cold War, the way it ended (on largely American terms), and the legacies it left behind (subjects that are analysed in the two chapters by Saull and Dumbrell) we will not be able to grasp what has happened to United States over the last two decades.

The second large theme—related to the first—concerns the complex relationship between foreign policy understood here as a set of short-term aims and America's

longer-term goals and interests. As Rowley and Weldes point out, the notion of interest is a problematic one and cannot be separated from how actors construct identity and how that identity in turn impacts upon perceptions of interest. Still, American foreign policy elites over time have been remarkably consistent in the ways they have tended to think about the world in general and what kind of world would best serve the United States. Naturally, there has been some room for debate and disagreement, but overall policy makers have assumed that the international order that would best advance American interests would be composed in the main of democratic states (in the belief that democracies do not go to war with another), open markets (on the grounds that they raise living standards, foster cooperation, and generate wealth), and self-determining nations (on the assumption that formal empires were not only antithetical to freedom but more likely to exclude American influence). Of course, the United States has not always been able to pursue these goals at all times, or in all places together at the same time. Thus what may have worked in relationship to postwar Europe—a region whose importance to the United States is assessed by Smith—has not always worked when it comes to its complicated, unequal relationship with Latin America, a theme developed by James Dunkerley in his chapter. Nor is it easy to conclude that US relations with Africa (the subject of Patman's chapter) were always motivated by such clearly defined or lofty goals.

That said, there are certain constants in the way America has related to the international system, although, as Toby Dodge points out in his contribution, consistency has not always been a feature of the way in which the United States has dealt with the Middle East since it first became seriously involved with the region midway through the twentieth century, and the recent 'Arab Spring' has added to this complex dynamic. Nor, as Rutland and Cox point out in their contributions on Russia and Asia-Pacific respectively, has the United States always achieved all of its ambitious goals in the 'post-communist' world. Obama may have reset that proverbial button determining Washington's relationship with Moscow, and the US continues to be viewed as a key actor in Asia. Still, as both authors show, Russia and China when taken together are bound to pose formidable problems for the United States in the years ahead. A third big theme developed here is the central importance of the 'domestic' in shaping US foreign policy choices. Here the book affirms the well-known truth that what the United States does abroad will be determined as much by factors at home—the influence of interest groups, the role of institutions, and the power of ideas—as it will be by external opportunities and threats. It is perhaps too much of a cliché to say that all politics is domestic and that all foreign policy merely a reflection of what happens domestically. But as many of the chapters here reveal, there is no Chinese wall dividing the international from the internal, the global from the specifically local. This is why the book has commissioned a number of original chapters to think about this large problem, one of which (by Michael Foley) deals squarely with the relationship between Congress and the President, a second (by Piers Robinson) assesses the impact of the media and public opinion on the making of US foreign policy, and yet a third (by Peter Trubowitz) advances the original claim that if we are to make sense of US foreign policy we should deconstruct the notion of the United States itself and assess its foreign policy as the by-product of shifting regional coalitions and not some eternal notion of what may or may not constitute the American national interest. Furthermore, as the Gowan and Stokes chapter reminds us, foreign policy is not merely a reflection of domestic politics but economic capabilities too, perhaps more so than ever in an increasingly globalized world economic system where power is not only measured in terms of how many weapons one might possess, but also by one's ability to innovate and compete. Foreign policy can never be reduced to economics as some seem to believe. But any study on US foreign policy that ignored material power and economic pressures—which many more conventional texts appear to do—would be seriously incomplete in our view, especially in the wake of the global financial crisis of 2008. This does not mean however, that US power in its totality can be reduced to either military or economic power, and as the Nye chapter on soft power and the Obama administration shows, the symbolism of America is as important as its capacity to project 'hard' power across borders.

This brings us then to the issue of perspective or what is sometimes referred to as 'balance'. As we suggested at the outset, US foreign policy over the past few years has been the subject of intense political debate. Everybody it seems has an opinion on the United States, even, possibly especially, those who have never studied the subject in any great depth. This is not something that can be said about the many expert authors gathered together here.

Many, it would be fair to say—Paul Rogers being amongst them—are critical of the way the Bush administration defined the war on terror. Some (including Brian Schmidt in his chapter on theory) are also deeply concerned about the impact that Bush's apparent abandonment of realist thinking in favour of dreams of empire will have on the United States and the world over the longer term. None of the authors, however, seeks either to denounce the United States or cast it in the role of the world's biggest 'rogue state', in spite of its fairly abysmal record in one of the key challenges confronting the international system—global environment (a topic dealt with by Eckersley in her chapter). Still, having strongly held views, as all the authors here most obviously do, does not preclude them from seeking to explore in depth how US foreign policy is made, why policy makers arrive at the decisions they do, and with what consequences. Indeed, it could be argued that only by approaching the subject with sufficient critical distance is it possible to engage in any meaningful—and engaging—way with their respective topics.

Finally, the authors here all accept the self-evident fact that whatever one might think of the United States past, present, or future, it is simply too important to be ignored. As the different perspectives provided by Wolhforth, Brooks, and Layne show, there is a huge debate that continues to rumble on concerning the future of American power and whether or not the US can remain hegemonic for ever. There is no easy answer to this very big question. Still, whether one is a radical critic, a conservative defender, liberal supporter, or of the opinion that American hegemony is a threat to world peace, it is absolutely vital to find out how the United States, with its vast national security apparatus, remarkably dynamic economy, complex array of alliances, and highly exportable popular culture will shape what some are now calling a 'post-American' world. During the seemingly predictable years before 1989, and the optimistic decade that followed, the task of understanding the United States was difficult enough. In the altogether different world we live in now with its political uncertainties and economic insecurities, it has become even more so, thus the need for a volume on such an important subject in our view. Ideas we are often told matter a great deal. This is true. But material facts like states matter as well—none more so than the United States, whose policies in the future (as much as its decisions in the past) are bound to impact on us all, for good or ill, well into the twenty-first century.

1 Theories of US foreign policy

Brian Schmidt

Chapter contents

Introduction

This chapter examines some of the competing theories that have been put forth to explain American foreign policy. In the quest to explain the foreign policy of the United States, a number of competing theories have been developed by International Relations scholars. Some theories focus on the role of the international system in shaping American foreign policy while others argue that various domestic factors inside the United States are the driving force. Still others attempt to combine both external and internal sources. The chapter begins with an introduction to some of the obstacles to constructing a theory of foreign policy. The following section provides a general survey of some of the competing theories of American foreign policy. The next section turns to the theoretical debate over the origins of the Cold War. The chapter concludes by examining the debate over the most appropriate grand strategy that the United States should follow in the post-Cold War era.

The task of explaining American foreign policy is infinitely complex. Part of the difficulty arises from the fact that there are so many diverse factors at play that it is often difficult to determine the underlying reason for a given policy. President Obama's decision to withdraw from Iraq and commit additional troops and resources to the war in Afghanistan clearly reveals a complex array of factors that led to this foreign policy. The problem confronting the foreign policy analyst is what set of factors to focus on in order to explain the external behaviour of the United States. Should one focus on the personality of President Obama and the members of his inner circle of advisors? Should one focus on the alleged threat that the Taliban and al-Qaeda pose to the United States and regional stability in Central Asia? Or should one look inside the United States to see how the values of liberty and freedom shape the goals that America attempts to achieve in its external relations with other states in general, and Afghanistan in particular?

As a result of this complexity, most of those who attempt to explain American foreign policy have recognized the centrality of theory. Theory is both necessary and unavoidable when it comes to understanding international politics. Unavoidable because both policy-makers and scholars approach the world from a specific paradigm or world-view that in turn generates specific theories. Theories are necessary in that they tell us what to focus on and what to ignore. We need theories to help us organize all the information that can overwhelm us on a daily basis. While students of foreign policy recognize the centrality of theory, the goal of achieving an over-arching theory to explain the foreign policy behaviour of the United States has proven to be illusive. Instead we have a number of competing theories that focus on different levels of analysis to account for the behaviour of the United States.

An insightful attempt to construct a theoretical framework for identifying the main sources of a state's foreign policy was developed by the renowned political scientist James N. Rosenau (1971). Rosenau identified five potential sources that influence a state's foreign policy: the external environment of the international system, the domestic/societal environment of a nation state, the governmental structure that specifies the policy-making process, the bureaucratic roles occupied by individual policy makers, and finally the personal characteristics and idiosyncrasies of individual foreign policy officials and government elites (see Figure 1.1). Each of these five sources can be considered independent variables that either individually or collectively help to explain the foreign policy behaviour of the United States, the dependent variable.

The external or systemic sources of foreign policy draw our attention to the point that the formulation of American foreign policy does not take place in a vacuum, rather the United States, like any other country, must take account of, and respond to, events taking place in the realm of international politics. The terrorist attacks against the United States on 11 September 2001 dramatically illustrate how an event perpetuated by an external actor, in this case by the al-Qaeda terrorist network spearheaded by Osama bin Laden, elicits a foreign policy response. The terrorist attacks against the World Trade Center in New York City and the Pentagon in Washington, DC did not determine the specific course of action that the United States decided to take—the global war on terrorism—but the event itself did necessitate a response. On any given day numerous developments take place around the world that American foreign policy officials must respond to even if they were previously preoccupied with a different region or issue area. Moreover, as we will see, the systemic source also highlights the underlying distribution of power in the international system and the effect this has on American foreign policy.

However, many analysts insist that the domestic sources of foreign policy are more important than external sources. The societal source accentuates the non-governmental aspects of a country's society that influences its foreign policy behaviour. The national character and value orientation of a country cannot be discounted as many believe that foreign policy should seek to promote the core values and ideology of the domestic political system. Many have observed that this view has been especially strong in the case of the

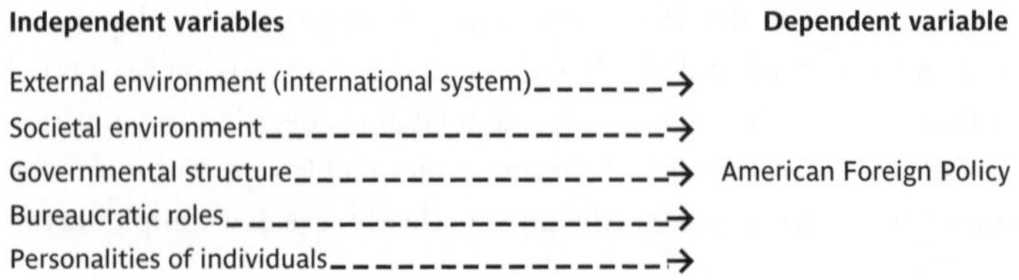

Independent variables   **Dependent variable**

External environment (international system)- - - - - - →
Societal environment- - - - - - - - - - - - - - - - - →
Governmental structure- - - - - - - - - - - - - - - - →   American Foreign Policy
Bureaucratic roles- - - - - - - - - - - - - - - - - →
Personalities of individuals- - - - - - - - - - - - - - →

Fig. 1.1 The multiple sources of American foreign policy.

United States as reflected by America's liberal, democratic character and by its desire to promote this political ideology around the world (Smith 1994). Indeed one alleged contributing factor to the decision to wage war against Iraq was the desire by the United States to spread liberty and democracy to the Middle East.

In addition to the societal sources of American foreign policy, there is also the particular governmental structure of the United States that plays a key role in the formulation and implementation of foreign policy. The Constitution of the United States establishes an elaborate, and some would argue cumbersome, framework for the formulation of foreign policy. The constitutional separation and division of power between the executive and legislative branches has led to what some refer to as 'an invitation to struggle' over the shaping of American foreign policy. Compared to other political systems, the United States political system allows for a vast array of actors to have a role in the formulation of American foreign policy. This includes the President, cabinet officials such as the Secretary of Defense, Secretary of State, and the Secretary of Commerce, advisors to the President such as the National Security Advisor and the Director of the Central Intelligence Agency, members of the United States Congress, lobbyists, both foreign and domestic, and interest groups. This is only a partial list and one can identify a host of additional actors that have a role in the formulation of American foreign policy.

The actors who are involved in the formulation of foreign policy draw our attention to the role played by large bureaucratic agencies such as the Department of Defense, the State Department, and the Central Intelligence Agency. Those who study the behaviour of bureaucratic organizations often make the point that the individuals who work for a particular agency are socialized to reflect their own agency's interests and needs. In a sense, the characteristics of the bureaucracy are more important than the characteristics and personality of the individuals. Thus even when an individual gains access to the foreign policy-making process, role theory suggests that a person's influence is circumscribed by the policy-making roles they occupy. The basic insight of the role source is captured by the adage, 'where you stand depends on where you sit'. Thus the position that a person takes on an issue of foreign policy depends on the bureaucracy that they represent.

The individual source category argues quite simply that individuals—their personality, past experiences, upbringing, personal convictions—matter greatly. Since American foreign policy behaviour follows from decisions made by elites, and often by decisions made by the President of the United States, the individual source prompts us to investigate the personal characteristics of the decision maker. The thesis is that the idiosyncratic characteristics of leaders influence American foreign policy behaviour. For many, it seems impossible to explain the direction of American foreign policy without highlighting the personality traits and beliefs of the current President.

Rosenau's framework is a simplifying device that helps us to identify the multiple sources of American foreign policy. In this sense it fulfils one of the core functions of theory: it helps us to identify what to focus on in our attempt to explain foreign policy. But Rosenau did not provide a full-blown theory of foreign policy, rather he offered what he termed a 'pre-theory' of foreign policy. He did not specify how each of his five sources directly influences foreign policy behaviour nor did he assess the relative influence of each of the sources. Ideally we want to know which of the sources is most important, because if we needed all five we would not have a parsimonious theory, that is, one that uses the fewest variables but nevertheless offers the most explanatory power. We might have a good description of a state's foreign policy, but we would not really have an explanatory theory. Those who have attempted to construct a theory of foreign policy have disagreed about the most important source of a state's external behaviour. We now turn to some of the theories that have been put forth to explain American foreign policy.

KEY POINTS

❑ The task of explaining foreign policy is infinitely complex.

❑ In order to explain foreign policy we need theory.

❑ James Rosenau identified five sources that influence a state's foreign policy: the international system, the societal environment of a nation-state, the governmental setting, the bureaucratic roles played by policy makers, and the individual characteristics of foreign policy elites.

> **KEY QUOTES 1.1:** Competing theories of international relations

Realism has no place for an expectation that democracies will not fight each other. To the degree we establish that peace between democracies is a fact, and are able to explain it theoretically, we build an alternative view of the world with great import for expectations and for policy.

(Russett 1993: 24)

The sad fact is that international politics has always been a ruthless and dangerous business, and it is likely to remain that way. Although the intensity of their competition waxes and wanes, great powers fear each other and always compete with each other for power.

(Mearsheimer 2001: 2)

Self-help and power politics are institutions, not essential features of anarchy. Anarchy is what states make of it.

(Wendt 1992: 396)

Theories of American foreign policy

The previous section argued that theory is essential to the task of explaining American foreign policy. Yet even if we agree that theory is necessary, this does not establish that it is possible to construct a theory of foreign policy. Kenneth Waltz (1996), one of the leading American scholars of international politics, argues that given the complexity of the foreign policy-making process, and the fact that foreign policy is shaped by both domestic and international factors, it is impossible to construct a theory of foreign policy. According to Waltz, the best that we can hope to achieve is a theory of international politics; that is, one that 'describes the range of likely outcomes of the actions and interactions of states within a given system and shows how the range of expectations varies as systems change' (Waltz 1979: 71).

Many scholars, however, want more than this—they also want to be able to explain the specific foreign policies of particular countries. These scholars have ventured to create a theory of foreign policy, one that seeks 'to explain what states try to achieve in the external realm and when they try to achieve it' (Rose 1998: 145). Compared to a theory of international politics, which is interested in explaining general patterns of behaviour such as the causes of war, a theory of foreign policy seeks to explain why a particular state pursued a specific policy at a certain point in time. A theory of foreign policy is dedicated to answering the question of what causes a state to adopt a specific type of foreign policy.

Systemic theories

As a first cut, we can divide theories of American foreign policy into those that accentuate external or systemic factors versus those that emphasize internal or domestic factors. Here we have a profound theoretical debate over whether American foreign policy should be understood as shaped primarily by the external environment or primarily by the internal environment of the United States. Those that emphasize systemic factors argue that the most important influence on American foreign policy is the international system and specifically the relative amount of power that the United States possesses. According to this view, which Fared Zakaria (1992) associates with the concept of the *Primat der Aussenpolitik* (the primacy of foreign policy), a state's foreign policy is a consequence of pressures emanating from the distribution of power in the international system. In other words, the international distribution of power is an autonomous force that has a direct influence on the behaviour of states.

Defensive realism and offensive realism are two theories which argue that systemic pressures play a decisive role in shaping the foreign policy behaviour of the United States. Both theories share a number of similar assumptions about the international system that they believe greatly impacts the foreign policy behaviour of all states. First, defensive and offensive realists agree that the international system is anarchic, meaning that there is no higher, centralized authority above states. This follows logically from the second assumption that the most important actors in the international system are sovereign states. The attribute of sovereignty means that each state regards itself as the highest authority and can order its domestic affairs according to how it sees fit. A third assumption is that states act on the basis of self-help, meaning that they each must take the appropriate steps to ensure their own survival. Fourth, because both defensive and offensive realists believe that states must take the necessary steps to ensure their own survival, they argue that power is the main currency of international politics. Systemic theories argue that the key to understanding a state's foreign policy rests with its relative amount of power. The amount of power that the United States possesses at a particular time in history compared to other states in the international system largely determines the character of its foreign policy. For realists it is a truism that capabilities (power) largely determine interests. Thus after the Second World War, as the power of the United States increased relative to that of other states, so did its interests. Many argue that this trend of an expansion of American power and interests continues to this day.

Defensive realism

What effect does the international distribution of power have on the behaviour of a state's foreign policy? According to defensive realists, states are fundamentally security maximizers. The international system, according to defensive realists, only provides incentives for moderate behaviour, and expansionistic policies to achieve security are generally not required and often prove to be counterproductive. This means that in order to ensure its own survival in the self-help, anarchic international system, a prudent foreign policy for the United States is only to seek an appropriate amount of power. Defensive realists argue that expansionist and aggressive behaviour most often results in other states forming a counterbalancing coalition. As a result of the belief that states are strongly inclined to balance against aggressive powers, they are, in Joseph Grieco's terms, 'defensive positionalists' and 'will only seek the minimum level of power that is needed to attain and to maintain their security and survival' (Greico 1997: 167). According to many defensive realists, a direct consequence of the expansionistic foreign policy that the United States pursued in the aftermath of 9/11 is that we are beginning to see an active attempt by other states to balance American power. The recent character and extent of balancing behaviour against the United States is further discussed in Controversies 1.1. In addition to balancing inhibiting an excessive power-seeking foreign policy, defensive realists introduce the concept of the offence–defence balance and argue that as a result of variables such geography, technology, and, most importantly, military doctrine, conquest rarely pays and that security can be readily achieved under anarchy.[1]

While defensive realism predicts that the foreign policy behaviour of the United States should be one of restraint, especially since America, partly owing to geography, enjoys a high degree of security, one could argue that the history of American foreign policy belies this prediction. Writers such as Noam Chomsky (2004) have argued that the United States has pursued a policy of hegemony and has frequently sought opportunities to increase its power relative to other states. As a fallback position, defensive realists posit that a variety of domestic pathologies can prevent a state from conforming to the imperatives of the international system.[2] Thus when the United States or any other state over-expands or pursues empire, defensive realists argue that the cause of this behaviour is rooted at the domestic level.

Offensive realism

Offensive realists like John Mearsheimer reach a different conclusion about the effect that the distribution of power has on the foreign policy behaviour of states. Rather than security maximizers, offensive realists argue that states are power maximizers, meaning that they are continually searching for opportunities to gain more power relative to other states. Unlike defensive realists,

CONTROVERSIES 1.1: Balancing against the United States?

For realists, the balance of power is an enduring feature of international politics. Although various meanings have been attributed to the concept of the balance of power, the most common definition holds that if the survival of a state or a number of weak states is threatened by a hegemonic state or coalition of stronger states, they each seek to increase their own military capabilities (internal balancing) or join forces, establish a formal alliance (external balancing), and seek to preserve their own independence by checking the power of the opposing side. The mechanism of the balance of power seeks to ensure an equilibrium of power in which case no one state or coalition of states is in a position to dominate all the others.

Today, the controversy is whether the United States is so powerful that the balance of power is no longer an operating principle of international politics. Some argue that the United States enjoys such an overwhelming abundance of power relative to other states that counterbalancing is prohibitively costly (Brooks and Wohlforth 2008). In addition to the preponderance of power argument is the liberal claim that the United States is a benign hegemon and that as a result of a number of institutional constraints, other states do not find

American power to be threatening (Ikenberry 2002). According to these two perspectives, states are not actively seeking to counterbalance the United States.

Other scholars argue that as a result of both unprecedented American power and its recent aggressive unilateral foreign policy behaviour, states are beginning to counterbalance against the United States. The best evidence of this might not be traditional 'hard balancing' in the form of countervailing alliances, but rather in the form of 'soft balancing', which Robert Pape defines as 'nonmilitary tools to delay, frustrate, and undermine aggressive unilateral US military policies' (2005: 10). Some interpret the refusal of the Permanent Members of the Security Council to pass a resolution authorizing the use of force against Iraq as an example of soft balancing. This action did not prevent the United States from invading Iraq, but it did complicate the mission and certainly increased the costs of the war. And while states like China, France, and Russia have so far only adopted institutional and diplomatic strategies to constrain US power, proponents of soft balancing do not rule out the possibility of states turning to hard balancing; especially if the United States unilaterally takes militarily action against additional states.

offensive realists do not believe that security in the international system is plentiful. They also do not believe that balancing behaviour is as frequent and efficient as defensive realists contend. According to Mearsheimer, the anarchical international system and the uncertainty that exists about the current and future intentions of other states such as China compels the United States to maximize its relative power position. For Mearsheimer, the logic of offensive realism leads states to 'understand that the best way to ensure their survival is to be the most powerful state in the system' (2001: 33). Global hegemony, according to offensive realism, is the highest goal of every state's foreign policy. Unfortunately, however, Mearsheimer argues that it is impossible because of the 'stopping power of water', which makes it impracticable for any state to project its power over vast distances and to conquer and hold distant territory. While global hegemony is impossible, regional hegemony is not and Mearsheimer argues that the United States is the only state in history to achieve this esteemed position. In light of the nineteenth-century history of American

foreign policy as it expanded across North America and acquired a number of offshore territories in wake of the Spanish-American War (1898), Mearsheimer concludes that the United States is 'well-suited to be the poster child for offensive realism' (Mearsheimer 2001: 238). Once America achieved regional hegemony in the western hemisphere, offensive realism predicts that its main foreign policy goal was to prevent the emergence of a hegemon in other regions of the world. According to this theory, the United States has actively sought to prevent the emergence of a hegemon in either Europe or Asia. Offensive realists favour an 'offshore balancing' grand strategy and, according to Mearsheimer, this is largely the strategy that the United States has followed since the end of the Second World War. While many realists endorse an offshore balancing grand strategy, it is certainly debatable whether this is the strategy that the United States has followed. For realists and non-realists alike, it is not self-evident that water has prevented the United States from achieving the position of global hegemon (Layne 2006).

Internal, domestic theories

Theories that accentuate domestic factors are sceptical of the ability of systemic theories to explain American foreign policy. These theories follow the tradition of *Innenpolitik* and emphasize the influence of internal, domestic factors on foreign policy. Rather than an outside–in explanation, these theories reverse the chain of causation to an inside–out explanation. Pressures from within a state determine the character of its foreign policy. Elections, public opinion polls, the condition of the domestic economy, and the degree of national unity are all factors that foreign policy officials, and especially the President, must take into account when pursuing foreign policy objectives. Rather than the international system determining the foreign policy of the United States, the political and economic structure of the American polity is argued to be of fundamental importance to explaining America's external behaviour.

Liberalism

Liberalism is one of the most prominent domestic theories of American foreign policy. This should not be surprising because the United States is a quintessential liberal state (Hartz 1991). The logic of liberalism dictates that America's foreign policy should replicate the liberal democratic character of the American polity. According to liberalism, one of the core objectives of American foreign policy is to promote the expansion of individual liberty across the globe. This is argued to be beneficial both to the United States, in that its own security is enhanced by the presence of a large number of like-minded liberal states, and to the rest of the world as liberalism is a political ideology that champions the rights and liberties of all individuals. While liberals agree that American foreign policy should be a manifestation of its domestic political values, there is disagreement on the best way to promote liberal democracy.

For many, liberalism is most closely associated with the foreign policy of President Woodrow Wilson (1913–21). Indeed the association is so close that liberalism and Wilsonianism are almost interchangeable terms. On the eve of the United States' belated decision to enter the First World War, Wilson articulated a new vision of the world, and America's role in it, that was informed by ideas that constitute the essence of a liberal theory of foreign policy. Most fundamentally, Wilson rejected the so-called timeless principles of realism by arguing that common interests needed to replace the focus on national interests and called for a collective security system to replace the flawed balance of power system. More specifically, Wilson advocated democratic forms of government, freetrade, the creation of international institutions to help maintain the peace, and the self-determination of peoples. In order to realize these ideals, liberals from Wilson to the present have argued that the United States must take the lead in actively promoting them. This is frequently referred to as liberal internationalism whereby the United States, as a liberal democracy, must take on the role of world leadership and actively construct a peaceful liberal order through multilateral cooperation and effective international organizations.

Today, democracy promotion is one of the main elements of a liberal theory of American foreign policy. Not only does democracy promote the advancement of liberty, but it has been proven that democratic states do not fight other democratic states. Liberals argue that it is in the national interest of the United States to promote the spread of democracy. The notion that democratic states do not fight wars with other democracies is what proponents term the democratic peace.[3] If one accepts the empirical finding that democracies do not fight one another, then the issue becomes the best way to encourage democratization so as to enlarge the club of democratic states. Different presidential administrations have been torn between, on the one hand, indirectly promoting democracy through leading by example, foreign aid to support pro-democracy movements, diplomatic encouragement, and, on the other hand, directly promoting democracy by using military force to remove dictators and bring about regime change. Democracy promotion was one of the rationales put forth by the George W. Bush administration to justify the 2003 invasion of Iraq. A democratic Iraq, it was argued, would remove the alleged threat Saddam Hussein posed to the United States and help jump-start democratic transitions throughout the Middle East. This is one of the reasons why many liberals supported the Iraq War while realists, who are not only suspicious of the so-called democratic peace but also critical of crusading foreign policies to re-make the world in America's image, were generally opposed to the war.

The promotion of free trade and the belief that international institutions help to facilitate international cooperation are two of the other main pillars of a liberal theory of American foreign policy. For a liberal thinker such as G. John Ikenberry, each one of the elements—democracy, free-trade, and international institutions—are mutually reinforcing and simultaneously help to advance American interests and contribute to a pacific world order (Ikenberry 2000). Thus liberals are strong supporters of free-trade agreements such as NAFTA, as well as membership of international institutions such as the United Nations. We will return to the three cornerstones of liberal internationalism in the section on American grand strategy.

Marxism

Marxist theories are another example of an inside–out explanation in that they emphasize the economic determinants of American foreign policy. Rather than accentuating the structure of the domestic political system, Marxism underlines the capitalist economy of the United States and the pressures that it exerts on an expansionistic and imperialistic foreign policy. By one account, the foreign policy of the United States simply serves the interests of the capitalist class and the large corporations that they own. Proponents of this theory argue that most of the interventions, covert or otherwise, that the United States has perpetrated in Latin America, the Caribbean, the Middle East, and elsewhere all stem from the needs of the American economy for markets and cheap sources of raw materials, for example oil

(Kolko 1969). Marxist theories interpret the history of American foreign policy as one of imperialism and empire building, and locate the source of this behaviour in the capitalist economic system of the United States (Chomsky 2004). The American economy, like that of other capitalist economies, is prone to crises—unemployment, over-production, downturns—and Marxists argue that elites attempt to solve them by searching for new sources of capital, raw materials, and markets abroad. In order to satisfy the interests of the capitalist class, Marxists argue that American foreign policy promotes their interests by providing a stable international environment for the expansion of capitalism. Marxists argue that the military power of the United States and the wars that it has fought in places like Vietnam, Bosnia, and Iraq are meant to provide the international stability that capitalists require in order to invest in foreign lands and accrue greater rates of profit.

The Open Door school of American diplomacy, which was largely inspired by a non-dogmatic Marxism, holds that the mainspring of United States foreign policy has been the search for markets and the desire to integrate the entire world into an open, free-trade economic system. The most famous proponent of the Open Door interpretation of American foreign policy was William Appleman Williams in his classic book *The Tragedy of American Diplomacy* (1972). According to Williams, the United States has attempted to solve its domestic economic problems by expanding abroad in search of overseas markets, cheap raw materials, and investment opportunities. Expansion was deemed to be the answer to America's woes and Williams argues that the foreign policy of the United States is determined by domestic factors. For policy makers who embraced the Open Door outlook on the world, America's prosperity at home depended on access to markets abroad. For Williams, the result of the United States pursuit of an Open Door foreign policy was the creation of an American empire. These views became the bedrock of the revisionist interpretation of the Cold War, which held that America's Open Door economic interests, and not Soviet expansionism, were largely responsible for US intervention in the third world.

Toward a synthesis: neoclassical realism

We would be amiss if we did not mention attempts to combine systemic and domestic factors into a comprehensive theory of foreign policy. A recent example of this undertaking is the theory of neoclassical realism. According to neoclassical realism the only way to explain the foreign policy of the United States is to consider the manner in which systemic and domestic factors interact with one another. Systemic factors, especially the relative amount of power that a state has, are important for establishing the broad parameters of foreign policy; they help to establish what is and what is not possible. Yet the distribution of power alone cannot, according to neoclassical realism, explain the particular foreign policy behaviour of the United States. Neoclassical realists argue that domestic factors are needed to explain how systemic factors are actually translated into specific foreign policy decisions. Stephen Walt explains that the causal logic of neoclassical realism 'places domestic politics as an intervening variable between the distribution of power and foreign policy behavior' (Walt 2002: 211). Two important intervening variables that neoclassical realism highlights are decision makers' perceptions of the distribution of power and domestic state structure. In other words, for neoclassical realists, both individual decision makers and domestic politics, including the governmental structure, matter in understanding the foreign policy of the United States.

Constructivism

Whereas the previous theories all tended to emphasize material factors to explain American foreign policy, constructivists accentuate the role of ideas and identity that they argue play a major role in foreign policy. Constructivists treat identities and interests as malleable social constructions and are interested in the social processes that lead foreign policy officials to regard America as an 'exceptional' state or a 'virtuous city on the hill'. National identity, according to constructivism, should be the starting point of foreign policy analysis. The identity of the United States is, in part, a function of both its domestic self-image and foreign policy. Constructivist scholars note that identity is never self-referential, but rather is always relational and emerges by differentiating oneself from others. Thus the identity of the United States during the Cold War as the defender of liberal democracy and freedom was, in part, derived by juxtaposing itself to the evil and totalitarian Soviet Union. Constructivists can point to the role of ideas in fostering these identities in documents such as NSC-68, which outlined the United States Cold War policy of containment and sharply differentiated the national identities of the United States and the Soviet Union.

One of the reasons why constructivist approaches to the study of American foreign policy consider identity to be so important is because contructivists argue it is the basis of interests that greatly affect the formulation of foreign policy. Contrary to theories such as realism, which consider interests to be a function of material capabilities, constructivists argue that they are largely a function of ideas. The ideas that American foreign policy officials hold about the United States form the basis of the American national interest. From a constructivist point of view, one way to understand the United States global war on terror is in terms of the identity of America as the global guardian of liberty and freedom. And this interest of defending liberty and freedom in order to preserve the identity of America obviously has important implications for the conduct of foreign policy. Yet American foreign policy is always susceptible to change because identities and interests are malleable. According to constructivists, the interests of the United States are derived endogenously through the process of social interaction. This helps to explain why the United States behaves one way when interacting with other liberal democracies and another way when interacting with non-democracies. By emphasizing ideas, norms, and the social construction of identity, constructivists have a keen interest in explaining the sources of change in American foreign policy (Dueck 2006).

The origins of the Cold War

The theoretical controversy over whether American foreign policy should be understood as shaped primarily by the external or internal environment has impacted the debate on the origins of the Cold War. A number of different answers have been given to the question of who was responsible for the Cold War. This period of American foreign policy (1945–89) has been a subject of intense interest for political scientists and diplomatic historians. The conventional wisdom is that American foreign policy underwent a tremendous transformation between the time the United States entered the First World War in 1941 following the Japanese attack on Pearl Harbor and when the United States and the allies emerged victorious over Germany and Japan. This is often described as a change from isolationism to globalism in which the United States used its preponderant power to assert itself on the world stage. Yet throughout the post-Second World War period American power was challenged by the Soviet Union, which resulted in a tense Cold War that was most dramatically illustrated by the nuclear weapons arms race between the two countries. A key question shaping the historiography of the Cold War is what led the United States and the Soviet Union to go from allies during the Second World War to bitter rivals locked in a global struggle for power from 1945 to 1989?

External explanations

From a purely systemic viewpoint, neither the United States nor the Soviet Union is to blame for the Cold War. The Second World War created a vacuum of power in Europe that was filled by the only two great powers that remained standing: the United States and the Soviet Union. According to this view, the ensuing rivalry and competition between the United States and the Soviet Union can be simply explained in terms of the bipolar distribution of power that existed after 1945. One problem with this account is that there is no agency; there are no villains in which to assess blame and responsibility for the origins of the conflict.

Another external, realist explanation of the Cold War holds that in addition to a bipolar distribution of power after 1945, one of the two poles, the Soviet Union, was an expansionist power that was bent on world domination. According to this view, United States foreign policy throughout the Cold War was a successful response to the threatening and expansionist behaviour of the Kremlin. Within diplomatic history, this is referred to as the orthodox account of the origins of the Cold War and, not surprisingly, is popular with many American historians. The orthodox explanation places the blame for the Cold War squarely on the shoulders of the Soviet

Union and its leader Joseph Stalin. The United States, in documents such as the famous NSC-68, interpreted Soviet intentions as inherently aggressive and a direct threat to American national security. Given this interpretation of Soviet intentions, the United States had no choice but to respond to this threat and actively check the power of the Soviet Union. This formed the basis of the American policy of containment that is often credited to George Kennan, who was a prominent diplomat stationed in Moscow. On the basis of Kennan's understanding of the Soviet's ideology, he argued 'it is clear that the main element of any United States policy toward the Soviet Union must be that of a long-term, patient but firm and vigilant containment of Russian expansive tendencies' (Kennan 1984: 119).

Internal explanations

As the Cold War dragged on a new set of historians arose that challenged the notion that American foreign policy was simply a response to the alleged threat posed by the Soviet Union. Instead of assigning responsibility to the bipolar distribution of power and to the expansionistic ideology of the Soviet Empire for America's behaviour throughout the Cold War, the revisionist school of historians looked inside the United States. And when they closely examined the domestic interests of the United States, the revisionists argued that since at least the late 1800s the overriding goal of American foreign policy was to promote the spread of capitalism so as to ensure a world of free markets that would provide access to American goods and services. This economic thesis was most eloquently put forth by William Appleman Williams (1972), who argued that the promotion of an Open Door world whereby other states embraced America's liberal ideology and opened their markets to US economic expansion was a constant pattern of behaviour in American foreign policy. Thus for the revisionists, especially those writing during and after the Vietnam War, the United States' expansionistic and even imperialist behaviour was responsible for the onset of the Cold War. The only threat that the Soviet Union posed after the Second World War was that it openly challenged America's vision of an open, liberal economic world run and managed by the United States. Here Williams went beyond a Marxist analysis

as he also underlined the liberal ideological dimension of US foreign policy whereby American policy makers believed that domestic prosperity and tranquility at home depended on continuous expansion overseas.

Neoclassical explanations

A neoclassical explanation holds that both external and internal factors are necessary to understand the origins of the Cold War. The starting point for a neoclassical explanation is the distribution of power that existed in the international system after the Second World War. Here neoclassical realists such as Chris Layne concur that in 1945 the United States held a significant power advantage over all the other states in the international system. This favourable distribution of power provided the opportunity for the United States to expand its interests around the globe. But for Layne (2006), it is domestic factors, namely Open Door economic and ideological imperatives, which explain why the United States chose to expand its interests and deliberately pursue a Cold War with the Soviet Union from 1945 to 1989. Layne puts forth an extraregional hegemony theory to argue that even if the Soviet Union had not existed after the Second World War, 'America's Open Door aims on the Continent would have led to the establishment of US hegemony in Western Europe' (Layne 2006: 70).

KEY POINTS

☐ Different answers have been given to the question of who was responsible for the Cold War.

☐ External explanations emphasize the bipolar distribution of power that existed after the Second World War and argue that the Soviet Union was inherently expansionistic and the United States attempted to contain the spread of communism.

☐ Internal explanations argue that the United States' economic expansionistic and even imperialist behaviour was responsible for the onset of the Cold War.

☐ Neoclassical explanations argue that the United States' favorable position in the international system coupled with the domestic imperatives of the Open Door explain why it pursued a Cold War with the Soviet Union.

Grand strategy

Grand strategy is defined as the overall vision of a state's national security goals and a determination of the most appropriate means to achieve these goals. Competing grand strategies provide different views about the character of international politics and the role that the United States must play in order to achieve its core national security interests. Since the end of the Cold War, there has been a general consensus that the United States has been pursuing a grand strategy of primacy. Yet, for many, the grand strategy of the Bush administration differed greatly from that of President Clinton's. With the election of President Obama in 2008, many are expecting that US grand strategy will once again change. The aim of this section is to provide an overview of three different grand strategies—primacy, liberal internationalism, and offshore balancing—and to underline the theory of American foreign policy that informs each of these competing strategies.

Primacy

A grand strategy of primacy seeks to preserve America's position as the undisputed preeminent power in the international system. Peace among the great powers and American security are held to rest on a preponderance of US power. The goal of, but certainly not the quest for, primacy was stymied by the existence of the Soviet Union. In the aftermath of the Cold War, the United States has occupied the unique position of being the sole super power in the international system. Proponents of primacy view this as an extremely advantageous position and argue that America's grand strategy should be one of preventing any future great powers from challenging the power of the United States. Thus the United States should militarily outspend other states to preserve its military dominance, continue to station troops in, and underwrite the security of, countries such as Germany and Japan, and actively work to prevent the rise of states such as China that could pose a challenge to American primacy.

In order to preserve American primacy, the United States not only needs to be more powerful than anyone else, but it must also exercise leadership. While recognizing that multilateralism has certain advantages, proponents of primacy argue that unipolar powers have the benefit of being able to act unilaterally to advance their own interests regardless of what other states think. Thus when the situation warrants, such as when dealing with rogue states armed with weapons of mass destruction, advocates of primacy do not hesitate to recommend that the United States act alone. Institutions such as the United Nations are regarded with a degree of suspicion as they are largely viewed as restraining rather than enabling American power. Finally, proponents of primacy do not believe that the promotion of democracy should trump other vital US interests. Primacy is largely informed by a power-maximizing version of structural realism that does not give much weight to the character of domestic regimes. Thus if the promotion of democracy in a country such as Iraq erodes US power relative to other great powers such as China, proponents of primacy would conclude that this is antithetical to American national interests. Yet some proponents of US primacy, such as neoconservatives in the Bush administration, argue that democracy promotion is a vital component of American grand strategy.[4] All advocates of US primacy, however, agree that keeping America in its preeminent position and the rest of the world off balance is the core national interest.

The Bush Doctrine embodied important elements of a strategy of preserving America's dominant position in the international system (see Major debates and their impact 1.1). The Bush Doctrine explicitly embraced America's commitment to preserving its unipolar position. The 2002 *National Security Strategy* declares that the US military will be 'strong enough to dissuade potential adversaries from pursuing a military build-up in hopes of surpassing, or equaling, the power of the United States'. The Bush Doctrine also declares America's willingness to act unilaterally, which is most evident in its controversial policy of preemptive and even preventive war. The Bush administration's unsympathetic view of international institutions was revealed by its decision to invade Iraq without the authorization of the United Nations

Security Council. Critics contend that the strategy of primacy is ultimately self-defeating as the US inevitably succumbs to the imperial temptation of overextending itself by fighting unnecessary wars and by other states actively seeking to counterbalance American power (see Controversies 1.1).

Liberal internationalism

Many associate a liberal internationalist grand strategy with President Clinton as evidenced by his *National Security Strategy of Engagement and Enlargement* (The White House 1995). Proponents of liberal internationalism agree that it is in the United States' interest to preserve its preeminent position in the world, but disagree with the policies that the Bush administration pursued to keep America number one. The Bush Doctrine, with its call for unilateral preemptive war, distain for multilateralism, and disregard for reigning rules and norms, is seen by many liberals as a bold new grand strategy that is destined to fail (see Major debates and their impact 1.1). By pursuing its interests unilaterally and shunning key international institutions, liberals argue that America's prestige and ability to lead has faltered. Throughout the second-half of the twentieth century, the United States, as a liberal hegemon, played a vital role in maintaining international order that directly benefited both the United States and much of the rest of the world. Ikenberry (2002) argues that in addition to the realist-based containment order that existed after the Second World War, the United States also established a liberal democratic order that was based on economic openness, international institutions such as the United Nations and the Bretton Woods system, and democracy. While the United States played a key role in the creation of these multilateral institutions, the argument is that they continue to serve American interests by providing legitimacy and a rule-based setting for its foreign policy behaviour. Liberals such as Ikenberry argue that before the Bush administration, most states did not fear US power because of its institutionalized, legalized, and democratic character. Liberals conclude that it makes strategic sense for the US to continue to adhere to the institutions and rules that it helped to build after the Second World War and a key issue for the Obama administration is whether the United States can return to a liberal internationalist grand strategy.

It should be self-evident that a liberal internationalist grand strategy is firmly anchored to the theory of liberalism. Most fundamentally, the strategy calls on America to promote the spread of democracy and liberty around the world. This is viewed as both a moral duty and a strategy that actually improves American security. The United States is better able to pursue its interests and reduce security threats when other states are also democracies. Closely related to the argument about the pacifying effect of democracy is the liberal idea that the promotion of free trade increases the prosperity of more and more people, which, in turn, creates the conditions for democratic governance. Free trade is believed to foster greater interdependence

---

 MAJOR DEBATES AND THEIR IMPACT 1.1: Bush Doctrine—realist or liberal?

There has been a great deal of debate and controversy regarding the Bush Doctrine. One debate centres on whether the doctrine is based more on the principles of realism or liberalism. For many, it seems self-evident that the doctrine is based on a muscular version of realism. The call for the preservation of American primacy, the willingness to use force against enemies who challenge US power and interests, and the enthusiasm to pursue a go-it-alone strategy in order to secure American interests in a hostile world seems to fit comfortably in a realist world view. Yet many realists are critical of the Bush Doctrine, especially with respect to how it justified the Iraq War. Realists point to a fourth component of the Bush Doctrine: democracy promotion. A key rationale for the invasion of Iraq was that regime change was necessary in order to install a democratic government in Iraq. Liberals who supported the war argued that democracy in Iraq would help to spread freedom and liberty throughout the Middle East, which would be beneficial to the US since democratic states do not fight democratic states. Thus rather than being based on the principles of realism, some argue that the Bush Doctrine is grounded on liberal Wilsonianism or what John Mearsheimer describes as 'Wilsonianism with teeth'.

among states that diminishes the economic gains that any state could expect to incur by going to war. Thus the greater degree of economic interdependence between the United States and China is believed to lessen the chance of conflict. Finally, the creation of international institutions and norms are viewed as the best mechanisms for managing the array of political, economic, and environmental problems that arise in an interdependent world. In this manner the three key ideas of liberal theory—democracy, interdependence, and institutions—are vital elements of a liberal internationalist grand strategy.

Offshore balancing

Apart from a few proponents of neo-isolationism, those advocating an offshore balancing grand strategy are the only ones who question both the wisdom and viability of preserving America's preeminent position in the international system. Rather than trying to preserve the impossible, namely unipolarity, many realists advocate a policy of offshore balancing that attempts to maintain America's relative power and protect its national interests in an emerging multipolar world. An offshore balancing grand strategy is firmly rooted in a realist balance of power theory. According to this theory, any state that attempts to make a bid for hegemony will be opposed by a coalition of other states that will seek to restore a rough balance of power. Moreover, as evidenced by the actions of the United States since the end of the Cold War, states that possess a preponderance of power are prone to misuse it.

By embracing multipolarity, proponents of offshore balancing argue that the United States will accrue a number of important geostrategic benefits. First, by giving up the quest to dominate the entire international system, the United States can actually preserve, if not augment, its relative power position in the international system. This can be achieved by requiring other countries, such as Germany, South Korea, and Japan, rather than the United States, to provide for their own security. Second, it allows the United States to distance itself from the power struggles in Europe and Asia, and focus on its own domestic and international interests. Third, offshore balancing circumscribes

America's national interests and limits its involvement to areas of the globe that are of vital strategic importance. Fourth, offshore balancing augments American national security by allowing it to take advantage of its insular geographical position in the western hemisphere and heed the advice of George Washington to steer clear of permanent alliances. Finally, by eschewing primacy, the United States would be able to put the break on the liberal world order building project that has entailed fighting unnecessary wars in the hope of promoting democracy and preserving the American empire.

Given the serious budget deficit and financial problems that America currently faces, it is uncertain whether the US can any longer afford the ambitious and expensive grand strategy it has been following. Proponents of offshore balancing also question whether primacy has in fact made America more secure. Rather than overwhelming power being the appropriate strategy to achieving American security, Benjamin Schwartz and Chris Layne consider the ironic possibility 'that the very preponderance of American power may now make us not more secure but less secure' (2002: 36). With respect to the threat of terrorism, an offshore balancing strategy recommends that the United States exercises restraint, reduces its overseas military presence, and refrains from meddling in the affairs of other states.

KEY POINTS

- ❑ Debates about grand strategy are explicitly related to different theories of American foreign policy.
- ❑ Primacy argues that the overriding goal of US grand strategy should be to preserve indefinitely America's position as the undisputed preeminent power in the international system.
- ❑ Liberal internationalism advocates continued American leadership of the world through multilateral institutions and the promotion of democracy and free trade.
- ❑ Offshore balancing is a grand strategy for a multipolar world and argues that the US must exercise greater constraint and shift some of its burdens to other states.

Conclusion

This chapter has attempted to demonstrate that the study of American foreign policy is dependent on theory. At the same time, there are a variety of different theories that attempt to explain American foreign policy. Some theories accentuate the impact that external, systemic factors have on American foreign policy while others highlight the influence of internal, domestic factors. And there are also those that attempt to combine systemic and domestic factors. Theories of American foreign policy are important for understanding past debates such as the origins of the Cold War as well as for the contemporary debate over American grand strategy. While complex, theory is unavoidable when it comes to the task of attempting to explain American foreign policy.

? Questions

1. Which of the five sources of American foreign policy identified by James Rosenau do you believe is the most important for understanding the external behaviour of the United States?
2. How would you explain the United States' decision to invade Iraq in light of each of the five sources of American foreign policy outlined by Rosenau?
3. Do you agree or disagree that it is impossible to construct a theory of American foreign policy?
4. What are the main sources of disagreement between offensive and defensive realists?
5. Compare and contrast 'inside–out' with 'outside–in' explanations of American foreign policy.
6. Whose interpretation of the origins of the Cold War do you believe is most persuasive?
7. Is Chris Layne's explanation of the Cold War able to bridge the divide between internal and external accounts of the Cold War?
8. Which of the three grand strategies do you believe the US should be following today?
9. Do you agree or disagree that states are attempting to counterbalance the US?
10. Which theory do you believe the Bush Doctrine is based on?

» Further Reading

For a general survey of the main theories in the field

Dunne, T., Kurki, M., and Smith S. eds (2010), *International Relations Theories: Discipline and Diversity*, 2nd edn (Oxford: Oxford University Press).

Snyder, J. (2004). One world, rival theories, *Foreign Policy*, **145**: 53–62.

On the Cold War

Gaddis, J. L. (1997), *We Now Know: Rethinking Cold War History* (Oxford: Oxford University Press).

LaFeber, W. (2002), *America, Russia, and the Cold War, 1945–2000*, 9th edn (Boston: McGraw-Hill).

On grand strategy

Ikenberry, G. J. (2001), *After Victory: Institutions, Strategic Restraint, and the Rebuilding of Order After Major Wars* (Princeton: Princeton University Press).

Mearsheimer, J. J. (2001), *The Tragedy of Great Power Politics* (New York: W.W. Norton).

Endnotes

1. For a discussion of the offence–defence balance, see Jervis (1978) and Lynn-Jones (1995).

2. Snyder (1991) and domestic pathologies.

3. On the theory that democratic states do not fight wars against other democratic states see Russett (1993). For a criticism of this theory see Layne (1994).

4. For an informative discussion of neo-conservativism and American foreign policy see Schmidt and Williams (2008).

For a range of additional resources to support your learning visit the Online Resource Centre that accompanies this book at www.oxfordtextbooks.co.uk/orc/cox_stokes2e/.

2 American exceptionalism

Daniel Deudney and Jeffrey Meiser

Introduction: American difference and exceptionality

Since its founding almost a quarter of a millennium ago, the United States of America has thought of itself as, and been widely perceived to be, exceptional. The United States is unlike other nation states in myriad ways. Most obviously, the United States is different from other states and nations because it is by far the most successful great power in late modern times. This success is manifest in its current unprecedented status as the world's sole superpower. It is the seat of the world's largest economy. And it is the ideological leader of the most powerful, appealing, and successful form of political, economic, and social organization in modern times: liberal capitalist democracy. Because of its extraordinary success as a great power, the United States has the capabilities to shape the world in a variety of ways that reflect its preference for how the world should be ordered, a preference rooted ideologically in its conception of itself and its special mission. Extraordinary success also has greatly magnified the effect of every aspect of America on the world, from the sublime to the shameful. This success and influence makes an understanding of the United States and its agenda vital to understand major features of contemporary world politics. Understanding how America is different and how it is exceptional is, for better or worse, essential for understanding not just US foreign policy, but major aspects of contemporary world politics.

Success makes the United States different and influential in far-reaching ways, but the core reason the United States is widely viewed as exceptional is because of its intensely liberal character. America is exceptional, both in fact and perception, because more than any other state in history it has embodied and advanced an ideological vision of a way of life centred upon freedom, in politics, in economics, and in society. Prior to the last half of the twentieth century, what were then called republics were very rare in world politics, and the American founding and expansion marked a decisive turning point in the long and largely tragic story of free and democratic government. Convinced they embodied, in the words of President Abraham Lincoln, 'the last best hope of mankind', Americans have been audacious, at times reckless, innovators in turning the abstract and lofty Enlightenment goal of a fully free society into a practical working arrangement. This project has been marred by contradictions, seedy opportunism, and startling blunders. But over nearly twenty-five decades it has relentlessly progressed and come far closer to realization than even the founders dared to imagine. From the outset, this anomalous and experimental polity saw itself not just as liberalism in one country but as the model, the vanguard, and at times vital facilitator of a universally appealing and universally realizable way of life. This vision of an eventual liberal republican end of history, as the German philosopher Immanuel Kant called it, has been deeply attractive, even intoxicating, to many, while being a frightening threat and a writ for upheaval and imperialism to others.

Given its influence in the world and its highly developed sense of itself as the embodiment of a universal and revolutionary ideology, the claim that the United States is exceptional is highly charged with contentious ideological connotations. In contemporary American and world politics, the expression 'American exceptionalism' means very different things to different people. For some it is a vision, for others a sham, and for others a nightmare. For some Americans, particularly recent neo-conservatives, intoxicated with power and righteousness, American exceptionalism is a green light, a legitimizing rationale and an all-purpose excuse for ignoring international law and world public opinion, for invading other countries and imposing governments, and for routinely identifying particular and often provincial and pedestrian American interests with the universal pursuit of progress and freedom. For others, American exceptionalism is code for the liberal internationalist aspiration for a world made free and peaceful not through the assertion of unchecked American power and influence, but rather through the erection of a system of international law and organization that protects domestic liberty by moderating international anarchy. This vision sees all states, and particularly large and powerful states, as inherently dangerous and seeks checks, both domestic and international, to restrain the worst impulses of all nations, including the United States. For liberals and internationalists American exceptionalism provides a standard against which much of American history is found wanting in various ways. It is a reminder that much remains to be done and is a perpetual call to action to bring American practices ever closer to American ideals.

Difference, exceptionality, and success

Exceptionality and the hard test of realism

The indispensable baseline for assessing the effects of any domestic factors, such as American liberal republicanism and the exceptionalist ideology associated with it, is the simple realist model of security, power, and interests. In this view, states above all seek security, and they need and seek power to achieve security.

They in turn use their power to realize various interests, particularly economic interests, which in turn enhances their power and thus their security. This baseline realist model poses the vital first question: what in actual American behaviour *cannot be explained* by the pursuit of security, power, and interest? Only if this simple model fails to explain do we even need to consider the possible influences of other factors, among them ideology, on American behaviour. However, applying this simple model to any state, particularly a large and powerful state, is rarely a straightforward task. What security requires, what the contours of power look like, and what content interests actually have are often ambiguous and fraught with misperception and debate, not only by actors in the heat of actual political decision making, but also among scholars making after-the-fact evaluations. Furthermore, as constructivist theorists remind us, identity, ideas, and ideology shape what are understood as threats and interests, and also powerfully shape, in both positive and negative ways, the capacity of states to mobilize power for the pursuit of security, power, and interest.

Applied to the United States, the simple realist model has considerable explanatory power, but also important blindnesses and limitations. Well-articulated through American history in varying degrees of clarity, and richly developed in recent decades by international theorists, the realist view is that the United States is not in any significant way fundamentally different from other states. This conclusion provides the basis for the routine dismissal of the entire discourse of American exceptionality. Realists hold that all the main steps in the trajectory of American foreign policy such as relentless continental expansion against weak adversaries, regional hegemony in the New World often exploited for economic gains, global great power balancing and alliance leadership against predatory revisionist states, and then Western and global hegemony are essentially what any state (seeking security, power, and interest) would have done if it were in the thoroughly enviable position of the United States in the international system.

The realist view of the United States does, however, clearly recognize that the liberal republican character of the United States has two significant distinguishing manifestations: early isolationism and later internationalism. For realists, liberalism has indeed mattered for US foreign policy, but in largely negative ways. For realists, the early American posture of isolationism was made possible by the relative isolation of the United States from the great powers of Europe. But as the industrial revolution unfolding in the twentieth century brought about the end of this isolation, the United States clung for too long to an isolationist foreign policy, with nearly disastrous consequences for the preservation of the balance of power in Europe. Forced to deal with the world,

the United States sought to transform the world through the realization of its liberal internationalist programme for democracy promotion within states and international law and organization between them. For realists, this agenda, particularly in its more urgent and crusading forms, entails an unrealistic and utopian hope for human improvement and political change, and is seen as a cloak for raw American power interests. Its pursuit is seen as a chronic source of mischief and disorder, and realists aspire for the United States to abandon its exceptionalist pretences and behave like a normal great power.

Yet the realists' critical and dismissive posture toward the liberal elements that sit at the core of American exceptionalism fails to do full justice to liberalism and its internationalism. The realists correctly see that the American liberal internationalist project has an agenda that is revolutionary to a Westphalian version of world order and to the types of states traditionally associated with this order. But they fail to appreciate the extent to which the extraordinary levels of peace, prosperity, and freedom that prevail within the core of the American system of the Western liberal democratic states are in significant measure the realization of the American liberal internationalist project. Realists also fail to see that this internationalist agenda (which is increasingly best advanced by Europeans rather than Americans) holds the key to whatever hopes there are to address the myriad real and significant global problems that are being produced by rising levels of global interdependence.

The dark side of American exceptionalism

The landscape of argument about American exceptionalism is further complicated by the fact that the United States is not purely a combination of the very standard realist goals and behaviours and liberal elements, but is also shaped, like all other states, by idiosyncratic factors of national identity rooted in ethnicity, religion, and race. Here are factors that at times powerfully compromise and subvert the liberal democratic vision of the American Creed, and their net effect has been to add streaks of stark eccentricity and blatant hypocrisy to American pretensions to embody the overall liberal project of human freedom (Lieven 2004).

These non-liberal and anti-liberal aspects of American identity and behaviour are distinct from another contemporary view, widely held in Europe, of American exceptionalism as a marker for a cluster of retrograde and dangerous American tendencies. The pro-American liberal narrative of exceptionality emphasizes the historically progressive and internationally indispensable role of the United States as the standard bearer of the liberal cause. But this has been and is being challenged, not just by the realists, but also by an older line of conservative anti-liberal European thinking and by a contemporary pro-liberal European position. The old European conservative line, echoed today in harsh terms by Islamicists, is that America's liberalism is a licence for popular anarchy and cultural levelling. For non-Western traditionalists, American liberty is a writ for the libertine, and the United States is the leading purveyor of 'westoxification' (Katzenstein and Keohane 2007).

Perhaps even more telling is the contemporary sceptical view of European liberal democrats, which has grown rapidly more widespread in reaction to the policies of the second Bush administration. At times, for such critics, it seems as if the United States has become something like the world's greatest and most dangerous rogue state. This new European view of exceptional America as liberal laggard emphasizes the ways in which more messianic and crusading aspects of the American liberal agenda, most manifest in contemporary American neo-conservativism, have linked up with some of the more parochial anti-liberal American religious and cultural tendencies to serve as the ideological façade for the exercise of a blatant and short-sighted pursuit of American power and interest. Given the vastness of American power, particularly military power, claims of American exceptionalism take on a frighteningly imperial character.

American success and its sources

The single most distinguishing feature of the United States has been its extraordinary success. This fact may not be universally liked, but it is universally recognized. Over the roughly two and half centuries since its founding, the United States of America has been by far the most successful state in the international system. This

success is the indispensable basis for the vast influence the United States has had on the world and it has nourished the widespread sense among Americans of their special world role.

The United States has been uniquely successful among the great powers over the last century, dubbed by the influential publisher Henry Luce 'the American Century'. The great powers of Europe, most notably Britain, Germany, and France, emerged from the First and Second World Wars either in ruins or ruinously sapped in strength, while the United States emerged largely unscathed. During the second half of the twentieth century, marked by the bipolar Cold War struggle between the Western capitalist democracies, led by the United States, and the socialist–communist coalition led by the Soviet Union, the United States and its allies also emerged victorious after the unexpected (and unexpectedly peaceful) Soviet collapse. Due to this outcome, the United States stands at the turn of the twenty-first century in a position of military ascendancy unprecedented in the modern European and global state systems. As the world's sole superpower, the USA spends more on its military than most of the rest of the world combined and holds something approaching worldwide military supremacy.

Success requires power and power is based, particularly in the industrial era, on wealth. The United States has been the world's largest economy for over a century. Even in the wake of rapid economic growth in large previously underdeveloped countries over the last several decades, the American economy is larger than the next two countries combined. And the United States has sustained its economic leadership across recessions, depressions, and a dizzying succession of technological transformations.

America's economic liberalism—its robust capitalism—has also significantly contributed to American success. The strong commitment to individual achievement and obsession with economic accumulation is supportive of technological innovation and economic growth generally. These ideas are exemplified by the Horatio Alger myth: nobody's class position is fixed by birth, everyone has an equal opportunity for economic success (Hartz 1991: 62–3, 11–3, 219–24). From this perspective, a liberal society can win the allegiance of even the poorest members because of the promise of becoming rich. Regardless of

Chapter 2 American exceptionalism   25

whether the Alger myth is real, Americans believe it, and so do many people around the world. Economic opportunity and prosperity have been self-reinforcing. The lure of economic opportunity was a major factor in the ability of the United States to attract skilled and hard-working immigrants.

In sum, the belief in American exceptionalism is based upon a number of core realities, including American military primacy, economic dynamism, and political diversity.

In order to further explore and assess the diverse conceptual landscape of what is at stake in the assertion of American exceptionalism, the remainder of this chapter is divided into four parts. The first part considers the meaning of exceptionalism, the critics of American exceptionalism, and the roots of American success. The second part examines the liberalism that makes the United States exceptional. The third part examines peculiar American identity formations of ethnicity, religion, and 'race', which interact with and often subvert the liberalism of America. Part four examines the role of American exceptionality across the five major epochs of American foreign policy, from the founding to the present.

Liberal exceptionalism

The free world project of American liberal republicanism

The fact that the United States has been so successful makes it different. But the fact that it has been so liberal is what makes it exceptional. A liberal republic, in the language of the Enlightenment, which originally conceptualized it, is a distinctly modern type of political regime, composed of a complex matrix of related elements, some of which are in perpetual tension with each other. A liberal republic, a polity liberal in the full and broad sense of the term, is animated and ordered by a set of values, institutions, and practices. The components of a modern liberal republic are individual freedom and institutionalized civil rights, popular sovereignty, limited government specified in a constitution, multiparty electoral democracy, private property and market capitalism, rule of law and independent courts, and religious liberty and separation of church and state. These ideas are codified in the founding documents of the republic: the Declaration of Independence, the US Constitution, individual state constitutions, and the Bill of Rights. It is common to speak of the 'American Creed' as a distillation of liberal democratic values: 'liberty, egalitarianism, individualism, populism, and laissez-faire' (Lipset 1996: 19) or 'liberty, equality, democracy, individualism, human rights, the rule of law, and private property' (Huntington 2004: 46). Each of these elements is complex and Americans, like citizens of other modern liberal democracies, are in perpetual ferment about their secondary features and the tensions among them. So important has liberal republicanism been to the United States and the United States to liberalism that it is impossible to understand the one without the other.

The American project of freedom did not, of course, spring fully formed out of the historically thin (if bracing) air of the New World. It was initially almost entirely an import of English institutions, practices, and values from the revolutions of the seventeenth century, which were then richly nourished by the moderate European Enlightenment in the eighteenth century. But unlike the long-established polities of Europe, where the traditional hierarchies of the crown and church held sway, and only slowly and reluctantly yielded to popular pressures over the last two centuries of reform, revolution, and war, the United States was born far more fully, and uncontestedly, liberal than any modern Europe state.

Anti-statism, state building, and militarism

Anti-statism is deeply rooted in liberal thinking. The United States is different and exceptionally liberal compared to other liberal democracies in the degree to which this anti-statism has been institutionalized and made the object of sustained popular pressure and shaped its foreign policy. Anti-statism and the fear of despotism led the American founders to create a state structure that is fragmented, decentralized, and accountable. Separation of powers allows different branches of government to 'check and balance' one another. The United States exhibits the foreign policy tendencies of both a democracy and a weak state. The open structure of Congress and its frequent elections provides access to individuals and groups that seek to affect foreign policy. Aversion to taxation, another aspect of American anti-statism, has made state building difficult and led to a consistent under-funding of the public sector. Mobilization of the state has been dependent upon outside security threats, or similar systemic shocks.

Anti-statism is integral to liberal republicanism because strong states, governmental apparatuses large in size and amply equipped with violence capabilities and uncontestedly authoritative, are seen as inherent threats to popular security and liberty. American anti-statism sometimes spawns ridiculously paranoid suspicions. For example, as the internationalist project started to bear fruit, popular anti-statism has produced a strong fear and hostility toward international organizations, thought to be seeds of a dark end of history in one-world despotism. In this view, world governance and organization, being big and further away, are less accountable and less checkable, and therefore intrinsically undesirable.

Over time, American anti-statism has been severely compromised by the need to combat foreign threats. The state and war feed on one another, and the single most important factor in overcoming the institutional and attitudinal barriers to American state building has come from war. The Civil War, and then the First World War, produced a great rise in the size and capacities of the federal government, which then quickly declined with the return of peace. But beginning with the mobilization for the Second World War and extending through the long and perilous decades of the Cold War, the United States built a permanent strong state structure, heavily centred on military capability, that went far beyond the vision and constitutional architecture of the founders. The erection of this American National Security State has been largely popular, often wildly so, at the same time as many Americans still voice severe doubts about its longer-term impact on limited government (Johnson 2004).

Over this long war, a peculiarly American style of militarism has arisen. The cumulative weight of a high

and enduring mortal foreign threat, a vast military and military industrial complex, and large numbers of politically active veterans has combined to produce increasing militarism in American culture and national life. This has also been fed by the extraordinary 'gun culture' in the United States, marked by widespread firearms ownership, chronic domestic gun violence, as well as the widespread conviction that gun possession is not only necessary as a check on criminals, and possibly even foreign invaders, but also on the US government itself, making gun possession the most basic right of a free society. These features of the American cultural landscape loom large in the increasing scepticism of liberal Europeans and others about the United States. But this militarism may have much more bark than bite because it coexists with an extreme reluctance to have Americans killed in battle, and a startling willingness to abandon wars that become more costly in blood than anticipated. Popular theatrical militarism is also tempered by the extreme reluctance of the US military to go to war except in overwhelmingly important and readily winnable conflicts.

American capitalism and prosperity

Among major states, the United States is the most distinctly pro-capitalist, and one of its most distinctive features is high levels of economic growth and widely distributed prosperity. America was capitalist or proto-capitalist from the beginning, a utopia of Lockean liberalism. This pervasive capitalist individualism has figured prominently in the seminal interpretations of the American experience, from Tocqueville in the middle of the nineteenth century to Louis Hartz in the middle of the twentieth. Because the United States was so purely capitalist, American political development has been profoundly different from Europe's, and many of the major features of European life, most notably the feudal stage with its *ancien régime* and working-class socialist movements, are almost completely absent in the United States.

Much of the attractiveness of freedom in the United States has been associated with the freedom to own and accumulate property. The early success of liberal capitalism in the United States was made possible by the availability of large quantities of cheap rich agricultural land.

The social mobility produced by economic advance fostered by abundant land in early America reinforced the belief that individual effort would lead to individual achievement, and helped account for the widespread economic equality, which was in stark contrast to the extreme socio-economic stratification virtually everywhere else. This widespread economic opportunity also reinforced American anti-statism by creating widespread strata of prosperous property owners attached to capitalist ideas, hostility to both a large and intrusive state and socialist redistribution.

America's deep commitment to capitalism and private property has had a significant impact on US foreign policy. American expansion in the nineteenth century was propelled by Americans seeking new and more abundant land for private ownership. Since the late nineteenth century, the United States has intervened abroad to protect American property beyond its borders (Kinzer 2006: 9–108) and has repeatedly sought to 'open' other countries to trade and investment. And much of twentieth-century American foreign policy, from the Spanish American War to the Marshall Plan and the erection of GATT and the WTO, is intimately connected to the interests of American corporations. This deep support for capitalism and private property also contributed to the strong American opposition to third world nationalists. In Guatemala, Iran, and Chile and elsewhere, the US government supported violent coups of right-wing groups to overthrow left-leaning regimes (Kinzer 2006: 111–216), contradicting American support for democracy and any government, whether elected or not, which favoured the seizure of foreign property ('nationalization') and redistribution. The Soviet Union seemed so threatening to Americans not just because it was a very powerful great power, but also because it was the central base of a worldwide movement to eliminate private property.

Trade policy is the most consequential domain where American capital has sought to strengthen and use state power, rather than oppose it. American trade policy has changed several times in major ways and from the beginning trade policy has been a central political topic, pitting different interests and regional 'sections' against one another. Initially, under the sway of Jefferson's vision of a decentralized agricultural polity of free proprietor yeomen farmers, and in the interest of the vast majority of Americans who lived and worked on farms, the United States pursued a low-tariff policy, and during this period the United States was part of the colonial 'periphery' in the capitalist world system. Like Brazil, Canada, and Latin America, the United States was mainly an exporter of unfinished raw materials and importer of manufactured goods from Europe. But the alternative economic vision of protectionism had been articulated from the beginning, most notably by the first Secretary of the Treasury, Alexander Hamilton, in his Report on Manufacturers (1790). This

---

 MAJOR DEBATES AND THEIR IMPACT 2.1: Exceptionalism and ideology

To what extent is American exceptionalism a reality or an ideology that justifies imperial behaviour? Throughout history, many states, both great and small, have claimed some degree of 'specialness' and exceptionalism. In fact, it is exceptional to find a state or a people that does not feel that they are in some ways special. This is especially the case when that historical state has been strong and/or had expansionist tendencies. One only has to think of Ancient Rome, or the Greek city state of Sparta.

In a sense, then, exceptionalism as an ideology has run throughout history and has often coincided with an imperial foreign policy that serves to justify conquest and overseas expansion. The exceptionalism of the imperial state can be justified in a number of ways that may include a claim to cultural or civilizational greatness (Christianity, democracy, or a civilizing mission) or it may instead rely upon a claim to economic development (capitalism as the end point of history). In some extreme cases, exceptionalism as an ideology may reside in the exceptional state's military preponderance and this can be married to a racial narrative of superiority. Nazi Germany would be a good example of this, and in a lesser sense imperial Britain with its superiority of arms and sense of 'white man's burden'. The central debate then is what comes first, exceptionalism as an ideology or exceptionalism as material fact? As Weber argued, do the cultural enabling conditions and self-belief precede the state of exceptionality or do the economic, political, or strategic conditions have to be in place before the ideology of exceptionalism develops? Ask yourself, would America regard itself as exceptional if it were a middle-ranking power on the world stage?

protectionist programme was fully implemented during the Civil War when the new Republican Party (in a congressional supermajority with the South absent) established a national currency, a national banking system, and a high tariff to protect American industry. Behind this tariff wall, progressively raised across the decades of Republican Party ascendancy, the United States rapidly industrialized and grew into the world's economic colossus.

Yet another reversal—back to free trade—was triggered by the Great Depression, and the realization that the United States, as the world's largest and lowest-cost industrial producer, could gain from free trade. This shift in economic interest combined with the realization that the spread of capitalism was vital to securing weak democracies against communist domination. With this new power and agenda the United States became, from Franklin D. Roosevelt's presidency through to the present, the leader in the worldwide effort to lower tariffs and other trade barriers. This effort not only helped trigger fifty years of global economic growth, but also produced the GATT (now WTO) and ancillary pro-capitalist global organizations and institutions such as the International Monetary Fund (IMF) and the World Bank.

The American state has sought to pursue an 'open door' policy of opening up the global economy to American inward investment and has opposed governments that have sought to resist American expansionism.

Peculiar Americanism

Ethnicity, immigration, and foreigners

The full story of immigration to the United States is very complex, but a broad pattern, identified by the political historian Michael Lind as the 'three American nations', captures much of it. The first American nation, 'Anglo-America', was composed of settlers and their descendants mainly from England and Scotland, and this group and its mores continue to provide the base template of American ethno-national identity. Anglo-America was white Protestant and English-speaking, and these traits, combined with an affiliation for Britain and other British settler colonies, have remained prominent features of the American scene. The second American nation, 'Euro-America', resulted from the immigration of a vast tide of people, from the early 1800s to the early 1900s, from all over Europe, particularly Germany, Ireland, Italy, and eastern Europe. Not speaking English, often Catholic, and poor, these new Americans largely, but not completely, 'assimilated' to the traits of the earlier Anglo nation.

Finally, beginning in the 1960s, with the reform of immigration laws to permit more Asians, Africans, and Latin Americans, combined with sudden influxes of political refugees from revolutions and wars in places like Cuba and Vietnam, there has emerged the third American nation, 'global America'. As earlier, the new wave of immigrants are partly assimilating, but also retain far more active contact, through modern air transport and communications, with extended networks of people in the countries from which they emigrated.

Religion

The desire to practise freely their religious beliefs and realize their religious ideals inspired the founding of several of the early English colonies. American religion has been floridly diverse, benefiting from robust freedom of religion and the 'separation of church and state'. Various strands of Protestant Christianity have been particularly prevalent and influential, in ways both direct and subtle. The overall Christian theme of equality reinforced democracy and the overall Protestantism theme of individualism reinforced liberalism and capitalism. Both the Calvinist and evangelical Baptist tendencies of early American religious sects, such as the Puritan founders of Massachusetts Bay Colony, have also infused American life and foreign policy with a messianic sense that the United States was, in the often-quoted words of the seventeenth-century Puritan preacher John Winthrop, a religiously special place, a 'city upon a hill' that would inspire and help lead mankind from wickedness. Overall, American religious participation helped compensate for the sharper edges of capitalism and provided large numbers of Americans with an intense experience of community otherwise absent in the starkly individualistic society. Periodic religious revivals of fervour and inspiration also motivated major movements of social reform such as the Abolitionist attack on slavery and the Temperance Movement's attack on alcohol consumption, as well as the recent movement for African–American civil rights (Morone 2003).

Religiously inspired social reform and messianism in America has also directly spilled into the international arena. Throughout the nineteenth century, when the United States government was small and inward-looking, American missionaries were actively prose-lytizing around the world, but also providing services such as basic education and medical care and promoting human rights and foreign aid (Mead 2001: 141–7). Yet at the same time, religious leaders provided a rationale for American imperialism as part of an effort to spread Christianity to heathen peoples, and missionaries also served as the vanguard of American imperial military and economic expansion (LaFeber 1963). In recent decades Protestant evangelicals and Catholics have been active and influential in opposing abortion and contraception services, as well as in mobilizing opposition to extreme human rights abuses, such as the genocide now occurring in the Darfur region of Sudan. Various American Christian groups have also become increasingly active and influential in supporting the United States' pro-Israel policy in the Middle East, and their theme of 'crusades' has become another volatile element in the current war on terrorism against violent Islamic fundamentalism.

Race

The inheritance from Europe with which the United States was born was not purely liberal, but also included a radically illiberal system of African slavery, whose presence and eradication profoundly shaped American politics and foreign policy. As part of the colossal global predation and audacious outburst of mercantile, imperial, and colonial activities that brought the global economy and state system into existence in the early

modern period, the Europeans coercively moved millions of people, mainly from Africa, across the oceans to labour in the New World's plantations and mines. This brutally coercive economic system was legitimized by, and in turn legitimized, virulently racist attitudes that remained long after slavery was abolished. Tocqueville caught the stark reality when he observed that each of the three 'hostile races' of North America 'follows a separate destiny' and that 'two unlucky races [i.e. Africans and Amerindians] suffer the effects of tyranny, and, though their afflictions are different, they have the same people [i.e. whites] to blame for them' (Tocqueville 1988: 317).

African slavery and white racism stand as the greatest exception to the exceptionally liberal character of the United States. The fact that this brutal system of slavery and racism was so thoroughly capitalist underscores the fact that markets are not inherently free but can be compatible with extreme conditions of unfreedom unless they are embedded in a fuller matrix of political and civil rights. Throughout the nineteenth century, racist ideas of Anglo-Saxon superiority shaped and legitimized 'manifest destiny', providing a convenient justification for the displacement of Indian tribes and Mexicans. The racism of America's dominant white populations, nourished by various 'scientific' Darwinist theories, reached its climax in the oppressive and bloody conquest and rule of the Philippines in the early years of the twentieth century (Kramer 2006).

The slow and halting but cumulatively largely successful struggle to eradicate first slavery and then institutionalized racism over the history of the American republic has had wide-ranging effects. During the first decades of the American republic conflicts over slavery touched upon everything, and part of the reason the American Constitution created such a weak state was that slave owners, the dominant economic and political group in the southern states, feared that too strong a government could potentially jeopardize their peculiar institution. Catalysed by growing liberal Abolitionist sentiment in the non-slave states in the North, slavery was only abolished by the Union victory in the major bloodbath of the Civil War (1861–5), by far the most destructive war in American history. The second lengthy phase of African–American liberation began after the Union armies left the South in 1876 and the white southerners quickly erected an elaborate system of legalized, or de jure, segregation of so-called 'Jim Crow' laws. Struggles against this domestic regime of racial oppression stretched across decades and it was only in the middle years of the twentieth century when landmark liberal Supreme Court rulings combined with a mass mobilization of African Americans and their white liberal allies in the Civil Rights Movement that formal equality was achieved. Throughout the era of segregation, white southerners, operating as a political bloc and occupying key positions in Congress, not only resisted pressure for domestic change, but also vigilantly opposed US participation in any international human rights regime or organization asserting universal rights, fearing they might weaken the South's system of discrimination. As late as the 1980s, the United States, while serving as the leader of the free world against communist tyranny, was also, embarrassingly, a principal ally of the white apartheid regime in South Africa and this was only reversed by sustained international pressure and the mobilization of a boycott of corporations doing business there.

In the twentieth century, America's growing global role also contributed to the weakening of racial barriers and the delegitimization of racism. As part of the national mobilization for the Civil War and the world wars, African Americans were drawn into military service in large numbers, increasing the ability of African Americans to claim full citizenship. During the Cold War racial segregation was seen as an embarrassment and liability in the battle for 'hearts and minds' in the third world, a major battleground of the struggle. American segregationist policy, in contrast to the official communist hostility toward racism, meant that racism had become a national security liability. The first important step toward desegregation was the integration of the US Army through an executive order from President Truman at the close of the Second World War. The Civil Rights Movement eventually succeeded in ending lawful segregation in the United States and domestic race relations have continued to slowly improve. Racism is now much less powerful a factor than in early periods of American history, a change reflected in the rise in legal emigrants from third world nations.

Race, religion, and immigration have served to make America a 'melting pot' that has been infused with successive cultural waves.

This form of regeneration and vibrancy has added to the sense of American exceptionalism.

KEY POINTS

❑ American liberal exceptionalism has pushed US foreign policy in directions that contradict and transcend the imperatives of power politics. The effect of exceptionalism is visible in American impulses toward the seemingly contradictory positions of isolationism during times of weakness, and internationalism during times of relative strength.

❑ The American founding was a manifestation of the original American internationalism. Following the War of Independence, thirteen sovereign states replaced their *ad hoc* confederation with a 'states-union' in order to replace international anarchy with binding law and organization.

❑ Throughout most of the nineteenth century the USA adopted an isolationist posture fostered by national weakness relative to European powers and the republican ideological belief that the United States should serve as a model for the rest of the world and focus on internal progress rather than external interactions.

❑ The twentieth century marked a major departure in American foreign policy: the rise of the USA to world power status under the strategy of liberal internationalism. As changes in technology shrank the globe, the United States sought to remake the world in its own liberal image while at the same time generating sufficient state capacity to prevent the eclipse of the free world by the twin totalitarian threats of Nazi Germany and the Soviet Union.

❑ The end of the Cold War and subsequent collapse of the Soviet Union produced an American-led global liberal hegemony. This 'moment' of liberal triumphalism has seemingly been undermined by the Bush administration, suggesting an uncertain future for liberal internationalism and America's exceptional effect on the international system.

Exceptionality and foreign policy

Liberalism, exceptionalism, and US foreign policy

Various strands of American particularistic national identity, whether ethnic, religious, or racial, have been omnipresent and often influential on American foreign policy. But in the overall trajectory of American foreign policy they are ultimately less central to the story of American exceptionalism than the truly central axis of the story, which derives both in fact and in perception from the liberal republican core of the American polity. And in turn these liberal influences on US foreign policy have been bounded by the exigencies of great power politics because the United States, like all states living in international anarchy full of uncertain threats and opportunities, has been by necessity keenly attentive to the requirements, often arduous, of the great power balance of power politics. The USA did not emerge so successfully through its long succession of wars by ignoring the demands of power and interest, but by being exceptional in their mastery. But the USA is not simply another great power with a particularly outstanding track record. Its deeply liberal character has powerfully shaped its foreign policy. Sometimes the influence of its liberal democratic polity has worked in ways that contradict the dictates of realpolitik and, even more importantly, in ways that escape and transcend it. What is exceptionally liberal about American foreign policy can be captured in two seemingly contradictory patterns: isolationism and internationalism.

At first glance isolationism and internationalism appear to be unrelated, indeed almost opposite, approaches to foreign policy. Isolationism is introverted, and seeks as much non-involvement as possible. Internationalism is extroverted and seeks to make the world more like the United States. In reality, of course, American foreign policy has never been purely isolationist or internationalist. At times it has been an odd mixture of both, and has also exhibited other unrelated tendencies.

In the American context, however, isolationism and internationalism are profoundly linked. They can best be viewed as different strategies to achieve the same essentially liberal ends, but in different circumstances.

Isolationism served liberal ends when the United States was relatively isolated (and isolatable) and weak. Internationalism serves liberal ends when the United States is inescapably interdependent with other states and when it is strong enough to influence a larger sphere beyond its borders (Deudney 2007).

In order to examine the actual roles that American exceptionalism, both liberal and illiberal, has played in the overall trajectory of American foreign policy, it is necessary to study these roles in the different major epochs of American foreign policy, and to see how they have intertwined with the pursuit by the United States of security, power, and interest in the often harshly competitive international system. Five periods, partially overlapping, deserve closer examination: the Founding (1774–87), Hemispheric Isolationism (1787–1917), Great Power Rivalry and World War (1900–91), Liberal Internationalism (1919–present), and Unipolarity, the War on Terrorism, and Unilateralism (1991–present).

Original American federal internationalism

Narratives of American foreign policy commonly begin after the founding of the government of the United States by the Constitution of 1787. In reality, however, the founding itself was not solely a 'unit-level' event of 'state formation' but rather had far-reaching 'international' aspects, with deep connections to what would later come to be called liberal internationalism. Although it is commonly held that American internationalism is largely a phenomenon of the twentieth century, and particularly the later post-Second World War part of it, in reality the United States, as a state, had extensive 'international' internal features that were pronounced at its founding and in the decades that followed. The deep historical roots of internationalism in the American political experience are often overlooked by international theorists, particularly realists, but they provide a template for twentieth-century liberal internationalism.

The founding of the United States took place through a process of confederation and federation among thirteen separate states. The organization of the British colonial activity in the New World was highly decentralized and colonies had a significant measure of local autonomy. After banding together to reach their common goal of independence, the thirteen states then formed a more substantial union with a weak central government. This negotiated union was a 'peace pact' that created the 'Philadelphian System' as an explicit antithesis to the Westphalian system of hierarchies in anarchy that marked European politics (Deudney 1995; Hendrickson 2003). The small professional army, minuscule national bureaucracy, and substantial state militias prevented the resolution of state and sectional conflicts through coercion.

The politics of antebellum America was one of internal sectional rivalry, between the 'free' and slave states. The vexed question of western expansion, potentially upsetting the intersectional balance within the union, was dealt with by diplomatic settlements, the so-called 'Great Compromises' of 1820, 1833, and 1850, that were negotiated between the sections, much like the diplomatic deals of European nation states with each other. When the issue of slavery could be finessed no longer, the sections fought a war that was largely conducted as an international or interstate war between clashing uniformed armies that largely followed the European laws of interstate war, belying its label as the 'Civil War'. The Union victory in the War of Southern Succession saved the Union from dissolution and deepened its liberal character by eradicating slavery. But the Union victory and the assumption of authority and capacity by the central government also marked the evolution of the states-union quasi-international system into something resembling a federal national state. Despite this change, the idea that the United States is, or at least was, as much a liberal 'states-union' as a 'liberal state' continues to serve as an inspiration and model to liberal internationalist aspirations to replace international anarchy with binding international law and organization.

The isolationist liberal republic

During its first century of existence, the United States' foreign policy centred on North America and to a lesser extent the western hemisphere. Americans were largely inward looking, highly focused on issues of internal development. The United States was relatively isolated and therefore had the option of pursuing a policy of isolationism. As the United States was weak, excessive interaction with European states would be on unfavourable terms, and would risk corrupting the American experiment. Instead of taking an active role in international politics, the United States would seek to be an example for the rest of the world to follow by perfecting its own liberal democratic political system and avoiding the corrupting influences of European war and diplomacy. Avoidance of foreign entanglements was a guidepost of American foreign policy. Despite this aspiration, the United States was in an international political and military system that it could neither fully escape nor significantly control. Because it had to fear European predation, the United States necessarily had to pay close attention to European politics and the balance that kept its powerful states in some degree of check. Because of its integration into the world economy centred in Europe, trade and the protection of trade played major roles in US foreign policy, and these economic connections drew the United States into war with European states during both the Quasi-War of the 1790s with France, and the War of 1812 with Britain.

Isolationism also appealed to Americans because of their fear of a large standing army derived from republican ideology and reinforced by recent experience leading up to the War of Independence. It was thought that international engagement would inevitably lead to conflict and war. Furthermore, war would require large-scale extraction of societal resources to fund a large standing army. High taxes and military dictatorship would become necessary to effectively compete within the European state system. therefore isolationism had beneficial implications for the American constitutional project.

In 1823, the Monroe Doctrine extended isolationism to the western hemisphere with the declaration that the United States would not allow European powers to involve themselves in the domestic affairs of New World republics. This approach had an imperialistic dimension, in that Central and South American states were assumed to only have partial sovereignty, but the main effect was to assert separation between Europe and the Americas. Within a general framework of isolationism, the United States pursued an abbreviated policy of imperialism in the Spanish–American War of 1898. This brief, one-sided war also marked a step toward the abandonment of isolationism. While ejecting Spain from the western hemisphere was the unfinished business of the Monroe Doctrine, the war also led to an expansion of American interests deep into the Pacific Ocean and East Asia with the occupation of the Philippines and annexation of Hawaii in 1898. Americans were, however, highly conflicted about the occupation of the Philippines and the counter-insurgency warfare against Philippine nationalists that followed. Many also felt that imperialism was inconsistent with the Constitution.

Great power rivalry and world war

The second century of American foreign policy was very different from the first. Isolationism became increasingly unworkable as America's relative isolation was diminished by the new industrial technologies of communication and transportation. With the 'abolition of distance' as it was referred to in the later nineteenth century, Europe and its great powers and their wars were now no longer buffered and distant from the United States. Beginning between 1890 and 1914, and abruptly ending in 1989–91, the United States was drawn into a series of world wars and struggles that profoundly shaped not only international politics, but the position of the United States in the system. Drawn

late into the First World War, the United States, after proposing a largely aborted scheme for an international peacekeeping league, pulled back into a semblance of hemispheric isolation. Initially also uninvolved in the wars in Europe beginning in 1939 and in Asia in 1936, the United States was inexorably drawn into the conflict and was able to serve as the most successful combatant due to the rapid military mobilization of its massive industrial base. With the war having two main victors, the Soviet Union and the United States fell into a struggle for global mastery that lasted over four decades and saw both sides deploy vast nuclear arsenals of global-range strike weapons, whose even partial use would have wiped out much of urban-industrial civilization on the planet. These total stakes seemed raised even further because the two blocs represented the vanguard of radically opposing socio-economic and political systems, which both sides believed were destined to become globally universal.

For America as an 'exceptional' state, these conflicts had two quite contradictory consequences. On the one hand, the specialness of the United States in the project of freedom as Americans understood it became greatly magnified. The United States became the leader and protector of liberal democracies everywhere, and had it not been for American power and purpose between 1940 and 1990, liberal democracy might well have been eliminated from the planet. The United States was no longer simply the leading exemplar of

---

 CONTROVERSIES 2.1:   Idealism in American foreign policy

One of the exceptional features of US foreign policy is the extent to which values affect it. A consistent debate in American foreign policy is what role values should play in foreign policy decision making. One perspective is that values should be the driving force in determining the policies that the USA pursues. From this perspective, US foreign policy should be based on a sincere commitment to values such as democracy, human rights, rule of law, and economic opportunity. The rationale for this approach is that American values are attractive to the rest of the world and policies based on these values enhance American legitimacy and increase the soft power of the United States. A second approach is that values should play no role in the decisions made by American leaders. Instead, US foreign policy should

be based on a 'realistic' appraisal of national interests. These interests included pursuing policies that increase American power, such as gaining access to foreign markets, and maintaining military and economic superiority. Scholars, policy analysts, and politicians that follow this approach often condemn US foreign policy as being overly moralistic and unrealistic. A third way of conceptualizing the role of ideas is to view them as instrumental. In other words, values are a means of achieving a goal. For example, some international relations theorists argue that the American people will only support an internationalist US foreign policy if they feel it is consistent with American values. Thus, American leaders must frame their preferred policy in terms of how it fosters American values.

the project of freedom, but the indispensable 'leader of the free world' whose every major action seemed ripe with world historical significance. On the other hand, the rigorous exigencies of these struggles forced the United States to become what it had always claimed to fear becoming: a polity with a vast standing military and state security apparatus, and a vast panoply of allies, clients, and protectorates. Its grand strategy, while still wrapped in the rhetoric of liberal purpose, was in actuality first and foremost about survival and success in the global great power system, and guided by the precepts of realism. While democracy survived, and in some ways even thrived alongside the National Security State, and while American lack of interest in formal territorial annexation kept its imperial presence from crossing over the line, at least as historically defined, into empire, there was no escaping the fact that the United States had become in important ways quite ordinary as a state, rather like the European national states that the founders had believed to be the antithesis of a republic.

Internationalist liberalism and world order

As impressive as America's success in the great power rivalries of the twentieth century is, what is most exceptional in American foreign policy is not its ascent from a weak regional state to the top of the global great power system, but rather the ways in which it has sought to remake the world according to a liberal vision. This vision is in its logic an extension of the principles of the original American internationalism of the founding. The trigger for the articulation and pursuit of the liberal one-world vision was the same as the move to great power global balancing, namely the realization that as the world shrunk the survival of the United States Constitution required a foreign policy of global scope. As outlined by President Woodrow Wilson and progressive theorists in the early years of the twentieth century, the American liberal internationalist project has two overall aims: to abridge international anarchy through the erection of binding international law and organization, and to change the other units in the system away from hierarchy toward constitutional democracy. Of course this

project has never been the sole aim of US foreign policy, which has been, by necessity, focused on the balance of power among the great powers. Many Americans have been ambivalent or hostile to it, and the United States has not always been a consistent adherent to the international arrangements it has played such a major role in creating. Nor has this project been pursued without or against power, but rather as the aim of power.

This basic vision has produced a wide array of efforts, whose real-world impact has ranged from abject failure to stunning success. In the early years of the twentieth century, the United States was the leading force behind the creation of a World Court to arbitrate disputes among states. At the end of the First World War, Wilson's ambitious proposal for a League of Nations was a key, if ultimately unsuccessful, part of the settlement of the Versailles Conference. In the wake of the near disaster of the Great Depression and the Second World War, the United States made a much more serious, sustained, and successful effort to erect a new liberal international order, with measures such as the establishment of the United Nations, the Bretton Woods institutions (IMF and World Bank), the multilateral free trade regime under the auspices of GATT, numerous proposals for bilateral and multilateral nuclear arms control (the Baruch Plan, Atoms for Peace, the Nuclear Non-Proliferation Treaty, and the Strategic Arms Limitation Treaties of the Nixon era), and the emergence of a range of global international regimes, varying greatly in almost every regard. These measures, taken as a whole, provided a greater degree of world public order and governance than ever before in history.

Unipolarity, war on terrorism, and unilateralism

The fifth, and still unfolding, period of US foreign policy was inaugurated with the unexpected collapse of the Soviet Union, an event which shifted the overall international system from Soviet–American bipolarity to American unipolarity. The period since the end of the Cold War has been short, is still unfolding, but has been unexpectedly marked by great inconstancy in the direction of US foreign policy.

The first part of this period, stretching from the end of the Cold War to the two Clinton administrations, is in many ways the historical high-water mark of American power and influence, and was accompanied by an array of remarkably progressive developments in world politics. The heady optimism and sense of breakthrough and potential of this period found expression in notions that the long-envisioned liberal 'end of history' was at hand. The collapse of the Soviet Union and the communist project it had spearheaded meant that for the time in history the liberal coalition of states was unmistakably hegemonic globally. The first Bush administration, following in the steps of Reagan's breakthrough diplomacy with Soviet reform leader Mikhail Gorbachev, negotiated a set of far-reaching nuclear arms reduction agreements, the Soviet withdrawal from eastern Europe, and the reunification of Germany as a liberal democracy. Throughout the 1990s, the liberal cause globally relentlessly pushed forward, as dozens of previously authoritarian or totalitarian states moved rapidly to try to become democracies, as the European Union both widened its membership and deepened its institutional capacities, as NATO expanded to encompass many former Soviet satellites in eastern Europe and beyond, as the liberal international trading regime was both strengthened with the establishment of the WTO and widened with the admission of many previously communist or socialist economies. The United Nations also seemed to have new possibilities without the Cold War deadlock, and under its auspices members of the international community made increased efforts to deal with humanitarian crises, failed states, and ethnic cleansing and genocide, and establish a permanent international court for crimes against humanity.

Somewhat unexpectedly, however, the administration of George W. Bush took US foreign policy on very different paths, marked by a near reversal of American leadership to strengthen international law, organizations, and regimes. 9/11 and the Bush administration's responses to it greatly amplified the intensity and impact of this new foreign policy direction. Even before 9/11 the administration had assumed a largely new American role as the leading opponent and critic of most international organizations and regimes, and

the leading laggard in dealing with issues arising from global interdependence, perhaps most notably global warming. The administration withdrew from landmark arms control treaties, sought to impede the establishment of the ICC, effectively scuttled the Kyoto Protocol, and simply walked away from an almost completed negotiation to strengthen the Biological Weapons Convention.

Observers of this American turn against the liberal internationalist agenda emphasized the new tendency for the United States to act unilaterally. Of course all states, particularly large and powerful ones, routinely act unilaterally, and US foreign policy in the nineteenth century was largely unilateral. But against the twentieth-century American role as multilateral alliance leader and institution builder, this turn (or return) marked a sharp departure from the policies of every administration since FDR.

The 9/11 terrorist attacks on the World Trade Center and the Pentagon seemed to draw an even sharper closure to the optimism and progress of the years after the fall of the Berlin Wall. Initially, with world public opinion solidly behind it, the United States executed a quick and bold campaign to overthrow the Taliban regime in Afghanistan that had sponsored and sheltered the al-Qaeda leaders of the 9/11 attacks. But the Bush administration saw the attacks as harbingers of further far more serious attacks, possibly employing nuclear or biological weapons, and set in motion a far-reaching reconfiguration of American state capacities and foreign policy. On the domestic front, a giant new Department of Homeland Security was created, and the Bush administration began to claim (and act) as if the President, as commander-in-chief of the armed forces, was free to act in wartime outside the limits of international law and constitutional constraints.

Internationally, the initial success in Afghanistan was followed by the United States' invasion of Iraq. This invasion seems to have been motivated by several goals: to preclude the emergence of a revisionist and anti-American nuclear power, to sustain American hegemony and alliances in the Middle East oil-producing region vital to the entire world economy, and perhaps even to catalyse the emergence of democratic states in the region. Whatever its purposes, the

American occupation of Iraq proceeded to bleed American strength and strengthened the radical Islamic regime in Iran, which had previously been held partially in check by the Saddam Hussein dictatorship in Iraq. As a result of this, and the growing backlash against many measures of Bush's open-ended 'global war on terrorism', by the end of his second term both domestic and international support for the administration and its novel policies had almost completely evaporated.

In one sense the sudden turn of the United States in the Bush years marked a serious diminution of the exceptionalist liberal strand in US foreign policy. While still bellowing its claims to special status as the global palladium of liberty, the United States now acted with an updated version of the simple realist script, doing what immediate security threats seem to make necessary, with little regard for their cost or international institutional fallout.

Conclusion: Obama—new turn?

With the election of Barack Obama as President in 2008, the story of American exceptionalism, difference, and peculiarism has taken another series of new turns. Obama campaigned on a criticism of neo-conservative interventionism and the Iraq War, in support of renewed American commitment to nuclear arms control, and leadership in addressing global climate change. More generally, Obama promised to seek the extension of the domestic new liberal programme advanced by the New Deal and the Great Society, while also expansively affirming the need for American leadership in solving global problems.

Despite these hopes, Obama's Presidency has been most marked by a growing sense of American limits. There has been a growing realization that American economic primacy, the wellspring of America's great difference in success as a Great Power, is inevitably waning, with profound implications for the future of American foreign policy. With the rise of China and India, along with the European Union, the overall international system is not unambiguously unipolar, but is rather increasingly multipolar. The recent global Great Recession, triggered by a combination of under-regulated financial institutions and over-extended consumers, produced increased unemployment and diminished national output, and has reduced the attractiveness of the American model of capitalism and the resources available to sustain America's far-flung security commitments. When job training is being reduced in Detroit, it is hard for Congress to justify

funding job training for former Taliban fighters in Afghanistan. Faced with these growing constraints, the foreign policy of the Obama Administration has been much more modest in its objectives and its willingness to undertake further burdens and commitments.

Internationally, the immediate effect of Obama's election was what pollsters refer to as 'the Obama effect', a marked increase in the positive perception of the United States by foreign public opinion. Obama's receipt of the Nobel Peace Prize during his first year in office highlighted the great expectations that his election and programme elicited abroad, particularly among European progressives. Hard realities, both at home and abroad, have made the realization of these promises and expectations much more difficult than his supporters anticipated.

Ironically, Obama's immense popularity abroad also is a partial indicator of the waning of America as exceptional in its overall liberalism. The very extent of the success of liberal democratic capitalism, propelled to global pre-eminence in part by the American model and muscle, meant that the United States was now part of a much larger community of liberal democracies, and no longer an outlier in a world of non-liberal or anti-liberal states. Would the United States thus become a normal state or would it become exceptional in new ways?

Admired abroad for largely symbolic reasons, Obama at home has been subject to relentless attack for essentially symbolic reasons. The overall tenor of

American political discourse has become increasingly shrill, fueled by a furious, at times hysteric, assault on Obama by a phalanx of populist conservative commentators, many with voices amplified by sponsorship from the Australian media mogul Rupert Murdoch. These critics equated twentieth-century American liberalism's use of state power to achieve democratic and egalitarian goals, and regulate the externalities associated with industrial society's interdependence with socialism, communism, and totalitarianism. For these critics, the post-Second World War order of Europe was a model of statism run wild, a model to be avoided not emulated. In effect these angry American libertarians and anti-statists want to undo the legacies of the Progressive era, the New Deal, and the Great Society, returning the United States to the late nineteenth century.

Obama has also become a lightning rod for cultural anxieties rooted in America's ethnic, religious, and racial peculiarisms. The fact that Obama's father was a Muslim (from Kenya), his middle name (Hussein) has Muslim origins, and he lived for a few years in Indonesia, an overwhelmingly Muslim country, has sparked an orgy of Islamophobic conspiracy theories and fantasies. This virulent anti-Obama hatred is particularly strong among white Evangelical Christians, whites who resist and resent the progress achieved by African Americans in obtaining full rights as citizens, and those fearful of immigrants, both illegal and legal, from the global south.

Taken together, the rise of domestic partisan rancor, economic malaise and rising inequality, and the shift of the international system raise serious doubts about the continued ability and willingness of the United States to play its historic post-Second World War role in the international system, and how the legacies of American exceptionalism and peculiarism will evolve in these new circumstances remains to be seen.

> **KEY QUOTES 2.1: The origins of American exceptionalism**

The United States, almost from its start, has had an expanding economic system. The nineteenth-century American economy, as compared to European ones, was characterized by more market freedom, more individual landownership, and a higher wage income structure—all sustained by the national classical liberal ideology. From the Revolution on, it was a laissez-faire country par excellence.

(Lipset 1996: 54)

Hence there was a strong family likeness between all the English colonies as they came to birth. All, from the beginning, seemed destined to let freedom grow, not the aristocratic freedom of their motherland, but a middle-class and democratic freedom of which the world's history had not previously provided a complete example.

(Tocqueville 1988: 34)

The English colonies—and that was one of the main reasons for their prosperity—have always enjoyed more internal freedom and political independence than those of other nations; nowhere was this principle of liberty applied more completely than in the states of New England.

(Tocqueville 1988: 39)

I have already said enough to put Anglo-American civilization in its true light. It is the product (and one should continually bear in mind this point of departure) of two perfectly distinct elements which elsewhere have often been at war with one another but which in America it was somehow possible to incorporate in to each other, forming a marvelous combination. I mean the spirit of religion and the spirit of freedom.

(Tocqueville 1988: 47)

There is therefore at the bottom of democratic institutions some hidden tendency which often makes men promote the general prosperity, in spite of their vices and their mistakes, whereas in the aristocratic institutions there is sometimes a secret bias which, in spite of talents and virtues, leads men to contribute to the afflictions of their fellows. In this way it may come about that under aristocratic governments public men do evil without intending it, and in democracies they bring about good results of which they have never thought.

(Tocqueville 1988: 235)

? Questions

1. Is America an exceptional country?
2. To what extent is US foreign policy characterized by either isolationism or internationalism?
3. How do we measure exceptionality and is it an 'objective fact'?
4. Is the belief of exceptionalism an ideological construct?
5. Are exceptionalism and imperialism two sides of the same coin? Explain your answer.
6. What is the basis of American exceptionalism?
7. To what extent was the belief in American exceptionalism rooted in American cultural history?
8. American exceptionalism is a logical outcome of its commitment to free markets and its victory in the Cold War. Critically discuss.
9. Ethnic, religious, and racial difference have given the USA its exceptional nature. Critically discuss.
10. To what extent is the USA a liberal power within world politics and in what ways does this influence the belief in exceptionality?

» Further Reading

Deudney, D. (2007), *Bounding Power: Republican Security Theory from the Polis to the Global Village* (Princeton: Princeton University Press).

Deudney 'brings America back in' to international relations by showing how the construction of the American states-union in 1789 succeeded in preserving democracy in a system populated by predatory monarchical, despotic, and totalitarian nation states. Only against the backdrop of the long tradition of republican security theory can the importance of the USA fully be realized.

Hartz, L. (1991), *The Liberal Tradition in America: An Interpretation of American Political Thought since the Revolution* (San Diego: Harcourt Brace Jovanovich).

American exceptionalism emerges from a political culture dominated by 'absolute and irrational Lockean liberalism'. This conformist and unique national identity limits the effectiveness of American foreign policy by fostering a sense of intolerance toward different political, cultural, and economic systems.

Lieven, A. (2004), *America Right or Wrong: An Anatomy of American Nationalism* (New York: Oxford University Press).

American identity is a composite of civic nationalism based on universalistic liberal values and chauvinistic nationalism based on religious and ethnic particularities. These two aspects of American exceptionalism foster contradictory impulses in US foreign policy: civil nationalism encourages a moderate internationalism while chauvinistic nationalism fosters isolationism, messianism, and, most ominously, imperialism.

Lipset, S. M. (1996), *American Exceptionalism: A Double-Edged Sword* (New York: W. W. Norton).

As the most prominent contemporary advocate of the idea that America is qualitatively different from other countries, Lipset presents an analysis of how the American Creed—'antistatism, individualism, populism, and egalitarianism'—fosters exceptionalism in American politics, policy, and culture. One important finding is that American exceptionalism is 'double-edged', meaning that the USA is different to, but not necessarily better than, other countries.

Mead, W. R. (2001), *Special Providence: American Foreign Policy and How it Changed the World* (New York: Routledge).

American foreign policy is an expression of four sometimes complementary and sometimes contradictory traditions: Hamiltonian economic realism, Jeffersonian republican isolationism, Jacksonian populist militarism, and Wilsonian religious moralism. American foreign policy works best when it draws on the strengths of each tradition.

Nau, H. R. (2002), *At Home Abroad: Identity and Power in American Foreign Policy* (Ithaca, NY: Cornell University Press).

The exceptionalist American identity prevents the United States from establishing a stable, moderate, internationalist foreign policy. Only when the USA realizes that American values have in large part come to dominate the international system will it finally feel 'at home abroad'.

Tocqueville, A. de (1988), *Democracy in America*, trans. G. Lawrence (New York: Perennial Library, Harper & Row).

Writing in the 1830s, Tocqueville studied the USA in the context of failed European social revolutions. He saw the USA as an exceptionally successful democracy rooted in mores, laws, political decentralization, and most importantly social equality.

 For a range of additional resources to support your learning visit the Online Resource Centre that accompanies this book at www.oxfordtextbooks.co.uk/orc/cox_stokes2e/.

Section 1
Historical Contexts

3 The US rise to world power, 1776–1945

Walter LaFeber

Introduction

Americans like to think of themselves as a powerful nation and a vibrant democracy. At pivotal points in their history, they have also thought of the United States as an *empire*—that is, a collection of various tribes, states, or nations which their central government controlled. That they held this view is somewhat surprising. After all, in 1776 Americans opened a new chapter in world history by successfully rebelling against an empire—the great British Empire.

From the beginnings of United States history, then, empire should have been a bad word. But it was not. Having grown up within the British Empire, George Washington, Thomas Jefferson, and other founders easily thought of their new nation as an empire—although,

of course, a decent, democratic, and just empire, quite unlike the British model, which they condemned for having corrupt kings and exploited colonies. Once free to conduct their own foreign policies, Americans rapidly grew into a continental power stretching from the Atlantic Ocean to the Pacific. The Civil War of 1861–5 interrupted this era of landed expansion. But the war between North and South also cleared the way for triumphant northern capitalists to create by 1900 the world's number one industrial and agricultural power. Producing far more than they could consume, Americans naturally looked overseas for new markets. The search led them into economic competition with the great imperial powers (Great Britain, France, Germany, Russia, and Japan), and into military competition as well. Not surprisingly, in the late 1890s Americans began to think again of themselves as an empire, only this time as an overseas (not merely a continental) empire.

But, as in 1776, they again also thought of themselves as different from the other imperialists. They saw themselves as representing middle-class order, democracy, and capitalistic success. And, as they demonstrated in the First and Second World Wars, they could build a highly efficient military to ensure their success. In 1945, that military power included the first atomic bombs.

Out of this stunning economic–military combination appeared the US foreign policies which dominated the post-1945 years. By 1991, the United States and its allies had defeated Russian communism to win the four-decades-long Cold War. Before as well as after the 9/11 terrorist attacks on New York City and Washington, DC, many Americans again thought of themselves as living in a nation which headed nothing less than a global empire—an empire now occupying some 700 military bases around the world, and with its economic and cultural power penetrating all corners of the globe (Johnson 2004; Ferguson 2004). This post-1991 version of American empire can only be understood by viewing it as the result of the previous two and a half centuries.

Some widely noted authors thought this post-1991 US empire was good for both Americans and, indeed, the entire globe. Just as Americans had settled and developed a continent before 1945, these authors argued, so they could now bring order and development to crucial parts of a suffering, supposedly less civilized, world. Americans in the mid-nineteenth century had followed what they believed to be a 'manifest destiny' (a term first used in New York City and Midwestern newspapers during the 1840s to indicate the right given by God to Americans to populate and develop the continent from the Atlantic to Pacific oceans). After 1917 and especially after 1991, they followed what they believed to be a new manifest destiny to stabilize, democratize, and profit from many parts of the globe.

From colonies to continental empire, 1776–1865

From their earliest days of independence, and even during the darkest days of their often-sputtering war against the British, Americans thought of their fortune in imperial terms. As the Revolution ground down to its end in 1783, US soldiers, long unpaid by a bankrupt Congress, threatened to overthrow that Congress and install their commander, George Washington, as a virtual monarch. The General quickly stopped the uprising and possibly saved what was to be an American republic. He passionately condemned anyone 'who wickedly attempts to open the floodgates of civil discord and deluge our rising empire in blood' (Van Alstyne 1960: 1–20). Washington had no doubt that it was a 'rising empire'.

In 1787, representatives from the thirteen states met in Philadelphia to write a constitution, one that, among other things, created a strong presidency which could protect them in international economic struggles. Those struggles had not only exploited the weaker Americans, but easily turned into murderous wars. The Constitution appeared just in time. The French Revolution erupted in 1789, then in 1793–4 exploded into a wide-ranging conflict between France and Great Britain. Presidents Washington and John Adams deftly manoeuvred throughout the 1790s to protect US trade and prevent the Americans from being sucked into the European killing fields.

During these years a golden rule of US diplomacy became fixed in American minds: never tie up the country in alliances, especially with stronger European powers who could dictate terms. Instead, keep your complete freedom of action so you can seize all opportunities for expanding the nation's territory and providing security. Washington uttered a classic definition of this principle in his famous 'Farewell Address' of 1796: 'The great rule of conduct for us, in regard to foreign nations, is in extending our commercial relations to have with them as little *political* connection as possible.' When he became President in 1801, Jefferson provided an equally famous pronouncement in his First Inaugural Address: 'Peace, commerce, and honest friendship with all nations, entangling alliances with none' (Gardner et al. 1976: i. 56–65). If only Americans could maintain freedom of action, Jefferson concluded, there were few limits to their empire. '[I]t is impossible not to look forward to distant times, when our rapid multiplication will expand itself beyond [present] limits, and cover the whole northern, if not the southern continent,' he wrote a friend in 1801, 'with a people speaking the same language, governed in similar forms, and by similar laws' (Jefferson 1903: x. 296).

Jefferson and his fellow Americans, obviously, did not think small. But the grave dangers inherent in building empires nearly overwhelmed the Virginian at the beginning of his presidency. In 1801, France's ruler, Napoleon Bonaparte, was pushing Spain out of New Orleans and the vast Spanish holdings west of the Mississippi River. Napoleon intended to create a New World empire for France which would dwarf all others. Jefferson and Secretary of State James Madison immediately saw that by controlling the port of New Orleans, Napoleon could dominate access to the Mississippi River, which drained the port.

Madison quickly identified the grave danger to the American empire. Perhaps the most influential member of the 1787 Constitutional Convention, he had constantly argued that Americans needed ever more territory because they produced so many children. Madison accurately did the arithmetic for his American multiplication table, as it became known (note Jefferson's use of 'multiplication' above). He concluded that the US population was actually doubling every 21–22 years. These families of six to twelve, and more, could not be allowed to overcrowd and corrupt eastern cities. They had to be encouraged to find their own space and income for their families in the west. Once in the west (or, as it is now known, the Midwest), these families would depend on the magnificent river system linked to the Mississippi. If Napoleon held New Orleans and, consequently, controlled the Mississippi, it would be only a matter of time before those thousands of American settlers might have to become citizens of Napoleon's French empire.

Jefferson and Madison exerted intense diplomatic pressure on the French. They even mobilized the small US Army for a possible attack on New Orleans itself. Faced with Jefferson's growing opposition, Napoleon decided his better opportunity lay in reopening war against the British and attempting to conquer much of

Europe. He consequently stunned Jefferson by offering in early 1803 to sell for $15 million not only New Orleans, but all of the former Spanish empire which reached from the Mississippi to the Rocky Mountains—and possibly beyond, although few at the time actually knew what lay in the Rockies and beyond. Americans suddenly more than doubled their territory, drove out the French, established complete control over the Mississippi, and gained their first vague claims to lands bordering the Pacific Ocean.

Now Jefferson confronted the central problem which would haunt US leaders from 1787 until the early twenty-first century, and no doubt long thereafter. Having obtained a territory which, he told a friend, would become an 'empire of liberty' for untold generations of Americans, how could the President maintain order and safely govern such a huge, distant holding (Ferguson 2004: ii. 30–7)? New Orleans, for example, held criminals and others who had fled from the United States. They wanted no part of a US-controlled government. In 1776, Jefferson's Declaration of Independence had trumpeted the belief that people held 'inalienable rights'. In late 1803 as he had to deal with Louisiana, however, he ditched that belief. The President set up military control, not a democratic system, over New Orleans and the surrounding territory.

Jefferson believed in democracy, but he did not believe that all people could be trusted to make democracy work properly. Democracy, he knew, was not merely casting a vote. It required, among other things, a fair code of laws, the people's faith that their economic system properly functioned, and the settlers' allegiance to the central and state governments which made all this work.

Louisiana was thus made a part of the growing American empire, if not immediately given a democratic system. Then another severe danger loomed. As Britain and France again went to war after 1803, a series of crises between London and Washington on the high seas and along the US–Canadian border finally exploded into war in 1812.

Madison, now the President, planned not only to stop the British mistreatment of American ships and commerce. He also ordered the invasion of Canada in the hope of expanding US landed empire northward.

Many Canadians, however, had left the United States in the 1770s because they preferred living under London's rule. They fought back, virtually wiping out the US invaders. In 1814, British forces invaded and burned down Washington, DC. James and Dolly Madison fled in such a hurry that they left plates and utensils set for dinner on the Executive Mansion's dining table. A potential catastrophe was avoided only by several US naval victories, skilful American diplomacy at the peace negotiations in late 1814, and—especially—British pre-occupation in the last months of their victory in Europe over Napoleon.

By 1815, with some twenty years of European wars finally ended, Americans seized the opportunities to expand their growing trade with now-peaceful Europe and also Latin American nations which were declaring their own independence of European colonialism. In 1823, Madison's successor, President James Monroe, declared that henceforth the United States would not tolerate any attempt by Europeans to restore their hold on these New World nations. This Monroe Doctrine was historic not because Americans had the military needed to keep Europeans away from the Americas. Such power would not appear until the 1890s. The Doctrine was a turning point because it announced the US belief that henceforth the Old World should no longer attempt to dominate the New. Three hundred years of European colonialism in the western hemisphere were over.

Or, to look at Monroe's announcement from another perspective (as many Europeans and Latin Americans certainly did), it was a declaration that since the United States was the most powerful of New World nations, its people would hereafter have the dominant voice in defining the western hemisphere's affairs. Monroe and his Secretary of State, John Quincy Adams, had already demonstrated this dominance. Adams is ranked as the greatest Secretary of State in American history, a ranking due in large part to his shrewd negotiations with a declining Spain between 1819 and 1821. Adams talked the Spanish into selling Florida (where many Americans had already settled) and giving the United States Spain's claims on the Pacific coast. Known as the Continental Treaty, Adams's brilliance provided, finally, the formal, internationally recognized claim of Americans to that coast.

Adams barely missed taking Texas from Spain as well. But the American multiplication table took care of that. By the 1830s, Mexico (which then included the present state of Texas) had become independent of Spanish rule. Thousands of Americans moved into the weakly governed Texas region. Mexico had prohibited slavery, but slaveholders from US Southern states easily moved west to establish Texan plantations. When Mexican officials tried to reassert their authority (and anti-slave laws), the new settlers fought back. Despite having 187 settlers wiped out at the battle of the Alamo, the rebels won a series of battles and established an independent country in 1836.

In 1845, newly elected President James K. Polk, a Tennessee slaveholder, worked out a deal in Congress to annex the region. Polk then used a dispute with Mexico over Texas's southern boundary as an excuse to declare war, invade Mexico itself, and demand what he most wanted: the Mexican northern regions, an area now including the states of California, Arizona, New Mexico, Nevada, and Utah. Polk, in other words, launched a war of aggression. The conflict dragged on through 1847 as Mexico refused to surrender. Worst of all, the seemingly never-ending conflict ripped open a debate in Washington. That debate raged around a central question: whether slaveholders should be allowed to take their human property into the newly seized territory.

The seemingly inevitable (even in some minds, apparently blessed-by-God) rise of the United States to world power had become intimately tied to the question of whether this success story required the continual expansion of slavery as well. It was the slaveholders, after all, who exported an ever increasing amount of cotton and tobacco, which enriched the US economy. Congressional compromises in 1850 and 1854 tried to quiet the question by allowing the new states to decide on their own whether to be free or slave.

At first glance, these compromises seemed to be the answer. Indeed, giving the people at the grass roots the power to make such fundamental decisions (that is, by exercising their democratic rights) seemed happily American. But in the 1850s an ever larger number of those Americans violently disagreed with such a grass-roots, democratic solution. Living largely in the northeast and Midwest, they believed it was evil to expand slavery, regardless of how it might be justified. Northern, non-slaveholding farmers especially thought it evil if they lost the chance to buy and exploit good western soil simply because slaveholders were protected by state law as they snapped up the land.

The slaveholders saw it quite differently. Correctly figuring that their multiplication table was not multiplying as rapidly as the North's, southerners believed it was only a matter of time until they would be outnumbered—and thus outvoted in Congress whenever issues involving slavery arose. They also needed new land to replace the soil which cotton and tobacco growing depleted. Southerners thus demanded the annexation of possible slave lands to the south, particularly Cuba (where Spain had installed a vicious slave system for the sugar industry) and Central America.

At this point, Abraham Lincoln entered American history. By 1860 the 51-year-old Illinois politician was a leading figure in the new Republican Party. The Republicans had been founded in 1854–5 to oppose the expansion of slavery. Lincoln was direct in declaring he would not interfere in states where it already existed. Given their dependence on continued expansion into Latin America, however, southerners bitterly condemned his and the Republicans' position of no more slave expansion. When Lincoln won the presidency in 1860, the slaveholding states prepared to leave the Union. A last-minute compromise tried to avert civil war. One part of the deal attempted to pull the southerners back in by guaranteeing federal protection for slavery south of the Kentucky–Missouri boundary lines. Lincoln rightly understood that this provision opened the way for seizing and extending American slavery into areas as far

south as Cuba and other Caribbean nations. He rejected the compromise. And so the killing began.

Lincoln became the first President to say no to the continued expansion of Washington's and Jefferson's landed empire. Throughout the 1830s to 1850s, Americans liked to believe this expansion was part of what they termed manifest destiny: an expansion, that is, watched over by a God which blessed the spread of American democracy and capitalism. By 1864–early 1865, however, after three years of terrible war, Lincoln was questioning why this God, claimed as the President noted by both North and South, would allow the nation to suffer such horrible bloodshed.

After his assassination in April 1865, and as the war finally ended, few of his fellow Americans picked up Lincoln's tortured, fundamental question: if the remarkable US expansionism of both territory and a democratic system was manifest destiny, why did it climax in the Civil War?

KEY POINTS

❑ Driven by their quests for both more territory for their multiplying families and wealth and security for themselves, Americans set out after their War for Independence to establish a continental empire.

❑ Jefferson called this an 'empire for liberty', but he carefully did not give democratic rights to the freshly acquired New Orleans region, and by the early nineteenth century the United States had become part of an empire containing human slavery.

❑ Lincoln determined to stop the territorial expansion of this slavery and thus helped bring about the Civil War.

From old empire to new empire, 1865–1913

The North's victors had happier subjects to think about after 1865. When the southerners left Washington in 1861, the northerners who now controlled Congress quickly passed a series of laws which created a foundation for the American industrial and financial complexes that soon dominated world affairs. The legislation

included, for example, a much higher tariff to protect northern producers against cheap European goods. Such a tariff had long been opposed by southerners, whose plantation owners wanted access to the cheapest (that is, British) industrial products. Now protected by the ever rising tariff, northern steel makers such as Andrew Carnegie joined the creators of other new industries, such as John D. Rockefeller's Standard Oil Company, to build an industrial complex which became the world's most productive by 1900. A new, overseas economic empire was being developed by Americans.

Landed expansion did continue. In 1867, Alaska was bought for $7.5 million from Russia. By 1875, trade deals were made with Hawaii, deals which led some twenty-three years later to the annexation of those islands. But this post-1865 landed expansion was radically different from the pre-1860 expansionism. The earlier expansion was one of settlement across adjoining territory. When native Indian tribes occupied those lands, or at times tried to fight back against the white settlements, the Indians were killed or forced to live on reservations. The new, post-1865 expansion, however, was not the movement of settlers across the land, but of traders and financers across the oceans. Americans had once viewed these oceans as great walls which helped protect them against foreign invasion. They now viewed them as great highways on which they could ship ever larger amounts of their farm and industrial goods to foreign markets.

Americans continued to follow the advice of Washington and Jefferson not to form any overseas political alliances. The resulting freedom of action allowed the United States to stay out of squabbles in Europe and Asia, while selling goods to all sides. It also led newly wealthy American families to marry their daughters and sons to European, especially British, aristocratic families. The Europeans thus obtained American money, the Americans obtained European class. These links even helped determine which side Americans would favour, and finance, in later wars.

Fuelled by the industrial revolution of the late nineteenth century, which produced the first telephones, automobiles, aeroplanes, and steel complexes as well as the transatlantic marriages, US foreign policy's focus moved from the North American continent to the markets of Europe, Latin America, and Asia. This was nothing less than a 'new empire', as one influential observer termed it at the time (Adams 1902). In this new empire, landed expansion aimed primarily not to find new areas for Americans to settle. It instead intended to develop naval bases, an isthmian canal in Central America, and coaling stations to protect and accelerate US overseas trade.

In 1874, the United States also embarked on this new era when, for the first time, it began consistently to sell more goods overseas than it bought. (This favourable balance of trade lasted more than seventy-five years until the expenses of the Cold War created steady deficit trade balances in the 1960s and after.) US international commerce generated such great profits that New York City was becoming a world financial centre. By 1904–5, some of the city's financiers even helped determine the outcome of the Russian–Japanese War by providing vast sums of money to help Japan—and thus to oppose the Russians, who were both clashing with US economic interests in Asia and deeply angering many Americans by conducting bloody campaigns against Russian Jews.

The economic foundation for this new empire was thus laid in the 1860 to 1890s era. The new empire's political structure strikingly appeared on this foundation between the 1890s and 1913. In 1895, Cubans rebelled against their Spanish rulers. Some $50 million of US investments in Cuba were endangered in the conflict. In April 1898, President William McKinley, a Republican, decided he had to go to war against Spain. Especially important in his thinking was a fear that the Cuban revolutionaries were winning their rebellion against Spain and, if triumphant, might threaten US property while ignoring American interests.

McKinley thus moved in the War of 1898 to drive Spain out of Cuba and, as well, to ensure that the Cuban revolutionaries would not control their country. As Jefferson had severe doubts about allowing democracy in New Orleans during 1803, so McKinley doubted that democracy was best for American interests in Cuba in 1898. In what Secretary of State John Hay called 'a splendid little war', US forces defeated Spain in less than three months. Cuba and Puerto Rico were taken from Spain, along with the Philippine Islands in the southwest Pacific. The Philippines were a prize McKinley and Hay wanted because control of the Filipino ports for the US fleet would suddenly make the United States a force in Asia and its vast markets. McKinley also annexed the Hawaiian Islands in 1898, thus setting up another link between Americans and Pacific markets. Cuba finally received what was termed independence, but Americans controlled the country and took over a potentially superb naval base at Guantánamo.

In 1899–1900 Hay issued two historic *open door* notes which defined the main principles for the new empire: China (then under attack by European and Japanese colonial powers) must remain whole, united, and under Chinese control, Hay proclaimed, so the entire country would be open to US trade and missionaries. His open door notes opposed colonialism and vigorously supported open foreign markets (in which the new American economic dominance could compete successfully against anyone). These two principles dominated US foreign policy into the twenty-first century.

In 1903, President Theodore Roosevelt helped Panamanians revolt successfully against Colombia, then seized a 10-mile-wide area through Panama. He began building an isthmian canal, which opened in 1914. Given its economic power and great battleship fleet (now one of the world's four largest), the United States could even act as a New World policeman. Indeed, Roosevelt actually announced in 1904–5 with his own corollary to the Monroe Doctrine that Americans would be the region's cop on the beat. The irrepressible TR, moreover, won the Nobel Peace Prize for mediating in

> **KEY POINTS**
>
> ❑ The reunification of the country after the Civil War, and the industrial revolution which followed, turned the United States into the world's leading economic power by the early twentieth century.
>
> ❑ McKinley, Hay, and Roosevelt used that power to build both a great battleship fleet, which was the beginning of the modern US Navy that later dominated twentieth-century waterways, and the Panama Canal, which linked two of those great oceans.
>
> ❑ The objectives of the new empire after 1865 were the taking of strategic naval bases in the Caribbean and Pacific, while trying to ensure that such potentially great world markets as China, North Africa, and Latin America would not be colonized by Europeans or Japanese, but remain open to US goods.

1905 a settlement between Russia and Japan after their war. The United States had become a major international power.

Wilson's empire of ideology—and the bitter reaction, 1913–33

In 1917 the United States finally dropped its long-held refusal to become involved in European affairs. It joined the British and French in their war against Germany and Austro-Hungary. By this time, the world was not only gripped by war but by massive class revolution in such vital areas as Russia and China. President Woodrow Wilson tried to set out plans to deal with both the world war and the spreading revolutions. He and his allies won the conflict. But they could not agree on peace terms or stop the revolutions. During the 1920s Americans tried to build the foundations for peace, especially through their economic power. In 1929 that power collapsed in an economic panic which dragged down much of the world and helped create the Japanese and German militarism that took the world into another, much greater, world war.

The first great era of *globalization* (that is, the ever closer linking of the world's peoples through economic ties and technology) developed between the 1860s and 1914. Faster, oil-driven ships, then primitive aeroplanes, automobiles, and global telegraph lines shortened time and distance. By 1910, widely read authors predicted that because peoples were becoming so closely linked, major international wars were impossible.

In the summer of 1914 that conflict nevertheless began. The First World War broke out because of misunderstandings and miscalculations between the Allies (British, French, Russians, and Japanese) and the Central Powers (led by Germany and Austro-Hungary). Both sides had believed that civilized nations, like themselves, would never allow the mass killing now possible with modern arms in a full-scale war, so they felt safe in taking chances. Within months, thousands of lives were being snuffed out in a single day on the blood-drenched fields of France and Russia. Great Britain, France, and Germany, three of the world's wealthiest nations, suddenly had to mobilize such immense forces that, to their surprise, they were going bankrupt.

This brought the United States into the picture. President Woodrow Wilson (1913–21) had demanded at the war's beginning that Americans remain neutral in thought and action. Meanwhile those Americans could profit by selling food and war supplies to both sides. As bankruptcy threatened the belligerents, however, they begged Wilson for help. He initially resisted. The President rightly feared becoming too closely tied economically to either side. But for three centuries Europe had been the most important market for Americans. As that market began to be unable to pay cash for US goods, and as economic depression threatened the United States, Wilson changed his mind. He allowed his nation's bankers to offer both sides dollars and credits so they could continue to purchase American products. The Allies, helped by long-time British ties to New York and Boston banks, borrowed $2.5 billion between 1915 and 1917. This was ten times the amount Germany and Austro-Hungary could obtain.

Wilson's decision to loan vast amounts of money was legal, but it turned out not to be neutral. As ships carrying US goods headed for British and French ports, Germany's submarines sank increasing numbers of those vessels and claimed hundreds of American lives. Wilson recognized the historic right of the British surface fleet, which controlled the oceans, to stop goods headed for the Central Powers. But no firm international law dealt with Germany's new weapon, underwater U-boats, so the President insisted that the submarines' attacks on US ships cease. The Germans complied until late 1916. In January 1917, however, they determined the American shipments to the Allies had to be stopped. The submarines again attacked US ships. In April 1917, the United States declared war on the Central Powers.

Americans now not only found themselves immersed in the bloodiest conflict in human history, but in a world racked by revolution. The twentieth century was to be shaped by these revolutions. Americans grew to hate and oppose them. The first major upheaval had occurred in Mexico after 1911. As that outbreak threatened US lives

and interests (especially oil holdings), Wilson several times sent in troops. Instead of taming the revolution, however, the President's military intervention helped make Mexicans both more radical and more anti-United States. At the same time, the great Chinese Revolution erupted. Preoccupied with Mexico, Europe, and the Caribbean, where outbreaks also threatened, Wilson could do relatively little in China.

When, however, the Russian Revolution of February–March 1917 exploded, the world changed for everyone, including Americans. Devastated and impoverished by fighting against Germany, the Russians overthrew their tsarist rulers, then rapidly moved to the left until in November 1917 a communist regime led by Vladimir Lenin seized power. The Soviet leader moved to place private property under state control and to close religious sanctuaries—two acts which shocked the West. Lenin further stunned the Allies by pulling bankrupt Russia out of the fight against Germany. The new leader in Moscow also angered Wilson by threatening to spread communism throughout Europe. It was not an empty threat. The Austro-Hungarian Empire was fragmenting. Peoples in Africa and Asia ruled by British and French colonial officers began to demand independence. The entire globe seemed to be flying apart in 1917–18 and offering communism golden opportunities.

Wilson moved to control the revolutionary outbreak by demanding that the new nations be governed by American-style democracy, not by Leninist-style communism. In doing so, the President set in motion the US challenge to Russian communism—a challenge which characterized American–Russian relations for nearly the whole of the twentieth century. He was determined, as he said, 'to make the world safe for democracy'. Wilson vowed to end, 'once and forever', the centuries-long 'old order' of international affairs which had tried to maintain peace by what 'we used to call the "balance of power"—a thing in which the balance was determined by the sword' (Gardner 1984: 2).

Peaceful voting, the American way, was to replace bloody swords as the method for making changes. Europeans, including the British and French with whom Wilson fought, had little use for his version of democracy. They pointedly noted that in destroying or isolating the Indian tribes and Mexicans who had once populated large parts of North America, US officials had waged war—not conducted elections to see how the Indians and Mexicans might vote. Nor had the North decided the results of the Civil War by holding democratic voting.

The British and French knew, moreover, that elections in Africa and Asia would quickly end their own colonial empires. On this question, Wilson seemed at times to agree with his allies. A Virginia-born racist who as President presided over the segregation of African Americans in Washington, DC, Wilson doubted that many Asians and Africans, or some Latin Americans, could be trusted with democracy. The President even successfully opposed a Japanese effort to write a clause in the post-war peace agreements which would support racial equality.

Wilson, it became apparent, had never thought through these dangerously complex problems in regard to democracy. He and his associates in London and Paris won the First World War, but they divided and lost the peace. They could not figure out how to deal with (that is, remove) Lenin. In 1918, Wilson had actually joined with the British and French in sending military forces into Russia to try to weaken the communist regime. The intervention backfired as Russians supported Lenin's government against the foreign invasion.

The President's dreams of democracy also turned to nightmares at home. As the leader of the Democratic Party he made pivotal mistakes in 1918 which helped lead to a Republican victory in that year's congressional elections. Republican leaders had grave doubts about Wilson's peace plans, above all his famous proposal to create an international organization, the League of Nations, to maintain the post-war peace. The President, of course, saw the United States, under his leadership, as shaping and leading the new League. For nearly 120 years, however, Americans had steadfastly followed the advice of Washington and Jefferson to stay clear of international alliances. As they prepared to debate the post-war treaty and the League in 1919, Republican leaders in the US Senate decided to oppose Wilson's plans. The President fought back by beginning a gruelling speaking trip across the country. In Colorado, he was stricken by a massive stroke which made it nearly impossible for him to speak. The post-war debate was over. The United States would not join the League of Nations. Wilson's vague, often contradictory, plans for making the world safe for democracy disappeared—at least for a while.

Americans instead set out on their own to help economically reconstruct the war-torn world. In this way they could both make some money and help insure those areas against the seductive promises of communism. Their booming industrial, banking, and farm complexes made impossible any isolation from world markets.

When a military spending race to build battleships threatened to break out after the war, US officials called a conference in Washington for 1921–2. With imagination and bravado, Secretary of State Charles Evans Hughes worked out a Five-Power Treaty with the British, French, Italians, and Japanese (the Russians of course were not invited), which sharply limited naval spending and even forced the signatories to destroy some of their ships. Hughes also seized the opportunity to work out a Nine-Power Treaty. This pact set out a peaceful approach to handling revolutionary China, including an agreed-upon open door approach to the vast Chinese markets. The 1921–2 Washington Conference was the greatest American diplomatic success in the era between the two world wars.

US officials also enjoyed success in helping rebuild Europe. In 1923 the German economy had begun to spin out of control. The war had devastated it, and the Paris Peace Conference in 1919 had then forced Germany to pay billions of dollars in penalties for the war's destruction of property. France tried to grasp the opportunity by seizing territory long disputed between itself and the Germans. A crisis loomed, not least for US bankers and exporters. They long had understood that Germany was the most powerful industrial nation on the continent. If Germans were not economically healthy then all of Europe could sink into depression. The United States consequently quickly convened a conference in 1924 to deal with the crisis. Led by US Vice-President Charles Dawes, a former Chicago banker, the conference worked out a solution. The so-called Dawes Plan proposed massive private loans from US banks to rebuild the German economy. France retreated from its land grab. Europe seemed finally to be at peace and safe from communist infections.

But appearances were deceiving. The economic centre of Europe, Germany, and the most powerful nation in Asia, Japan, heavily depended on US banks for needed capital. By 1928 and early 1929, however, the American economy began to stumble. The immediate cause was the New York Stock Exchange. Its stock prices had ridden the booming economy upward until in 1929 over-speculation and corrupt investment practices set in motion a sharp downward spiral of those prices. Capital began to disappear. Between October 1929 and mid-1931, the New York Exchange's stocks suffered the single greatest loss in history to that time. Some suddenly bankrupt investors chose to commit suicide. As the economy continued to sink in 1932–3, unemployment doubled during those years to an unheard-of number of 25 million. Little help came from most states or the federal government.

The two most important regional powers, Germany in Europe and Japan in Asia, had been supported (as in the 1924 Dawes Plan, noted above) by the dollar. When that currency began to weaken after 1929, so did German and Japanese ties to the United States. The civilian-based governments in Germany and Japan declined along with their economies. A militarily dominated regime emerged in Japan and then, in 1933, Adolf Hitler's Nazi Party seized power in Germany.

The meaning of all this for US foreign policy was immediate—and catastrophic. The United States was unable either to help Tokyo or stop its military plans. The Japanese invaded Manchuria in September 1931.

US President Herbert Hoover (1929–33) refused to try to stop Japan. He was frightened of anything that might threaten the long US–Japanese friendship. He also preferred that if someone were going to exploit weakened, revolution-racked China, it would be Japan and not the neighbouring Soviet Union.

Moments occur in US history when events, usually catastrophic events such as the Civil War, the 1929–33 crash, or the 2001 attacks on New York City and Washington, should force Americans to rethink a world they thought they knew well. Such rethinking is incredibly difficult, especially if the years before the catastrophic events were marked by American successes, and in every instance (before the Civil War, the 1929–33 crash, or the 2001 attacks) that had indeed been the case. In 1861 Abraham Lincoln provided the rethinking by stopping centuries-long American expansion in order to kill the institution of slavery.

After the 1929 crash, no Lincoln appeared. President Herbert Hoover had considerable international experience, both as a successful engineer in Asian mining ventures and as a close adviser of Woodrow Wilson's between 1917 and 1920. But he was unable to deal with the failures of the nation's economic system. He largely stood immobile as prices collapsed and unemployment soared. Nor could Hoover fundamentally reconsider the foreign policies of the 1920s, which had rested on US economic power and cooperation with Japan and Germany. And so, along with the British and French, he did little as Japan invaded Manchuria and China and as Germany slid downwards into Nazism.

KEY POINTS

❑ The globe was shaken after 1911 not only by the First World War (1914-18), but by revolutions which struck, among others, Mexico, China, and Russia.

❑ The United States was swept into the First World War by its historic ties to the British and French, and by President Wilson's hope that he could help create a world safe for democracy, not revolution.

❑ Wilson and other victors failed to create this world at the Paris Peace Conference (1919), and Americans refused to join the League of Nations.

❑ Americans thus retained their freedom of action, but because of economic and security interests, they had to take the lead with the Washington Conference (1921-2) to limit military spending, and with the Dawes Plan (1924) to rebuild Germany.

❑ The American economic system, however, sank into depression between 1929 and 1933 to help trigger a global depression that created conditions for the emergence of a militarist regime in Japan and the Nazis in Germany.

The road from economic depression to the Cold War, 1933–45

In 1933, Hoover was replaced in the White House by New York Governor Franklin D. Roosevelt (1933–45). The new President spent his first six years in office trying to end the economic depression at home. Conditions seemed slowly to improve, but for some months in 1938 the nation suddenly suffered one of the steepest economic downturns in its history. Within a year, however, Roosevelt's greatest concern was not the economy but the outbreak of the Second World War in Europe. Indeed, new military spending after 1939 finally lifted the nation out of the depression. In late 1941, the United States entered the conflict. The President spent the next four years not only winning the war, but trying, with much less success, to work out a post-war peace with the other two victors, Great Britain and the Soviet Union.

Roosevelt, much like Hoover, was an internationalist, an Assistant Secretary of the Navy under Woodrow Wilson, and a young vice-presidential nominee for the Democrats in the 1920 election who had strongly favoured joining the League of Nations. In dealing with the 1930s economic crisis, however, FDR moved away from internationalism. His domestic, so-called New Deal, programmes tried to clean up and regulate the stock markets and banking system, while providing direct, immediate federal governmental help to out-of-work Americans. By 1936, the nation's economy had slightly improved, employment rose, and Roosevelt won a second term.

But he had accomplished this improvement at home with little rethinking of American foreign policy. Roosevelt believed he could best raise prices in the United States only through internal manipulation, not difficult international negotiations with trading partners. The President's isolationist (that is, having maximum freedom of action, free of overseas political and also many economic commitments) foreign policies were driven in part by his desire to have an unrestrained hand to revive, quickly, his nation's economy. His policies were also shaped by an isolationist Congress which wanted to concentrate on the domestic crises, not foreign developments. The desire of Americans to stay free of overseas commitments intensified as Hitler's Germany began a series of military aggressions which seized Austria and parts of Czechoslovakia in 1937–8, and as Japanese militarists renewed their invasion of China in 1937.

In 1938, the British and French weakly went along in an international conference at Munich to allow Hitler to seize parts of Czechoslovakia which contained large German populations. Roosevelt agreed with this policy of appeasement (allowing an aggressor—Hitler, in this case—to take territory in the hope it would satisfy the aggressor and bring about long-term peace). Hitler, however, absorbed the slice of territory granted by the British and French, then, to the shock of Americans and the rest of the world, also seized the remainder of defenceless Czechoslovakia. Appeasement and 'Munich' became dirty words in US and international politics, then and after 1945 (Record 2006: 8).

By the summer of 1939, Hitler was prepared to attack other parts of Europe. But he first wanted to neutralize his most important military opponent, the Soviet Union headed by dictator Josef Stalin. Throughout the 1933 to 1935 era, Stalin, deeply frightened of Hitler, had asked Roosevelt, along with British and French leaders, to cooperate in stopping the German aggression. The Westerners were not prepared to do so. They also doubted whether it was possible to work with a communist such as Stalin. In August 1939 the Soviet dictator stunned the West by making a deal with Hitler to stand aside while Germany attacked Poland. The Soviets and Germans then divided Poland between themselves. On the first day of September 1939, the Second World War began with that German invasion. The British and French declared war against Hitler, but the Americans remained neutral in the hope that they could somehow avoid the spreading flames.

By mid-1940 France and most of continental Europe had fallen under Nazi control. President Roosevelt, however, made only measured responses. London and other major British cities were being struck every night by Nazi planes in the so-called Battle of Britain, while a German invasion seemed imminent. The new

British leader, Winston Churchill, begged Roosevelt for help. The President responded with large amounts of economic assistance. Equally important, he secretly ordered US warships to track and if necessary sink any German submarines which threatened to interrupt the growing US trade with Great Britain.

But the greatest help for the British came, in a stunning surprise, from the Soviet Union. Hitler was growing tired of dividing up parts of Europe with Stalin and hoped to obtain badly needed petroleum by seizing Soviet oil fields. In June 1941 the Nazi leader launched the largest military operation in history with his invasion of the Soviet Union. His armies soon approached the Russian capital, Moscow, and the Soviet oil fields. Despite encountering considerable opposition, especially in Congress, Roosevelt quickly began sending large amounts of war matériel to Russia. FDR and Churchill agreed that the Soviet dictator was not the person they would most like to work with, but Stalin was certainly to be favoured over Hitler. By autumn 1941, several encounters between American ships and Nazi submarines indicated it was only a matter of time before the United States would go to war, much as it had in 1917.

Instead, war surprisingly struck Americans from the opposite direction. Throughout 1940, Japan had moved into China and South-East Asia in a quest for regional domination and, especially, badly needed oil fields. By mid-1941, as the Japanese seized control of French Indochina, US officials responded by shutting off American petroleum shipments to Japan. In a series of talks, no settlement could be reached between Japan and the United States in regard to the oil or—more importantly—China. Roosevelt refused to recognize Japanese domination of parts of China. Such recognition would have surrendered the historic US open door policy in that country.

Japan's military-dominated government secretly decided to launch a surprise attack on the American naval base in Hawaii, Pearl Harbor. Japanese officials hoped to destroy enough of the US Pacific fleet so Roosevelt, also faced with possible war in Europe, would be willing to meet most of Tokyo's demands in Asia. Japanese planes devastated Pearl Harbor on Sunday 7 December 1941. The attack stunned Americans, but instead of considering a settlement, as the Japanese hoped, Congress, at Roosevelt's request, declared war against Japan. On 11 December, Japan's sometime partner, Hitler, declared war against the United States.

The early months of American involvement in the Second World War were among the darkest in the nation's history. Japan seized a number of US bases in the Pacific, including the strategic Philippines, and threatened to invade Australia. US naval victories, especially in mid-1942 at the Midway Islands, finally began to turn the tide of battle. In Europe, Hitler's offensive continued until mid-1943 when Stalin's armies were able to stop the Nazi advance. Fighting the Second World War, the Soviets paid a horrible price of at least 25 to 30 million dead. Throughout 1942–3, Stalin desperately asked Roosevelt and Stalin to help by opening a second military front in France, and thus force Hitler to shift troops away from Russia.

The US and British leaders refused to open that second front until June 1944. Their refusal came in part from FDR's belief that Anglo-American armies were not prepared for such an invasion of France, and in part from Churchill's determination to fight first in the Mediterranean, where the British Empire had major interests. Thus US and British forces invaded not France, but German-controlled North Africa in 1942 and then Italy. Stalin grew suspicious that his allies were hoping his armies would exhaust themselves fighting Hitler and thus not be in a position to threaten US and British plans after the war.

The United States was beyond question becoming the world's greatest power. British, Russian, Japanese, and western European industries and cities were largely reduced to smoking ashes between 1941 and 1945. But untouched US industrial production shot up by 90 per cent. Americans came to understand what this meant: they no longer needed to fear becoming politically involved with the world because now, they believed, they finally held the raw power to control and run that world. For example, in 1942, when Roosevelt announced a new United Nations organization which was to replace the failed League of Nations, most Americans immediately accepted the UN because they believed they (unlike Wilson with the League in 1919) would be able to control it. (And they did—until the 1960s and 1970s when membership in the UN of many new African and Asian nations threatened US control. Then Americans cooled considerably toward the UN.)

A consensus emerged among US leaders during the conflict that they would hold post-war power. But for what purpose? What kind of world should Americans try to construct? Here Roosevelt and Truman encountered the haunting problem which, finally, doomed Americans' post-war hopes and swept the nation into a forty-five-year Cold War—and beyond.

On the one hand, they were determined to construct an open, integrated post-war world in which trade could move freely. War-torn nations were to be rebuilt rapidly. There was to be no more high-tariff and other forms of economic warfare which had destroyed international relations in the 1930s and climaxed in the Second World War. Roosevelt first moved against his own ally, Great Britain. The British had tried to preserve their empire by setting up trade walls around it during the 1930s. In return for providing all-important US military help in 1941, Roosevelt asked Churchill to promise that after the war the British would remove those walls (and allow Americans, for example, to trade freely with such parts of the British Empire as India, Canada, and South Africa). The British leader complained bitterly, and tried to add reservations, but he had no choice except to give in to the Americans if he expected US help.

Washington officials followed this up in 1944 by establishing the economic side of the new United Nations: the World Bank and International Monetary Fund (IMF). The World Bank was to provide international cooperation in investment to rebuild the post-war world. The IMF was to create international financial cooperation so the deadly economic wars between nations which had marked the 1930s could not be repeated. Because Americans controlled half the world's wealth in 1945, there was no doubt who would provide the financial resources for these two institutions—and thus control the institutions themselves.

Ominously, the Soviet Union refused to join the World Bank or the IMF in 1945–6. Stalin refused to allow any international organization controlled by the United States to examine Soviet records or try to shape the Russian economy. The dictator's refusal to cooperate with the US policy of an open economic world was also linked to the failure of the Russians and Americans to agree on how the post-war world should be rebuilt politically. Through three wartime summit conferences (at Tehran, Iran, in 1943, the Soviet city of Yalta

in February 1945, then Potsdam, Germany, in July 1945), the US, British, and Soviet leaders failed to reach agreement on the crucial European question: how to rebuild a defeated Germany. Roosevelt at first was willing to make the Germans pay by stripping them of all industry (a position Stalin happily agreed with). But FDR then changed his mind when he realized Europe could never be quickly rebuilt and kept open unless its long-time economic power centre, Germany, was rebuilt first. Stalin's armies finally took the decision out of Roosevelt's hands by reaching the German capital of Berlin ahead of US and British forces, and then holding on to eastern Germany. While the leaders debated, the Soviets stripped eastern Germany of all the resources they could ship back to Russia. Germany would remain divided for the next forty-five years.

The German and other central post-war issues had not yet been fully decided on 12 April 1945, when Roosevelt suddenly died of a massive stroke. FDR, however, had worked hard to stay on good terms with Stalin (recall his sending of massive US aid to the Soviets in mid-1941 even before the Americans entered the war), although the relationship was in decline during the months before Roosevelt's death. His successor, Vice-President Harry S. Truman, was a parochial Missouri politician who knew little about foreign policy, nor did FDR ever try to help him understand the deteriorating relationship with the Russians in early 1945.

Understandably highly insecure personally, as well as unprepared, Truman quickly tried to show he was tough by demanding that the Soviets back down from their control of Poland and hold open elections in that country. The new President privately bragged that he had given the Russians 'the straight one-two to the jaw' (Sherwin 1975: 72; Stimson and Bundy 1949: 609). Stalin responded with a one-two of his own, which turned out to be more effective. He pointed out that he did not protest US and British policies in countries close to those two nations' interests (such as Italy, Belgium, France, and Mexico)—so Americans should understand that the Soviets had comparable interests in eastern Europe, through which, after all, the Germans had twice invaded Russia in just twenty-seven years. Stalin determined there would not be a third invasion.

Truman attended his first summit with Churchill and Stalin at Potsdam in July 1945. The President believed he had a secret weapon which would help him pressure Stalin to cooperate on American terms. That weapon, the atomic bomb, was first tested while Truman was in Potsdam. He told Stalin about the successful test. The Soviet leader seemed unimpressed. (He had learned a good deal about the bomb's development from Russian spies.) Despite the President's pressure, the Soviets refused to back down on Germany or eastern Europe.

Stalin did renew his earlier pledge to Roosevelt that the Russians would enter the war against Japan about 8 August. Truman, however, was by now little interested in having the Soviets involved in Japan. The United States dropped the first atomic bomb on Hiroshima on 6 August 1945, instantly killing more than 80,000 Japanese. On 8 August, the Soviets declared war on Japan. The next day the President dropped the second bomb on Nagasaki which quickly killed more than 65,000 people. Within a week, Japan surrendered. Truman believed he had avoided the terrible bloodshed which would have resulted from an invasion of the Japanese home islands. The President rushed occupation teams into Japan so he would not have to share final control of the occupation with either the British or Soviets.

The struggle against Hitler and the Japanese militarists had ended in triumph. But a new war had erupted

---

KEY POINTS

❑ During the 1930s the United States could neither solve its own economic depression nor cooperate with those nations concerned about the rise of Hitler in Germany or militarism in Japan.

❑ When the United States entered the war after being attacked by Japan in 1941, US officials began extensive planning for an open post-war world free of both British colonialism and Soviet occupation.

❑ Neither Roosevelt nor Truman, however, could find the means to force Stalin to retreat from eastern Germany and eastern Europe—two areas the Soviets believed were fundamental for assuring their own security.

---

between the United States and Great Britain, on the one hand, and the Soviets on the other. The conflict was over the question of whether the world was to be open to trade, investment, and cultural influences (which the virtually untouched American society, enriched by the war, could command), or whether strategic areas of the globe, particularly central and eastern Europe, which had recently given birth to two world wars, were to be controlled and closed off by victorious Soviet armies. The Cold War had begun.

Conclusion

In the early 1830s (that is, as Americans were convinced they were manifestly destined to build a North American continental empire), a shrewd French visitor, Alexis de Tocqueville, wrote a two-volume work, *Democracy in America*. It is perhaps the best analysis ever made of the nation's society—and its destiny. Tocqueville predicted that although both peoples were only beginning to be players on the international stage, Americans and Russians were each 'marked out by the will of heaven to sway the destinies of half the globe' (Tocqueville 1948: i. 434). In the 1940s, Tocqueville's prediction of 110 years before seemed to be coming true.

Americans had seldom doubted their own destiny. They began with thirteen colonies on the western rim of the Atlantic Ocean, then, less than eighty years after

achieving independence, spread their system, which their leaders called an 'empire', from the Atlantic to the Pacific. The landed expansion was in part based on, and profited from, the institution of human slavery. In 1861, Lincoln stopped any further landed expansion which might benefit those who owned slaves. The result was the war which took more American lives than any other in the nation's history.

When the Civil War ended with the North's victory, a forcefully reunited nation proved so effective in exploiting and developing the continent that a new empire had to be developed after 1865. It was an empire of global markets, protected by naval bases in such places as Panama and the Philippine Islands, which could absorb the extraordinary production spewing out of American farms and factories. By 1900, the United States had become by many measurements the world's number one producer. Its interests swept it into two world wars. Faced in 1917–20 with a dangerously revolutionary world, Woodrow Wilson tried to organize that world by replacing radical revolution with his determination to 'make the world safe for democracy'. He failed, as did later American leaders who falsely assumed that political institutions arising out of centuries of American and British history could easily be translated into similar institutions in, say, Asia, the Middle East, and Africa, whose history and traditions were vastly different.

Indeed, the American system itself broke down in 1928–9 and helped trigger a global depression which in turn gave birth to military regimes in Japan and Germany. By 1941, Franklin D. Roosevelt was concerned not with expanding democracy but stopping Japanese and German expansion. The United States finally won the Second World War, but only with the help of the British and, especially, Soviets. Of the 13 million Germans who perished in the war, Stalin's armies killed more than 10 million, although at the cost of probably three times

that number of Russian lives. The Soviet dictator determined to hold eastern Europe and part of Germany as a security area for the Soviet Union.

US officials could not accept such results of the war. They believed the world had to be open and developed economically along capitalist lines (thus the creation of the World Bank and International Monetary Fund in 1944–5), while the globe was also being opened, decolonized, and slowly integrated politically (thus the creation of the United Nations between 1942 and 1945). When he issued his prophecy in the 1830s, Tocqueville had noted that although they were each destined to create an empire dominating half the globe, nevertheless the Russian and American 'starting point is different and their courses not the same' (Tocqueville 1948: i. 433–4). The Frenchman was correct. The Americans' view of why they had become the world's greatest power in 1945, and why they now had to fight that Cold War, can only be understood by understanding how they developed their continental empire and then their new empire over the previous 170 years. They were, and continue to be, the products of their own, long history.

? Questions

1. What were the major characteristics of the first American 'empire'?

2. When and why did the first American 'empire' transform into a 'new empire'?

3. Jefferson is famous as a father of American democracy, so why did he deny democracy to the New Orleans region after he bought Louisiana in 1803?

4. Why did American expansion across the continent, which was supposedly blessed by 'manifest destiny', lead to the outbreak of the Civil War?

5. Why do the War of 1898 and its immediate results exemplify a new era, a 'new empire', in American history?

6. In 1918, much of the world (outside the Soviet Union) saw Woodrow Wilson as its greatest hope. Why, then, did Wilson fail to 'make the world safe for democracy' between 1918 and 1920?

7. Why was the US stock market crash of 1929 such a blow to the American foreign policies which had been forged, with considerable success, between 1921 and 1929?

8. With the world facing increased danger during the 1930s from Japanese and German military aggression, why did President Franklin D. Roosevelt follow isolationist foreign policies which offered little resistance to that aggression?

9. What were the major differences between the Soviet Union and the United States which developed when they were allies between 1941 and 1945 and led them into the post-1945 Cold War?

10. Why did the United States follow an 'open door' policy throughout much of its post-1890s foreign relations and, notably, in its planning during the Second World War for the post-war peace?

11. Given their history to 1945 of trying to expand democracy, should Americans make the expansion of democratic institutions throughout the world a central principle of their diplomacy?

» **Further Reading**

Cohen, W. I. (2000), *The American Response to China*, 4th edn (New York: Columbia University Press).

This excellent survey of the entire US–China relationship includes useful reading guides.

Cole, W. (1983), *Roosevelt and the Isolationists, 1932–1945* (Lincoln, Nebr.: University of Nebraska Press).

Cole's volume is the best overall analysis of isolationism in the period and Franklin D. Roosevelt's relationship to it.

Gardner, L. C. (1984), *Safe for Democracy: The Anglo-American Response to Revolution, 1913–1923* (New York: Oxford University Press).

A superb, detailed analysis of Woodrow Wilson's response to the revolutions, this volume also provides important perspective by comparing Wilson's with the British response before, during, and after the First World War.

Hunt, M. H. (1987), *Ideology and American Foreign Policy* (New Haven: Yale University Press).

In a splendid post-1780s overview, Hunt emphasizes the role of race and anti-revolutionary sentiment in the formulation of US foreign policies.

Iriye, A. (1993), *The Globalization of America, 1913–1945* (New York: Cambridge University Press).

A provocative overview, this volume includes most helpful bibliographical references.

LaFeber, W. (1993), *The American Search for Opportunity, 1865–1913* (New York: Cambridge University Press).

An overview emphasizing the American role in stimulating revolution, as well as opposing it, the book also has extensive lists for further reading.

Langley, L. (1990), *America and the Americas: The United States in the Western Hemisphere* (Athens, Ga.: University of Georgia Press).

A valuable survey, with most helpful guides for further reading, this book notes the Latin American developments as well as US policies toward the southern hemisphere.

Perkins, B. (1993), *From Sea to Sea, 1776–1865* (New York: Cambridge University Press).

Written by a leading scholar of the era, this detailed overview has important interpretations as well as select lists of books and articles for further research.

Weinberg, A. K. (1935), *Manifest Destiny* (Baltimore: Johns Hopkins University Press).

A classic work of writing, scholarship, and interpretation, Weinberg's analysis is notably important for its questioning and, at times, its sarcasm.

Wilkins, M. (1970), *The Emergence of Multinational Enterprise: American Business Abroad from the Colonial Era to 1914* (Cambridge, Mass.: Harvard University Press).

This is the pioneering work on US financial expansion overseas and, although it is not identified as such, on the first great age of globalization between 1860 and 1914.

 For a range of additional resources to support your learning visit the Online Resource Centre that accompanies this book at **www.oxfordtextbooks.co.uk/orc/cox_stokes2e/**

4 American foreign policy during the Cold War

Richard Saull

Chapter contents

Introduction

This chapter seeks to provide a theoretically informed overview of American foreign policy during the Cold War. It will cover the main historical developments in US policy: from the breakdown of the wartime alliance with the USSR and the emergence of the US–Soviet diplomatic hostility and geopolitical confrontation through to the spread of the Cold War beyond Europe and US military interventions in the third world, and the US role in the ending of the Cold War. The chapter will discuss these historical developments through drawing on different theoretical explanations of US foreign policy; those that focus on the role of geopolitical, ideational, and/or socio-economic factors. It aims to highlight the duel concerns of US foreign policy—one based on the geopolitical–ideological threat from the USSR and wider communist world, and the other based on the US role in the international capitalist economy and the evolving and sometimes contradictory relationship between these two areas and how they were resolved by US policy makers.

The discussion of American foreign policy during the Cold War has been dominated by three sets of analytical questions: (1) the role of the US in emergence of the Cold War; (2) what factors best account for US foreign policy during the Cold War; and (3) the role of US policy in the collapse of Soviet communism and the end of the Cold War. Within the scholarly literature on US foreign policy two theoretical responses have tended to dominate the discussion of these questions. The first has emphasized the role of material or geopolitical factors in accounting for American foreign policy. Simply put, US policy was concerned with addressing the geopolitical and military threat to its security from the Soviet Union. The second response, whilst recognizing the significance of the geopolitical challenge to American security and international interests, has focused much more on the ideological characteristics of US foreign policy; meaning that it was the communist ideological character of the USSR that was as much of a concern to US policy makers as the geopolitical threat, and, further, the fact that the domestic liberal-democratic characteristics of the US also informed the ends and implementation of foreign policy.

This 'mainstream' debate on American foreign policy during the Cold War has done much to illuminate our understanding of both the Cold War and the character of American foreign policy. However, it rests on a contestable assumption as to what the Cold War was about, namely the post-war bipolar US–Soviet relationship. This—what could be considered as the—conventional account of the Cold War and US foreign policy within it has tended to overlook the socio-economic dimensions of US foreign relations. This refers to the place of economic actors and processes in American foreign policy, as well as the wider concerns—extending beyond the Soviet threat—to include other (communist states) and radical and revolutionary movements that confronted the US after 1945, and which came to inform the decisions and policies of the US foreign policy bureaucracy during the Cold War. Further, the conventional account has not sufficiently addressed the relationship between the US and its Cold War allies—in western Europe in particular—and how these relations contributed to the overall dynamic of the Cold War.

What I intend to do in this chapter is to provide a theoretically informed overview of American foreign policy during the Cold War covering the main historical developments within the evolution of the Cold War. As well as addressing the arguments within the mainstream debate on US foreign policy in the Cold War, I will also engage with a wider academic literature, particularly those scholars who draw on an analytical framework informed by a Marxist understanding of international relations, to provide a historically richer and more theoretically informed survey of American foreign policy during the Cold War.

The rest of the chapter is organized in the following way: first, I will provide a brief overview of the main theoretical frameworks accounting for American foreign policy during the Cold War; secondly, I will move onto a survey of the history of US foreign policy in the Cold War, weighing up the explanations offered by each theoretical framework.

The Cold War and theorizing American foreign policy

Realism

There are two strands to realist explanations of American foreign policy during the Cold War. On the one hand there are those 'Cold War realists' (Kennan 1984; Kissinger 1961, 1994; Lippman 1947; Morgenthau 1951) who sought to account for the emergence of the Cold War and, later, became public critics of US foreign policy during the Cold War and, on the other hand, there are international relations theorists (Mearsheimer 2001; Waltz 1979), who have addressed the bipolar relationship and the US role within it. What links these two sets of scholars is their common concern with what they regard as the shifting geopolitical contest between the US and the USSR for ascendancy over post-war Europe and other strategically important areas (the Middle East and east Asia) after the war, and the way in which concerns centred on geopolitical and military power—security—guided US foreign policy. These scholars, then, have—in different ways—questioned the ideological motivations (of anti-communism and/or the upholding and expansion of liberal-democratic values) on US policy.

Where they differ is in their respective emphasis on US policy in the Cold War. Thus, Mearsheimer and Waltz emphasize the stability of the Cold War encapsulated in Gaddis's (1987) term, the 'long peace', highlighting how US power countered or balanced Soviet power after 1945 and through the mutual deterrence of nuclear weapons reduced the likelihood of geopolitical competition triggering war. In this sense the Cold War was relatively stable because US policy was driven by geopolitical concerns.

This view contrasts with the public criticisms of US foreign policy voiced by Cold War realists, who regarded US foreign policy as too dependent on a militarized form of containment (Kennan 1984) and too influenced by an ideological commitment to spreading liberal democratic (Wilsonian) values in its foreign policy (Morgenthau 1951). The consequence of these failings according to these critics—of not being realist enough—was that the US became involved in areas of the world, such as Vietnam, where it had few if any strategic interest in becoming embroiled in costly wars that did not best serve the national security interests of the US. Consequently, whilst the Cold War realists agreed with the orthodox view on the origins of the Cold War—that the US had no choice but to react to aggressive moves by the USSR in east-central Europe after 1945 with the doctrine of containment—they disagreed with the orthodox claim that Soviet policy was driven by communist–ideological expansion (Feis 1970) rather than traditional Russian great power manoeuvring. The Soviet threat and the key concern of US policy, then, was the Red Army's military presence in east-central Europe (and the wider expansion of Soviet geopolitical power throughout the Cold War) rather than the declared revolutionary aims of Moscow as the centre of the international communist movement.

Ideational approaches

In opposition to realist arguments ideational explanations of American foreign policy during the Cold War (Crockatt 1995; Lebow 1994; Schlesinger, Jr. 1967) dwell on the way in which US foreign policy decision making was to a significant extent conditioned by the prevailing political values and ideological frameworks located within American domestic politics. According to these scholars, the liberal democratic characteristics of the American polity and the way in which American policy makers viewed themselves—what it meant to be an American and what American values were—influenced not only the foreign policy objectives of the United States, but also how those objectives were realized.

Such accounts emphasize the dismay and revulsion of American leaders towards Soviet political practices in east-central Europe after the war and the way in which an ideological commitment to liberal democratic political and economic values conditioned US policies towards western Europe after the war. Some scholars, such as David Campbell (1998), go as far as stressing how US foreign policy in the Cold War and the representation (and manipulation) of a Soviet threat was a key factor in the construction of a post-war American national identity based on the idea of 'freedom' as a uniquely American characteristic in contrast to the 'foreign' and 'hostile' ideas and values of socialism, equality, and collectivism.

In contrast to realism's emphasis on the supposedly impersonal and objective geopolitical interests as the guiding principle informing foreign policy, scholars within the ideational–constructivist school give greater analytical purchase to the way in which a clash of ideological mind-sets and world views between Soviet communism and American liberalism after the war was played out. This was reflected in the manner in which each superpower related to each of the two halves of divided Europe and the nature of the political institutions each sought to establish. Thus, these scholars argue that whereas the Marshall Plan and NATO reflected and institutionalized liberal-democratic values, the institutions created by the USSR in east-central Europe bore the hallmark of communist dictatorship.

With regard to the origins and evolution of US foreign policy during the Cold War, ideational approaches have tended to reflect on the language and principles guiding US actions towards the USSR. Briefly, although the US was obviously concerned with the Soviet geopolitical presence in Europe this became a Cold War because of the way in which that presence was combined with the articulation and institutionalization—through the imposition of communist rule—of a conflicting ideological vision of the post-war world (Schlesinger, Jr. 1967) in opposition to liberal-democratic principles.

Further, as Mervyn Leffler (1994) has argued, US policy towards the USSR after 1945 was strongly influenced by a deep-rooted institutional and wider societal mentality of suspicion and hostility towards the ideology of communism dating from the 1917 Bolshevik Revolution and the way in which this—in some respects—virulent anti-communism made recognition of what some scholars regarded as 'legitimate' Soviet defensive security interests in east-central Europe after the war difficult. This approach also suggests that US policy makers were unable—as the Cold War progressed—to recognize that communism was not as centrally dominated by Moscow as the prevailing ideological mindset of the US national security bureaucracy believed (LaFeber 1989; Barnet 1972). The failure to compromise or engage the USSR at certain moments in the Cold War, then, is regarded as reflecting the way in which ideational assumptions about communism informed US foreign policy. Such assumptions continued into the closing stages of the Cold War as a number of senior figures in the Reagan and Bush administrations continued to harbour ideologically determined reservations and suspicions (Risse-Kappen 1994) about Gorbachev's policies and commitment to fundamentally reforming Moscow's relations with Washington.

Socio-economic approaches

Those scholars that focus on the way in which socio-economic structures and processes are central to explaining American foreign policy making during the Cold War (Cox 1984; Halliday 1986; Horowitz 1967; Kolko 1969; Saull 2001, 2007) have been concerned with the specifically capitalist properties of American foreign policy. These scholars highlight two dimensions to the capitalist character of American foreign policy. First, is that both American (economic) actors— businesses, corporations, and individuals (and trade unions)—and processes—production, investment, trade, distribution, and consumption (as well as conflicts between capitalists and workers)—located within the sphere of the market economy played an important role in the international relations of the United States during the Cold War. In particular, these actors and processes conditioned the implementation and impact of American foreign policy towards other capitalist states with respect to the way in which such processes helped promote stability, co-operation, and economic development within and amongst these states, as well as furthering American national security interests.

As much as American foreign relations during the Cold War, then, were concerned with physical security encapsulated in military power and strategic alliances, so they were also concerned with issues of economic security and prosperity, particularly with respect to the way in which international economic processes influenced the health and prosperity of the domestic political economy of the United States. Simply put, the upholding of a liberal, open, and capitalist American economy was, in part, conditional on the existence of a wider international capitalist system that was also characterized by liberal principles of openness.

The second capitalist dimension of American foreign policy is that the American state is capitalist; meaning that its institutional structure, jurisdiction, and policies not only rest on the relative separation of the sphere of the state (politics) from the economic activities of production, exchange, investment, and consumption located in the market, but that the policies of the American state seek to uphold this particular organization of society. According to these scholars, then, when we refer to American foreign relations we are in fact referring to something more than the formal diplomatic relations between states but also other (socio-economic) actors and processes committed to preserving and expanding capitalist relations of production and exchange.

This approach to American foreign policy is as much concerned to account for US relations with other capitalist states as it is the bipolar relationship after the war and the way in which capitalist *social* or class interests pervaded US national security policy. Consequently, for these scholars the Soviet threat was not primarily because of its geopolitical presence within east-central Europe but rather that this geopolitical presence was based upon a different and antagonistic set of socio-economic arrangements encapsulated in the communist organization of society and politics.

It was not then—as suggested by ideational scholars— mainly a concern with the different ideological values of the Soviet leadership and the way in which this challenged US post-war goals, but rather the fact that the socio-economic organization and reproduction of the Soviet type of society (and its expansion into east-central Europe and beyond) removed a

KEY POINTS

❏ Three main theoretical approaches to American foreign policy during the Cold War: realists, ideational, and socio-economic.

❏ Two aspects to realist approaches to US foreign policy in the Cold War: (1) Cold War realists who accounted for the origins of the Cold War and later became critics of US policy and (2) international relations theorists concerned with the US role in the post-war bipolar relationship.

❏ Both concerned with the role of geopolitical factors in US foreign policy towards the USSR and have tended to downplay the ideological motivations in determining US policy.

❏ Ideational approaches stress the role of liberal-democratic ideas and values in determining the objectives of US foreign policy during the Cold War and how those objectives were realized.

❏ Ideological assumptions about the nature of communism conditioned US foreign policy at the start of the Cold War

and influenced Washington's assumptions about Soviet policy (making compromise and negotiation difficult). Such assumptions also influenced US policy during the Reagan and Bush administrations during the closing stages of the Cold War.

❏ Socio-economic approaches focus on the capitalist character of American foreign policy: the role of socio-economic actors and processes in US foreign policy; and the way in which American foreign policy has been concerned with internationalizing the domestic–capitalist character of US society.

❏ This approach focuses on US relations with other capitalist states and how US policy tried to condition domestic political and economic developments within these states, as well as the way in which the USA was concerned with the threat to international capitalism from other revolutionary movements and states, not just the USSR.

geo-economic space from involvement in capitalism, cutting off potential markets for US and international capital, as well as claiming to be a societal alternative to American-led capitalism. Further, it was not only the case that the USSR threatened the international (and domestic American) social reproduction of a capitalist kind of society, but that other revolutionary states— that emerged throughout the history of the Cold War—extended this threat, as well as those revolutionary and communist social and political movements active throughout the Cold War who were committed

to overthrowing capitalist social arrangements (Halliday 1986; Saull 2001, 2007).

Now that I have provided an overview of the main theoretical perspectives on explaining American foreign policy during the Cold War, giving a flavour of their main theoretical arguments, I will spend of the rest of the chapter examining the key historical developments in American foreign policy during the Cold War, interspersing the historical narrative with reflections on the varying analytical strengths of each of the three approaches outlined above.

The origins of the Cold War and containment

The debate on the origins of the Cold War

The analysis of American foreign policy in the early period after the Second World War has been dominated by the debate over the US role in causing the breakdown of the wartime alliance and the triggering of diplomatic hostility and geopolitical confrontation between Washington and Moscow. This has been framed in the so-called 'orthodox–revisionist debate on the origins

of the Cold War'. Whilst the 'orthodox interpretation' of the origins of the Cold War sees US diplomacy as rather passive and reactive in the face of acts of Soviet aggression in east-central Europe (Kennan 1947; Feis 1967; Schlesinger, Jr. 1967) highlighted by the creeping Sovietization of the region between 1945 and 1948, the alternative, revisionist view, stresses the conservative (rather than revolutionary) and defensive character of Soviet policy and the more proactive and expansionist policies of Washington.

CONTROVERSIES 4.1: The orthodox–revisionist debate on the Cold War

The orthodox argument:

- The origins of the Cold War are found in Marxism–Leninism and its doctrine of class struggle leading to world revolution.
- The USSR was hostile to capitalist states and pursued policies to undermine the authority of these states.
- After the war the USSR was committed to extending Soviet power over Germany as much as east-central Europe.
- Roosevelt and Truman misjudged the expansionist nature of Soviet policy, naively harbouring vain hopes about integrating the USSR into a post-war liberal-democratic world order.
- US leaders did not have a clear vision of the post-war world and they were prepared to make political concessions (over east-central Europe) to Moscow for short-term military gains.
- Despite evidence of increasing Sovietization of east-central Europe the Truman administration continued to make concessions to Moscow (e.g. proposing, in the Baruch Plan, joint US–USSR control over the production of nuclear weapons, and inviting the USSR and east-central European states to participate in the Marshall Plan in 1947).
- Soviet hostility and aggression forced the USA to change policy by coming to the aid of western Europe and accepting the division of Germany.
- The Soviet response was further aggression in east-central Europe highlighted by the Czech coup of February 1948.
- With the Berlin blockade the US finally realized that it had to make a military commitment to the defence of western Europe with the creation of NATO.

The revisionist argument:

- Rejects the orthodox account as misreading Soviet actions and objectives, and overlooking the expansionist character of US policy.
- The USSR cannot be held responsible for the Cold War by highlighting the impact of the war on the USSR and the military (monopoly on nuclear weapons) and economic advantages (massive increase in the economic power of the USA through the war) of the USA after the war.

- Soviet policy after the war was concerned with domestic economic reconstruction (after the devastation caused by the war) and ensuring that Germany would never again pose a military threat.
- The Cold War emerged out of the needs of the American capitalist system to expand into new markets as a way of overcoming the problem of overproduction within its domestic economy.
- The expansion of American economic influence resulted in the spread of American political power.
- Because the USA was the leading economy after the war, inevitably it would benefit most, and policies of 'free trade' and 'equal opportunity' in all foreign markets would lead to US domination.
- The decisive reason for US involvement in the war was the aim to maintain and expand its influence in the world economy over other capitalist states.
- During the war and in negotiations afterwards, the USA was primarily concerned with breaking up the British Empire and ending the policy of imperial preferences that discriminated against American producers.
- When the 'open door' of American economic expansion was applied to east-central Europe, the USSR saw a threat to its legitimate security interests and was forced to act to prevent the spread of US economic and political influence.
- The Truman administration applied economic pressure to the USSR (ignoring Soviet requests for economic aid after the war, abruptly ending lend-lease deliveries at the end of the war, refusing to grant German reparations to Moscow at the Potsdam Conference) to try to extract concessions from Moscow over the future of east-central Europe and Germany.
- The Marshall Plan was an attempt to impose liberal-capitalism on east-central Europe, thus expelling Soviet influence.
- It was US policy that caused the division of Europe. When it became clear that the USA could not force changes in Soviet policy, by 1946 it pursued a policy of containment and division, which forced Moscow to act.

In this account revisionist scholars (Horowitz 1967; Kolko and Kolko 1972) argue that the US used its post-war economic power and dominance to not only try to undermine Soviet influence in east-central Europe through drawing these states into a US-led international economic system decoupling them from economic links with the USSR, but also used this power to pressure other capitalist states (in western

Europe and Britain in particular) to agree to and adopt the policies that would realize a distinctly American vision of how the post-war international economy should be organized—a vision that would have forced these states to not only open up their economies to US investment, but to dismantle their imperial trading blocs that had closed off access to American capital.

This debate has generated a huge scholarly literature (Ambrose and Brinkley 1997; Gaddis 1987, 1997; Leffler and Painter 1994; Paterson 1988) that has benefited from and expanded with the post-Cold War opening of Soviet diplomatic archives. I don't have the space to address many of the issues discussed in this literature nor provide a historical narrative of the key events in the move from alliance to confrontation. Instead, I will make reference to some of the key historical developments that each of the three different theoretical approaches highlight to assess their relative merits in explaining US foreign policy in the early Cold War and, in doing so, highlight the relative strengths and weaknesses of the orthodox and revisionist accounts of the early Cold War, respectively.

As suggested, above, in my survey of the different theoretical perspectives on US foreign policy each approach emphasizes one or other set of factors to account for American behaviour: geopolitical, ideational, and/or socio-economic. To what extent, then, can we explain the shift in US foreign policy towards Cold War through a focus on each of these factors? The end of the war saw Europe and—though to a lesser extent—the world beyond continental Europe structured around the geopolitical dominance of the United States and the Soviet Union—the superpowers. This geopolitical outcome was coloured by the differing political and ideological values associated and institutionalized within each superpower; on the one hand liberal democracy and on the other communist dictatorship. Further, these differences in ideology and political values were matched by the very different forms of societal organization and socio-economic structure that characterized the USA and the USSR respectively.

❝ KEY QUOTES 4.1: 'X': the sources of Soviet conduct

[W]e are going to continue for a long time to find the Russians difficult to deal with. It does not mean that they should be considered as embarked upon a do-or-die program to overthrow our society by a given date . . .

In these circumstances it is clear that the main element of any United States policy toward the Soviet Union must be that of a long-term, patient but firm and vigilant containment of Russian expansive tendencies. It is important to note, however, that such a policy has nothing to do with outward histrionics: with threats or blustering or superfluous gestures of outward 'toughness.' While the Kremlin is basically flexible in its reaction to political realities, it is by no means unnameable to considerations of prestige. Like almost any other government, it can be placed by tactless and threatening gestures in a position where it cannot afford to yield even though this might be dictated by its sense of realism. The Russian leaders are keen judges of human psychology, and as such they are highly conscious that loss of temper and of self-control is never a source of strength in political affairs. They are quick to exploit such evidences of weakness. For these reasons, it is a sine qua non of successful dealing with Russia that the foreign government in question should remain at all times cool and collected and that its demands on Russian policy should be put forward in such a manner as to leave the way open for a compliance not too detrimental to Russian prestige. . . .

In the light of the above, it will be clearly seen that the Soviet pressure against the free institutions of the Western world is something that can be contained by the adroit and vigilant application of counterforce at a series of constantly shifting geographical and political points, corresponding to the shifts and manoeuvres of Soviet policy, but which cannot be charmed or talked out of existence. The Russians look forward to a duel of infinite duration, and they see that already they have scored great successes.

(*Foreign Affairs*, July 1947)

The emergence of containment

What is clear is that this post-war geopolitical arrangement did not immediately settle into the fixed and frozen division and strategic competition that was to characterize the Cold War. Initially, at least, the US did not automatically see the geopolitical outcome of the war as a *necessary* cause for diplomatic and geopolitical hostility to develop with Moscow. It was to be the combination of Soviet actions in east-central Europe and the American response to them that would trigger confrontation. In this sense both orthodox and revisionist arguments contain elements of truth. Soviet policy was perceived as aggressive and against the spirit, if not the letter, of the Yalta and Potsdam agreements over the future of post-war Europe by the US, whilst US policies, particularly towards western-occupied Germany, were seen as hostile to Soviet security interests. The key analytical issue here is that issues of perception, interpretation, and, crucially, domestic politics within the United States were to play an important role in determining the response to Soviet actions in east-central Europe, something which both orthodox and revisionist approaches do not sufficiently recognize.

The 'Sovietization' of east-central Europe and the particular way that this was carried out—through the gradual elimination of non-communist political forces and the coercive economic integration of east-central Europe into the Soviet economic system between 1945 and 1948—was crucial to shifting US perspectives on how the post-war international system would be organized. These developments and their militarized character not only entrenched the geopolitical consequences of the war but also appeared to threaten the political security of western Europe and other areas (Iran and Turkey) that bordered the Soviet Union. The illiberal and undemocratic character of Soviet policies were, then, important in colouring the geopolitical outcome of the war. Simply put, for US leaders, Soviet actions communicated that Moscow could no longer be seen as a partner or ally, but rather a competitor and foe committed to establishing a very different if not antagonistic set of post-war arrangements over east-central Europe.

However, this change in the geopolitical outlook of the post-war world recognized by Truman and his advisors in the early months after the end of the war needed to be conveyed to the American public and Congress, who had to be persuaded to support a shift in US policy to a more forthright opposition to Soviet actions. In this regard Soviet policies, notably the rigged elections in Hungary and Poland in 1947, the coup in Czechoslovakia in February 1948, and the Berlin blockade later that year, provided helpful ammunition for the struggle to persuade the American public, but it took a campaign of speeches, publicity, and, to some extent, manipulation, exaggeration, and propaganda waged by US government agencies and sympathetic newspapers and other opinion formers to mobilize public and Congressional support behind a policy of containment and confrontation.

The Truman Doctrine

What is also significant in the move towards the containment of the USSR is that two crucial developments, which triggered policy responses that became landmarks in the onset of the Cold War, did not directly involve or concern the USSR. Thus, although US policy was directed towards the USSR, in some cases US policy was in *response* to actions carried out by other communist or revolutionary states or movements. In this sense, US foreign policy in the beginning of the Cold War—as it was to be throughout the Cold War—was as much concerned with responding to the actions of non-Soviet forms of communist power, as it was to Soviet actions.

The first development concerned the situation in Greece, where communists were fighting a civil war against a right-wing pro-Western government supported by British troops. It was the decision by the British government to end its support of the Greek government in February 1947—due to economic exigencies—that raised the spectre of communist victory. Such a development was seen as posing a threat to the security of not only Turkey, but also the wider Middle East, and it was this that led Truman to deliver a speech—what became known as the 'Truman Doctrine'—in early March to both houses of Congress, and to the wider audience of the American public calling on the American people to shoulder the burden of 'support[ing] free peoples who are resisting attempted subjugation by armed minorities or by outside pressures'.

Although Congress took further convincing to grant Truman's demands for aid to Greece this was to

> **KEY QUOTES 4.2: The Truman Doctrine**

President Truman's address before a joint session of Congress, 12 March 1947

The peoples of a number of countries of the world have recently had totalitarian regimes forced upon them against their will. The Government of the United States has made frequent protests against coercion and intimidation, in violation of the Yalta Agreement, in Poland, Rumania, and Bulgaria. I must also state that in a number of other countries there have been similar developments.

At the present moment in world history nearly every nation must choose between alternative ways of life. The choice is too often not a free one.

One way of life is based upon the will of the majority, and is distinguished by free institutions, representative government, free elections, guarantees of individual liberty, freedom of speech and religion, and freedom from political oppression.

The second way of life is based upon the will of a minority forcibly imposed upon the majority. It relies upon terror and oppression, a controlled press and radio; fixed elections, and the suppression of personal freedoms.

I believe that it must be the policy of the United States to support free peoples who are resisting attempted subjugation by armed minorities or by outside pressures.

I believe that we must assist free peoples to work out their own destinies in their own way.

It is necessary only to glance at a map to realize that the survival and integrity of the Greek nation are of grave importance in a much wider situation. If Greece should fall under the control of an armed minority, the effect upon its neighbor, Turkey, would be immediate and serious. Confusion and disorder might well spread throughout the entire Middle East.

Moreover, the disappearance of Greece as an independent state would have a profound effect upon those countries in Europe whose peoples are struggling against great difficulties to maintain their freedoms and their independence while they repair the damages of war.

It would be an unspeakable tragedy if these countries, which have struggled so long against overwhelming odds, should lose that victory for which they sacrificed so much. Collapse of free institutions and loss of independence would be disastrous not only for them but for the world. Discouragement and possibly failure would quickly be the lot of neighboring peoples striving to maintain their freedom and independence.

(*Public Papers of the Presidents* 1963: 176)

become the first step in America's political and military commitment to the security of western Europe and, later, a global commitment to containing communist expansion. The significance of this for our understanding of American foreign policy was that US policy was in response to how the prospect of a local communist revolution could have geopolitical consequences—by extending communist power allied to the USSR—and, further, the crucial role played by politics, perception, and, to a not insignificant degree, personality in determining what the US did.

The Marshall Plan

The other key development concerned the economic future of post-war Europe and how this related to US concerns to organize the post-war international economy in such a way that would not only prevent the likelihood of another global economic crisis—as occurred in the 1930s, which provided an important context for the origins of the Second World War—but would also allow the US to best realize its economic interests. The framework for organizing the post-war international economy was decided—under the guidance of the US Treasury—at the Bretton Woods conference in New Hampshire in 1944. The agreement laid out a framework for a liberal and open international trading system, that is, a framework that not only tended to reflect US political and ideological interests and values, but also that would ensure significant economic benefits would flow towards the US as western European economies (and their imperial possessions) would be opened up to take American goods. The Bretton Woods agreement, then, seemed to bear out Revisionist claims and, more broadly, socio-economic approaches, to a significant degree, with respect to explaining the importance of socio-economic interests—that of American exporters and the American economy as a whole—on US foreign policy.

However, the original Bretton Woods blueprint was to be short-lived, as a combination of developing geopolitical tensions with Moscow and mounting economic difficulties within western Europe through 1946–7 caused a US rethink. The growing economic crisis in western Europe raised two prospects of concern for the US. First, that an economic crisis in western Europe would force these economies to move towards protectionist economic policies, thus closing off their economies from meaningful international economic exchange and scuppering the hopes and plans of the US. This would not only have had negative consequences on the US economy—depriving US exporters of foreign markets—but would have also removed a source of leverage over the post-war political future of western Europe and the wider international economy, as these economies would have removed themselves from American influence.

The second concern was that communist and other pro-Soviet forces in western Europe would take advantage of any crisis to seize power and push western Europe in a pro-Soviet direction. In this case the US was concerned less with Soviet policies and more with how potentially revolutionary domestic political developments within western European states could have geopolitical consequences favourable to the USSR. The US response to the growing economic difficulties in western Europe and the possibility of one or other of the two possible future scenarios emerging was the Marshall Plan, announced by the US secretary of state, George Marshall, in a speech at Harvard University in June 1947.

The Marshall Plan was aimed at aiding European economic recovery, thus thwarting economic crisis, but also drawing those states in receipt of Marshall Aid into closer economic links with the US and implementing policies—revised from Bretton Woods—that the US found acceptable. Further, the diplomatic and institutional framework that the US developed to deliver Marshall Aid—through the Organization of European Economic Co-operation (OEEC)—would provide a vehicle for developing links with east-central European countries. On this point, revisionist arguments have some substance. Any moves by east-central European states to join the Marshall Plan framework would have not only integrated them into a pro-US liberal institutional and political framework, but would have also fundamentally challenged Soviet economic and security interests in the region by weakening the ability of the USSR to determine internal political and economic developments within these states. Consequently, Moscow compelled east-central European states to reject such overtures.

The Marshall Plan is significant for understanding US foreign policy in the early Cold War for a number of reasons. It highlights how US foreign policy was concerned with developments within the domestic politics of other capitalist states, particularly in western Europe. Thus, contrary to orthodox (and realist) approaches, it was not only the case that the US did meddle in the domestic affairs of western European states in the early Cold War—and after—as a way of influencing political developments in a way compatible with US interests, but that this was also a crucial area of concern for US foreign policy.

This suggests that the Cold War was not, then, just about international diplomatic and geopolitical relations between the superpowers, but also concerned political and economic developments within the domestic politics of other capitalist states (Rupert 1995). In this respect, whilst the USSR was a geopolitical threat, the flow of political developments, conflict, and economic instability and crisis within other capitalist states was—throughout the history of the Cold War—a socio-economic challenge to the US, as the possibility remained that a government could come to power and not only oppose US economic interests, but also alter the geopolitical relationship with the USA by opting for neutrality or withdrawal from alliance with the US (Colás 2006: 12–17). The fact that this never occurred does not mean that it was not a constant concern for the US or that the US did not implement policies to ensure that it didn't happen.

Whilst Marshall Aid provided an economic means for the US to realize its foreign policy objectives of preventing economic crisis as well as tying west European states into closer diplomatic relations with the US, this concern with domestic political developments saw the US—or, more precisely, the newly created CIA—play an important role in thwarting the constitutional political ambitions of the communist party in Italy in the 1948 elections. The Marshall Plan also alerts us to the *form* of US foreign policy. Whereas the formal machinery of diplomacy was utilized to introduce the Marshall Plan, as a number of scholars have highlighted (Carew 1987; Rupert 1995; Saull 2007) Marshall Aid was organized through a broader coalition of private, non-governmental agencies. US companies and trade unions (the American Federation of Labor—Conference of Industrial Organizations) played a key role in 'selling' Marshall Aid to European trade unionists and workers, and encouraging the establishment of anti-communist trade unions.

The analytical significance of this goes beyond how we think about the nature and delivery of the Marshall Plan; it also highlights the socio-economic or class dimensions of Marshall Aid and American foreign policy more generally. The foreign policy of the US (or any other state for that matter), then, is likely to have uneven socio-economic consequences, not only for the society that a policy is directed at, but also for the 'home' society where the policy is made. Thus, whilst the US did have to make revisions to its original blue-print regarding the character of the post-war international economy, it was a price worth paying in that private property rights were protected and the interests of capital tended to take preference over those of workers (Cox 1987; Rupert 1995: 43–9). In sum, then, the Marshall Plan could be seen as reflecting an attempt to promote a particular form of societal organization within western European states that maintained a balance of promoting economic stability, thus social peace and political alliance with Washington, founded on the privileging of capitalist socio-economic interests.

The twin pillars of US Cold War foreign policy

By early 1948, then, the US had established the key pillars of its Cold War foreign policy. On the one hand was the military–geopolitical dimension of containment highlighted in its commitment through the Truman Doctrine to the defence of 'free peoples' facing 'communist subversion and aggression'. Once this threshold had been crossed, it became much easier for Truman and future presidents to persuade Congress and the American public to shoulder further and heavier burdens in the struggle against Soviet and communist expansion. Thus, in April 1949 the implicit commitment to the military defence of its west European allies in the Truman Doctrine was formalized with the establishment of NATO.

However, in recognizing this we also need to acknowledge the dynamic within the relationship of not only Soviet policy, but also—as will become clearer below—of other communist movements and states and the way in which the US leadership was unable—for much of the history of the Cold War—to differentiate the diplomacy of Moscow from the policies of other communist states and the actions of communist movements. This highlights the strengths of ideational approaches to understanding US foreign policy, that is, how political developments in other states were *interpreted* as having negative international consequences for the United States.

Further, we also need to recognize the way in which US foreign policy decisions—in the early period (and throughout) of the Cold War—were influenced by the behaviour of its key allies. In this regard the US decision to make a political and military commitment to the defence of western Europe was conditional on the policy decisions of these states. Geir Lundestad's (1998) phrase 'empire by invitation' nicely captures the character and dynamic within the relationship between the US and its western European allies after 1947. Western European states, spurred on by Churchill's 'iron curtain speech' of March 1946, which called for a western Alliance against what he regarded as a growing Soviet threat, effectively requested and welcomed US diplomatic and military support and protection.

Thus, whilst recognizing the hierarchy and distribution of political and military power within the Atlantic Alliance during the Cold War we also need to recognize the way in which the US made efforts to accommodate the interests and concerns of its allies. This has already been mentioned with regard to the Marshall Plan and the way it was organized and delivered through the multilateral OEEC, but it goes beyond this in that the ruling elites within western Europe tended to share the concerns of US policy makers to a significant degree, thus assisting the implementation of US policy and facilitating the legitimacy of institutions such as NATO and the basing of tens of thousands of US troops in western Europe.

The second element concerned the economic framework governing the international capitalist economy and US relations with the other advanced capitalist states.

Here, the US was forced to make concessions to the economic and social needs of other capitalist states, even if that meant—in the short-term—tolerating economic policies it found questionable. Further, and in contrast to the revisionist argument over the aim of US foreign relations, US policy contributed to the economic growth of the other capitalist states, to such a degree that by the late 1960s these states—Germany, Japan, and France in particular—were beginning to eat away at US post-war economic ascendancy in the production of manufactured goods. However, whilst recognizing the economically benign consequences of US policies we also have to acknowledge the way in which these arrangements also rested on a rather uneven distribution of social or class power within these states, reflected in the disproportionate flow of benefits to the owners and managers of capital.

Korea, NSC-68, and the militarization of US foreign policy

Thus far I have focused on US policy towards Europe in the early period after the war. The relations with both

its allies and its Soviet foe were to remain relatively stable after 1949. With the seeing off of the attempt by the

Soviets—through the almost year-long (June 1948–May 1949) blockade of Berlin—to thwart Western policy towards divided Germany, the division of Germany and Europe into two opposing zones was sealed. This division was soon to become highly militarized with the stationing of massed divisions of tanks and troops on either side of the divide, which effectively froze the European Cold War, ushering in a period of military-enforced stability until the late 1980s. However, the momentum of events in Europe and the direction of US policy were to be influenced by events elsewhere—in Asia—which would result in a much greater militarization of US foreign policy and containment.

Two events would propel the US towards a much bolder and ambitious containment policy, thus assisting those tendencies within the US polity that favoured such a posture and making it easier to convince Congress and the American public of the need to militarize containment. The two events were the communist revolution in China in 1949 and the outbreak of the Korean War in June 1950 with the invasion of the pro-Western South by the Communist North. The significance of these developments was to be profound. They were to inaugurate US military interventions in the former colonial or third world, which would culminate in the intervention in Vietnam between 1965 and 1973. As the dynamic of Soviet policy in Europe conditioned and triggered US responses there, rather than the US having a grand design (as suggested by revisionists) regardless of Soviet actions, so developments involving other communist movements and states would provide the key factors in the shaping of containment, leading to the involvement of the US in a number of 'hot wars' in the third world.

The failure of US policy towards China, what critics of the Truman administration called 'the loss of China' was a major strategic setback (Paterson 1988: 54–75) as US post-war planning had always assumed that China would be a source of post-war stability and alliance in Asia. It also had consequences for US policy towards Japan, as Japan now became much more central to US security in the Pacific and with China going communist, more at risk from communist expansion.

Following the pattern towards Europe and the move towards post-war demobilization of its military forces at the end of the war in the Pacific, US policy was fil-tered through local agents, specifically the anti-communist Kuomintang government. Here, US policy was characterized by ineffectiveness and frustration despite providing significant financial and military aid to the Kuomintang in its struggle with the Chinese communists. Unable to intervene themselves—the scale of any intervention in a country the size of China would have required tens of thousands of troops, as well as contradicting Washington's commitment to decolonization and national self-determination—the US was reliant on the incompetent, corrupt, and feckless Kuomintang.

The Korean War

However, despite the shock of the communist victory in China it was to be the North Korean invasion of South Korea—what the US interpreted as an act of aggression across a recognized international boundary—that would be the defining event in shifting containment from a policy of diplomatic threats to the construction of a major military alliance in NATO and Japan (with the 1951 Mutual Defense Treaty) and active military interventions in the third world, beginning with the dispatch of US combat forces to the Korean peninsula soon after the invasion. Whilst the 'loss of China' was a much greater strategic set-back, this came through the result of an internal civil war. This contrasted with Korea where—despite the fact that the boundary dividing the north and south of the peninsula had no legal basis—the communist invasion appeared to signal a new brazenness and aggression in communist policy. The invasion appeared to bear out the arguments of anti-communist hardliners in the US government, who interpreted events in Korea as part of a co-ordinated pattern of communist expansion directed by Moscow, rather than as a local civil war only cautiously supported by the Soviets and Chinese (Cumings 1981/1990).

NSC-68

Other than the decision to send troops to repel North Korean forces, the defining decision relating to the war was Truman's approval of the proposals outlined in National Security Council Report number 68 (NSC-68) in September 1950. Truman's decision moved the US towards a containment of Soviet and communist advances

> **KEY QUOTES 4.3:** NSC-68

VII. Present risks

A. GENERAL

[T]he integrity and vitality of our system is in greater jeopardy than ever before in our history. Even if there were no Soviet Union we would face the great problem of the free society, accentuated many fold in this industrial age, of reconciling order, security, the need for participation, with the requirement of freedom. We would face the fact that in a shrinking world the absence of order among nations is becoming less and less tolerable. The Kremlin design seeks to impose order among nations by means which would destroy our free and democratic system. The Kremlin's possession of atomic weapons puts new power behind its design, and increases the jeopardy to our system. It adds new strains to the uneasy equilibrium-without-order which exists in the world and raises new doubts in men's minds whether the world will long tolerate this tension without moving toward some kind of order, on somebody's terms . . .

The risks we face are of a new order of magnitude, commensurate with the total struggle in which we are engaged. For a free society there is never total victory, since freedom and democracy are never wholly attained, are always in the process of being attained. But defeat at the hands of the totalitarian is total defeat. These risks crowd in on us, in a shrinking world of polarized power, so as to give us no choice, ultimately, between meeting them effectively or being overcome by them . . .

B. SPECIFIC

It is quite clear from Soviet theory and practice that the Kremlin seeks to bring the free world under its dominion by the methods of the cold war. The preferred technique is to subvert by infiltration and intimidation. Every institution of our society is an instrument which it is sought to stultify and turn against our purposes. Those that touch most closely our material and moral strength are obviously the prime targets, labor unions, civic enterprises, schools, churches, and all media for influencing opinion. The effort is not so much to make them serve obvious Soviet ends as to prevent them from serving our ends, and thus to make them sources of confusion in our economy, our culture, and our body politic. The doubts and diversities that in terms of

our values are part of the merit of a free system, the weaknesses and the problems that are peculiar to it, the rights and privileges that free men enjoy, and the disorganization and destruction left in the wake of the last attack on our freedoms, all are but opportunities for the Kremlin to do its evil work . . .

Since everything that gives us or others respect for our institutions is a suitable object for attack, it also fits the Kremlin's design that where, with impunity, we can be insulted and made to suffer indignity the opportunity shall not be missed, particularly in any context which can be used to cast dishonor on our country, our system, our motives, or our methods. Thus the means by which we sought to restore our own economic health in the '30's, and now seek to restore that of the free world, come equally under attack. The military aid by which we sought to help the free world was frantically denounced by the Communists in the early days of the last war, and of course our present efforts to develop adequate military strength for ourselves and our allies are equally denounced . . .

At the same time the Soviet Union is seeking to create overwhelming military force, in order to back up infiltration with intimidation. In the only terms in which it understands strength, it is seeking to demonstrate to the free world that force and the will to use it are on the side of the Kremlin, that those who lack it are decadent and doomed. In local incidents it threatens and encroaches both for the sake of local gains and to increase anxiety and defeatism in all the free world . . .

The risk that we may thereby be prevented or too long delayed in taking all needful measures to maintain the integrity and vitality of our system is great. The risk that our allies will lose their determination is greater. And the risk that in this manner a descending spiral of too little and too late, of doubt and recrimination, may present us with ever narrower and more desperate alternatives, is the greatest risk of all. For example, it is clear that our present weakness would prevent us from offering effective resistance at any of several vital pressure points. The only deterrent we can present to the Kremlin is the evidence we give that we may make any of the critical points which we cannot hold the occasion for a global war of annihilation.

(Foreign Relations of the United States 1950)

KEY POINTS

- Significance of the spread of the Cold War to Asia on US policy towards western Europe and the increasing militarization of containment after 1950.
- 1949 communist revolution in China seen as a failure of US policy by critics of the Truman administration. US failure due to its dependence on the corrupt and incompetent Kuomintang government.
- The communist victory in China undermined US plans for the post-war future of east Asia, increasing the importance of Japan to US interests, as well as making Japan more vulnerable to communist influence.
- Despite the shock of the Chinese Revolution the key turning point for US policy came with North Korea's invasion

of South Korea in June 1950. This was perceived as an act of aggression across a territorial border, triggering US military intervention in defence of the South and ushering in a policy of US military interventions in third world conflicts.
- As well as dispatching troops to the Korean peninsula, the US initiated a massive programme of rearmament—as proposed in NSC-68—instigating the militarization of containment.
- The Korean War also saw a major increase in US aid for French forces fighting communist forces in Indochina and the USA agreeing to the rearmament of West Germany within NATO.

---

by military means, primarily because the Truman administration—and later US administrations—regarded Soviet/communist advances as occurring through military aggression, across territorial boundaries, rather than, as in the case of Korea (and other later cases) the result of internal political, socio-economic, and military dynamics. With US troops engaged on the ground against Soviet and Chinese-backed communist invaders (and after the Soviets had detonated an atomic device in August 1949 earlier than the US had anticipated) the perception of a much more threatening global context led to momentous changes in US foreign policy.

In the following months and years the US moved towards implementing the recommendations of NSC-

68—something much less likely without the events of June 1950. US troop numbers in Europe were strengthened and NATO was to be given much greater military bite with the decision—supported by the US—for the rearmament of western Germany in May 1955. By 1953 US military production was seven times that of 1950, the army grew by 50%, and the US also doubled the number of air groups to ninety-five (Ambrose 1997: 122; Leffler and Painter 1994: 118). Another key consequence of the Korean War was the stepping-up of US military aid to French forces in Indochina fighting communist-led anti-colonial forces. This was the first step in what would eventually become the Vietnam War.

Cold War in the third world

As indicated in the previous section, the US military intervention in the Korean civil war from 1950 initiated what would become a dominant and increasingly controversial aspect of US foreign policy in the Cold War—military interventions in support of allied governments and/or against revolutionary states.[1] The outstanding case in this regard was the US military intervention in Vietnam between 1965 and 1973. The scale and length

of the US intervention in Vietnam (which actually began in 1950 through its support for the French and then, after, through its support of the attempts to create a post-colonial independent anti-communist state in the south of Vietnam from 1954) contrasted with numerous other interventions in Latin America, the Caribbean, sub-Saharan Africa, the Middle-East, and other parts of Asia through smaller-scale military and covert interventions involving the CIA and/or the funding, training, arming, and directing of local anti-communist forces waging forms of armed struggle against revolutionary states.[2]

I don't have the space to detail these many interventions and the specific reasons for the US decisions to mount them. Instead, I will focus on the Vietnam War as reflective of a broader US concern about the spread of communism in the third world and, with it, the political and geopolitical expansion of Soviet global power.

Vietnam

In Vietnam, as in many other parts of the third world—with the exception of Cuba after the 1959 revolution and Chile between 1970 and 1973—US economic interests were rather marginal as a direct cause of US intervention because in most cases revolutionary seizures of power did not tend to result in major setbacks for the direct national economic interests of the United States. Further, and as highlighted by the Cold War realists mentioned earlier, many of the countries and regions were not regarded—at least by some high-profile realist thinkers (Morgenthau 1969)—as being of strategic interest to the United States.

Thus, whilst the Korean War could be seen as reflecting a geopolitical challenge to the United States, for some realists at least this was less the case with Vietnam and the many other US interventions in the third world. How, then, do we explain the US intervention in Vietnam and what does this tell us about American foreign policy towards the third world (and revolutionary political change) more generally throughout the Cold War? To address this question we have to look at the actual steps leading up to the intervention—a basic narrative of events—and then assess the reasons for the intervention and the role of different factors and explanations.

In the case of Vietnam, US intervention proceeded in a step-by-step fashion conditioned by developments on the ground in Vietnam, the wider regional and global context of the Cold War, and, finally, the complexion of political opinion within the United States. As I have already mentioned, the initial US intervention—in support of the French between 1950 and 1954—was largely determined by the wider regional context of war and

communist expansion across geographical borders. It was this that gave rise to the idea of the 'domino theory' whereby those countries neighbouring a newly-created revolutionary or communist state would become 'infected' with the 'communist contagion' and would fall over like dominoes—becoming communist. Hence, the importance of those countries—like (South) Vietnam and South Korea—in the frontline of the struggle to contain the spread of communism.

With the departure of the French and the division of Vietnam into a communist North and anti-communist South in 1954, the US picked up where the French had left off in providing financial and military support for the construction of an independent South Vietnamese state. In this sense the US was following the pattern established in Korea—a divided peninsula after the 1953 armistice—with the US committed to supporting the construction of a strong pro-Western and capitalist regime in the South. From this point on, having made a political commitment to the future of South Vietnam, the flow, implementation, and success of US policy became dependent on its relationship with its local ally and the social and political forces associated with the South Vietnamese ruling elite.

In a similar fashion to its relationship with the Chinese Kuomintang between 1945 and 1949, between 1954 and 1973 US policy was concerned with not only with addressing the escalating communist political and military threat—especially after 1960 when the communist-led National Liberation Front (NLF) launched its struggle in the South—but also with getting its local ally to pursue policies that the US favoured and regarded as the best way of constructing a stable and credible non-communist state in the South.

With the launching of the NLF offensive in 1960 (after the Saigon regime had arrested, tortured, and assassinated thousands of communists and suspected communists in the South in the preceding months) the US commitment to Vietnam became increasingly militarized, resulting in a steady increase in the number of US troops and advisers dispatched to Vietnam.[3] The key point here is that it was the actions of the Saigon government that triggered the upsurge in guerrilla activity in the South and it was to be this dynamic—the policies and failures of the South Vietnamese—that would effectively drive US policy on the ground. This was particularly so as the Saigon regime's military inepti-tude and political and economic incompetence and corruption quickly showed itself to be unable to effec-tively deal with the NLF offensive, and its economic and agrarian policies—in spite of US advice and pressure for reform—actually aggravated the political and security situation in the countryside.

Faced with this situation as 1965 approached, and as US troop numbers and involvement increased (along with casualty figures), the US had two options. First, it could withdraw and leave Saigon to deal with the com-munist threat with the likelihood that it would prob-ably fail and the South would go communist. Such an outcome would have had dramatic consequences for US standing in the world, questioning the will of the US to meet communist threats, potentially undermin-ing the regional security of other US allies in the region, and questioning the effectiveness of US policy. Such a dilemma has confronted the US leadership in other scenarios where it has launched military interventions, including the most recent cases in Afghanistan (2001) and Iraq (2003). In these two cases the concern hasn't been over how a 'precipitous withdrawal' of military sources might have resulted in a communist victory but rather in civil war and the disintegration of the state in the case of Iraq, and a return to power of the Taliban Islamist militia in Afghanistan. Second, the US could become much more involved, effectively taking over responsibility for directing the war in the countryside against the NLF.[4]

The US chose the latter and, as in the case of those other key moments in modern US history where the US has decided to take on a much bigger military commit-ment likely to have a significant impact on US domestic politics (Pearl Harbor, Korea, 9/11), a *casus belli*—an 'unprovoked' act of aggression on the US or its forces—was required that would be used to convince the Amer-ican public of the need to take on a military burden involving the dispatch of large numbers of troops over-seas to fight.

This was 'provided' with the 'Gulf of Tonkin inci-dent' where US ships were supposedly[5] attacked by North Vietnamese forces. This apparent 'act of aggres-sion' highlighting the involvement of the North in the war in the South provided the basis for the infa-mous 'blank cheque' granted by Congress—the Gulf of Tonkin Resolution—to the Johnson administration to intensify the war through increasing the numbers of US troops in South Vietnam (reaching a peak of just under half a million in 1968) and through launching bombing raids—Operation Rolling Thunder—on the North.

After 1965, then, the US became involved in a drawn-out and bloody war in the jungles of south-east Asia, propping up an autocratic, ineffective, and corrupt state and—in spite of the huge and horrific levels of bombs (and chemical weapons) dropped on the peoples of Vietnam—south and north—and along with killing far more Vietnamese than the combined communist forces were able to kill US troops, failed to deliver the knock-out blow to win the war. Instead, as the war went on and, particularly after the political debacle and humiliation of the 1968 NLF Tet Offensive—when NLF guerrillas seized control of the US embassy in Saigon—American domestic politics began to play a much more important role on US policy as the campaign for withdrawal gath-ered pace in the US.

Although the anti-war movement did not force the US to withdraw it played a key role in ending the pol-icy established under Johnson after 1965, highlighting, again, the importance of domestic political opinion on US foreign policy. With the election of Richard Nixon in late 1968 US policy changed as it sought an exit from Vietnam.

Although the US commitment to Vietnam was sin-gular, what does the US experience in and with Viet-nam suggest about American foreign policy towards the third world? As recognized by the Cold War real-ists, US involvement was not—primarily—driven by geopolitical concerns. However, although Vietnam and the many other sites of US intervention were not—in themselves—of geopolitical significance, whether or not communist expansion took place within them was.

Although not in all cases, in enough case revolution-aries (not just communists) coming to power did tend to open up avenues for the expansion of Soviet influence and power, and the expansion of communist and Soviet influence did tend to have an impact on wider regional international relations and the security of neighbouring states. This is not to suggest that the 'domino theory' was to be born out in South-East Asia after the 1975 communist victory in Vietnam, but it does suggest that revolutions had international repercussions that had an impact on the international and domestic politics of neighbouring states even if they did not succumb to revolution.[6]

The international and geopolitical consequences of revolutionary change were most evident in developments in Cuba after the 1959 revolution, which led to the 1962 Missile Crisis through the attempt by Moscow to alter the strategic balance of power by deploying nuclear missiles on Cuba. Whilst we might argue that openings to Moscow only occurred because of US hostility to revolutionary change (highlighted in its sponsorship of the ill-fated Bay of Pigs invasion by counter-revolutionaries in April 1961), we still

---

> **KEY QUOTES 4.4:** The Gulf of Tonkin incident and resolution

President Johnson's Message to Congress, 5 August 1964

Last night I announced to the American people that the North Vietnamese regime had conducted further deliberate attacks against U.S. naval vessels operating in international waters, and I had therefore directed air action against gunboats and supporting facilities used in these hostile operations. This air action has now been carried out with substantial damage to the boats and facilities. Two U.S. aircraft were lost in the action.

After consultation with the leaders of both parties in the Congress, I further announced a decision to ask the Congress for a resolution expressing the unity and determination of the United States in supporting freedom and in protecting peace in southeast Asia.

These latest actions of the North Vietnamese regime has given a new and grave turn to the already serious situation in southeast Asia . . .

The threat to the free nations of southeast Asia has long been clear. The North Vietnamese regime has constantly sought to take over South Vietnam and Laos. This Communist regime has violated the Geneva accords for Vietnam. It has systematically conducted a campaign of subversion, which includes the direction, training, and supply of personnel and arms for the conduct of guerrilla warfare in South Vietnamese territory. In Laos, the North Vietnamese regime has maintained military forces, used Laotian territory for infiltration into South Vietnam, and most recently carried out combat operations—all in direct violation of the Geneva Agreements of 1962.

In recent months, the actions of the North Vietnamese regime have become steadily more threatening . . .

As President of the United States I have concluded that I should now ask the Congress, on its part, to join in affirming the national determination that all such attacks will be met, and that the United States will continue in its basic policy of assisting the free nations of the area to defend their freedom.

As I have repeatedly made clear, the United States intends no rashness, and seeks no wider war. We must make it clear to all that the United States is united in its determination to bring about the end of Communist subversion and aggression in the area . . .

Joint Resolution of Congress RES 1145, 7 August 1964

Resolved by the Senate and House of Representatives of the United States of America in Congress assembled,

That the Congress approves and supports the determination of the President, as Commander in Chief, to take all necessary measures to repel any armed attack against the forces of the United States and to prevent further aggression.

Section 2. The United States regards as vital to its national interest and to world peace the maintenance of international peace and security in southeast Asia. Consonant with the Constitution of the United States and the Charter of the United Nations and in accordance with its obligations under the Southeast Asia Collective Defense Treaty, the United States is, therefore, prepared, as the President determines, to take all necessary steps, including the use of armed force, to assist any member or protocol state of the Southeast Asia Collective Defense Treaty requesting assistance in defense of its freedom.

Section 3. This resolution shall expire when the President shall determine that the peace and security of the area is reasonably assured by international conditions created by action of the United Nations or otherwise, except that it may be terminated earlier by concurrent resolution of the Congress.

(*Department of State Bulletin*, 24 Aug. 1964)

KEY POINTS

❑ Initial US intervention in Vietnam (Indochina) between 1950 and 1954 was conditioned by wider regional (the Chinese Revolution and Korean War) and international (formation of NATO) developments.

❑ Role of the 'domino theory'—that states surrounding a newly created communist state would become 'infected' with communism and at risk of communist subversion—in US policy towards Vietnam.

❑ After 1954 the USA committed itself to building a stable anti-communist state in South Vietnam, the success of which was dependent on its relations with local political forces in South Vietnam.

❑ Increasing US (military) involvement in South Vietnam after 1960 due to the failings of the South Vietnamese government. By the mid-1960s the US faced a dilemma: to pull out of Vietnam and see a likely communist victory or become more involved, effectively running the war.

❑ The significance of the Gulf of Tonkin incident in 1965 in justifying the escalation of US military involvement in Vietnam.

❑ The prolonging of the war and the humiliation caused by the NLF's 1968 'Tet offensive' meant that American domestic politics became much more influential on American policy, leading to the eventual withdrawal of US troops by 1973.

❑ The significance of revolutionary change in the third world is that it opened up avenues for the expansion of Soviet geopolitical power, as well as the way new revolutionary regimes threatened to undermine the political stability of neighbouring states.

❑ The geopolitical consequences of revolutionary change were most evident in how the 1962 Cuban Missile Crisis developed out of the 1959 Cuban Revolution.

have to recognize the very different and antagonistic domestic and foreign policy priorities of most, if not all, revolutionary states during the Cold War with respect to US priorities and interests.

The threat of revolution, then, could be seen in geopolitical terms. However, US responses to revolutionary change were also a product of the prevailing anti-communist ideational mindset within the US national security bureaucracy, which also pervaded wider US society. Simply put, most if not all revolutionary changes tended to be seen as communist inspired or—in one or another—involving Moscow. This was obviously not the case as revolutionary change carried out by nationalist movements—mainly against European colonial powers—in the third

world was a product of very local political and economic developments with little or nothing to do with Moscow. Consequently, on one level, we could see the struggles of nationalist movements for political and economic independence in the third world as being separate from the Cold War. This highlights a further layer of complexity in surveying American foreign policy as US policy was concerned not only with the USSR and other communist states, but also with thwarting the domestic and international ambitions of a number of third world states not because they were communist, but because they refused to accept or involve themselves in American-constructed international security and economic frameworks.

Ending the Cold War

The discussion of the role of American foreign policy in the ending of the Cold War has focused on the policies of the Reagan administration and, in particular, the claims by some scholars and former members

(Weinberger 1990) of the Reagan administration that 'Reagan won the Cold War'. The claim, then, is that Reagan's arms build-up and policy of confronting the USSR and its allies in the third world (after a spate of revolutions during the 1970s that saw an expansion of Soviet power) through supporting anti-communist guerrilla movements forced the USSR into making strategic and political concessions that effectively ended the Cold War between 1987 and 1989. So, did Reagan's policies of confrontation force Soviet concessions, effectively ending the Cold War?

In assessing the impact of Reagan's policies most scholars tend to highlight the differences between the first and second terms. Whilst the first term was characterized by a more aggressive and confrontational stance towards the USSR, the second term—in part reflected in the turnover in key personnel and a more assertive Congress—saw a gradual shift away from confrontation and, with Gorbachev's accession to the Soviet leadership in 1985, an opening to negotiations with Moscow.

In terms of timing, then, Reagan's policies did *not* force Soviet concessions as the developments that realized the end of the Cold War confrontation emerged out of a rather different political and geopolitical context. Further, for as long as the US kept the pressure on, Moscow continued to—in the main—meet its international commitments and, further, did not move towards making concessions to the US (Halliday 1994; Saull 2007: 165–79). This was the case even in the early stages of the Gorbachev leadership during 1985–6.

We do not know what might have happened had the second term Reagan administration continued with the hard-line policies of the first term, but the reduction of international tensions certainly made it easier for Gorbachev to usher in the changes that he made in Soviet foreign and domestic policies that broke the geopolitical and ideological framework that had dominated US–Soviet relations since 1945. Further, it was only in this altered—more benign—geopolitical context that the Soviet leadership could tolerate the developments in east-central Europe in 1989, which saw the collapse of communist power within these states and the dissolution of the Warsaw Pact.

However, in recognizing the paradoxical role played by Reagan's policies in ending the Cold War we also need to take stock of the longer-term consequences of US geopolitical hostility towards the USSR and the economic burdens that this posed on the USSR. Thus, whilst the Reagan doctrine may not have forced the USSR to end the Cold War, the longer-term impact of US policy towards the USSR and international revolution, more generally, posed huge burdens that could only undermine the domestic political and economic legitimacy of the USSR and its allied regimes—thus bearing out Kennan's prognosis in the 'The Sources of Soviet Conduct' that the US should contain Soviet power until the domestic problems within the USSR forced political change—particularly through the way in which economic resources were channelled towards maintaining the military–geopolitical balance with the US. In this regard, the wider international capitalist socio-economic dimensions of US power and the way in which the US took advantage of economic resources beyond the national economic space of the United States proved to be a defining factor in the long-term struggle with the USSR.

Conclusion

This chapter has provided a historical survey of American foreign policy during the Cold War covering a number of major developments and changes in US policy. It has sought to account for US policy by drawing on and evaluating contrasting theoretical arguments that stress the role of geopolitical, ideational, and/or socio-economic factors on US foreign policy. The chapter has demonstrated the explanatory uses and limitations of each approach. Its main conclusions are that the making of US foreign policy during the Cold War was centred on the how external developments involving the USSR and other revolutionary states and changes in the international capitalist economy were mediated through the institutions of the US state and domestic political debates involving the American people and their political representatives.

> **KEY QUOTES 4.5: REAGAN'S 'EVIL EMPIRE' SPEECH**

President Reagan's 'evil empire' speech to the House of Commons, 8 June 1982

From Stettin on the Baltic to Varna on the Black Sea, the regimes planted by totalitarianism have had more than thirty years to establish their legitimacy. But none—not one regime—has yet been able to risk free elections. Regimes planted by bayonets do not take root . . .

If history teaches anything, it teaches self-delusion in the face of unpleasant facts is folly. We see around us today the marks of our terrible dilemma—predictions of doomsday, antinuclear demonstrations, an arms race in which the West must, for its own protection, be an unwilling participant. At the same time we see totalitarian forces in the world who seek subversion and conflict around the globe to further their barbarous assault on the human spirit. What, then, is our course? Must civilization perish in a hail of fiery atoms? Must freedom wither in a quiet, deadening accommodation with totalitarian evil? . . .

The decay of the Soviet experiment should come as no surprise to us. Wherever the comparisons have been made between free and closed societies—West Germany and East Germany, Austria and Czechoslovakia, Malaysia and Vietnam—it is the democratic countries that are prosperous and responsive to the needs of their people. And one of the simple but overwhelming facts of our time is this: of all the millions of refugees we've seen in the modern world, their flight is always away from, not toward the Communist world. Today on the NATO line, our military forces face east to prevent a possible invasion. On the other side of the line, the Soviet forces also face east to prevent their people from leaving . . .

The objective I propose is quite simple to state: to foster the infrastructure of democracy, the system of a free press, unions, political parties, universities, which allows a people to choose their own way to develop their own culture, to reconcile their own differences through peaceful means . . .

What I am describing now is a plan and a hope for the long term—the march of freedom and democracy which will leave Marxism–Leninism on the ash heap of history as it has left other tyrannies which stifle the freedom and muzzle the self-expression of the people. And that's why we must continue our efforts to strengthen NATO even as we move forward with our zero-option initiative in the negotiations on intermediate-range forces and our proposal for a one-third reduction in strategic ballistic missile warheads . . .

(*Public Papers of Ronald Reagan*, 1982, available at www.reagan.utexas.edu/archives/speeches/1982/60882a.htm)

KEY POINTS

❏ The role of American foreign policy in the ending of the Cold War has focused on the claims by some scholars and former members of the Reagan administration that Reagan's hard-line policies forced the USSR into making concessions that ended the Cold War.

❏ Most scholars highlight the differences between the first and second terms of the Reagan presidency. Whilst the first term was dominated by confronting the USSR in the third world and imposing an economic burden on Moscow through a massive arms build-up, the second term saw Reagan move towards negotiations with Moscow.

❏ Historical evidence suggests that Reagan's hard-line policies had little impact on changing Soviet behaviour during his first term.

❏ It was the changed circumstances (and policies) of Reagan's second term that made Gorbachev more willing and able to implement his reform programme, which ended with the collapse of communist power and the dissolution of the Warsaw Pact.

❏ Whilst Reagan's hard-line policies may not have 'won' the Cold War, the long-term costs imposed on the USSR by containment played a very important role—as suggested by Kennan—in undermining the political and economic legitimacy of communist rule in the USSR and east-central Europe.

In this sense the realm of domestic politics and the prevailing ideational and ideological currents within state institutions and wider society were crucial in determining the US response to geopolitical changes and challenges and in responding to changes in the international capitalist economy. Further, the chapter has tried to expand our intellectual gaze beyond the traditional focus on US diplomatic and inter-state relations through highlighting the connections between geopolitics and international economic relations.

US foreign policy then and now has been preoccupied with these two concerns—geopolitical and socio-economic—and in this regard the re-ordering of the international economy after the war based on US leadership and a US model of political economy could be seen as the transformation in world politics after the war now that the Cold War has ended. The interesting point for the future of US global power is that the Cold War was integral to those post-war international economic arrangements.

? Questions

1. In what ways did domestic political developments influence American foreign policy during the Cold War?
2. Critically assess the orthodox–revisionist debate on the origins of the Cold War. Which account do you find more convincing and why?
3. 'Throughout the history of the Cold War the United States used and manipulated the Soviet threat to secure its leadership over the Western world'. Discuss.
4. How useful is the concept of imperialism in explaining American foreign relations during the Cold War?
5. Why did the United States intervene in Vietnam? Why was it unable to overcome communist forces?
6. 'American policy towards third-world revolutions was as much about misperception as it was about confronting communist expansion'. Discuss.
7. To what extent was US foreign economic policy of a case of 'containment by other means'?
8. Did the US cause the 'new' Cold War?
9. Did Reagan 'win' the Cold War?
10. What impact did the end of the Cold War have on American foreign policy?

» Further Reading

Chomsky, N. (1991), *Deterring Democracy* (London: Verso).

A survey of American foreign policy from one of its leading radical critics.

Gaddis, J. L. (1997), *We Now Know: Rethinking Cold War History* (Oxford: Clarendon Press).

An important study of the Cold War, drawing on the interpretation of de-classified Soviet documents.

Garthoff, R. (2006), *A Journey Through the Cold War: A Memoir of Containment and Coexistence* (Washington D.C.: Brookings Institution Press).

A personal survey of Cold War history from a leading diplomatic historian of the Cold War.

Kolko, G. (1988), *Confronting the Third World: United States Foreign Policy, 1945–1980* (New York: Pantheon Books).

A survey of American foreign policy towards the third world from a leading Cold War revisionist.

Lebow, R. and Risse-Kappen, T. (eds) (1995), *International Relations Theory and the End of the Cold War* (New York: Columbia University Press).

A collection of articles drawing on different theoretical perspectives debating the end of the Cold War.

Pollard, R. (1985), *Economic Security and the Origins of the Cold War: The Strategic Ends of US Foreign Policy, 1945–1950* (New York: Columbia University Press).

An excellent analysis of the role of economic considerations in US foreign policy after the war.

Young, M. (1991), *The Vietnam Wars, 1945–1990* (New York: HarperCollins).

An excellent survey of the US military intervention in Vietnam.

Endnotes

1. Prior to this the US had shown itself committed to using force—through numerous interventions—against revolutionary movements and states in the western hemisphere in the early decades of the twentieth century. See Horowitz (1969).

2. Many of which formed the basis of Presidential national security doctrines throughout the Cold War.

3. Between 1961 and 1962 the number of US military personnel in South Vietnam more than tripled from 3000 to 11,000, increasing to over 16,000 in 1963 and more than 23,000 before the formal introduction of combat troops in March 1965. By the end of 1965 there were 184,000 US military personnel in South Vietnam. See Young (1991: 332–3).

4. See Saull 2001: 189–99, 2007: 109–112, 120–7 for a detailed analysis of US policy in Vietnam.

5. An alternative view is provided by in the 'Pentagon Papers' which states that the US deliberately provoked the North Vietnamese attack on the two US vessels—the *Maddox* and *Turner Joy*. See Sheehan (1971) and Prados (2004).

6. This was evident in Indonesia in the mid-1960s and the growing power of the Indonesian Communist Party. The result was a pre-emptive counter-revolutionary *coup d'état* by right-wing and pro-American elements within the armed forces—led by General Suharto—that overthrew the radical nationalist government in 1966, ushering in the massacre of tens of thousands of communists and other leftists by the military regime over the following months.

 For a range of additional resources to support your learning visit the Online Resource Centre that accompanies this book at www.oxfordtextbooks.co.uk/orc/cox_stokes2e/.

5 America in the 1990s: searching for purpose

John Dumbrell

Chapter contents

Introduction: post-Cold War American internationalism

Between the late 1940s and 1989, the guiding principle of American foreign policy was straightforward. The underlying principle of those years was the containment of Soviet international power. With the collapse first of the Berlin Wall and subsequently of Soviet communism itself, the United States stood in need of a new way of grounding its internationalist engagement. A lengthy debate ensued as to the proper scope and purpose of this new foreign policy. Post-Cold War foreign policy was developed under the contrasting leadership of President George Herbert Walker Bush and Bill Clinton. This chapter surveys and evaluates US foreign policy debates and policy management under the direction of these two presidents.

The current chapter discusses the 'long 1990s', the era between the benevolent external shock of 1989 (the fall of the Berlin Wall) and the malevolent external shock of 9/11. The 'long 1990s', the immediate post-Cold War era, appears with hindsight a distinct phase in the history of US foreign policy. It had its own characteristic preoccupations, priorities, and processes. Derek Chollet and John Goldgeier (2008: xiv) have likened the period between 1989 and 2001 to the years between the two world wars, when 'with no common threat to unite them, Americans couldn't come together to define the national interest'. Policy elites were preoccupied by questions of international disorder and the proper role for the United States to take in containing disorder. Debates swirled in the 1990s over the possibility of successful military intervention to promote humanitarian ends. Long-standing arguments about the relationship between ideals and interests in US foreign policy were transformed and re-energised in this new, post-Soviet international environment. Washington continued to be centrally concerned with Russia's place in the new order, but was also increasingly exercised by the rise of China, the communist country whose political system had survived the upheavals of 1989–90 more or less intact.

Following 1989, US policy makers came to appreciate the degree to which the disappearing Cold War system had promoted a form of international stability, however brittle and inherently dangerous. The apparent international triumph of liberalism seemed to point away from the kind of global geopolitical/ideological intermixture which had defined the Cold War. Norman Ornstein (1994: 114) wrote in 1994: 'Geoeconomics increasingly drives geopolitics, compared to a Cold War agenda where geopolitics drove geoeconomics.' In the 1990s, economic foreign policy constituted a kind of operational cutting edge, providing purpose and coherence to wider strategies

of US international engagement. The 1990s also witnessed the emergence of new agendas, often 'old' issues transformed by circumstance and perception. New agendas centred on what the Clinton administration came to call 'borderless threats' such as environmental problems and the rise and transmogrification of international terrorism. The 'long 1990s' were years of intense democratic possibility. Yet from Rwanda to Bosnia, they were also years of atavistic negativity and irrationality. How should the USA respond to a world which was apparently both rapidly integrating and rapidly disintegrating?

Perhaps, above all, at least from the point of view of our concern here with the course of US foreign policy, the post-Cold War era saw a conscious and complex debate, conducted at both elite and public levels, about the very point and purpose of American internationalism. Should America continue to lead? Was leadership, or even sustained global engagement, good for America?

BOX 5.1:   Chronology of key events, 1989–2001

1989 January: inauguration of President George H. W. Bush	October: 18 US military personnel killed in Somalia
June: Tiananmen Square massacre in Beijing	November: NAFTA (North American Free Trade
November: fall of Berlin Wall	Agreement) approved by the US Congress
December: Bush–Gorbachev Malta summit	**1994** April: US forces leave Somalia
US invasion of Panama	May: Presidential Decision Directive 25
1990 May–June: Bush–Gorbachev summit in Washington	September: US invasion of Haiti
and Camp David	October: North Korean nuclear agreement
Superpower agreement on reunification of Germany	**1995** January: Republicans assume leadership of both
August: Iraq invades Kuwait	houses of the US Congress
September: Bush's New World Order speech	US rescue operation for the Mexican *peso*
November: European conventional force levels	July–August: Congress votes to lift the arms embargo
treaty signed	on the Bosnian government
1991 January: Congressional Gulf War debate	August: US diplomatic initiative in Bosnia
January–February: Operation Desert Storm: liberation of Kuwait	November: Dayton Peace Accords agreed
	1996 November: Clinton re-elected
July: First START (superpower strategic arms treaty)	**1997** May: NATO–Russia Founding Act signed
signed	**1998** April: Good Friday (Belfast) Peace Agreement
August: failed coup in Moscow	August: missile attacks on Sudan and Afghanistan
Soviet parliament bans the Communist Party	December: US–UK air strikes on Iraq
December: USSR replaced by 'Commonwealth of	**1999** March: NATO air strikes on Serbia begin
Independent States'	April: NATO 50th anniversary summit: formal admission of Poland, Hungary, and the Czech Republic
1992 June: Washington summit: Russia recognized as the	
'successor state' to the USSR	October: US Senate fails to ratify the Comprehensive
December: Operation Restore Hope begins in Somalia	Nuclear Test Ban Treaty
1993 January: inauguration of President Bill Clinton	**2000** July: Israel–Palestine peace talks begin at Camp David
June: air assault on Iraq	November: George W. Bush wins the presidential
September: Oslo Declaration of Principles on Middle	election
East peace	

Searching for purpose: the 'Kennan sweepstakes'

Post-Cold War options

Beginning in the late 1980s, the American foreign policy community was exposed to a sometimes bewildering and prolonged national meditation on possible options for an America without a Soviet threat. During the first year of Clinton's presidency, the debate became known in administration circles as the 'Kennan sweepstakes': a conscious effort to find a post-Soviet statement of purpose to rival George Kennan's early Cold War concept of 'containment' of communism (Brinkley 1997; Dumbrell 2009: 41–5). The debate was at first deeply influenced by the notion, inherited from the years following the end of the Vietnam War, of American decline. Perceptions of decline were, however, even in the early 1990s, undercut by the contemporary advances for liberal democracy, not only in former communist countries, but also in Latin America and South Africa. Commentators began to develop the notion of the 'democratic peace', an idea derived from Enlightenment philosopher Immanuel Kant which was profoundly to influence the foreign policy thinking of the Clinton administration (Russett 1993; Doyle 1995). Moreover, as the Soviet Union imploded, American military eminence became obvious. Even before the formal break-up of the USSR, neo-conservative commentator Charles Krauthammer (1991) was discussing the 'unipolar moment'. From a liberal perspective, Joseph Nye (1991 and 2004) developed the idea of 'soft power', involving the ability to co-opt rather than coerce, to set the assumptions, even the organizational framework, for international behaviour. The United States seemed, above all nations, to combine formidable amounts of economic, military, and 'soft' power.

The range of options on offer in the early 1990s was conveniently arranged along a spectrum leading from strong internationalist assertion (to the point of actual imperialism) at one end, to contractionism (to the point of isolationism) at the other (Crabb, Sarieddine, and Antizzo 2001). The major fear in elite discourse was that of a new isolationism. With the Soviet threat extinguished at last, perhaps America really was homeward bound? Ronald Steel (1995: 85) discerned 'a chasm between a foreign policy establishment mesmerized by notions of American leadership and "global responsibilities" and an American public concerned by drug trafficking and addiction, jobs, illegal aliens' and other domestic issues. By 1998, Samuel Berger, Clinton's second National Security Adviser, was arguing that the real danger came from 'those who would "talk the talk" of internationalism, but "walk the walk" of isolationism' (Berger 1998: 188). Successful internationalism, in this line of argument, required the nerve to spend money and to take risks even when America was not directly threatened.

President Bush Senior and 'the vision thing'

President Bush was actually an unlikely post-Cold War visionary. He famously denied any skill with 'the vision thing'. In the frenetic immediate post-Cold War climate, he was not short of advice. Former Defense Secretary Robert McNamara (1989) urged him to cut defence spending by 50 per cent. At the other extreme, the 1992 Defense Planning Guidance, written in his Department of Defense and leaked to the press in April 1992, reflected neo-conservative thinking. It envisaged

---

KEY POINTS

❑ Both the George H. W. Bush and the Clinton administrations wrestled with the problem of deciding on a clear, publicly defensible, strategy for US foreign policy in the new era.

❑ Debates prior to 1995 were affected by perceptions of American decline.

❑ Post-Cold War options ran a gamut from expansionist/imperialist to contractionist/isolationist.

MAJOR DEBATES AND THEIR IMPACT 5.1: The 'end of history' and the 'democratic peace'

'End of history'

What we may be witnessing is not just the end of the Cold War, or the passing of a particular period of post-war history, but the end of history as such: that is, the end point of mankind's ideological evolution and the universalization of Western liberal democracy as the final form of human government. . . .
(Fukuyama 1989)

Fukuyama predicted the end of ideological conflicts, not history itself, and the triumph of political and economic liberalism. That point is correct in a narrow sense: the secular religions that fought each other so bloodily in the last century are now dead. But Fukuyama failed to note that nationalism remains very much alive. Moreover, he ignored the explosive potential of religious wars that has extended to a large part of the Islamic world.
(Hoffman 2002)

The 'democratic peace'

The end of ideological hostility matters doubly because it represents a surrender to the force of Western values of economic and especially political freedom. To the degree that countries once ruled by autocratic systems become democratic, a striking fact about the world comes to bear on any discussion of the future of international relations: in the modern international system, democracies have almost never fought each other.
(Russett 1993)

Just as neighbors who raise each others' barns are less likely to become arsonists, people who raise each others' living standards through commerce are less likely to become combatants.
(Bill Clinton, American University speech, February 1993)

❝❞ KEY QUOTES 5.1: The New World Order

Out of these troubled times . . . a new world order can emerge . . . Today, that new world order is struggling to be born, a world quite different from the one we have known, a world where the rule of law supplants the rule of the jungle, a world in which nations recognize the shared responsibility for freedom and justice, a world where the strong respect the weak.
(President George H. W. Bush, 11 September 1990)

'World Orders, Old and New': the rule of the 'rich men of the rich societies . . . assisted by the rich men of the hungry nations who do their bidding'.
(Chomsky 1994)

Using force makes sense as a policy where the stakes warrant, where and when force can be effective, where no other policies are likely to prove effective, where its application can be limited in scope and time, and where the potential benefits justify the potential costs and sacrifice.
(President George H. W. Bush, 5 January 1993)

an America which would enjoy permanent and unremitting military primacy.

Bush's natural caution was tempered by the demands of occupying the White House as the Cold War order expired. His advice to aides included the injunction to 'think big', as well as to 'work as a team' under close presidential direction (Kolb 1994: 6). An August 1990 speech in Colorado represented an early effort to map out a post-Cold War foreign policy. The USA needed to meet new, unspecified threats, 'wholly

unrelated to the earlier patterns of the US–Soviet relationship'. Only 'a strong and engaged America' could respond adequately to threats which might emerge in any corner of the globe (Melanson 1996: 219).

The elder Bush's main contribution to post-Cold War role setting was the concept of a New World Order, outlined to Congress following the 1990 invasion of Kuwait by Saddam Hussein's Iraqi army. Although it contained a general commitment to democratic idealism, the New World Order was far from an American-led campaign for global democracy. It represented rather a brand of 1990s internationalism which was closely attuned to a keen awareness of the limits of American power. Following the 1991 victory in the Gulf against Iraq, Bush famously, and rather prematurely, boasted of having buried the 'specter of Vietnam' in 'the desert sands of the Arabian peninsula' (Tucker and Hendrickson 1992: 72). Yet, just as the New World Order was no unabashed call to arms, Bush's farewell speeches at the close of his presidency emphasized constraints as well as opportunities. At West Point military academy in January 1993, Bush rhetorically reserved the use of force for occasions 'where its application can be limited in space and time, and where the potential benefits justify the potential costs and sacrifice' (*Public Papers* 1993: 2229).

Bill Clinton

Clinton's 1992 presidential campaign was dominated by domestic issues; indeed a major Clinton criticism of Bush was that the latter had become excessively oriented towards foreign policy. By the time Clinton entered the White House, however, it was clear not only that an entry had to be found for the 'Kennan sweepstakes', but that Bush's New World Order had to be recast. Clinton was now looking for a vision that combined a commitment to geo-economics, and an awareness of limits, with moral purpose. The key task was to delineate the conditions for engagement, military or diplomatic. Various administration spokespeople advanced notions of 'assertive humanitarianism'. Undersecretary of State Peter Tarnoff promoted a highly restrained version of 'assertive mulilatarianism', based on a 'case by case decision to limit the amount of American engagement' (Brown 1994: 609). As they developed in the early phase of Clinton's presidency, the 'tests' or conditions for engagement seemed to centre on the domestic

overspill from regional conflict, alliance obligations, and demonstrable US economic interest.

The administration's prize entry in the 'Kennan sweepstakes' was 'democratic enlargement', defended and defined by National Security Adviser Tony Lake in September 1993. Lake made it clear that 'democratic enlargement' had economics at its heart. The replacement for anti-communist containment would be 'a strategy of enlargement . . . of the world's free community of market democracies' (Brinkley 1997: 116). 'Democratic enlargement' never gained wide currency as a slogan, and was superseded in later declarations of purpose by the formula 'engagement and enlargement'. Yet, 'democratic enlargement' did capture what was to become the central, integrating purpose of the Clinton foreign policy: to position the USA at the head of economic globalization.

As it developed in the mid-and late 1990s, Clinton administration 'big thinking' on post-Cold War foreign policy reflected both a new confidence and a new caution. Confidence derived from the retreat of declinism. By mid-decade, the computer revolution, growth in global free trade, and the US consumer spending boom had transformed the recessionary economic climate which had affected the election of 1992. The reversals in Somalia, however, raised doubts about the future of 'assertive humanitarianism'. From January 1995, Clinton had to share power with a Republican congressional majority which was contemptuous of anything resembling naive altruism in foreign policy. One expression of the post-Somalia mood was Presidential Decision Directive (PDD) 25, drafted in May 1994. The document laid out conditions for US participation in UN peacekeeping operations. It was actually a little less cautious than similar directives from Bush. Under PDD 25, the USA would contribute across its full range of capabilities, not just its 'unique' ones. However, US troops would support UN operations only if risks were 'acceptable' and objectives clear (Daalder 1996).

Administration thinking in the second Clinton term focused on the desired globalization of market democracy, a concept encapsulated in the Clintonite phrase, 'family of nations'. Excluded from the family were 'rogue' or 'backlash' states, later dubbed 'states of concern'. Such states included familiar international 'bad boys': Iraq, Iran, Cuba,

North Korea, Libya. The post-Cold War 'democratic peace' was to be extended and protected by exposing and marginalizing the rogues (Lake 1994). Against Republican arguments that 'Americanism' and narrowly defined national interest should guide foreign policy, second-term Clintonites argued for the US role as 'indispensable nation'. For Clinton's second term Secretary of State Madeleine Albright (2003: 420), the final decade of the twentieth century was 'the global era, a time characterized by heightened interdependence, overlapping national interests, and borders permeable to everything from terrorists and technology to disease and democratic ideals'. The USA would not and could not do everything; yet it could guide and shepherd the global progress towards market democracy. Democratic idealism was still part of the administration's conceptual apparatus in the second term. However, it was

an idealism which had by this time been severely tested against the stubborn refusal of traditional security concerns to disappear, even in the era of post-communism. The 'security agenda', especially in relation to the Korean peninsula, Russia, and China, appeared to subsume 'global freedom' in a major foreign policy address in San Francisco in February 1999 (McCormick 2005: 192).

KEY POINTS

❑ Clinton's post-Cold War vision shifted from 'democratic enlargement' to 'engagement and enlargement'.

❑ Clinton increasingly looked towards extending the sway of market democracy and to marginalizing 'rogue states'.

❝ KEY QUOTES 5.2: The Clinton administration: globalization, democracy promotion, and rogue states

With NAFTA, we'll be creating the biggest trading block in the world right at our doorstep, and led by the United States.

(President Bill Clinton, radio address, 18 October 1993)

. . . our policy must face the reality of recalcitrant and outlaw states that not only choose to remain outside the family but also assault its basic values. There are few 'backlash states': Cuba, North Korea, Iran, Iraq, and Libya. For now they lack the resources of a superpower, which would enable them to seriously threaten the democratic order being created around them. Nevertheless, their behaviour is often aggressive and defiant. The ties between them are growing as they seek to thwart or quarantine themselves

from a global trend to which they seem incapable of adapting.

(Lake 1994; Anthony Lake was Clinton's first US National Security Adviser)

The world is no longer divided into two hostile camps. Instead, we are building bonds with nations that once were our adversaries. Growing connections of commerce and culture give us a chance to lift the fortunes and spirits of people the world over. And for the very first time in all of history, more people on this planet live under democracy than dictatorship.

(President Bill Clinton, second inaugural address, 20 January 1997)

Foreign policy making in the new order

Policy making under Bush and Clinton: executive organization and legislative prerogatives

In the early 1990s, there was a wide consensus to the effect that the form as well as the content of US foreign policy would change in the new world. At one level, so

it was argued, the USA needed to develop and embed policy processes which reflected the requirements of a globalizing world economy, increasingly shaped by

---

BOX 5.2: The USA and Somalia, 1992–4

The Bush intervention, 1992

In December 1992, shortly after his defeat in the presidential election, President George H. W. Bush announced, during a congressional recess, the start of Operation Restore Hope, involving some 28,000 US troops in a humanitarian aid intervention in Somalia, a country torn apart by civil conflict. The original intention was to have US troops withdrawn before Clinton's inauguration. A United Nations authorization in December recognized that the force would be commanded by the United States. Divisions quickly opened between the USA and the UN, while domestic opinion focused on the possibility of 'another Vietnam'. The troop commitment took place with a minimum of reference to the 1973 War Powers Resolution. When the first US Navy SEAL commandos landed in Somalia on 8 December, they were greeted by the television lights and cameras of the international media.

Clinton and Somalia

Following some initial apparent success, the intervention developed into a messy crash landing for Clinton. The new President made references to his need to inform Congress under the War Powers Resolution, but held that continued deployment of US forces was a function of his 'inherent powers' as commander-in-chief of the armed forces. The situation deteriorated sharply after the UN Security Council, prodded by US Ambassador Madeleine Albright, adopted a 'nation-building' brief for the mission. US forces were tasked with arresting Mohamed Farah Aideed, the Somalian warlord blamed for the murder of twenty-three Pakistani peace-keepers in June 1993. Eighteen US military personnel were killed in a Mogadishu firefight in October. By this time, the

intervention was unpopular and beginning to stimulate congressional calls for withdrawal. The Democratic leadership in Congress, however, effectively protected the new Democratic President from any radical assault on his authority. Clinton announced, following the Mogadishu killings, that all US troops would be withdrawn by April 1994. Congress raised the prospect of a funding cut-off thereafter, though it allowed limited troop deployment until early 1995.

Rationale and significance

Bush's decision to commit troops to a region without significant immediate security interest for the United States was, in effect, the New World Order in action. Here was the USA acting as chairman of the international board of post-Cold War peace and order imposition. Moreover, this was an intended demonstration that Vietnam-era constraints on US military action had now evaporated. Bush's decision was rooted in a genuine concern to advance humanitarian interventionism in the new order, as well as to compensate for his administration's perceived inability to affect the worsening security and humanitarian situation in the former Yugoslavia. The deployment reflected the 'CNN effect': the putative ability of media coverage of post-Cold War humanitarian disasters to shape Washington's agenda. Clinton was bequeathed something of a poison pill. The shift in purpose, from humanitarian relief to nation building, indicated the dangers of 'mission creep' in the new international environment. The Somalian failure illustrated the shallowness of the US public and legislative commitment to the kind of expansive internationalism envisaged by Bush's New World Order.

---

the dynamics of free trade (Paarlberg 1995). America's domestic political process appeared likely to become increasingly decentralized, less hierarchical, and more open to legislative and domestic interest group pressure. With the integrating force of immediate threat removed, the line between foreign and domestic policy seemed about to become even more blurred than previously. Presidents would no longer be able to assert authority under the cover of perpetual international crisis. Even state and local governments appeared to be getting in on the act, as they developed quasi-independent trade strategies (McHenry 1994).

Despite all this, the foreign policy process under President George H. W. Bush retained more of a Cold War than a New World Order aspect. The practical efficiency of the Bush foreign policy team was impressive. It coped well with much of the 'high politics' management, notably the reunification of Germany, which accompanied the end of the Cold War. Inside the White House, Bush operated a closely structured National Security Council (NSC) committee system, deferring always to the President. Many key decisions were made by ad hoc groups chaired by Bush himself. The President and his foreign policy elite were unenthused by the possibility of post-Cold War legislative resurgence, a development they managed to keep at bay. The congressional debate which preceded the 1991 Gulf War was a set-piece for the articulation of legislative war-making prerogative; narrow victories were achieved for the presidential line in both houses. As with the Panamanian invasion of 1989, the 1991 Gulf conflict nevertheless proceeded with a minimum of legislative involvement.

Policy making in the Clinton years did provide evidence of a decentralized post-Cold War process. East European ethnic lobbies in the USA, for example, played an important role in energizing the presidential commitment to the eastward expansion of NATO, the North Atlantic Treaty Organisation (Asmus 2002: 80). In post-Soviet conditions, policy towards Cuba lost its high-security profile and became influenced by congressionally oriented expatriate anti-Castro lobbies in Florida, notably the Cuban–American National Foundation (Kiger 1997; Haney and Vanderbush 1999). Clinton made important bureaucratic changes, designed to recognize the newly central international economic agenda. The National Economic Council (NEC)—originally headed by Robert Rubin and later by Laura Tyson—was established in order to raise economic foreign policy to the same status as foreign diplomatic policy.

The early Clinton foreign policy operation was hampered by the President's own preoccupation with domestic policy. The post-1992 foreign policy team was not as effective as that associated with Clinton's predecessor. At times, especially in relation to Balkans policy before 1995, the process was in frank disarray (Bert 1997). By 1995, Clinton was concentrating more clearly and effectively on foreign policy, and continued to do so during the second term. Republican challenges on domestic issues, effectively ending the prospects for a successful presidential reform agenda, made a contribution here. Despite all the difficulties, the key Clinton players—Warren Christopher and Tony Lake in the first term; Madeleine Albright, Sandy Berger, and (Republican) Secretary of Defense William Cohen in the second—worked reasonably well as a team, avoiding the conspicuous public disagreements that had damaged previous administrations.

The post-1994 Republican Congress quickly asserted itself in regard to policy in Bosnia. During the second term, Clinton suffered defeats when the Senate refused to confirm the Comprehensive Nuclear Test Ban Treaty in 1998, and when Congress subsequently removed the presidential 'fast track' trade-negotiating authority. Battles were fought over foreign aid, economic aid to Mexico, and reorganization of the State Department. Yet policy initiation remained firmly in the White House. Clinton achieved Senate ratification in 1997 of NATO expansion. When the USA began its air bombardment of Yugoslavia in 1999, Congress was 'consulted' rather than substantively included in decision making (Hendrickson 2002: 122).

Public opinion

Bush's New World Order was, among other things, an effort to sell a reordered American globalism to a sceptical American public. The notion of a post-Cold War 'homeward bound' public, even of a neo-isolationist 'new populism', profoundly influenced the foreign policy debates of the 1990s. 'New populist' candidate Pat Buchanan made waves in the 1992 and 1996 Republican primary elections, arguing for a foreign policy based on narrowly defined national interest. Following the 1994 elections, Senator Jesse Helms of North Carolina, inveterate opponent of foreign aid and of the United Nations, headed the Senate Foreign Relations Committee. The 'new populism' had to be taken seriously.

There was little public encouragement in the 1990s for the USA to become actively engaged in apparently remote regional conflicts. Foreign aid and 'global altruism' slipped down all polled lists of public priorities (Rosner 1995–6; Bacevich 1996). The gap, identified by Ronald Steel and referred to above, between elite and public perspectives—global leadership versus domestic concerns—was evident, for example, in Chicago Council on Foreign Relations polling in the mid-1990s (Rielly 1995).

Yet truth was more complex. The 'new populism' was itself as much an expression of electoral opportunism as of mass preference. Would-be 'new populist' leaders of the right (notably Pat Buchanan) and left (such as Democrat Jerry Brown) attacked globalization and elite free trade policies in the name of the ordinary American. The post-1994 congressional Republicans certainly had a 'new populist' tinge;

KEY POINTS

❏ The 1990s saw a widespread expectation that foreign policy making would become more decentralized and less dominated by presidents.

❏ The post-Cold War presidents were, to varying degrees, able to resist the decentralizing dynamic and, in particular, showed scant regard for congressional war powers.

❏ 'Homeward bound' public opinion was a major potential constraint on executive policy making in the new era.

they showed considerable distaste for 'entangling alliances' and tended to favour unilateralism in foreign policy. However, post-Cold War public opinion *per se* was complex. It retained from the earlier post-Vietnam War era a prudent attitude towards military intervention, especially if goals were vague and American interests indistinct (Jentleson 1992). Post-Cold War public introversion had its limits. The saliency of foreign policy to the US public certainly decreased in the 1990s; yet there was little public enthusiasm for quitting international bodies such as the United Nations and NATO (Kull 1995–6). Both Bush and Clinton were able to lead America along the internationalist path, with the latter conspicuously succeeding in eliciting public approval for troop commitments to Bosnia in 1995–6.

US foreign policy in the post-Cold War era

President Bush Senior, 1989–93

Despite the centrality of 'big thinking' in the 1990s, much foreign policy leadership remained as it had always been: the management of complex international interactions, especially in the context of more or less unexpected crises and emergencies. George H. W. Bush's main concern in 1989–90 was how to manage the extraordinary, and largely unexpected, transformations that were taking place in Russia and eastern Europe. The hallmarks of the Bush approach were procedural deftness, restraint, and caution (Zelikow and Rice 1995; Hurst 1999; Bush and Scowcroft 1998). At times, strategic caution resembled stasis. Bush offered a process of 'testing' both Soviet premier Mikhail Gorbachev's good faith and his security in office. Washington sought also to integrate a reforming USSR into Western capitalist economic and political networks. The collapse of communism in eastern Europe was greeted in official Washington with diplomatic equanimity, with Bush famously declining 'to dance on the Berlin Wall'.

The Bush policy, as it evolved between November 1989 and the extinction of the Soviet Union just over two years later, was one of attempting to bolster Gorbachev's domestic position where possible, but also of stopping well short of complete commitment to the Soviet reformer. There was to be no 'grand bargain', wherein Soviet reform might be underpinned by massive American aid. At the Malta summit in late 1989, Bush effectively promised that Washington would not 'create big problems' if Moscow intervened to pacify the Baltic republics (Beschloss and Talbott 1993: ch. 7). The unpredictability of Soviet politics was underlined by the failed anti-Gorbachev coup of August 1991. Bush supported Boris Yeltsin, the leader of the newly independent Russia, throughout 1992, although again with relatively little in the way of concrete aid. Although criticized for its hesitancy, Bush's Soviet/Russian policy had much to commend it. Two superpower strategic arms (START) treaties were signed by early 1993. Above all, the huge shift in the geopolitical landscape had been managed, at least beyond the immediate disorder in the former Yugoslavia, in a way broadly congruent with the White House's desire to avoid violent disintegration of the Soviet state system. Bush's pragmatic conservatism applied also to relations with China, with only muted criticism being offered following the 1989 massacre of student activists in Tiananmen Square, Beijing.

Bush's policy elsewhere was notably more incautious. In December 1989, the USA invaded Panama. The invasion followed the 'voiding' of elections by Panamanian dictator Manuel Noriega. The White House offered a range of justifications for the action: 'to safeguard the lives of Americans, to defend democracy in Panama, to combat drug trafficking, and to protect the integrity of the Panama Canal' (Maechling 1990: 123). It was rather remarkable that this invasion, the first such use of military force in what were (just) post-Cold War conditions, had very little basis in international law (Fisher 1995: 145–8). Noriega, one-time US intelligence 'asset', had become a severe embarrassment to Washington. The invasion served as an indication of Washington's resolve to act decisively in the new international era, especially in its own hemisphere.

In contrast to Panama, the US response to Iraq's illegal August 1990 invasion of Kuwait was strongly backed by the United Nations. Saddam Hussein, like Noriega, was a former recipient of American aid who was now seen by Washington as an international menace. The US diplomatic and military response to the Kuwaiti invasion, Operations Desert Shield and Desert Storm, however, was multilateral and measured. As Freedman and Karsh (1994: 441) argued, the 1991 ouster of Iraq from Kuwait 'saw the return of the United States to a self-confident and an effective role at the heart of international affairs'. Bush's justification for action, centring on international law and on the threat the Iraqi action mounted to oil supplies, was internationally persuasive. Controversy extended to the way in which mission goals—defending Saudi Arabia from attack, expelling the illegal invader, at times even destroying the Iraqi regime—shifted. The US commitment noticeably expanded following the 1990 midterm elections. The US attacks on virtually defenceless retreating Iraqi troops at the war's end were also highly controversial. Bush's reasons for allowing Saddam to remain in power—primarily concern for the integrity of the allied Gulf coalition and for the limited UN mandate, as well as the desire to avoid involvement in prolonged and unpredictable Iraqi nation

> **KEY POINTS**
>
> ❑ Bush's management of the geopolitical convulsions which accompanied the end of the Cold War was generally sure-footed, if rather uninspired.
> ❑ The 1989 Panamanian invasion and the 1991 Gulf conflict were transformative assertions of post-Cold War US military force.

building—were coherent. The raising and subsequent disappointing of the hopes of the Shi'a population of southern Iraq, that the USA would intervene further in Iraq itself, profoundly damaged the prospects of a successful invasion by American troops in 2003.

President Clinton, first term, 1993–6

Much of the early Clinton foreign policy agenda centred on issues inherited from the momentous Bush years: ratification of the North American Free Trade Agreement (NAFTA) between the USA, Canada, and Mexico, attempting to achieve a post-Cold War settlement with Russia, continuing Bush's moves towards a military posture appropriate for the new era, and developing a credible policy for the disintegrating Yugoslavia.

The November 1993 congressional endorsement of NAFTA (234–200 in the House; 61–38 in the Senate) was a major victory for the President and for the principle of regional free trade. It was a defeat for protectionist and 'new populist' forces, including those represented by Ross Perot, whose 19 per cent national support in the 1992 presidential election had done so much to usher Clinton into the White House. The NAFTA vote set the foundation of a presidential record that was to be distinguished by its commitment to both bilateral and multilateral free trade policies. The administration set its sights on 'big emerging markets', including China, India, Brazil, and South Africa. The interpenetration of global security and economics was exemplified in the administration's policy of free trade with China, more or less without regard for Beijing's human rights record.

Policy towards Russia combined various elements, some of them mutually irreconcilable: a recognition of Boris Yeltsin as the only credible leader of the former superpower, a generalized commitment to Russian and east European democratization, the real need to control and decommission nuclear weapons in various parts of the old USSR, a concern to marginalize Russia as a future international security player, and the playing of a central role in the over-rapid marketization of the Russian economy (Clark 2001: 103–7; Talbott 2003; Marsden 2005). Policy towards Russia was also complicated by what was to become a major achievement of the Clinton administration: the expansion of NATO into eastern Europe. The result of these competing policy concerns was a stance towards Russia which continually risked provoking either a nationalist counter-reaction or a capitulation to the 'new oligarchs' who came to dominate the Russian economy. Regarding the post-Cold War military, Clinton continued the Bush dynamic of resetting capabilities. In 1993, it was announced that, by 1998, defence spending as a percentage of GNP would be less than half what it had been in the era of the Vietnam War. The US defence posture would be organized around the ability to fight two near-simultaneous major regional conflicts.

Clinton's early Bosnian policy continued the Bush administration's unwillingness to accept the need for direct US involvement in what Warren Christopher called in 1993 a 'European situation' (Hendrickson 2002: 73). Deadlock was broken only in 1995, with the threat of a Republican takeover of Bosnian policy, and with the massacre at Srebrenica. Richard Holbrooke, Assistant Secretary of State for European Affairs, began a diplomatic offensive which led within a few months to the Dayton Accords.

The Somalian disaster cast a long shadow. The Rwandan genocide of 1994 proceeded with a minimum of attention from either the UN or the USA. Clinton was later to describe relative non-involvement in Rwanda as the greatest shame of his administration. Military action did occur in Iraq, initially as part of the policy of 'keeping Saddam in his box' and of the commitment to 'dual containment' (of Iraq and Iran). Clinton emerged as an enthusiastic and frequent user of small-scale military force. Iraq was attacked from the air in 1993,

---

KEY POINTS

- ❏ Until 1995, Clinton struggled to develop a credible and consistent policy towards the former Yugoslavia.
- ❏ Clinton's first term was dominated by free trade agendas and by efforts to operationalize the policy of 'selective engagement'.

1994, 1996, 1997, 1998, and 1999. In 1994, the USA launched what was to be a virtually bloodless invasion of Haiti. Designed to restore the rule of elected leader Jean-Bertrand Aristide, the invasion followed domestic pressure, associated particularly with the large refugee influx from Haiti.

Reviewing the first Clinton term, Secretary of State Warren Christopher (1995: 8) asked: 'What would the world be like without American leadership just in the last two years? We might have four nuclear states with the breakup of the Soviet Union instead of one; a North Korea building nuclear bombs; a rising protectionist tide rather than rising trade flows... brutal dictators still terrorizing Haiti and forcing its people to flee; and Iraqi troops very likely back in Kuwait, threatening the world's oil supplies.' Christopher's summary was a reasonable one, despite the conspicuous omission of Bosnia, Somalia, and Rwanda from his survey.

President Clinton, second term, 1996–2001

As is the case with most presidencies, Clinton's second term witnessed a noticeable shifting of gear. The shift proceeded partly from the 1995 transformation in policy towards Bosnia. With declinism now a philosophy of the past, the post-1995 White House exuded greater confidence in America's ability to exercise global leadership. Above all, the Republican Congress began to make its presence felt, pressing the executive towards unilateralist foreign policy options, and towards a new commitment to military spending. The second term witnessed important presidential reverses at the hands of the Congress, as well as international failures such as the failure to prevent India and Pakistan becoming viable nuclear powers.

The later security agenda extended also to Taiwan, where in 1996 Clinton moved to deter the threat of a Chinese invasion, to Iraq, to international terrorism, and to the Balkans. Regarding Iraq, the containment of the Baghdad regime gave way to willingness to countenance the possibility of 'regime change' (Ritter 2005). The international terrorist threat climbed swiftly up the bureaucratic tree. According to Sandy Berger, by 1995 Osama bin Laden 'was on the radar screen; in 1998 he was the radar screen' (Zegart 2007: 24; Branch 2009: 511). Attacks on US embassies in East Africa and the 2000 assault on the USS *Cole* kept these issues firmly on the agenda. The charge of insouciance towards terrorism has frequently, and unjustly, been levelled at the Clinton administration. The 9/11 Commission (2004: 340) offered a more balanced judgement. According to the Commission, the Clinton people 'took the threat seriously, but not in the sense of mustering anything like the kind of effort that would be gathered to confront an enemy of the first, second, or even third rank'. The missile attacks on putative terrorist targets in Sudan and Afghanistan were ineffectual and counter-productive.

In March 1999, NATO forces, led by the USA, instituted a seventy-eight-day bombing campaign against Serbia. The action, which Clinton dubbed 'the first ever humanitarian war' (DiPrizio 2002: 130), was taken following Serbian leader Slobodan Milosevic's refusal to sign the Rambouillet Agreement, setting terms for a cessation of violence against the Albanian minority in the Serbian region of Kosovo. The action led to Serb government capitulation and the entry of NATO forces into Kosovo. The bombing was hailed by sympathetic observers not just as the first humanitarian war, but also as the first war ever to be won by air power alone, albeit with a (more or less) credible threat of ground invasion. The war was waged outside any UN remit; Russia would almost certainly have vetoed the action in the Security Council. The willingness of the administration to follow unilateralist or quasi-unilateralist paths was evidenced further in its opposition to American involvement in the International Criminal Court, a position which Clinton reversed in his very final days in office. Republican pressure, along with administration re-evaluation of

US military preparedness, led also to defence spending increases. Particularly conspicuous here was the revival of anti-missile defence, a cherished Republican cause harking back to President Reagan's Strategic Missile Defence programme.

Clinton's final year in office was dominated by the effort to achieve a Middle East peace settlement, building on the 1998 Wye River Accords between Israel and the Palestinians. Clinton's activism in Irish issues had been an important factor in achieving the Northern Irish peace deal (the Good Friday, or Belfast, Agreement) in 1998. Clinton looked to replicate Irish peace promotion in the even more difficult conditions of the Middle East (Dumbrell 2009: 88–92, 146). Clinton's sponsorship of Israeli–Palestinian peace negotiations in 2000 achieved significant concessions on both sides of the conflict. Palestinian negotiators accepted that some Israeli settlements, with Israel providing security, could continue in the West Bank, and that Jewish areas of east Jerusalem could be part of Israel. Israelis accepted various logistic positions on the viability of a new Palestinian state (Ross 2004). Major issues, however, notably the Palestinian refugee question, remained unresolved. The process failed, ultimately, to overcome decades of distrust and also the unwillingness or inability of Palestinian leader Yasser Arafat to move beyond long-held positions.

President Clinton continued, indeed confirmed, the willingness of the USA to use military force in ways that would have been familiar to many pre-Cold War presidents. In his last year in office, for example, the USA greatly extended its commitment to intervention against guerrilla movements in Colombia. Clinton's main concern was to find a foreign policy that reconciled expansive internationalism with the contractionist climate of the 1990s. As Stephen Walt put it, Clinton sought 'hegemony on the cheap' (Walt 2000: 78–9).

KEY POINTS

❑ Clinton's second term involved a noticeable turn towards unilateralism and remilitarization.

❑ The 1999 Kosovo campaign involved a denial of traditional notions of national sovereignty.

CONTROVERSIES 5.1: Evaluating the presidents

Evaluating presidents and their foreign policy leadership

Evaluation of presidential performance is plagued by problems of subjectivism. Regarding presidential performance as a whole, congressional success scores and the achievement of 'landmark' legislation are often regarded as key indicators of presidential success. In foreign policy, where legislation is less central than in the domestic arena, 'objective' congressional voting success scores are much less helpful. Successful foreign policy leadership seems to reside in the following:

- Clarity of purpose and 'vision': this was especially important if policy was not merely to drift following the end of the Cold War.
- Effective procedures and skilled foreign policy management.
- Maintenance of a domestic foreign policy consensus.
- Protecting US security and international economic interests.
- Observing the requirements of domestic and international law.
- Avoiding manifest foreign policy disasters.

Evaluating G. H. W. Bush and Clinton

Both presidents struggled with the development and articulation of a post-Cold War foreign policy 'vision' for the United States. Bush's procedural management was generally sure and effective. Clinton's management was less sure-footed, but bears comparison with that of most presidents. Despite setbacks, both presidents managed to maintain a general domestic consensus behind at least a moderately expansive American internationalism. American global power—military, economic, and cultural—skyrocketed throughout the 1990s. Both presidents were committed to multilateralism in pursuit of American international interests, although Clinton's later foreign policy was marked by a move towards unilateralism. Both Bush and Clinton followed a 'presidentialist' foreign policy, with relatively little concern for the rights and prerogatives of Congress. Foreign policy 'disasters' on the model of the Vietnam War did not occur in the 1990s, despite missed opportunities (for example, in the Balkans before 1995), outright failures (as in Somalia), and misjudgements (such as the assault on Sudan in 1998).

Conclusion

The two presidents of the 'long 1990s' differed considerably in temperament and in their understanding of the possibilities of American internationalism. President George H. W. Bush is conventionally regarded as a conservative realist, an 'American tory' (Polsby 1990). President Barack Obama praised the elder Bush's cautious realism during the 2008 presidential election campaign. Clinton is usually seen as developing aspects of the Bushite New World Order, but as more inclined to 'assertive humanitarianism' and as more wedded to the agenda of economic globalization. Such generalizations are not especially insightful; they certainly tend to collapse when we consider Bush's far-from-cautious decision to send troops to Somalia in 1992. Whatever the differences between the two presidents, foreign policy leadership in the immediate post-Cold War period showed considerable unity of purpose. Bush's New World Order and Clinton's various formulations—'assertive humanitarianism', 'selective engagement', 'democratic enlargement', 'assertive multilateralism', 'engagement and enlargement'—were all attempts to keep expansive US internationalism alive in the post-Soviet environment. They were also efforts to articulate a foreign policy which looked beyond narrowly conceived national interest. The 1990s were years in which US leaders bolstered their internationalism with an optimistic commitment to democratizing purpose.

In general, while they recognized limits to US global ambition, the 'long 1990s' presidents managed to restrain the more extreme variants of neo-isolationism and 'new populism', sometimes by deliberately exaggerating the strength of those forces. US foreign policy leaders in the 1990s sought to manage transition, to infuse short-term crisis management with longer-term vision, to reset the diplomatic compass. Between them, Bush and Clinton, for good or ill, bequeathed to post-9/11 presidents a continuing commitment to American global hegemony, with the associated risk of over-extension (Mearsheimer 2011). Bush Sr. and Clinton also handed on, contrary to the expectations of the immediate post-Cold War years, strong executive control of the foreign policy process. Both bequests—hegemonic commitment and continuing executive domination of the foreign policy process—set up dynamics and problematics which continued to reverberate into the second decade of the twenty-first century.

? Questions

1. To what extent was the 'long 1990s' (1989–2001) a distinct phase in the history of US foreign policy?

2. What foreign policy options were available to foreign policy leaders in the immediate post-Cold war period?

3. How coherent was President Bush Sr.'s vision for post-Cold War US foreign policy?

4. How coherent was President Clinton's vision for post-Cold War US foreign policy?

5. To what extent did the 1990s see a reassertion of congressional influence over US foreign policy?

6. How influential was the 'new populism' in the making of 1990s US foreign policy?

7. What were America's objectives in the 1991 Gulf War and how comprehensively were they achieved?

8. How successful was President Bush Sr.'s foreign policy management?

9. How successful was President Clinton's foreign policy management?

10. To what extent did American leaders in the 'long 1990s' bequeath an unsustainable commitment to US global hegemony to their successors?

» Further Reading

Brands, H. (2008), *From Berlin to Baghdad: America's Search for Purpose in the Post-Cold War World* (Lexington: The University Press of Kentucky).

Reliable and lively history of post-Cold War foreign policy.

Bush, G. and Scowcroft, B. (1998), *A World Transformed* (New York: Alfred A. Knopf).

Memoir of the Bush management of the geopolitical changes of the 1990s.

Chollet, D. and Goldgeier, J. (2008), *America Between the Wars: From 11/9 to 9/11* (New York: Public Affairs).

Interweaves US domestic debates and post-Cold War foreign policy.

Cox, M., Ikenberry, G. J., and Inoguchi, T. (eds) (2000), *American Democracy–Promotion: Impulses, Strategies and Impacts* (Oxford: Oxford University Press).

Essays covering vital themes in post-Cold War US foreign policy.

DiPrizio, R. C. (2002), *Armed Humanitarians: US Interventions from Northern Iraq to Kosovo* (Baltimore: Johns Hopkins University Press).

Survey of 'assertive humanitarianism' under Bush and Clinton.

Dumbrell, J. (2009), *Clinton's Foreign Policy: Between the Bushes* (London and New York: Routledge).

Defence of Clinton's foreign policy in the context of post-Soviet US internationalism.

Hendrickson, R. C. (2002), *The Clinton Wars: The Constitution, Congress, and War Powers* (Nashville: Vanderbilt University Press).

War powers debates from Somalia to Kosovo and Iraq.

 For a range of additional resources to support your learning visit the Online Resource Centre that accompanies this book at **www.oxfordtextbooks.co.uk/orc/cox_stokes2e/.**

6 Obama and smart power[1]

Joseph S. Nye, Jr.

Introduction

Barack Obama inherited a fraught foreign policy agenda in January 2009: a global economic crisis, two difficult wars, erosion of the non-proliferation regime by North Korea and Iran, and deterioration of the Middle East peace process. Obama's dilemma was how to manage this difficult inheritance while creating a new vision of how Americans should deal with the world that had been central to his 2008 campaign. He also needed to adapt American foreign policy to the new context of power in the twenty-first century.

Through a series of symbolic gestures and speeches in Prague, Cairo, Accra, the United Nations, and others, Obama developed his new narrative about America's role in the world. In doing so, he helped to restore American soft or attractive power. As a Pew poll reported, in many countries opinions of the United States became as positive as they were at the beginning of the decade before George W. Bush took office.

Power involves setting agendas and creating others' preferences as well as pushing and shoving. Soft power alone rarely solves hard problems. That is why the Obama administration referred to its foreign policy as 'smart power', which successfully combines hard and soft power resources in different contexts. And in sending additional troops to Afghanistan, his use of military force in support of a no-fly zone in Libya, and his use of sanctions against Iran, Obama showed that he was not afraid to use the hard components of smart power.

Critics portrayed Obama as a rock star who won a Nobel prize in 2009 on the basis of promise rather than performance. But in addition to words there have also been some important deeds. First and foremost was the handling of the economic crisis. When Obama came into office, he was told by his economic advisors that there was one chance in three of a 1930s style Depression. If he had not avoided that disaster, all else would have paled. This required not only an economic stimulus package at home, but international coordination. Obama used the crisis to accomplish what many had suggested for years, the transformation of the G-8 into a broader institutional framework of a G-20 that includes the emerging economies.

Closely related to the economic crisis was Obama's handling of relations with China, whose rise is one of the most important foreign policy challenges of the twenty-first century. Obama broadened the Treasury-led economic meetings to a strategic dialogue co-chaired by the State Department with an agenda that includes climate change as well as multilateral issues, and had many face-to-face meetings with Chinese President Hu Jin Tao. At the same time, Obama maintained close alliances with Japan, Korea, and Australia, and good relations with India to help maintain the hard power capabilities that help shape the environment for a rising China.

Obama also sought to reframe the issue of nuclear non-proliferation, which many experts saw as in crisis at the end of the Bush era. By embracing the long-term goal of a non-nuclear world (although perhaps not in his lifetime), Obama reiterated a long-time American commitment to reduce the role of nuclear weapons that is written into Article 6 of the Non-Proliferation Treaty. Moreover, he followed up by negotiating with Russia a replacement of the Strategic Arms Reduction Treaty that further cut the American and Russian strategic arsenals. He has raised the non-proliferation issue on the agenda of both the UN and the G-20, and developed multilateral support for sanctions on Iran for failing to meet its international obligations regarding its nuclear programme.

In December 2009, Obama decided to increase American troops in Afghanistan, and later achieved a NATO consensus that the alliance would train Afghan forces with the intent of handing over primary responsibility for security to them by 2014. And in March 2011, he worked with the Arab League, the UN, and NATO to develop support for the use of force to protect civilians in Libya (see Controversies 6.1). At the same time, during the Arab Spring of 2011, the Obama Administration struggled to combine the hard power of military assistance to governments like Egypt with a soft power narrative of democracy and reform that would appeal to the next generation of protesters in Tahrir Square.

As authoritarian Arab regimes struggled with Twitter and Al Jazeera inflamed demonstrations, Iran tried to cope with the cyber sabotage of its nuclear enrichment programme, and American diplomats struggled to understand the impact of Wikileaks, it became increasingly clear that smart foreign policy in an information age would need a more sophisticated understanding of power in world politics. Traditionally, the mark of a great power was its ability to prevail in war. But in an information age, success depends not just on whose army wins, but also on whose story wins.

Obama was faced with the two types of historical power shifts that are occurring in this century: power transition and power diffusion. Power transition from

---

> ### KEY QUOTES 6.1: Competing theories of international relations

Our power grows through its prudent use; our security emanates from the justness of our cause, the force of our example, the tempering qualities of humility and restraint.

> (Barack Obama, inaugural address, 20 January 2009)

America cannot solve the most pressing problems on our own, and the world cannot solve them without America. We must use what has been called 'smart power', the full range of tools at our disposal.

> (Hillary Clinton, confirmation hearing for Secretary of State, 13 January 2009)

I am here to make the case for strengthening our capacity to use soft power and for better integrating it with hard power.

> (Robert Gates, Secretary of Defense, Landon Lecture, Kansas City, 26 October 2007)

Secretaries Clinton and Gates have called for more funding and more emphasis on our soft power, and I could not agree with them more. Should we choose to exert American influence solely through our troops, we should expect to see that influence diminish in time.

> (Mike Mullen, Chairman of the Joint Chiefs of Staff, Landon lecture, 2010)

one dominant state to another is a familiar historical event, and in adjusting American policy Obama resisted the misleading metaphor of American decline but accepted the rise of emerging powers such as China, India, Brazil, and others. Power diffusion, however, is a more novel process and more difficult to manage. The problem for all states in today's global information age is that more things are happening outside the control of even the most powerful states. These were the major changes in the context of global politics that Obama was trying to cope with in developing his policy of smart power.

Power in a global information age

Power is the ability to obtain the outcomes one wants, and in behavioural terms that can be done in three ways: through threat of coercion (sticks), through payments (carrots), and through attraction and persuasion. That third way is soft power, and a state that could use soft power can save on carrots and sticks.

In foreign policy, some goals are impossible to achieve with soft power, but others are more susceptible to soft than hard power. Arnold Wolfers once distinguished between what he called possession goals—specific and often tangible objectives—and milieu goals, which are often structural and intangible. For example, access to resources or basing rights or a trade agreement are possession goals while promoting an open trade system, free markets, democracy, and human rights are milieu goals. Focusing solely on hard power may mislead us about how best to promote such goals. For example, military means alone are less successful than when combined with soft power approaches in promoting democracy—as the United States discovered in Iraq.

American foreign policy debate tends to focus on hard power because of political culture and institutions. No politician wants to appear 'soft', and Congress finds it easier to boost the budget of the Pentagon than the State Department. That bias has been reinforced by the prevailing theory of 'realism' with its distinguished lineage stretching back to Thucydides and Machiavelli. Realists come in many sizes and shapes, but all tend to argue that global politics is power politics. In this they are right, but some limit their understanding by conceiving of power too narrowly. A pragmatic or common sense realist takes into account the full spectrum of power resources, including ideas, persuasion, and attraction. Many classical realists understood the role of soft power better than some of their modern progeny.

A state can wield global power by engaging and acting together with other states, not merely acting against them. John Ikenberry has argued that American power after the Second World War rested on a network of institutions that constrained the US but were open to others and thus increased American power to act with others (Ikenberry 2006). This is an important point in assessing American foreign policy in the current international system. For example, if the US is involved in more communication networks, it has a greater opportunity to shape preferences in terms of soft power. A smart power foreign policy needs to consider preference formation and agenda framing as means of shaping the environment before turning to hard power. There are costs to policy if one fails to do so.

Realism represents a good first cut at portraying some aspects of international relations. But states are no longer the only important actors in global affairs, security is not the only major outcome that they seek, and force is not the only or always the best instrument available to achieve those outcomes. Indeed, these conditions of complex interdependence are typical of relations among advanced post-industrial countries such as the US, Canada, European countries, Australia and Japan. Mutual democracy, liberal culture, and a deep network of transnational ties mean that anarchy has very different effects than realism predicts. In such conditions, a smart power strategy has a much higher portion of soft power in the mix.

It is not solely in relations among advanced countries, however, that soft power plays an important role. In an information age, communications strategies become more important, and outcomes are shaped not merely by whose army wins, but also by whose story wins. In combating terrorism, for example, it is essential to have a narrative that appeals to the mainstream and prevents recruitment by radicals. In battling insurgencies, kinetic military force must be accompanied by soft power instruments that help to win over the hearts and minds (shape the preferences) of the majority of the population.

Smart strategies must have an information and communication component. States struggle over the power to define norms, and framing of issues grows in importance. For instance, while CNN and the BBC framed the issues of the first Gulf War in 1991, by 2003, Al Jazeera played a large role in shaping the narrative in the Iraq War. Such framing is more than mere propaganda. In describing events in March 2003, one could say that American troops 'entered Iraq', or that American troops 'invaded Iraq'. Both statements are true, but they have very different effects in terms of their power to shape preferences. Similarly, if one thinks of international institutions, it makes a difference if agendas are set in a group of eight with a few invited guests or a group of twenty equal invitees. The spectrum of power behaviours is represented in Figure 6.1.

In general, the types of resources that are associated with hard power include tangibles like force and money, while the resources that are associated with soft power often include intangible factors like institutions, ideas, values, culture, and perceived legitimacy of policies. But the relationship is not perfect. Intangible resources like patriotism, morale, and legitimacy strongly affect the capacity to fight and win. And threats to use force are intangible, but a dimension of hard power. If one distinguishes between power resources and power behaviour, one realizes that resources often associated with hard power behaviour can also produce soft power behaviour

depending on the context and how they are used. Since attraction depends upon the minds of the perceiver, the subject's perceptions play a significant role in whether given resources produce hard or soft power behaviour.

For example, naval forces can be used to win battles (hard power) or win hearts and minds (soft power), depending on who the target is and what the issue is. The American navy's help in providing relief to Indonesia after the 2004 East Asian tsunami had a strong effect on increasing their attraction toward the United States, and the Navy's 2007 Maritime Strategy refers not only to war fighting but additionally to maritime forces that will be employed to build confidence and trust among nations.

Some critics complain that the definition of soft power has become fuzzy through expansion 'to include both economic statecraft—used as both a carrot and as a stick—and even military power. . . . Soft power now seems to mean everything' (Gelb 2009). But these critics are mistaken because they confuse the actions of a state seeking to achieve desired outcomes with the resources used to produce them. Many types of *resources* can contribute to soft power, but that does not mean that soft power is any type of *behaviour*. The use of force and payment (and some agenda setting based on them) is hard power. Agenda setting that is regarded as legitimate by the target, positive attraction, and persuasion are the parts of the spectrum of behaviours included in soft power. Hard power is push; soft power is pull. Fully defined, soft power is the ability to affect others to obtain preferred outcomes by the co-optive means of framing the agenda, persuasion, and positive attraction. Smart power is the combination of hard and soft power resources into successful strategies in various contexts.

| Hard   Soft |
| Command>   Coerce Threat Pay Sanction   Frame Persuade Attract   <Co-opt |

Fig. 6.1 The spectrum of power behaviours.

KEY POINTS

❑ The resources that produce power are changing in a global information age. While hard military and economic power remains important, the soft power of attraction and persuasion is becoming increasingly important.

❑ Realists are correct in arguing that global politics is power politics, but they sometimes mistakenly restrict their definitions of power to hard power alone.

❑ Smart power is the ability to combine hard and soft power resources into successful strategies in different contexts.

Soft power in American foreign policy

Sometimes attraction and the resulting soft power it engenders require little effort. The effects of values can be like the light from 'a city on the hill', the phrase originally coined by the seventeenth-century Puritan John Winthrop and adapted for twentieth-century American foreign policy by President Ronald Reagan. At other times, efforts to create attraction and soft power are more complicated, and soft power can work directly and indirectly. In the direct form, leaders may be attracted and persuaded by the benignity, competence, or charisma of other leaders. It is reported, for example, that President Obama's arguments at a G-20 meeting persuaded other leaders to increase food aid. More common, however, is an indirect model in which publics and third parties are influenced, and they in turn affect the leaders of other countries. In this case, soft power has an important indirect effect by creating an enabling environment for decisions. Alternatively, if an actor or action is perceived as repulsive, it creates a disabling environment.

Judging direct causation requires careful process tracing of the sort that good historians or journalists do, with all the difficulties of sorting out multiple causes when trying to trace whether a given influence effort was an important part of achieving a preferred outcome. With indirect effects, public opinion polls and careful content analysis can help provide a first estimate of the existence of an enabling or disabling environment. Even though polls can measure the existence and trends in potential soft power resources, they are only a first approximation for behavioural change in terms of outcomes, since it is elites that make decisions.

Student and leadership exchanges are a good example of direct effects that do not go through public opinion. Forty-six current and 165 former heads of government are products of US higher education. Not all of the nearly 750,000 foreign students who come to the US annually are attracted by the country, but the large majority are. 'Research has consistently shown that exchange students return home with a more positive view of the country in which they studied and the people with whom they interacted', and foreign educated students are more likely to promote democracy in their home country if they are educated in democratic countries (Atkinson 2009). The results can be dramatic. For example, Mikhail Gorbachev's embrace of perestroika and glastnost was influenced by ideas learned at Columbia University by exchange student Alexander Yakovlev, even though they took two decades to come to full fruition. And while the end of the Cold War involved multiple causes, there is ample testimony by former Soviet elites about how Western ideas interacted with Soviet economic decline.

With the indirect model, public opinion affects elites by creating an enabling or disabling environment for specific policy initiatives. For example, in regard to Iraq in 2003, Turkish officials were constrained by public and parliamentary opinion and unable to allow the American 4th Infantry Division to cross their country. The Bush Administration's lack of soft power in Turkey hurt its hard power. Similarly, Mexican President Vicente Fox wished to accommodate George W. Bush by supporting a second UN resolution authorizing invasion, but was constrained by Mexican public opinion. When being pro-American is a political kiss of death, public opinion has an effect on policy that the sceptics do not capture.

As noted above, in addition to specific goals, countries often have general 'milieu goals' such as democracy, human rights, and open economic systems. Here the target of soft power *is* broad public opinion and cultural attitudes. After the Second World War, American power to promote such goals in post-war Europe was strongly affected by the attraction to its culture and ideas. While governmental programmes such as the Marshall Plan were important, historians of the period stress the impact of non-state actors as well. 'American corporate and advertising executives, as well as the heads of Hollywood studios, were selling not only their products but also America's culture and values, the secrets of its success, to the rest of the world' (Pells 1997). As one Norwegian scholar argued, 'federalism, democracy, and open markets represented core American values. This is what America exported'. That made it much easier to maintain what he called an 'empire by invitation' (Lundestad 1998).

Today, the challenges to American foreign policy are different. Non-state actors use terrorism to create a climate of polarization in which an extremist narrative can spread to wider parts of the Muslim world. Misuse of hard power may play into the hands of the terrorists. It is estimated that the American invasion of Iraq, for example, helped al-Qaeda to recruit new members. Soft power becomes essential in helping to win the hearts and minds of the mainstream.

The 'city on the hill' or values effect of soft power should not be exaggerated, particularly in its impact on specific rather than milieu goals. An interesting 'natural experiment' can be seen in the 2008 election of Barack Obama, which helped to dispel negative stereotypes of a closed American political system. In 2009, polls showed an impressive revival of America's global image in many parts of the world, reflecting confidence in the new president. One poll-based assessment of brand values even suggested the Obama effect was worth two trillion dollars in brand equity (Anholt 2009). But in areas like Pakistan and the Palestinian territories where American policies were unpopular, ratings of Obama were only marginally better than the abysmal ratings

accorded to Bush. In constructing narratives, deeds matter as well as words.

Interestingly, American military analysts trying to understand the problems they faced dealing with the counter-insurgency in Iraq developed doctrines that recognized the importance of soft power. In the words of General David Patreus, 'we did reaffirm in Iraq the recognition that you don't kill or capture your way out of an industrial-strength insurgency' (Gamel 2008). Or as the American commander in Afghanistan noted, when we resort to expedient measures, 'we end up paying a price for it ultimately. Abu Ghraib and other situations like that are non-biodegradable. They don't go away. The enemy continues to beat you with them like a stick' (Berger 2010).

Except at the tactical level, the military options for the use of soft power have to been seen in a larger policy context. As the Australian expert David Kilcullen noted, 'This implies that America's international reputation, moral authority, diplomatic weight, persuasive ability, cultural attractiveness and strategic credibility—its "soft power"—is not some optional adjunct to military strength. Rather, it is a critical enabler for a permissive operating environment . . . and it is also the prime political competence in countering a globalized insurgency.'

Narratives and public diplomacy

Soft power is difficult for governments to wield. Sustained attraction—being a 'city on a hill'—requires consistency of practice with values. Going further to project attraction, frame agendas, and persuade others is even more difficult. The causal paths are often indirect, the effects often take time to ripen, some of the general goals to which it is directed are diffuse, and the government is rarely in full control of all the instruments. That is true of efforts to create soft power through the practice of public diplomacy—or actions designed to affect public opinion in other states. Classical diplomacy, sometimes called cabinet diplomacy, involved messages sent from one ruler to another, often in confidential communications. But governments also find it useful to communicate with the publics of other countries in

an effort to influence other governments through the indirect model.

The United States began to incorporate public diplomacy into its foreign policy in the First World War. In 1917, President Woodrow Wilson established a Committee on Public Information directed by his friend the newspaperman George Creel, who described his task as a vast enterprise in salesmanship. Creel insisted that his office's activities did not constitute propaganda and were merely educational and informative. But the facts belied his denials. Among other things, Creel organized tours, churned out pamphlets on 'the Gospel of Americanism', established a government-run news service, made sure that motion picture producers received wartime allotments of scarce materials, and saw to it that the films portrayed

America in a positive light. The office aroused sufficient suspicions that it was abolished shortly after the return of peace.

The advent of radio in the 1920s led many governments into the arena of foreign language broadcasting, and in the 1930s communists and fascists competed to promote favourable images to foreign publics. In addition to its foreign language radio broadcasts, Nazi Germany perfected the propaganda film. By the late 1930s, the Roosevelt Administration became convinced that America's security depended on its ability to speak to and win the support of people in other countries, particularly in Latin America. By 1941, the United States was broadcasting around the clock.

What became known as the Voice of America (VOA) grew rapidly during the Second World War. Modelled after the BBC in approach, by 1943 it had 23 transmitters delivering news in 27 languages. With the growth of the Soviet threat in the Cold War, the VOA continued to expand, but so did a debate about how much it should be a captive purveyor of government information or an independent representative of American culture. Special radios were added, such as Radio Liberty and Radio Free Europe, which used exiles to broadcast to the Eastern bloc. More generally, as the Cold War developed, there was a division between those who favoured the slow media of cultural diplomacy—art, books, exchanges—that had a 'trickle-down effect', and those who favoured the fast information media of radio, movies, and newsreels, which promised more immediate and visible bang for the buck.

Throughout the Cold War, these two approaches struggled over how the government should invest in soft power. The tough minded did not shy away from direct propaganda while the tender minded argued that changing foreign attitudes is a gradual process that should be measured in years. There were also struggles over how directed and how free government-supported programmes should be. There was a thin line between information and propaganda. During the Cold War, some cultural and information activities were financed by the Central Intelligence Agency, but when these activities were disclosed in the early 1970s, they lost their credibility.

These struggles persisted despite various reorganizations of American institutions for public diplomacy over the years. The tension between how directly or indirectly the government should try to control its instruments of soft power can never be fully resolved because both sides make valid points. In 1999, the United States Information Agency (USIA) was abolished and its functions absorbed into the State Department, where it would be closer to policy, while VOA and other specialized stations were put under a new bipartisan Broadcasting Board of Governors.

With the end of the Cold War, Americans were more interested in budget savings than in investments in soft power. From 1963 to 1993, the federal budget grew fifteen- fold, but the USIA budget grew only six and a half times. Soft power seemed expendable. Between 1989 and 1999, the budget of USIA, adjusted for inflation, decreased 10 per cent. While government-funded radio broadcasts reached half the Soviet population every week and between 70 and 80 per cent of the populace of Eastern Europe during the Cold War, at the beginning of the new century, a mere 2 per cent of Arabs heard the VOA. Resources for the USIA mission in Indonesia, the world's largest Muslim nation, were cut in half. From 1995 to 2001, academic and cultural exchanges dropped from 45,000 to 29,000 annually, while many accessible downtown cultural centres and libraries were closed. In comparison, the BBC World Service had half again as many weekly listeners around the globe as did the VOA. Soft power had become so identified with fighting the Cold War that few Americans noticed that with an information revolution occurring, soft power was becoming more rather than less important. Only after September 2001 did Americans rediscover the importance of investing in the instruments of soft power.

The Bush administration did not totally neglect soft power in its response to the terrorist attacks on 9/11, but its emphasis on unilateralism, hard power, and the invasion of Iraq undercut American soft power. Polls showed a precipitous drop in the attractiveness of the United States in Europe, Latin America, and particularly the Muslim world. The president's stirring rhetoric about a freedom agenda was better designed for domestic than for foreign audiences, which heard it as hypocritical. Moreover, the Administration's approach tended towards a centralized 'selling' of the American message that was often discounted as propaganda and thus not credible to foreign audiences.

Polls showed a considerable rise in the attractiveness of the United States after the election of Barack Obama, even before the new administration came into office. The idea that the United States could elect an unknown African-American senator with a strange sounding name helped to restore faith in American democracy. At the same time, Secretary of State Hillary Clinton made a point of using her personal political presence to directly address foreign audiences during her travels, and turned to a greater use of the internet in public diplomacy at the State Department. The effect on American soft power was noticeable, but in the long term the durability of the Obama effect will probably depend upon the success of his policies, not merely his rhetoric and style. In the long term, even in the creation of soft power, actions speak louder than words.

Problems in wielding soft power

Governments trying to utilize public diplomacy in the twenty-first century face new problems. Promoting attractive images of one's country is not new, but the conditions for trying to create soft power have changed dramatically in recent years. For one thing, nearly half the countries in the world are now democracies. In such circumstances, diplomacy aimed at public opinion can become as important to outcomes as the traditional classified diplomatic communications among leaders. Information creates power, and today a much larger part of the world's population has access to that power. Technological advances have led to a dramatic reduction in the cost of processing and transmitting information. The result is an explosion of information, and that has produced a paradox of plenty. Plentiful information leads to scarcity of attention. When people are overwhelmed with the volume of information confronting them, it is hard to know what to focus on. Attention rather than information becomes the scarce resource, and those who can distinguish valuable information from background clutter gain power.

Politics has become a contest of competitive credibility. The world of traditional power politics is typically about whose military or economy wins. As noted earlier, politics in an information age 'may ultimately be about whose story wins' (Arquila and Ronfeldt 1999). Narratives become the currency of soft power. Governments compete with each other and with other organizations to enhance their own credibility and weaken that of their opponents. Information that appears to be propaganda may not only be scorned, but it may also turn out to be counterproductive if it undermines a country's reputation for credibility. Exaggerated claims about Saddam Hussein's weapons of mass destruction and ties to al-Qaeda may have helped mobilize domestic support for the Iraq war, but the subsequent disclosure of the exaggeration dealt a costly blow to American credibility. Under the new conditions more than ever, a soft sell may prove more effective than a hard sell.

The centralized mass media approach to public diplomacy still plays an important role. Governments need to correct daily misrepresentations of their policies as well as to try to convey a longer term strategic message. The main strength of the mass media approach is its audience reach and ability to generate public awareness and set the agenda. But the inability to influence how the message is perceived in different cultural settings is its weak point. The sender knows what she says, but not always what the target(s) hear. Cultural barriers are apt to distort what is heard.

The greater flexibility of non-governmental organizations in using networks has given rise to what some call the 'new public diplomacy', which is no longer confined to messaging, promotion campaigns, or even direct governmental contacts with foreign publics serving foreign policy purposes. It is also about building relationships with civil society actors in other countries and about facilitating networks between non-governmental parties at home and abroad. In this approach to public diplomacy, government policy is aimed at promoting and participating in rather than controlling such networks across borders. Indeed, too much government control or even the appearance thereof, can undercut the credibility that such networks are designed to engender. The evolution of public diplomacy from one-way communications to a two-way dialogue model treats publics as peer-to-peer co-creators of meaning and communication.

Much of a country's soft power or attraction is produced by its civil society rather than the government. For the United States to succeed in the networked world of the new public diplomacy, it is going to have to learn to relinquish a good deal of its control, and this runs the risk that non-governmental civil society actors are often not aligned in their goals with government policies or even objectives. For example, in 2011 after the pastor of a tiny church in Florida burned a Koran, riots in Afghanistan led to the deaths of UN workers.

The State Department has taken advantage of the new technologies of social networking, with employees licensed to use Facebook and Twitter, and Secretary of State Clinton has made major speeches about the importance of free speech on the internet.

The domestic political problems of the new public diplomacy are real, but the international effects can be beneficial. The presence of dissent and self-criticism is likely to enhance the credibility of messages, as well as to create a degree of attraction to the society that is willing to tolerate it. When Wikileaks released secret cables from American diplomats in 2010, one international reaction was embarrassment, but another was praise for the fact that even in secret cables the United States seemed to evidence genuine concern for human rights. Criticism of government policies can be awkward for a government, but it can also cast a society in a more attractive light and thus help to create soft power. The paradox of using public diplomacy to generate soft power in a global information age is that decentralization and diminished control may be central to the creation of soft power. As public diplomacy is done more *by* publics, governments find themselves facing a dilemma, but here the open nature of American society may prove more helpful to its soft power than the orchestrated campaigns by authoritarian governments.

To be credible, American efforts to project soft power will have to avoid the dangers of an over-militarized and state-centric approach. Power becomes less hierarchical in an information age, and social networks become more important. That means that two-way communications are more effective than commands. As a young Czech participant in an exchange programme during the Cold War observed, 'this is the best propaganda because it's not propaganda'. Interactive discourse fits with empowering choices. It involves recognition that the sharing of values can be interactive and binding on the US as well as others. To a large extent, the future of American soft power in the twenty-first century will depend upon accepting rather than rejecting such multilateral and civil society approaches.

CONTROVERSIES 6.1: Obama and Libya

Obama's decision to support a no-fly zone in Libya is a useful case study of the controversies surrounding smart power policies. When President Obama delayed intervening in Libya for weeks, he was criticized for failing to lead. Many of his critics, however, remained captive of narratives about American leadership that envisaged the Lone Ranger riding into a town and shooting the bad guys. Unlike George W. Bush in Iraq, Obama did not plunge ahead decisively with the use of force, but while Bush was more decisive in Iraq, he also turned out to be decisively wrong about the presence of weapons of mass destruction and the ease of creating a democratic polity in Iraq. The result was a sharp drop in America's international standing.

In designing his strategy for Libya, Obama showed awareness of both hard and soft dimensions of power in ways that many of his critics did not. First he was careful to limit both American objectives and commitments. Humanitarian interests are important but not vital in the sense of national survival. Moreover, there is always a danger of good intentions leading to unintended bad consequences, as happened after George H.W. Bush intervened in Somalia in 1992. Thus, while Obama correctly said that the United States wanted to see Qaddafi overthrown, he made it clear that would have to be done by means other than American military action. Second, Obama was careful not to create a global narrative of a third American military attack on a Muslim country, which would have reverberated from Morocco to Indonesia. Instead, he waited until the Arab League and UN Security Council resolutions provided a narrative of a legitimate enforcement of a humanitarian responsibility to protect civilians. Third, he encouraged France, Britain, and other allies to share in the lead, and also encouraged the devolution of the operation of the no-fly zone to NATO, a multilateral institution.

The outcome in Libya remained far from certain and involved considerable risks of a stalemated civil war. Obama established a basis for avoiding a slippery slope and being drawn into ownership of a nasty problem that advocates of the Lone Ranger narrative demanded. Some realists questioned Obama's initial decision to be involved in a humanitarian action at all, but in terms of balancing interests and values while limiting risks, Obama provided a lesson in smart leadership.

Conclusion

Smart leadership in a global information age is less about being the king of the mountain issuing commands that cascade down a hierarchy than being the person in the centre of a circle or network who attracts and persuades others to come and help. Both the hard power of coercion and the soft power of attraction and persuasion are crucial to success in such situations.

A smart power narrative for America in the twenty-first century is not about maximizing power or preserving hegemony. It is about finding ways to combine resources into successful strategies in the new context of power diffusion and the 'rise of the rest'. As the most powerful country, America remains the most important leader in global affairs, but the old twentieth-century narrative about American hegemony and primacy, or alternatively narratives of American decline are both misleading about the type of strategy that America needs. As mentioned earlier, in a global information age it is not always who has the biggest army that determines success, but also who has the best story. A large part of Obama's foreign policy has focused on combining the elements of hard and soft power into what his administration called a smart power strategy.

? Questions

1. What were the major foreign policy problems that Obama faced when he came into office in 2009?
2. What did the administration mean by its reference to smart power?
3. What is power? What is the difference between hard and soft power? How can they be combined?
4. How is power changing in a global information age?

5. Were Obama's responses to these changes appropriate?

6. What is public diplomacy? How does it differ from traditional diplomacy? How has it changed over time?

7. What are the difficulties involved in deploying soft power?

» Further Reading

Boulding, K.E. (1989), *Three Faces of Power* (London: Sage Publications).

A lively and thoughtful exploration of the many dimensions of power.

Chief of Naval Operations (2007), *A Cooperative Strategy for 21st Century Seapower* (Washington, DC).

An illustration of the way hard and soft power can be combined in naval strategy.

Gaventa, J. (2007), Levels, spaces, and forms of power. In F. Berenskoetter and M. J. Williams (eds) *Power in World Politics* (London: Routledge).

Various ways of approaching the questions of power in world politics.

Guzzini, S. (1993), Structural power: The limits of neorealist power analysis. *International Organization*, 47, 443–79.

A good critique of the inadequacy of overly simple formulations of realism.

Ikenberry, G. J. (2006), *Liberal Order and Imperial Ambition* (Cambridge: Polity).

A liberal view of the successful use of power in American foreign policy.

Lukes, S. (2005), *Power: A Radical View*, 2nd edn (London: Palgrave).

A classic exploration of the three faces of power.

Schelling, T. C. (1960), *The Strategy of Conflict* (Oxford: Oxford University Press).

One of the great books on strategy that has aged well over the decades.

Slaughter, A. M. (2009), America's edge: Power in the networked century. *Foreign Affairs*, 88, 94–113.

A thoughtful exploration of the importance of networks to American power in an information age.

Taylor, A. J. P. (1954), *The Struggle for Mastery in Europe, 1848–1918* (Oxford: Oxford University Press).

A classic account of power in the nineteenth century and the importance of military force.

Wolfers, A. (1962), *Discord and Collaboration: Essays on International Politics* (Baltimore: Johns Hopkins University Press).

Timeless essays on power and world politics by one of the great classical realists.

Endnote

1. Parts of this essay draw upon my book, *The Future of Power* (New York: Public Affairs Press, 2011).

 For a range of additional resources to support your learning visit the Online Resource Centre that accompanies this book at www.oxfordtextbooks.co.uk/orc/cox_stokes2e/.

Section 2
Institutions and Processes

7 The foreign policy process: executive, Congress, intelligence

Michael Foley

Chapter contents

Introduction

The United States system of government was originally conceived to be a complex model of power sharing and reciprocal restraint. In many respects, the foreign policy process reflects that initial design but it also reveals the effects of political, institutional, and constitutional evolution in which the distribution of decision making has changed in favour of a more centralized and functional matrix. The emphasis upon rationality, specialization, and management has increased along with the expansion of the United States as a global superpower with a profusion of international interests requiring supervision. The presidential office has been at the centre of this transformation but it has also acted as a catalyst for periodic revivals of constitutional fundamentalism in which systemic indictments lead to demands for greater democratic participation in the service of republican values.

Foreign policy as a primary agency of governmental adaptation

It is often acknowledged that the creation and design of the American republic in 1787 was based upon the establishment of a federal constitution that instituted a set of separate yet interlocking powers with the aim of ensuring coherence and constraint. What is usually overlooked in this process of state formation is the central importance of the geopolitical context and security anxieties in the priorities of those who founded the new constitutional arrangement. It was these concerns in an era of imperial power politics and expansionist force projection that is thought to have allowed the incorporation of an element of strategic ambiguity into the constitution's republican system. Partly to reverse several defeats in the Constitutional Convention, the more nationalist minded of the Founders secured an agreement in which a set of foreign policy powers that had originally been reserved to the Senate were transferred to the presidential branch. In doing so, it offered the new federal government an enhanced executive framework for national cohesion in the face of several pre-existing state sovereignties. Whether by political circumstance or by conscious design, the embryonic executive branch was afforded a potential for integrated governance that was to become closely related not only to the federal government's own formative processes but also to the generative forces of international affairs in the expansion of federal authority and in the construction of the modern structure of foreign policy making.

The dominant theme in the history of US foreign policy making has been the extent to which this initial potential has been fulfilled. It is customary to regard the field of foreign policy as having been the subject of a transformative process that has paralleled the republic's rise from an isolated small power to that of a global hegemon. The predominant pattern to have emerged over American history has been the rise of the presidential office in the formulation of foreign policy and in the responsibility for American lives and interests abroad. This has been, and remains, a controversial development in a system of government specifically designed to be one of limited powers and reciprocal restraints. But over the course of the republic, the presidency has been able to claim the existence of a synergy of development between the executive office and the policy sector of foreign policy. Together they have provided the main agency not only for constitutional change but for altering the fabric of American society and ultimately the nature of the world order. Foreign policy issues have been instrumental in the evolutionary transformation of American government into what is widely seen to be an extensive and centralized system of administration relating to the resources and actions of a world power. In like manner, the development of the presidency has been closely tied to the numerous and urgent demands of the international sphere and to the need of the United States to have the capacity to attend to them with the appropriate levels of decisiveness and judgement (Hargrove 1974: 98–174; Corwin 1957: 170–262).

In one sense, it is a measure of the influence assigned to the federal government's responsibilities in foreign policy that this sector has been able to generate such substantial changes to the scale of the federal government and to the internal distribution of power within it. In another sense, the integrity of the Constitution and its derivative processes has always been a subject of great sensitivity in a polity whose identity is closely bound up with the tradition and legitimacy of its governmental processes—and in particular its ability to address the litmus test issue of restraining executive power. The net effect has been a largely continuing tension between need and law, between security and due process, and between unified executive direction and the claims to a rightful and productive pluralism.

Very often the executive has prevailed and it can be claimed that these instances and even periods of executive dominance have led to a definite and irreversible historical drift towards an executive-centred policy process. But such a conclusion not only overlooks the developmental contingencies of constitutional change, but also diminishes its contested nature. What appear to be historically settled patterns of foreign policy making can on occasion experience seismic shifts of complaint based not just on the substance of the policy output but, more significantly, on the structure and authority of the policy process (Schlesinger 1974: 208–419). It is on these occasions that the constitutional and political basis of United States foreign policy can be seen as being far from settled in favour of presidential government. It is against such a background, and with this caveat in mind, that we must attempt to account for the rise to prominence of the presidency in this field—and for the conditioning factors in such a position of conspicuous responsibility.

The executive as the lead agency of systemic evolution

The primary focus of America's foreign policy-making systems lies with an executive infrastructure of departments and agencies whose roots and authority are drawn from the initial grant of constitutional power to the presidential office. Of all the Framers' creations, the presidency is the one structural feature of the Constitution that can only be fully comprehended, and satisfactorily accounted for, by reference to a process of development. And this emphasis upon precedent, continuity, and jurisdictional sensitivity remains central to a branch of government whose resources have had to be claimed and rationalized through time, rather than through definitive and final grants of power. It is true that the Constitution did assign to the presidency a number of specific roles in relation to foreign affairs. But in time it became increasingly evident that presidents were being placed in positions where they had to supplement their enumerated functions with additional roles that were occasioned by changing conditions, issues, and requirements that were not clearly reducible to the minimalist

features of the Constitution. Whether this was seen as filling in the gaps or taking up the slack of a short and tersely composed constitution, the net effect was that presidents quickly assumed the central position in a dynamic that conjoined the presidency with issues of peace and security in the furtherance of constitutional evolution (Pious 1979: 332–415; Fisher 2007).

This is not to say that the presidency's rise to prominence has been uncontested or that the office has been immune to the American system of checks and balances. Nevertheless, presidents have been able to exploit their associations with concepts like the national interest and the popular will, along with the themes of public safety and social stability, to make persuasive cases in support of an expansive role. Apart from the instrumental argument of executive responsiveness to palpable need, presidents have been effective in advocating the property of executive virtue that gathers power in support of causes considered to be just.

BOX 7.1: Expansive presidents up to and including the inception of the modern presidency	
Presidents who played an active role in expanding the scope of the office in national security and foreign affairs, and who have had lasting effects on the development of the presidency in these areas of policy making.	James Polk (1845–1849)
	Abraham Lincoln (1861–1865)
	Theodore Roosevelt (1901–1909)
Thomas Jefferson (1801–1809)	Woodrow Wilson (1913–1921)
James Monroe (1817–1825)	Franklin D. Roosevelt (1933–1945)
Andrew Jackson (1829–1837)	

Through an accumulation of precedents, the presidential office has in many respects introduced a common law ethos into the 'black letter' formalism of the Constitution. In doing so, the presidency has not only pushed the specified powers of Article II into new meanings through the aggregation of usage, but also pursued the logic of an executive office in a system of government otherwise burdened with complex countervailing dynamics. As a consequence, presidents have injected an instrumental realism, and often a utilitarian spirit, into the framework of government. Presidents, and especially those designated as 'great' or expansive, have used the issue of national security and international relations to widen the parameters of the executive branch and the federal government as a whole.

Expansionist presidents have coincided with various expansionary features of the United States not just in terms of state formation and social integration, but also in respect to its status as an international power. The presidential office has provided a means by which the federal government has been able to provide a centre of responsive and timely decision making. It has done so by exploring the opportunities for power accumulation within the political order and by developing a linkage between external challenges to the system as a whole and the need for some agency of responsive adjustment. In no field has this inventiveness been more evident than in the area of war. The prospect, or actual condition, of a supreme emergency has been particularly significant in disclosing the full rationale of the president's position in the constitutional framework of the US government. It is not simply that war tends to transform political and social institutions into a different configuration. It is that issues of war and peace open up the interior properties and implicit premises of the executive function in a much more explicit manner than is usually the case in other less urgent areas of public life.

Executive prerogative

Even though the United States is renowned for its reliance upon a sovereign constitution whose logic ensures that all its components are reducible to its central provisions, the issue of security has always been particularly problematic. In the main this is because a society's need to maintain itself against threats generates demands for

an exceptional sphere of authority that will not necessarily be wholly derived from the explicit framework of the Constitution. The authority in question is the mercurial theme of executive prerogative. In the British constitution, the crown prerogative allows for the remaining elements of the monarchy's original authority to be exercised by ministers. Given the self-professed republicanism of the Founders, the US Constitution allows for no express provision for any notion of prerogative powers.

Nonetheless, the Framers would have been aware of the difficulty of confining all state activities and responsibilities to the forms of due process and representational consent. Even John Locke (1632–1704), whom many of the Founders regarded as their philosophical mentor, found it difficult to liberalize the state to the point where it would no longer be necessary to have any recourse to an executive prerogative operating in the absence of law, or even contrary to its enactments. At one level, it would appear that the US Constitution is purposefully devoid of such discretionary powers. But constitutions invite interpretations of their defining logic and operating principles. They also depend upon usage and precedent to accumulate meanings. In the case of the United States Constitution, it is clear that presidents have sought to make explicit what in their view was implicit in the very creation of an executive branch of government: namely a responsibility to act in the nation's self-interest.

The possession of the physical means of coercion, as well as its functional capacity of initiative and decisiveness, has permitted the creation of a set of powers that are interpreted as being implied by the Constitution's original construction of an executive. Just as presidents have often been in a position to claim such powers, so other centres of power have often been prepared to acquiesce in the emergency nature of such presumptions (Pious 1979: 47–84; 2007). Aware of the possible weaknesses of democratic government described by Alexis de Tocqueville (1805–59), other branches have not always disputed the rights and judgements of presidential leadership in an area of governance rich in the potential for prerogative privilege. On the contrary, they have had a pronounced tendency to defer to the asserted realism and pragmatism of executive-led decisions over military action.

Judicial recognition of inherent executive power

This outlook of pragmatic acquiescence has been evident in the limited number of Supreme Court cases relating to the president's responsibilities in foreign policy. The general absence of cases in this area is itself significant. It not only demonstrates a disinclination on the part of the judiciary to involve itself in this field of policy, but reveals the ambiguous relationship between the principles of constitutionalism and the realism of executive prerogative. For example, in *The Prize Cases* (1863), the Court was asked to consider whether President Lincoln had any authority to blockade southern ports at the outset of the Civil War (1861–5). According to the Constitution, a state of war could only exist if Congress had formally declared war, but in this instance the President had acted without such express authorization. Although the Supreme Court is tasked to protect the integrity of the Constitution, on this occasion it saw fit to affirm the president's judgement in superseding the precise demands of due process. The very nature of the emergency created its own momentum for executive action and prompted a recognition that under certain conditions executive prerogative possessed a legitimacy that was not reducible to the Constitution:

> [T]he President is . . . bound to resist force with force. He does not initiate the war, but is bound to accept the challenge without waiting for any special legislative authority. And whether the hostile party be a foreign invader, or states organized in rebellion, it is none the less a war . . . [In] this greatest of civil wars . . . [t]he President was bound to meet it in the shape that it presented itself, without waiting for Congress to baptize it with a name. (*The Prize Cases* 1862: 669)

Another keynote decision was prompted by the growing instability of the international order during the 1930s. The rise of international tensions and the threat of war led the Supreme Court to make a concerted case in favour of presidential authority and, in doing so, to incorporate the theme of executive prerogative firmly within the Constitution. In the case of *United States* v. *Curtiss–Wright Export Corporation* (1936), the Court went to great lengths in underwriting the need for executive authority in the conduct of foreign relations. The decision was based not merely upon the powers implied in the Constitution but also on the authority vested in the executive by virtue of the fact that it was an executive office. The president's powers therefore were not strictly limited to the Constitution's provisions, or

---

BOX 7.2: *United States* v. *Curtiss–Wright Export Corporation*

Not only, as we have shown, is the federal power over external affairs in origin and essential character different from that over internal affairs, but participation in the exercise of the power is significantly limited. In this vast external realm, with its important, complicated, delicate and manifold problems, the President alone has the power to speak or listen as a representative of the nation. He makes treaties with the advice and consent of the Senate; but he alone negotiates. Into the field of negotiation the Senate cannot intrude; and Congress itself is powerless to invade it . . . .

It is important to bear in mind that we are here dealing not alone with an authority vested in the President by an exertion of legislative power, but with such an authority plus the very delicate, plenary and exclusive power of the President as the sole organ of the federal government in the field of international relations—a power which does not require as a basis for its exercise an act of Congress, but which, of course, like every other governmental power, must be exercised in subordination to the applicable provisions of the Constitution. It is quite apparent that if, in the maintenance of our international relations, embarrassment—perhaps serious embarrassment—is to be avoided and success for our aims achieved, congressional legislation . . . must often accord to the President a degree of discretion and freedom from statutory restriction which would not be admissible were domestic affairs alone involved. Moreover, he, not Congress, has the better opportunity of knowing the conditions which prevail in foreign countries, and especially is this true in time of war. He has his confidential sources of information. He has his agents in the form of diplomatic, consular and other officials. Secrecy in respect of information gathered by them may be highly necessary, and the premature disclosure of it productive of harmful results.

to statutory grants from Congress. They were supplemented by a range of supports that arguably were not strictly constitutional in nature (e.g. historical tradition, force of circumstances, threat levels, executive skills, and the nature of international negotiations). The judgement in this landmark case represented an extraordinary piece of constitutional metamorphosis. It could be claimed that this set of extravagant—and arguably extra-constitutional—propositions represented a departure from constitutional government. The principle of shared and concurrent powers, which lies at the heart of American constitutionalism, had been largely replaced in the area of foreign policy by one of condoned presidential primacy under the pressure of external developments.

The *Curtiss–Wright* judgment became the linchpin of presidential claims to extraordinary legitimacy and to a widening remit of executive prerogative. Its implications quickly became evident during the Second World War, which witnessed the establishment of an entire defence infrastructure in American society. The logic of a sustained emergency continued with the Cold War, when global conditions and the advent of nuclear arsenals ensured that even greater power flowed to the centres of executive direction. The need for sophisticated structures of decision making, intelligence assessment, and crisis management led to the 'national security state', to the further enhancement of the president's own Executive Office (e.g. the National Security Council),

> **KEY POINTS**
>
> ❏ Foreign policy became increasingly recognized as an exceptional issue area in the governing responsibilities of the USA.
> ❏ The requirements of foreign policy were a powerful motive force in the adaptive capacity of the federal government.
> ❏ The presidency has acted as the chief agency and main beneficiary of governmental evolution in response to foreign policy needs.
> ❏ Executive prerogative and inherent powers—especially in relation to war—have marked the emergence of presidential power and the rise of the USA as a world power.

and to the formal establishment of a range of intelligence resources (e.g. the Central Intelligence Agency (CIA)) (Nathan and Oliver 1987: 21–105; Hart 1995; Andrew 1996; Inderfurth and Johnson 2004). References to an emergent and necessary form of 'presidential government' seemed prosaic as the executive prerogatives of foreign policy had become as self-evident as the international threat to American security (Burns 1973; Koh 1988). Even after the Cold War, the scale of the executive establishment in this area continued to grow so that by 2006 the USA accounted for 48 per cent of the world's military expenditures, with the president as commander-in-chief of the world's most lethal form of force projection.

Congress and the challenge of co-equality

In the field of foreign policy, the United States system of government is distinguished by an extraordinary mixture of movement and stasis; of evolutionary modernity and fixed tradition. Nothing better illustrates this dualism than the continued presence of Congress as a formal co-equal constitutional partner in the sphere of public policy. In most respects, Congress represents a traditional order of governance that is rooted in a strict formal sequence of government process, whereby laws are first enacted by legislative assent and subsequently implemented by the executive. It has already been noted that the requirements of foreign policy do not fit easily into

such a formulaic process and that the presidency has had to lead the way in recalibrating the process of government in line with the exigencies of the international sphere. As a result, Congress has often had to resort to a rearguard strategy of adaptation and repositioning in order to maintain a meaningful role in the area of foreign policy. In this it has been able to call on the support of the Constitution and the principle of the rule of law as well as different sectors of the public and various elements of the executive. The net effect has been one of ambiguity and dispute, which has generated a host of repercussions throughout government and the policy process.

Congress as a model of compliance

It is possible to view the role of Congress in foreign policy as something of an anomaly in that it is suggestive of an *ancien régime* of a simpler age when governments were altogether smaller in size and scope, and when the United States had the option of keeping the world at bay through geographical and political isolation. The heyday of congressional activism in foreign policy is often cited as the 1930s when the legislature sought to prevent President Roosevelt from implicating the United States in international disputes by a series of enactments intended to secure American neutrality in the face of rising European fascism and growing Japanese expansionism. The congressional position of isolationism may have been a politically responsive position, but in retrospect it was seen as thoroughly misguided, shortsighted, and dangerous. Congress's efforts to maintain security through appeasement became so discredited that they ushered in the rise of presidential initiative, executive judgement, and specialist foresight in the formulation of American foreign policy. The mindset of the Cold War merely intensified the transition of Congress into something of a support agency for executive action against communism as well as an institutional embodiment of America's social consensus against the communist threat (Spanier 1981; Sundquist 1981: 91–126).

According to this perspective, Congress was an institution that was simply too big, too decentralized, and too disorderly to be a responsible partner in the conduct of foreign policy. To much of its membership, Congress could neither compete with the executive's sources of information, nor challenge its expertise in the way it was appraised and acted upon. Just as the executive accepted the responsibility of setting the agenda, so Congress in many ways believed that the virtues of institutional responsiveness and political responsibility were based upon the merits of public affirmation and strategic compliance. Policy initiatives and constitutional powers were delegated to the executive (Schlesinger 1974: 127–207). Presidential pre-eminence afforded executive discretion to expand the usage of 'executive agreements' between states in place of the legal formalities of the treaty process. Furthermore, the sharing of war powers was gradually superseded through the commander-in-chief's capacity to deploy the armed forces in the absence of any formal declarations of war. When Congress was asked for its support, it was customary to give it in extravagant terms such as the Gulf of Tonkin Resolution of 1964 (see Key quotes 4.5). Anything less may have been construed as questioning the executive's action in a crisis, which in turn could be interpreted as signifying a lack of national resolve in confronting an adversary.

Congress as a model of assertion

This picture of model compliance and institutional subordination has become a well-established impression of Congress in the sphere of foreign policy. And yet, whilst acknowledging the inherent structural deficiencies of such a body, it is possible to arrive at quite a different estimation of Congress's contribution to this area of policy making—and with it a more balanced perspective of the nature of foreign policy making in general. An alternative view can be drawn from three main sources.

First, the characterization of Congress as a collectively supine branch always amounted to something of an overstatement. Even during the Cold War, representatives remained attentive to, and active within, a number of international areas (e.g. trade, transport, communications, immigration, foreign aid) and were often prepared to assert their positions in the form of legislative enactments. In addition to its influence upon the structural configuration of the military's distribution of resources, therefore, Congress was, and has remained, far from passive in a range of issue areas relating to foreign policy.

Second, as the intensive nature of the Cold War subsided in the 1970s and 1980s, the basic imperatives of executive-centred foreign policy diminished in scale. When this relaxation in Cold War disciplines was combined with the onset of greater congressional decentralization and with increased budgetary pressures upon federal expenditures, the effect was to bring many aspects of foreign policy under closer scrutiny. It was during this period that the differentiation between foreign policy and domestic policy began to erode as international dimensions intruded increasingly upon domestic issues and as constituency concerns began to be extended to America's policies abroad. The net effect was that more members of Congress found that they had more discretion in challenging the executive in its positions and judgements (Lindsay 1994). Congress also became better positioned to involve itself more deeply in the bureaucratic politics of the executive branch, particularly as its specialized subcommittees were increasingly embedded in the policy communities, or sub-governmental networks, that incorporated private sector interests, legislative connections, and agency agendas.

Third, the mystique that had conjoined foreign policy with executive sophistication in the Cold War was seriously compromised in the circumstances surrounding the Vietnam War. The level of misrepresentation, concealment, and deception in the highest reaches of government, the ambiguous nature of the commitment undertaken by the United States, and the volume of casualties and costs incurred by a war that America found it could not win were all factors in the public's disenchantment with the conflict. But more significantly for the processes of governance, the Vietnam War aroused a deep-set American reaction over the conduct of its politics in having allowed US forces to become so embroiled in an Asian land war. In essence, the war stimulated a fundamentalist response that proceeded on the basis that Vietnam was not simply the consequence of mistaken intelligence or poor decisions by a particular administration but instead indicated a dysfunctional imbalance within the structure of government (Schlesinger 1974: pp. vii–x, 208–419).

The notion of systemic defect that had permitted what was widely interpreted to be an abuse and even a usurpation of power prompted Congress into a series of direct countermeasures to correct the perceived imbalance. In an atmosphere of heightened republican fervour and Constitutional revival, Congress engaged in a quantum leap of foreign policy activism. Its challenge ranged from 'end the war' amendments and war budget cuts to critical appraisals of weapon system projects and military performance indicators; from investigations into the conduct and legitimacy of intelligence agencies to interventions into areas of high strategic and diplomatic value (e.g. nuclear non-proliferation, human rights, regional security); and from the establishment of procedures enabling Congress to acquire information and to underpin its rights of consultation and participation in the formulation of foreign policy (e.g. arms sales, military assistance,

executive agreements) to measures challenging the presidency's acquired prerogatives in the field of war powers.

Collectively, this release of political energies represented a radical shift both in attitudes and in the ecology of institutional relationships. The forcible intrusion of Congress into international affairs appeared to run counter to a pattern of precedents that had come to be seen as entrenched and geared to the logic of an ineluctable executive hegemony. Although Congress was more structurally fragmented and atomized in outlook than ever, its indiscipline allowed it to offer the prospect of critical oversight and to create an impression that foreign policy was now as amenable to legislative politics as it had been to bureaucratic politics.

The resurgence of Congress into the foreign policy field has sometimes been referred to as such an emphatic reversal of power away from the executive that it constituted a 'revolution' in Washington politics (Franck and Weisband 1979; Sundquist 1981: 238–314; Ripley, Lindsay, and Farrell 1993). But in the same way that it is important not to exaggerate the diminished status of Congress during the Cold War, so it is equally important that Congress's contemporary role is not overstated (Hinckley 1994). The general position lies in the intermediate area between the two extremes of an 'imperial presidency' and an 'imperial Congress'.

Congress as a mixed model

Throughout the 1980s and 1990s, Congress continued to depend upon the executive for the day-to-day responsibilities of foreign policy, but at the same time it retained its right to intervene on a selective basis, in order to draw attention to an issue, to reorder a set of priorities, or to challenge a policy direction. President Reagan, for example, expended considerable political capital in long-running disputes with Congress over the issue of economic sanctions on South Africa, and over American military assistance to the contra rebel forces in Nicaragua. President Clinton also struggled with Congress over foreign policy issues (e.g. NATO enlargement and the commitment of US troops to peacekeeping in former Yugoslavia).

Congress has devised new ways to ensure greater consultation and transparency in the conduct of foreign policy (e.g. conditional authorizations, reporting requirements). Further developments in congressional organization mean that legislative initiatives in foreign policy have the effect of often circumventing the traditional channels of influence away from the previous centres of dominance towards new bases of influence. The Senate, for example, with its constitutional powers over treaties and appointments, together with the prestige of its Foreign Relations Committee, has traditionally been central to the legislature's capabilities in foreign policy. Now, in many ways, the emphasis has shifted to the usage of budgetary devices in influencing foreign policy which has given the House of Representatives greater leverage than the Senate in the international politics surrounding the US government's appropriations process.

Congress has continued to benefit from an expanded licence to contest foreign policy with executive departments. Its oversight role has also been enhanced by the contemporary proliferation of special interest groups in the area of international relations, which has ingested an ever growing number of economic, social, ethnic, religious, regional, and global concerns ranging from multinational business organizations to values-based advocacy outfits and consultants operating openly on behalf of foreign governments. Whatever their basis of political leverage, the trend has been one of a deepening synergy between organized interest group activity and Congress's representational role. James Lindsay has observed the

---

 CONTROVERSIES 7.1: Presidential leadership

The emphasis given to presidential leadership in foreign policy is not to deny, or even to diminish, the significance of other actors, agencies, or influences upon the policy process. The literature on the formulation of America's position in international affairs correctly refers to the importance of such generic elements as international, societal, governmental, and bureaucratic factors—as well as to the more specific factors such as particular regional histories and individual crises. Nevertheless, the presidency does retain a close association with foreign policy. It is largely a matter of supply and demand. In many of the most important and conspicuous areas of foreign policy, American society requires a focal point of national unity to give material form to the idea of solidarity and patriotism in the face of possible adversity. For their part, presidents naturally gravitate towards the illustrious roles and political theatre of international affairs where the office's constitutional status as head of state and its capacity for political symbolism receive their maximum expression. For example, it is presidents who are the chief instigators, and the primary embodiments, of the 'rally-round-the-flag' effect (Mueller 1973; Hetherington and Nelson 2003). This refers to those occasions when the American public is mobilized in response to an international crisis involving the United States. It is the president who benefits from these public reactions not just because of being personally involved in an international event but because of the presidency's representational significance as the only nationally elected office in American democracy.

The president's leadership role is discernible in a wide variety of contexts from imposing a particular imprint upon the management of the national security structure to shaping the posture and future planning of America's relationship with the rest of the world; from giving public expression to the purposes and values of American foreign policy to the issue of whether and when to commit US forces abroad. Just as US strategic positions become defined as presidential 'doctrines' (e.g. the Truman Doctrine, the Nixon Doctrine, the Bush Doctrine), so American military interventions tend to become known as presidential wars. The intimate connection of significant foreign policy issues with the presidency has become part of a high-exposure form of governance in which presidents continually seek to enhance their national credentials but also to cultivate a direct relationship with the public in a process that has been likened to a permanent election campaign (Ornstein and Mann 2000).

The shift toward a 'public presidency' (Kernell 2007) of maximum engagement and outreach can relate well to the more traditional role of national leadership. But at the same time the drive to widen the support base can also lead to an erosion of more institutional foundations to presidential power. This can in turn result in presidents becoming increasingly exposed in terms of personalized blame and accountability. Just as 'rally-round-the-flag' incidents tend only to lead to short-term gains in presidential support, so the decline and fall of many presidential leaderships have been marked by public reactions to what are perceived to be foreign policy failures (Mueller 2005). In this way, foreign policy can become the access point for presidential critique and the means by which a president's reputation for leadership and even for competence can be undermined.

dynamic leading to the surge in legislative activism: 'With more groups active on more foreign policy issues, members find themselves under greater pressure to address foreign policy. At the same time, the rise of interest group activity means that suddenly members stand a good chance of benefiting politically by undertaking detailed legislative work on foreign policy' (Lindsay 1994: 29).

While it is true that congressional involvement in foreign policy issues has increased, it remains the case that its participation is variable across different sub-fields of foreign policy and that it is the presidency which retains the mainline obligation of coordinating and overseeing America's position in the international sphere. The office possesses enormous reserves of influence in foreign policy not just because of the prodigious resources that are available in the federal bureaucracy but also because of the executive privileges of secrecy, initiative, and rapid response. On this basis, the president can offer to provide a leadership role in a system that arguably requires its force, and denies its legitimacy, in equal measure. Even in a post-Cold War setting, Congress still suffers from chronic problems in matching the presidency as a co-equal partner in foreign policy. It is not simply that congressional attempts to restrict the presidency by legislative means have often led to the White House reinterpreting them as sources of authorization. It is that Congress's own determination in following through on its own conditions and pre-requirements has often been less than robust.

The relationship between the Congress and presidency continues to be a changeable mix of conflict and cooperation, of legislative enquiry and assertion coexisting with executive discretion and residual responsibility. On occasions, the relationship can amount to a complex interdependency of mutual trust that works towards reconciling the principle of open enquiry with an executive rationale of secrecy and operational discretion in what remains a highly sensitive area of decision making (Johnson 1991, 2004; Jeffreys-Jones 1998; Zegart and Quinn 2010). Congress cannot be an exact equivalent of the presidency in such a field but what it can do on occasions is to reveal the contested nature of foreign policy and to ensure that policy issues in the international arena are forced onto the political agenda. Arguably, its role can be said to have a much wider significance. Congressional oversight can serve to underline the importance not merely of what policy decisions are made and how they are arrived at, but also the values that have informed both the process and outcomes of policy production.

Policy making in a congested space

The nature of these two central institutions and the changeable relationship between them underscores the often unsettled and contingent properties that characterise the policy-making process in this area. During the Cold War, a widely held conception of the political and jurisdictional configuration of foreign

---

KEY POINTS

❑ Congress represents not only its electorates but also traditional precepts of democracy, the rule of law, due process, and constitutional government.

❑ Although a formal co-equal in status, the legislature faces considerable political and technical difficulties in matching the executive in foreign policy.

❑ Fluctuations occur in the relationships between the two institutions in this litmus test area of governmental responsibilities and political legitimacy.

❑ While global integration has increased congressional interest in more foreign policy sectors, it still suffers from serious disadvantages in the more strategic areas associated intelligence information, executive agreements, and military deployments.

BOX 7.3: The foreign policy environment

Federal Executive

Amongst the array of federal departments, independent agencies, government corporations, boards, commissions, and advisory committees that have responsibilities for foreign and national security policy, the following are usually identified as prominent:

Department of State (1789): organization of the foreign service; responsible for embassies, consulates, travel, passports, and visas; centre of diplomatic resources; specialist competence in international politics; foreign policy formulation and implementation; local onsite knowledge; lead in the negotiation of treaties; traditionally inclined towards supportive engagements with international organizations, key allies and the 'international community'.

Department of Defense (1947): provision and maintenance of military forces to defend US citizens and interests; source of information and assessment on key security issues; force projection and deterrence; heavy economic footprint in contracts, bases, and employment; inter-service rivalries between army, navy, air force, and marines; key element in national security strategy and planning.

Department of Homeland Security (2002): a compendium organization drawn from various pre-existing agencies and programmes following the 2001 terrorist attacks; responsibilities in the areas of counterterrorism; border security; emergency planning; disaster management; immigration enforcement; cybersecurity; committed to defending US from acts of terrorism both inside and outside its borders.

Central Intelligence Agency (1947): traditionally the key agency tasked with the collection, analysis and co-ordination of information concerning not only the behaviour and intentions of adversaries, but also the state of more generic conditions around the world that have an actual or potential impact upon American interests. Despite its civilian status, the CIA has not been confined to purely passive intelligence work concerning threat levels and warnings to policy makers, but has conducted special operations and covert actions in support of policy objectives.

National Security Council (1947): elite White House unit designed to be the principal source of presidential advice on foreign, military, and domestic issues relating to national security; primary means of policy co-ordination across the executive branch. Among the statutory or regular participants are the Vice President, Secretary of State, Treasury Secretary, Defense Secretary, Assistant to the President for National Security Affairs, Chairman of the Joint Chiefs of Staff, and Director of National Intelligence. A Homeland Security Council was formed in 2002 as the centre of presidential advice on home security and counter-terrorism but this was merged into the National Security Council in 2009 under the aggregate name of the National Security Staff.

US Congress

Extensive committee and subcommittee systems in both the House of Representatives and the Senate afford specialist oversight of policy formulation and implementation, investigative hearings, appropriations and budgetary reviews, multiple access points for the representation of social, economic, and bureaucratic interests.

Notable examples

House Committees on Armed Services, Foreign Affairs, Homeland Security, Intelligence, Energy and Commerce, Financial Services, and Appropriations.

Senate Committees on Foreign Relations, Homeland Security and Governmental Affairs, Intelligence, Armed Services, Commerce, Science and Transportation, Energy and Natural Resource, and Appropriations.

Non-governmental bodies

Republican and Democratic parties; economic interest and lobby groups; think tanks; social advocacy movements; campaigning non-governmental organisations (NGOs); religious, ethnic or nationalist/regional organizations; specialist information gathering/dissemination groups; international monitoring and opinion formation centres; policy communities and sub-governmental networks.

Media/Public opinion

Channels of political communication; provision/consumption/mediation of political information; news agendas; media framing of issues and policies; rise of multiple platforms; dependency relationships; public attitudes/values; agenda formation; opinion polling; political marketing; construction of narratives; societal influences; 'multiple publics'.

BOX 7.3: (*continued*)

'Intermestic issues'

Rising number and intensity of transnational problems and issues that have an international dimension, including trade, terrorism, health security, biological and nuclear security, gender issues, migration, capital flows, regional integration, nuclear proliferation, criminal behaviour (trafficking, slavery), sustainable development, energy resources, environmental degradation, food security and climate change as well as themes relating to overseas practices, international inequality, and global justice.

External players

Allies/partners; treaty obligations; economic pressures; global governance; international institutions and organizations; international norms and legal codes; competitors, adversaries, and threats; global order issues; weak/failed states; foreign assistance programmes; human rights issues; international NGOs; regulatory frameworks.

---

policy making was the 'two presidencies' thesis. In sum, this posited the coexistence of two entirely different and separate spheres of policy formulation, one for foreign policy and one for domestic policy. While the former was characterized by the unifying drives of presidential primacy, the latter was depicted by Congress and its representation of society's multiple interests and cleavages. A key element of the thesis was the way that political pluralism in the field of foreign policy was not considered to be really relevant. In effect, the normal dynamics of cross-cutting divisions had been displaced or in some way switched off either by the force of active consensus, or by a passive deference to the technical expertise required for the complexities of international power politics.

After the Cold War, the position appeared to undergo a radical change as foreign policy was opened up to the challenges of an altered ecology in terms of issues, players, and attitudes. In some ways the change was marked more by an opening up of government agencies and interests that had been in existence all along but were now more able to express their particular positions with greater vigour to outside audiences. In other ways, the shift was marked—and continues to be characterized—by a transformative process in which no settled pattern of policy making has emerged and arguably is not likely to do so in the near future. The net effect has been a more crowded, contested, and

volatile environment that is marked as much by its variability as it is by its expansive contours. A brief overview of this increasingly complex topography is given in Box 7.3.

One conclusion that can be drawn from such a matrix is a marked dependency within government upon increasingly specialist resources and embedded experience in the analysis and assessment of problems that are complex and multi-dimensional in scope. Another conclusion would assign the high level of structure and continuity within the foreign policy-making process less to the existence of a settled perspective of world politics amongst key elites and more to a condition of stasis arising from a profusion of power centres engaging in a continual process of bureaucratic politics and positional competition within a system designed to generate continuity through reciprocal constraints. An alternative perspective would view the usually calm and deep waters of foreign policy as a derivative of the sheer scale not only of world politics and the international system at large but also of a superpower's necessarily cautious and calibrated engagement with such an interdependent context. Notwithstanding this reputation for systemic equilibrium, the condition of US foreign policy can occasionally be disrupted by a shock event that can suddenly galvanize a previously stable process into one marked by conspicuously different patterns of behaviour and priorities.

9/11, the war on terror, and new tensions

Notwithstanding the unprecedented nature of the terrorist attacks on the United States in 2001, the overall configuration of the policy processes and disputes surrounding America's reaction revealed a marked resemblance to previous foreign policy crises. In the aftershock of the attacks, American society looked to the White House for a focal point of national consciousness and collective solidarity. President Bush was adept at using the 'rally around the flag' effect for the purposes of framing the issue of international terrorism and shaping political support for the selected reactions. Governments have long been able to use fear and insecurity to mobilize resources and to accumulate powers on a scale that would be inconceivable without the stimulus of aroused public anxiety. The Bush administration was no exception in making full use of the transformative energies of a crisis. The president was able to secure the accelerated passage through a compliant Congress of the Patriot Act, which not only radically reshaped the federal government's structure of internal security, but dramatically increased its powers of surveillance and detention. In effect, the Cold War apparatus of the national security state was deepened and combined with a homeland security society that reached into areas previously protected by civil liberties and constitutional limitations (Brzezinski 2005; Arnold 2006; Amnesty International 2007).

Although the initial reaction of the Bush administration had been cautious in respect to overseas retaliation, the White House used the issue of international terrorism to reaffirm its prior scepticism of international institutions and multilateral processes. This set the stage for a new form of international coalition building that would bypass established processes in favour of an *ad hoc* task force dedicated to a 'war on terror'. Bush's populist disregard for traditional diplomacy and institutional formalities was prompted by the nature of the threats against the United States, by the mercurial character of terrorist organizations like al-Qaeda, and by the calculation that urgent action was required to pre-empt the danger of the USA being attacked through groups covertly acquiring and deploying weapons of mass destruction. To the administration, the special character of the

danger required a different kind of warfare and a different set of executive prerogatives to go with it.

The initial military response by America was seen as reasonable by the international community. The intervention in Afghanistan (2001) was widely supported. Because the Taliban regime had given sanctuary within its borders to al-Qaeda groupings, the United States was easily able to organize a broad-based coalition that included NATO forces. But when President Bush extended his anti-terrorism agenda to include Iraq as part of the 'axis of evil', the level of international support suddenly diminished, leaving an increasingly unilateralist White House reliant upon its option of a 'coalition of the willing' (Bush 2002). The objections lodged by the traditional channels of international governance found very little resonance inside the United States. On the contrary, supported by high public approval ratings, by solid congressional support, and by a generalized fear of further attacks, President Bush was able to establish a public perception that Iraq was not only implicated in the attacks on 9/11 but possessed weapons of mass destruction (WMD) that would be passed on to Islamic extremists. In a move that was strongly suggestive of the need to compensate for the intelligence failures surrounding 9/11, the White House projected intelligence information and its assessment to the forefront of its adopted causes of war against Iraq. The intelligence-led linkage between Iraq, 9/11, WMD, and terrorism was clearly evident in the congressional resolution authorizing the threat posed by the regime of Saddam Hussein.

After the initial success of the invasion and the removal of Saddam Hussein, United States-led coalition forces became increasingly involved in a costly campaign of establishing security against a backdrop of sectarian violence and social disintegration. As the temporary intervention turned into a long-term occupation and a war of attrition against insurgents, the Bush presidency came under severe pressure. The issues of terrorism, national security, and regional stability, which had boosted his political influence in 2001–3, were transmuted into an instrument of indictment during his second term of office. The claims and assumptions made by the Bush White House in support of both the war and the president's own

---

BOX 7.4: Authorization for use of military force against Iraq Resolution of 2002

The Joint Resolution, authorizing the use of United States armed forces against Iraq, was passed by the House of Representatives (296–133) on 11 October 2002, and by the Senate (77–23) on 12 October 2002.

- Whereas the attacks on the United States of September 11, 2001, underscored the gravity of the threat posed by the acquisition of weapons of mass destruction by international terrorist organizations;
- Whereas Iraq's demonstrated capability and willingness to use weapons of mass destruction, the risk that the current Iraqi regime will either employ those weapons to launch a surprise attack against the United States or its Armed Forces or provide them to international terrorists who would do so, and the extreme magnitude of harm that would result to the United States and its citizens from such an attack, combine to justify action by the United States to defend itself; …

- Whereas the President and Congress are determined to continue to take all appropriate actions against international terrorists and terrorist organizations, including those nations, organizations, or persons who planned, authorized, committed, or aided the terrorist attacks that occurred on September 11, 2001, or harbored such persons or organizations;

Sec. 3. Authorization for use of United States armed forces.

The President is authorized to use the Armed Forces of the United States as he determines to be necessary and appropriate in order to (1) defend the national security of the United States against the continuing threat posed by Iraq; and (2) enforce all relevant United Nations Security Council resolutions regarding Iraq.

---

rights to determine policy were increasingly subjected to critical review in light of what was being interpreted as a policy failure. In the forefront of the critiques was the charge that the Bush administration had politically manipulated the intelligence on Iraq for the purposes of mobilizing public support for the war. In misrepresenting intelligence materials over WMD, the president was accused not only of misrepresenting the causes of war but of misappropriating the legal processes relating to decisions over entering into a state of war.

The White House had previously aroused anxieties over the magnitude of its constitutional assertions. For example, it claimed a unilateral power to initiate wars without any congressional approval, and it assumed it could interpret, terminate, or suspend international treaties at its discretion (Yoo 2005). The protracted nature of the Iraq War allowed these concerns to resurface as part of a more general reaction against the style of the Bush presidency. Under Bush's leadership, the administration had authorized the detention of prisoners without trial at Guantánamo, placed 'illegal combatants' beyond the scope of the Geneva Conventions, claimed that Congress could not restrict the president's authority in instituting harsher methods of interroga-

tion, and insisted that the inherent powers of the presidency permitted the National Security Agency to breach the provisions of the Foreign Intelligence Surveillance Act (1978) and to monitor the phone call records of millions of Americans. All these positions came under critical review not least by the Supreme Court, which broke its customary reticence over considering foreign policy issues in *Hamdan* v. *Rumsfeld* (2006). In the case, the Court declared that the administration's plan to try terrorist suspects at Guantánamo by military commissions denied them not only the protection of the Geneva Conventions but the rights of due process that would be afforded by a court martial or a civilian tribunal.

Prior to the Iraq action, Congress had been complicit in what was retrospectively seen as a rush to war. Louis Fisher concluded that in authorizing military action by a measure comparable to the notorious Gulf of Tonkin Resolution, the legislature had failed in its constitutional duty: 'instead of acting as the people's representatives and preserving the republican form of government, they gave the president unchecked power' (Fisher 2003: 405). But following the 2006 mid-term elections when the Democrats regained control of the House and Senate, Congress became much more vocal in its assaults upon the presidency in the key area of war powers. As institutional and political interest in the venerable dogmas of the separation of powers revived, so public scepticism of the war and the Bush presidency intensified. Personal culpability for individual judgements and choices was directed to the White House but, in line with American traditions of political accountability, responsibility was not confined to President Bush. The issue of causality was characteristically widened into that of a systemic failure of the decision-making structure—stretching from bureaucratic disarray and confused agendas to intelligence mismanagement and the abandonment of checks by alternative centres of political and media opinion (Ricks 2006; Gordon 2007). These in turn led to calls not for new frameworks of governance but for a return to the fundamentals of a balanced constitution. However, as we have seen, the comforting prospect of

---

KEY POINTS

❑ Terrorist attacks, and further threats of international terrorism, prompt President Bush into new kinds of warfare and new claims of inherent executive powers.

❑ Sweeping powers of surveillance, arrest, detention, and interrogation raise issues over the relationship of security to civil liberties.

❑ The use or misuse of intelligence in mobilizing support for the war on terror, combined with the outcome of the 2006 mid-term elections, revive interest in the constitutional balance between the presidency and the Congress.

---

constitutional certainty is a chimera, for the only precision afforded by its provisions remains that of strategic ambiguity.

The Obama presidency

The world that President Obama inherited from his largely discredited predecessor was one marked not only by the aftershock of President Bush's global war on terror but also by the onset of new international priorities (e.g. climate change) as well as the continuation of more familiar global and regional agenda items. In the 2008 presidential campaign, Obama promoted himself as an antidote to the Bush administration and its reputation for aggressive unilateralism, preventive war, force projection, and regime change. He associated his presidency with a drive to reconfigure the United States' posture towards the world in a more positive and constructive light. He looked to restore confidence in the security community among the leading powers through a greater emphasis upon soft power, international organization, cultural diplomacy, and multilateral co-operation. Notwithstanding these intentions, Obama quickly found that his discretion in reconstructing American foreign policy was heavily constrained by what he discovered to be an area of activity that was marked by a rising trajectory of interconnected dimensions, cross-cutting jurisdictional issues, and proliferating players. The nature of this increasingly

intricate predicament can be illustrated by the following set of brief examples.

● The intelligence failures associated with the attacks on 9/11 and with the issue of WMD in Iraq had prompted the Bush administration to re-organize intelligence resources to secure better co-operation and sharing of information between key agencies. The main structural change was the creation of a Director of National Intelligence. This position was tasked with providing a strategic overview of US intelligence, including responsibilities for setting intelligence budgets and priorities with the aim of transforming US intelligence resources into a fully functional collaborative enterprise. The death of eight CIA employees from a bomb attack in Afghanistan (December 2009), the intelligence failures surrounding an attempted suicide bombing on a Northwest Airlines plane over Detroit (December 2009), and the discovery on a cargo plane of explosive materials addressed to locations in Chicago (December 2010) provoked concerns over the reliability of US security systems. In particular, the incidents illustrated the continuing problems associated with the levels of coordination within what had remained a sprawling intelligence community consisting of sixteen agencies each with developed linkages to different departmental hierarchies and Congressional units (Dombey 2010). The incidents helped to reveal continuing turf struggles—most notably between the relatively new Office of the Director of National Intelligence centred in Washington and the traditional primacy of the CIA with its overseas field stations and experience in covert activities. The security incidents not only represented an embarrassment to the administration, but allowed critiques of the presidency to be extended to the issue of managerial competence and, more seriously, to Obama's personal commitment to counterterrorism.

• While the Obama administration inherited the war in Afghanistan, the president soon found that he faced a difficult dilemma over the future course of the engagement, namely whether to concede to military pressures in favour of increasing the US presence by 40,000 troops, or to follow his political instincts in seeking to wind down the war through graduated troop withdrawals. The heated debates between key policy makers on this highly contentious issue found their way into the public domain through various political conduits and media channels. While some interpretations depicted President Obama as being distracted by a mainly domestic agenda, other perspectives saw him as interested primarily in achieving sufficient military disengagement to preserve his status amongst liberal and Democratic Party constituencies, as well as his re-election prospects in 2012. In the end, he was damaged by an outwardly reluctant commitment in December 2009 to raise troop levels by 30,000 but only on condition that the additional commitment would be geared to the overall position of securing phased withdrawals by July 2011 (Woodward 2010). Apart from the central anomaly of opting for a temporary surge of ground forces in order to strengthen a necessarily long-term counterinsurgency strategy, the disarray surrounding the Afghanistan review revealed the difficulties of a president seeking to arrive at authoritative decisions in a multi-structured, media-rich and increasingly interconnected environment—a context that ultimately led to the resignation of General Stanley McChrystal, the Commander of US and international forces in Afghanistan, over allegations of unauthorized briefings, media leaks, and insubordination.

• Another example of the increasing interconnectedness not only between different sectors of foreign policy but also between the international and domestic spheres lies in the area of US trade policy. The Obama administration has had to engage with a widening trade deficit between the US and China as well as with a deepening dependency upon China's foreign currency holdings for international financial stability. While the White House remains firmly committed to a free trade position as central to the development of the global economy, others in both the main parties view the relationship with China as being detrimental either to American employment or to US security. President Obama therefore has had to tread a difficult line between seeking to gain concessions from China in such areas as market access, intellectual property rights, copyright law, and currency policy, while at the same time not provoking the Chinese leadership into jeopardising the prospects of American economic recovery by disrupting the main source of low-cost goods and high-volume credit. While domestic pressures—especially from the unions within his own party—can make trade deals with China and other countries politically problematic, the situation is further strained by China's growing geopolitical footprint, which has implications stretching across many key aspects of US foreign policy (e.g. nuclear non-proliferation, North Korea, Burma, Iran, Pakistan, Sudan, climate change).

Barack Obama had secured the presidency on the basis of a culturally transformative platform that pivoted upon a renewal of American values that would occasion not only a 'new politics' at home but also a repositioning of the United States in relation to the world outside. However, the Obama presidency quickly acquired the position of an ongoing negotiation between the idealism of the campaign and the hard-edged realism of largely intractable issues at home and abroad (Grimmett 2010; Hendrickson 2010; Kupchan 2010; Traub 2010). It can be argued that this was a necessary learning process that all modern presidents have had to encounter in office—and most especially in the field of foreign policy. Nevertheless, it is possible to argue that the Obama administration has been confronted not merely by the normal run of constraints, frustrations, and reversals, but by an emergent array of shifting dynamics within the sphere of foreign policy politics.

First is the deepening tension between on the one hand the premises of US sovereignty along with its concomitant traditions of international leadership in respect to the shape and security of the global order, and on the other hand the need to accommodate itself to the rising prominence of those institutions, organizations, processes, and norms associated with the structures and ethos of global governance. The conspicuous position of the presidency means that while the office-holder still has the ability to publicise issues and advocate responses to increasingly large audiences, the inferences of direction and autonomy are variously compromised by the intricacies and containments of global institutions, international NGOs, and multilateral regulatory frameworks. In essence, President Obama has by political necessity and personal conviction propounded a more inclusive and integrationist international posture but by doing so he has had to contend with damaging counterclaims that assert not merely a failure to determine or to deliver beneficial outcomes, but also a complicity with an ascribed process of American decline.

Second, as the interdependency of domestic and international sectors becomes tighter, it is more difficult for presidents to use the recourse to foreign policy as a strategic change of focus in response to domestic difficulties and electoral setbacks. Many of President Obama's predecessors had been able to divert attention from domestic agendas to international challenges as part of an often general osmosis towards an identification of presidential roles with the external realm of foreign policy responsibilities. Obama has found that this aspect of 'presidential time' has become highly attenuated. Because foreign policy factors now line the point of entry to the White House, the processes of adjustment to international issues have become accelerated beyond the point where they can be selected by a president with an inclination to change priorities. In a deep global recession, the real or attributed influence of other players in what are increasingly international

markets and integrated economies underlines both the processes of political prioritisation but also the immediacy of presidential discomfort in such a mercurial sphere of multiple interactivities.

Third, although Obama's presidential campaign had adopted highly sophisticated techniques of public outreach and voter mobilisation through new media channels in the field of political communication, the new president has found it difficult to maintain the initiative in these new areas of political projection, most of which have an international dimension of one sort or another. For example, the Obama administration has been subjected to a concerted assault by a profusion of highly critical websites and digital networks which have had a significant impact upon the president's political standing. President Obama has experienced great difficulty in confronting or even engaging with an expanding blogosphere within which an internet-based commentariat persistently seeks to establish a perceptual linkage between the president and his agenda, the state of the economy, and the levels of public dissatisfaction and anxiety over the United States' position in the world. These new forms of mass communication serve to underscore the ways in which the convergence of domestic and foreign policy can be used to political effect. Just as widely circulated critiques of Obama's social policy agenda can serve to erode his political and professional standing in the US, so both these critical narratives can shift perceptions overseas, leading to a lack of traction in key foreign policy areas. In other words, persistent and ramifying media portrayals of a president under political and personal challenge—along with international access to polling trends and analysis—have direct repercussions overseas and especially on the political calculations made by other actors in the international arena.

Finally, the foreign policy sector has become more intensively politicised over the course of the post Cold War era. Apart from the increased incursion of interests and stakeholders into the equation of foreign policy making, the sector is now more vulnerable than ever to a proliferation of alternative centres of international analysis, assessment, and activism. These can vary from think tanks and broad spectrum NGOs to more specialized advocacy groups and representations of corporate interest. When these myriad competitors for public and international attention become conjoined with the impact of a 24/7 multiple-platform media environment then, as President Obama has discovered, the net effect can be one of unremitting challenge in the very area of policy that used to be thought of as a presidential preserve.

Far from offering an alternative dimension to conventional politics, the foreign policy sphere has increasingly become a device by which to engage in generic assaults upon presidential conduct, competence, and judgement across the board. To a growing extent, the structural and operational critiques that have traditionally been applied to the US political system in domestic affairs are now routinely extended to the foreign policy sphere, leading to claims that even in this area of policy making the system can be categorized as febrile, dysfunctional, and broken. The pace of these indictments had noticeably quickened under his predecessor (Skelley 2006; Wiarda 2009; Hook 2010). President Obama has sought to create a disjuncture between himself and President George W. Bush by recalibrating the posture of the United States towards the world and by devising a more inclusive approach to foreign policy both at home and abroad. In doing so—or at least in giving that impression—the president has not established a break with the past so much as progressed further along a continuum of congestion and complaint. Set against the clamorous background

> **KEY POINTS**
>
> ❏ President Obama's election raises the prospect of a reconfiguration of US foreign policy but his first term shows the internal and external problems associated with any transformative processes in an increasingly congested policy space.
>
> ❏ The deepening cross currents between domestic and international politics along with the growing fusion of their respective audiences generate new challenges to presidential leadership.
>
> ❏ Disputed narratives concerning America's role in the twenty-first century world—combined with the widening scope of claims relating to the structural inadequacies of the its constitutional arrangements—encourage fresh concerns over a trajectory of national decline.

of these contemporary developments within America's policy-making context, the issues of control, direction, and coherence are likely to remain considerable challenges not just for the rest of his presidency but also for his political successors in the White House. Far from assuming the mantle of a redeeming corrective to an otherwise chronically fragmented system, the foreign policy sphere in Washington has increasingly come to imitate the very properties of multi-polarity that have come to characterize the world itself.

? Questions

1. Describe and evaluate the significance of presidential leadership in the area of foreign policy.

2. How can Congress influence the formulation of foreign policy?

3. What is meant by the term 'rallying round the flag' and how important is it to presidential leadership in times of crisis?

4. Examine the challenges to democratic principles posed by the requirements of foreign policy.

5. What conclusions do you draw from the wording of the Gulf of Tonkin Resolution (1964) and the Authorization for Use of Military Force against Iraq Resolution (2002)?

6. Is secrecy a necessary and indispensable element of effective policy making? What problems does the intelligence community pose for the processes of foreign policy governance?

7. Is it accurate to describe the foreign policy process in the United States as a continual struggle between Congress and the presidency?

8. Has President Obama managed to create a foreign policy that is distinguishable from his predecessor?

9. Examine the political, constitutional, and international difficulties of ending a war.

» **Further Reading**

Cronin, T. E. and Genovese, M. A. (2009), *The Paradoxes of the American Presidency*, 3rd edn (New York: Oxford University Press).

By exploring the presidency through the analytical device of paradoxes, Cronin and Genovese are able convey the way that the office attracts increased expectations at the same time as the system restricts the resources and power that would enable the presidency to fulfil the promises of effective governance.

Fisher, L. (2004), *Presidential War Power*, 2nd edn (Lawrence, KS: University Press of Kansas).

A leading congressional scholar navigates his readers through the complex and contentious debates over the allocation of war powers. By locating the disputes in their historical, political, and constitutional contexts, Fisher is able to reach a critical appreciation of the trend lines in presidential war making and the need for an institutional balance to be restored.

Inderfurth, K. F. and Johnson, L. (eds) (2004), *Fateful Decisions: Inside the National Security Council* (New York: Oxford University Press).

Karl Inderfurth and Loch Johnson guide the reader through the structures and processes of the National Security Council. Their team give an array of valuable insights into the origins, workings, strengths, and weaknesses of the NSC. The book not only assesses the contribution of the NSC over the period 1947 to 2003, but offers reform proposals to improve the Council's performance.

Mann, T. E. and Ornstein, N. J. (2006), *The Broken Branch: How Congress is Failing America and How to Get it Back on Track* (New York: Oxford University Press).

A study that is illustrative of the critiques levelled at Congress and of the need for reform. It argues that the recent developments of high partisanship and procedural arbitrariness have led it to become increasingly dysfunctional.

Wittkopf, E. R. and McCormick, J. M. (eds) (2008), *The Domestic Sources of American Foreign Policy: Insights and Evidence*, 5th edn (Lanham MD: Rowman & Littlefield).

This collection of readings takes full account of the domestic influences on the formulation and conditioning of US foreign policy. It is organized on the basis of three levels of analysis, namely the societal, institutional, and individual levels. This framework allows for a very wide variety of observations and discussion points relating to systemic, ideational, and personal aspects of foreign policy decision making.

 For a range of additional resources to support your learning visit the Online Resource Centre that accompanies this book at **www.oxfordtextbooks.co.uk/orc/cox_stokes2e/**.

8 Military power and US foreign policy

Beth A. Fischer

Chapter contents

Introduction

How has military power been reconceptualized over time in the United States? For what purposes has the United States deployed its military? How effective is military power in achieving political objectives? This chapter will consider the rise and use of American military power since 1945. It will also consider important debates regarding containment, deterrence, preemption, and the limits of military power.

Rise of American military power 1945–91: containment and deterrence

The United States emerged from the Second World War as a military great power. It had the largest navy in the world and, more importantly, it was the only state to have the atomic bomb. This military capability grew throughout the Cold War. By the time the Soviet Union collapsed in 1991 the United States' military power was unrivalled. Two concepts governed US military power and strategy throughout the Cold War: containment and deterrence.

The military implications of containment

Containment was the foundation of American foreign policy throughout the Cold War. Each administration had its own version of containment, but the ultimate goal remained the same: to contain the spread of Soviet communism. Containment sought to prevent Soviet expansionism.

During the 1950s the United States sought global containment. That is, it sought to aid all those resisting communism throughout the world. All countries were considered vital to American interests in the belief that if one country fell to communism, its neighbours would be destabilized and fall to communism as well. This analogy is known as the domino theory.

These perspectives led to American military involvement in Korea between 1950 and 1953. In this case the United States went to war to prevent communist North Korea from controlling democratic South Korea. American policy makers feared that if North Korea could gain control of the south, it would lead to further communist expansion throughout Asia. Although the Korean War ended in 1953, US troops remain posted along the border between North and South.

The desire to contain the spread of communism in Asia led to another war, this time in Vietnam. Although the political objective was the same, the Vietnam War was a different type of conflict. The Korean War had been a traditional war fought between massive, organized armies with relatively clear front lines. The Vietnam War was less traditional: the front lines were often unclear, battles often took place in muddy jungles, and, most importantly, Vietnamese civilians engaged in guerilla-style attacks on US forces. The US military was ill-prepared to counter this kind of insurgency. It was structured, trained, and equipped to fight a large-scale conventional war. The United States originally sought to fight a 'limited war'. However, throughout the late 1960s the White House incrementally increased the number of US troops in Vietnam. By late 1968 there were over half a million US troops in the region and Washington was spending $35 billion per year on the conflict.

Nonetheless, the United States was unable to win the war. By the time a cease-fire was signed in January 1973 58,000 US soldiers had been killed, along with countless Vietnamese. American involvement truly ended in April 1975 when Saigon fell to the North Vietnamese and all remaining Americans were evacuated. Despite the fact that the United States was a military superpower, it had suffered a humiliating defeat.

The Vietnam War was both unpopular and devastating for Americans. It led to an era in which Americans lost faith in their political and military leaders. The Vietnam War had several important implications for the way in which military power was conceptualized in the United States.

For one thing, the loss in Vietnam led Americans to reject containment on a global scale. Many believed that the United States had overextended itself: the United States did not have the resources to protect all peoples fighting communism. President Nixon reflected these views in 1970 when he declared that the United States would continue to provide military and economic assistance to friends, but those nations must be responsible for their own security. Nixon implicitly acknowledged that there were limits to American military power and what it could achieve. This decision to scale back containment became known as the Nixon Doctrine.

Secondly, the defeat in Vietnam has led to what some call a Vietnam Syndrome. In this view Americans have been so haunted by the loss that they have sought to avoid involvement in other wars at almost all costs. Thus, although American military power has been growing for the past 30 years, there has also been a strong reluctance to actually use this power. The Vietnam Syndrome is wrapped in both fact and myth. While Americans continue to be scarred from Vietnam, the US has, in fact, repeatedly deployed its military power since 1975, as will be discussed.

The experience in Vietnam has also led US military leaders to revamp military strategies. Some contend that the attempt to fight a limited war in Vietnam contributed significantly to the United States' defeat. In this view the gradual increase in troop deployments did not allow the United States to make maximum use of its military capabilities. Consequently, in future wars the United States must deliver massive force right from the outset. This perspective is often called the Powell Doctrine, after General Colin Powell, who served as Chairman of the Joint Chiefs of Staff for the first President Bush, and as Secretary of State for the second President Bush. General Powell had spent a career in the military, including two tours of duty in Vietnam. In his view, in order to address the mistakes of Vietnam future military deployments must meet three criteria: the aim of the mission and the rules of engagement must be clear, the United States must send overwhelming force right from the outset, and there must be a clear exit strategy to avoid mission creep. Powell also emphasized the need for strong public support for such operations (Powell 1992–3).

The military implications of deterrence

At the conclusion of the Second World War the United States was the only state with an atomic weapon. Although the Soviet Union had a larger conventional army, American leaders believed the US monopoly on nuclear weapons was the 'great equalizer', that is, the destructive capacity of nuclear weapons made up for the relative weakness in conventional (non-nuclear) military power.

In August 1949 the Soviet Union tested an atomic weapon of its own. This event profoundly changed the nature of the Cold War. The US responded to the Soviet test with a policy review, called NSC-68. This document claimed the United States was now in a dangerously inferior position. Consequently, it needed to build up its own military strength so that it surpassed that of the Soviet Union. The United States needed to achieve and maintain a position of military superiority. NSC-68 led to a dramatic increase in US defence spending, as well as to a global network of US military bases and alliances. The Cold War was no longer simply an ideological and political contest—it now involved an arms race of epic proportions.

The United States also adopted a strategy of deterrence. Deterrence involves dissuading an enemy from attacking by convincing him that the costs of an attack would far outweigh any benefits. During the Cold War the United States deterred the Soviets from launching a nuclear attack by threatening to respond in kind. In other words, if the Soviet Union were to launch a nuclear strike against the US or its allies, the United States would respond with a retaliatory nuclear attack on the Soviet Union. Such retaliation would bring unacceptable damage to the

USSR. In effect, a nuclear attack on the US would have been suicidal for the Soviets. This strategic doctrine was called mutual assured destruction, or MAD.

MAD generated a *nuclear* arms race. In order to effectively deter the Soviet Union from launching a nuclear attack, the US needed to be able to maintain a nuclear arsenal that was large enough to withstand the initial attack, with enough weapons left over for a devastating retaliatory strike. But how many nuclear weapons were enough? How many weapons could a Soviet attack be expected to destroy? Because the destructive effects of a nuclear attack could only be speculated, each side could never be certain that it had enough weapons for a retaliatory strike. The logic of MAD created an impetus to continually increase the size and destructive capability of each arsenal. Thus, the Soviet and American arsenals grew into the tens of thousands not because strategic planners believed this many weapons were necessary in order to subdue the enemy, but rather because they assumed a significant portion of the arsenal would be destroyed during a first strike. The goal was to have enough nuclear weapons standing after the first strike to be able to launch a devastating retaliatory strike (see Figure 8.1).

Neither the Soviet Union nor the United States has ever had a comprehensive defensive system to protect itself against a nuclear attack (although the Soviet Union has a limited defensive system around Moscow). Throughout the Cold War, the logic of MAD dictated that defensive systems were destabilizing and therefore to be avoided. For example, imagine that the USSR built a defensive system that protected Soviet territory against a nuclear attack. Moscow would then be able to launch a first strike against the US without fear of a reprisal. According to the logic of MAD, there would be nothing to deter the Soviets from initiating a nuclear war. Consequently, in 1972 both the United States and the Soviet Union signed the Anti-Ballistic Missile (ABM) Treaty, which outlawed the construction of new systems designed to defend against nuclear attack. In essence, the superpowers agreed that mutual vulnerability would lead to mutual security.

Owing to this nuclear stand-off, superpower conflicts were fought primarily through proxies in the Third World. Throughout the Cold War the superpowers supported and assisted adversaries throughout Asia, Africa, Latin America, and the Middle East. Indeed, the

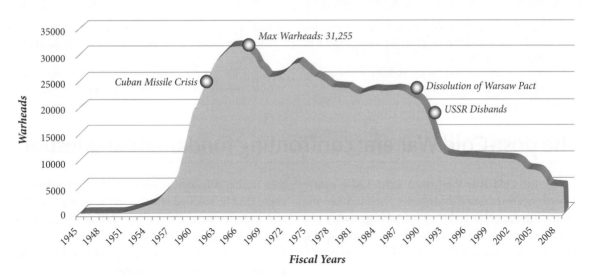

U.S. Nuclear Weapons Stockpile, 1945-2009*

Includes active and inactive warheads. Several thousand additional nuclear warheads are retired and awaiting dismantlement.

Fig. 8.1 US nuclear weapons stockpile, 1945–2009 (includes active and inactive warheads—several thousand additional nuclear warheads are retired and awaiting dismantlement).

Source: Department of Defense, May 3, 2010 http://www.defense.gov/npr/docs/10-05-03_fact_sheet_us_nuclear_transparency__final_w_date.pdf.

most blood was spilled not in Europe or North America, but in Latin America.

Questioning deterrence and ending the arms race

For much of the Cold War many experts believed that MAD had prevented the superpowers from engaging in direct conflict with one another. However, during the 1980s there was a significant change in both American and Soviet thinking. President Ronald Reagan and Soviet leader Mikhail Gorbachev both abhorred MAD. Each leader believed that the reliance on mutual destruction was not only nonsensical, but irresponsible. Moreover, Reagan and Gorbachev were both concerned about the possibility of a nuclear accident. Both leaders sought to shift away from nuclear deterrence and to eliminate nuclear weapons.

In 1987 Reagan and Gorbachev signed the landmark Intermediate Nuclear Forces (INF) Treaty. This treaty stipulated that the superpowers would eliminate intermediate-range nuclear missiles from Europe. The treaty was significant because it was the first time the superpowers agreed to actually eliminate nuclear weapons. All previous arms agreements had simply limited the rate at which nuclear arsenals could grow.

By 1990 the superpowers were making substantial progress in dismantling the arms race that had been a cornerstone of the Cold War. In June 1990 Washington and Moscow pledged to destroy a significant percentage of their chemical arsenals by 2002, as well as to accelerate discussions on reductions in strategic nuclear weapons and conventional weapons. In November the US and its NATO allies and the USSR and its Warsaw Pact allies concluded the Conventional Armed Forces in Europe (CFE) Treaty, which substantially reduced the amount of conventional forces in Europe. In the summer of 1991 the US and the USSR also signed the Strategic Arms Reduction Treaty, or START. This treaty was the first to reduce the superpowers' long-range nuclear arsenals. In short, by the time the Soviet Union collapsed in December 1991 the superpower arms race had already become defunct.

KEY POINTS

- During the 1950s the United States sought to stop the spread of communism throughout the world. This led to wars in Korea and Vietnam.
- The loss in Vietnam led the US to question its military commitments abroad and revamp military strategy.

- Mutual assured destruction (MAD) generated a nuclear arms race and led the superpowers to forego defensive systems.
- During the late 1980s the US and the USSR shifted away from deterrence and began to dismantle the arms race.

The post-Cold War era: confronting fundamental questions

During the Cold War the United States had a clearly defined enemy and established alliance systems. When the USSR collapsed in December 1991 US foreign policy lost its focal point. Washington had to confront fundamental questions about its role in the world and its military power.

How much to spend on the military?

After the Cold War concluded Americans debated how much of the federal budget should be devoted to military expenditures. Some argued that defence spending should be slashed because the United States was no longer 'at war' with the Soviet Union. The United States could reduce its global responsibilities and deployments, thus cutting military expenditures. This 'peace dividend' could then be invested at home, in things like education and infrastructure. Others argued that drastic reductions in defence spending were not possible. The United States was the sole remaining superpower, they noted, and with this power came responsibility. There would be more demands on the United States in the post-Cold War world, not fewer. Moreover, the United States would confront a proliferation of threats from a variety of sources.

Although US military expenditures did decrease during the 1990s, the US defence budget has grown significantly since the attacks of September 2001. In 2011 total (proposed) military spending will be $720 billion, an increase of about 67 per cent since 2001 (Olson 2010).[1] This constitutes approximately 46% of total global military expenditure, and is more than the next nine countries combined.

Table 8.1 Military spending 2009[2] (figures in 2009 US dollars and exchange rates)

Country	Spending ($ billion)	Approximate world share (%)
United States	661	43
China[*]	100	7
France	64	4
United Kingdom	58	4
Russia[*]	53	3.5
Japan	51	3
Germany	46	3
Saudi Arabia[**]	41	3
India	36	2
Italy	36	2

[*]Estimated figures
[**]The figure for Saudi Arabia includes expenditure for public order and safety, and therefore might be an overestimate.

For what purpose should the US military be deployed?

For what purpose should US military forces be sent abroad and under what conditions? Throughout the Cold War the United States had focused almost exclusively on the threat of Soviet expansionism. After the USSR collapsed, American leaders sought to envision the threats, challenges, and responsibilities of the post-Cold War world. Establishing priorities was difficult, particularly for a generation of military and political leaders who had gained their expertise during the Cold War.

As indicated in Table 8.2, the US deployed its military repeatedly during the post-Cold War era for a variety of purposes. Between 1990 and 2001 the United States deployed military forces abroad 21 times. These deployments involved anywhere from a few military advisers to over a half million troops. Nine of these twenty-one deployments involved evacuating American citizens from unstable countries. Five more—Somalia, Haiti, Bosnia, East Timor, and the latter part of the Kosovo mission—involved operations intended to foster political stability. (However, the Somalia operation began as a humanitarian mission.) In only one instance during this period did the United States engage in a major conventional war—the Persian Gulf War.

The Persian Gulf War (1990–91) and its aftermath

In August 1990 Iraq invaded Kuwait. The Iraqi leader, Saddam Hussein, calculated that the United States would condemn the invasion, but that Washington would take no action. He reasoned that the Vietnam Syndrome still prevailed in the US, that is, he believed that after the United States' humiliating loss in Vietnam, Americans would not have the stomach to become involved in another foreign war.

Saddam Hussein calculated wrongly. President George H. W. Bush did not interpret the invasion in terms of the Vietnam War. Rather, he and British Prime Minister Margaret Thatcher considered the invasion to be akin to Hitler's invasion of Poland at the outset of the Second World War. While the lesson of Vietnam may have been to avoid foreign military involvement, the lesson from the Second World War was that aggression must be stopped at the outset. Consequently, President Bush and Prime Minister Thatcher were determined to eject Iraq from Kuwait. Bush's resolve grew when it appeared that Saddam Hussein intended to invade Saudi Arabia as well. If allowed to gain control of Saudi Arabia's oil fields, Saddam would control nearly 40% of the world's oil supplies, thus allowing him to dictate world oil prices.

President Bush considered Hussein's actions the first test of the 'new world order', and advocated a multilateral solution that centred on the United Nations. First, the White House worked through the UN to pass a series of resolutions calling on Iraq to withdraw from Kuwait, and placing economic sanctions on Baghdad until it did so. The administration also built an alliance of over thirty states to place further pressure on Iraq. Finally, President Bush deployed military forces to Saudi Arabia to deter Saddam from invading that country.

When Saddam Hussein failed to withdraw his forces from Kuwait by the UN deadline of January 1991, the United States and its allies launched Operation Desert Storm. This operation was conducted in accordance with the principles of the Powell Doctrine. First, there was a clear military objective: the coalition was to eject Iraqi forces from Kuwait. Second, the United States employed overwhelming force. The US sent half a million troops to the region—approximately the same amount of troops that had been deployed at the peak of the Vietnam War. Finally, there was a clear exit strategy: US and coalition forces would withdraw once Iraqi forces had left Kuwait.

The Persian Gulf War lasted 42 days and was a clear military victory for the US and its allies. It began with a high-tech bombing campaign, and ended 100 hours into a ground war. It was a large-scale conventional war for which the United States military was well-structured, equipped, and trained. However, over time Americans increasingly questioned whether the Persian Gulf War was a political victory. Although the coalition forces had succeeded in ejecting Iraqi forces from Kuwait, Saddam Hussein remained in power after the cease-fire. Indeed, he remained in power far longer than President Bush or Prime Minister Thatcher. Bush administration officials repeatedly pointed out that the UN resolutions only called for Iraqi forces to be ejected from Kuwait. They argued that if the United States had sought to remove Saddam Hussein from power, such actions would have violated the UN resolutions and international law, and

Table 8.2 US military deployments, 1990–2001

Date	Location	Objective
1990	Liberia	Assist evacuation of US embassy in Monrovia
1990–1	Saudi Arabia/Iraq	Operation Desert Storm: Eject Iraqi forces from Kuwait. Limited US forces deployed to northern Iraq in May 1991 to provide emergency humanitarian relief to Iraqi Kurds.
1992	Kuwait/Iraq	US forces monitor Iraq–Kuwait border and no-fly zones in southern Iraq. US and British air forces engage in sporadic, limited battles in the no-fly zones throughout 2003.
1992–4	Somalia	Operation Restore Hope, which began as a US-led UN humanitarian mission. After May 1993 US forces continued to participate in the successor UN operation, UNOSOM, which sought political reconciliation in that country. This mission entailed limited military action to quell local violence.
1993–2001	Bosnia	US participation in NATO air actions to enforce UN efforts to stop Bosnian Serb violence against Muslims in the region. By the end of 1995 US troop deployments were increased as part of a NATO mission to enforce the Dayton Peace Accords. US participation gradually reduced.
1994	Rwanda/Burundi	Evacuate US citizens and other third parties. Assist in humanitarian aid.
1994	Haiti	Restore democratically elected leader to power. Began as naval embargo, but evolved to include troop deployments to restore and maintain stability.
1996	Liberia	Evacuate US citizens and other foreign personnel.
1996	Central African Republic	Evacuate US citizens.
1997, 1998	Albania	Evacuate US citizens and enhance security at US embassy.
1997	Congo and Gabon	Evacuate US citizens.
1997, 2000	Sierra Leone	Evacuate US citizens.
1997	Cambodia	Possible evacuation of US citizens.
1998	Guinea-Bissau	Evacuate US citizens and other foreigners.
1998	Kenya and Tanzania	Disaster assistance and security personnel deployed to US embassies bombed by al-Qaeda.
1998	Afghanistan and Sudan	Airstrikes against suspected al-Qaeda sites in response to bombings of US embassies in Kenya and Tanzania.
1998	Iraq	Operation Desert Fox. Bombing campaign (with the UK) against military targets and industrial facilities suspected of producing weapons of mass destruction. No-fly zones enforced more strictly.
1999	Yugoslavia/Albania/Kosovo	NATO air campaign to stop ethnic cleansing of Albanian Muslims.
1999	East Timor	Limited support for UN stability force.
2000	Yemen	Disaster response assistance after terrorist attack.
2001	Various regions	In response to 9/11 terrorist attacks forces deployed to a number of nations in the Central and Pacific Command areas of operations.

would have caused the US to lose the support of most of its coalition partners. However, the president's characterization of Saddam Hussein as an evil dictator had raised expectations that he would be removed from power.

After the war concluded the United States adopted a policy of containment toward Iraq. Small contingents of US forces remained stationed in the region to deter the Iraqi leader from further invasions. Two no-fly zones were also established in the northern and southern sections of the country to prohibit Iraqi forces from aerial attacks on the Kurds and Shi'ites living in these regions. American and British air forces monitored these no-fly zones, which covered 40 per cent of the country. The United Nations and member states placed sanctions on Iraq, and UN inspectors were deployed in an attempt to prohibit Iraq from developing weapons of mass destruction (WMD). However, in October 1998

Saddam Hussein ejected these inspectors. This prompted the US and Britain to launch Operation Desert Fox. This four-day mission consisted of 650 sorties against security targets in Iraq, which significantly undermined Iraqi military capability. Afterward, US and British forces began to enforce the no-fly zones more strictly, which led to sporadic skirmishes. In addition, the Clinton administration sought to modify the sanctions regime so as to place more pressure on Saddam, yet limit the negative effects on the Iraqi people. Moreover, Congress passed, and President Clinton signed, a bill calling for regime change in Iraq.

What role for nuclear weapons?

In the post-Cold War world are nuclear weapons still useful?

MAJOR DEBATES AND THEIR IMPACT 8.1: What role for nuclear weapons?

It is time—well past time, in my view—for the United States to cease its Cold War-style reliance on nuclear weapons as a foreign policy tool. . . . I would characterize current US nuclear weapons policy as immoral, illegal, militarily unnecessary, and dreadfully dangerous. The risk of an accidental or inadvertent nuclear launch is unacceptably high. . . . How destructive are these weapons? The average US warhead has a destructive power 20 times that of the Hiroshima bomb. Of the 8,000 active or operational US warheads, 2,000 are on hair-trigger alert, ready to be launched on 15 minutes' warning. . . . What is shocking is that today, more than a decade after the end of the Cold War, the basic US nuclear policy is unchanged. It has not adapted to the collapse of the Soviet Union. . . . At minimum, we should remove all strategic nuclear weapons from 'hair trigger' alert. . . . That simple change would greatly reduce the risk of an accidental nuclear launch. It would also signal to other states that the United States is taking steps to end its reliance on nuclear weapons. . . . I have worked on issues relating to US and NATO nuclear strategy and war plans for more than 40 years. During that time I have never seen a piece of paper that outlined a plan for the United States or NATO to initiate the use of nuclear weapons with any benefit for the United States or NATO. . . . To launch weapons against a nuclear-equipped opponent would be suicidal. To do so against a nonnuclear enemy would be militarily unnecessary, morally repugnant, and politically indefensible.

(McNamara 2005; Robert S. McNamara was US Secretary of Defense 1961–8 and president of the World Bank 1968–81)

[O]ver the last decade the nature of the nuclear threat has fundamentally changed, from large-scale attack to the use

of one or a few nuclear devices by a rogue nation or subnational group against the United States or one of its allies. Countering the proliferation of nuclear weapons. . . has thus become as high a priority as deterring major nuclear attacks. . . . [W]ith its overwhelming conventional military advantage, the United States does not need nuclear weapons for either war fighting or for deterring conventional war. It should therefore scale back its nuclear activity significantly. . . . The United States should not, however, abandon effective nuclear forces, and it should even leave open the possibility of certain limited kinds of nuclear tests. . . . [N]uclear weapons continue to play a key role in US security. After all, there is no guarantee that geopolitical circumstances will not change dramatically, and the emergence of a more militant China or Russia's return to totalitarianism might compel the United States to place greater reliance on its nuclear forces. Moreover, Washington's commanding nuclear posture still works to limit the nuclear ambitions of other countries. US allies, most notably Germany and Japan, have forsworn establishing their own nuclear programs in exchange for protection under the US security umbrella. . . . Ultimately, Washington must strike a balance between conflicting goals: maintaining a modern nuclear weapons posture, on the one hand, and curbing the spread of nuclear weapons, on the other.

(Deutch 2005; John Deutch was Deputy Secretary of Defense, chairman of the Nuclear Weapons Council, and director of Central Intelligence during the Clinton administration. He was also an Undersecretary of Energy during the Carter administration)

In the 1990s some American military and political leaders began calling for the elimination of nuclear weapons. These so-called nuclear abolitionists contend that the US should eliminate its nuclear arsenal for numerous reasons. For one thing, the United States has such overwhelming conventional military power that the introduction of nuclear weapons into any conflict is not militarily necessary. Moreover, the implicit threat that the United States could introduce nuclear weapons during a conventional conflict is simply not credible. The use of nuclear weapons would be morally repugnant, thereby eliminating them as a serious policy option. Third, maintaining such a large nuclear arsenal raises the probability of a catastrophic nuclear accident. Furthermore, nuclear weapons are expensive to develop, maintain, and store safely. Since they have little military utility in the first place, it makes little sense to continue to fund them, abolitionists argue.

Others disagree, however, and believe that the United States must continue to retain a nuclear weapons capability. Few have called for a *build up* of American nuclear arsenals since the ending of the Cold War, but many contend that it is necessary to retain at least a more limited arsenal. For one thing, they argue, nuclear weapons continue to be necessary in order to deter attacks against the United States. In addition, the knowledge of how to make nuclear weapons cannot be destroyed. Thus, it is

---

KEY POINTS

❑ During the post-Cold War era the US deployed its military abroad repeatedly, and for a variety of purposes.

❑ The Persian Gulf War was a conventional war conducted according to the principles of the Powell Doctrine. It was a clear military victory, although some have questioned whether it was a political victory.

❑ Some believe nuclear weapons continue to be a useful deterrent, while others maintain they should be abolished.

---

likely that there will be more nuclear states—and possibly nuclear enemies—in the future. The United States would be dangerously vulnerable should it completely destroy its arsenal.

The administration of President George W. Bush has agreed with this latter perspective. In the administration's view, it is essential for the US to retain a nuclear capability, although a significantly smaller capability is sufficient. Towards this end Bush and Russian President Vladimir Putin signed a treaty in May 2002 to reduce nuclear weapons down to a level of 1700–2200 warheads each by December 2012. This agreement, known as the Moscow Treaty, or the Treaty on Strategic Offensive Reductions (SORT), will reduce stockpiles to their lowest total since the 1950s.

Responding to terrorism

President George W. Bush came to office during the post-Cold War era, when the United States was still trying to figure out its national security policy for the new international system. During the 2000 presidential campaign Bush's foreign affairs adviser, Condoleezza Rice, outlined the candidate's approach to national security in an article in *Foreign Affairs* (see Key quotes 8.1). Rice called for the United States to place greater emphasis on its national interest, and emphasized the need for overwhelming military strength. These capabilities should be reserved for fighting major wars, not for engaging in humanitarian missions or state-building. Military power, she wrote, 'is a special force. It is lethal and it is meant to be....[I]t is most certainly not designed to build a civilian society.' Nonetheless,

the Bush administration deployed US forces to fight two major wars–and to build democratic states in both Afghanistan and Iraq.

Prior to 9/11 the United States viewed terrorism primarily as a crime. Crimes are dealt with through a legal process: suspects are captured, put on trial, and, if found guilty, imprisoned. The Bush administration took a different approach. It declared the terrorist attacks of 9/11 to be an act of war. It stressed that Osama bin Laden had specifically called for a war against the United States and American citizens, and had engaged in large-scale violence toward this end. President Bush then invoked the United States' right to self-defense under Article 51 of the United Nations Charter. In this understanding, states have the right to defend themselves against

> **KEY QUOTES 8.1:** Condoleezza Rice

The United States has found it exceedingly difficult to define its 'national interest' in the absence of Soviet power. . . . In a democracy as pluralistic as ours, the absence of an articulated 'national interest' either produces fertile ground for those wishing to withdraw from the world or creates a vacuum to be filled by parochial groups and transitory pressures. . . .

Power matters, both the exercise of power by the United States and the ability of others to exercise it. Yet many in the United States are (and always have been) uncomfortable with the notions of power politics, great powers, and power balances. . . . The reality is that a few big powers can radically affect international peace, stability, and prosperity. . . . America's military power must be secure because the United States is the only guarantor of global peace and stability. . . .

[T]he next president will be confronted with a prolonged job of repair[ing US military power.] Military readiness will have to take center stage. . . . [T]he next president should refo-cus the Pentagon's priorities on building the military of the 21st century rather than continuing to build on the structure of the Cold War. US technological advantages should be leveraged to build forces that are lighter and more lethal, more mobile and agile, and capable of firing accurately from long distances. In order to do this, Washington must reallocate resources, perhaps in some cases skipping a generation of technology to make leaps rather than incremental improvements in its forces.

The president must remember that the military is a special instrument. It is lethal, and it is meant to be. It is not a civilian police force. It is not a political referee. And it is most certainly not designed to build a civilian society.

(Rice 2000; these extracts outlined what Bush's foreign policy would be should he win the 2000 presidential election. Condoleezza Rice was the National Security Adviser during President George W. Bush's first term in office, and the Secretary of State during his second term)

an attack through retaliatory military action. Consistent with this view, for the first time in its history NATO came to the defense of one of its members. Within 24 hours of the attacks NATO deployed aircraft and ships in support of the United States.[3]

The Bush administration's post-9/11 foreign policy was outlined in the 2002 National Security Strategy (NSS), and reiterated in the 2006 NSS. Two principles outlined in the 2002 NSS have implications for military strategy.

First, the NSS declared that the United States would 'make no distinction between terrorists and those who knowingly harbor or provide aid to them'. Thus, the scope of the war on terror is very broad.

Second, the NSS also introduced the policy of preemption. 'We will cooperate with other nations to deny, contain, and curtail our enemies' efforts to acquire dangerous technologies [and WMD]', the document states. 'And, as a matter of common sense and self-defense, America will act against such emerging threats before they are fully formed.' The NSS goes on to state that the US 'must be prepared to stop rogue states and their terrorist clients before they are able to threaten or use WMD against the US, our allies and friends'. In short, the Bush administration seeks to prevent adversaries (or potential adversaries) from developing WMD. Although it uses the term 'preemption', the policy is more accurately termed 'prevention'.

Thus, the Bush administration rejected the idea of containment, which had been the foundation of US national security policy for decades. In the post-9/11 era containing threats was no longer possible, it reasoned. Instead, the United States would seek to prevent threats from developing in the first place.

It has long been accepted that each state has the right to act preemptively in the face of an *imminent* threat. That is, if faced with an imminent attack, a state has the right to use military action so as to forestall that attack. However, the Bush administration's version of 'preemption' is not focused on such imminent threats. It seeks to prevent potential adversaries from *developing the capability* to launch an attack on the US. It seeks to forestall *long-term* threats to its security, rather than imminent attacks.

This doctrinal shift is most striking when compared to US policy during the Cold War. Throughout the Cold War Washington feared and loathed Soviet nuclear weapons, but it implicitly accepted Moscow's right to develop them. The White House sought to contain the

Soviet threat; it never asserted a right to prevent the USSR from building WMD in the first place.

Three days after the 9/11 attacks Congress passed a joint resolution authorizing the president to use armed force against those responsible. The resolution gave the president authority 'to use all necessary and appropriate force against those nations, organizations, or persons, he determined planned, authorized, committed or aided the terrorist attacks… [or who] harbored such organizations or persons….' Within a month US forces were deployed to Afghanistan.

The war in Afghanistan (2001)

On 7 October 2001 the United States launched Operation Enduring Freedom in Afghanistan. This war had several aims. First and foremost, it sought to close down al-Qaeda training camps in that country, and to capture al-Qaeda operatives. The operation also sought to disrupt and end support for terrorism. Additionally, the United States sought to topple the Taliban regime, which had been providing a safe haven for al-Qaeda.

The US invasion of Afghanistan met with little international criticism. For one thing, the Taliban regime was broadly perceived to be illegitimate. Only three countries recognized the Taliban as the official government of Afghanistan, and it had been denied the right to take Afghanistan's seat at the United Nations. Second, the Taliban had one of the worst human rights records in the world, and was particularly harsh toward females. Moreover, diplomatic attempts to resolve the problem had proven fruitless. During the 1990s Washington and the international community had been in talks with the Taliban trying to get them to turn over Osama bin Laden, and to close down the terrorist training camps. The Taliban repeatedly refused. Sanctions had proven futile as well. Finally, many agreed with the Bush administration's assertion that the 9/11 attacks had been an act of war.

The war in Afghanistan was the most high-tech war the United States had ever conducted. Sixty per cent of the bombs dropped during the campaign were guided by lasers or satellites, and early estimates indicated that 75 per cent of the bombs dropped were accurate (BBC 2002).[4] Other technological innovations were also on display, such as unmanned aerial vehicles (UAVs), or drones, called Predators, which proved extremely effective in tracking and destroying targets.

Despite these new technologies, the US military found that some of its most effective forces were distinctly low-tech. Special operations forces, which consisted of a dozen or so elite troops or CIA operatives, proved especially useful. Often travelling by horseback, these units blended into local environments and gathered important intelligence information about enemy movements and targets.

In November 2001 the US war in Afghanistan ended with a clear military victory. al-Qaeda training camps were largely destroyed, the network was severely disrupted, and the Taliban regime was replaced with a new, more humane government. However, subsequent political developments have been troublesome. For example, during the war the United States captured approximately 5000 people suspected of abetting terrorism. While most of these individuals were released, many remain in detention centres under questionable conditions. These detentions have raised questions about the ethics of US foreign policy. Moreover, opium production in Afghanistan has soared, running the risk that it will devolve into a 'narco-state'. Profits from the opium trade also fuelled a growing insurgency in the southern sections of the country. By 2006 both the Taliban and al-Qaeda were regrouping under new leadership along the Afghan–Pakistan border. In an effort to quell this growing instability, President Obama announced in 2009 that the United States would send an additional 30,000 troops to Afghanistan. The American aim is to create a period of stability to allow the Afghan government to improve its security capabilities. The United States will then begin to draw down its forces in mid-2011.

The war in Iraq (2003)

The war in Iraq, which began in March 2003, was the second phase of the Bush administration's war on terror. Whereas there had been international support for the war in Afghanistan, the US war in Iraq was broadly condemned.

Why did the United States invade Iraq? The Bush administration provided several reasons. First, it argued that Saddam Hussein had repeatedly violated UN Resolutions which required Iraq to open its military facilities to international inspections. This assertion was undeniable. Hussein had ejected UN weapons inspectors from Iraq in 1998. Second, it contended that Saddam Hussein was seeking to develop WMD. This assertion seemed plausible at the time, since the Iraqi dictator had previously tried to develop such capabilities. Third, and most controversial, the administration charged that Iraq harboured terrorists. It repeatedly implied that Saddam Hussein had links to al-Qaeda. President Bush suggested that Saddam Hussein had to be overthrown so as to prevent him from transferring WMD to terrorists.

The war in Iraq was the first test of the Bush administration's preemption policy. That is, the aim was to prevent Iraq from developing a WMD capability and to prevent it from transferring that capability to terrorist groups. (The Afghanistan war was not an example of preemption, as the military operation was launched *after* al-Qaeda had attacked.)

The war in Iraq was divisive for many reasons, not least of which was over military strategy. Within the Bush administration there were several important debates. One centred on whether the US should go to war with Iraq at all. Secretary of State Colin Powell and others argued that the US should remain focused on fighting al-Qaeda in Afghanistan. In this view, a war in Iraq would be a potentially dangerous diversion from the war on terror. Others disagreed. Secretary of Defense Rumsfeld, Vice President Cheney and others insisted that the Iraqi dictator had to be removed from power.

Once it became clear that the president was heading towards war another debate developed. Powell argued that the United States should try to cobble together a multilateral coalition, similar to the way in which the first President Bush conducted the 1991 Persian Gulf War. In Powell's view, the United States could topple Saddam's regime alone, but it could not single-handedly build a new Iraq. It would need allies to do so. Others disagreed. They preferred a unilateral approach, claiming that multilateralism would slow the process down and perhaps derail it altogether.

A third debate centred on the amount of force the United States would deploy to Iraq. Some believed the war should be conducted in accordance with the Powell Doctrine, that is, the US should deploy overwhelming force right from the outset. According to some estimates, this would entail 400,000 or so troops. Powell and others maintained that high troop levels would be needed to maintain order after the regime fell and during the period of reconstruction.

Secretary Rumsfeld disagreed. Rumsfeld believed the US goal should be to invade, depose Saddam Hussein, and withdraw as quickly as possible. A large US force would not only appear to be an imperialist occupier, he reasoned, it would take longer to exit Iraq. The longer US forces remained in Iraq, the more anti-American resentment would arise. Consequently, Rumsfeld favoured sending just enough troops to depose Saddam and exit quickly.

In short, whereas one group envisioned a long-term state-building project, the other envisioned a lightning war in which the US would decapitate the existing regime and rapidly depart to allow the Iraqis to rebuild themselves.

Ultimately, the Secretary of Defense's vision prevailed. The United States launched Operation Iraqi Freedom in March 2003, deploying approximately 140,00 troops in the process. Once again, American technology allowed the United States to topple the existing regime quickly. The Defense Department made even more extensive use of Special Operations Forces, and refined much of the technology it had used in Afghanistan, thus making it even more effective.[5]

This initial military success became tempered, however. Although the United States has overwhelming military power and the most technologically sophisticated military, it found itself bogged down fighting a low-tech, urban insurgency in Iraq. While the US army is adept at fighting large-scale conventional wars, guerilla-style combat proved far more challenging.

Political success has been even more elusive. Efforts to build a stable democracy in Iraq were halting, at best, creating growing instability. Terrorism flourished. Moreover, the war called into question the whole concept of preemption. The Bush administration launched the war to prevent Saddam Hussein from transferring WMD to terrorists. After the invasion it became evident that Saddam did not have

WMD, nor did he have substantive links to al-Qaeda. In order for preemption to be a viable policy, a government must have accurate intelligence information on both the capabilities and the intentions of potential adversaries. In this case, US intelligence was mistaken on both counts.

In February 2009 President Obama announced that US combat missions in Iraq would end by August 2010. The US mission in Iraq would change from combat to supporting the Iraqi government and its security forces as they take the lead in securing their country. The drawdown will be accompanied by increased diplomatic efforts to support the Iraqi government promote stability. All US troops will be removed from Iraq by the end of 2011.

KEY POINTS

❑ The Bush administration considered the September 11 attacks to be an act of war.

❑ The US invaded Afghanistan in response to al-Qaeda's attacks in September 2001. The US stated it was acting in self-defence and this position was widely supported around the world.

❑ The policy of preemption entails denying an adversary the ability to develop WMD. This policy was first tested in the war in Iraq. The war in Iraq was controversial both at home and abroad.

❑ The wars in Afghanistan and Iraq were quick military victories. However, political victory has proven elusive.

Conclusion

US military power has grown since the end of the Second World War. Today, US military power is unequalled throughout the world. The United States has used its military power in a variety of ways: to counter the spread of communism, to deter attacks, to promote peacekeeping, to assist in humanitarian disasters, to counter terrorism, to promote democracy, and to counter the spread of WMD, among other aims.

This chapter highlights a central paradox: although the US has the most powerful military in the world, there are limits as to what military power can achieve. The war in Vietnam was neither a military victory nor a political victory. US military strategists learned from this defeat and adapted. Consequently, the Persian Gulf War, the war in Afghanistan, and the war in Iraq were all military victories. In all three instances enemy forces were quickly defeated.

However, it is questionable whether these wars were political victories for the United States. Saddam Hussein remained in power far longer than the first President Bush, and continued to threaten his people and the region throughout the 1990s. In Afghanistan, the Taliban was quickly ousted, but the country remains unstable. This instability has spilled over into neighbouring countries. Political victory has also proven elusive in Iraq. Although Saddam Hussein was overthrown with relative ease, the United States had great difficulty building a democratic state that can maintain order. This political failure has been destabilizing, both for the country and the region. The on-going conflicts in Afghanistan and Iraq highlight another conundrum: although the US has the largest military force in the world, this force is not well-suited to fighting insurgencies and terrorism, the central threats to American security today.

? | **Questions**

1. Why did the United States become involved in the Korean War and the Vietnam War?
2. What is the Powell Doctrine and how has it influenced military operations?
3. What is mutual assured destruction (MAD)?
4. For what purposes has the United States deployed its military? To what effect?
5. What are the military implications of containment and how have they changed over time?

6. Do nuclear weapons have a role to play in US security?

7. Why is national missile defence controversial?

8. How can a large conventional army effectively counter terrorism and insurgencies?

9. What are the implications of the Bush administration's policy of preemption?

10. Can military power be used to achieve political victories in Iraq and Afghanistan?

» Further Reading

Blackwill, R. D. and Carnesale, A. (eds) (1993), *New Nuclear Nations: Consequences for US Policy* (New York: Council on Foreign Relations).

This volume systematically analyses a multitude of diplomatic and military means for coping with nuclear proliferation.

Clark, W. K. (2001), *Waging Modern War: Bosnia, Kosovo and the Future of Combat* (New York: Public Affairs Books).

Clark, a US general and former NATO Supreme Allied Commander, draws upon his experiences in the Kosovo war to offer lessons about fighting terrorism and asymmetrical warfare.

FitzGerald, F. (2000), *Way Out There in the Blue: Reagan, Star Wars and the End of the Cold War* (New York: Simon and Schuster).

A detailed, yet engaging book on the Strategic Defense Initiative and national missile defense.

Gordon, M. R. and Trainor, B. E. (2007), *Cobra II: The Inside Story of the Invasion and Occupation of Iraq* (New York: Vintage).

An account of the invasion plans and the manner in which they led to the insurgency.

Kaplan, R. D. (2006), *Imperial Grunts* (New York: Vintage).

An on-the-ground account of numerous military missions throughout the globe.

Larson, J. A. and Wirtz, J. J. (eds) (2001), *The Rocket's Red Glare: Missile Defense and the Future of World Politics* (Boulder, CO: Westview Press).

This volume provides a reasonably balanced view of many of the key debates surrounding national missile defense.

Woodward, B. (2004), *Plan of Attack: The Definitive Account of the Decision to Invade Iraq* (New York: Simon and Schuster).

An in-depth account of the Bush administration's decision to go to war in Iraq and the development of its plans for invasion.

Endnotes

1. See also the Stockholm International Peace Research Institute (SIPRI), www.sipri.org/yearbook/2010.

2. Adapted from the Stockholm International Peace Research Institute (SIPRI), The 10 major spender countries, www.sipri.org.

3. www.nato.int/issues/terrorism/index.html (accessed 1 March 2007).

4. This figure will probably be revised downwards over time.

5. See Woodward (2004, 2006), Gordon and Trainor (2007), and Risen (2006).

 For a range of additional resources to support your learning visit the Online Resource Centre that accompanies this book at **www.oxfordtextbooks.co.uk/orc/cox_stokes2e/**.

9 Regional shifts and US foreign policy

Peter Trubowitz

Chapter contents

Introduction

American statecraft has been in flux during the past two decades. External events—the end of the Cold War, the terrorist attacks of 9/11, the wars in Afghanistan and Iraq—have been primary drivers of shifts in strategy. But domestic developments have also been shaping the conduct of US foreign policy. Indeed, political polarization has been shaking the domestic foundations of US foreign policy, sorely testing bipartisan support for liberal internationalism—the overarching strategy that guided the United States from the Second World War through the end of the Cold War.

This is not the first time that America has been deeply divided over foreign policy. Deep fault lines surfaced in the 1890s and 1930s, and debates over foreign policy took on strongly emotional and moral overtones, just as they do today. In each period, the conventional wisdom that politics in the United States 'stops at the water's edge' was betrayed by protracted and divisive conflicts over how the country should respond to the breakdown of the old international order, and to the emergence of new strategic realities and economic challenges. Questions of foreign policy became enmeshed in the nation's electoral politics. In each period, America's leaders experienced great difficulty in articulating a vision of the national interest that commanded broad domestic support.

Why do America's leaders find it so difficult to mobilize broad-based support for their foreign policies? Why is the nation's foreign policy so conflict prone? Some scholars locate the source of conflict in America's political culture. They argue that Americans hold divergent images of what their nation is, or what it should be, and that these differences invariably give rise to profound disagreements over how and when America should use its power. Other scholars argue that America's divided constitutional order is the source of conflict over foreign policy. The 'weakness' of the American state, manifest in the sharing of foreign policy-making powers between the White House and Congress, is considered to be, in Edwin Corwin's famous phrase, 'an invitation to struggle' for control over the authority to make foreign policy.

Despite their many and important differences, both approaches assume that the appropriate level of analysis is national: the focus is on *national* political traits or structures. They ignore what for many scholars of American politics is fundamental: regional difference. All politics may not be local, but as V. O. Key pointed out long ago, in the United States regions are the 'building blocs' of national politics (Key 1964: 229). Like E. E. Schattschneider before him, and Walter Dean Burnham after him, Key underscored the sectional dimension of national politics in the United States (Schattschneider 1960; Burnham 1970). These scholars showed that many of the great struggles in American history over domestic policy were also conflicts between *subnational* coalitions advancing conflicting regional agendas.

This chapter builds on this insight by showing how regionalism also impacts foreign policy. In contrast to accounts that grant primacy to ideas or institutions, it identifies America's *regional* diversity as the most important source of tension and conflict over foreign policy. I show that conflicts over the purposes of American power, as well as the constitutional authority to exercise it, are fundamentally conflicts over the

distribution of wealth and power in American society among coalitions with divergent interests and claims on the federal government's resources. They are regional in nature, and they grow out of the uneven nature of the nation's economic development and integration into the world economy.

This argument is developed by analysing debates over American foreign policy in three different periods: the 1890s, the 1930s, and the current era. During the 1890s, the 'Great Debate' over imperial expansion in Latin America and the Pacific Basin pitted the industrial North-East against the agrarian South, with the West playing a decisive 'swing' role. A quarter of a century later, the urban North-East and the South found common ground in an 'internationalist' foreign policy agenda and waged a fierce battle against their 'nationalist' rivals in the rural West. At issue was whether the United States should assume a more assertive role in checking the spread of fascism in Europe and in promoting global economic recovery.

Today, sectional conflicts divide the nation again. What many define as a fight between 'liberals' and 'conservatives' over how to respond to the challenges posed by globalization and terrorism is more usefully understood as a conflict between two broad coalitions of interest: one based in the South and Mountain West; the other grounded in the North-East and Pacific Coast. This pattern of regional polarization, which developed long before 9/11, reflects a deepening division of the electoral map into so-called 'red' states that benefit from military spending, export promotion, and import liberalization, and 'blue' states that do not. Those differences go a long way toward explaining why two decades after the end of the Cold War, the United States is still debating how it should define and pursue its interests in the world.

Regional interests and foreign policy

Regionally based political competition and conflict is one of the most distinctive features of American politics. Frederick Jackson Turner first identified the significance of regionalism in the United States, and since then a large literature has developed on its sources

and impact on national policy. A common theme in this literature is that regionalism in American politics is rooted in the geographically uneven nature of economic growth and development.[1] In other industrialized nations regional economic differentiation is often

---

BOX 9.1: American exceptionalism? Sectionalism American style

In many countries, regionalism is associated with ethnic or religious difference. These political systems are typically studied within a centre–periphery perspective, where regionalism manifests itself in the form of protest by culturally distinctive peripheries against political and economic exploitation by the centre. While ethnic and religious diversity is also an important feature of American politics, it is most conspicuous and salient at the 'microregional' (neighbourhood and city) level. At the 'macroregional' level, the absence of the kinds of cultural cleavages present in other nations has meant that in the United States sectionalism is usually grounded in conflicts of economic interest.

---

coterminous with ethnic or religious difference (see Box 9.1). While ethnic and religious difference is also an important feature of American politics, at the regional level political conflicts are grounded in conflicts of economic interest.

Scholars identify a number of factors to explain these regional differences. Some emphasize geographic disparities in resources, markets, and the costs of factors of production. Others focus on the role that the federal government plays in shaping patterns of uneven regional growth and development. There is also an important literature on how the spatially decentralized structure of political representation in the United States reinforces regional differences that arise from uneven growth. Historically, when the nation's political parties have been rooted in sections of the country with significantly different economic interests, domestic competition over public policy at the national level has intensified. Popular images like 'Red America' and 'Blue America' capture this interplay of party and region. In the past, much of this literature focused on domestic policy. However, in recent years the effects of regionalism on foreign policy making have received increased attention. A central finding in this work is that regions that stand to benefit, politically as well as economically, from the projection of American power are likely to support more ambitious, expansionist foreign policies.[2] Politicians from these regions are the ones most apt to favour a strong American presence abroad and a powerful chief executive at home. Conversely, regions whose income, profits, or political standing at the national level depend on the home market, or are threatened by international competition, are less likely to support the 'overhead charges'

of maintaining international openness: a powerful military, easy credit for foreigners, an open domestic market, and so on. Elected officials from these regions are the ones who are most likely to make the case for a more retrained and cost-conscious foreign policy and stress domestic priorities and needs.

Explaining deep and persistent conflict over US foreign policy requires some mapping of the nation's economic geography.[3] Functional position alone, however, is too blunt an instrument to explain fully how regional competition over foreign policy is played out in the national political arena. As mentioned, party politics also plays a role. Party leaders have a long if inglorious record of playing politics with the national interest. Within the structures of a two-party system, they have often used foreign policies to mobilize electoral support and marginalize political opponents. As I show in the cases below, explaining how regional foreign policy coalitions form also requires some attention to electoral geography and party politics.

KEY POINTS

❑ Regionalism is one of the oldest and most distinctive features of American political life.

❑ Regions that benefit, politically as well as economically, from the projection of American power are likely to support more ambitious, expansionist foreign policies.

❑ Historically, when the national parties have been rooted in regions with significantly different stakes in international openness, partisanship has intensified.

The great debate over expansionism

Few periods in American history had a more profound impact on the nation's foreign policy, or have enjoyed more attention by American diplomatic historians, than the 1890s. Having created a continental empire in the nineteenth century, Americans set their sights on more distant frontiers. As every textbook on American diplomatic history states, in the 1890s the United States became a great power, shedding its isolationist past and embracing a more assertive, outward-looking foreign policy geared to opening new markets in Latin America and Asia. America built a modern battleship navy, transformed its protective tariff into a bargaining tool to open foreign markets, and extended its strategic reach through the acquisition of foreign lands.

America's turn toward empire

This shift in American foreign policy is often viewed as the inevitable result of the nation's rise as a world power. Such interpretations begin with the obvious: the country was growing at a spectacular rate. Between the end of the Civil War in 1865 and the beginning of the Spanish–American War in 1898, the population of the United States more than doubled, and the gross national product nearly trebled. As the national economy expanded, so did Americans' financial and commercial interests overseas. Once highly dependent on foreign capital, America's leading banks and corporations now aggressively looked overseas for investment opportunities. Even more impressive was growth in America's commercial trade. Between 1865 and 1898, exports expanded from $281 million to roughly $1231 million. While much of this increase came from agriculture, by the 1890s manufactures were rapidly closing the gap. The bulk of the industrial export trade went to less developed nations in Latin American and Asia. Industrial exports to Europe also increased but not nearly as much; agricultural goods, especially cotton and wheat, made up the single largest class of exports to the Old World.

Fears of overproduction and colonial encirclement fuelled Americans' interest in overseas expansion. Severe depressions in the 1870s and 1890s, and a somewhat milder contraction in the 1880s, contributed to the perception that foreign markets were essential to American well-being. Overproduction was seen as the cause of these crises, and each one sent more and more farmers and manufacturers in search of new markets to sell their surplus goods. The discontent and turmoil engendered by these economic downturns led many to view foreign markets the way an earlier generation had looked to the national frontier: as a 'safety valve' for economic and social problems. There was a growing conviction in the 1890s that continental expansion had reached an end, and this only underscored the sense of urgency that many felt about the 'export solution'.

Great power rivalry was also a source of great concern to many Americans. For most of the nineteenth century, the world economy had revolved around Great Britain. The world's banker, workshop, and policeman, Great Britain used its power to establish an international economic order which, at its peak, emphasized free and open trade. Beginning in the 1870s, this system started to fall apart. Economic crises in Europe and Asia led Germany, France, and Japan to contest British hegemony and turn to mercantilism and imperialism to revive their slumping economies and pacify domestic discontent. While great power rivalry, and the 'scramble for empire' it kicked off, did not pose an immediate threat to American security, it did raise questions about the country's ability to guarantee access to its budding export trade to South America and Asia in the near and long term.

These were fundamentally questions about means. If most Americans by the 1890s favoured the goal of commercial expansionism, they disagreed sharply about the appropriate methods: would the acquisition of foreign lands (e.g. Hawaii, Cuba, the Philippines) and a larger navy be needed to promote expanded trade or could America's foreign trade expand without political and military burdens? Should new economic opportunities be sought in underdeveloped or advanced regions, in South America and Asia, or Europe? On these questions of means, consensus gave way to intense domestic conflict and political rivalry. The critical fault line ran along sectional lines. On one side stood the industrial North-East, and on the other, the agrarian South. In between, lay the West.

Sectional bases of the conflict

Many factors explain why expansionism divided the country so sharply along sectional lines, but one was central: the economy. The northern and southern economies differed enormously. Despite the development of a *national* economy after the Civil War, the United States in the 1890s remained in many ways a single nation state with two distinct regional economies: one specializing in manufacturing, the other in agriculture. This meant that these regions had very different things to sell on the world market. It also meant that their elected representatives in Washington had quite different ideas about where America should cultivate commercial ties. Seeking outlets for its surplus manufactures, the industrial North-East looked primarily to non-industrialized areas of the globe, particularly South America and Asia. By contrast, the agrarian South was highly dependent on industrial markets for selling its raw materials. It looked to Europe for expanded trade.

Where to expand was one thing; *how* to expand was yet another. For the Republicans, who dominated the North-East, a neo-mercantile strategy that put a premium on overseas bases and naval power had distinct advantages. For starters, the Republican North-East was home to the country's most powerful industrial, financial, and commercial interests—the very interests that had the biggest stake in securing greater access to, and control over, markets in Latin America and Asia. They viewed territorial expansion and naval power as two sides of the same coin. Naval power, Republicans argued, was needed to promote the spread of American commerce overseas; establishing a strategic presence in places like Hawaii, Cuba, and the Philippines was needed to enhance the Navy's ability to project power. The Republican case for imperial expansion was thus both economic and strategic.

It was also a way for northern Republicans to advance partisan interests. Empire building was a way of addressing the needs of hard-pressed workers. The modernization of the Navy meant jobs for northern workers, which in turn meant votes for northern politicians. A strategy of territorial expansion also helped Republican leaders to shore up and consolidate political support among industrialists, bankers, and merchants who were interested in expanded trade and investment. Additionally, northern Republican leaders found the issue of expansionism helpful at the ballot box, using jingo nationalism to mobilize their partisans at election time and silence discontents. It certainly was not the first time in American history that elected leaders played politics with the national interest.

Expanding the capacity of the federal government to project power abroad also helped to expand the Republican Party's electoral base at home. Republicans used the lure of naval expenditures to win support along the Pacific Coast. In the rural West, efforts to open markets in Latin America through tariff reform served to enhance the Republicans' appeal among hard-pressed western farmers, who viewed Latin America as an outlet for their surplus foodstuffs. Expansionism had a hard edge as well. Republicans used it to split the western and southern branches of the radical agrarian movement known as the Populists—the most serious political threat to Republican rule in the 1890s.

BOX 9.2: Quo bono? The great debate over American imperialism

Debates over foreign policy are not just about the world 'out there'. They are also about the balance of political power inside the United States. In the 1890s, as during other periods of the nation's history, politicians viewed foreign policy issues against a larger political canvas. The issues of naval spending, territorial expansion, and tariff reform were debated in terms of their impact on each region's overseas commercial interests and on post-bellum political arrangements that continued to make the agrarian South a 'colony' of the industrial North-East. Who stood to gain politically and economically from an expansionist foreign policy, and who stood to lose, was the central question.

All of this helps to explain why the South so vigorously opposed the North-East's foreign policy agenda. While the North-East and parts of the West could hope to realize gains from a strategy of imperial expansion, the agrarian South could not and, in fact, did not. The South was more dependent on international markets than any other region in the country. Not surprisingly, southern politicians were among the most vocal proponents of expanded trade. For the South, however, there was a key difference: the Democratic South required industrial markets for their goods and thus had powerful reasons for avoiding policies that might provoke or exacerbate great power tensions and, thereby, threaten American access to the great industrial markets of Europe among the industrial nations there. Policies that challenged British commercial dominance in the southern half of the western hemisphere raised potential risks for the South.

For the North and South, the decline of British hegemony and the rise of imperial rivalry meant very different things: for the former, it opened up possibilities for commercial expansion; for the latter it threatened an already-weakened liberal trading order on which the South was vitally dependent. This is why southern lawmakers in Washington advocated free trade and also helps to explain why they opposed building a powerful navy. A more powerful military posed other risks for the South as well. Twenty-five years after the end of the Civil War, the South was still very much a 'colonial append-age' of the North. Many of the region's leaders viewed military expansionism as a way to keep the South in tow. Others saw anti-expansionism as a means to deflect the Populist appeal to southern farmers. For every northern Republican who reminded Populists that foreign markets were the answer to their woes, there was a southern Democrat claiming that the seizure of 'tropical lands' like Hawaii would mean an influx of 'cheap coolie labour' that would threaten their livelihoods. Preaching the doctrine of 'white supremacy' was one way to deflect the Populists' appeal to southern farmers.

Expansionism abroad; hegemony at home

America's emergence as a great power was forged in the crucible of domestic political struggle (see Box 9.2). Often depicted as a contest between competing visions of America's purpose in the world, the conflicts over expansionism in the 1890s were bred on conflicts of interests. The stakes were high. Those in the North-East who stood to gain the most faced the challenge of mobilizing a domestic political coalition broad and stable enough to overcome the South's resistance. The key to success lay in the West and this was not lost on Republican leaders. Indeed, the Republicans' foreign policy agenda is best seen as part of a larger electoral strategy in the 1890s that was designed to exploit sectional differences in the agrarian periphery and to prevent an alliance against the North-East.

Southern Democrats, well practised in the art of sectional politics, were wise to the game. Being able to do something about it was another matter. In politics, as in war, there are objective realities, and in the late 1890s the possibilities for a southern–western alliance over foreign policy were remote. The West was not as dependent on foreign markets as the South; its principal market was at home, not abroad. Policies that challenged British dominance were thus less risky for the West than the South. Moreover, because it was not as dependent on foreign markets as the South, western lawmakers could us their votes in Congress on issues of importance to the North-East—naval spending, foreign bases, tariff reform—to win concessions on domestic policy matters such as currency reform, railway regulation, and monopoly control that were of great importance in the trans-Mississippi West.

So it was that the West threw its weight behind the Republican North-East's foreign policy agenda. The story of America's rise as a great power is thus also a story about how the Republicans established hegemony at home. With the exception of Woodrow Wilson's presidency, Republicans would control the machinery of national government for the next thirty years. Indeed, it took the full force of the Great Depression to destroy the regional alliance between the North-East and the West that formed the backbone of Republican political power. The depth and breadth of Franklin Delano Roosevelt's stunning victory in the 1932 presidential contest created new possibilities for a sectional alliance spanning the Mason–Dixon line and, in so doing, offered a new opportunity to redefine the purposes of American power.

The struggle over internationalism

The 1930s were years of upheaval and change in America's foreign relations. During this tumultuous decade
of depression and war, the United States went from a
country that defined its interests in largely hemispheric
terms to a nation that saw itself as a global power, with
far-flung interests and international responsibilities.
The raw, assertive nationalism that had so often characterized America's foreign policy during the preceding
quarter-century was abandoned in favour of a new role
for the United States, where Washington took the lead
internationally in liberalizing the world economy and
guarding against the kind of international breakdown
that had led to one of history's longest depressions and
one of its worst wars (see Box 9.3).

America's internationalist turn

No figure looms larger in this transition to internationalism than Franklin Roosevelt. Often remembered as a
great innovator on the domestic front, Roosevelt was
also an extraordinary statesman. Certainly, few in the
1930s had a better appreciation of the perilous international situation confronting the United States. As early
as 1933, Roosevelt began urging that he should be given
the authority to impose economic sanctions to deter
German and Japanese military intimidation and expansionism. The new president also lost little time experi-
menting with ways to revive the world economy and
promote foreign trade. As the political crisis in Europe
and Asia deepened in the 1930s, again it was Roosevelt
who made the case for giving Britain and others the

military means to defend themselves against the Axis
powers and rearming the United States itself.

In all cases Roosevelt would have his way with Congress, but not before the country endured one of the
most bitter fights over foreign policy in its history. From
Japan's seizure of Manchuria in 1931 to Mussolini's invasion of Ethiopia in 1935, to the Nazi occupation of
France in 1940, America's leaders fiercely debated *how*
the United States should respond. Policy differences
in Washington became less tractable and debates over
how the nation should respond to international events
became hopelessly embroiled in fights over means.
Were the new governmental mechanisms Roosevelt
was proposing needed to restore the world economy
and safeguard against another breakdown? Should the
United States assume a more assertive role in deterring
expansionism and checking aggression? These were the
questions that divided America in the 1930s.

As in the 1890s, fights over foreign policy in the
1930s were inextricably linked to domestic conflicts of
interest. So were debates over 'entangling' America in
foreign rivalries. Once again, arguments for and against
an assertive foreign policy had direct implications for
the domestic distribution of wealth and power. What
changed, and dramatically so, was *who* lined up on each
side of the battle line. This time, it was the West, not the
South, that led the fight against the projection of American power—a battle that it, like the South in the 1890s,
would lose. In the 1930s, the South favoured a vigorous
assertion of US leadership in world affairs, a position it
ironically now shared with the North-East.

BOX 9.3: Franklin Roosevelt and the great transformation

When Franklin Roosevelt was inaugurated in March 1933, twelve years of Republican-dominated foreign policy came to an end. During the 1920s, laissez-fairism was America's credo in foreign as well as domestic policy. Instead of looking for ways to capitalize on America's tremendous power after the First World War, Republican presidents throughout the decade looked for ways to minimize American involvement in the affairs of other countries, especially in continental Europe. Although Washington would continue to promote commercial expansion abroad, as it had since the 1890s, the Republican administrations of Warren Harding, Calvin Coolidge, and Herbert Hoover maintained a low political-military profile overseas and for the most part eschewed the kind of multilateralism that Franklin Roosevelt and the Democrats would champion in the 1940s.

Depression, militarism, and the North–South alliance

Once deeply divided over foreign policy, North and South found common cause in the 1930s fight against economic nationalism, military intimidation, and imperial expansion. However much northerners and southerners might disagree on the rights of Negroes and organized labour, sectional rivalry stopped at the water's edge. What explains the rise of a new foreign policy coalition that crossed the once impenetrable Mason–Dixon line? Why did the once-powerful alliance between the North-East and West break down? Although many factors contributed to this domestic realignment over foreign policy, much is explained by a single development: by the late 1920s, the North-East was far more deeply integrated in, and deeply dependent on, the world economy, than it had been in the 1890s.

America's dramatic rise as a mature industrial and financial power in the first quarter of the twentieth century is largely a story of the North-East. The First World War had transformed the world economy and America's place in it. As a result of the war-inflated economic boom, the national trade surplus climbed to over $3.5 billion in 1917, with manufactured goods accounting for over 60 per cent of total exports. Foreign direct investment also grew rapidly. The nations of Europe needed foreign capital to fund their recovery from the ravages of the First World War; American investors needed foreign outlets to dispose of surplus capital. America's largest corporations kept pace with the nation's big Wall Street banks. Once relatively insignificant in the American economy, the nation's overseas assets had become equal to over one-fifth of the gross national product by the time of the 1929 Wall Street crash. Although less dramatic, the growth of America's overseas trade was also important. More significant, the composition of this trade changed radically. In the past, the United States had been chiefly an exporter of primary goods to Europe. While cotton remained the leading export commodity, by the 1920s industrial sectors such as automobiles, machinery, and iron and steel had a considerable stake in foreign markets.

As the country's position in the world economy changed, America's leaders reassessed the nation's role in world affairs. Incentives to do so were especially strong in the North-East, where most of the wealth and prosperity generated by the rapid economic growth in the country's overseas trade, investment, and lending was concentrated. With roughly half of the national population, the region stretching from southern New England to the Potomac and west to the Mississippi produced over two-thirds of all manufacturing jobs in the country. More impressive still was the region's productivity. Seventy-five per cent of the total value added in manufacturing came from the manufacturing belt, and most of that was concentrated in the region's powerful industrial and financial centres: Baltimore, Boston, Chicago, Cleveland, Detroit, Philadelphia, Pittsburgh, and New York.

Once a part of the country that depended on economic protection from foreign imports, America's 'manufacturing belt' was now the core region of the world economy, eclipsing the great 'iron triangle' in Europe that ran from Stuttgart to Antwerp to Paris.

Hitler's barter system in *Mitteleuropa* and Japan's drive for a Greater East Asia Co-Prosperity Sphere promised nothing good for a region whose representatives now favoured freer trade, open access, and capital mobility. It is thus not surprising that the urban North-East was at the vanguard of support for reviving and liberalizing the world economy, or that its elected officials in Congress now looked to their colleagues from the Deep South rather than the trans-Mississippi West to build a domestic coalition strong enough to sustain a change in international direction.

By any measure, the South was more committed to a vigorous assertion of American power overseas than any other part of the country. Opinion polls consistently showed southerners to be more internationalist and interventionist than non-southerners. The vast majority of the region's newspapers endorsed Roosevelt's foreign policy, even though many took exception to his domestic policies. Southerners even led the country in volunteer enlistment in the armed services. These sentiments were widely shared by the region's representatives in Washington. No region of the country more avidly supported a 'get tough' strategy toward the Nazis than the South.

Southern support for a more ambitious and decisive foreign policy sprang from multiple sources. Party politics tell part of the story. Roosevelt was remarkably popular among southern voters, and he swept the South by huge margins in each of his runs for the presidency. Yet party loyalty and Roosevelt's personal charm alone cannot explain southern policy choices. The South was a region that depended heavily on exporting commodities, especially cotton, to world markets, and in this regard little had changed since the 1890s. And this explains why most southerners viewed the spread of economic nationalism in the 1920s and 1930s with alarm. For them, the collapse of the liberal European-oriented world system presented a fundamental threat. 'However else the crisis of that world might have been viewed by others,' writes one scholar, 'the articulate South saw Nazi aggression as a dagger thrust at the heart of this system.'[4] If Germany defeated Britain, Hitler and his Axis partners would establish economic hegemony over the European continent and divide the world into exclusive spheres of influence. If Hitler were

not stopped, he would close the doors of Europe to American exports and move against US commercial interests elsewhere.

If internationalism was the credo of the agrarian South, isolationism was the ideology of the West. The same polls that ranked southerners as Roosevelt's strongest supporters on foreign affairs showed westerners to be his toughest critics. Westerners were generally more sceptical than other Americans about the virtues of foreign trade, military preparedness, and aid to Britain, and they were less willing to spend American blood and treasure to check Germany's or Japan's drive for hegemony in Europe and Asia. Isolationism reigned supreme in the 1930s in the Great Plains and Mountain West. Western isolationists, steeped in the region's agrarian traditions, looked above the Mason–Dixon line and found allies in other parts of rural America.

Western views were well represented on Capitol Hill. No elected officials defended isolationism more passionately than those from the rural West. Often attributed to ignorance, backwardness, and parochialism, westerners opposed internationalism for very concrete reasons. Unlike the agrarian South, the rural West looked primarily to the domestic market for its prosperity. Wheat growers, who produced the region's leading farm export, sold less than 20 per cent of their crop abroad each year. Producers of other leading crops in the West were even less dependent on overseas markets. Having less at stake in Europe than the South or the urban North-East, it is thus not surprising that the rural West also felt comparatively less urgency in aiding the Allies or expanding the nation's capacity to project military power overseas.

Politics reinforced western scepticism toward internationalism. No part of the country was more susceptible to claims that American and British bankers had dragged the United States into the First World War. The vast majority of the region's farmers held Wall Street in low repute, and London's standing in the region was not much higher. Few westerners attached much credence to the notion that American and European security interests were interdependent, or to the idea that Britain was America's 'first line of defence'. In western eyes, such talk was nothing more than self-serving British propaganda and Ivy League sophistry. Calls for military mobilization were greeted with the same suspicion.

One consequence is that the Republican Party's hold on the region weakened during the 1920s. The national parties were always held in low repute by large numbers of western voters, many of whom viewed the parties as instruments of powerful eastern interests. The Republican Party had carried the region in most presidential contests since the 1890s, but the West's support was always fragile and variable. As the Republican-dominated North-East moved in the direction of internationalism in the 1920s, it became increasingly difficult for the party's leaders to broker intra-party compromises over foreign policy. In fact, Herbert Hoover's efforts to do by pursuing 'semi-internationalism' only exacerbated tensions within the party. By the time Franklin Roosevelt took office in March 1933, the Republican Party was in tatters: deeply divided along regional lines and incapable of offering a programmatic response to the economic and political dislocations caused by the Great Depression.

Internationalism as party building

Republican losses were Democratic gains. Just as the internationalization of the urban North-East weakened the sectional bases of the Republican coalition, it created new possibilities for political alliance that Roosevelt and the Democrats were quick to exploit. In the past, Democratic politicians faced an uphill battle in the staunchly protectionist and Republican North-East. By the 1930s, however, internationalist principles like free trade and collective security were no longer anathema in the region's big urban metropolises. On the contrary, as Roosevelt came to realize, internationalism could be used to broaden the Democratic base in the North-East and to weaken the Republican Party by exacerbating sectional rivalry within it. Economic nationalism, once the Republican elixir, now divided the party. Still heavily Republican, the eastern Establishment advocated liberal internationalism. Western Republicans were nationalism's staunchest supporters.

For Roosevelt there were thus huge political advantages in moving decisively toward internationalism. The Democrats were now well positioned to reap the rewards of the urban North-East's internationalization and the internecine struggles within the Republican Party it touched off over international trade. Because core elements of the Democratic and Republican parties now stood to benefit politically as well as economically from a commitment to maintain order, stability, and openness on the Eurasian landmass, their elected representatives had a strong incentive to support Roosevelt's efforts to stabilize the world economy and prevent the spread of nationalism and militarism overseas. In sum, America's internationalist turn rested on political facts *inside* as well as *outside* the United States.

American efforts to stabilize the international environment began in the 1930s. An even greater effort occurred after the Second World War. From the late 1940s onward, American policy makers sought to rebuild the world economy along liberal lines. They also worked to ameliorate Europe's chronic geopolitical troubles by encouraging economic integration, interdependence, and growth. The Marshall Plan, the General Agreement on Tariffs and Trade (GATT), and the North Atlantic Treaty Organization (NATO) were all part of this larger effort aimed at liberalizing the world economy and preventing the kind of international breakdown experienced in the 1930s. Under US leadership, new governmental mechanisms were created to regulate the world economy, new institutions and agencies were established to disperse American economic relief, and new military means were developed to strengthen the nation's presence overseas and to deter other nations, most conspicuously the Soviet Union and China, from taking advantage of political instability on the Eurasian landmass.

The domestic political viability of America's liberal internationalism depended on the alliance between the North-East and the South that Roosevelt forged in the 1930s. From the Second World War to the Korean and Vietnam wars this alliance afforded America's presidents, Republican and Democratic alike, considerable latitude in managing the nation's foreign policy. Then, around the 1970s, the first cracks in the domestic foundations of liberal internationalism appeared. While it would not be until later that the regional and party battle lines would be redrawn, the international and domestic processes that fractured the North–South alliance made it increasingly difficult to manufacture consensus over foreign policy.

KEY POINTS

❑ During the Great Depression, the key question was whether or not America should assume an active role in rebuilding the world economy and checking the spread of fascism in Europe and Asia.

❑ Internationalists from the urban North-East and the agrarian South favoured active American international leadership. Because this coalition spanned the Mason–Dixon line and included Republicans as well as Democrats, it overwhelmed nationalist opposition in the West and formed the foundation of the Cold War consensus to come.

❑ In the 1930s, as in other periods of American foreign policy, politicians from different parts of the country sought to equate regional interests with the national interests. Foreign policy issues were debated in terms of their immediate impact on regional prosperity and their longer-range regional political and economic consequences.

American primacy and the 'new sectionalism'

With the end of the Cold War, that domestic challenge only became more difficult. While the United States enjoyed unrivalled power internationally, its political ability to convert its power into influence rapidly diminished. Political fissures over foreign policy that opened up two decades earlier became more acutely partisan after the collapse of the Soviet empire. Republicans from the 'red' states of the South and Mountain West espoused fundamentally different views about the purposes of American power from elected officials from 'blue' states in the North-East and along the Pacific Coast. Contrary to all expectations, those foreign policy differences have only hardened since 9/11. Indeed, today Republicans and Democrats are more divided over foreign policy matters than at any time since the Second World War.

End of consensus

For nearly three decades after the Second World War, the nation's foreign policy was based on an alliance between the North-East and the South. These regions were the earliest and largest beneficiaries of the policies of foreign aid, forward defence, and liberal trade that were aimed at promoting an open, interdependent world economy, and at the Cold War isolation or 'containment' of nations that threatened it. Because this coalition was rooted in the regional power base of the Democratic Party and the powerful eastern wing of the Republican Party, it provided an institutional framework for a bipartisan foreign policy. Party politics did not stop at the water's edge during the Cold War years; rather, shared interests kept partisanship in check (see Box 9.4).

That bipartisan coalition lasted until the 1970s, when it began to fall apart under the combined weight of three developments: mounting social tensions triggered by the Civil Rights Movement and the Vietnam War, the economic decline of the industrial North-East and the rise of the so-called 'sunbelt' states of the South and West, and the shift in the Republican Party's centre of gravity from the North-East to the Mountain West. The first two drove North and South apart. The third created opportunities for coalition building between West and South. As the Republican Party aligned itself with the rapidly growing states of the Mountain West, it searched for allies in the country's other late developer, the South.

During the 1970s economic activity began to shift from the North-East to the South and West. Many factors contributed to this process: the diffusion of large-scale, high-technology production, lower transportation costs, regional disparities in labour costs, energy prices, and local tax rates. No less important were the uneven consequences of the erosion of American commercial power in the international economy. The North-East suffered disproportionately from the rise of Europe and Japan in the

---

BOX 9.4: The Cold War consensus

American leaders were able to mobilize broad domestic support for their foreign policies during the quarter century that followed the Second World War. Presidents enjoyed considerable latitude, if not deference, on matters of foreign policy—certainly more than they did on domestic policy issues. The absence of foreign policy conflict during this period did not mean that politics stopped at the water's edge. Rather the Cold War consensus rested on a bipartisan alliance that spanned one of America's great political fault lines: the Mason–Dixon line. Northern and southern lawmakers found common cause in Cold War policies aimed at containing the Soviet Union and promoting international economic openness. As that political alliance began to come apart in the 1970s, America's leaders, Republican and Democratic alike, found it increasingly difficult to mobilize and sustain bipartisan support for their foreign policies.

1970s as economic competitors. Spatial disparities in federal spending and federal tax policies also played a role in accelerating, if not encouraging, this regional shift in power. Federal expenditures and tax policies spurred the growth of sunbelt cities such as Atlanta, Miami, Houston, and Phoenix while exacerbating economic difficulties in the older north-eastern centres of Boston, Chicago, Detroit, and New York. The migration of industries, jobs, and people from the manufacturing belt to the sunbelt created 'structural conditions' conducive to political alliance between West and South. Republican stratagems made it a reality. Beginning in the late 1970s western Republicans like Ronald Reagan aggressively pushed domestic and foreign policies that were now antithetical to the interests of the declining North-East. In foreign policy, the Republicans' long-standing commitment to anti-communism was grafted onto a 'new' foreign policy agenda that favoured less international regulation, a strong national defence, and 'bolder, more assertive' leadership. By playing on these and other issues (such as race), Republicans wrought havoc in the Democratic Party. Southerners left the party in droves.

In the 1980s the Democrats' electoral stronghold narrowed to the ageing North-East. No longer restrained by the demands of coalition building, the Democratic leadership adopted a foreign policy strategy that played well in the northern 'rustbelt' and along the Pacific Coast: retrenchment. While most Democratic leaders continued to favour American participation in international institutions, they urged greater restraint in the use of military force and a smaller defence establishment. On foreign economic policy, Democrats edged away from their long-standing commitment to free trade, capital mobility, and equal access. Demands for 'fairer trade', job retraining, and industrial policy became as obligatory in Democratic politics as demands for freer trade, 'fast track procedures', and 'FTAs' (free trade agreements) were in Republican circles.

Red America versus Blue America

By the time the Berlin Wall fell in 1989, the domestic underpinnings of liberal internationalism had given way. In its place arose two new coalitions: one, centred in the South and Mountain West, that was dedicated to the projection of American power and the primacy of national security; the other, based in the North-East and Pacific Coast, committed to reducing America's geopolitical footprint and investing greater resources on the domestic side of the ledger. Much of the struggle over foreign policy since the end of the Cold War originates here, in the deepening divide between what political pundits dubbed 'Red America' and 'Blue America' (see Box 9.5). In contrast to what happened in the 1890s and 1930s, when new hegemonic blocs arose out of the struggles set in motion by uneven growth, the regional and partisan divisions that emerged before the end of the Cold War only intensified afterwards.

Economic trends in the 1990s generally reinforced this 'new sectionalism'. Higher tax rates, labour costs, and energy prices in the North-East made it harder for elected officials from 'blue' states to find common ground on foreign and domestic policy with 'red' state officials who had competing economic concerns. So did the uneven effects of globalization. The outsourcing of American jobs hit the ageing industrial centres of the North-East especially hard. Well-paying, unionized jobs in manufacturing were the first to be lost as production lines were moved abroad and cheap imports arrived from low-wage economies. The North-East moved to the forefront of efforts to rein in America's commitment to free trade. Free trade's most reliable advocates came from the South and, especially, the Mountain West: ironically, the one part of the country that consistently opposed Roosevelt's efforts to liberalize trade in the 1930s.

The South and the West also provided the surest support for foreign policies that put a premium on military power. Some analysts attribute these regional differences to strategic subcultures: southerners are said to be more nationalistic and less willing to accept the constraints on national autonomy that accompany institutionalized multilateralism. Whatever the merits of such claims, changes in the economic and political geography of military spending and production made it harder for politicians from different parts of the country to find common ground on national security policy. Since the 1970s, Pentagon spending on military procurement and research and development benefited the South and West at the expense of the North-East, contributing to the decline of the manufacturing sector in the North. In addition, the southern and western states that make up the so-called 'gunbelt' have consistently received a larger share of the resources spent on military bases and personnel.

Seen in this light, the fights between Republicans and Democrats about how America should respond to 'rogue states' like Saddam Hussein's Iraq, or China's rise to great powerdom, or the outsourcing of American jobs to India take on new meaning. They are battles in a larger, political war for control of the national political economy. This is why Republicans took exception to Bill Clinton's efforts to slow the growth of defence spending and why Democrats opposed the

unilateral turn foreign policy took during George W. Bush's presidency. Foreign policies that put a premium on military power and free trade resonate in the southern and western areas Republicans represent. Conversely, foreign policies that shift some of the burden of 'leadership' to other nations and international institutions help Democrats politically in the North-East and Pacific Coast.

To be sure, this gap between Republicans and Democrats is not solely explained by uneven growth or electoral geography. American primacy has also had an effect. For all of its pathologies and shortcomings, the Cold War had a disciplining effect on America's politics. Public anxieties about Moscow's geopolitical ambitions and 'the bomb' also made consensus building easier by forcing politicians to the centre. With the collapse of the Soviet empire Republicans and Democrats have found it easier (i.e. politically safer) to use foreign policy to pursue narrower political ends. This is especially true of those elected officials who hail from the 'red' and 'blue' districts and states whose voters are overwhelmingly Republican and Democratic.

The widening gyre

For all it changed, 9/11 did not reverse this trend. The initial surge in bipartisan unity in Washington and beyond that followed the attacks on the World Trade Center and the Pentagon quickly subsided.[4] And as the partisan debate over the war in Iraq demonstrates, Republicans and Democrats today are in strong disagreement about the proper mix of power and diplomacy in foreign affairs. Meanwhile, the war on terrorism has done little to quell partisan strategizing and electioneering on Capitol Hill over trade policy, foreign aid, and even homeland security. According to one widely used index, Congress is today more politically fractious and polarized than at any time in the last one hundred years.[5]

George Bush's combative governing style clearly contributed to this state of affairs, but the sources of today's foreign policy divide run deeper. Indeed, while many foreign policy analysts predicted that Barack Obama's election would restore bipartisanship to foreign policy, the anticipated 'post-partisan' era in foreign policy has

BOX 9.5: Regionalism redux: 'red' America versus 'blue' America

America is today experiencing the return of important regional divides; partisan differences are again running along regional lines, making it more difficult for the country's leaders to mobilize broad and consistent support for their foreign policies. One regional coalition, centred in the South and Mountain West, is dedicated to the projection of American power and the primacy of national security; the other, based in the North-East and Pacific Coast, is committed to reducing America's geopolitical footprint and investing greater resources in domestic programmes. In contrast to the 1890s and 1930s, when new hegemonic blocs arose out of the regional struggles set in motion by uneven growth, the contest between what pundits call 'red' America and 'blue' America intensified during the presidency of George W. Bush and has not abated under Barack Obama's leadership.

KEY POINTS

❑ Today, Republicans and Democrats are more divided over foreign policy matters than at any time since the Second World War. Partisan differences are again running along regional lines, with the so-called 'red' states of the South and Mountain West on one side and the 'blue' states of the North-East and Pacific Coast on the other side.

❑ Politicians from 'red' America champion foreign policies that put a premium on American power. Those who hail from 'blue' America favour greater reliance on international institutions and multilateral diplomacy.

❑ These divisions hardened during George W. Bush's presidency and have not eased on Barack Obama's watch. But the process of regional restructuring that gave rise to them began before 2001.

not materialized. Try as he might to reach across the aisle, Obama's calls for renewed bipartisanship have gone unanswered (Kupchan and Trubowitz 2011). Congress remains deeply divided over foreign policy.

Meanwhile, public opinion polls reveal striking gaps between Republican and Democratic voters on issues ranging from the war on terrorism, to Pentagon spending, to free trade.

Conclusion

Most accounts of American foreign policy making focus on national ideologies and institutions. This reflects the widely held belief among foreign policy analysts that politics in the United States has become increasingly 'nationalized' and divorced from place-specific interests. The regional nature of struggles in America's early years that shaped the political debates over 'non-entanglement' in European affairs and continental expansion is assumed to have withered away in the twentieth century, with the closing of the 'national frontier', the rise of American power, and the nation's

steady integration into the world economy. Sectionalism is viewed as a relic of America's past, a primitive impulse that has been displaced by the march of time.

The view of American development confuses a process with an outcome. Despite decades of economic convergence, the American economy is marked by high degrees of regional specialization and differentiation. Moreover, the nation's spatially decentralized system of political representation offers ample opportunity for regional differences to find political expression at the national level, and sometimes as party conflicts, as in the 1890s and again today. Once again, Republicans and Democrats are advancing fundamentally different visions of American power that are shaped in significant ways by the regional interests these parties represent. Republicans who hail from 'red' America contend that American power depends primarily on the possession and use of military might. By contrast, Democrats who represent 'blue' America maintain that the nation's power depends more on persuasion than coercion, and on domestic investments in infrastructure and education.

Which vision will dominate American foreign policy in the years ahead? Making predictions is always hazardous, but short of a major political realignment that gives the Democrats or Republicans effective control over the national political economy, the most likely outcome is continued conflict and polarization. America's two parties are so deeply entrenched regionally, and so evenly divided nationally, that bipartisan coalition building is likely to continue to be *ad hoc*, fragile, and short-lived (Trubowitz and Mellow 2011). America may enjoy unrivalled power internationally, but today it lacks the domestic political will needed to convert that power into programmatic policy.

? Questions

1. Why is the foreign policy-making process in the United States so conflict ridden?

2. Why are some regions of the United States more prone to expansionist foreign policies than others?

3. When are sectional differences over foreign policy most likely to find expression as partisan conflicts? Use historical examples to support your answer.

4. Why did the industrial North-East favour a policy of imperial expansion in the 1890s? Why did the agrarian South oppose expansionism?

5. Why did the North-East and the South find common cause in internationalism in the 1930s?

6. Why were politicians from western states more prone to nationalism and isolationism before the Second World War?

7. Why is the foreign policy-making process in the United States so much more partisan today than it was at the height of the Cold War?

8. How have the North-East's views of free trade changed over time? What explains the shifts in the region's attitudes toward trade?

9. In the 1890s, southern leaders opposed a large peacetime military establishment. Today, southerners are the Pentagon's biggest backers in Congress. What factors contributed to this change in the South's attitude toward military power?

10. Why have Barack Obama's calls for bipartisanship gone unfulfilled?

» Further Reading

Brzezinski, Z. (2007), *Second Chance: Three Presidents and the Crisis of American Superpower* (New York: Basic Books).

A critical examination of American statecraft since the fall of the Berlin Wall.

LaFeber, W. (1993), *The American Search for Opportunity, 1865–1913* (New York: Cambridge University Press).

A stimulating account of America's rise as a great power and its international consequences.

Reynolds, D. (2001), *From Munich to Pearl Harbor: Roosevelt's America and the Origins of the Second World War* (Chicago: Ivan R. Dee).

An insightful study of America's turn toward liberal internationalism.

Trubowitz, P. (2011), *Politics and Strategy: Partisan Ambition and American Statecraft* (Princeton: Princeton University Press).

A systematic analysis of how presidents make foreign policy.

Endnotes

1. See, for example, Agnew (1987), Bensel (1984), and Markusen (1987).

2. See Trubowitz (1998), Silverstone (2004), and Narizny (2007).

3. In the discussion below, I utilize the classic tripolar grouping that divides America's states into three 'great regions', divided roughly along the courses of the Mississippi and Ohio rivers: the North-East, South, and West. The North-East refers to states in New England, the Middle Atlantic, and the Great Lakes areas: Connecticut, Delaware, Illinois, Indiana, Maine, Maryland, Massachusetts, Michigan, New Hampshire, New Jersey, New York, Ohio, Pennsylvania, Rhode Island, Vermont, and Wisconsin. The South includes states from the South-East and South-West: Alabama, Arkansas, Florida, Georgia, Kentucky, Louisiana, Mississippi, North Carolina, Oklahoma, South Carolina, Tennessee, Texas, Virginia, West Virginia. The West refers to states from the Great Plains, Mountain West, and Far West: Alaska, Arizona, California, Colorado, Hawaii, Idaho, Iowa, Kansas, Minnesota, Missouri, Montana, Nebraska, Nevada, New Mexico, North Dakota, South Dakota, Utah, Washington, and Wyoming.

4. See Trubowitz and Mellow (2005).

5. http://voteview.com/.

10 Media and US foreign policy

Piers Robinson

Chapter contents

Introduction

The attacks of 11 September 2001 transformed the foreign policy agenda of the United States and ushered in a global 'war on terror'. The events themselves were communicated by the world's media almost instantaneously and had a profound impact upon both US and global public opinion. Within weeks, and with overwhelming support from both US media and public, the Bush administration invaded Afghanistan. Then, in a short period of time, the US government mobilized the support of both the US media and public to back the invasion of Iraq. Since then, US strategies in Iraq and Afghanistan have caused controversy both internationally and within the United States. The increase in US casualties across both war zones, scandal over the treatment of Iraqi prisoners at Abu Ghraib, and a growing perception that US policy is 'failing' have generated significant levels of media criticism and public dissent in the USA. In short, US foreign policy since 9/11, under both the Bush and Obama administrations, has been conducted under the glare of media and public attention both within the United States and globally. But what roles have public opinion and media played during these events? To what extent have the US media and public been manipulated by the US government, and to what extent, conversely, have public opinion and media shaped US foreign policy during these tumultuous times? Moreover, what are the consequences of public opinion and media for US power in the twenty-first century? Such questions are the subject matter of this chapter.

This chapter introduces students to the range of debates that have dominated research into the relationship between US public opinion, media, and foreign policy. Before grappling with these academic debates, we will discuss the nature of US media and public opinion, including a consideration of democratic expectations of mass media and public opinion. This initial section sets the grounds for a discussion of pluralist and elite models of the public opinion/media/foreign policy nexus. The pluralist model emphasizes both the independence and power of US media and public opinion and their ability to influence US foreign policy. The elite model, discussed next, adopts a different understanding of this nexus and highlights the ability of US political elites to shape both media and public perceptions. The chapter then moves to a discussion of public and media diplomacy aimed at projecting US power abroad. Throughout, attention is paid to the ways in which public opinion and media can be understood as a source of power for, and as a constraint upon, US foreign policy. In conclusion, the chapter discusses contemporary debate concerning the impact of technological developments, including the internet and the rise of global media such as Al-Jazeera, upon US power and influence. First, however, we need to introduce basic concepts regarding media and public opinion.

Concepts

When discussing *media*, academics are, more often than not, referring to mainstream media outlets such as TV news channels, newspapers, and cable networks such as CNN and Fox News. Whilst other components of US media, such as the film and light entertainment industry, are important with regard to political information (Baum 2003), it is these traditional mainstream news media sources that are understood to be the crucial sites upon which political information is mediated and communicated to the American public. For the sake of brevity, in this chapter the term 'media' is used to mean news media. Key US network television media outlets include CBS, NBC, and ABC, and significant cable channels are CNN and Fox News. All these outlets communicate news to a national audience. US newspaper coverage of international affairs is largely led by the *New York Times* and the *Washington Post* (and to a lesser extent the *Los Angeles Times*). As with other US newspapers, these are regionally based, albeit with a minority nationally based readership, but they do have a significant influence upon the remainder of the US press.

In terms of journalistic norms, mainstream US media claim to be objective in their approach to covering the news. Even in relation to international affairs coverage, mainstream media disavow suggestions of their news coverage being distorted by patriotism and national bias. Whilst acknowledging a focus on US interests, these media maintain a commitment to telling US citizens the truth about international events. As such, mainstream media in the USA are supposed to function as the central component of the US public sphere within which informed, open, and free-ranging debate can occur. Media are also expected to perform a watchdog role whereby both government and powerful interests are held to account by media. Examples such as the Watergate scandal in the 1970s, when journalists Bob Woodward and Carl Bernstein uncovered political corruption by the Nixon administration, are often cited as seminal examples of watchdog journalism. More recently Seymour Hersh's watchdog journalism highlighted issues surrounding the treatment of Iraqi prisoners at Abu Ghraib in Iraq. The independence of the media from political power is in theory guaranteed through US media operating according to the free market model; that is to say media outlets are privately owned and run as a business in order to make profit. As a consequence, US media are not controlled by government and are, in theory, protected from undue influence and pressure. Public service broadcasting, whereby media is funded through public money and regulated by the state, does exist in the USA (e.g. PBS, the Public Broadcasting Service) but has a small viewership and minimal influence. As such, the dominance of commercial media in the USA is exceptional, as most Western democracies have developed mixed media systems that contain a greater proportion of public service broadcasting. Overall, the key point here is that the assumption underlying the free market model is that power is sufficiently devolved so as to enable a free and independent media. As such, US media are expected to conform to the pluralist model whereby all groups in US society, from government through to business to the public, have access to, and are represented in, the US public sphere.

With respect to public opinion and international affairs, research has traditionally identified two distinct orientations amongst US citizens. The first is the *isolationist* sentiment, the second the *internationalist* sentiment. Isolationists are opposed to the USA taking an active role in world affairs. Beyond guaranteeing the security of the USA, isolationists believe that the USA should avoid both involvement in international organizations such as the United Nations and attempts to influence the affairs of other states. For example, prior to the attack by Japan on Pearl Harbor in 1941, majority US public opinion was isolationist and, therefore, opposed to becoming directly involved in opposing Nazi Germany's expansionist war. Internationalists, conversely, support a more active role for the USA in global affairs including US involvement in international organizations such as the United Nations. Internationalists support the deployment of

> **KEY POINTS**
>
> ❑ Political communication research focuses upon the analysis of mainstream media outlets such as television news and newspapers.
> ❑ As a whole, US mainstream media are expected to provide US citizens with a full range of relevant viewpoints and opinions.
> ❑ US citizens are often categorized as either *isolationist* or *internationalist*.

US forces around the world and attempts to promote values such as democracy and free market economics. For example, since the 9/11 attacks it is likely there has been an increase in internationalist sentiment with the US public supporting an interventionist foreign policy in order to combat threats and secure US interests. Whilst more recent studies have sought to develop more nuanced descriptions of US public beliefs regarding foreign policy (e.g. Wittkopf (1990)), the isolationist/internationalist distinction remains a useful analytical tool.

The pluralist model

The pluralist model makes a number of important assumptions. The first is that power is sufficiently dispersed throughout society (including across government, media, and the public) so that no one set of interests is able to prevail. Rather, the political process, including media debate and public opinion formation, is the outcome of a range of competing positions negotiated through an open political system and a free media, and underpinned by a public that has access to sufficient information in order to develop an independent opinion. More specifically, the pluralist model assumes, first, that the US public are capable of rationally processing news information in order to form their own, independent, opinion. Second, the pluralist model maintains that mainstream media are sufficiently independent from political power to allow them to present a diverse range of political perspectives. Third, the pluralist model assumes the US political system is

sensitive to, and therefore influenced by, public opinion and media.

Having clarified what is meant by *pluralism*, we now turn to consider pluralist accounts of the public opinion/media/foreign policy nexus. I will first examine pluralist accounts of the relationship between public opinion and foreign policy, and then pluralist accounts about the relationship between media and foreign policy.

Public opinion and foreign policy

Historically, tension exists between *realist* and *liberal-democratic* perspectives on the role of public opinion in US foreign policy formulation. Realists traditionally resist public input to the complex task of foreign affairs. Conversely, liberal approaches advocate greater levels of public involvement in the process of foreign policy making (see Major debates and their impact 10.1). But, what influence does the US public actually wield on foreign policy formulation?

For some academics and many politicians, public opinion is a force to be reckoned with. Perhaps the clearest articulation of this claim can be found in the Vietnam Syndrome (otherwise referred to as *casualty aversion*). During the United States war in South-East Asia, aimed at preventing the defeat of the South Vietnamese government to communist forces, the US government suffered a significant, albeit gradual, decline in public support for the war. With the eventual defeat of US forces, a perception emerged within some quarters of the US foreign policy establishment that negative public reaction to US casualties was fundamental in draining the commitment of the US government to fight in Vietnam. Belief in the Vietnam Syndrome is so prevalent within military and political circles that it is regularly invoked during debates over US military operations, for example in Somalia in 1992–3, in Kosovo in 1999, and in recent US operations in Afghanistan and Iraq. Unless military victory can be achieved with minimal loss of life, erosion of public support will ultimately contribute to military defeat. According to the Vietnam Syndrome, public opinion acts as a *constraint upon US power*.

Whether or not the Vietnam Syndrome exists as a reality, as opposed to a belief, is subject to substantial debate. In fact, evidence exists supporting an inverse relationship between US casualties and public support for war. For example, in War, *Presidents and Public Opinion*, John Mueller (1973) examined opinion polls and casualty counts during the Korean and Vietnam wars, and found that public support for these wars declined at first rapidly, and then more slowly, as US casualties mounted: overall he argues that public support declined *inexorably* as the death toll of American soldiers increased. However, whilst casualties might decrease public support for war, the extent to which this then influences politics is less clear-cut. For example, there exists some evidence that foreign policy issues do have a major impact upon how the US public votes (e.g. Aldrich, Sullivan, and Borgida 1989). However, even if foreign policy issues influence voting and, in turn, impact on a US president in electoral terms, this does not necessarily mean that actual

policy is then influenced. For example, the Republican Party suffered significant losses in the 2006 congressional elections, which many analysts put down to the Iraq War. However, the resulting impact of those losses on the Bush administration did not necessarily influence its decisions regarding policy in Iraq. Indeed, research documenting the impact of public opinion on actual foreign policy decisions is relatively scarce (see Holsti (1992) for an overview). Part of the problem lies in gathering evidence from meetings that are held in secret. And, even when documentary evidence exists from such meetings, the researcher is still confronted with the task of inferring from this data what was actually going on in the minds of policy makers. A more complicated issue confounding attempts to *measure influence* is the difficulty of disentangling one factor influencing policy making, public opinion, from the multitude of factors that may be relevant.

Overall, however, a perception persists that US public opinion does influence US foreign policy. The actual empirical evidence to support this perception is less certain. Whilst evidence points toward the importance of foreign affairs *vis-à-vis* voting, there is less to support the claim that foreign policy decisions are then influenced as a result. At most, public opinion is one factor amongst many shaping policy decisions. Perhaps of greater importance, however, is the tendency of the public opinion–foreign policy literature to ignore a crucial intervening variable—that of media. In the broadest sense, whilst public opinion might be formed along isolationist/internationalist lines, the details of particular foreign policy issues have to be communicated via mainstream media. In turn, the question of how public opinion is shaped regarding specific issues is linked to the way in which US media present those issues. At the same time, officials use media both as a source of information and as a guide to 'perceived public opinion' whereby policy makers use the agenda and tone of media reports as a guide to public opinion (Entman 2000: 79). In terms of understanding influences upon US foreign policy, it is equally important to examine the way media reports on international affairs. And it is to pluralist accounts of the relationship between media and foreign policy that we now turn.

MAJOR DEBATES AND THEIR IMPACT 10.1: Realist and liberal-democratic views on public opinion and foreign policy

The liberal-democratic perspective

The idea that public opinion should influence foreign policy formulation has a long history. In the early twentieth century, President Woodrow Wilson articulated the importance of public scrutiny of foreign affairs in his famous 'Fourteen Points'. Here he called for 'Open covenants of peace, openly arrived at, after which there shall be no private international understandings of any kind but diplomacy shall proceed always frankly and in the public view'. More specifically, a key component of liberal theory is the *democratic peace thesis*. This thesis maintains that liberal democracies are war-averse because, at least in part, the consent of the public is required. As people generally prefer peace to war, public opinion can act as a powerful constraint upon elected leaders and, therefore, the external behaviour of a state. In order for this to occur, public opinion should be able to influence foreign policy. Overall, the liberal-democratic perspective maintains that public opinion can contribute to sound foreign policy, as well as acting as a check against corrupt political elites, incorporating public concerns increases the range of opinions and arguments available to policy makers. As a result, more rational and well-thought-out policies can be devised.

The realist perspective

The realist perspective that foreign policy should be immune from public influence also has a long history. Writing in reference to US public opinion during the early part of the Cold War era, Walter Lippman claimed that '[t]he Unhappy truth is that the prevailing public opinion has been destructively wrong at the critical junctures' (Lippman 1955: 20) (see also Key quotes 10.3). In part, the claim underpinning the realist perspective is that foreign policy elites are best placed to decide what should be done in order to further US national interests and, at the same time, that the US public are largely ignorant and/or ill-informed about international affairs and, therefore, ill-equipped to think about the complexities of foreign policy. But the realist claim is also now underpinned by the neorealist position that policy makers react to events in the international system, such as emerging threats and shifts in the balance of power, and not to internal factors such as the desires and wishes of the US public. Overall, realism argues that policy makers should remain detached from the pressures of public opinion, formulating foreign policy in response to external events in the international system, and not in response to internal domestic politics, including public opinion.

To a large extent, these two competing normative positions on the role of public opinion and media are reflected throughout both policy debate and academic research. For example, some policy makers from a realist perspective have complained that public opinion and media wield too much power *vis-à-vis* foreign policy formulation, and that this prevents rational policy making. In the case of Vietnam, the apparent impact of public opinion and media suggested to realists that these had prevented the USA from winning that war. For academics, these normative positions are often spoken to in the research questions that they pursue. For example, some research into the *CNN effect* analyses this phenomenon in order to assess whether policy elites have 'lost control' over the policy process. As such, this research is of direct relevance to policy makers, who seek to minimize media impact on policy.

Media and foreign policy: from the Vietnam syndrome to the CNN effect

It was the Vietnam War, again, that elevated interest in the power of media to mould both public opinion and foreign policy. Whilst arguments surrounding the Vietnam Syndrome focused upon the impact of US casualties on public opinion, a parallel argument emerged concerning the role of US media, in particular during 1968 Tet Offensive. This offensive involved an uprising throughout South Vietnam organized by communist forces. During this crisis, widespread fighting occurred across major cities in South Vietnam and in full view of US journalists. A war that had been presented by the US military as one that was being won, suddenly appeared out of control. For some, relentlessly adversarial and critical journalism

> **KEY QUOTES 10.1:** Richard Nixon on media and the Vietnam War
>
> The Vietnam War was complicated by factors that never before occurred in America's conduct of a war . . . More than ever before, television showed the terrible human suffering and sacrifice of war, whatever the intention behind such relentless and literal reporting of the war, the result was a serious demoralization of the home front, raising the question whether America would never again be able to fight an enemy abroad with unity and strength of purpose at home.
>
> (Nixon 1978)

revealed the horrors of the Vietnam War, both fuelling anti-war sentiment and forcing the hand of policy makers. As with public opinion and the Vietnam Syndrome discussed earlier, the perception was created that media had acted as a powerful constraint, effectively limiting the use of US military power (see Key quotes 10.1). Since that time, the quantity of studies asserting the influence of media on foreign policy has steadily increased. Two developments, in particular, underpinned the thesis that the US media was beginning to wield greater power. The first concerned the arrival of 24-hour news broadcasting epitomized by Cable News Network (CNN). As a news channel attempting to compete with traditional media, CNN promised an orientation toward international news and took advantage of developments in communication technology to provide dramatic real-time reporting from around the world. Largely due to CNN, events such as the collapse of communism, symbolized by the fall of the Berlin Wall, and the 1991 Gulf War were experienced in real time by many US citizens. The effect of this development, according to some commentators (e.g. Hoge (1994)), was to increase the exposure of both the US public and foreign policy establishment as major crises around the world were reported instantaneously. Some spoke of foreign policy being driven by CNN, the so-called 'CNN effect'. The second development understood to have increased media influence was the end of the Cold War. During this period world events had been dominated by the ideological clash between communism and capitalism that had created an ideological bond between US journalists and policy makers. In short, US journalists and US policy makers viewed global events through the same Cold War prism of anti-communism and journalists were disinclined to

question their government when under threat from the 'red menace'. Released from the ideological prism of the Cold War, US journalists had, it was argued, become freer to cover the stories they wanted to and criticize their government. Overall, these developments in media (24-hour, real-time news) and global politics (the ending of the Cold War) have been understood by some as ushering in an era of unequalled media power (e.g. Entman (2000)).

Further impetus was given to the CNN effect claim by an increase in interventions during humanitarian crises (see Key quotes 10.2). Following the 1991 Gulf War, when the USA led a UN-authorized war to reverse the invasion of Kuwait by Iraq, uprisings occurred in northern and southern Iraq aimed at the overthrow of Saddam Hussein's regime. When these were suppressed by Saddam Hussein a major humanitarian crisis developed and, in northern Iraq, Iraqi Kurds became trapped in the mountainous region of northern Iraq attempting to escape Saddam's forces. Following weeks of critical media coverage, the USA intervened by creating safe areas in northern Iraq. For many this represented an unprecedented instance where the USA had been moved by media and public pressure to intervene in the internal affairs of another state in order to protect human rights. Further US involvement during crises in Somalia in 1991–2 (see Box 10.1), Bosnia in 1995, and Kosovo in 1999, all of which received extensive attention from the US media, seemed to confirm the power of media to drive foreign policy formulation (Robinson 2002). Overall, the idea of the CNN effect dovetails with liberal-democrat arguments (see Major debates and their impact 10.1) that favour a democratic and open foreign policy agenda shaped by media and public opinion. Furthermore, for some liberal advocates of humanitarian intervention, media are a source of power

> **KEY QUOTES 10.2:** Michael Mandelbaum on humanitarian intervention

For the United States, however, what lies behind intervention in the post-Cold War era is neither gold, nor glory, nor strategic calculation. It is, rather, sympathy. The televised pictures of starving people in northern Iraq, Somalia, and Bosnia created a political clamor to feed them, which propelled the US military into those three distant parts of the world.

(Mandelbaum 1994)

in terms of helping to build public support for humanitarian operations. At the same time, many realists who oppose US involvement in humanitarian operations perceive this influence as damaging to US interests. But how true is the CNN effect?

In fact, rather than confirming the impression of an all-powerful media, a large body of research into the CNN effect conducted over the last fifteen years has suggested the existence of a far more subtle range of effects, most of which indicate that claims

> **BOX 10.1:** Case study: US intervention in Somalia, 1992–93

The US intervention (Operation Restore Hope) during the crisis in Somalia 1991–2 was a seminal event both in terms of intervention during a humanitarian crisis and the role of media in US foreign policy formulation. The crisis in Somalia had developed due to civil war, the collapse of central government, and ensuing mass starvation. By 1992, the crisis was attracting a significant degree of international attention and the USA started to become increasingly involved. By December 1992, 28,000 US troops were deployed in Somalia in order to support the provision of aid. As well as apparently cementing a new norm of humanitarian intervention, the intervention was a major news event remembered perhaps most for the graphic images of starvation and conflict in Somalia and the images of US marines being greeted on the beeches of Mogadishu, not by hostile gunmen, but by the world's press. By the end of the operation, with the worldwide broadcast of a dead US marine being dragged through the streets of Mogadishu, the intervention was indelibly etched on US memory. As a case study in media, public opinion, and US foreign policy, the intervention highlights the various roles media and public opinion might play. In terms of the initial intervention, many have argued that the decision to intervene was caused by the CNN effect whereby graphic and emotive images of starving people created a cry to 'do something' from the American public, thereby compelling US policy makers to take action (e.g. Kennan (1993)). Others have claimed that the attention of US media to the suffering in Somalia helped to build a domestic constituency for the intervention which policy makers were then able to draw upon to support the intervention (Robinson 2002: 59–62). As such, the media and public opinion had an enabling effect with respect to the decision to intervene. Once the intervention was under way, US media coverage helped to mobilize support amongst the US public for the operation by portraying US actions in a positive light, emphasizing the role US soldiers and aid workers were playing in saving Somali lives (Robinson 2002: 59–62). By mid-to-late 1993, however, the operation had evolved beyond supporting aid delivery to include military action against specific factions within Somalia. The now infamous 'Black Hawk Down' incident, which involved the deaths of 18 US soldiers and up to 1000 Somalis, was a pivotal moment *vis-à-vis* the perceived failure of the intervention and US withdrawal from the country. In particular, images of a dead US combatant being dragged through the streets of the Somali capital Mogadishu were broadcast on US media and generated, according to some (e.g. Kennan (1993)), a political imperative to withdraw from the country. As such, at this stage of the intervention media may have come to have an impediment effect on policy makers whereby images of dead US soldiers turned public opinion against involvement in Somalia. Beyond the specifics of the intervention and withdrawal, and any role public opinion and media played in these, the Somalia intervention and its ignominious end have become embedded in US foreign policy thinking as an example of US military failure in the context of humanitarian intervention.

of a media-*driven* foreign policy are exaggerated and that media effects are narrower and more conditional than is often claimed to be the case (Gowing 1994; Robinson 2002). For example, Gowing (1994) argues that media influence is limited to largely cosmetic and tactical policies such as the airlifting of a few injured children out of Sarajevo during the 1992–95 war in Bosnia or the use of limited airstrikes during that same war. Also, Robinson (2002) and Livingston (1997) argue, respectively, that media influence is limited to situations of elite uncertainty and relatively low-cost and uncontroversial policies (such as helping aid agencies deliver food and medical supplies). Rarely has research demonstrated significant media impact on major foreign policy matters although, as described in Box 10.1, which describes the case of US intervention in Somalia, many still believe that media plays a significant role in foreign policy formulation.

Procedural criticism versus substantive criticism

In concluding our discussion of pluralist accounts, it is important to note that whilst claims about the influence of public opinion and media abound, academic research suggests actual influence wielded is more subtle and nuanced than is commonly assumed. As discussed, the influence of public opinion upon foreign policy, whilst receiving empirical support, needs to be moderated by the acknowledgement of the multitude of factors influencing policy making. At the same time, notions of a CNN effect need to be moderated through acknowledgement that its scope is more conditional and moderate than is often claimed to be the case. Whilst it would be churlish to argue that media and public carry no influence, the question of whether that influence is sufficient from a liberal-democratic perspective is debatable.

More significantly, much research on media influence suggests that it occurs most often at the procedural level, rather than at a substantive level (Althaus 2003). The term *procedural* describes criticism and influence that relates to debate over the implementation of foreign policy. The term *substantive* is used to describe criticism and influence that relates to the underlying justification and rationale for particular foreign policies. For example, the Vietnam War was criticized by US media and public more often at a procedural level whereby the central question revolved around whether the USA was winning or losing the war. Criticism, however, rarely raised the more substantive question of the justification for US involvement in Vietnam. As we shall see in the next section, when we discuss elite/critical accounts of the public opinion/media/foreign policy nexus, the primary focus of concern is precisely this lack of substantive debate over US foreign policy.

Criticisms of the pluralist model

The claim that the relationship between US public opinion, media, and foreign policy can be described as pluralist is often subject to four major criticisms. The first relates to the tendency of pluralists to overestimate agency, that is the ability of individuals to influence and change politics, whilst underplaying the importance of political and economic structures that serve to constrain and direct individuals. For example, whilst US journalists are 'independent' and guaranteed the right to free speech, both the political system within which they operate and the commercial company their media are a part of are likely to exert an influence upon what the journalist thinks and writes. Second, the pluralist model can be criticized for overplaying both the knowledge levels of the US public *vis-à-vis* foreign affairs as well as the actual responsiveness of the US government to public and media influence. Here, a tendency to measure the more plentiful procedural-level criticism and influence, as opposed to the rarer substantive-level criticism, leads to overestimates regarding the pluralist credentials of the US system. A third and related problem is a tendency for advocates of the pluralist model to focus on relatively rare events, such as the Watergate scandal, as evidence of public and media power when, in fact, these are very much exceptions to the rule. Finally, the pluralist model tends to ignore the financial and material resources that are employed by the US government in order to influence media and public opinion. Here, a substantial public relations apparatus serves to promote official viewpoints via press briefings, information packs, off-the-record briefings, and the careful packaging (or 'spin-doctoring') of policy. As such, the flow of information between government and public is not a two-way street, as assumed by the pluralist model, but heavily weighted in favour of the US government.

KEY POINTS

❏ The liberal-democratic perspective maintains that public opinion and media should influence foreign policy.

❏ The pluralist model argues the public are capable of both rationally assessing foreign policy and influencing foreign policy.

❏ The pluralist model argues media have a significant impact upon foreign policy formulation.

❏ Media criticism of, and influence upon, foreign policy can be categorized according to procedural and substantive categories.

The elite model

Compared to the pluralist model, the elite model of the public opinion/media/foreign policy nexus works with different assumptions. Whilst the pluralist model assumes that power is dispersed throughout the political system and society, the elite model argues that relatively small groups within the USA wield power. With respect to US foreign policy, groups with power include the combination of foreign policy officials, think tanks, and representatives of large business interests. Those who are not included, according to the elite model, are the bulk of the American public. Consequently, the political process, including media debate and public opinion formation, is the outcome of elite interests and agendas that dominate media and public debate. Specifically, the elite model maintains that the US public are not only influenced by what they see and hear in the news, but are also directed to think about issues in a way congenial to elite interests. Following on from this, the elite model maintains that media are closely located to elite groups in both political and financial terms. Consequently media are a propaganda tool for elites. Finally, the elite model maintains that the US political system is largely immune from non-elite influence.

Having introduced the elite model, and following the section on the pluralist model, I will first examine elite accounts of the relationship between public opinion and foreign policy, and then discuss elite accounts of the relationship between media and foreign policy. But first we need to briefly discuss the differing normative stance of realist and critical perspectives.

Realists and critical perspectives

Unlike the liberal-democratic perspective, which advocates public involvement in foreign policy formulation, realist approaches caution against allowing public opinion to influence foreign policy (see Major debates and their impact 10.1). Beyond the realist perspective, critical accounts share a similar empirical position to that of the realist; i.e. that elites control the foreign policy process and are immune from public influence. The critical perspective, however, does not share the normative assumption of the realist perspective that this state of affairs is right. Rather, critical accounts develop a moral critique of elite domination of US foreign policy (see Controversies 10.1). To recap, both realist and critical perspectives maintain that foreign policy is conducted by elites, largely free from the pressures of public opinion. Where the two perspectives differ is on whether this is right, as argued by realists, or wrong, as is claimed by critical approaches.

Public opinion and foreign policy

It was largely early research that laid the ground for realist hostility toward the US public. Gabriel Almond's (1950) *The American People and Foreign Policy* argued that only a small proportion of the US public, which

> **KEY QUOTES 10.3:** Walter Lippman on public opinion

The people have impressed a critical veto upon the judgements of informed and responsible officials. They have compelled the government, which usually knew what would have been wiser, or was necessary, or what was more expedient, to be too late with too little, or too long with too much, too pacifist in peace and too bellicose in war, too neutralist or appeasing in negotiations or too intransigent . . . It has shown itself to be a master of indecision when the stakes are life and death.

(Lippman 1955)

he labelled as an 'attentive public', possessed knowledge sufficient to hold a valid position on foreign policy issues. The broader mass public held non-attitudes whereby individuals responded irrationally to foreign affairs issues and held unstable, rapidly changing opinions. Associated with Almond's position was a significant stream of research maintaining public opinion had little impact on foreign policy. Together, the idea that public opinion was both irrational and possessing of little influence became known as the 'Almond–Lippman Consensus' (see Key quotes 10.3). For example, Bernard Cohen's (1973) *The Public's Impact on Foreign Policy* asserted that foreign policy officials discounted public opinion and maintained that public opinion should rather be shaped by government. Whilst pluralist challenges have emerged (as discussed in the previous section), plenty of examples abound to support the Almond–Lippman Consensus. For example, in relation to knowledge levels of the US public and the 2003 Iraq War, some opinion polls showed that a significant number of the US public believed the Iraqi President Saddam Hussein was involved with Osama bin Laden in conspiring to attack the USA.[1] An example that policy elites regard the US public as something to be led is that of President Bush's speech writer Michael Gerson, who asserted that the 9/11 attacks provided the Bush administration with a 'plastic, teachable moment' (Woodward 2004: 84) whereby the US public could be persuaded to support Bush's war on terror and other foreign policy initiatives.

Whilst the realist perspective highlights the inadequacy of public knowledge and understanding, critical accounts point towards the ways in which public knowledge and understanding are shaped by mainstream media. Contrasting with pluralist accounts, critical accounts argue that the extent to which the US public are able to consume news and form independent opinions is more limited than suggested by the pluralist model. Here, the concepts of *agenda setting* (McCombs and Shaw 1972), *priming* (Iyengar and Kinder 1987), and *framing* (Entman 1991) clarify the ways in which public opinion can be shaped. In his seminal study *The Press and Foreign Policy*, Bernard Cohen (1973) argued, '[t]he press may not be successful much of the time in telling people what to think, but it is stunningly successful in telling its readers what to think about'; that is to say, media are able to set the agenda by getting the public to think about certain issues and not others. Priming refers to the ability of media to direct publics to the issues upon which they should judge their leaders, whilst framing refers to the ways in which the presentation of news information helps to shape how people think about specific issues. For example, analysing the 1991 Gulf War, Iyengar and Simon (1994) demonstrate that media focus on the Gulf crisis led to the public defining the crisis as the most important political issue at the time. Media had set the agenda and directed the public as to what was the most important issue to think about. Their analysis also demonstrated that the US public were, accordingly, primed to judge US President George Bush Sr. on how well he handled the war. Finally, Iyengar and Simon argue that media coverage of the war was framed in terms of event-driven news (*episodic news*) that focused upon military matters, such as military technology and the progress of the war, and tended to downplay *thematic news* dealing with diplomatic issues and issues related to the rationale and justification for war. According to their analysis this framing of news increased viewers' support for military action, as opposed to alternative diplomatic solutions.

Thus far, it is clear that elite accounts (both realist and critical) perceive the US public as either ill-informed, a 'bewildered herd' as the famous political commentator Walter Lippman (1922) once asserted, or as dependent upon media in terms of their opinion formation. But what role do the US media play in creating this state of affairs? With this in mind, it is to elite accounts of media we now turn.

Media and foreign policy

At the core of elite accounts of mainstream US media lies the claim that the media agenda, and the framing of issues, is usually highly compatible with the agenda and perspective of US political elites. A significant and powerful early critique of US media was developed by Daniel Hallin (1986) in his analysis of US media coverage of the Vietnam War, *The Uncensored War*. Directly challenging claims (noted earlier) that US media adopted an adversarial stance toward the war, Hallin's analysis found that coverage was actually very supportive of the war right up until 1968. At this point, however, communist forces launched the Tet Offensive, and fighting that had, hitherto, been confined to rural parts of the country spilled over onto the streets of major cities, including the capital Saigon. Whilst this event produced some of the most graphic and infamous images of the war, and did precipitate an increase in media criticism, Hallin finds that this only occurred after the US political establishment had become divided over whether or not the war in Vietnam could be won at a cost that was bearable for the United States. Importantly, according to Hallin, the media rarely reported in positive terms the views of the US anti-war movement, which maintained that the war was immoral and unjustified. As such, the US media, throughout the war in Vietnam, merely followed the contours of elite opinion as journalists relied upon privileged, Washington-based news sources. Consequently, when the US establishment was in agreement on policy, media operated within a *sphere of consensus* and coverage was supportive of the war. When the US establishment became divided over the war, the US media reflected this debate by reporting within the *sphere of legitimate controversy*. However, the US media rarely reported upon those with views outside the boundary of *legitimate controversy* (such as

the anti-war movement) which, according to Hallin, lay within a *sphere of deviance*. As such, media criticism of the Vietnam War remained at a procedural and tactical level, reflecting debate over whether current policy was winning the war, and did not extend to substantive questioning of the legitimacy of US involvement in Vietnam.

Further conceptual clarification of the elite model came with Bennett's influential *indexing hypothesis*. According to Bennett (see Key quotes 10.4), media deference to US elites can be explained through the propensity of journalists to index news coverage to public officials in Washington. In part this is because journalists see it as their democratic responsibility to consult publicly elected officials when reporting the news. But it is also a function of the tremendous quantity of information (press briefings, public statements, etc.) that is produced by US centres of government which helps to feed media demands for a constant flow of news stories. Perhaps most significantly, Bennett notes that the indexing norm helps to keep 'news compatible with the shifting political and economic interests of the state' (Bennett 1990: 109).

Overall, the net result of the close proximity between US mainstream media and the foreign policy establishment is, according to elite perspectives, that the US public is rarely presented with news information that does anything other than 'manufacture consent' (Lippman 1922; Herman and Chomsky 1988), via processes such as *agenda setting* and *framing*, for

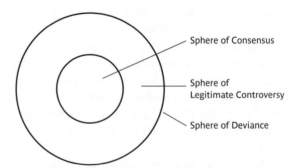

Fig. 10.1 Spheres of consensus, controversy, and deviance. *Source*: By permission of Oxford University Press Inc. Originally published in Daniel C. Hallin (1986), *The Uncensored War: The Media and Vietnam* (New York: Oxford University Press), 117.

KEY QUOTES 10.4: Lance Bennett and indexing

In this ironic twist on the democratic ideal, modern public opinion can be thought of as an 'index' constructed from the distribution of dominant institutional voices as recorded in the mass media. By adopting such an opinion index, the media have helped create a political world that is, cul-turally speaking, upside down. It is a world in which governments are able to define their own publics and where 'democracy' becomes whatever the government ends up doing.

(Bennett 1990)

 CONTROVERSIES 10.1: Herman and Chomsky's (1988) propaganda model

In *Manufacturing Consent: The Political Economy of the Mass Media*, Herman and Chomsky set out their propaganda model, which describes how mainstream US media function as a tool to mobilize public support for elite policy preferences (see Key quotes 10.5). According to this model, five filters function to shape news media output. First, the 'size, ownership and profit orientation of mass media' and their shared 'common interests . . . with other major corporations, banks, and government' create a clash of interest between the media's supposed role as a watchdog of the elite and the interests of that elite (Herman and Chomsky 1988: 3, 14). Consequently, news stories that run contrary to those vested interests are less likely to surface than those consistent with the world view of major corporate conglomerates. Second, media reliance on advertising revenue introduces a further constraining link between the news media and the interests of commerce. This reliance shapes media output in order to appeal to affluent audiences, in whom the advertisers are most interested. It also limits the amount of critical and controversial programming because advertisers generally want 'to avoid programs with serious complexities and disturbing controversies that interfere with the "buying mood"' (Herman and Chomsky 1988: 17). Third, journalists rely heavily on official sources when constructing the news. The need to supply a steady and rapid flow of 'important' news stories combined with the vast public relations apparatus of government and powerful interests more broadly means that journalists tend to become heavily reliant on public officials and corporate representatives when defining and framing the news agenda. Fourth, whenever controversial material is actually aired it generates a disproportionate degree of 'flak' from individuals connected with powerful interests, including 'corporate community

sponsored . . . institutions' (Herman and Chomsky 1988: 27) such as the Center for Media and Public Affairs, Accuracy in Media (AIM) and government 'spin doctors'. Such criticism serves to caution editors and journalists against putting out news stories that are 'too' controversial. Finally, Herman and Chomsky highlight the importance of an ideology of 'anti-communism as a control mechanism' that provided journalists, at least during the Cold War, with a ready-made template with which to 'understand' global events, and provided the political elite with a powerful rhetorical tool with which to criticize as unpatriotic anyone who questioned US foreign policy (Herman and Chomsky 1988: 29). At the core of the critique developed by Herman and Chomsky (1988) is the claim that mainstream US media perpetuate an image of the United States as inherently benign, peaceful, and committed to high moral standards when, in fact, its foreign policies are riddled with self-interested economic and political objectives that often lead the USA to support violent and illiberal policies. As such, US media are not free and autonomous but, rather, mobilize—through deception—US citizens in support of the actions of their government. For instance, in support of their case, Herman and Chomsky (1988) document how US media functioned to promote anti-communism by highlighting human rights abuses committed by communist states and downplaying similar abuses committed by allies of the United States during the 'struggle against communism'. Overall, Herman and Chomsky present a profound and forcefully argued thesis that raises fundamental questions about the democratic credentials of US society and politics.

For discussions sympathetic to the propaganda model see Herring and Robinson (2003). For critical discussion of the propaganda model see Lang and Lang (2004).

> **KEY QUOTES 10.5:** Edward Herman and Noam Chomsky on manufacturing consent

The mass media serve as a system for communicating messages and symbols to the general populace. It is their function to amuse, entertain, and inform, and to inculcate individuals with the values, beliefs, and codes of behaviour that will integrate them into the institutional structures of the larger society. In a world of concentrated wealth and major conflicts of class interest, to fulfil this role requires systematic propaganda.

(Herman and Chomsky 1988)

policy-making preferences that are decided in Washington. Even when the news *appears* to be critical and adversarial, it is kept within the bounds of elite-legitimized controversy. As Bennett describes: 'the media have helped create a world that is, culturally speaking, upside down. It is a world in which governments are able to define their own public and where "democracy" becomes whatever the government ends up doing' (Bennett 1990: 125). Of course, for realists, this state of affairs is to be welcomed as it ensures that foreign policy remains debated and decided by those who have the skills to do so. From this perspective, a compliant and therefore supportive public and media become a source of power for US foreign policy, with media helping to mobilize the US public in support of US foreign policy objectives. From the critical perspective, this state of affairs is to be challenged as an affront to the democratic principles of the United States and its claimed commitment to human rights and justice (see Controversies 10.1).

Criticisms of the elite model

The empirical claims put forward by advocates of the elite model are subjected to five main criticisms. First, that they overemphasize the idea that political and economic structures limit the autonomy and agency of both journalists and the US public. Here, the argument is advanced that journalists and citizens actually have a good deal of independence from political and economic power, and are capable of forming opinions that are distinct from the viewpoints of elite groups. Associated with this is a second criticism, based upon audience reception studies, that individuals have been shown to be capable of resisting dominant messages and frames promoted by political elites. For example, whilst US elites, and indeed media, promoted the value of the Vietnam War, some claim that significant sections of the US public rejected the legitimacy of the action throughout the war. Third, elite accounts are criticized for exaggerating both the level of agreement and the consistency of shared interests that exists between elite groups in society. Here, the idea is advanced that, in reality, there are divergent interests between, for example, US government and big business, which means that elite groups as a whole are far weaker than implied by the elite model, often 'fighting' amongst themselves and rarely succeeding in promoting a unified dominant message to media and public. Fourth, the elite model is also sometimes criticized for treating 'the media' as a unified and monolithic entity, effectively acting as a well-honed propaganda wing of the US state when, in fact, there is a good deal of diversity across different US media outlets. Finally, the elite model is sometimes criticized for failing to pay attention to circumstances where elite influence might be disrupted and spaces opened up for a more critical and independent media. For example Regina Lawrence (2000) argues that unexpected and newsworthy events that occur beyond the control of government can lead to opportunities for previously marginalized, non-elite, groups to influenced media reporting (see Box 10.2).

BOX 10.2: Beyond the elite/pluralist dichotomy: new approaches to theorizing the public opinion/media/ foreign policy nexus

Whilst elite and pluralist perspectives continue to influence academic debate, recent research has attempted to develop models that capture both these theoretical perspectives and, therefore, provide a more nuanced and differentiated understanding of media–state relations. For example, many academics now argue that both elite dissensus (Hallin 1986) (when there exists disagreement within the political and foreign policy establishment) and unexpected events (Lawrence 2000) that occur beyond the control of governments can considerably open up the boundaries of media criticism and influence. So, for example, during the build-up to and the invasion of Iraq in 2003, debate occurred amongst politicians and within the foreign policy community in the UK over the justification for the war. As a consequence, media coverage was more critical and perhaps influential in terms of shaping public and elite perceptions of the war (see, for example, Robinson et al. (2010)). At the same time, unexpected or uncontrolled events (such as the abuse of Iraqis by coalition forces) that spread through the world's media meant that the UK and US governments were subjected to varying levels of criticism and dissent from their respective domestic medias. Other recent accounts that attempt to bridge the elite/pluralist divide include Wolfsfeld's (1997) *political contest model*

and Robinson's (2002) *policy-media interaction model*. These models emphasize variables such as levels of policy certainty (Robinson 2002) and control over the political environment (Wolfsfeld 1997). For example, when a government is uncertain over policy, media and public opinion can exert greater influence on policy formulation. Alternatively, when policy is set in place, the potential for media influence wanes. Wolfsfeld argues that sometimes a government can lose control of the political environment, which in turn leads to a more critical media and space for non-elite challenges. He demonstrates how the Israeli government lost control over the political environment during the 1987 Palestinian uprising, the *intifada*; as a consequence media mobilized support for the Palestinians and criticized Israeli policy (see Key quotes 10.6). And finally, Baum and Groeling present a novel theoretical work in their work *War Stories* (2010) in which the elites are understood to dominate the media and public environment during the early stages of a war, but that overtime elite discord and the reality on the ground (casualties and costs of war) endow media and publics with greater autonomy from, and power over, a US government and its war policy. In short, the applicability of the elite and pluralist models varies across time and circumstance.

❝ **KEY QUOTES 10.6: Gadi Wolfsfeld and political contest**

The competition between authorities and challengers over the news media is as fascinating and unpredictable as politics itself. In some ways the central arena resembles the modern sports facility that can be converted into several structures, each designed for a different type of event. Sometimes the arena is used for lavish spectacles in which officials show off

their most colourful costumes and weapons. At other times it is a place for fierce contests in which challengers and authorities square off in brutal combat. And at yet other times it becomes a theatre-in-the-round putting on tragic morality plays about the plight of the oppressed and the need for social change.

(Wolfsfeld 1997)

KEY POINTS

❑ The realist perspective argues that media and public opinion should not influence foreign policy.

❑ Critical accounts argue that the failure of media and public opinion to influence foreign policy is wrong.

❑ The elite model argues that the public are ignorant of international affairs and have little influence.

❑ The elite model argues that media mobilize support for government policies.

Public and media diplomacy

Thus far, the focus of this chapter has been the relationship between foreign policy, media, and public opinion with respect to the United States and domestic politics. An important area of research, however, has analysed the ways in which the US government attempts to project power and influence by both influencing non-US public opinion, or world opinion, and shaping the news agendas of non-US media. At the heart of these policies lies the concept of *soft power* (Nye 1990), a term that refers to non-coercive (and non-military) approaches to projecting US power and influence in the world. At this point in time, with the continuing global war on terror and the desire to 'win hearts and minds', particularly amongst non-Western and Muslim audiences, the role of public and media diplomacy is perhaps more central than ever to US foreign policy. Indeed, the current Obama administration has set out to work hard at better communicating US viewpoints to global audiences, both to improve support for US supply and to rectify some of the perceived deficits arising from controversies surrounding the Bush administration, including the war in Iraq, Guantanamo Bay, and Abu Ghraib.

Public diplomacy has a long history. For example, *Voice of America* first started radio broadcasts in 1942 aimed at promoting democracy and, in time, came to be broadcast in forty-five languages with over 100 million listeners worldwide (Gilboa 1998: 58). Again, in 1953, the United States Information Agency was created in order to 'coordinate the combat against the spread of communist ideas' (Taylor 2006: 5). Overall the aim of public diplomacy has been to attempt to influence the citizens of foreign nations in ways conducive to US interests so that they can in turn influence their respective governments accordingly. As Gilboa (1998: 58–67) describes, public diplomacy (conducted through both

media and other fields, including cultural and educational initiatives) has been aimed at long-term influence of target audiences around the world, functioning very much at an ideological level by both promoting US values (such as democracy, human rights, and capitalism) and attempting to persuade peoples of the world that the USA is the leading example of such values. Media diplomacy, conversely, has been more narrowly focused upon both promoting US interests *vis-à-vis* specific issues, such as peace initiatives, and attempting to promote a US agenda throughout the world's media. More recently, the intensity and resources committed to these aspects of US diplomacy have increasingly adopted the style and approach of the marketing industry, whereby policies are packaged and sold as if they were commercial products. For example, following the toppling of Saddam Hussein's regime in 2003, President George Bush alighted upon a US aircraft carrier against a banner that read 'Mission Accomplished': it is likely that the event was carefully crafted so as to produce images that offered a symbol of success to the America public and send a powerful signal *vis-à-vis* US military prowess to the governments and peoples of the world.

The belief amongst many is that the development of political marketing (or spin as it is commonly described) techniques is a central tool in promoting US interests in today's world of global media. Moreover, the prevalent belief by those involved with public and media diplomacy is that, so long as the message is correctly packaged and communicated, the USA can indeed project power through winning the hearts and minds of world opinion. The extent to which this is true, given the rise of non-US-based global media such as the Arab-based Al-Jazeera and the nature of the current war on terror, is a question to which we now turn.

KEY POINTS

❑ *Soft power* refers to the power to influence international affairs via persuasion.

❑ The US government devotes considerable resources to the projection of soft power.

❑ Soft power is projected through the promotion of US culture and values, in part, to non-US publics and the global media.

Conclusion: new technology and US power

Pluralist and elite models of the public opinion/ media/foreign policy nexus, and attendant liberal, realist, and critical debates, continue to dominate academic discussion. However, recent debate has increasingly revolved around new developments in communication technology and both their potential and actual impact upon these existing theoretical frameworks and debates. In this closing section, I set out the key features of this debate, which are, principally: (1) the extent to which developments in communication technology have empowered US public opinion and media, and (2) the impact of these technological developments on global US power and influence, in particular in the context of the current war on terror.

The rise of the internet and global media

On the one hand, the proliferation of new communication technology, such as portable satellite broadcasting equipment and the emergence of digital cameras contained within mobile phones, appears to create a degree of transparency of events around the world that is unprecedented. Potentially, any event can be captured on 'camera' and that information then passed around the world instantaneously via the internet or global media. In addition, the rise of global media, such as CNN and now the Arab-based network Al-Jazeera as well as the internet, means that such images (and their story) can be communicated both to US citizens and to the peoples of the world. Received wisdom claims that such developments have a radically pluralizing effect by bringing information and news to people quicker and, in turn, creating greater difficulty for the US government in influencing (or manipulating) news agendas. The recent and ongoing controversy over the *Wikileaks* website, which has disseminated online large quantities of secret US government documents regarding the wars in Iraq and Afghanistan, as well diplomatic cables, epitomizes the apparently limited capacity the US government has to control information flows in the internet era.

These developments offer, at first glance, evidence to suggest that the pluralist model has greater validity today. That is to say, developments in communication technology have indeed increased the independence, and therefore power, of the US media and public. Following on from this, the elite model is less valid and cogent, as the US government has found it harder to direct news agendas and to mould US public opinion. For realists, who advocate elite control of foreign affairs, this is a worrying and perhaps catastrophic development which means that the ability of the USA to protect and promote its interests is being undermined by increased media and public criticism of US foreign policy. From the liberal-democratic perspective, these developments could be seen as potentially positive in terms of strengthening the quality and quantity of both public and media input into the foreign policy-making process. And yet, even liberal US scholars often appear to believe that perhaps too much power and influence has been handed over to the US media and public (see Key quotes 10.7). Overall, if the thesis that developments in communication technology have indeed transformed the US public sphere is correct, then a question can be raised as to the ability of US foreign policy elites to both communicate important issues to the US public and maintain support for US foreign policy (the realist position). As we shall see next, current evidence suggests that claims of a transformation in the US public sphere are exaggerated, and that it is important to differentiate between domestic US audiences and global audiences.

In fact, the argument that US public/media/foreign policy relations have been significantly pluralized is very much open to challenge (Domke 2004; Bennett, Lawrence, and Livingston 2006; Livingston and Bennett 2003). Since 9/11, and the emergence of the war on terror as the primary framework within which US foreign policy is formulated, US media and public opinion have been remarkably supportive of the US executive. For example, during the run-up to the 2003 invasion of Iraq, the US government was apparently successful at persuading most of the US media and public of the relationship between Saddam Hussein's regime and al-Qaeda (even though the majority

> **KEY QUOTES 10.7:** Joseph Nye on the impact of new communication technology

The free flow of broadcast information in open societies has always had an impact on public opinion and the formulation of foreign policy. But now the flow has increased in volume and shortened news cycles . . . The so-called CNN effect makes it hard to keep items that might otherwise warrant a lower priority off the public agenda. Now, with the added interactivity of groups on the Internet, it will be harder than ever to maintain a consistent agenda.

(Nye 1999)

of expert opinion challenged such a link). Again, in what could be seen as a public relations disaster for the Bush administration, the dreadful images of Iraqi prisoners detained by the US military at Abu Ghraib in Iraq were, according to recent research (Bennett, Lawrence, and Livingston 2006), in fact reported in a manner conducive to the official White House line. This was done by the US media echoing the White House line that the events represented abuses by a few soldiers rather than the result of a policy of torture. Finally, whilst public opposition to, and media criticism of, the wars in Iraq and Afghanistan has escalated as the number of US casualties has increased, the jury is still out as to the extent to which this has reflected the increasing elite dissensus over the course of the war that has emerged across both the Republican and Democrat divide. Overall, the question of whether traditional patterns of media–public opinion–state relations really have been dramatically transformed, and in doing so reduced the ability of US elites to coordinate US foreign policy in the war on terror, is very much open to contestation.

Less contentious, however, is the impact of technological developments in terms of global media and public opinion. Here, the USA has arguably suffered a public relations or propaganda disaster certainly in terms of winning 'hearts and minds' in the war on terror. In part this is due to the 'problems' surrounding the invasion of Iraq in 2003 and the diplomatic crises that have emerged as the Bush administration attempted, unsuccessfully, to persuade governments and global public opinion of the legitimacy of their actions. The material fact that the aftermath of the toppling of Saddam Hussein has not led to a peaceful, democratic, and flourishing Iraq has increased hostility and resentment

toward the USA.[2] As noted above, the current Obama administration is working hard to improve the image of the US around the world. At the same time, US public diplomacy and media diplomacy are significantly challenged by the rise of new global media such as Al-Jazeera, which effectively limit the degree to which the USA can influence broader global opinions. Put quite simply, non-Western audiences will access news sources that are largely independent of the influence of Western governments. Moreover, the internet further compromises influence over global communication flows and, for example again, the infamous images from Abu Ghraib flow freely through the internet and world media who, unlike the US media, will often use such images without qualification with the White House line.

Overall, transformations in the global information environment of today mean that there is a significant shift in the balance of soft power, which poses a direct challenge to the ability of the USA to project power internationally. Perhaps of greater importance is the fact that, as I have discussed, at the domestic level media and public debate tends to remain limited to a procedural level, rarely questions the fundamentals of US foreign policy, and significant capability lies with US foreign policy elites in terms of leading public and media debate. And yet opinion outside the US domestic public sphere (i.e. global public opinion within the global public sphere) is increasingly disillusioned, in particular with America's war on terror. Whether or not these two increasingly isolated public spheres can be bridged, especially in a time when US public and media diplomacy are compromised by the emerging forms of media, and mainstream US media is reluctant to facilitate debate beyond the procedural level, remains to be seen.

? Questions

1. What influence, if any, does the US public have on foreign policy formulation?
2. In what ways, and to what extent, can media influence public opinion?
3. Assess the relative cogency of elite and pluralist models of media–state relations.
4. To what extent do you agree with the realist perspective on media and public opinion?
5. To what extent do you agree with the liberal-democratic perspective on media and public opinion?
6. Critical accounts argue that US mainstream media and public opinion are manipulated by elite interests. To what extent do you agree?
7. What impact has new technology had on the public opinion/media/foreign policy nexus in the USA?
8. To what extent *should* public opinion and media shape US foreign policy?

» Further Reading

Baum, M.A. and Groeling, T.J. (2010), *War Stories: The Causes and Consesquences of Public Views of War* (Princeton and Oxford: Princeton University Press).

A sophisticated and up-to-date analysis of the complex relationship between media, public opinion, and US elites during war.

Entman, R. (2004), *Projections of Power: Framing News, Public Opinion and US Foreign Policy* (Chicago: University of Chicago Press).

Comprehensive introduction to the concept of framing, detailing its impact upon both public and foreign policy.

Herman, E. and Chomsky, N. (1988), *Manufacturing Consent: The Political Economy of the Mass Media* (New York: Pantheon).

Provocative and widely read example of the elite model, arguing that US media function to mobilize support for elite interests.

Robinson, P. (2002), *The CNN Effect: The Myth of News, Foreign Policy and Intervention* (London: Routledge).

Provides a contemporary theoretical and empirical analysis of the CNN effect debate, highlighting the contrasting roles media can play in policy formulation.

Wolfsfeld, G. (1997), *The Media and Political Conflict* (Cambridge: Cambridge University Press).

A rich and nuanced analysis of how media can come to act as champions for non-elite groups, and how at other times media serve the interests of governments.

Endnotes

1. For opinion poll data on US belief in an al-Qaeda–Hussein link see Milbank and Deane (2003).
2. For extensive information on changing international attitudes toward the USA, see the Pew Global Attitudes Project, http://pewglobal.org/.

 For a range of additional resources to support your learning visit the Online Resource Centre that accompanies this book at www.oxfordtextbooks.co.uk/orc/cox_stokes2e/.

11 Identities and US foreign policy

Christina Rowley and Jutta Weldes

Chapter contents

Introduction

Conventional (e.g. realist) explanations of foreign policy invoke national (i.e. state) interests as the primary factor driving US foreign policy. In contrast, this chapter examines the central role of identity in *constructing* US foreign policy. It adopts a critical social constructivist approach and argues that particular conceptions of US identity constitute US interests, thus providing the foundations for US foreign policy. After introducing central analytical concepts, the chapter examines US presidents' articulations of US state identity and US foreign policy over the last 60 years.

On 20 September 2001, in discussing the attacks on New York and the Pentagon, US President George W. Bush (2001c) raised the question of US identity—of who or what 'the US' is—asking 'Why do they hate us?'[1] Couched in terms of 'us' ('Americans') and 'them' ('terrorists'), this question places identity at the centre of US foreign policy. Bush's answer is also about US identity: '[t]hey hate what they see right here in this chamber—a democratically elected government.... They hate ... our freedom of religion, our freedom of speech, our freedom to vote and assemble and disagree with each other.' 'They'—'terrorists', 'murderers', 'enemies of freedom'— hate 'us' for who 'we' are. Bush's narrative highlights the importance of identity to US foreign policy. To illustrate what we mean by identity, we begin with three exercises.

Exercise 1: If you had to describe yourself, what would you say? Would you mention your gender, religion, ethnicity, social class, fashion sense, favourite food, or film genre? Would your answers be the same if you were talking to a prospective employer, an elderly neighbour, a blind date? If not, how might they differ? How might your answers change over the course of your life?

Exercise 2: Think about the country in which you live. How would you describe its 'national' identity? Which features do you think are characteristic, or important? What words, concepts, images, and sounds do you associate with it?

Our identities constitute our sense of selves: who we are, how we think and act. This is true of individual and collective identities. We feel a sense of belonging with fans of 'our' football team or with others who enjoy the same music. We join churches or political parties. Often we feel that we share a 'history in common' with people of the same nationality, and people often generalize about 'national character', of both their own and others' states. Benedict Anderson (1991) has referred to nations as 'imagined communities'. Nationalists often claim that nations (should and do) share a certain degree of homogeneity (sameness).

Exercise 3: Think about 'the other', someone seemingly very unlike yourself or people in your country. What do they look like? What are they like? (Think about your answers to previous exercises.) Where does this image of 'the other' come from? From meeting such people? School? Talking with family and friends? News media, films, the internet?

As we discuss below, the self is never constituted solely in relation to itself. Rather, it is always constituted in relation to others. Self and other are relational terms. Sometimes these relations are oppositional, like 'democratic' versus 'totalitarian' or 'freedom loving' versus 'terrorist'; sometimes they are complementary, like 'us' and 'our allies' or 'our friends'. In all cases, these relations underpin individual, state, and other collective identities.

Interests and US foreign policy

The concept of interest—preferences held by individual or collective actors—has been central to explanations of state action in general and of US foreign policy in particular because 'interest' is thought to capture the motives that drive states to act. Accounts citing interests as an explanatory factor in foreign policy analysis vary widely.[2] We briefly examine the most prominent one as a counterpoint to our focus on identity.

States' interests—incorrectly labelled 'national interests'[3]—are central to a theoretical approach called political realism. Realism prides itself on addressing hard truths of power and (in)security in world politics. In realist accounts, international politics differ from domestic politics primarily in their anarchic character. Anarchy—the absence of suprastate authority—places states in a security dilemma (Herz 1951): an inevitable, perpetual, and potentially deadly competition for survival. The most fundamental interest of any state is thus always to protect its sovereignty—independence and decision-making authority—and its territoriality—physical control over its territory—against encroachments from other states.

On this view, a state rationally and objectively assesses the threats it faces. Because power supplies the means for states to protect sovereignty and territoriality in a world in which other states are actual or potential threats, decision makers and analysts must realistically assess power relations in order to determine their interests. Every state, in short, must pursue its national interest 'defined in terms of power' (Morgenthau 1993: 5). Through the need for sovereignty and territoriality, 'interest' connects the nature of world politics—anarchy and the ubiquitous search for power and security—with states' policies and actions.

The concept of a rational actor is a key assumption of interest-based explanations. A rational actor can be a state, an organization, or an individual, which ranks its interests and preferences in order of priority and calculates costs and benefits in order to maximize its outcomes for the least effort. The central problem with interest-based explanations is that they treat interests as exogenous—as pre-determined, given, and external to the explanation being offered. In realism, the basic interest in preserving sovereignty and territoriality is determined by the anarchic nature of the international sphere. Interests are assumed to be obvious—they follow from external, objectively identifiable threats and are thus directly accessible to policy makers and analysts alike, who behave as rational actors when assessing these threats and deciding on appropriate courses of action.

The difficulty with this assumption is that objects and events do not present themselves transparently to observers, however 'realistic' they may be. Rather than being self-evident, threats, states' interests, and possibilities for action are fundamentally matters of *interpretation*. For example, it is not the physical fact that nuclear weapons can pulverize whole cities that makes them

> **KEY POINTS**
>
> ❑ Realists assume that states are the central actors in world politics and that states' interests are determined by the objective threats states face.
> ❑ Interest-based explanations assume rational actors with predetermined interests.
> ❑ Threats and problems facing states are products of interpretations. Interests are also products of interpretation.

threats to US security. US and British nuclear weapons are not seen as threats. Only when such weapons are interpreted as dangerous—e.g. because they are wielded by 'communists' or 'rogue states'—do they become threats, and only then does it become in the US 'interest' to prevent their development or seek their removal.

Critical social constructivism

Rather than taking interests as exogenously given, critical social constructivism understands interests as constituted in relation to identity. Critical constructivism foregrounds the role of identity in the construction of state interests and thus of state action. This approach has three central analytical commitments: (1) reality is socially constructed, (2) constructions entail naturalized power relations, and (3) naturalized power relations can and should be denaturalized (Weldes et al. 1999: 13–21). We discuss these commitments as the theoretical framework for introducing discourse and the role of processes of articulation and representation in constituting identity. We then discuss the conceptualization of identity in more detail, briefly consider possible data sources for investigating state identity, and highlight the importance of insecurity, threats, and crises to the (re)production of state identity/identities.

The social construction of reality

Critical social constructivism assumes that reality is socially constructed. All 'things'—states, subjects, objects, feelings, interests, processes, practices, relationships—

only come to have meaning through the linguistic, visual, and other symbolic signifiers—words, photographs, sounds, signposts, musical notes—that we use to describe, represent, and understand these things (Hall 1997a: 1; Shapiro 1986: 193). As Terrell Carver puts it, 'we use language to inscribe meanings into the world—whether into or onto objects, or experiences—and then we read those meanings back to ourselves as if they had always resided in the objects or experiences' (2002: 50).

This means that the world is constituted (constructed) through meaningful practices and that people act on the basis of the meanings that 'things' have for them. These meanings are fundamentally cultural: they are made possible by discourses—systems of meaning production (see below)—which provide the categories through which the world is understood. There is no universal or objective 'view from nowhere' from which we can understand the world. We are always already situated within (many) different discourses. Meaning is a social phenomenon: meaning resides in the practices and categories through which people engage with each other and with the world.

> ### ❝ KEY QUOTES 11.1
>
> [I]nsecurities, rather than being natural facts, are social and cultural productions . . . insecurity is itself the product of processes of identity construction in which the self and the other, or multiple others, are constituted. . . . The constitution of identities is often a reciprocal process. As each subject seeks to perform its identity, it threatens others, whose identities are consolidated in response.
>
> (Weldes et al. 1999: 10, 15)
>
> '[A]bsolute' objectivity—*no* interference from value-laden subjectivity—is an incoherent claim. To make a *meaningful* claim, one is always already in a value-laden (intersubjective) context that necessarily includes power relations. The relationship between knowledge and power becomes central—and political.
>
> (Peterson 2003: 28, emphasis in the original)

One such discursively constituted category is 'terrorist'. Rather than being self-evident, a 'terrorist' must be discursively constructed as such. While much twentieth-century US discourse constituted the Irish Republican Army (IRA) as patriotic nationalists valiantly fighting a foreign (British) occupation, British state and media discourse constituted the IRA as terrorists. These two discourses constituted the same object differently. Similarly, George W. Bush's statements in the war on terror constitute the US as rational, as an innocent victim of Islamic terrorism, and as fighting a virtuous struggle, while constituting al-Qaeda as murderous and irrational barbarians with whom one cannot do anything except fight (Bush 2005b). Osama bin Laden's statements, on the other hand, construct Muslims as innocent victims of the US's terrorist foreign policy, and the US as murderous and irrational barbarians against whom one can do nothing but fight (Agathangelou and Ling 2004: 521–4).

Discourse

The concept of discourse is essentially open-ended and can be used to refer to a variety of levels and types. There are academic, legal, medical, and cinematic discourses. More narrowly, we might refer to sociological or anthropological discourses within academia, specific genres within cinema, or neo-realist or feminist discourses of world politics. More than one account of US foreign policy can be constructed, depending on what one wishes to highlight. Institutions are often seen as having their 'own' discourses, such that we may talk of World Bank or United Nations discourse(s). At a broader level, we can apply the term to Western philosophy, science, modernism, Islam, or Judaeo-Christianity.

Discourses both enable us to speak/think/imagine and constrain what we can say/think/imagine. First, they enable us to speak/think/imagine at all because they provide the discursively constituted objects and categories that we require to communicate, e.g. physics provides a discourse to understand the constitution of the physical universe. They therefore enable us to make specific statements, e.g. within physics we can talk about 'atoms', 'quarks', and 'strings'. Second, discourses constrain by attempting to fix meaning, e.g. to present their knowledge claims as 'truth' rather than as socially constructed. They therefore render certain statements false or, more importantly, meaningless, e.g. contemporary physics discourse does not permit explanations in terms of 'angels', while a Christian discourse might.

We are always—whether consciously or not—manipulating discourses and representations when we communicate, in order to tell a persuasive story or to find the most accurate or expressive verbs and adjectives. Discourses can also be deployed more instrumentally, however. Spin-doctoring, propaganda, public relations exercises, and speech-writing are examples that occur in the construction of US foreign policy. Nevertheless, a constructivist argument is *not* the claim that all discourse is propaganda because 'truths' and 'falsehoods' are both socially constructed.

Articulation

Articulation refers to the process through which meaning is produced from existing socio-cultural and linguistic resources—the terms, symbols, and ideas that are already present within a culture. Extant linguistic resources are articulated (connected together, discursively linked) to produce representations of the world (Hall 1997a: 1–5). In this way, meaning is created and temporarily fixed, on which action is then based, and justified. Phenomena, whether objects, events, or social relations, come to connote (invoke) one another and are thereby welded into associative chains. '9/11' is an example of articulation, functioning as a kind of cultural 'shorthand' that stands for a series of discursively linked concepts: 'World Trade Center', 'New York', and 'aeroplanes' have been articulated with 'Islamic', 'terrorists', and 'war', as opposed to, say, 'murder', 'crime', and 'police'. The attacks of 11 September 2001 thus appear *inevitably* to require a military response rather than a domestic and/or international policing effort to apprehend the criminals responsible for planning the attacks. Conversely, deaths from road traffic accidents in the US in 2001 exceeded 40,000 (National Highway Traffic Safety Administration 2011) and each year far outnumber the deaths caused by terrorist attacks (which have been minimal since 2001), but road safety is rarely if ever articulated as a national security concern.

With their successful repeated articulation, representations come to seem as though they are inherently or necessarily connected and the meanings they produce as natural and an accurate description of reality. Despite this apparent naturalness, however, the chains of association established are socially constructed and historically contingent rather than logically or structurally necessary. The non-necessary, contingent character of any particular articulation means that these connections can be contested. This contestability has two important consequences. First, it means that specific

> ### KEY POINTS
>
> ❑ Reality is socially constructed: 'things' only have meaning through the signifiers used to represent them.
> ❑ Discourses are systems of meaning production which both constrain and enable what can be said and imagined.
> ❑ Articulation produces meaning by discursively linking symbols and ideas already present within a culture.
> ❑ Articulations are neither natural nor permanent, but dynamic and constantly in need of rearticulation and reinforcement; other articulations are always possible.

articulations are never simply produced 'once and for all'. Instead, to prevent them from becoming unglued, or from being forcibly pried apart, they have always to be reproduced. Second, it means that any articulation can be uncoupled and the resulting component parts rearticulated in different, and perhaps novel, ways. Put simply, alternative representations are always possible.

To the extent that such a rearticulation is successful— i.e. persuasive—the result is a very different description of US foreign policy. If the events of 11 September are contextualized through the decades of interventionist US foreign policy in the third world (Blum 2003), or the US's role in funding and supplying the Israeli state and thus sustaining the occupation of Palestinian territory (Chomsky 2003), or the influence of US foreign policy on Arab states during the Cold War, then 9/11 may appear as 'retaliation', a violent reaction to US foreign policy, not the proverbial 'bolt from the blue' to which US foreign policy is always appearing to respond.

Discourses as productive

Power

Social constructions reflect, produce, and reify— treat as natural—relations of power. Discourses are sites of social power in at least two important ways. First, discourses bring with them the power to define and thus to constitute the world. Such constructions successfully become common sense when they are treated as naturally or transparently reflecting reality. In this way social constructions are naturalized,

and both their constructedness and their specific social origins are obscured. Conversely, anything outside of this common sense is rejected as implausible, 'ideological',[4] or spurious. When US discourse successfully articulates the IRA as patriotic nationalists fighting a passé European empire, funding them makes sense—despite the 'special relationship' between the US and the UK—and condemning them as 'terrorists' becomes unintelligible and thus unsustainable.

Likewise, articulating al-Qaeda or Iraqi insurgents as irrational Islamic fanatics who simply hate 'American' freedoms creates a situation in which military force is appropriate and necessary. In contrast, articulating them as rational Arab militants who use 'weapons of the weak' (Scott 1987) in order to oppose US foreign policy and make intelligible political demands—e.g. withdrawal of US military forces from Iraq and Saudi Arabia, and of Israeli forces and settlers from Palestinian territory in the West Bank (Barkawi 2004)—would reconfigure them as political actors with whom one could (and should) potentially negotiate.

Second, some discourses are more powerful than others because they partake of institutional power. Certain elites, or powerful institutional actors, play privileged roles in the production and reproduction of discursive constructions. State foreign policy discourses are a prominent example. State officials' representations have immediate prima facie plausibility because these officials are themselves constructed as speaking for 'us' and 'our state'. They have legitimacy, especially in the construction of foreign policy, because the national interest is understood to be quintessentially the business of the state and the identification of threats to state interests is thus a task rightly belonging to its officials. US presidents are, in this sense, the US's interpreters-in-chief (Stuckey 1991). Dominant discourses, like those of the state, become and remain dominant because of the power relations sustaining them. When there is little or no challenge to dominant discourses, they become hegemonic—that is, they receive (sometimes passive) assent from most, if not all, of the public.

Identity

One hegemonic discourse in relation to identity is liberal individualism. It is 'common sense' in Western society that each body houses one self-contained individual with a stable and coherent identity. However, identity is a complex concept. Think back to the exercises at the start of this chapter: we listed several subject positions, or 'identity markers': race, class, gender, sexuality, ethnicity, and so on. Although we assume a stable, single, and unitary 'I' when we speak about ourselves, individuals are embedded in many identities; the notion of a singular 'core identity' is in fact a complex interplay of multiple subject positions. Marysia Zalewski (2000: 23) uses apples and onions as

metaphors representing these opposing liberal and constructivist views of identity: an apple has a vital core, but when you peel away the layers of an onion, there is nothing there at the end. For instance, accounts of ourselves as gendered beings look very different from accounts in which we privilege our racial or class identities; no aspect of identity is in principle more 'fundamental' than any other, although, as we note below, aspects of identity are variously salient in different situations. We also tend to assume that identities are only relevant when they deviate from the white, masculine, heterosexual, able-bodied, middle-class norm (Hearn 2004). We thus often act as though only non-white people have ethnic identities and only female bodies are gendered.

Similarly, analysing identity in US (or, indeed, any state's) foreign policy requires undermining the notion that the nation-state is a natural phenomenon or possesses a unitary identity. An immense amount of ideological labour goes into constructing nations/states (Smith 1991) and the notion that the state is 'an' or 'the' actor in international relations (Enloe 1996). Other identities must be marginalized, silenced, or denied: 'America, love it or leave it' is an illustration of how any dissent from dominant US foreign policy discourse is considered 'un-American' or even 'anti-American', despite the belief that free speech is a cornerstone of US identity. Dissent is almost always understood in terms of aiding and abetting terrorists. In the statement 'support our troops', what is denied/silenced is the argument that withdrawing US troops can be understood as a form of support, by removing them from potential danger and terminating an immoral occupation.

Furthermore, identities are not fixed and stable but are constantly in flux, changing as people grow older (as states and nations change over time) and experience new things. Thus interests, which derive from identities, are not fixed, exogenous, or permanently given, but are also dynamic and unstable. US practices at Guantánamo Bay on Cuba provide an excellent example. On the one hand, US identity is constructed as unwaveringly freedom-loving, committed to the rule of law, and opposed to cruel and unusual punishments. On the other hand, when needs be, US identity as providing national security and protecting the innocent US (and other) public overrides its identity as law-abiding, thus allowing its interests to be served by the psychological intimidation and imprisonment of 'terror suspects' without trial. Torture—'enhanced interrogation techniques'—are warranted by the juxtaposition of an irredeemably evil terrorist threat with US leadership in the fight for Western freedoms.

We emphasize different aspects of our identities—perform our identities differently—depending on who or what we are identifying with (and against). The claim that we perform our identities, while sharing some connotations with actors in the theatre, is not exactly the same. Actors consciously choose to perform certain roles, whereas performance of identity is inescapable, occurring all the time, and usually at a much less conscious level. Nor do we have complete control over how we are defined—our identities are also largely constituted for us by others. For example, the US and its allies have the power to construct other state identities: Afghanistan and Somalia thus become 'failed states' (Rotberg 2002), and Iraq and North Korea become 'rogue states', 'rogue regimes' (Klare 1996; Rice 2000), or 'states of concern' (BBC News 2000). The US and the international community, rather than the states themselves, construct such identities for them.

Representation

To represent means to symbolize, to stand for (Hall 1997b: 16); representations can be pictures, models, signs, words. Discourses and discursive articulations manifest themselves—and identity is produced—in concrete representations. However, representation is also a discursive *practice*. Thinking of representation as a practice reminds us that representation only takes place when interpretative labour is being performed. When we generalize about other people or cultures, we represent them in particular ways. We decide that certain features are important and others are less valid or relevant. Generalizations, simplifications, abstractions—all are inherently *political* processes of representation. The generalizations that women in burkas are oppressed and that US women are liberated (Smeeta and Shirazi 2010) are two examples.

Often, representations are woven into narratives. Narratives are basically stories: fairy tales, history, this chapter, the 'good versus evil' storyline articulated by George W. Bush after 9/11 (2001b) are all different types of narrative. Tropes—devices such as figures of speech, metaphors, and analogies—are common representational practices that appear in these narratives. The repeated references, explicit and implicit, to the lessons of Munich 1938 and the dangers of appeasement drawn from the Second World War that can be seen in Cold War and post-Cold War US foreign policy rhetoric are tropes.

BOX 11.1: Strategies of representation

Infantilization

Attributing childlike or immature characteristics and behaviours to individuals or groups (e.g. 'developing' states): 'Filipinos were regarded as precocious children who had assimilated the superficial aspects of US culture but had failed to grasp its more fundamental implications. . . . The ostensibly nurturing relationship invoked by the parent/child opposition obscured and justified practices of domination' (Doty 1996: 88–9).

Feminization

Attributing feminine characteristics to something or someone: '[w]hat is different about [1980s Vietnam war] films and the cultural revisionism that accompanies them is the depiction of the US government as feminine. And it is precisely its femininity that is seen to have caused the loss of the Vietnam War' (Jeffords 1986: 189). *Masculinisation* occurs in similar ways (e.g. Hooper 2001).

Bestialization

Using animal metaphors to describe individuals/groups. President George W. Bush used this strategy in the war on terror (Jackson 2005: 5) when referring to Afghanistani and Iraqi militants as 'parasites' that 'leech' onto 'host' countries (2001d,e, 2002a, 2004) and depicting 'suicide bombers' as '*burrowing* into our society' (2001b [emphasis added], 2006a).

Demonization

Representing someone/something as monstrous or evil: the 'creation of monsters [h]as [been] a continuing feature of American politics' (Rogin 1987: xiii). President Reagan used this strategy in speeches about Nicaragua and the Soviet 'evil empire' in the 1980s (Rogin 1987: p. xv). President George W. Bush's 2002 State of the Union Address on the 'Axis of Evil' (Bush 2002a) articulates a concept from the Second World War ('Axis' powers) with the war on terror.

KEY POINTS

- ❏ Constructions entail naturalized power relations. Constructions successfully become common sense when treated as transparently reflecting reality.
- ❏ Elites play privileged roles in the (re)production of discursive constructions. When there is little or no challenge to dominant discourses, they become hegemonic.

- ❏ Individuals and states are embedded in many identities; the notion of a singular 'core identity' masks a complex interplay of multiple subject positions.
- ❏ Identities are constituted in/through discourse. Discourses manifest themselves in concrete representations.
- ❏ Generalizations, simplifications, and abstractions are inherently political processes of representation.

Just as individuals are assigned gendered identities, gendered characteristics can also be assigned to states, institutions, and concepts. Peterson and Runyan (1999: ch. 2) discuss how stereotypes of men's and women's behaviours, roles, and preferences are organized around binaries that link the concepts male/female, strong/weak, active/passive, rational/emotional, international/domestic, public/private such that, in each binary, the first term is masculine and privileged over the second, feminine term. Shepherd (2006) has demonstrated how articulations of US identity and foreign policy after 11 September were explicitly gendered. US identity was represented as masculine, in contrast to both the aggressive and irrational hyper-masculinity of al-Qaeda and the Taliban, and the feminization of the 'Afghanistani women', who, in needing to be 'saved', provided justification for the intervention. The US masculine self-image, in contrast, as strong, rational, heroic and restrained, was embodied in the fire-fighters and policemen repeatedly photographed assisting 9/11 victims and in authority figures such as George W. Bush and New York Mayor Rudy Giuliani.

Critical social constructivism as critique

Denaturalization

'Critique' is not synonymous with 'criticism' or negativity. Critical social constructivism is expressly 'critical' in that it assumes dominant constructions can, and ought to, be denaturalized. The process of denaturalization seeks to defamiliarize—literally, to make strange—common-sense understandings and so to make their constructedness apparent. Exposing 'what-goes-without-saying' (Barthes 1973: 11) exposes the ideological labour that is required to produce and maintain such meanings. Constructivist approaches examine (among other things) the ways in which discursive representations constitute state identity and thus interests and actions. This leads, in turn, to uncovering possibilities for the transformation of common sense and facilitates the imagining of alternative worlds and ways of being.

It ought to be emphasized that discourses are not 'merely' rhetoric', nor is critiquing them about 'political correctness'. 'Rhetoric' is sometimes used to mean ornamental or strategic language deliberately designed to persuade, rather than to describe reality. In contrast, a constructivist approach is committed to the view that *all* language is rhetorical—all language use is designed to persuade. Since language thus does not transparently reflect the world, the linguistic constructions we use *matter* (Weldes 1999a: 117). 'Political correctness' is usually invoked in order to imply that language is unimportant. However, language is the medium through which we think and act. Thus, linguistic constructions are not merely a veneer, and critiquing these representations does not mean stating that they are false.[5]

The idea that social 'facts'—identities like 'terrorist' and 'freedom fighter'—are constituted in discursive representations implies neither artificiality nor dispensability (Griffin 2007: 227). Constructions are not 'false', nor can we do without them because we cannot escape discourse. Social facts exist only within wider discourses and through power relations and, importantly, they can be transformed. For example, the UK state made considerable, partially successful, efforts to transform US discourse about the IRA in order to undercut its moral and financial support amongst the US public. Similarly, soon after taking office, UK Prime Minister Gordon Brown announced a shift in UK foreign policy, declaring that the UK would no longer pursue a 'war on terror' but would instead treat terrorism as a criminal issue (*The Independent* 2007).

Elite discourse and popular culture

What data sources[6] are best for finding and analysing the identity/identities that drive US foreign policy? Most analysts turn immediately to the statements and actions of states or, more accurately, the decision makers who act in their name. Governmental representations of US identity and interests are contained in formal policy documents such as the US *National Security Strategy* (The White House 2010), speeches and other statements by decision makers, congressional hearings, government reports, and the like. Elite representations generally provide the dominant interpretation of US identity and interests. Data abounds in other elite sources, including the news media—newspapers, television news, magazines—which both reproduce and occasionally contest these official discourses, particularly in times of controversy and crisis (Hallin 1989; Herman and Chomsky 1988).

> ### KEY POINTS
>
> ❑ Naturalized power relations can and should be denaturalized.
> ❑ Claiming that the world is socially constructed does not mean it is false or that the world does not exist.
> ❑ The social construction of reality means that although the world exists independently of our knowledge of it, we cannot access this knowledge except through discourse(s).
> ❑ Critiquing discourses is not about political correctness; language is not 'merely rhetoric'. Language matters because it is the primary medium through which we make sense of the world.
> ❑ Representations of identity and foreign policy can be investigated using official/elite and popular cultural discourses, among others.

Often neglected in foreign policy analysis, but central to the discursive constitution of state identity, is popular culture, as Box 11.2 shows.[7] Representations in popular culture, *precisely because* they are treated as 'just entertainment', contribute to the background knowledge through which people understand state identities and foreign policy. When policy makers want to persuade the public of the validity or importance of a particular foreign policy decision or action, they construct their arguments from the cultural resources already present in society. These understandings 'are produced not only in state officials' rhetoric but also, and more pervasively, in the mundane cultures of people's everyday experiences'. This implicates popular culture in the manufacture of consent for states' foreign policies (Weldes 1999b: 119). Conversely, in order to be plausible, popular cultural texts also need to resonate with people's prior expectations about the real world.

Identity in US foreign policy

US identity and the Cold War

In the dominant US foreign policy narrative, the bipolar Cold War conflict—intense rivalry between the two superpowers—is understood as a global struggle: the USSR vs. the USA, 'East' vs. 'West', 'communism' vs. 'the free world', 'totalitarianism' vs. 'democracy'. During the Cold War, US foreign policy was framed by the grand strategy of containment (Gaddis 1982): the US led 'the free world' in preventing Soviet/communist expansion

---

BOX 11.2: Articulations of US identity in popular culture

Reader's Digest (1922–)

Reader's Digest, the largest-circulation general-interest Cold War-era US magazine, 'might offer the single most important voice in the creation of popular geopolitics in America in the twentieth century' (Sharp 2000: ix). It created an imagined geography of the world and the US place therein by creating, and then naturalizing, representations of 'America' in opposition to the Soviet 'evil empire'. *Reader's Digest* constructed models for people in the US 'of how the world works, of what America could and should do as a major player in this international political geography, and of what the individual American could and should do to help this national mission' (xv).

24 (2001–2010)

24 routinely showed its hero, Jack Bauer, torturing terrorist suspects, a practice justified by *24*'s classic 'ticking time bomb' narrative. In 2006 US Army Brigadier General Patrick Finnegan met with the show's creative team to express concern that the show's 'central political premise—that the letter of US law must be sacrificed for the country's security' influenced West Point cadets to view torture, which is illegal in US law, as both legitimate and efficacious (Mayer 2007).

'Diamonds from Sierra Leone' (2005)

KanYe West articulates the 'bling' culture of US hip hop with both drugs and the illegal smuggling of conflict diamonds out of Sierra Leone: 'Though it's thousands of miles away, Sierra Leone connect to what we go through today, over here [US] it's the drug trade, we die from drugs, over there [Sierra Leone] they die from what we buy from drugs, the diamonds'. He encapsulates how actions seemingly connected only to one's personal identity have international repercussions.

Avatar (2009)

Avatar represents the US/humanity as greedy, exploitative, and militaristic, perpetrating the social and environmental destruction of an alien community in order to secure mineral deposits considered essential to human technological development. Audiences are encouraged to identify with the aliens and empathize with their way of life. However, the Na'vi's victory over the human colonizers, orchestrated by a US marine, perpetuates the old Western myth of white civilization's superiority over native others. Furthermore, victory is ultimately secured through the use of force as a 'last resort', which resonates with US self-conceptions of its foreign policy decisions.

---

into non-communist regions of the world, and in preserving freedom—free markets, free elections, and, later, human rights—through interventions particularly, although not exclusively, in the so-called third world.

However, other stories can be told about the Cold War. In one alternative narrative, on which we focus here, the Cold War was largely an enterprise of US empire, through which US (and Western) neo-imperial relations—that is, domination from a distance through unequal economic exchange rather than through direct colonial administration—were extended to ever larger parts of the world. On this view, the US established an empire in Latin America with the 1823 Monroe Doctrine, broadened it in wars against Spain (1898) in Cuba and in the Philippines (1899–1902), and sought to expand its domination into Europe and elsewhere through a globalizing free trade system, global US military deployments, and a global alliance structure. US empire was driven not by anti-communism, but by

the underlying US drive to establish a capitalist—private property-based—global free market (Cox 1984; Williams 2004).

How does one story—global US intervention in the Cold War to contain communism and preserve freedom—become hegemonic (i.e. accepted as common sense/true) and the other marginalized? In the remainder of this section we provide an introductory discourse analysis[8] of the tropes and narratives of US identity articulated by US presidents to show how these representations continually operate to reinforce and naturalize the state-centric 'freedom' Cold War narrative while marginalizing representations of US imperialism.

Historical parallels and references/analogies to the Second World War are among the most significant representations articulated in US presidential speeches. The Second World War has been constructed as the most noble war ever waged (at least, by the US and its Allies) and 'Munich conditioned the thinking of every Cold War administration from Truman to George H. W. Bush'

(Record 2007: 165). Kennedy (1961) refers to the US having fought for Berlin before; Truman (1950: 610), Kennedy (1962: 67), and Carter (1980) all invoke the clear 'lesson' of history learned from the 1930s and the rise of Nazism. Truman (1950: 610) uses the word 'appeasement' in describing policy alternatives with regard to the Korean conflict. Articulating Cold War events with the Second World War, then, served to legitimize US intervention and provided continuity for the US's role as leader of the 'free world' against all forms of 'totalitarianism'—previously fascist, now communist.[9]

When 'totalitarianism' is invoked, through its association with Nazism, it simultaneously carries with it connotations of 'expansion' and 'aggression'. The main enemy/threat to the US, its allies, and global stability in US Cold War discourse is 'communism', whether embodied in the Soviet Union, in other communist states like China and Cuba, or in an 'international communist conspiracy' guided from the Kremlin. The identity of the communist 'other' is represented as a threat in several ways. For example, Truman (1950: 610) and Carter (1980) emphasize the USSR's massive size in comparison with the small countries it threatens. Eisenhower (1961: 236), Kennedy (1962: 67, 68), and Carter (1980) use words such as 'aggressive' and 'hostile'. The dominant theme, occurring in almost every Cold War speech, is a communist conspiracy based on betrayal and deception (Kennedy 1961; 1962: 68), undertaken by an enemy who violates agreements and whose claims are false (Carter 1980), whose methods are ruthless and insidious (Eisenhower 1961: 236), and whose aims are subversion, infiltration, and world conquest (Truman 1950: 609).

The US is constituted in opposition to this evil and dangerous 'other'. US actions are always represented as benign and defensive, and only ever as *responses* to objective and external (communist) threats; the US is never the aggressor. The predicates (qualities) most commonly articulated with the US are leadership, freedom, strength, and commitment. The US is represented as decisive and united;[10] it has 'courage', 'determination' (Kennedy 1962: 67, 68), shoulders 'responsibilities' (Carter 1980), carries 'burdens', and makes 'sacrifices' (Eisenhower 1961) in order to preserve freedom and fulfil its commitments to protect other (weaker) states. US credibility is based on this role as the world's

policeman: an attack on any state is an attack on the US (Carter 1980; Kennedy 1961; 1962: 67) and nations look to the US for leadership in international affairs (Truman 1947), thus providing a clear moral basis for US intervention. However, the US also works in partnership with other states to defend liberty (Truman 1947; Carter 1980).

Constructing the US as strong, benign, determined, and defending freedom, in contrast to the USSR defined as 'a slave state, duplicitous and secretive, despotic and aggressive' (Laffey and Weldes 2004: 29), creates a warrant for action in US foreign policy. It makes some policies and actions possible, legitimate, and necessary, while rendering others unlikely or even unthinkable. It 'permits the US to engage in certain practices, e.g., "noble causes," and precludes others, e.g., "aggression" or "coercion"' (Doty 1993: 310–12).

These representations enable the US construction of the 1962 Cuban missile crisis as a scenario in which the US defended 'the free world' from Soviet missiles placed in Cuba, which were understood as creating a communist bridgehead in the Americas. From the dominant US perspective it was not possible to understand the missile deployment—as the Cubans and Soviets did—as a legal and internationally acceptable defensive measure taken to protect a small, vulnerable island from sustained US imperial aggression, including the 1961 Bay of Pigs invasion (Weldes 1999a: 21–40).

US identity and the New World Order

The fall of the Berlin Wall and collapse of the USSR signalled the Cold War's abrupt and unexpected demise. The disappearance of the Soviet/communist 'other'/threat and US containment policy's resultant irrelevance triggered a crisis in US identity and foreign policy. As they had after the Second World War, US policy makers understood the international system as fundamentally altered. On 11 September 1990, President George Bush Sr. announced a 'New World Order' that would be free from old Cold War threats and insecurities (1990a: 1219). Multilateralism (working in concert with the international community and international organizations) and humanitarian intervention (the threat or use of military force to prevent human rights violations) were the new US strategy for the New World Order. President Clinton's 1993 speech about the downing of a Black Hawk helicopter in Somalia provides an explicit example.

Alternative narratives continued to construct US foreign policy as imperialist. Post-Cold War foreign policy, on this view, was about the defence and expansion of US empire. The New World Order was a unipolar system—dominated by a single global power—and the US was intent on expanding its political and economic reach into former Soviet and communist bloc areas. The Persian Gulf War (1990–1), for instance, was understood as an imperialist war in which the US sought to maintain Western access to Middle Eastern oil (Chomsky 1991; Said 1991). Through what representational mechanisms did the conventional narrative become hegemonic and the imperial alternative marginalized?

Despite the post-Cold War world being 'quite different', the New World Order is also immediately represented as sharing continuities: 'the world remains a dangerous place' (Bush Sr 1990b: 1092). US foreign policy discourse proliferated threats and insecurities. 'In the post-Soviet era', Les Aspin (then Chairman of the US House Armed Services Committee) argued, 'threats to American security will be broader and more diverse, and the security environment will be murkier, more ambiguous, and more fluid' (1992: 4). Insecurities include residual threats from the USSR/Russia, regional aggressors (Iran, Iraq, Syria, Libya, North Korea, China, and Cuba), the proliferation of nuclear weapons and other weapons of mass destruction, terrorism, hostage-taking, and drug-trafficking, among others. Post-Cold War 'others' are 'renegade regimes and unpredictable rulers', 'rogue states', 'thugs', and 'cynical leaders' full of 'poisonous' 'hatred', who engage in systematic repression, brutality, and mass killing (e.g. Bush 1990b: 1092; Clinton 1993, 1999).

Threats are 'launch[ed]', 'unleash[ed]', and 'arise suddenly, unpredictably, and from unexpected quarters', which 'require' responses and to which 'we all react' (Bush 1990b: 1092; Clinton 1993, 1999). The US is again represented as benign and defensive, acting decisively and effectively, creating security, and saving lives. Unlike Somali men, who starve children, the US distributes food. Unlike Yugoslavia, which oppresses Kosovar Albanians, the US has 'shed racism' and its 'sense of

superiority'. The 'New World Order' is a place where 'freedom and democracy have made great gains', where nations can 'prosper and live in harmony' (Bush 1990a: 1219) and pursue 'economic progress' because the US is doing the 'morally right thing' (Clinton 1999) by protecting freedom.

The US is strong and committed in the face of these threats. Strength is equated with military force, and military intervention is presented as inevitable, as the only way in which threats can be countered. Both Clinton (1999) and Bush Sr. (1990a) refer to international cooperation and shared responsibilities, and Clinton emphasizes that US intervention in Somalia is part of a UN humanitarian mission, but US leadership continues to be presented as natural: 'people are looking to America', to 'American leadership and America's troops', to get the job done (Clinton 1993).

References to the Second World War continue to appear in post-Cold War US foreign policy representations. At a ceremony commemorating Second World War veterans, Clinton (1999) articulates the impending NATO intervention in Kosovo with the Allied struggle against the Nazis. In the 1990–1 Gulf War, representations of Iraq/Saddam Hussein are (as with representations of the USSR during the Cold War) modelled on narratives and tropes about the Nazis/Hitler/the Second World War (Record 2007). However, all history of US and Western imperialism in the Middle East is erased. Through the rhetoric of humanitarian intervention and through discursive articulation with the Second World War and the Cold War, the US continues to construct world politics in such as way that it is authorized to act in defence of freedom, democracy, and human rights. In contrast, the imperialist narrative, in which the US continues to engage in exploitative economic practices, political intervention, and military action in and against other states, is obscured (Blum 2003).

US identity and the war on terror

9/11 was represented as another major rupture in world politics and US foreign policy, creating a new geostrategic reality that directly challenged US identity. In the face of a transnational terrorist threat, Bush articulated a 'war on terror', a(nother) global battle between good and evil, civilization and barbarism. The non-state version of this narrative, focusing on an amorphous network of terrorist organizations and cells, was quickly replaced by a more conventional state-centric narrative, one that manifested itself in the wars in/on Afghanistan and Iraq.

Alternatively, the war on terror can be represented as the further expansion of, and a new guise for, US imperialism. The events of 9/11 provided a tool for the implementation of an imperial US strategy in the twenty-first century, already articulated by the Project for the New American Century (www.newamericancentury.org/; Bennis 2003), in which the Bush administration used 9/11 to legitimize the broadening of US empire as the means for securing long-term global US military and economic supremacy.

Interestingly, this imperial argument is no longer the sole preserve of the left (Hardt and Negri 2000; Ignatieff 2003; Stokes 2005; Layne and Thayer 2007), and is no longer easily dismissed or entirely marginalized. Conservative politicians and commentators have begun to rearticulate the notion of 'American empire' as a fundamentally positive goal of the right (rather than as a critique from the left) and, further, as a necessity in a dangerous world (Boot 2002; Mallaby 2002). 9/11 and the war on terror have brought new and overt support for US empire from policy makers, analysts, and media pundits alike.

In US discourse after September 2001, terrorists, and their allies and sponsors, are claimed to be unlike anything the world has ever seen, forming an irredeemable axis of evil. They are barbaric and brutal, fanatical extremists who operate through totalitarianism, tyranny, and aggression (Bush 2002a,b, 2004, 2005a, 2006b). They are both cowardly and predatory; plotting in secret, running for cover, retreating, hiding; and resorting to propaganda, blackmail, and terror whenever and wherever the opportunity arises (Bush 2001a, 2005b). In their lack of 'regard for conventions of war or rules of morality', they are 'outlaw regimes' (Bush 2003) and the US must, again, respond to this new and unprovoked attack and ongoing threat from a brutal enemy (Bush 2004).

Similar to Cold War and New World Order rhetoric, this threat is posed not just to the US, but to the whole world: the enemy struck at all 'freedom-loving people' (Bush 2001b). US identity is articulated to/conflated with both the 'innocent and unsuspecting' victims of the 9/11 attacks and with 'freedom and democracy'

everywhere. As in previous eras, the US has the 'responsibility' of being the leader of a global coalition fight for freedom, defending itself, its friends, and its allies. The US 'continue[s] to be steadfast', 'patient', 'persistent', 'determined', and 'focused', with strength, commitment, and resolve to pursue its objectives and defeat the terrorists (Bush 2001d,e, 2002a).

Bush also invokes historical parallels, articulating 9/11 with Pearl Harbor (2006a) and the Holocaust (2001e), and the war on terror with the fight against fascism, Nazism, and the Japanese, as well as against communism in the Cold War (2001c, 2002c, 2005a, 2006b). He claims that the terrorists cannot be 'appeased' (2001e, 2005b, 2006a), and the rhetoric of the axis of evil is itself a reference to the Axis powers of Germany, Japan, and Italy in the Second World War.

The pervasive rhetoric of good vs. evil, dark vs. light, civilization vs. barbarism that underpins US policy in the war on terror makes possible both interstate wars in/on Afghanistan and Iraq and the global torture system (manifest in Abu Ghraib and Guantánamo) of disappearances, extraordinary renditions, indefinite incarceration without trial, psychological intimidation and abuse of prisoners, and the undermining of civil rights in the US, all in the name of 'freedom'. The articulation of 'we' the US as 'innocent and unsuspecting' erases the history of US actions in the Middle East, its complicity in the imperial origins of most Middle Eastern states and in repeated military and covert political operations, and its support of Israel against the Palestinians (Kolko 1988).

This rhetoric also serves to construct a 'fundamental' difference between, on the one hand, intentionally targeting civilians in the World Trade Center, a Bali nightclub, or car bombs in Iraqi towns and cities, and, on the other, killing many tens of thousands of civilians as a 'side effect' of security measures in Iraq and Afghanistan. The terrorists' attacks are 'deliberate and deadly', in contrast to Allied-caused deaths, which are merely 'collateral damage'.[11] Crucial to US identity is the notion that these latter deaths are simultaneously unplanned and unavoidable, and that the US is just as morally blameless for these deaths as for those in September 2001.

Within the Bush administration's narrative, 9/11 is constructed as a radical disjuncture in US foreign

KEY POINTS

❏ Constructions of identity in dominant US foreign policy discourse marginalize other interpretations of US identity and foreign policy, such as the US as imperialist and interventionist.

❏ In all three eras analysed, the primary characteristics associated with 'the US' are leadership, freedom, strength, and commitment/determination.

❏ Predicates most commonly attached to the 'other' in Cold War US discourse represent the USSR as totalitarian, aggressive, deceitful, and subversive.

❏ After the Cold War, the dominant threat is articulated as 'rogue states', often through the use of analogies to Hitler/Nazism/the Second World War.

❏ In the war on terror, terrorists are articulated as evil and irrational, while the US continues to be represented as defensive, strong, and committed to defending freedom.

❏ The US's and others' identities interact and constitute discourses of US foreign policy in complex and multifaceted ways.

❏ It too early to tell how Obama administration discourse fits within post-Second World War US foreign policy discourses.

policy. Seen in the context of US imperialism, however, 9/11 represents a continuation of the rhetoric, tropes, and narratives—most prominently, analogies with the Second World War—identifiable in US foreign policy discourses from earlier eras.

We have deliberately omitted a discussion of Barack Obama's rhetoric in the discourse analysis provided above. We have done so because it remains too early to tell whether the Obama administration will offer new ways of thinking about US identity or ultimately align itself with conventional understandings of US identity and foreign policy. There is evidence of both possibilities in Obama's rhetoric thus far.

In his address at Cairo University, Obama (2009) noted the colonial oppression experienced by Muslims, and the mistrust and fear that exists between the US and Islamic societies, thus signalling the importance of identity. Instead of creating an image of Islam as 'other', he highlighted similarities between US and

Muslim values—their identities as complementary rather than in opposition. He also noted that 9/11 led the US 'to act contrary to our traditions and ideals', acknowledging that Iraq was a 'war of choice' and promising to withdraw US combat troops (completed in August 2010 [Msnbc.com 2010]) and close the Guantánamo Bay detention camp (which he has as yet been unable to achieve). However, Obama also deployed the same representations as previous US presidents: the US acts 'boldly' and with 'resolve', has 'responsibilities' and 'commitments', meets 'challenges' and acts in multilateral concert with other nations. The US has no imperial ambitions, but rather 'has been one of the greatest sources of progress that the world has ever known'. While terrorists and extremists are ruthless and kill innocent civilians, the US still only ever *re*acts out of necessity, to defend its national security and 'to protect the American people' (Obama 2009).

Conclusion

In this chapter we have shown how processes of identity construction and representations of foreign policy are mutually constitutive. US identity is a complex phenomenon, and is constantly being articulated and rearticulated, maintained, contested, and transformed in the face of revised representations of supposedly external and objective threats. Each new articulation of US identity in US foreign policy is based on recurring themes and representations that have been articulated by previous generations of policy makers.

Transformations in world politics—e.g. the shift to the Cold War, its subsequent evaporation, 9/11—generally appear to policy makers and analysts as fundamental challenges to US identity and the attendant US role in the world. Such developments force policy makers to rearticulate the nature of threats and insecurities so as to be able to reconstitute a (seemingly) stable US identity. As we have argued here, this has meant reproducing and representing US leadership in a global fight for freedom against a variety of mutating threats.

We have also presented a different narrative, that of US imperialism, in order to demonstrate how both of these discourses are socially constructed. If we examine US foreign policy from different vantage points, other aspects of US identity come to the fore. Scholars have examined how models of masculinity influenced US Cold War policy makers (Dean 2001), how religion and 'family values' are articulated through Bush's war on terror discourse (Kline 2004), how gender and race were deployed in the build-up to the 1991 Gulf War (Farmanfarmaian 1992; Niva 1998) and after 9/11 (Kimmel 2003; Shepherd 2006; Nayak 2006).

Countless other stories about identity and US foreign policy remain untold. In particular, it should be evident that we have chosen to focus on the US's own constructions of (US and others') identities in articulations of US foreign policy, and have not examined other states' representations. No doubt an analysis of identities in US foreign policy from the perspective of, say, Iranians, Palestinians, or Venezuelans would look very different from what we have outlined here, not to mention the interstate and supra-state organizations, as well as non-state actors, who also construct representations of their own and others' identities.

We have also only briefly discussed how these representations also exist outside elite policy discourses, in music, films, TV shows, and other popular cultural sites and texts. However, while it is impossible to give a comprehensive account of all of the facets of identity in US foreign policy, we hope we have provided some insights into what such analyses might look like and, more importantly, that we have unpacked the assumptions upon which these analyses are based and the concepts with which such analyses can be conducted.

Finally, we want to point out that it is not only political and cultural/media elites who construct representations of US identity; academic elites—lecturers, authors, researchers—are also involved in these processes of identity construction.

Exercise 4: **How are identities articulated and represented in the approaches and chapters in this textbook?**

? Questions

1. What do we mean by identity?
2. In what ways does the concept of identity help us to understand US foreign policy?
3. In what ways is social constructivism a useful framework for analysing US foreign policy?
4. What is the relationship between identities, values, and interests?
5. Has US identity changed or remained constant over time?
6. What is the relationship between identity, insecurity, and threats?
7. In what ways are 'others' represented in discourses of US foreign policy?
8. What roles do race and religion play in representations of US foreign policy?
9. In what ways are narratives and representations of US foreign policy gendered?
10. What is the relationship between capitalism, US identity, and US foreign policy?
11. Think about your own foreign policy preferences; in what ways are these values constituted through, and connected with, your identity?

» Further Reading

Bennis, P. (2003), *Before & After: US Foreign Plicy and the War on Terrorism* (Moreton-in-Marsh: Arris Books).

Bennis critically assesses the major foreign policy decisions made by the Bush administration in the aftermath of 9/11, arguing that 9/11 allowed that administration unilaterally to implement a long-standing right-wing foreign policy agenda.

Campbell, D. (1998), *Writing Security: United States Foreign Policy and the Politics of Identity*, rev. edn. (Minneapolis: University of Minnesota Press).

Campbell argues that the identities and foreign policies of states are performatively constituted in representations of danger.

Croft, S. (2006), *Culture, Crisis and America's War on Terror* (Cambridge: Cambridge University Press).

Croft understands the war on terror as a cultural phenomenon that has permeated US everyday life. He explores the ways in which this discourse has become 'common sense', expressed through news media, film, and TV as well as in novels, jokes, and people's religious practices.

Dean, R. (2001), *Imperial Brotherhood: Gender and the Making of Cold War Foreign Policy* (Amherst, MA: University of Massachusetts Press).

Examining the McCarthy era and the war in Vietnam, Dean shows how elite conceptions of male identity—particularly a deeply ingrained sense of upper-class masculinity—fashioned the course of US foreign policy in the Cold War.

Drinnon, R. (1990), *Facing West: The Metaphysics of Indian-Hating and Empire-Building* (New York: Schocken Books; first pub. 1980).

Drinnon's searing critique examines the history of Anglo-American expansion across North America and beyond, from the first Puritan confrontation with Native Americans through twentieth-century US interventions in the Philippines and Vietnam.

Hunt, M. (2009 [1987]), *Ideology and US Foreign Policy*, with a new afterword (New Haven, CT and London: Yale University Press).

Hunt argues that US foreign policy has, since its inception, been based on a persistent ideology comprised of three components: an extroverted conception of national greatness, a detailed racial (and racist) hierarchy, and an abiding hostility toward social revolution.

Jackson, R. (2005), *Writing the War on Terrorism: Language, Politics and Counter-Terrorism* (Manchester: Manchester University Press).

Jackson critically examines US war on terror discourse to illuminate how it has become the dominant political narrative in the US, justifying and normalizing a global counter-terrorist campaign.

Weber, C. (2006), *Imagining America at War: Morality, Politics, and Film* (London: Routledge).

Weber examines the political functions of film in the 'war on terror', arguing that filmic representations are intimately connected to US identity and foreign policy.

Weldes, J. (1999), *Constructing National Interests: The United States and the Cuban Missile Crisis* (Minneapolis: University of Minnesota Press).

Weldes re-examines the Cuban missile crisis from a critical constructivist perspective.

Williams, W. A. (2004), *The Tragedy of American Diplomacy*, new edited edn. (New York: W. W. Norton; first pub. 1962).

Williams examined US–Cuban relations 1898–1961 in order to defend the thesis that the US had long had an expansionist and economically imperialist foreign policy, thereby undermining US claims that it defends self-determination and democracy abroad.

Endnotes

1. Using the noun 'America' for the US or the adjective 'American' to describe its citizens or inhabitants is problematic. People from Chile, Mexico, and Cuba are also 'American'. Throughout this chapter, we use 'US' as noun and adjective to describe the state, its citizens, and inhabitants.

2. Other interest-based explanations focus on the rational decision making of various sorts of actors—whether bureaucrats (Allison and Zelikow 1999), interest groups (Terry 2005), public opinion (Entman 2004), or electoral politics (Gaddis 1982).

3. 'Nation' and 'state' are commonly hyphenated based on the assumption that each nation coincides with a territorial state. However, there are no ethnically or culturally homogeneous 'nation-states'.

4. The term 'ideological' is commonly used pejoratively (negatively), to connote something that is based on ideas about how the world works, rather than on the 'truth'. We problematize this notion below (see Purvis and Hunt 1993).

5. Maps provide a useful way for us to think about these issues because maps are neither 'true' nor 'false', but rather are ways of *representing* the world. Different maps serve different purposes and they represent (construct) the world in different ways.

6. As scholars we do not simply 'find' data waiting for us in the world, even in the natural sciences. Data sets are always *constructed*: the boundaries between what is interesting/relevant and what is discarded as less (or un)important are defined by the analyst, in the assumptions underpinning the research design and methods.

7. Popular cultural texts are also constructed by elites, albeit not generally policy elites. For overlaps between these two elites, see Robb (2004) and Valantin (2005).

8. See Milliken (1999) for other examples of discourse analytic research.

9. This discourse analysis is based on a few key presidential speeches. The themes and tropes we identify can be found in many policy documents (see, for example, The American Presidency Project).

10. A common theme in US politics is that, however the two political parties (and the public) may be divided on domestic issues, the country must unite behind its foreign policy, which should enjoy bi-partisan support (survival and national security are 'prior to' domestic politics).

11. See Collins and Glover (2002) on language in the war on terror, and Cohn (1987) on the rhetorical function of terms like 'collateral damage' in US nuclear policy.

 For a range of additional resources to support your learning visit the Online Resource Centre that accompanies this book at **www.oxfordtextbooks.co.uk/orc/cox_stokes2e/**.

Section 3

The United States and the World

12 US foreign policy in the Middle East[1]

Toby Dodge

Chapter contents

Introduction

This chapter assesses the main dynamics that have transformed United States foreign policy towards the Middle East over the last eighty-five years. First it discusses the applicability of realist, Marxist, and constructivist theories of international relations. It will then assess the role that the Cold War, oil, and Israel have played in shaping American foreign policy. In each of these three areas the United States' tactical approach to the Middle East has produced unintended consequences that have increased resentment towards America, destabilized the region, and undermined its long-term strategic goals. The chapter goes on to discuss the Bush Doctrine, launched after 9/11 and the resultant invasion of Iraq. It concludes by assessing President Barack Obama's attempts to overcome the tensions and suspicion causes by previous US foreign policy in the Middle East.

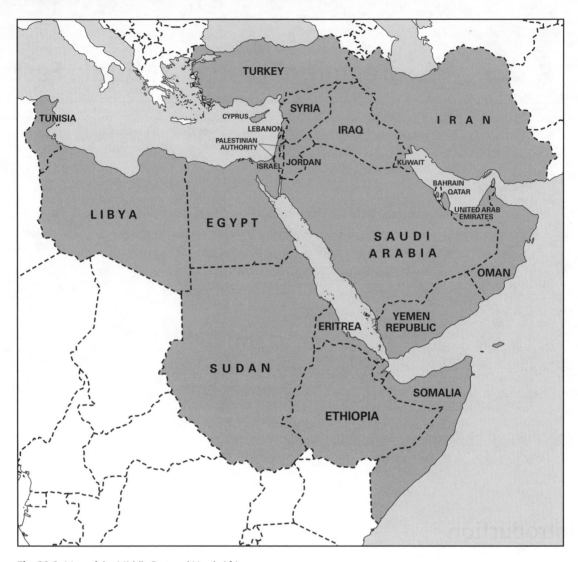

Fig. 12.1 Map of the Middle East and North Africa.

The evolution of the United States' early relationship with the Middle East was shaped by the demise of both the Ottoman and the British empires. The Ottoman Empire collapsed in the wake of the defeat it suffered during the First World War. The United States consequently intervened to limit the imperialist ambitions of both the French and British. In the aftermath of the Second World War, America was increasingly drawn into the Middle East, first to replace the rapidly declining power of the British Empire but also to counter the military and ideological influence of the Soviet Union.

The end of the Cold War has seen American foreign policy dominated by what Fred Halliday labelled 'the greater West Asian crisis': instability, radicalism and violence that dominates a region including the Middle East, Pakistan and Afghanistan. Ever since the attacks of 9/11 this region has sat at the top of Washington's list of grave concerns (Halliday 2005, 130).

The growing importance of the Middle East to US foreign policy since 1945 has been driven by geostrategic, economic, and domestic concerns. Geostrategically the region sits at the junction of three continents, in close

BOX 12.1:   Important dates and events in relations between the states of the Middle East and the United States of America

1917   April: the United States of America enters the First World War.

2 November: the Balfour Declaration. British Secretary James Balfour in a letter to Lord Lionel Walter Roth-schild says Britain (with US acquiescence) would support the creation of a Jewish homeland in Palestine.

1918   8 January: the American President, Woodrow Wilson, issues the 14-point statement of its reasons for joining the war and what it expects the peace to look like.

1919   January–June: the Paris Peace Conference draws up the international agreement to run the world after the First World War. It results in the formation of the League of Nations.

1947   12 March: US President Truman addresses Congress and launches the Truman Doctrine, asking for permission to aid Greece, Turkey, and then Iran against the Soviet threat.

1948   May: the founding of the state of Israel.

The first Arab–Israeli War.

1955   24 February: the formation of the Baghdad Pact: an anti-communist regional alliance with Iraq, Turkey, Iran, and Pakistan as members.

September: Egypt's arms deal with Czechoslovakia.

1956   26 July. Nasser announces the nationalization of the Suez Canal.

July–November: Suez crisis and the second Arab–Israeli War. Britain, France, and Israel collude to invade Egypt and attempt to remove President Nasser. US President Eisenhower refuses to offer military, diplomatic, or financial support, thus forcing a humiliating withdrawal.

1958   15 July: the first Lebanese civil war erupts; 15,000 US troops are sent to Beirut to stop radicals taking control of the country.

1962   September: left-wing officers in Yemen overthrow Imam Mohammed al-Badr and invite Nasser to send troops to help them consolidate power.

1966   22 February: the British government announces a large-scale reduction of troops in the Middle East, drawing their military out of territory east of Suez Canal in Egypt.

1967   5 June: the third Arab–Israeli War. Israel launches a pre-emptive strike against Egypt, Syria, and Jordan as they prepare for war. The 'Six-Day War' ends with Israel occupying the Sinai Peninsula and the Gaza Strip previously held by Egypt, the Golan Heights formerly held by Syria, and the West Bank previously held by Jordan.

1972   September: the Munich Olympics massacre. Seven Palestinian terrorists belonging to the Black September group kill eleven Israeli athletes during the Olympic games in Germany.

1973   6 October: the fourth Arab–Israeli War. Egypt and Syria launch a surprise attack against Israel during the Jewish holiday of Yom Kippur.

In retaliation for United States support of Israel during the war, the Organization of Arab Oil-Producing States impose an oil embargo on exports to America, to try and force territorial concessions from Israel. It lasts until 1974 by which time oil prices have quadrupled.

1974   16 June: Richard Nixon is the first US President to visit Israel.

1977   19 November: Egyptian President Sadat flies to Israel in an attempt to make peace.

1978   April: the communists seize power in Afghanistan in a bloody coup.

1979   March: Egyptian President Sadat and Israeli Prime Minister Begin sign a peace treaty in Washington. Israel agrees to withdraw from Sinai and to commence Palestinian autonomy talks within three years in exchange for a formal peace treaty with Egypt.

February: the Shah of Iran is overthrown by the Islamic revolution.

24 December: the Soviet Union invades Afghanistan.

1980   22 September: the Iraqi air force attacks Iran and a land invasion begins at several points along the Iran–Iraq border.

1981   6 October: Anwar Sadat gunned down in Cairo by the 'Islamic Group'.

1982   June: Israel invades Lebanon and lays siege to its capital Beirut in what becomes a bloody military stalemate.

1983   23 October: the US marine compound at Beirut airport is destroyed by a suicide bomber: 241 are killed.

1984   7 February: President Ronald Reagan announces the retreat of US forces from Lebanon to American war-ships offshore.

1987   December: the Palestinian uprising or *intifada* begins in the West Bank and Gaza Strip.

1988   July: the eight-year Iran–Iraq War ends.

1990   2 August: Iraq invades Kuwait.

BOX 12.1: *(continued)*

1991   16 January: Operation Desert Storm. Allied air attacks against Iraqi troops in Kuwait begin.

24 February: the Allied ground offensive against Iraq begins.

27 February: President George Bush announces hostilities with Iraq will cease at midnight, hours after the liberation of Kuwait City.

1993   September: the Oslo Accords are signed between the PLO and Israel.

2000   September: the second Palestinian uprising or *intifada* begins.

12 October: USS battleship *Cole* is attacked by al-Qaeda in Aden harbour, Yemen, killing 17 US sailors.

2001   11 September: Al-Qaeda uses passenger planes to attack the World Trade Center in New York and the Pentagon in Washington, DC.

2003   20 March: the invasion of Iraq begins shortly after a 48-hour deadline for Saddam Hussein to leave the country expires.

9 April: US marines help crowds to topple a giant statue of Saddam Hussein in Firdous Square, central Baghdad. Widespread looting breaks out unhindered in the Iraqi capital.

2009   4 June: President Barack Obama gives a speech in Cairo designed to launch 'a new beginning' for relations between the United States and the Muslim world.

2011   17 March: The UN Security Council passes Resolution 1973 authorizing a no-fly zone over Libya to project the Libyan population from the government's troops.

31 December: All US troops to be removed from Iraqi soil under an agreement signed between Baghdad and Washington.

 CONTROVERSIES 12.1:   The influence of the 'Israeli Lobby' on United States foreign policy

In March 2006, two respected professors, John Mearsheimer and Stephen Walt, published the 'Israeli Lobby' in the *London Review of Books* (Mearsheimer and Walt 2006) and a subsequent book (Mearsheimer and Walt 2007). The article caused an explosion of controversy and debate across the United States. Mearsheimer and Walt, two of the most influential realists working in international relations, argued that America's support for Israel ran counter to US national interests. They examined Israel's role as an ally in the war against terrorism, its vulnerability to attack by its neighbours, and the moral case for American support. They concluded that after the Cold War, Israel had become a strategic and political burden and US support for it had directly damaged American interests.

They went on to examine why, given what they saw as the high costs of this support, it continued. They concluded that an Israeli lobby, a 'loose coalition of individuals and organisations who actively work to steer US foreign policy in a pro-Israel direction', was responsible. Given the highly polemical nature of debates in the United States surrounding the Middle East in general and Israel in particular, it was no surprise that the article ignited an extended and at times bitter response. Amongst their most trenchant critics was Alan Dershowitz, along with Walt a professor at Harvard (Dershowitz 2006). Dershowitz argued that the paper was 'filled with errors and

distortions', with quotations 'wrenched out of context', facts mis-stated, and 'embarrassingly poor logic'. Given what he saw as the poor quality of the scholarship and analysis, Dershowitz went on to question Mearsheimer and Walt's motives, implying that they were driven by anti-Semitic motives.

The controversy that the 'Israeli Lobby' caused indicates the passions and sensitivities surrounding the issue in US foreign policy circles. However, some sections of Mearsheimer and Walt's arguments were factually incorrect. They also attributed a unity of viewpoint to an ideologically diverse set of organizations. One of the central accusations of the article, that the Israeli lobby played a key role in driving the USA to invade Iraq, takes a complex and multifaceted issue and reduces it to a single cause. This is not an academically sustainable explanation. However, Michael Massing, in a much stronger and more thoughtful paper, sets out in detail the manner and extent of the influence those organizations seeking to persuade the US government to pursue a pro-Israeli policy have (Massing 2006). It is Massing's reasoned and well-sourced argument that needs to be debated in a calm and analytical fashion at the heart of US foreign policy making. One of Mearsheimer and Walt's key criticisms was that anyone seeking to question the American–Israeli special relationship was intimidated by accusations of anti-Semitism. Dershowitz's response went a long way to proving that point at least.

proximity to the Mediterranean, the Persian Gulf, and America's main rival during the twentieth century, the Soviet Union. As the Cold War intensified, the USA came to regard the Middle East as second in order of strategic importance to Europe. Economically the region supplies 32 per cent of the world's oil and has 58 per cent of the globe's proven reserves (Shlaim 1995: 35). Although the United States' own dependence on Middle Eastern oil has slowly increased during the twentieth century, American policy towards the region has been shaped by a keen appreciation of the global economic significance of its oil reserves. The creation of the state of Israel in 1948 and its long-running conflict with its Arab neighbours has likewise dominated US foreign policy. For strategic, ideological, and domestic political reasons, Israel has enjoyed a very strong alliance with the USA. Strategically it has been perceived as a reliable ally at the centre of the Middle East from the Cold War onwards. In domestic American politics, lobby groups supporting Israel have always had the ability to organize public support in favour of a very close and supportive relationship.

Within Washington, the president is primarily responsible for shaping America's policy in the region. However, both houses of Congress, the Senate and the House of Representatives, are empowered to oversee foreign policy and have historically provided an influential point of access for those individuals, companies, lobby groups, and countries seeking to shape US policy. Washington is overflowing with think tanks and policy experts whose sole purpose is to influence the US government's development of foreign policy generally and Middle Eastern policy specifically (Hudson 2005: 296). The high level of politically motivated intra-and interstate violence in the region has forced it to the forefront of US media coverage. This in turn has caused Middle Eastern politics to loom large in the foreign policy concerns of the educated and mobilized section of American public opinion. Middle East policy is hence developed in the full glare of the media spotlight, subject to intense discussion, lobbying, and analysis. A US president neglects this fact at his or her electoral peril.

The transformation of US foreign policy towards the Middle East: from Wilson to Obama

The United States' relations with both the states and societies of the Middle East have been transformed during the twentieth century. The extent and nature of this change can be gauged by comparing the tone, content, and reception of three landmark speeches that have had far-reaching consequences for the region. On 8 January 1918, as the First World War drew to an end, American President Woodrow Wilson addressed a joint session of the United States Congress in Washington, DC (Wilson 1918). The USA, under Wilson's leadership, had been drawn into the war against its better judgement and the president was determined to shape the peace settlement in a way that would make another world war impossible. Wilson faced two major obstacles in securing this goal. The first was the conflict's main protagonists; the European states themselves. For Wilson, they represented all that was wrong with international relations; indulging in secret, even conspiratorial, agreements amongst themselves while simultaneously competing to expand the territorial extent of their non-European

empires to dominate other nations for their own benefit. The second emerging challenge was represented by the new ideology of Bolshevism, personified by the Russian Communist Party's seizure of power in Moscow.

Wilson's attempt to meet these challenges combined ambition with idealism. He outlined a fourteen-point agenda that would shape America's post-war diplomacy. The speech called for transparent public diplomacy, open markets, and collective security. However, it was the twelfth point of Wilson's speech that led directly to the transformation of the Middle East. He demanded that the non-Turkish-speaking nationalities that had been ruled by the now defeated Ottoman Empire 'should be assured an undoubted security of life and an absolutely unmolested opportunity of autonomous development'. These words were seized upon by Arab nationalists across the region. Wilson's promotion of self-determination for previously oppressed nations became a touchstone for those Arabs seeking to escape the imperial ambitions of the Ottomans, then the British and French troops who controlled the region. The subsequent formation of the League of Nations under Wilson's direction placed direct limits on the imperial ambitions of both France and Britain. In effect, Wilson can be seen as the father of the modern independent state in the Middle East (Dodge 2005: pp. xii–xix).

Eighty-four years later on 29 January 2002, President George W. Bush addressed Congress, giving his annual State of the Union Address. It had only been four months since al-Qaeda launched its devastating attacks on the World Trade Center in New York and the Pentagon in Washington. Like Wilson before him, Bush invoked the powerful imagery of a nation at war, a 'war against terror' which 'is only beginning'. Bush stressed that America faced two enemies in this war, the 'terrorist underworld' responsible for 9/11 and the allied states who were seeking to develop weapons of mass destruction. These allies were grouped in 'an axis of evil' whose 'regimes pose a grave and growing danger' (Bush 2002a). Two of the three members of this axis, Iraq and Iran, were key Middle Eastern states.

This speech heralded what developed into the Bush Doctrine, a potentially revolutionary approach to international relations. It forged weapons of mass destruction and terrorism into one homogeneous threat to the continued security of the American people that was primarily located in the Middle East. George W. Bush, unlike Woodrow Wilson, saw that the best way to meet this threat was to restrict the right to sovereignty of errant Middle Eastern states. All means necessary were to be deployed to ensure rogue regimes did not support terrorism or develop weapons of mass destruction. In a startling contrast to Woodrow Wilson's fourteen-point speech and his promotion of self-determination, the Bush Doctrine was greeted with widespread hostility across the Middle East. President Bush's attempt to link the fight to the promotion of democracy was largely dismissed and the Bush Doctrine rejected as a new form of American imperialism (Harvey 2003; Bush 2002b). The logic of the Bush Doctrine led directly to the invasion and regime change in Iraq. The ongoing insurgency and ensuing civil war this caused has greatly destabilized the Middle East and all but dissipated the genuine empathy felt for the American people in the wake of the 9/11 attacks. Whereas Wilson's ambitious and idealist approach to the Middle East increased the prestige and standing of the United States in the region, the Bush Doctrine and the cataclysmic aftermath of the Iraqi invasion has driven anti-American sentiment to new levels of hostility.

Seven years after President Bush addressed Congress, his successor, Barack Obama, gave a speech at Cairo University on 9 June 2009 specifically designed to undo the damage he thought President Bush had done to US relations with the Middle East and the wider Muslim world. Obama recognized that US policy during the Cold War had treated Muslims as proxies, ignoring their own concerns and aspirations. Obama went on to define the Arab–Israeli conflict as a major source of tension. He set out to explain America's 'unbreakable bond' with Israel but then acknowledged the suffering that Palestinians had gone through in struggling to gain their own homeland. The solution, he argued, was that both the Israelis and Palestinians should have their own states and to obtain this, the Israelis had to stop building settlements on occupied Palestinian land. Finally, he explained the 'enormous trauma' caused to the US by the attacks of 9/11 but accepted this had led to mistakes and committed himself to closing down the American prison at Guantanamo Bay in Cuba, which had become synonymous with American prisoner abuses during the 'war against terror'. In his speech Obama was signalling to the Muslim world that the US had made a number of mistakes since the Cold War, especially in its relations with the Middle East. He was calling for dialogue, understanding, and a new start in relations. However, by placing the solution of the Arab–Israeli conflict at the centre of his new approach, he was setting a very high and almost certainly unobtainable measure of success for his administration to attain.

KEY POINTS

❑ US foreign policy towards the Middle East has been dramatically transformed over the twentieth century.

❑ President Woodrow Wilson, in 1918, organized US foreign policy around the promotion of self-determination for previously oppressed people.

❑ President George W. Bush, after 9/11, sought to constrain the sovereignty of Middle Eastern states in an attempt to promoted democracy and limit the spread of weapons of mass destruction and terrorism.

❑ Woodrow Wilson's foreign policy greatly enhanced the standing of the USA in the Middle East.

❑ The Bush Doctrine and the invasion of Iraq have fuelled the rise of a powerful anti-Americanism across the region.

International relations, United States foreign policy, and the Middle East

The period between these two momentous speeches encompasses sixteen American presidents and their relations with a diverse group of states that spread from Morocco in North Africa, west to Iran, and from Turkey south to Yemen. The radically different policies towards the Middle East pursued by Wilson and Bush indicate how the United States' relations with the region have been transformed over the twentieth century. International relations theory needs to be deployed to assess what has driven this changing policy agenda. This theory is both descriptive and prescriptive. It allows those studying the actions of decision makers to investigate their motivations and perceptions. In addition, different approaches to international relations guide or constrain the politicians and diplomats themselves, offering the categories and units of analysis used to understand a complex world.

Realism, the USA, and the Middle East

Three different and competing approaches to international relations can be usefully deployed to assess the United States' changing relations with the Middle East: realism, Marxism, and constructivism. Against the background of the Cold War realism rejected any appeal to morality as a dangerous diversion. It stresses the anarchical nature of international relations, ungoverned as it is by any higher power to adjudicate between competing states, all seeking to maximize their power in an uncertain world. For Hans Morgenthau decision makers 'think and act in terms of interest defined as power', allowing for predictability and a common understanding of state behaviour (Morgenthau 1985: 5). Morgenthau's approach appeared to explain the evolution and comparative stability of the Cold War, a world divided into two multi-state alliances, where each superpower dominated its weaker allies. Realism's descriptive and predictive abilities apply equally to the Middle East, with one of the longest running conflicts in modern diplomatic history, the Arab–Israeli dispute, the eight-year Iran–Iraq War, and Iraq's invasion of Kuwait in 1990.

The Marxist approach

However, a series of damaging critiques of the methodological assumptions underpinning realism have shaped two useful alternatives, constructivism and Marxism. Marxist approaches to international relations argue that the states that realists see as their central unit of analysis have to be placed in a much wider context. This stresses the socio-economic dynamics within which the state and the international system itself were formed. Marxists argue that there are three levels of analysis operating within international relations (Cox 1986: 220). The determinant level shows how a society organizes its economic production. This, Marxists argue, shapes power relations within societies: who owns the means of production and who they employ to work for them. This in turn frames how political and military power is structured to protect the economic organization of society. It also defines how people within that society think about their lives and roles.

From a Marxist perspective, the Cold War was not primarily about two states maximizing their own power but a clash of two very different modes of production attempting to impose their specific economic model on the rest of the world (Halliday 1994: 103). Marxists certainly recognize the importance of the political and military power of the state, but argue that it has been created within a specific set of socio-economic circumstances, determined in the last instance by the mode of production. First, states are dominated and act in the interests of those who own the mode of production; in advanced capitalist countries it is the bourgeoisie. It is these economic entrepreneurs who, in search of new markets and resources, use state power to move across the world, imposing a capitalist mode of production upon weaker societies as they travel.

BOX 12.2: US Presidential doctrines and the Middle East

Doctrines are developed by specific presidents to map out a grand strategy to deal with pressing foreign policy issues. The aim is to focus governmental resources on the most serious problem or threat the president believes is facing the United States.

The Truman Doctrine

Announced on 12 March 1947, in a speech before Congress, it committed the USA to defend Turkey and Greece against Soviet aggression.

The Eisenhower Doctrine

Announced on 9 March 1957, it offered US military and economic aid to any Middle Eastern state threatened by international communism.

The Nixon Doctrine

On 25 July 1969, faced with the growing cost of the war in Vietnam, the USA aimed to develop regional allies to act as proxies in the Cold War struggle against the Soviet Union. In the Middle East these proxies were Israel, Iran, and Saudi Arabia.

The Carter Doctrine

Announced in the January 1980 State of the Union Speech, as a response to the invasion of Afghanistan, it committed the USA to deploy military force to counter Soviet intervention in the Persian Gulf.

The Clinton Doctrine

Announced by Martin Indyk, a senior official on the National Security Council, on 18 May 1993, it committed the USA to 'dual containment', placing sanctions on both Iran and Iraq.

The Bush Doctrine

Developed in response to the attacks of 9/11 and set out in the January 2002 State of the Union Address and *The National Security Strategy of the United States*, published in September 2002, it promised to fight terrorism and countries that developed weapons of mass destruction, and encourage democratization in the Middle East.

Finally, Marxists argue that the international system is structured by hierarchy not anarchy, by the dominance of a hegemon. Marxists would argue that Woodrow Wilson, in calling for open markets and the end of European imperial domination, was attempting to reorder international economic and political relations in a way that would be of primary benefit to the United States. From this perspective, US policy in the Middle East is designed to defend its economic and political domination of the region. A Marxist approach to international relations provides powerful insights into the motivation of the US government and the vulnerability of regimes in the region to American power. However, Marxists have a propensity to overstate the economic rationale shaping US policy to the exclusion of other incentives. There is a tendency to assume that the US government is always acting to further the interests of their multinational corporations. This can lead to a focus on oil and a reduction in the influence of ideology, belief, and perception in shaping the policy making. It is this tendency to neglect the influence of ideas and perceptions that has given rise to the final approach to international relations, constructivism.

Constructivism

Constructivism places great explanatory weight on the role that ideas, culture, and norms play in the policy decisions of politicians and diplomats. Preconceived ideas about the situation statespeople find themselves in then become a crucial variable that shapes how the policies are chosen. For constructivists, belief systems constrain and ultimately direct those at the pinnacle of state power. A state's collective understanding of its own identity is a key factor in how diplomats perceive their national interests (Wendt 1999: 20; Ruggie 1998: 14).

In the context of the United States' relations with the Middle East, American politicians' perceptions of the region are a crucial factor. Douglas Little persuasively argues that US policy towards the Arab world has been decisively shaped by three ideological dynamics. First, the United States' own collective self-image, which perceives America as selflessly reaching out to the region to share with it the benefits of its own political and economic system. Secondly, Little argues American popular culture has, over many years, perceived the Middle East to be backward looking, prone to

KEY POINTS

❏ Given the length of time under consideration and the diversity of states in the Middle East, international relations theory is needed to understand US foreign policy towards the region.

❏ Realism stresses the instability of the international system, with states maximizing their power in competition with each other. This helps scholars understand the Middle East as dominated by interstate war and conflict.

❏ Marxism perceives the international system as structured by hierarchy not anarchy. US foreign policy in the region is designed to defend its economic and political dominance and access to oil.

❏ Constructivism stresses the role that ideas and norms play in foreign policy making. US interaction with the Middle East is thus structured by its own self-image and what policy makers see as the 'backwardness' of Middle Eastern societies.

violence, and dangerously unstable. Finally, this negative perception is reinforced by a contrastingly positive perception of Israel. Little argues this has fuelled a mutual incomprehension between the Middle East and the United States that has given rise to mistrust and violence (Little 2002: 2–33).

The United States, the Cold War, and the Middle East

The dominant global dynamic shaping the United States' relations with the Middle East has been the Cold War, from its origins in the aftermath of the Second World War to the collapse of the Soviet Union in 1989. On one level, realists would argue, the demands of the Cold War simplified diplomacy for the United States. The preferences and even personal morality of individual statespeople could be subsumed within what Henry Kissinger has termed 'the ethic of responsibility'. United States interests under this rubric were straightforward: it must maximize its interests, defined as power, in the face of the Soviet threat (Gaddis 1987: 221). The Middle East became one of many arenas within which global struggle ensued. It was divided between the two superpowers as they each struggled to build the largest stable alliances possible.

However, the realist simplicity of rolling the Middle East into a global struggle for allies and dominance had a number of unintended consequences. The complexities of struggles based within the Middle East subsystem itself did not always sit well within the Cold War mindset that dominated thinking in Washington. Often ideologies originating within the region, Arab nationalism and Islamic radicalism for example, were co-opted into the struggle against the Soviet Union, which had profound ramifications for the domestic politics of the Middle East. Alternatively, they were simply misdiagnosed as a tool or product of Soviet interference. The unintended consequences and misperceptions of US foreign policy during the Cold War still haunt the region's politics today.

The Middle East became an early venue for the opening stages of the Cold War. The Soviet Union had stationed troops in Iran during the Second World War but had agreed to withdraw them at the end of hostilities. However, by 1945 it looked increasing reluctant to do so. In addition it encouraged locals to establish an autonomous government in the Iranian province of Azerbaijan, north-west of Tehran. US alarm increased when Stalin's attention focused on Turkey, attempting to pressure Ankara into sharing control of shipping through the Dardanelles. The US administration concluded that the Soviets' central aim in the region was to gain control of Turkey. Their unease increased when evidence came to light of Soviet meddling in the Greek civil war. President Truman sought to meet this challenge in March 1947 by announcing the Truman Doctrine, a $400 million package of economic and military aid for Greece and Turkey. However, Truman appears to have overestimated Stalin's interests and goals in the region. Stalin regarded Arab nationalist politicians as unreliable bourgeois nationalists (Brown 1984: 199). The Soviet Union under Stalin treated the Middle East as a sideshow.

Eisenhower and the Middle East

United States–Soviet competition over the Middle East and the problems this caused increased with Stalin's death and the Eisenhower presidency. Nikita Khrushchev, the new leader of the Soviet Communist Party, announced a new policy towards the third world during the Congress of the Communist Party in 1956 at which he denounced Stalin (Westad 2005: 68). It resulted in 'rubble diplomacy', a substantial programme of economic aid directed at third world states, including Egypt.

The Eisenhower administration, developing Truman's fears of Soviet encroachment through Turkey, colluded with Britain to organize the 'northern tier' of the Middle East in an anti-Soviet alliance, the Baghdad Pact. This grouped Iraq, Turkey, Iran, and Pakistan in a mutual defence agreement, strengthened by US military assistance. Eisenhower further escalated US involvement and Cold War tensions in the Middle East in 1957. Worried that a reduction in British influence in the region would be exploited by the Soviet Union, he countered with a promise of direct US military intervention and economic aid in support of any state which felt under threat from communist aggression. Congress voted to support what become known as the Eisenhower Doctrine in 1957. However the only intervention sanctioned was to send marines to stop the eruption of the Lebanese civil war of 1958. This was a purely regional conflict, not connected to the Cold War.

Increasing US involvement in the Middle East under Eisenhower drove growing resentment amongst Arab nationalists, who were battling to defend their newly won independence and minimize outside interference in the region. In spite of US political rhetoric stressing freedom from Soviet domination, Arab politicians found it increasingly difficult to distinguish between the dying days of a British imperialism justified in terms of progress and development, and a militarized US presence promoting capitalism and democracy. It was this sentiment that caused the Baghdad Pact to be denounced by both Syria and Egypt as an attempt to sustain foreign domination rather than the protection of its members.

It was a bloody military coup in Iraq in July 1958, orchestrated in the name of Arab nationalism and freedom from foreign domination, that overthrew the British-installed monarchy and broke the Baghdad Pact. The rising tide of Arab nationalism, primarily driven by the remnants of British imperialism, was continuously mistaken by Washington during this period as a stalking horse for international communism. Egypt's radical president, Gamal Abdul Nasser, became the personification of this problem. In 1955 he struck a major arms deal with Czechoslovakia. However, this transaction had more to do with his military confrontation with Israel than a desire to join the Czechs as a member of the Communist International. When the US government reversed a promise to help fund the building of the Aswan dam in 1956, Nasser announced the nationalization of the Suez Canal. This triggered a wave of economic nationalism across the third world that was driven by a desire for economic sovereignty and development, not international communism.

Britain and France, in a secret compact with Israel, attempted to reverse the nationalization of the Suez Canal and remove Nasser from power by invading Egypt in October 1956. Public opinion across the Middle East saw the Suez crisis as the personification of European imperialism, an illegal conspiracy using military force to reverse Arab independence. For President Eisenhower the invasion of Egypt coincided with Soviet tanks crushing the Hungarian uprising in Budapest. The US deployed financial and diplomatic pressure to force France and Britain into a humiliating withdrawal, turning Nasser into a hero across the third world and making Arab nationalism the dominant ideology in the Middle East.

Nixon, Kissinger, and the 1973 war

The next presidential doctrine to have significant consequences for the Middle East was developed by Richard Nixon. Inheriting an increasingly unpopular and costly war in Vietnam from his predecessor President Johnson, the Nixon Doctrine's goal was the empowerment of proxy states in the third world to replace the already overstretched United States. The application of the Nixon Doctrine to the Middle East encouraged Saudi Arabia and especially Iran and Israel to become regional policemen, enforcing an American policy agenda at second hand. The Shah of Iran seized upon his new-found responsibilities with gusto, demanding larger and larger amounts of sophisticated weaponry from Washington in return. Any doubts this raised within the US administration were placated, temporarily at least, by the Shah's help in destabilizing the Ba'athist regime in Iraq, who were in receipt of Soviet weaponry. The Shah's support for the Cold War reached its peak when he agreed to send 1200 troops to support the Sultan of Oman in his struggle against a Soviet-supported uprising in the restive province of Dhofar in 1973.

However, the nexus between an essentially regional conflict and a global Cold War created a crisis with the Arab–Israeli War of 1973–4. During 1969–70, the Soviet Union dramatically increased its military support for Egypt in the aftermath of the cataclysmic defeat of 1967. Although Egyptian President Sadat distanced himself from Moscow in 1972, the Soviets felt compelled to threaten direct intervention in the face of massive US support for Israel in the 1973–4 war. Nixon responded by putting US nuclear forces on DEFCON 3, the stage preceding all-out war. Although the Soviet Union backed down and the Arab states suffered another defeat at the hands of Israel, Cold War manoeuvring in an essentially regional conflict had very nearly brought the superpowers into direct confrontation in the Middle East.

Carter, Iran, and Afghanistan

It was Democratic President Jimmy Carter who inherited the fallout from Nixon's decision to give unconditional backing to the Shah of Iran. Throughout the 1970s, the Shah had become increasingly detached from Iranian society. His oil-fuelled development strategies and land reform backfired, causing rapid unplanned urbanization, inflation, and unemployment. US support for an increasingly autocratic and corrupt monarch only increased his unpopularity. This allowed the opposition to combine a powerful Iranian nationalism that portrayed the Shah as an American stooge with a religious moralism that focused on his family's decadence and corruption. It resulted in the 1979 Islamic revolution, which brought Ayatollah Khomeini to power and mobilized the population behind a radical manifesto of Islamism and anti-Americanism.

The Carter administration was further engulfed in a crisis of Middle Eastern origin when the Soviet Union airlifted thousands of troops into Afghanistan on Christmas Eve 1979. The invasion was almost certainly defensive, attempting to limit the threat that political Islam posed for the USSR's own Muslim population. However, Carter saw it in terms of the Cold War's balance of power. On 23 January 1980, during his State of the Union Address, the president announced the Carter Doctrine. Consciously modelled on the Truman Doctrine before it, Carter announced that 'the implications of the Soviet invasion of Afghanistan could pose the most serious threat to the peace since the Second World War'. Carter concluded by placing the region at the heart of the Cold War and stressing its centrality to US interests. In order to turn Afghanistan into the Soviets' Vietnam, the USA quickly built an unwieldy alliance of convenience. It brought together the logistical capacity of Pakistan's military intelligence with funding for the Arab Gulf states and, most damagingly, a motley group of Afghan and Arab Islamic radicals. It certainly succeeded in trapping the Soviet army in Afghanistan, fighting a long, costly, and unwinnable war of attrition. Their eventual ignominious defeat and withdrawal hastened the end of the Cold War and America's victory. However, the unintended consequence of Afghan war was to empower a transnational network of Islamic radicals, who, having defeated one superpower, were on 9/11 emboldened to strike at the other.

Reagan and Lebanon

If the empowerment of al-Qaeda under the auspices of the Carter Doctrine represents the worst unintended consequence of the United States Cold War policy in the Middle East, then the Reagan administration's involvement in Lebanon in the early 1980s indicates how a Cold War prism could distort the basis to policy making. With his focus on combating the 'evil empire' of Soviet communism, President Reagan placed the military threat of the Soviet Union at the core of his foreign policy. The Arab–Israeli conflict and regional dynamics more generally were downgraded in the face of a renewed Cold War. The Reagan administration's unquestioned support for Israel meant it backed Prime Minister Begin and Defence Minister Sharon's plans to invade Lebanon in June 1982 and drive Yasser Arafat's Palestine Liberation Organization from the Middle East. Ariel Sharon sold the plan to Washington by claiming it would weaken two of the USSR's main clients, the PLO themselves and Syria (Shlaim 1995: 55). However, the US military were drawn into the resultant conflict as peacekeepers. By analysing the violence in Lebanon through a Cold War lens, US military power was deployed to back one side of a largely indigenous civil war against another. As a result the USA became party to an increasingly bloody civil war. In retaliation a suicide bomber attacked US facilities in Beirut in 1983, killing 241 American marines and forcing the USA to leave Lebanon in trauma and defeat.

The realist approach to international relations that shaped US policy on the Cold War assumed that the conflict was global and that 'interests defined as power' could be deployed in a bipolar struggle. However, in the Middle East this approach led to profound miscalculations about which regimes to support and the consequences of that aid. The USA, under different presidents, twice intervened in the Lebanese civil war using the Cold War as justification. They took sides in a bitter and bloody civil war, paying a terrible price, and exacerbated the violence. In creating the coalition that funded a disparate group of Islamic radicals in Afghanistan, the country simply became another arena for the

> **KEY POINTS**
>
> ❑ The Cold War acted as the dominant issue shaping US relations with the Middle East. However, seeing the region simply as an arena for a global struggle had profound unintended consequences.
> ❑ The Cold War meant that ideologies originating from within the region, Islamic radicalism and Arab nationalism, were either seen as tools of Soviet influence or weapons with which to fight Soviet power.
> ❑ In 1947, as the Cold War took hold, President Truman announced his doctrine to meet the challenge of Soviet expansionism in the region. However, this overestimated Moscow's interest in the Middle East.
> ❑ President Nixon in 1973 faced the tension between the regional Arab–Israeli conflict and the Cold War, when the Soviet–American rivalry in the Middle East brought the world to the brink of a nuclear confrontation.

Cold War. Once the Soviets had left, the USA turned its back on Afghanistan and the organizations it had created, with tragic consequences. Afghanistan, largely ignored by the USA and the international community, become the launch pad from which the attacks of 9/11 were planned and executed, providing the most traumatic example of Cold War blowback in the history of US diplomacy.

The United States and Israel

The United States' alliance with Israel has grown progressively closer from the founding of the state in 1948 until today. The American government now gives Israel $3 billion a year in military assistance and economic aid (Hudson 2005: 289). However, it is the United States' supportive relationship with Israel that is most often cited as a cause of Arab and more generally Muslim anger towards American foreign policy. The founding of the state of Israel led to the dispossession of tens of thousands of Palestinians and six major wars. It is both the continued exile of a large diaspora of Palestinian refugees along with Israel's occupation of the West Bank of the Jordan River and the Gaza Strip that fuel resentment towards both Israel and the United States.

Despite the cost, in terms of Arab public opinion and diplomatic censure, the American–Israeli relationship shows few signs of weakening. Both realist and constructivist explanations can be usefully deployed to examine the enduring nature of this alliance.

Constructivism and the special relationship

Constructivist explanations focus on the ideas and perceptions that the American public and more importantly their politicians have about Israel. This, they argue, is the key to explaining the strength and durability of the alliance. The relationship is deeply anchored into both history and cultural affinity. First, the murder and suffering that the Jewish population of Europe were subjected to during the Holocaust forms the backdrop against which the Israeli state was built. The empathy generated by such horrors is the bedrock upon which the American–Israeli relationship is constructed. The argument that the Israeli state was founded as a safe haven for all Jews, both the survivors of the Holocaust and those facing persecution elsewhere, meets with deep approval in the United States. In addition Israel's supporters argue that since 1948 it has been surrounded and outnumbered by hostile neighbours bent on its destruction. These arguments in favour of American support of Israel are strengthened by the perceived similarities the US public sees between their own history and that of Israel. The USA, like Israel, is a settler nation created by waves of mass immigration from Europe. At the core of America's own myth of nationhood is a pioneering spirit. This self-perception of pioneers building a state and society from scratch is very close to Israel's own myth of formation. Central to America's identity in the wider world is its democracy, a democracy that Israeli politicians are keen to stress they share. Added to these cultural affinities are religious ones. Various forms of Christianity dominate American society and the idea of Jews returning to the holy land resonates with their own reading of the Bible. This potent mix of history, national self-identity, and religion has been carefully cultivated and deployed by those mobilizing public opinion and lobbying the American government to pursue policies that favour Israel.

The realist explanation of US–Israeli relations is much more straightforward. It downplays or even discounts ideological influences. Instead it stresses Israel's role as a staunch ally during the Cold War and its aftermath. Surrounded by Arab regimes with ties to the Soviet Union, realists would argue that Israel has

---

❝ KEY QUOTES 12.1: The Middle East through American eyes

Because of their own pioneer heritage, Americans were even more apt than Europeans to identify with lurid images of brave, outnumbered settlers of European stock taming an arid land in the face of opposition from ignorant, fanatical nomads—wildly distorted and unrealistic (albeit lasting) though these images were.

(Khalidi 2004: 119)

From the dawn of the Cold War through the twilight of the twentieth century, US policy makers insisted time and again that Islamic radicals, Israeli prime ministers, and Iraqi dictators had merely misunderstood America's good intentions and that better understanding would produce better relations. Over the years, however, critics from Tel Aviv to Tehran have retorted that they understood those intentions all too well and that the peculiar blend of ignorance and arrogance that characterised US policy would effectively prevent Americans from ever truly understanding the region and its people.

(Little 2002: 2–3)

... America saw the world in rather simple terms: on one side was the Soviet Union and militant Third World nationalism, which America regarded as a Soviet tool; on the other side was political Islam, which American considered an unqualified all in the struggle against the Soviet Union.

(Mamdani 2004: 120)

Iraq provided a blank screen on which Americans were free to project anything they wanted, and because so few Americans had anything directly at stake there, many of them never saw more than the image of their feelings. The exceptions of course, were the soldiers and their families, who carried almost the entire weight of the war.

(Packer 2005: 382, 385)

The failure of state-building in Iraq raises a series of profound questions about US foreign policy in the wake of 9/11. The decision to invade and remove Saddam Hussein was meant to signal a new approach to international relations. The 'war against terror' was constructed in the broadest possible terms, uniting the disparate themes of terrorism with weapons of mass destruction and the instability of postcolonial states. By justifying the invasion in terms of democratising the Middle East, President Bush evoked a renewed, if supercharged, spirit of Wilsonian idealism. The sovereignty of states in the so-called 'developing world' was now dependent upon their ruling elites meeting US-defined responsibilities.

(Dodge 2006: 198)

provided a reliable partner in an unstable region. The United States' interests were continually furthered by giving the strategic, diplomatic, and economic support Israel needed to prosper. Realists examine the strength of US–Israeli relations in terms of the geostrategic utility to America of Israel's position in the Middle East.

The final argument seeking to explain the longevity and strength of the alliance would point to domestic electoral calculations. There is a very well-organized lobby designed to ensure US policy is very supportive of Israel. The leading organization in this lobby, the American Israeli Public Affairs Committee (AIPAC), has a membership of 100,000 and a yearly budget of $47 million (Massing 2006). By deploying both realist and constructivist arguments and tactics AIPAC has successfully mobilized American public opinion in support of Israel.

A second electoral calculation is the Jewish section of American society. Although estimated to number only between 2 and 3 per cent of the electorate, as a group they have one of the highest voter turnouts, with 89 per cent living in electorally key states, with enough votes to return a president (Bard 1994: 81). However, it is easy to overstate the electoral significance of the Israeli lobby. The majority of Jewish voters have a tendency to vote Democrat, reducing their tendency to change their preference on the basis of Israeli policy. Secondly, a broad consensus exists in mainstream politics around the issue of Israel.

Harry Truman, the US president in 1948, set a pattern for the way future American presidents dealt with Israel. In reaction to the horrors of the Holocaust, Truman pushed for Jewish emigration to Palestine. He also deployed diplomatic pressure at the United Nations in favour of dividing Palestine between a Jewish and Arab state, and authorized the recognition of Israel as soon as it declared statehood on 15 May 1948. Truman, clearly influenced by a close presidential election that year, ignored State Department warnings about the negative effect recognition would have on US influence in the wider region.

Eisenhower and Israel

As the Cold War escalated, Truman's successor President Eisenhower became increasingly aware of the damage America's relations with Israel were causing in the Arab Middle East. This alarm reached its peak with the Suez crisis in October 1956. Eisenhower, because the Anglo–French–Israeli invasion of Egypt coincided with US presidential elections, came face to face with the electoral mathematics surrounding Israeli policy. Eisenhower, casting these concerns aside, pushed the United Nations to condemn the invasion and was re-elected with a landslide over the Democrats. He then went on to push for UN sanctions against Israel. Faced with a concerted public campaign to overturn this decision he confronted the issue directly in a television broadcast which resulted in an Israeli climb-down (Little 2002: 92).

Eisenhower, in the run-up to and during the Suez crisis, decided that US interests in the Middle East and its Cold War foreign policy more generally were directly harmed by its relations with Israel. With this foremost in his mind, he ignored the potential electoral risks, and took his argument directly to the American people, over the heads of the American–Israeli lobby, defending his policy. Eisenhower subsequently implemented the approach he thought best served America's interests and Israel was forced into a compromise.

The Arab–Israeli conflict descended into open warfare for the third time in 1967 under Lyndon B. Johnson's presidency. The stunning victory that Israel inflicted on its Arab neighbours confirmed in American public opinion the David and Goliath image of Israel fighting to win against all the odds. Johnson, who believed that Eisenhower had been far too lenient on Egypt during the Suez crisis, saw the discrediting of Nasser by the Israeli military as a welcome retort. The victory of America's ally Israel over Arab states supported by the Soviet Union was similarly perceived as beneficial to US power. The aftermath of the Six-Day War left Israel in occupation of Jordanian, Egyptian, and Syrian territory. It also cemented American–Israeli diplomatic and military relations, removing any ambiguity from the partnership.

Nixon and Yom Kippur

The Nixon Doctrine of developing regional proxies had strengthened Israel's status as a key ally in the fight against Soviet influence. The surprise attack launched by Syria and Egypt over the Jewish holiday of Yom Kippur placed that policy in doubt. The Arab armies made early gains, with Egyptian tanks crossing the Suez Canal and the Syrians threatening to retake the Golan Heights.

Israeli Prime Minister Golda Meir made a desperate plea to Nixon for help and the president responded with a massive airlift of 11,000 tons of military equipment and munitions that gave the Israeli military yet another victory. However, such sustained US support for Israel's success triggered a united Arab response; the oil embargo against America and western Europe.

For the Nixon administration, the 1973 war highlighted the destabilizing effect of the ongoing Arab–Israeli conflict on the region and America's interests. Nixon's foreign policy guru, Henry Kissinger, was assigned the task of defusing the conflict. Through 1974 and 1975 Kissinger flew back and forth to the region, first brokering a disengagement agreement and then persuading Israel to undertake a limited redeployment of troops in return for even greater American military assistance, oil supplies, and economic aid.

Following the Yom Kippur War, Kissinger was unable to secure a sustainable peace settlement because Israel was unwilling to embark on further territorial compromise. It was regional diplomacy that broke the stalemate, with Egyptian President Anwar Sadat boldly flying to Jerusalem in November 1977. By this time Jimmy Carter was in the White House and he had to structure a peace process that would capitalize on Sadat's statesmanship. It created the first sustainable peace settlement between Israel and one of its Arab neighbours. The signing in Washington of the March 1979 Treaty of Peace between Egypt and Israel ended thirty-one years of hostility between the two states and was built around the 'land for peace' formula originally suggested by the UN in 1967. Israel agreed to withdraw its troops from the Sinai Peninsula, which it had seized from Egypt. In return America compensated Israel economically and committed itself to continued generous financial and military support for both Israel and Egypt. Thus the United States underwrote the peace treaty with considerable economic incentives for both sides. However, for the hawkish Israeli Prime Minister, Menanchen Begin, this was not the beginning of a comprehensive peace deal with the Palestinians or Israel's Arab neighbours but the splitting of the Arab front. Vague references in the treaty to Palestinian self-rule were never acted upon and Israel was free to continue building houses for Israelis in the territory on the west bank of the Jordan River it had seized in 1967.

James Baker and the Oslo peace process

It took the ending of the Cold War in 1989, Iraq's invasion of Kuwait, and then defeat in 1990–1 to trigger another sustained American attempt to solve the Arab–Israeli conflict. President Bush's Secretary of State, James Baker, came face to face with Arab resentment at the continuing stalemate with Israel when building the diplomatic and military coalition needed to eject Iraq from Kuwait. In the aftermath of that victory he applied economic pressure to Israel and shuttle diplomacy to the wider region to set up a multinational peace conference in Madrid in October 1991. Despite the diplomatic fanfare surrounding the talks in Spain and the subsequent Palestinian–Israeli negotiations in Washington, no breakthrough was achieved. Like Sadat's initiative in 1977, it was direct interaction between the main protagonists, the Palestinians and Israelis, which delivered a breakthrough in 1993. The negotiations were tellingly hosted by Norway, who were judged a more neutral arbiter than the United States. The resulting Israel–PLO Declaration of Principles was signed in Washington under the watchful eye of President Clinton. But this was not a fully-fledged peace treaty but a set of guidelines and aspirations for further negotiations. Those negotiations delivered restricted Palestinian self-rule in Gaza and parts of the West Bank, but the turbulent and violent history of Palestinian–Israeli relations since 1993 shows the profound limitations of the Oslo process. The Oslo process was followed by a separate peace treaty between Jordan and Israel. Again, however, the deal was basically bilateral, representing the work of the two states who signed it, not the success of muscular American diplomatic intervention (Shlaim 1995: 120–40).

The presidency of George W. Bush proved to be just as pro-Israeli as the presidencies of Clinton and Reagan before him. Barack Obama, as indicated in his 2009 Cairo speech, attempted to push the peace process forward by demanding that the Israeli government freeze the building of settlements on occupied Palestinian land. This was seen as the bare minimum needed to restart meaningful negotiations. After agreeing to a nine-month freeze, the Israeli government renewed its building programme and in doing so made the chance of a major breakthrough in negotiations negligible. US policy towards Israel after the Cold War has been based on similar if not identical foundations to those which guided policy since 1948, with Israel's military superiority being maintained at all costs. This, it is hoped, will give Israel the confidence to negotiate with the Palestinians and the Arab states from a position of unchallengeable strength. However, with the brief exception of James Baker in 1991, US diplomacy has proven to be chronically unable or unwilling to put enough pressure on Israel to deliver the compromises needed to reach sustainable peace settlements. This would involve implementing the United Nations Security Council Resolution 242, passed in November 1967. Israel would give up enough land on the West Bank for the Palestinians to create a sustainable state. It would also give back to the Syrians all of the territory of the Golan Heights it seized in 1967 in return for a peace settlement.

Now that the dynamics of the Cold War are well and truly in the past it is the constructivist argument, stressing an ideological affinity between US policy makers, their population, and Israel, which best explains American–Israeli relations. US opinion, both at a policy-making level and across the public in general, favours Israel to such an extent it appears diplomatically unable to apply the pressure needed to force the Israeli government to compromise. With US backing, Israel is militarily and diplomatically strong enough not to have to enter into sustained or meaningful negotiations with either the Palestinians or Syria, facilitating an ongoing conflict with no end in sight. The United States' continued support for Israel has certainly fuelled resentment amongst Arab and wider Muslim public opinion. It also prohibits any viable solution to a violent conflict at the heart of the Middle East. The direct costs of this conflict

> **KEY POINTS**
>
> ❑ The United States' supportive relationship with Israel is most often cited as a cause of Arab and more generally Muslim anger towards American foreign policy.
>
> ❑ Constructivist explanations of this relationship focus on the empathy generated by the horrors of the Holocaust, the pioneering spirit of Israeli state builders, its democracy, and an affinity between US Christians and Jews returning to the Holy Land.
>
> ❑ As the Cold War escalated, President Eisenhower became increasingly aware of the damage America's relations with Israel were causing in the Arab Middle East and attempted to constrain Israeli foreign policy in the Suez crisis of 1956.
>
> ❑ During the Arab–Israeli War of 1967 President Johnson, on the other hand, saw the victory of America's ally Israel over Arab states supported by the Soviet Union as beneficial to US power.
>
> ❑ President Nixon's extended support for Israel in the 1973 war resulted in the Arab oil embargo that quadrupled the world price of oil.
>
> ❑ It took the end of the Cold War to see a major breakthrough in Israeli–Palestinian relations with the Oslo agreements of 1993 that delivered limited self-rule to the Palestinians.
>
> ❑ US policy remains focused on maintaining Israel's military superiority in the hope that this will give them the confidence to negotiate a substantive peace deal with both the Palestinians and Syria.

to the United States have been the destabilization of a region of great geostrategic importance to them and a continued sense of resentment and anger. It is this anger that al-Qaeda and Islamic radicals have continued to exploit for recruitment and justification.

The United States and oil

There is a tension at the heart of United States' policy towards the Middle East between two of its primary interests: first the almost unquestioning support for Israel, but secondly to maintain the flow of oil at the lowest price from the Gulf region. The Arab Gulf states have been historically the leading financial backers of the struggle against Israel. The USA, when faced with the deep antipathy between Israel and the Arab Gulf states, has struggled to keep its relations with the two separate and the Arab–Israeli conflict confined to the front-line states surrounding Israel.

In examining America's relations with the oil-rich states of the Middle East the Marxist approach to international relations provides a series of powerful insights. As the American economy's dependence upon oil increased after 1945, US government policy increasingly became concerned with the stability and pliability of the main oil-producing states in the region. US military power, both overtly and covertly, has been repeatedly deployed to remove troublesome governments or support those whose ruling elites are close to Washington. Marxists would argue this is a clear example of the United States' political and military power being deployed to further the economic interests of American multinational corporations.

The interests of major American oil companies in the Middle East have slowly grown since the First World War. President Wilson's 'open door' policy was perfectly suited to their needs, giving access to the oil-rich former territories of the Ottoman Empire coveted by British and French companies. As the United States economy rapidly expanded during and after the Second World War, the US government came to view access to Middle East oil fields as a crucial issue for national security. Diplomacy and the military power of the American state would be deployed to ensure US oil companies could operate in the region on the best possible terms. With the rise of strident Middle Eastern nationalisms demanding economic sovereignty, this aim often clashed with the policies of regional governments.

The USA, Iran, Iraq, and oil

Two post-1945 examples show the extent and nature of US government attempts to shape the Middle East oil industry to its own advantage. In April 1951, the Iranian parliament, dominated by nationalists led by Mohammed Mosaddeq, passed a law nationalizing the Iranian oil industry. This triggered a clandestine intelligence operation by the US Central Intelligence Agency and the British. In August 1953, this operation reached its peak when the Iranian army, trained and advised by the American military since the Second World War, launched a coup that removed Mosaddeq and placed the pro-American Shah back on his throne. In the aftermath of the coup, nationalization was halted and the American oil company ARAMCO gained a 40 per cent share in the industry (Khalidi 2004: 90–1, 104).

Similar motives drove US interference in Iraq between 1958 and 1963. In 1958, a coup by army officers, led by Colonel Abdel Karim Qassim, seized power in Baghdad in the name of Arab nationalism. The new government set about drafting a law to nationalize the Iraqi Oil Company, which was jointly owned by British and American businesses. The Kennedy administration saw in Baghdad a dangerously radical government with increasing ties to Moscow seeking to reduce American control and profits from Middle Eastern oil. The American embassy in Baghdad established ties with dissident officers in the Iraqi army and a second coup in February 1963 ousted Qassim just before the nationalization of oil took place.

US interference in both Iranian and Iraqi politics may have postponed oil nationalization but had dramatic unintended consequences. In Iraq, the 1963 coup and a counter-coup later that year sparked off a series of violent military takeovers, which resulted in the Ba'ath party coming to power in 1968. They eventually nationalized the oil industry and were only removed in April 2003 by a US invasion. In Iran, once reinstalled, the Shah ruled until 1979 but was similarly removed from power, this time by a violent revolution inspired by Islamism and anti-Americanism.

OPEC and Israel

The United States' ability to keep the Arab–Israeli conflict separate from its relations with the oil-producing states of the region also dramatically broke down in 1973. The growing influence of nationalism across the region began to define the oil policies of the Arab Gulf states. During the 1960s, these countries became increasingly disgruntled by the low price of oil on the world market. This frustration resulted in the formation of the Organization of Oil Exporting Counties (OPEC) in 1960. During the Arab–Israeli Yom Kippur War of 1973, the Gulf states became increasingly outraged at the United States' large-scale and overt support for Israel. In retaliation, OPEC's Arab members deployed the oil weapon against America. The price of oil was increased by 70 per cent and production was cut by 5 per cent a month with an embargo placed on exports to America until Israel made major territorial concessions. By December 1973, the price of oil was four times what it had been in October. After twenty-five years of support for Israel, America's policy had finally caused it a direct and painful economic cost.

President Nixon sent Henry Kissinger to the Middle East to directly intervene in the conflict and he persuaded Israel to make some limited territorial compromises. Even though he convinced OPEC to lift its embargo in 1974, the price of oil continued to rise, reaching a new height when the news broke that another staunch American ally, the Shah of Iran, had been removed by an Islamic revolution in 1979. The USA, in an attempt to limit the damage of Islamic radicalism in Iran, supported Iraq in the eight-year Iran–Iraq War. But Iraq's invasion of Iran in 1980 further pushed up the price of oil.

Oil prices did not substantially fall until 1985 but United States oil policy towards the Middle East is still haunted by the unintended consequences of its actions. This was personified on 2 August 1990, when Saddam Hussein, previously supported by the United States in his war with Iran, invaded Kuwait. President George Bush Sr.'s response to this breach of international law summed up over fifty years of US policy towards the Gulf:

> **"**An Iraq permitted to swallow Kuwait would have the economic and military power, as well as the arrogance, to intimidate and coerce its neighbours—neighbours who control the lion's share of the world's remaining oil reserves . . . We cannot permit a resource so vital to be dominated by one so ruthless. And we won't. (Bush 1990)**"**

Although the war to liberate Iraq was launched in the name of democracy and a post-Cold War New World

---

KEY POINTS

- ❑ United States support of Israel has often been in conflict with its policy of obtaining oil from the Gulf at the lowest possible cost.
- ❑ As the American economy's dependence upon oil increased after 1945, US government policy became concerned with the stability and pliability of the main oil-producing states in the region.
- ❑ In 1953 the USA supported a coup in Iran aimed at stopping the nationalization of the Iranian oil industry.
- ❑ In the aftermath of Iraq's invasion of Kuwait in 1990, the USA put together a multinational coalition to liberate Kuwait and stop Saddam Hussein dominating oil supplies from the region.
- ❑ The USA has repeatedly intervened in the Middle East to secure its economic advantage but its policy cannot be reduced to a focus solely on oil.

Order, the region and its ruling regimes looked very similar in the aftermath of the invasion to before. US policy, focused amongst other things on the security of its oil supplies, had once again chosen to back the regimes it was familiar with, in the hope that conservative stability would deliver oil at the best possible price. With this in mind, Marxist explanations of US policy do have strong analytical purchase. The USA has clearly and repeatedly intervened in the region to secure economic advantage. However, the danger of this approach is that economic motivations are promoted to the exclusion of all others. Clearly America's relations with the Middle East cannot simply be reduced to the quest for cheap oil and the creation and defence of pliant regimes to deliver it.

Barack Obama, US foreign policy, and the Arab Spring

At the start of Barack Obama's presidency, his approach to foreign policy was shaped by a desire to distance his administration from that of George W. Bush and try to reverse the damage done to the United States' international reputation by the unilateral policies of his predecessor. During his speech in Cairo in June 2009, Obama promised 'a new beginning between the United States and the Muslim world' (Obama 2009a). Three months

later, when he addressed the United Nations General Assembly in New York, he guaranteed 'a new era of engagement with the world' in which the US would strive to act within multinational coalitions and abide by international law (Obama 2009b). This prompted one observer to speculate that a nascent Obama Doctrine would focus on global rights, responsibilities, and reciprocal exchange between states. This was 'certainly optimistic, rational and practical' but would ultimately remain an 'empty vessel' until it was 'filled with the details of real life' (Ignatius 2009).

A closer examination of the people Obama chose to run his foreign policy indicates a deliberate attempt at balancing realists, pursuing what they perceive to be America's national interest with liberal idealists seeking to use America's power to enforce a global regime of human rights and democracy. Thomas Donilon, the National Security Advisor from October 2010 and Robert Gates, the Secretary of Defence Obama chose to inherit from the administration of George W. Bush, were both unapologetically realist. However, Obama also appointed high-profile liberal idealists to key positions within the foreign policy-making structure. These included Susan Rice, his ambassador to the United Nations, Michael McFaul, the senior director for Russian policy on the National Security Council (NSC), and Samantha Power, who also serves in a senior role on the NSC.

This balance between realism and liberal idealism saw the administration, on one hand, stress the centrality of national interests and an abhorrence of the ideologically driven foreign policy they thought had caused the previous administration so much trouble. As Secretary of State Clinton said in April 2009, 'Let's put ideology aside; that is so yesterday.' However, the liberal idealists in the NSC were also influencing policy. When Obama accepted his Noble Peace Prize in Oslo in 2009 he directly addressed how and when the United States should go to war. He certainly went to great lengths to stress the international standards that had to govern the use of force and promised that the US would now follow these standards in all future interventions. However, he also went out of his way to stress that 'force can be justified on humanitarian grounds'. The 'slaughter of civilians by their own governments', stopping civil wars, and genocide could all now justify the use of America's military might against other states (Obama 2009c).

In the aftermath of the Cairo speech, the Obama administration did attempt to push the Israeli–Palestinian peace process forward. It was however, also trying to move away from what it saw as previous administrations' dangerous obsession with the Middle East. America's foreign policy was now to be 'rebalanced' towards Asia, the Pacific region, and specifically China (Lizza 2011).

This move away from the Middle East and the careful balancing between realism and liberal idealism was thrown into doubt by the events surrounding the Arab Spring in 2011. The Arab Spring or new Arab Awakening was triggered by a tragic event in the Tunisian town of Sidi Bouzid in December 2010. Mohamed Bouazizi, a vegetable seller, set himself on fire after being harassed by allegedly corrupt Tunisian officials. His subsequent death caused outrage and mass demonstrations across Tunisia that, after 29 days of protest, forced the president Zine el Abidine Ben Ali to flee into exile after 23 years of rule. This unprecedented upsurge in popular protest against the corrupt, dictatorial, and sclerotic regimes of the Middle East soon spread across the whole region.

The Obama administration found it difficult to react to such an unprecedented and fast-moving situation. Demonstrations calling for the removal of Egyptian president Hosni Mubarak quickly dominated central Cairo. Obama, in his State of the Union speech on 25 January 2011, praised the success of the Tunisian demonstrations but failed to mention events in Egypt (Lizza 2011). Mubarak had been Washington's long-term and very valuable ally in the region. He had a close relationship with Israel and actively supported its attempts at breaking the power of Hamas, the Palestinian radical Islamists who governed in the Gaza Strip (Lynch 2011, 35). Finally, after increasing violence against the protestors and a series of belligerent speeches by Mubarak, Obama announced his support for the Egyptian president's removal, 'what I indicated tonight to President Mubarak—is my belief that an orderly transition must be meaningful, it must be peaceful, and it must begin now' (Obama 2011a).

However, after Mubarak was safely removed from power by the Egyptian army another even greater foreign policy crisis presented itself in Libya. This would test the careful balance between realists and liberal idealists around which Obama had built his foreign policy team. The protest movement against the dictatorial rule of Libyan president Colonel Muammar Gadaffi centred on the eastern city of Benghazi but quickly spread west along the coast towards the capital Tripoli. The United Nations, with American backing, responded to the regime's violent attempts to suppress the revolt by tightening sanctions on Libya and forcing the country into diplomatic isolation. However, Obama's own foreign policy team were divided about the best way to proceed. Defence Secretary Robert Gates advised that a proposed no-fly zone would have little effect and anyone suggesting that 'a big American land army' should be sent into the Middle East needed to 'have his head examined' (Gates 2011). But the liberal idealists in the administration, McFaul, Power, and Rice, backed up by Secretary of State Clinton, persuaded the President to push for a UN Resolution that would give authorization for a no-fly zone to protect the Libyan demonstrators against the regime. The result was UN Resolution 1973, adopted on 17 March and enforced by US, French, and British war planes. Obama, in a speech justifying the use of force against Gadaffi's regime, echoed his Nobel Prize acceptance speech, arguing that the US had spent thirty-one days working with 'our international partners to mobilize a broad coalition' and 'secure an international mandate to protect civilians' (Obama 2011b). Three times during this speech Obama justified military action by saying it stopped what would have become a massacre if Libyan troops had entered the city of Benghazi.

The use of American military force against the Libyan army raised a series of issues about Obama's foreign policy. First is the issue of consistency. After some hesitation, Obama called for the removal of the Egyptian president Hosni Mubarak and then used force against the Libyan government. However, at exactly the same time, the government of Bahrain, with the assistance of Saudi Arabian troops, used military force to suppress demonstrations calling for democracy. These demonstrators were much more peaceful than the comparable protestors in Libya. Although US diplomats unsuccessfully tried to broker a compromise, their criticism of the Bahraini and Saudi use of violence to suppress pro-democratic protests was very muted. No-one in

Washington suggested deploying diplomatic sanctions, let alone military force, against either government. Secondly, more analytically nuanced critiques of the 2003 US invasion of Iraq stressed not only its illegality but also its unsustainable presumption that the deployment of American military power could deliver a better life for Iraqis. Libya is one of the least institutionalized states in the Arab world. The deployment of American airpower may have temporarily stopped Libyan government forces from taking back control of Benghazi but it did not immediately removed Gadaffi from power and could not help reconstruct the Libyan state or guarantee the protection of the people's human rights or the rule of law in any post-Gadaffi future. This leaves President Obama open to similar criticisms to those levelled at President George W. Bush, that in listening to the liberal idealists in the NSC he was too quick to deploy military force, with little or no idea what the long-term consequences would be. In short, he tried to deliver on liberal idealist promises through the short-term application of military power without paying sufficient attention to the ramifications of his actions.

If the reaction of US administration to the Arab Spring heralds the birth of a fully fledged 'Obama Doctrine' then its promoters will argue that it was the time taken to build an international coalition and obtain a UN Security Council Resolution that marks it out from George W. Bush's previous forays into the Middle East in search of democratization. However, sceptics will counter by arguing that the problems faced by Obama's new policy in Afghanistan, centrally its inability to build the capacity of the Afghan state or guarantee democracy, were not helped and may well have been hindered by the international coalition and UN presence that accompanied it.

Conclusion: from Woodrow Wilson to Barack Obama: continuity and change in US foreign policy towards the Middle East?

The attacks on the United States by al-Qaeda on 11 September 2001 gave rise to an intense debate about the causes and consequences of America's relations with

the Middle East. Where had this radical ideology of violence come from? Who or what was to blame? The removal of the Taliban in Afghanistan, because they gave sanctuary to the senior leadership of al-Qaeda, was undertaken with speed. However, the longer-term goals of the Bush administration in the wake of 9/11 took some time to emerge. Eventually the Bush Doctrine committed the United States to fighting a global war against terror, stopping the spread of weapons of mass destruction in combination with the muscular promotion of democratization across the Middle East. The invasion of Iraq launched by George W. Bush appeared to combine all three motives. Saddam Hussein had defied United Nations sanctions for over a decade, was falsely thought to be committed to building weapons of mass destruction, and was undoubtedly a bloody dictator.

Marxist scholars were quick to identify the economic logic of oil underpinning the decision to unseat Saddam (Harvey 2003: 24–5). One realist, John Lewis Gaddis, supported the invasion, calling for a 'repeat of the Afghan Agincourt on the banks of the Euphrates' (Gaddis 2002). Interestingly, however, many more notable realists very publicly set themselves against the invasion, arguing that it was a miscalculation driven by ideology, not a rational assessment of US interests (Mearsheimer 2005; Bacevich 2005). It is the overtly ideological content of the Bush Doctrine which sets it aside from previous US foreign policies toward the Middle East. Repeatedly before and after the invasion itself, George Bush committed his government to spreading democracy throughout the Middle East (Bush 2003). The realist approach adopted by his predecessors, which supported dictators because they were allied with Washington, was jettisoned. Instead the goal was a transformation of the governing systems throughout the Middle East, if necessary using American military power to democratize the region. This represented a major point of departure from traditional US policy guided by the principles of realism, with its focus on the amoral maximization of power.

However, the dangers of US policy soon became apparent; there was a backlash from those who did not want to be dictated to by the world's sole remaining superpower. George Bush's vision of what Iraqis needed collided violently with realities on the ground in Baghdad.

One of the most far-reaching and bold attempts to change US foreign policy towards the Middle East since Woodrow Wilson resulted in tens of thousands of people dying (Dodge 2007). Barack Obama was in part elected to succeed George W. Bush because of foreign policy mistakes, most of them in Middle East, that Bush had made during his two terms in office. Although Obama's election campaign was driven by powerful idealist rhetoric, his foreign policy once in office sought unambiguously to return US foreign policy to its realist roots. Early on in his presidency, Obama did speed up the timetable for America troop withdrawal from Iraq. However, the rhetoric and promises placed at the heart of the speech he gave in Cairo were not delivered on and this is bound to further deepen the already powerful cynicism across the Middle East towards America's foreign policy goals and motives in the region.

KEY POINTS

❑ In the wake of 9/11 the Bush Doctrine committed the United States to fighting a global war against terror, stopping the spread of weapons of mass destruction in combination with the muscular promotion of democratization across the Middle East.

❑ The invasion of Iraq launched in March 2003 by George W. Bush appeared to combine all three motives.

❑ The majority of realist academics were against the invasion, arguing that it was a miscalculation driven by ideology not a rational assessment of US interests.

❑ It is the overtly ideological promotion of democracy that sets the Bush Doctrine apart from previous US foreign policies towards the Middle East.

❑ The US invasion of Iraq resulted in the collapse of the state, a violent civil war, and tens of thousands of deaths. It will almost certainly be viewed as a major defeat for the USA.

? Questions

1. What has been the balance between interests and ideology in the evolution of the United States' relations with the Middle East since the First World War?

2. What accounts for the differences of approach to the Middle East between President Wilson after the First World War and George W. Bush after 9/11?

3. Does a realist or constructivist approach best explain US foreign policy towards the Middle East?

4. What accounts for President Eisenhower's policy towards Israel?

5. What accounts for President Eisenhower's reaction to the Suez crisis of 1956?

6. Can the application of the Nixon Doctrine to the Middle East be judged a success?

7. Was the Carter Doctrine an overreaction to the Soviet Union's invasion of Afghanistan?

8. Was Ronald Reagan right to see the Lebanese civil war as an extension of the Cold War?

9. What accounts for the durability of America's special relationship with Israel?

10. Is Marxism the best approach to explaining the United States policy towards oil in the Middle East?

11. Did the OPEC oil embargo of 1973 represent a failure of US policy towards the Middle East?

12. To what extent is the Bush Doctrine a major departure from previous US foreign policy towards the Middle East?

» Further Reading

Cooley, J. (2002), *Unholy Wars: Afghanistan, America and International Terrorism* (London: Pluto Press).

A detailed discussion of the United States' relations with radical Islam.

Halliday, F. (2005), *The Middle East in International Relations: Power, Politics, Ideology* (Cambridge: Cambridge University Press).

Khalidi, R. (2004), *Resurrecting Empire: Western Footprints and America's Perilous Path in the Middle East* (London: I.B. Tauris).

A trenchant critique of the United States' relations with the Middle East by a renowned historian.

Little, D. (2002), *American Orientalism: The United States and the Middle East since 1945* (London: I.B. Tauris).

A detailed diplomatic history of the United States' relations with the Middle East, written from a constructivist point of view.

Packer, G. (2005), *Assassins' Gate: America in Iraq* (New York: Farrar, Straus and Giroux).

The best book yet written on the reasons for the US invasion of Iraq and its failure.

Quandt, W.B. (2005), *Peace Process: American Diplomacy and the Arab-Israeli Conflict since 1967* (Berkeley and Los Angeles: University of California Press).

A diplomatic history of America's role in trying to solve the Arab-Israeli conflict.

Shlaim, A. (1995), *War and Peace in the Middle East: A Concise History* (Harmondsworth: Penguin).

A wide-ranging historical account of US-Middle East relations.

Westad, O.A. (2005), *The Global Cold War: Third World Interventions and the Making of our Times* (Cambridge: Cambridge University Press).

A very detailed historical work on the relationship between Cold War and the third world, stressing the role of ideology.

 For a range of additional resources to support your learning visit the Online Resource Centre that accompanies this book at www.oxfordtextbooks.co.uk/orc/cox_stokes2e/.

Endnote

1. I would like to thank Clare Day and Tim Lynch for reading earlier versions of the text and recommending improvements.

13 The USA and the EU

Mike Smith

Chapter contents

Introduction

This chapter explores one of the key relationships in which the USA has been involved since the end of the Second World War: the transatlantic relationship with the European integration project. This is a relationship not with a single state, but with a densely institutionalized region, which has itself grown and become markedly more prominent in the world arena over the past half-century. American foreign policy makers have generally been consistent in their support for the integration project, but it has challenged US foreign policy in a number of important areas. The focus of the chapter is thus on the ways in which US policy makers have developed images of the European Community (EC) and now the European Union (EU) on the challenges posed by European integration for US policy processes and the uses of US power, and on the ways in which these challenges have been met in the very different conditions of the Cold War and post-Cold War periods.

This is a relationship with a history, and also one that has seen considerable change, both in the context within which it is conducted and in the content with which it is concerned. In terms of the context, US policies towards European integration have spanned both the Cold War and the post-Cold War periods, and have also contended with the growth of globalization and its consequences. In terms of content, US policy makers have had to adapt to a European project that has expanded both in scope and scale, and which has become a central feature in the foreign policies of individual European Union member states, some of whom are among the USA's oldest and closest allies.

The purpose of this chapter is to explore the ways in which American foreign policy makers have promoted or responded to these changes, and to point out some of the key areas of tension that have emerged from the changing relationship between the USA and European integration. The chapter begins with a review of key factors in the evolution of the relationship within US foreign policy up to the end of the Cold War, focusing especially on US images of the European integration processes and on responses to change. This is followed by an analysis of key trends and tensions during the period. The third part of the chapter then focuses on the ways in which the post-Cold War period has thrown up new changes and challenges, and the ways in which these have been dealt with by US policy makers, again with attention to images and responses. As with the analysis of the Cold War period, this is followed by an evaluation of trends and tensions in the period since 1990. The conclusions raise a number of questions about the capacity of the USA to shape and adapt to European integration, and thus about the future of the USA–EU relationship.

Fig. 13.1 Map of the European Union.

US foreign policy and European integration

Images and adaptation

As shown elsewhere in this volume (Chapter 4), the end of the Second World War ushered in a period of uncertainty in US foreign policy. The emergence of the US 'liberal order' was not a preordained outcome, and indeed the initial US position on continued involvement in western Europe was shaped by the desire to retreat to the American homeland. But the development and definition of the Soviet threat between 1945 and 1947 led to a redefinition of US policies towards Europe that had a profound effect on European integration (DePorte 1986; Grosser 1982; Heller and Gillingham 1996).

Central to this reorientation of US foreign policy was the Marshall Plan—the system of financial and other assistance that contributed to the recovery and stabilization of the western European countries, and thus, it can be argued, to the initiation of European integration itself. Secretary Marshall's speech made at Harvard University in June 1947 concentrated on the need for immediate economic assistance, but also had an explicitly political aim: to stabilize (or in some cases, to create) democratic institutions and free markets, which were seen as two sides of the same coin. Between 1947 and 1950, the European Recovery Programme (ERP) channelled $19 billion of US aid to those countries that accepted the ground rules, and by so doing also accentuated the Cold War division of Europe by excluding the countries of the developing Soviet bloc (Hogan 1987; Milward 1984). Because the aid was given explicitly on the basis that the European recipients would cooperate in its distribution and the associated planning processes, it is possible to see this as the seed of the eventual European integration process. When in 1950 Robert Schuman and Jean Monnet proposed the Schuman Plan for the creation of a European Coal and Steel Community (ECSC), this was generally welcomed in the US administration as a further step in the recovery and consolidation process. The ERP and the ECSC together, it can be claimed, expressed the US position in the political economy of western Europe and led to the 'Americanization' of large parts of European industry.

But this was not the whole story. Alongside the ECSC, US policy makers had come—in some cases reluctantly—to the conclusion that they needed a long-term commitment to European security, not just to economic and political recovery. This was what lay at the bottom of the North Atlantic Treaty (NAT) signed in 1949 by the USA and fourteen other members (western European plus Canada). It is important to note here that the NAT and subsequently the North Atlantic Treaty Organization (NATO) are not strictly 'European integration'—they were explicitly transatlantic, with a dominant US presence expressed in military and political structures. One immediate consequence, though, was a focus on the need to rearm West Germany in order for it to play its part in the defence of the 'western alliance'. This led the French to propose a further and dramatic step in European integration: the creation of a European Defence Community with a multinational structure and a common military command. Whilst not sponsored by the Americans, this was eventually accepted as a way to create a robust European 'pillar' of the Atlantic alliance. When in 1954 it was defeated, ironically by the French National Assembly, the Americans and the British stepped in to provide an alternative structure through which the West Germans could eventually join NATO and be rearmed as part of the Atlantic alliance (Fursdon 1980).

By the mid-1950s, therefore, it could be argued that the Americans had achieved all of their key goals in respect of European integration. They had fostered European cooperation in key industries, and had managed to get the West Germans integrated into the NATO command and political structure. Led by the State Department, US foreign policy elites saw European integration as an unquestioned and positive contribution to western security, and also to the development of a liberalized 'western' world economy centred on the Atlantic area. The Eisenhower administration wanted this to go further, through the entry into European institutions of Britain and other key NATO allies. Thus, when the original six member states of the ECSC set out in 1955 to create a European Economic Community (EEC), US policy makers saw this as positive, despite the fears of some that it might constitute a protectionist economic bloc that would damage American agricultural and industrial interests (Winand 1993).

It is important to note, though, that this position was not aligned with some of the emerging realities of life in the 'new Europe'. The British proved strangely reluctant to immerse themselves in what they saw as a second-rank organization, partly because of their perceived 'special relationship' with the USA itself. At the same time, the French saw US enthusiasm for British membership as a sign of a malign hegemony, which led them ever more strongly to emphasize the EEC's role as a point of resistance to US policies. President Charles de Gaulle, who held power in France from 1958 to 1969, was especially sensitive to the American threat, and made constant efforts to turn the West Germans and others away from their Atlanticist orientation. As a result, when in 1962 John F. Kennedy made a major speech calling for the development of a true 'Atlantic partnership' between the United States and a uniting Europe, this became a major point of friction rather than a rallying point. Throughout the remainder of the 1960s, the discourse among US policy makers about 'Atlantic partnership' or 'Atlantic community' was countered by calls from Paris for resistance to US domination and for the use of the EEC as a means of fighting back (Calleo 1970; Cleveland 1966). Ironically, this was accompanied by a substantial flow of US foreign direct investment into the EEC—a factor that was to contribute greatly to integration at the transatlantic level, and to become a significant influence on US foreign economic policy (Krause 1968).

The late 1960s, therefore, saw contradictory trends in US policies towards European integration. On the one side, there was the continuing rhetoric of 'Atlantic partnership' as part of the broader Cold War system—a rhetoric which defined the EEC as part of the 'western system' and as the economic equivalent of NATO. This rhetoric was strongly dedicated to the leading role of NATO in western security, and incidentally as a major source of US leverage over the countries of western Europe. On the other side, there was the rhetoric of 'adversarial partnership', focusing on the challenge posed by the French and on the danger of a developing 'third way' which might turn into a European form of neutralism or non-alignment. This second rhetoric was given added force by the economic turbulence of the late 1960s, by the loss of dynamism in the US economy,

and by the feeling that the Europeans had profited from US financial and military support without playing their full part in return.

In this context, the Nixon–Kissinger foreign policy conducted between the late 1960s and the mid-1970s played a crucial catalytic role. In economic terms, Nixon and Kissinger subscribed to the view that the USA was an 'ordinary country' which needed to defend its national economic interests and to protect itself against those who took advantage of the liberal international economy (Rosecrance 1976). In security terms, the Nixon Doctrine implied that America's allies would have to do far more to protect themselves and pay far more towards the costs of alliance, both in Europe and elsewhere. For European integration, this policy stance held important implications. It meant that they could no longer rely on the USA as a benign hegemonic force in the global economy, and that they could no longer count on the unqualified support of the USA for European defence. US policy makers came to see European integration as much more of a problem than a solution; the EEC's development of foreign policy cooperation, with its insistence that the Community was a 'civilian power', implied to US policy makers that the Community was a means of hiding from international obligations and developing a form of the non-alignment that they feared and despised. The entry of the British into the EEC in 1973 thus could be defined not as a triumph for US policy but as a worrying move that could lead to the loss of their most trusted ally. The Nixon–Kissinger response was characteristic: Kissinger proclaimed 1973 'the year of Europe' and called for the conclusion of a new Atlantic treaty in line with the administration's idea of the global 'structure of peace' (Cromwell 1978). But this initiative, which had not been discussed with any European governments, fell on stony ground in a year when the combination of EEC enlargement, conflict in the Middle East, and an accompanying oil price crisis preoccupied European policy makers.

US policies towards European integration during the early 1970s might thus be summarized as a form of wary containment, but this misses the point that the EEC had become a genuine economic rival to the USA in a number of major areas. Although the Community's plans for economic, monetary, and political union by 1980 came to little or nothing, the 1970s as a whole gave evidence of the fact that the Americans needed the

Community as much as the Community needed them. Thus the process of adjustment in US policy positions and policy rhetoric could be observed, especially during the Carter administration between 1976 and 1980: Europeans were seen as partners in interdependence and as a focus for cooperation within international institutions, although this was not without its own difficulties in a period of economic stagnation (Hoffmann 1978). European foreign policy cooperation was a source of worry, for example over the Middle East where the Community members were much more pro-Palestinian than was Washington, but as it became clear that European declarations would lead to little substantive policy change, this suspicion moderated (Allen and Smith 1983).

Much of this apparent reconciliation was dissipated by the events of the 'second cold war' and by the arrival of the Reagan administration in 1980. Reaganism attacked the Europeans on two fronts. First, it politicized and 'domesticized' American foreign economic policies, leading to a concentration on the needs of the US economy but also to a strong emphasis on the sin of 'trading with the enemy', in this case the Soviet bloc in particular. For some Europeans, this rhetoric and the subsequent application of 'extra-territorial' measures to restrict trade with the Soviet bloc was evident of US unilateralism and a form of imperialism; for others, such as the British, it was defined much more positively as a reassertion of US leadership. That is certainly the way the US administration saw it: the USA was the leader of the free world, and was assuming its responsibilities (Allen and Smith 1989).

The second area in which US foreign policy challenged European integration was in the development of the fledgling 'European' foreign and security policies. Here, we can see again the 'containment' aspect of the

---

> **KEY QUOTES 13.1:** US policy makers and European integration in the Cold War

The Marshall Plan Speech, 1947

It is evident . . . that, before the United States Government can proceed much further with its efforts to alleviate the situation and help the European world on its way to recovery, there must be some agreement among the countries of Europe as to the requirements of the situation and the part those countries themselves will take in order to give proper effect to whatever action might be undertaken by the Government. It would neither be fitting nor efficacious for this Government to undertake to draw up unilaterally a program designed to place Europe on its feet economically. This is the business of the Europeans. The initiative, I think, must come from Europe. The role of this country should consist of friendly aid in the drawing up of a European program and of later support of such a program so far as it may be practical for us to do so. The program should be a joint one, agreed to by a number, if not all, of Europe's nations.

(Marshall 1947; George C. Marshall was US Secretary of State)

'The Transatlantic Relationship: A Long-Term Perspective'

I have often discussed with European friends the different requirements for a nation with global responsibilities to those with more regional concerns. The use of the word global is not meant in any arrogant fashion. Nor is it to deny the interests that several European nations retain in areas of the world beyond their continent. But the sheer scope of American interests engages us in a different set of perspectives and imperatives. I am persuaded that despite periodic inconsistencies (mainly on our part) and even more frequent crises of policy disagreement (emanating frequently from the European side) members of the alliance can still forge a strong consensus on most issues of importance . . . [but] . . . now may well be the appropriate moment for all of us—Europeans and Americans—to take a new look at where we should be going together and how we should get there . . . The two pillars of a 'smarter' relationship, in my opinion, are: increasing respect for the differences in our alliance; and a more coordinated approach—across the board—to all political, economic and security issues with our European allies.

(Eagleburger 1984; Eagleburger was US Under Secretary of State for Political Affairs)

US stance *vis-à-vis* European integration. US policy makers felt strongly that they did not want the Community to develop in such a way as to erode NATO, or to reduce their capacity to form 'special relationships' with individual EEC member states. In pursuit of this stance, Washington was prepared to use its connections with the British and others to ensure that any new developments in the Community were moderated and always made subject to the primary role of NATO in ensuring European security (Treverton 1985; Joffe 1987). Thus during the late 1980s when the revival of the Western European Union created a platform for a distinct European defence identity, the White House was quick to emphasize the dire consequences of any attempt to duplicate or undermine NATO.

Trends and tensions

The review of US attitudes towards European integration up to the end of the 1980s reveals that the relationship as a whole was characterized by a number of overall trends and a number of persistent tensions. For US foreign policy, a key trend was the move from apparently unqualified hegemony to a position where leadership had to be justified and legitimized (see Box 13.1). Another associated trend was what might be called the problem of leadership and followership: by the end of this period, EC member states had become far less inclined simply to follow where the USA led, but at the same time there were areas where they could not collectively follow. A third trend was in the adaptation of US policy makers' images of the EC: not surprisingly, these images often said more about the needs and priorities of US foreign policy than they did about the evolving realities of the European project, and they were also 'sticky', that is, resistant to change. Finally, US policy makers' approach to European integration was clearly conditioned to significant degrees by events in US–Soviet relations, as Cold War tensions fluctuated and evolved in periods of détente or 'new cold war'. Thus, the European project could be seen as a pillar of the western alliance, as a breeding ground for neutralism or non-alignment, or as a source of often intense economic competition. In reality, of course, it was often all three of these at once, with consequent implications for the focus and direction of US policy.

Alongside these trends and tensions in the images held by US policy makers went another set of significant connections and interactions. From the outset, relations between the USA and European integration were an uneasy combination of the political, the economic, and the security related. Between 1950 and 1990, the balance and linkages between these three components of the relationship grew, shifted, and evolved, and this was a key issue for policy makers in Washington. Thus, during the 1950s and 1960s, it was tempting to see the integration process as somehow separate from the political and security dimensions of the relationship, and as somehow subordinate to the demands of NATO and of superpower diplomacy. In many ways this was never true, but the 1970s disposed of the myth in no uncertain terms. The politicization of economic issues (especially in the energy crisis), the use of economic sanctions (for example against Iran, or the Soviet bloc in the 'new cold war'), and the increasing attention to issues of high technology as matters of foreign or national security policy, all meant that US views of the 'economic' integration process needed to change. As noted above, these images were often 'sticky', and American policy makers found it difficult to adjust to the world of economic power, in which the preconditions for what later came to be termed globalization were being established. By the end of the 1980s, with the initiation of new stages of European integration through the Single Market Programme, and with discussion of economic and monetary union in the EC, the tensions were still observable and if anything more severe than before.

A third set of trends and tensions, strongly related to those described above, was in the stance of US foreign policy overall, as affected by and expressed in their relationship to European integration (Smith 2000). It can be argued that three central trends are observable in US policies towards the integration project. The first can be termed 'imperial': the integration project was subsumed willingly or unwillingly within the creation and maintenance of an American empire, in which transatlantic relations were a central component (Lundestad 1998). A subset of this trend is the exercise of hegemony, and the holding of hegemonic assumptions about the nature of US–EC relations, whether these relate to trade, to monetary relations, or to foreign and defence policies (Calleo 1987). In this trend, US policy makers assumed

---

BOX 13.1:   Trends and tensions in US–EU relations, 1945–80s

- *Images and reality*: move from US hegemony to questioning of leadership and legitimacy; problems of 'leadership and followership'; 'stickiness' of adjustment of images and expectations in US policy making; influence of fluctuations in US–Soviet relations.
- *Politics, economics, and security*: shifting balance and linkages; intersection of the three areas, and consequent 'politicization' of economic issues especially in the 1970s

(Middle East, 'new cold war'); impact of intensification of European integration in the 1980s.
- *Empire, alliance, and interdependence*: challenges to US assumptions of European dependence; US capacity to 'divide and rule' through 'special relationships'; tensions between 'imperial' assumptions, those of 'alliance', and those of 'interdependence', affecting policies, institutions, and 'rules of the game'.

---

that the European project was essentially dependent, that they held the power to make the rules within which integration proceeded, and that they could also detach key EC member states when the need for 'special relationships' overrode the need for a relationship with the EC as a whole.

Alongside the 'imperial' component of US policies towards European integration went two other, not always compatible, trends. One was what might be termed 'alliance', according to which the relationship with the EC was a part of the broader Western system and subject to rules and conventions about leadership and followership (Sloan 2005). As we have seen above, this dimension of US policy was consistent throughout the 1950–90 period, and the Europeans came increasingly to make their collective voices heard within the alliance structure. But this dimension was of course in tension with persistent 'imperial' tendencies, which might admit the need for alliance but also emphasize

American structural dominance in all of the areas that really mattered. Both 'imperial' and 'alliance' trends were in tension with the third dimension of the relationship: that of 'interdependence'. The growth of transactions, exchange, and institutions in the Atlantic area during the 1950s and 1960s created a dense region of interdependence, in which the actions (both domestic and external) of each of those involved had implications for all of the others (Cooper 1968). During the 1970s and 1980s this reality became more apparent, and US policy makers were faced with the need to incorporate interdependence thinking into their approach to European integration. Not only this, but they were compelled to go beyond interdependence into the realm of what some observers called 'interpenetration'—where US and European societies and economies were so closely linked that it was difficult to work out 'who is us' and 'who is them'. Not surprisingly, these views were more strongly rooted in some parts of the US administrations

---

KEY POINTS

- ❏ In the early years of the Cold War, the US position in Europe was consolidated, and the European integration process was part of this consolidation.
- ❏ Nonetheless, there were tensions in US policies about the extent to which on the one hand the European project should be part of the Cold War system and the 'western alliance', and on the other hand the basis for a more independent Europe. US policy makers' images were shaped not only by relations with the EEC, but also by Cold War priorities and by domestic needs.

- ❏ From the late 1950s onwards, US policy makers had to respond to change within the EEC, especially its continuing economic growth and the beginnings of political assertiveness. This created a kind of 'containment' policy on the part of the USA, alongside continuing support for the integration process as a whole.
- ❏ As a result, there were continuing tensions involving issues of US leadership, the linkage between political, economic, and security factors, and three strands in US policies: 'empire', 'alliance', and 'interdependence'.

than others, and in some administrations than others. Thus the Carter administration in the late 1970s played heavily on the interdependence theme, but this was not welcomed by those within the political system and US society more broadly who believed in the restoration of US dominance. Equally, the Reagan administrations of the 1980s emphasized the 'imperial' or hegemonic aspects of the relationship, but found themselves confounded at times by the impact of alliance politics and interdependence.

The United States and the European Union

The purpose of this section is to explore the ways in which the changing European integration project interacted with changes in US foreign policy after 1990, and thus to arrive at an assessment of the ways in which the central trends and tensions in the relationship changed during that period. As before, the chapter looks first at images and responses in US foreign policy, and then at trends and tensions.

Images and responses

As with the end of the Second World War, the end of the Cold War ushered in a period of uncertainty and fluctuation in US foreign policy. As shown in Chapter 5, the tension between triumphalism and caution in Washington, and in the country as a whole, was a key feature of the early 1990s, as was the tension between internationalism and 'domesticism'. These tensions were still present in the early years of the new millennium, as the search for an effective 'grand strategy' in US foreign policy evoked painful and often highly partisan debates. Our interest here is in the ways in which the EC and after 1993 the EU took their place in these debates, and in the images that US foreign policy makers deployed in their efforts to meet the challenge of renewed European dynamism.

For the George H. W. Bush administration that presided over the end of the Cold War, a number of key factors played into their redefinition of relations with European integration. One was that the end of the Cold War was a European process—albeit one with global reverberations. In consequence, it was tempting for the administration to see the EC as playing a new and special role in stabilizing and assisting the reconstruction of the eastern half of the continent (Smith and Woolcock 1993; Treverton 1992). James Baker, the Secretary of State, made this abundantly clear as early as December 1989, in the immediate aftermath of the fall of the Berlin Wall, when he underlined the EC's role in the 'New World Order'. For Baker, the EC should enlarge to the east, and quickly, to provide the anchor for the newly liberated states of the ex-Soviet bloc. This did not mean that the US position in Europe, and especially NATO, should be abandoned; it did mean, though, that the EC was seen as a major 'subcontractor' in the establishment of a new European order. Thus the Americans were willing to give the EC a lead role in providing aid to the ex-Soviet states and in coordinating the provision of reconstruction assistance at the continental level. They were also willing to envisage a new diplomatic and security role for the EC, giving it responsibility for more of the 'hard security' issues that were likely to emerge in the 'new Europe' and also for the broader range of 'soft security' issues arising from such areas as migration or the development of human rights regimes.

This US perception was buttressed to a large degree by the evident willingness of leading European states to take the lead in the new European order. During 1990 and 1991, the negotiations that led to the Treaty on European Union and to the establishment of a Common Foreign and Security Policy for the EU led many to believe that a new era of political and defence integration was just over the horizon. As during the Cold War, the development of these new areas of integration was broadly welcomed by Washington, for reasons especially of 'grand strategy' (see above), but the EC and its members proved rather less able (or in some cases, willing) to follow through with dramatic initiatives. One of the problems for Washington in dealing with the EC and then the EU has always been the question attributed to Henry Kissinger during the early 1970s: 'if I want to talk to Europe, who do I call?' In the conditions of Europe immediately after the end of the Cold War, this question was if anything more pressing than before but the answer was still not easy to discern.

For US policy makers, therefore, the early 1990s were years of frustration as well as expectation where the EU was concerned. The Europeans had agreed a treaty, but it took two years to get it ratified, and there were also strong limitations on the extent of EU collective action built into it. When the federation of Yugoslavia collapsed during 1991–2, with fierce fighting first between Serbia and Croatia and then between warring groups in Bosnia-Herzegovina, there were European leaders prepared to proclaim that 'this is the hour of Europe, not of the United States', and to call for a European solution to a European problem—a sentiment supported by a number of key figures in Washington (Smith and Woolcock 1993). But as the war in former Yugoslavia continued and intensified, it became apparent that the EU and its member states were singularly unprepared to deploy the 'hard power' that might have brought an early end to the conflict. As a result, the Clinton administration was eventually led to intervene, using NATO as a vehicle for the use of force against the Bosnian Serbs in 1994–5 and against the Milosovic regime in Belgrade during 1999 when the Serbs attempted a forcible solution to the problem of Kosovo.

US policy makers thus had good reason by the late 1990s to be cautious about claims of EU responsibility for major international conflicts, even when they took place in the Europeans' backyard. They also had their doubts about the speed with which the EU moved to enlarge its membership and thus contributed to the emerging new European order. The Clinton administration's National Security Strategy focused on 'engagement and enlargement' (see Chapter 5), and the EU was assigned a key role in this process with particular reference to the continent of Europe itself. But a combination of the complexities of the enlargement process, together with the reluctance of some member states to go for a 'big bang' enlargement to at least ten new members, created an understandable frustration in Washington as the 1990s unfolded (Peterson 1996; Smith and Woolcock 1994). Here there is a key cultural difference between US foreign policy and the nature of

policy making at the European level: for Europeans, the process is at least as important as the result, whereas for Americans the result is what matters. This basic difference underlines the key fact that all US foreign policy makers need to remember when dealing with the EU: despite its impressive institutional apparatus and economic weight, the Union is not a state. Nor would most US policy makers want it to be a state, since that might very well mean that it would be much more difficult to deal with on an everyday basis as well as on matters of grand strategy.

The Clinton administrations also had to deal with the impact of the EU's changing economic structure, and with its increasing influence in the global political economy. The Treaty on European Union consolidated the gains made in the EU's Single Market Programme, which by the mid-1990s had taken market integration to new levels (Hocking and Smith 1997). It also had to deal with the approach of economic and monetary union, which eventually led to the establishment of the 'Eurozone' and of the euro as a major international currency at the beginning of the new millennium. Alongside these 'internal' developments, the EU also became more active in leading international trade initiatives, in pursuing trade disputes with the USA in particular, and in taking on issues in the 'new agenda' of environmental issues, human rights, and the like. The fact that these were often intractable issues within the USA itself, and within the administration, frequently meant that the USA seemed less sure-footed than policy makers in Brussels—who were not slow to comment on this shift.

Towards the end of the Clinton years, a further challenge emerged from the EU. Partly as a result of the failures in Bosnia and Kosovo, in 1998 and 1999 the British and the French led a move to establish a European Security and Defence Policy. Whatever the motivations and expectations of those involved within the EU, the importance of this move for the discussion here is clear: this was a challenge to the idea that US priorities and NATO would automatically take precedence in matters of 'western security', and it promised the establishment of a second centre of military power within the western system (Howorth 2000, 2005). The response of the Clinton administration, through Secretary of State Madeleine Albright, was to caution the Europeans in terms of the 'three Ds'—no duplication of capabilities, no discrimination by Europe between third countries that would be unacceptable to the USA, and no decoupling of Europe from the USA. It was also noted that whilst the EU had been deeply involved in negotiations with potential new members since the early 1990s (see above), but had not yet enlarged, NATO had rapidly expanded to encompass many of the potential new EU member states as well as enlarging its broader role through devices such as the Partnership for Peace programme, which took it well into the former Soviet space (Webber 2007). At the same time, the administration continued to nurture its 'special relationships' with some of the EU member states most closely involved, especially Britain, who was its closest ally in the continuing confrontation with Iraq.

By the end of the 1990s, there was thus a dynamic and somewhat confused picture in US–EU relations. Since 1995, there had been a formal institutional link between the USA and the EU in the shape of the New Transatlantic Agenda (NTA) and its extensive action plan—an initiative taken by the USA and agreed by the Europeans for a combination of political and economic reasons, but which covered a very large number of 'new agenda' items with a global dimension (Philippart and Winand 2001; Pollack and Shaffer 2001; Steffenson 2005). But this formal link did not comprehensively or consistently cover key emerging areas of security policy, and for US tastes was rather limited in terms of the commitments made to support US policies outside Europe. Indeed, as time went on, the NTA captured less and less of what was important to key US policy-making groups, and covered more and more of those areas where the USA and the EU diverged quite strongly, for example the environmental issues surrounding the Kyoto Protocol. When this was combined with glacial progress on enlargement and the concerns aroused by the development of ESDP, there was much to be cautious about in US–EU relations (Gompert and Larrabee 1997).

The George W. Bush administration initially pursued policies much like those of the Clinton administration towards the EU, with some crucial differences in policy areas that 'flanked' but did not form part of the core of relations at the European level, for example ballistic missile defence or policies towards Russia. There was also a 'hardening' of policies on the environment and other areas where the Clinton foreign policy had

attempted to soften the edge of US domestic opposition. But the key event in shaping US policies towards the EU in the early part of the new millennium was—as in so many other areas of US foreign policy—the attack on New York and Washington on 11 September 2001. The immediate impact of 9/11 was to encourage EU member states collectively to support the USA, but it soon became very clear that the EU did not feature large in US policies undertaken on a predominantly unilateral basis or with key allies (many of them member states of the EU itself). US policy makers, led by Vice-President Cheney and Secretary of Defense Rumsfeld, simply did not see the use of an organization that depended so heavily on the generation of internal consensus, and which could mobilize almost nothing in the way of 'hard power'; whilst the Department of State and Secretary of State Powell were less resistant to the notion of 'civilian power' and multilateral diplomacy, their voices were much less loud and insistent. As a result, the initial stages of the war on terror in Afghanistan and elsewhere were predominantly led and coordinated by the USA and a few close allies. In the words of Donald Rumsfeld, 'the mission determines the coalition, not the coalition the mission', and the EU as a major focus of intense coalition politics was largely out of the game. Things were different, however, when the war on terror touched areas in which the EU had a substantial presence, such as financial sanctions, border security, and post-conflict reconstruction—all key elements in counter-terrorism cooperation; here, the Americans could not do without the EU and had to accept in large measure the complexities of dealing with Brussels (Peterson and Pollack 2003; Rees 2006).

When the Bush administration decided to move against Iraq in 2002–3, it was clear that the EU would not be a major factor in their deliberations. But a number of key long-standing EU member states were, including Britain, Italy, and Spain, as were a number of the eastern European states that were due to join in 2004. For US foreign policy makers, attention focused naturally on those who were either strongly with Washington, or—as in the case of France and to a lesser extent Germany—against it (Gordon and Shapiro 2004; Lindstrom 2003). During 2003–4, US policies were aimed essentially at dividing the EU, and at isolating the French, whose demands for fuller use of the United Nations process grated with the administration. The fact that the French lined up with the Russians to thwart US aims at crucial points only increased the tension. In this atmosphere, with Rumsfeld encouraging intra-EU frictions with talk of the division between 'old' and 'new' Europe, it was easy to draw a stark contrast between US unilateralism and EU multilateralism, and between the US role as a 'warrior' state and the EU's qualities as a 'trading state' and 'civilian power' (Smith 2004).

The argument earlier in this chapter should warn us against making sweeping and stark distinctions, though. Alongside the open conflicts of 2003–4, a great deal of US–EU cooperation persisted, disputes were managed, and the transatlantic networks in economic and social affairs were maintained. The definite change of style that the George W. Bush administration had brought to the relationship softened during 2005 and 2006, as a 'new multilateralism' seemed to spread in transatlantic relations (Andrews 2005; Zaborowski 2006). By 2007, the Americans even seemed to be warming to the EU's position on global environmental change, and to be more ready for compromise on a number of key trade and commercial issues. For US foreign policy, a number of questions remained open: how would the USA relate to the European Security and Defence Policy in 'normal' times rather than in the heat of war against Iraq? Could the political partnership between the USA and the EU be restored on the basis of mutual respect and awareness of each other's distinctive priorities and internal constraints? Could American policy makers accommodate the nature of the EU's 'normative power' with its focus on human rights and conflict prevention, as opposed to the US focus on hard power and pre-emption? Could the USA and the EU operate as 'partners in leadership' to address some of the most pressing questions in the global political economy, such as those linking environment and development?

These questions lead inexorably into an examination of the Obama presidency and its relationship with the EU. From 2007 onwards, the Europeans were preoccupied with two major sources of change or potential change in US–EU relations. On the one hand, they were waiting for the successor to George W. Bush, and as the presidential campaign proceeded, effectively waiting for Barack Obama. Not only the leaderships of most EU Member States, but also their publics saw Obama as a president who would be much more sensitive to the needs of Europeans, and more responsive to calls for multilateralism and coordination in challenging policy areas (de Vasconcelos and Zaborowski 2009). At the same time, the debate over the future of the EU itself was a key focus of political concern. The Constitutional Treaty put forward in 2006 was eventually rejected by referenda in the Netherlands and France, whereupon it was re-born in 2007 as the Reform Treaty (usually known as the Lisbon Treaty). After this treaty was in turn rejected in an Irish referendum, it was further amended and eventually entered into force in late 2009. The treaty provided for new foreign policy powers for the EU, and specifically for the strengthening of the role of the EU's High Representative for Foreign and Security Policy, who would be supported by a 'diplomatic service' (the European External Action Service) composed of elements drawn from the European Commission, the Council of Ministers and national diplomatic services (Duke 2009). It also provided for a semi-permanent President of the European Council, explicitly on the grounds that this person would have a role in representing the Union abroad (Joint Study 2010).

In the context of this chapter, the intimate details of the new EU foreign policy apparatus are less relevant than the interaction between a new US president and the 'new' EU. In this respect, the Obama presidency posed four challenges for the EU. First, the new presidency expected more of its international partners: whereas the George W. Bush administrations, until late in their course, had cultivated partnerships only where and when they were seen as unavoidable, the Obama administration offered the prospect of multilateralism but on condition that others played a full part in its pursuit. Second, and related, the administration practised a form of pragmatic realism that was designed to be adaptable to new challenges and opportunities, rather than to long-standing partnerships. Third, the administration confronted and responded to a changing constellation of global power, in which the EU was notably less salient or potentially challenging than China and other 'emerging powers'. Finally, the imperative demands of domestic economic and financial reconstruction in the wake of the 2008 financial crisis would inevitably form a key shaping force in US foreign policy, and thus in policies towards the EU (Smith 2011).

> **KEY QUOTES 13.2:   US policy makers and European integration after the Cold War**

James Baker's Berlin speech in December 1989

As Europe changes, the instruments for western cooperation have got to adapt. Working together, it is up to us to
design and generally to put into place what I refer to as a
new architecture for this new era . . . The future development of the European Community will also play a central
role in shaping the new Europe . . . As Europe moves toward
its goal of a common internal market, and as its institutions for political and security cooperation evolve, the link
between the United States and the European Community
will become even more important. We want our transatlantic cooperation to keep pace with European integration and
with institutional reform. To this end, we propose that the
United States and the European Community work together
to achieve, whether it is in treaty or some other form, a significantly strengthened set of institutional and consultative
links . . . We propose that our discussions about this idea
proceed in parallel with Europe's efforts to achieve by 1992
a common internal market, so that plans for US–EC interaction would evolve along with changes in the Community.
The United States also encourages the European Community to continue to expand cooperation with the nations of
the east. The promotion of political and economic reform
in the east is a natural vocation for the European Community . . . We see no conflict between the process of European
integration and an expansion of cooperation between the
European Community and its neighbors to the east and
west. Indeed, we believe that the attraction of the European Community for the countries of the east depends most
on its continued vitality. And the vitality of the Economic
Community depends in turn on its continued commitment
to the goal of a united Europe envisaged by its founders—
free, democratic and closely linked to its North American
partners.

(Baker 1989; James Baker was US Secretary of State)

**Madeleine Albright's warning to the EU on the
'three Ds' in 1998**

Our . . . task is working together to develop a European
Security and Defense Identity, or ESDI, within the Alliance
[NATO], which the United States has strongly endorsed. We
enthusiastically support any measures that enhance European capabilities. The United States welcomes a more capable European partner, with modern, flexible military forces
capable of putting out fires in Europe's own backyard and
working with us through the Alliance to defend our common

interests. The key to a successful initiative is to focus on practical military capabilities. Any initiative must avoid pre-empt-
ing Alliance decision-making by de-linking ESDI from NATO,
avoid duplicating existing efforts, and avoid discrimination
against non-EU members.

(Albright 1998; Madeleine Albright was
US Secretary of State)

Donald Rumsfeld on 'old' and 'new' Europe in 2003

Q: Sir, a question about the mood among European allies . . .
If you look at, for example, France and Germany . . . it seems
that a lot of Europeans rather give the benefit of the doubt to
Saddam Hussein than President George Bush. These are US
allies. What do you make of that?

A: What do I say? Well, there isn't anyone alive who wouldn't
prefer unanimity. I mean, you just always would like everyone
to stand up and say, Way to go! That's the right [thing] to do,
United States . . . Now, you're thinking of Europe as Germany
and France. I don't. I think that's old Europe. If you look at
the entire NATO Europe today, the center of gravity is shifting to the east. And there are a lot of new members... They're
not with France and Germany on this, they're with the United
States.

(Rumsfeld 2003; Donald Rumsfeld was
US Secretary of Defense)

The Obama Administration and the EU in 2010

. . . The European Union has become a global actor and a
critical US partner. The United States strongly supported the
Lisbon Treaty because we want the EU to play an increasing role on all of the most important economic and security
issues on the transatlantic agenda and beyond. The treaty
marked a milestone for Europe and its role in the world and
we hope it will guide the further evolution of the European
Union toward a more consistent, coherent, and effective
foreign policy. The EU represents the collective potential of
its twenty-seven member states: among the most prosperous and militarily-capable democracies on the planet. That is
why it is an essential partner and why this upcoming summit
will be a valuable opportunity for our leaders to meet and to
advance our common agenda.

This US–EU summit will be the first post-Lisbon US–EU summit and, while the agenda is not yet finalized, we hope to
pursue expanded partnership by:

1. promoting the recovery and growth of our economies through addressing regulatory barriers to trade
2. coordinating US and EU resources to meet the development needs of poorer countries, as well as those emerging from crises and disaster
3. identifying ways to enhance our efforts on counter-terrorism and security
4. working together on critical foreign policy issues such as Iran, the Middle East Peace Process, Pakistan, and Afghanistan.

(Gordon 2010; Gordon was Assistant Secretary, Bureau of European and Eurasian Affairs, Department of State)

This set of converging forces posed a challenge for the EU that was arguably as great—though less confrontational in style—as that posed by the George W. Bush administrations. Obama himself had visited Europe during his presidential campaign and made a much-heralded speech in Berlin during August 2008. But on the assumption of power, the administration's attention was inexorably dragged towards existing commitments in Iraq and Afghanistan, and towards the combined challenges posed by China and other rising powers and the domestic imperatives of the financial crisis. Thus, whilst a number of EU leaders cherished hopes for a 'new transatlantic bargain' at the beginning of the administration, these were soon lost in a complex web of issues to do with European contributions to the Afghanistan war, the emergence of the G-20 as a key channel for responses to the financial crisis (a channel in which the EU's influence was arguably diluted), and by the need for the Americans to pay attention to a wide range of new challenges. Tellingly, in late 2009, the White House cancelled plans for an EU–US summit in the spring of 2010 on the grounds that there was no significant agenda. Although the summit was eventually held in late 2010, in the context of Obama's visit to NATO and other European organizations, and the administration went to some lengths to identify the EU as an essential partner in its pursuit of cooperative solutions to global issues (see key quotes above), this was not the resounding endorsement of the EU's status that some had expected. Given that 2010 had seen extensive internal wrangling over the introduction of the EU's new foreign policy apparatus, which was only beginning to be resolved by the end of the year, it seemed clear that a combination of US preoccupation with events elsewhere and EU preoccupation with its own internal workings had at least postponed the 'new transatlantic bargain' that some had hoped for.

Trends and tensions

What can we now say about the changing nature of the US–EU relationship and its place in US foreign policy since the end of the Cold War, using as our starting point the sets of trends and tensions explored earlier in the chapter?

A first observation is that US policy makers have found it very difficult in the period since 1990 to generate settled images either of European integration or of the USA's own role in that process. At one end of the spectrum, US leaders have feared being excluded from the 'new Europe' as a result of decreased threat from the east and the declining need for US military involvement. As a result, there has been a desire to maintain both presence and leverage in the security affairs of Europe, and to resist the apparent threat of exclusion. At the same time, however, the progress of European integration has actually increased the American stake in Europe in the economic and political domains. The Single Market Programme and its successors have stimulated ever greater US foreign direct investment (matched, it must be noted, by major increases in investment by EU companies in the USA). The image of the EU held by major US corporations has often been at odds with that of the US administration, and in many ways this is not surprising.

But perhaps the greatest challenge to US images of European integration, and their own role in relation to it, has come from the ambiguities attending the increasing international assertiveness of the EU itself. In an increasing number of policy domains, especially those of the 'new agenda' such as environment or human rights, the EU has asserted its right to be heard and to take a leadership role. This exertion of 'soft power' and a form of 'EU exceptionalism' has been accompanied by persistent EU failings in the area of 'hard power' and military security—failings given added prominence in American eyes by the lack of collective support from EU member states over Iraq and in certain parts of the 'war on terror'. This issue of power has come to be seen in terms of two key interrelated images, largely but not entirely propounded by US policy makers or their close advisers. The first is the 'Mars/Venus' debate, in which European unwillingness to resort to or collectively deploy 'hard power' is seen as part of a fundamental cultural disconnect between the USA and Europe (Kagan 2003; Lindberg 2005). The second is the 'unilateral/multilateral' debate, through which the Europeans' commitment to multilateral institutions and rules of conduct in the international arena is contrasted to US unilateralism and willingness to take hard national decisions (Pollack 2003). In terms of US policy, it can readily be seen that these two areas of imagery express American ambivalence and uncertainty about the status and future of their EU partners, and to this extent they express starkly ideas that have been around in US–EC and US–EU relations for decades. The post-Cold War period may have highlighted and focused them, but it did not entirely create them (see Box 13.2).

The same can be said of the second set of trends and tensions: those between political, economic, and security dimensions of the US–EU relationship. There is no doubt that the post-Cold War period has both intensified and reshaped these forces, but the question is, how and with what effects? As we have seen, the breakdown of the Soviet bloc and of the Soviet Union itself was not merely a political event; it has had profound implications for economic and security processes, and has brought the need for 'comprehensive security' alongside that for purely military security. These trends were reinforced (but not created) by the events of 9/11 and the war on terror. As noted above, one consequence for US policy makers was that they found themselves having to deal more and more with the EU on matters of economic

and financial sanctions, on questions of counterterrorism, and on problems of what has been termed 'societal security', involving social and environmental standards (Pollack and Peterson 2003). This has been a challenge both for the institutional structure of US foreign policy and for the substance of policy itself. At the level of institutions, the EU poses the challenge of working across departmental boundaries and of coordinating policies at the transnational or the supranational level—a challenge to which not all US government departments have been fully responsive, and which has caused frictions within and between parts of the foreign policy community. At the level of policy substance, the EU demands close control of what is being said and done by US officials at the national and at the EU levels within Europe, and a strong capacity to undertake multidimensional negotiations with a variety of partners. This has not come easily to US policy makers even where they have wanted to pursue this kind of policy approach; others have rejected this kind of policy style in favour of strong action by the USA and certain favoured allies, but it is not clear that this has been successful in anything but the short term.

Finally, what can we say about the balance in US policies towards European integration between the underlying structures of 'empire', 'alliance', and 'interdependence' since the end of the Cold War? Discussion of the ways in which US foreign policy since 1990 has expressed a kind of liberal imperialism is of course much more broadly based than in US–EU relations alone (see many other chapters), but the rise of the EU has had its own distinctive impact. Indeed, there is some ground for the argument that the new continental scale of the EU has created or expressed a form of 'EU imperialism' based on its structural power within the continent and on its dominance of what the European Commission calls the 'new neighbourhood' (Zielonka 2006; Smith 2007). American policy makers have found this difficult to pin down or to deal with, since it is based on the form of 'civilian power' that is at least at odds with if not alien to US thinking about world order, and this difficulty has been compounded in some ways by uncertainty about the EU's foreign policy and diplomatic capacity following the Lisbon Treaty reforms. Whilst Washington has been able to continue its overall support for the stabilizing role and the economic benefits of EU enlargement, it has found itself at odds with the Europeans over how far this can be pushed. The most obvious example is that of Turkey, which American policy makers want to see as a member state of the EU but to which both the EU's enlargement processes and some existing EU member states are resistant. The EU has also been resistant to US pressure to deal more forcefully with the Russia of Medvedev and Putin as it has become more assertive within and outside Europe, and has acted in part as a competitor with the US in dealings with other emerging powers such as China, India, and Brazil. Alongside these primarily political contradictions, the EU has gained strength through the consolidation of the Eurozone and of the euro as an international currency. But the example of the euro (to which by 2011 only eighteen of twenty-seven member states belonged, and which had been placed in question by the continuing impact of the financial crisis) does still point to the lack of a fully collective EU policy in many areas—a feature that can be and has been exploited by American policy makers.

The jury is thus still out on the persistence of 'empire' or hegemony in US–EU relations. Equally, the 'alliance' dimension must be seen as still valid but still inconclusive. At times in the post-Cold War period, US–EU relations have appeared as a form of 'adversarial partnership', with structural constraints preventing a divorce but plenty of disputes and tensions within the transatlantic 'family'. The formal institutional commitments of the New Transatlantic Agenda are not legally binding, but they do form a powerful set of shaping factors in all but the hardest of 'hard security' areas. The development of the European Security and Defence Policy has also provided a new channel for communication on matters of military security, although this is often still mediated through NATO, using the so-called 'Berlin plus' arrangements for coordination of resources and planning (Howorth 2005, 2007). Yet there is no common perception of a transatlantic 'grand strategy' either for the global political economy or for the areas of 'hard security' that proved so troublesome in the early years of the new millennium (Sloan 2005). What there is, is a form of institutional pluralism in which mechanisms to adjust and deal with differences have grown up over the post-Cold War period, rather than a new 'transatlantic bargain' covering all areas of US–EU interaction. From a US foreign policy perspective, and from the point of view of Washington preoccupied with the rise of China, India, and other emerging regional or global powers, this may be the best that can be hoped for.

The forces of 'empire' and 'alliance' are thus still intermingled in US policies towards the EU. The same can be said for 'interdependence', the third of our underlying factors (see Box 13.2). The intensification of globalization, and the consistent growth of transactions between the USA and the EU, have been persistent shaping factors since the 1960s. But since the end of the Cold War there has been a growing tension between the various approaches to the management of these issues. The EU is the most highly developed form of regional interdependence—in fact, it goes beyond interdependence because of its dense institutionalization and the legal

---

BOX 13.2: Trends and tensions in US–EU relations, 1989–2007

- *Images and reality*: difficulty of generating settled images of European integration; fears of exclusion, desire to retain leverage; increasing assertiveness of the EU, debates over nature of EU and US power and over unilateralism/multilateralism.
- *Politics, economics, and security*: linkages intensify, assisted by collapse of Soviet bloc and processes of globalization; pressures on new dimensions of security, including 'societal security'; need for complex policy mix to match growing scope of EU.

- *Empire, alliance, and interdependence*: US as 'only superpower'—liberal imperialism; growing continental power of the EU; links to issues of European and world order; pressures on alliance from changes in EU, US, and world arena; new challenges of global governance created by globalization and interdependence; 'securitization' and institutionalization of many international issues, with implications for exercise of power in US–EU relations.

KEY POINTS

❑ The end of the Cold War had a major impact on US views of European integration, but has to be seen alongside other and more long-lasting factors in shaping US policies.

❑ US policy makers engaged in a redefinition of their views of European integration during the 1990s, especially in light of the change from EC to EU, but this was subject to a series of uncertainties and contradictions.

❑ Tensions between the USA and the EU over matters of European order (conflict in former Yugoslavia, enlargement) were a key feature of the 1990s.

❑ The EU also posed a broader challenge to US policy in the global political economy (through the Single Market and monetary union), and in matters of security and defence (through the European Security and Defence Policy from the end of the 1990s).

❑ Although there was a growth of new 'partnership' institutions between the USA and the EU, these did not eliminate tensions—rather they assisted with their management.

❑ The impact of 9/11 was substantial, but did not change everything in US–EU relations. Rather, it meant that existing issues were cast in a new light and given additional point. Longer-term processes such as globalization and new types of conflict were crystallized in 9/11 and later by Iraq.

❑ By the early 2000s, the tensions in US–EU relations caused by US policy makers' redefinition of their images, by linkages between political, economic, and security issues, and by underlying trends towards 'empire', 'alliance', and 'interdependence' were still apparent, but in radically changed conditions.

---

structures that sustain it, especially in economic activities. For US policy makers, this makes the EU a key partner in the management of interdependence not only in the North Atlantic area but also at the global level. US–EU competition and convergence strongly shape such bodies as the World Trade Organization, the International Monetary Fund, and the World Bank, not to mention a vast range of more specialized organizations within the global political economy (McGuire and Smith 2008). They also increasingly influence what goes on in a wide variety of newly 'securitized' organizations dealing with migration, asylum, transport, and other areas central to the challenge of terrorism. US policy makers have therefore had to adapt to dealing not with a number of independent interlocutors in Europe, but with governments and other groups who are themselves

constrained by membership of the EU. US foreign policy has thus faced conflicting pressures in dealing with the growth of interdependence between the USA and the EU—on the one hand, a pressure to act unilaterally and make others adjust to US preferences, on the other hand a realization that in the EU, this is not as easy as it might appear and that multilateral methods might be more effective. It would be too much to claim that dealing with the EU has changed the culture of US foreign policy, but there can be no doubt that the development of the EU since 1990 has provided a concentrated form of the interdependence to which all US foreign policies have had to adjust since the 1960s.

Conclusion

As noted in the Introduction, this chapter has explored one of the key relationships in which the USA has been involved since the end of the Second World War: the transatlantic relationship with the 'European integration project'. This is a relationship not with a single state, but with a densely institutionalized region, which has itself grown and become markedly more prominent in the world arena over the past half-century. American foreign policy makers have generally been consistent in their support for the integration

MAJOR DEBATES AND THEIR IMPACT 1.1: US policies towards European integration

The 'Mars/Venus' debate of the early 2000s

The controversies centring around US and EU responses to the war on terror and the war in Iraq during 2002–4 generated debate not only in policy circles but also in academic analysis. One of the key figures in this debate was the American policy analyst Robert Kagan, who in 2003 published his book *Of Paradise and Power: America and Europe in the New World Order*. Kagan's argument was that there was a deep difference over the interpretation and the uses of power between the United States and Europe, and that this reflected long historical experience as well as current events. To put it simply, the United States had evolved with a strong orientation towards the use of 'hard' military power and a strong position both on sovereignty and national security, as the result of its geopolitical location, its industrial and technological development, and the growth of an official culture in which military force was a central

means of implementing foreign policy. On the other side, Europe—best represented by the 'civilian power' promoted by the EU—had grown to focus on the use of 'soft power' and the building of institutions for the solving of international problems. This too reflected the relevant historical and cultural experiences: the disastrous history of the use of force in Europe up to 1945, and the conclusion drawn by ruling elites that military force was to be constrained and subjected to rigorous rules. But according to Kagan, it also effectively reflected the weakness of Europe, since if the EU or individual European countries had been able to match the USA in military terms, they would not have had to adopt this rationalization of their own inadequacies. This debate was of course centred on the war in Iraq, and it also adopted a sweeping view of both US and European positions—but how much can it be seen as reflecting a permanent underlying set of differences?

project, but it has challenged US foreign policy in a number of important areas. The focus of the chapter has thus been on the ways in which US policy makers have developed images of the EC and now the EU, on the challenges posed by European integration for US policy processes and the uses of US power, and on the ways in which these challenges have been met in the very different conditions of the Cold War and post-Cold War periods.

The chapter has shown that US foreign policy makers have consistently placed European integration at the core of their policies, but that this has not prevented persistent tensions, many of which express issues about the nature of US foreign policy itself and the US role in the world arena. We have seen that US policy makers have needed to develop an image of European integration, but that this has been made difficult by the nature of the integration process itself, by the 'stickiness' of US assumptions about the status and the role of the EC and then the EU, and by changes in the broader world arena, specifically those surrounding the end of the Cold War and the rise of globalization. We have also seen that US policy towards European integration has reflected the complex interaction of political, economic, and security forces, and that the

shifting balance between these three elements has made US policy formation problematic. Finally, we have seen that underlying tendencies in US foreign policy, towards 'empire', 'alliance', and 'interdependence', have coexisted more or less easily in dealing with the European integration, and that whilst conflicts between the three elements have been especially clear during the first years of the new millennium this is not the first time that such conflicts have been seen. Such is the nature of US–EU relations that one can safely say it will not be the last.

During the course of relations between US foreign policy and European integration, many have tried to identify key potential future trends. Over the years, the options that have been discerned can be broadly categorized into three schools of thought: convergence, and the development of a new and more integrated 'transatlantic bargain'; divergence, and the growth of tensions and contradictions; and drift, implying the growth of indifference and unevenness. The analysis in this chapter suggests, not surprisingly, that the future is likely to be a combination of all three of these tendencies, reflecting not only the nature of US–EU relations but also the turbulence of a changing global order.

CONTROVERSIES 13.1:   How has the US responded to European integration?

The US role in European integration: partnership, leadership, or hegemony?

This has been a continuous thread in the development of US–EU relations. US policy makers have found themselves constantly trying to balance their expectations about European dependence and the USA's right to exert its predominance against those that reflect the desire of Europeans to assert themselves—and of course, the Europeans can only really assert themselves against the USA, their 'most significant other'. This controversy also links to the key questions about the nature of power and its exercise that we have encountered at many points in the chapter.

The US adaptation to the development of European integration: adaptation or the pursuit of new dominance?

As the Europeans began to develop their own 'identity' and to strengthen their institutions during the 1980s, this meant that the Americans were forced to adjust. But this was quite a difficult process because of the 'stickiness' both of images and of institutional cultures in the USA. As a result, during the late 1980s and the 1990s, US policies towards European integration went through a series of partial adjustments, with no overarching grand strategy. This was also affected by the range of global challenges in which US foreign policy became embroiled, which in many cases deflected their attention from the EU. The George W. Bush administrations of the new millennium attempted to assert a new US predominance, but whilst this was possible in issues of 'hard power' and security, it was less possible in economic, cultural, and humanitarian issues. The Obama administration adopted a more pragmatic and realist position, which promised enhanced cooperation but at times threatened to marginalize the EU.

The US response to the European Union: cooperation or containment?

This is really a continuation of the 'controversies' above. The USA has pronounced its support for European integration from the start, and for the EU since it was established in the early 1990s. But many of the actions taken by US policy makers have accompanied that general support with a desire to contain the specific harm that a growing EU might do to US interests. Economically, this has meant vigorous use of the

World Trade Organization to raise complaints against the EU; politically, it has meant the desire by many US leaders to contain the development of a 'European foreign policy', and to put the EU in a subordinate position; and in security affairs, it has led to considerable ambivalence about the development of a European Security and Defence Policy. Often, this ambivalence in US policies has led Washington to try and exploit 'special relationships' with EU member states such as the UK, and to pursue a kind of 'divide and rule' strategy either explicitly or implicitly.

The USA, the EU, and the aftermath of 9/11: unilateralism versus multilateralism?

One of the key contrasts that has been drawn between the USA and the EU since the early 1990s has been the alleged preference of US policy makers for unilateral solutions, and thus the contrast with the EU's search for multilateral solutions through a range of international organizations. In the aftermath of 9/11, and especially in the build-up to war in Iraq, this seemed an important distinction to draw, but the question is, how much of this contrast is permanent, and how much is it the product of particular circumstances? Do the EU and the USA really inhabit different 'worlds' of international relations, or are they more alike than they are often presented as being? Certainly, in the economic field, the EU has armed itself with the same range of weapons as the USA, and shows a tendency towards unilateral actions where its 'targets' are relatively weak; the USA, on the other hand, has stuck with multilateral rules for the most part, even where they threaten its short-term interests. Kagan (see Major debates and their impact 12.1) would certainly argue that the EU's apparent promotion of multilateral solutions to political and security problems is a rationalization of its own weakness (although he would also argue that the USA's preference for unilateralism is a reflection of perceived power). Events such as 9/11 and the Iraq War can be seen as those most likely to underline the differences, although it must not be forgotten that the response to terrorism covers a wide range of activities in which the EU has major strengths, such as international financial and judicial cooperation. It might thus show the EU's strength as well as its weaknesses, and be more challenging to US policy makers than apparently simple issues of military force.

? Questions

1. What motivated US support for the early stage of European integration?
2. What is the importance of John F. Kennedy's 1962 speech on Atlantic partnership?
3. Why were US–EC relations especially difficult in the early 1970s?
4. Why did the 1970s see a new pattern of interaction between political, economic, and security issues in US–EC relations?
5. What was the impact of the 'new cold war' during the early 1980s on US policies towards European integration?
6. What events in the late 1980s created concern in the USA about the future impact of European integration?
7. What role did US policy makers envisage for the EC at the end of the Cold War?
8. What impact has the enlargement of the EU had on US perceptions of the European integration process?
9. Why did American foreign policy makers initially feel that the war in former Yugoslavia was a matter for the EU, and why did they have to change their minds?
10. What effect did the changing agenda of global economic and social issues have on US policies towards the EU in the late 1990s, and why?
11. Has the challenge of terrorism strengthened or weakened US support for European integration?
12. Why was it said in the early 2000s that 'Americans are from Mars, Europeans from Venus'? How does the distinction apply in the second decade of this millennium?

» Further Reading

There is a vast range of literature on the transatlantic relationship, both from an American and from a European standpoint. The following deal especially with the issues raised in this chapter.

Andrews, D. (ed.) (2005), *The Atlantic Alliance under Stress: US–European Relations after Iraq* (Cambridge: Cambridge University Press).

A strong collection of contributions from Americans and Europeans.

Bujajski, J. and Teleki, I. (2007), *Atlantic Bridges: America's New European Allies* (Lanham, Md.: Rowman and Littlefield).

Deals with the ways in which the new or newly liberated countries of central and eastern Europe relate both to the EU and to the USA.

Heller, F. and Gillingham, J. (eds) (1996), *The United States and the Integration of Europe: Legacies of the Postwar Era* (New York: St Martin's Press).

Strong collection on the foundations of US policy towards the European integration project between 1945 and 1960.

Hocking, B. and Smith, M. (1997), *Beyond Foreign Economic Policy: The United States, the Single European Market and the Changing World Economy* (London: Cassell Pinter).

Explores American responses to the new challenge of the Single Market, and places this in the context of broader global trends.

McGuire, S. and Smith, M. (2008), *The European Union and the United States: Competition and Convergence in the Global Arena* (Basingstoke: Palgrave/Macmillan).

Covers a wide range of EU–US relations, and links the political, economic, and security dimensions with an emphasis on shared challenges as well as competition and tensions.

Peterson, J. and Pollack, M. (eds) (2003), *Europe, America, Bush: Transatlantic Relations in the Twenty-First Century* (London: Routledge).

Charts the controversies of the early 2000s with a particular focus on the ways in which 9/11 and Iraq fed into them.

Philippart, E. and Winand, P. (eds) (2001), *Ever Closer Partnership: Policy-Making in US–EC Relations* (Brussels: PIE-Peter Lang).

Especially useful on the working of the New Transatlantic Agenda, but also on institutional and policy questions more generally.

Pollack, M. and Shaffer, G. (eds) (2001), *Transatlantic Governance in the Global Economy* (Lanham, MD: Rowman and Littlefield).

Major collection exploring the growth of institutions and multi-level politics in the transatlantic arena, including US policy responses.

Sloan, S. (2005), *NATO, the European Union, and the Atlantic Community: The Transatlantic Bargain Challenged*, 2nd edn (Lanham, MD: Rowman and Littlefield).

Places the US–EU relationship both into its historical context and into the context of security relations through NATO.

Smith, M. and Woolcock, S. (1993), *The United States and the European Community in a Transformed World* (London: Pinter for the Royal Institute of International Affairs).

Focuses on the nature of the transformations taking place in the early 1990s, and covers political, economic, and security dimensions.

Winand, P. (1993), *Eisenhower, Kennedy and the United States of Europe* (Basingstoke: Macmillan).

Substantial historical study of the ways in which US administrations dealt with European integration within their foreign policies between 1950 and 1963.

 For a range of additional resources to support your learning visit the Online Resource Centre that accompanies this book at www.oxfordtextbooks.co.uk/orc/cox_stokes2e/.

14 US foreign policy in Russia

Peter Rutland and Gregory Dubinsky

Chapter contents

Introduction

The end of the Cold War lifted the threat of nuclear annihilation and transformed the international security landscape. The United States interpreted the collapse of the Soviet Union as evidence that it had 'won' the Cold War, and that its values and interests would prevail in the future world order. However, the Russian Federation, which inherited half the population and 70 per cent of the territory of the former Soviet Union, was an unknown quantity. Would it become a friend and partner of the United States, a full and equal member of the community of democratic nations? Or would it slip back into a hostile, expansionary communist or nationalist power? Twenty years later, this debate is still unresolved. Russia has not fully joined the community of Western nations, but nor has it turned its back on them. The US foreign policy establishment is still divided

Fig. 14.1 Map of Russia and its neighbours.

over whether Russia is an 'evil empire' or a country with rational leaders with whom we can—and must—do business.

Back in 1991, the most pressing question for the US was the fate of the Soviet Union's 27,000 nuclear warheads and stocks of chemical and biological weapons. There was also concern about whether Moscow would act to defend the interests of the 25 million ethnic Russians who were now living outside the boundaries of the Russian state. Would Russia follow the example of Slobodan Milosovic, who was fighting to carve a 'Greater Serbia' out of the former Yugoslavia? Because

no catastrophes occurred, it is easy to forget that these were very real fears back in the early 1990s.

US–Russian relations have gone through several distinct phases since 1991. Initially, the hostility of the Cold War was replaced by a feeling of giddy cooperation, but that gradually eroded in the course of the 1990s. That was replaced by a sense of uncertainty about Russia's intentions, following Russia's hostile reaction to the US-led war over Kosovo in 1999 and the accession to power of Vladimir Putin later that year. Washington took a wait-and-see attitude towards the new Russian president, until the terrorist attacks on 11 September

> ❝ **KEY QUOTES 14.1:** Condoleezza Rice on the post–Soviet power vacuum
>
> The United States has found it exceedingly difficult to define its 'national interest' in the absence of Soviet power.
> (Condoleezza Rice, writing in 2000, shortly before she became National Security Adviser)

2001 led to a renewal of hope that a strategic alliance could be forged with Moscow. But this third phase was short-lived. Visions of partnership were dashed by the US invasion of Iraq in 2003 and Russia's slide into authoritarianism, signalled by the arrest of oil magnate Mikhail Khodorkovsky in October 2003. Relations continued to deteriorate, with talk of a 'new cold war', culminating in the August 2008 Georgian war. There was another about turn after the accession to the presidency of Dmitry Medvedev and Barack Obama, and their commitment to 'reset' the relationship, which bore fruit in the signing of a new arms control treaty, New START, in 2010.

In retrospect, the heady optimism of the early 1990s was unrealistic. At the same time, the notion of a 'new cold war' appears equally exaggerated. Despite differences of opinion between Russia and the USA—over the handling of regional issues in Iran, North Korea, and the former Soviet states—there continues to be substantial cooperation in areas of common interest, such as nuclear proliferation and the war on terror. The main uncertainty now revolves around the willingness of the United States to deal with a Russia that has an authoritarian political system and that is keen to assertively defend its perceived national interests.

The end of an era

The collapse of the Soviet Union on 25 December 1991 abruptly terminated a fifty-year-old struggle for global supremacy between the Soviet Union and the United States. That contest remained a 'Cold War' because nuclear weapons prevented the two superpowers from attacking each other directly.

The Soviet Union collapsed as a result of Mikhail Gorbachev's efforts to reform the archaic Soviet economy and political system. Historians argue over the extent to which Gorbachev was responding to internal causes or was reacting to the new aggressive policies of President Ronald Reagan. The debate over the extent to which the USA can influence developments inside Russia continued through the 1990s to the present day.

Most Americans see the United States as the clear victor in the Cold War. The Soviet collapse led to the triumph of American ideals of liberal democracy and market capitalism, and left the USA as the unchallenged sole superpower. But many Russians believe that both sides won the Cold War, since it ended by mutual agreement, and because both countries benefited from the removal of the threat of nuclear annihilation. After all, it was primarily Mikhail Gorbachev's initiatives that brought the confrontation to an end: the withdrawal from Afghanistan and the decision not to use force to hold onto Eastern Europe. The Cold War effectively ended in 1989—at the December Malta summit of Gorbachev and President G. H. W. Bush, shortly after the fall of the Berlin Wall on 9 November.

The new spirit of cooperation paid dividends in August 1990, when Secretary of State James Baker persuaded his Soviet counterpart Eduard Shevardnadze to support the US plan to drive Saddam Hussein out of Kuwait.

The Bush administration backed Soviet President Mikhail Gorbachev to the very end and spurned contacts with Boris Yeltsin, the leader of the democratic opposition. Bush did not meet Yeltsin until July 1991, one month after he was elected president of the Russian Federation. The USA was concerned above all about the Soviet nuclear arsenal and the 500,000 Soviet troops stationed in East Europe, both of which were still under Soviet President Gorbachev's control. In August 1991 hardliners launched an abortive coup in a desperate effort to maintain the

Soviet Union. Power then shifted from Gorbachev to Yeltsin, who personally brokered the break-up of the Soviet Union in December 1991.

The USA was delighted to see the end of the Soviet Union, but fearful of its consequences. The dissolution of the Soviet Union and Yugoslavia triggered a number of bloody regional conflicts that needed containing. The USA was concerned to prevent the proliferation of Soviet nuclear weapons to third countries or terrorist groups. Already in September 1991 President Bush unilaterally announced that the USA would destroy all its tactical battlefield nuclear weapons, and Gorbachev said the Soviet Union would do the same. Two US senators, Richard Lugar and Sam Nunn, introduced a bill pledging $400 million to help pay for the dismantling of Soviet nuclear weapons. The Pentagon opposed the Cooperative Threat Reduction programme, but the Senate approved the money in November 1991. By the end of the decade the USA had spent $5 billion, helping to destroy nuclear materials and paying Russian nuclear scientists to deter them from selling their expertise abroad.

At a meeting in Lisbon in May 1992 the USA managed to persuade Ukraine, Kazakhstan, and Belarus to give up the nuclear weapons located on their territory. Yeltsin's pro-Western foreign minister, Andrei Kozyrev, agreed with the need for radical cuts in both sides' nuclear arsenals. Bush and Yeltsin signed the Strategic Arms Reduction Treaty START II in January 1993, under which they promised to reduce their arsenals of some 10,000 strategic warheads to 3000–3500 each by 2003. Baker had some difficulty persuading the Pentagon to accept such large cuts. START II also committed both sides to eliminate multiple warheads on land-based missiles. Multiple-warhead missiles (MIRVs) were considered destabilizing

> **KEY POINTS**
>
> ❑ In December 1991, the Soviet Union ceased to exist as a geopolitical entity, and with its demise the central organizing principle for US foreign policy since the Second World War—containing the Soviet threat—no longer existed.
>
> ❑ During the break-up of the Soviet empire, a revolutionary figure named Boris Yeltsin came to the forefront of Russian politics and promised to lead his new country to a better and brighter future in cooperation with the West.
>
> ❑ The United States sought to limit the threats posed by the immediate transition, especially by persuading the newly independent states to relinquish their nuclear arsenals.

because there was an incentive to launch them pre-emptively in a crisis before they could be destroyed on the ground by a single incoming warhead. START II was ratified by the US Senate in 1996, but not approved by the Russian State Duma until 2000.

Russia experienced a profound economic crisis in the spring of 1992 as the government introduced radical reforms known as 'shock therapy'. Production plummeted while goods disappeared from the shelves and prices spiralled. The Bush administration was criticized for doing nothing as Russia fell into chaos. In response Bush announced in April 1992 a $24 billion international aid package, including $5 billion from the USA. But most of that was money already committed in the form of postponement of Soviet-era debts. The administration believed that Russia was too unstable to make use of a serious influx of new funds.

Bill and Boris

Bill Clinton took office in January 1993 with high hopes that a partnership with Russia could be the linchpin for America's role in the post-Cold War world. The goal was to transform Russia into what Clinton called a 'market democracy', while integrating it into international institutions. Clinton was influenced by the 'democratic

peace' theory, which was experiencing an academic revival. It was in America's best interests to ensure that Russia became a democracy, since democracies do not go to war with each other.

Clinton appointed his former Oxford roommate, Russia expert Strobe Talbott, point man for relations

CONTROVERSIES 14.1: Debates in US–Russian relations

Building market democracy in Russia

Yes: Russia had a good chance of becoming a stable market economy with democratic political institutions, and the United States had a responsibility to do all it could to bring that about.

No: American interference in Russia's domestic politics and economics was bound to fail and cause a negative reaction from Russian elites.

NATO enlargement

Yes: NATO is a defensive alliance and Russia had nothing to fear from its enlargement into eastern Europe.

No: By expanding NATO the western powers were effectively excluding Russia from the most important international security institution of post-Cold War Europe.

Relations with Putin

Yes: Russia is a great power due to its geographical presence in Eurasia, its seat in the United Nations Security Council, and its role as an energy exporter. The USA has to establish a good working relationship with whoever is in power in Moscow.

No: Putin is a dictatorial leader whose authoritarian rule will only bring instability to Russia. He cannot be trusted as a reliable partner.

Relations with Medvedev

Yes: President Medvedev is a liberal, pro-western reformer who deserves our support.

No: Medvedev is a puppet and Prime Minister Putin still controls Kremlin decision making.

---

with Russia. (Talbott served as counsellor and then Deputy Secretary of State from 1993 to 2000.) Talbott's close personal relationship with Clinton meant that Secretaries of State Warren Christopher and Madeleine Albright had a less prominent role in USA–Russia relations than one might have expected. National Security Adviser Anthony Lake was sceptical about the scope for democratic transition in Russia, but likewise deferred to Talbott.

Yeltsin and Clinton hit it off at their first meeting in April 1993, backslapping and bear-hugging. Both men declared their readiness to create a 'dynamic and effective Russo-American partnership'. Clinton promised a financial aid package of $1.6 billion, predicated on the assumption that Yeltsin was introducing reforms that would create a market democracy. Clinton visited Russia in January 1994, and by the end of his term the two men had met no less than eighteen times. Clinton was fully aware of Yeltsin's idiosyncrasies, telling Talbott on one occasion that 'Yeltsin drunk was better than most of the alternatives sober'.

The USA clung to this policy despite a series of events indicating that all was not well, such as Yeltsin's shelling of the opposition-controlled parliament in October 1993 and the invasion of the breakaway province of Chechnya in December 1994. New York University Professor Stephen Cohen ridiculed the Clinton administration's approach as a 'failed crusade' that strove to remake Russia in America's image. Russia expert Dmitri Simes argued that the United States was mistakenly treating Russia as if it were a 'defeated enemy'. Many Russians came to blame the chaos of the early 1990s on the capitalist reforms that they believed were forced on Russia at America's insistence.

While Talbott handled diplomatic and security issues, economic relations were handled by Larry Summers and David Lipton at the US Treasury. They focused their attention on macroeconomic stabilization and debt management. Despite earlier pronouncements, by 2001 the USA had sent only about $1 billion in aid to Russia, and two-thirds of that was spent on

---

❝ KEY QUOTES 14.2: The spinach treatment

Behind the façade of friendship, Clinton administration officials expected the Kremlin to accept the United States' definition of Russia's national interests. Talbott and his aides referred to it as the spinach treatment.

(Dmitri Simes, President of the Nixon Institute, 2007)

> **KEY QUOTES 14.3:** Russia's democratic prospects

A true and lasting transition to normalcy, democracy, and free markets in Russia is neither inevitable nor impossible. It is an open question.

(Secretary of State Madeleine Albright, October 1998)

KEY POINTS

❑ The relationship forged by the two leaders, Bill Clinton and Boris Yeltsin, was cemented by what Clinton saw as Yeltsin's commitment to reforms to modernize the Russian state and economy. The two men thought American assistance and expertise could transform Russia into a 'market democracy'.

❑ The reforms failed, and as Russia's economy shrank the quality of life for many Russians plummeted. The economy was dealt a further blow by the August 1998 financial crash.

❑ Yeltsin did manage to win re-election in 1996, which enabled the USA to continue in its commitment to building democracy in Russia.

---

nuclear-weapon-related programmes, managed by the Pentagon and Department of Energy. The main vehicle for influencing Russian economic policy was International Monetary Fund (IMF) loans, conditional on the introduction of specific reform policies. At the suggestion of the Russians, a special commission was created between Prime Minister Viktor Chernomyrdin and Vice President Al Gore to promote economic cooperation. It also handled some sensitive strategic issues such as Russian missile sales to Iran, cooperation in space launches, and a plan for the USA to process plutonium that had been removed from Russia nuclear warheads for use in civilian reactors.

The 1990s reforms produced few concrete results for US business interests. The privatization programme mostly excluded foreign buyers, and Russia took in only $3.7 billion in foreign direct investment over the decade. The European Union (EU) was Russia's main economic partner, accounting for more than half of Russia's foreign trade, while the USA accounted for less than 5 per cent.

After the communist victory in the December 1995 State Duma election, Yeltsin appointed former foreign intelligence chief Yevgenii Primakov as Foreign Minister. Primakov tried to move Russia away from its dependency on the United States, sometimes talking about a strategic triad of Russia, China, and India. But even Primakov realized that the USA was the dominant power.

Boris Yeltsin faced the daunting task of winning re-election in June 1996. He was deeply unpopular due to the ongoing war in Chechnya and the economy, which was in its sixth year of decline. Many of his advisers urged him to cancel the election, but he went ahead with the vote and managed to win a second term, thanks to a massive media campaign and an influx of IMF loans, used to pay off wage and pension arrears. Washington breathed a huge sigh of relief. A cancelled election—or a communist victory—would have been the end of the road for Clinton's democratic transition paradigm.

Russia was not yet out of the woods, however. The 1997 Asian financial crisis triggered a slump in world oil prices, hitting Russia's export earnings and government revenue. A growing fiscal deficit was covered by reckless external borrowing. Despite a last-minute $22 billion IMF rescue package, the ruble crashed in August 1998, losing 75 per cent of its value. The government went into default on its debts. The crisis forced the resignation of Yeltsin's new liberal Prime Minister, Sergei Kirienko, and his replacement by the conservative Primakov. The crisis shattered any illusions that Russia was in transition to stable market democracy.

NATO enlargement

The main problem in the USA–Russia relationship was the US plan to expand the North Atlantic Treaty Organization (NATO) into central Europe. NATO was created in 1949 to deter the Soviet military threat, so Moscow argued that since the Soviet Union and its military alliance, the Warsaw Pact, had dissolved

> **KEY QUOTES 14.4:** 'We had a deal'

I told Yeltsin that if he would agree to NATO expansion and the NATO–Russian partnership, I would make a commitment not to station troops or missiles in the new member countries prematurely, and to support Russian membership in the new G-8, the World Trade Organization, and other international organizations. We had a deal.

(President Bill Clinton, at a meeting in Helsinki in March 1997)

in 1991, NATO should follow suit. Yeltsin withdrew Russian troops from the Baltic countries and eastern Europe—but only after the USA promised funds to build housing for officers relocated to Russia. The USA radically cut its 300,000 troops stationed in Europe, but did not want to dismantle NATO—which it saw not only as a highly successful defensive alliance, but also a vehicle for projecting stability into eastern Europe.

Initially, the USA had hoped that the EU would take the lead in integrating the former socialist countries. But it was clear that preparing the central European countries for full EU membership would take many years. A sense of urgency was introduced by the first-place finish of the semi-fascist Liberal Democratic Party, led by Vladimir Zhirinovsky, in the State Duma elections in December 1993. This prompted Clinton to approve NATO enlargement in Prague in January 1994 ('not if, but when'). In September 1994 the enlargement plans were published, leading Yeltsin to warn of a 'cold peace'. Countries that were not candidates for membership in the immediate future would be offered a Partnership for Peace cooperation plan.

The year 1995 saw renewed fighting in Bosnia, culminating in NATO's airpower intervention on the side of the Bosnian Muslims and Croats. The US-brokered November 1995 Dayton Accords brought peace to Bosnia, and Russia was invited to send peacekeepers to join NATO's Implementation Force there.

Clinton delayed NATO expansion until after Yeltsin's hotly contested election battle in June 1996. In December 1996 the hard-line Madeleine Albright replaced Warren Christopher as Secretary of State. Countries joining the alliance would receive a cast-iron security guarantee: Article V of the NATO Charter pledges all signatories to come to the aid of a fellow member under attack. In July 1997 NATO's Madrid summit invited Poland, Czech Republic, and Hungary

to join the alliance. The three Baltic countries were worried that they were being excluded, so in January 1998 the USA signed the Baltic Charter pledging to help them in their bid for NATO membership. In April 1998 the Senate approved NATO expansion by 80 to 19. On 12 March 1999 Poland, Hungary, and the Czech Republic joined NATO, bringing the alliance to 19 countries.

NATO's expansion stoked fears of 'capitalist encirclement' among Russian communists and nationalists, and in protest the State Duma refused to ratify the START II treaty. In September 1996 Clinton and Yeltsin did initial a Comprehensive Nuclear Test Ban Treaty (including a ban on underground tests), but the US Senate rejected the treaty in 1999. In 1997 Russia started deploying a new intercontinental missile, the SSX-27 Topol-M, and introduced a new National Security Concept—one that seemed to show a greater willingness to be the first to use nuclear weapons.

In order to mitigate Russia's feeling of exclusion, in May 1997 the NATO–Russia Founding Act created a Permanent Joint Council in Brussels. Also, in June 1997, Yeltsin was invited to attend the Group of Seven (G-7) annual meeting of leaders of the foremost developed democracies. Russia was granted full

> **KEY POINTS**
>
> ❑ The Russians were severely disappointed by the US decision to expand the NATO alliance into countries that had once been part of the Soviet Union's Warsaw Pact security organization.
> ❑ To placate Russia it was allowed to join the G-7 group of leading economies, and the 1997 NATO–Russia Founding Act created a Permanent Joint Council in Brussels.
> ❑ In March 1999, Poland, Hungary, and the Czech Republic joined NATO.

membership in the G-8 in June 2002, one of the few Western organizations it was allowed to join. There was no progress with Russia's application to enter the World Trade Organization (WTO), which it submitted in 1993. Russia did join the Council of Europe in 1996, where its actions in Chechnya were sharply criticized. It continued as a member of the Organization for Security and Cooperation in Europe, which tried ineffectively to resolve the 'frozen conflicts' in Moldova, Georgia, and Azerbaijan.

For Clinton, NATO enlargement was an insurance policy that protected US interests in case Russia 'went bad'. The Kremlin eventually realized that it was powerless to stop the process. US–Russian relations soon faced the most severe test of the entire post-Soviet period, the Kosovo crisis.

The Kosovo crisis

On 24 March 1999, just two weeks after the three new members joined the alliance, NATO planes started bombing Yugoslavia. The West wanted President Slobodan Milosovic to accept international peacekeepers to halt violence in the rebellious province of Kosovo. The bombing commenced just as Prime Minister Primakov was flying to the USA to ask for more financial aid. Primakov ordered his aircraft to turn around mid-Atlantic and head back to Russia: a step that became symbolic of a new chill in US–Russian relations. Russia was incensed that the United States was using brute force to advance its political agenda in Europe—over Russian objections.

Moscow saw itself as having strong historical ties with the Serbs. But Moscow had little interest in tying itself to the sinking ship of Slobodan Milosovic. When the opportunity arose to play the peacemaker in June 1999, Moscow seized the chance. Ex-Prime Minister Chernomyrdin was sent to Belgrade to deliver the bad news—that NATO was preparing to launch a ground invasion, and Milosovic could not expect any more Russian support. If Milosovic agreed to withdraw his troops from Kosovo, he could preserve Yugoslavia's formal sovereignty over the province. In a curious footnote to the crisis, several hundred Russian peacekeepers drove down from Bosnia to seize the Kosovo airport before advancing British troops arrived. An armed clash was only averted thanks to the cool head of the British commander at the scene.

KEY POINTS

❑ The US decision to use military force against Yugoslavia met strong opposition from Moscow. The latter saw it as an unjustified use of force in its sphere of influence, and felt embarrassment at its seeming impotence in the face of US military might.

The 'Great Game' in Eurasia

The USA had a clear strategic interest in securing the viability of the newly independent states and preventing their possible reabsorption into a revived Soviet Union. US advisers and aid flowed into the region. The first priority was securing the removal of nuclear weapons from the non-Russian states. With that task accomplished, the Clinton administration turned to promoting the same kind of transition to 'market democracy' that was being attempted in Russia. The task was straightforward in the three Baltic states, but was much more challenging in the other countries, which had weak states and weaker economies, and lacked a tradition of self-rule. Civil wars raged in Tajikistan, Moldova, Azerbaijan, and Georgia, conflicts in which Russia was heavily involved. Former Communist Party leaders stayed on as authoritarian presidents in every Central Asian country except Kyrgyzstan, where a reformist president came to power.

The oil and gas reserves of the Caspian basin were seen as the key to securing the region's long-term development. Building pipelines to export Caspian oil and gas through Georgia and Turkey would increase the flow of hydrocarbons to world markets, while containing the influence of Iran and Russia. Moscow regarded the region as part of its exclusive sphere of influence, and despite US assurances it saw the rivalry for Caspian oil as a zero-sum game in which US advances would come at Russian expense.

Azerbaijan and Kazakhstan opened the doors to Western investors. In 1993 Texaco (now Chevron) entered Kazakhstan to develop the giant Tengiz oil field, and through the Caspian Pipeline Consortium built a new export pipeline to the Russian Black Sea port of Novorossiisk. In September 1994 BP signed 'the contract of the century' with Azerbaijan to develop offshore fields in the Caspian. Production started in 1997. BP wanted to build a 1100-mile oil export pipeline from Baku through Tbilisi to Ceyhan (BTC) on Turkey's southern coast. A complicating factor was the 1992–4 war over the disputed province of Nagorno-Karabakh, which left 15 per cent of Azerbaijan's territory in Armenian hands. The Armenian-American lobby persuaded the US Congress to enact section 907 of the Freedom Support Act in 1993, which barred direct US aid to the Azerbaijani government so long as it maintained a blockade and state of war with Armenia. (President Bush lifted section 907 in 2002, in return for Azerbaijan's cooperation in the war on terror.) Work started on the BTC pipeline in 2002 and it became operational in 2006.

Energy exports brought strong economic growth to Azerbaijan and Kazakhstan, although democracy is lacking in both countries, and Azerbaijan's stand-off with Armenia remains unresolved. The west would also like to export Kazakh oil and Turkmen gas by building pipelines across the Caspian Sea to Baku. Russia used a dispute over the legal status of the Caspian to block plans for an undersea pipeline in a bid to maintain its monopoly over Central Asian oil and gas exports, all of which flowed through Russian pipelines. Kazakhstan

> **KEY POINTS**
>
> ❑ The United States was quick to establish a diplomatic and economic presence in the new states of the Caucasus and Central Asia.
> ❑ Russia resented the projection of US influence into what it regarded as its own sphere of influence and tried to block US initiatives.
> ❑ The rise of the Shanghai Cooperation Organization, a multilateral security framework including China and Russia, has expanded Chinese influence in Central Asia.

and Turkmenistan subsequently built new pipelines to China to export oil and gas, respectively, reducing their dependency on Russia.

Under the Partnership for Peace programme, NATO held joint exercises in Uzbekistan in 1998, followed by extensive military assistance programmes in Georgia and Azerbaijan. The latter countries looked to western help to regain control over breakaway regions that had established de facto independence with Russian military support. Incursions by Islamic guerrillas into Uzbekistan and Kyrgyzstan in 1999–2001 threatened the stability of those regimes. China was also becoming more active in Central Asia, through the Shanghai Five, a multilateral security framework that with the addition of Uzbekistan became the Shanghai Cooperation Organization in 2001.

For most of the 1990s Ukraine showed enthusiasm for closer ties with NATO and the EU, but corruption and economic stagnation limited the scope for real reform. President Leonid Kuchma, who came into office in 1996, tried to follow a balanced course between Russia and the west, aware of Ukraine's dependence on Russian gas imports and the presence of 12 million ethnic Russians in east Ukraine. The scandal which erupted in 2000 after the murder of crusading journalist Heorhy Gongadze damaged Kuchma's credibility in the west.

A new face in the Kremlin—and the White House

In August 1999 fighting again broke out in Chechnya, which had been *de facto* independent since the

withdrawal of Russian troops in 1996. That was followed by several terrorist apartment bombings in Moscow a month later. To deal with the crisis Yeltsin appointed as Prime Minister Vladimir Putin, a seventeen-year KGB veteran who was heading the Federal Security Service. Putin launched a second full-scale invasion of Chechnya. Yeltsin resigned on New Year's Eve and appointed Putin 'acting president'. That cleared the way for Putin to win election as president in March 2000.

The United States watched these developments with resigned detachment. Washington no longer thought it could influence the outcome of Russian elections. Moscow was looking increasingly irrelevant to global affairs, saddled as it was by economic instability, corruption, and political instability. Russia was seen as incapable of providing domestic order, still less projecting power abroad.

Putin was an unknown quantity to Western leaders. His KGB background and ruthless prosecution of the war in Chechnya gave cause for concern. On the other hand, in personal meetings he impressed European leaders with his charm and intelligence. In his public statements, Putin signalled that he was well aware of Russia's debilitated condition. While moving quickly to restore the Kremlin's control over Russian society, Putin realized that integration within the global economy was essential to rebuild Russian state power.

Arms control was the main item on the agenda during President Clinton's farewell visit to Moscow in June 2000. The USA pushed for modifications in the 1972 Anti-Ballistic Missile Defense (ABM) treaty so it could begin testing a national missile defence system (NMD), intended to counter a possible nuclear strike from Iran, Iraq, or North Korea. Moscow was sceptical, fearing that successful deployment of NMD would lock in US global dominance. The US Senate approved the development of theatre missile defence in March 1999. In a bid to head off NMD, Putin persuaded the State Duma to ratify START II, signed in 1993, which they dutifully did in 2000.

Clinton could not offer deep cuts in strategic missiles in return for Russian approval of NMD: influential Senate Republican Jesse Helms made it clear that he would block approval of any such treaty. Clinton signed two minor agreements: to cut each country's weapons-grade plutonium reserves and to create a joint early warning centre in Moscow to reduce the risks of an accidental nuclear launch. (The centre never opened.)

USA–Russia relations were not a prominent issue in the November 2000 election campaign, although

---

❝ KEY QUOTES 14.5: Time for a new approach

The Clinton administration's embrace of Yeltsin and those who were thought to be reformers around him has failed... Support for democracy and economic reform became support for Yeltsin. His agenda became the American agenda. The United States certified that reform was taking place where it was not, continuing to disburse money from the International Monetary Fund in the absence of any evidence of serious change. The realities in Russia simply did not accord with the administration's script about Russian economic reform... Frustrated expectations and 'Russia fatigue' are direct consequences of the 'happy talk' in which the Clinton administration engaged... US policy must concentrate on the important security agenda with Russia. First, it must recognize that American security is threatened less by Russia's strength than by its weakness and incoherence.

(Condoleezza Rice, Bush's top foreign policy adviser, November 2000)

❝ KEY QUOTES 14.6: Bush's impression of Putin

I found a man who realizes his future lies with the West, not the East, that we share common security concerns, primarily Islamic fundamentalism, that he understands missiles could affect him just as much as us. On the other hand he doesn't want to be diminished by America.

(President George W. Bush, talking of Vladimir Putin in July 2001)

the Republicans attacked the Clinton administration for its naive pro-Yeltsin policy. The Republican candidate Bush denounced Russia's pervasive corruption—in one presidential debate he even charged former Prime Minister Chernomyrdin with pocketing Western loan money. In an autumn 2000 essay in *Foreign Affairs* Condoleezza Rice, Bush's top foreign policy adviser, laid out a strongly critical assessment of Clinton's Russia policy, in which Democratic candidate Al Gore was deeply implicated, as Vice President.

US–Russian relations did not get off to a good start with the new Bush administration. It appeared that Washington was not treating Moscow as a serious player on the global stage. Condoleezza Rice, Bush's national security adviser, argued that 'It would be foolish in the extreme to share defenses with Moscow as it either leaks or deliberately transfers weapons technologies to the very states against which America is defending.' In a February 2001 interview in *Le Figaro,* Rice commented that 'I believe Russia is a threat to the West in general and to our European allies in particular.'

As the USA was ignoring Moscow, Putin was flexing his diplomatic muscles, making a flurry of visits to countries in Europe and Asia. Iranian President Muhammad Khatami visited Russia in March 2001 to discuss arms sales, and Putin reiterated Russia's intention to help complete the long-stalled Bushehr nuclear power plant. Putin stepped up military and political cooperation with China, and Russia's economic recovery meant it was no longer begging for extensions on its foreign debts, as it was throughout the 1990s. In 2006 it paid down its entire $22 billion debt to the IMF ahead of schedule. A huge scandal erupted following

the February 2001 arrest of FBI agent Robert Hanssen, who had spied for the Russians for fifteen years. In response, the USA ejected fifty Russian diplomats: the largest number of expulsions since 1986. The Russians reacted by expelling an equivalent number of American officials.

It was not until June 2001 that the two leaders finally met, in Ljubljana, Slovenia. President Bush famously 'looked the man in his eye' and 'was able to get a sense of his soul'. Bush said, 'I am convinced that he and I can build a relationship of mutual respect and candor', and promised support for Russia's entry into the WTO. Putin said he and Bush had forged a 'very high level of trust', and referred to the American president as a 'partner' and 'a nice person to talk to'. But the drama and sense of historical importance that characterized the past two presidential relationships was gone; in the new century, Russia simply did not capture the focus of the US strategic mind. The Ljubljana summit did prepare the ground for closer US–Russian cooperation. And then came 9/11.

KEY POINTS

❑ The ailing economy, the war in Chechnya, and the weakness of the state were the priorities on Vladimir Putin's agenda as he assumed power in 1999.

❑ President George W. Bush saw Russia as in a weakened state, and relations with Moscow were not a priority for the new administration.

❑ The United States and Russia attempted to find common ground on arms control, but Putin was opposed to the US national missile defence effort.

❝❞   KEY QUOTES 14.7: Partners in the war on terror

We affirm our determination to meet the threats to peace in the 21st century. Among these threats are terrorism, the new horror of which was vividly demonstrated by the evil crimes of September 11 . . . We have agreed that the current levels of our nuclear forces do not reflect the strategic realities of today. . . . We support the building of a European–Atlantic community whole, free, and at peace, excluding no one, and respecting the independence, sovereignty and territorial integrity of all nations.

(Joint US–Russian statement after the presidential summit in Crawford, Texas, November 2001)

A strategy for a New World

The terrorist attacks on the World Trade Towers and the Pentagon had a major impact on US–Russian relations. Putin was the first leader to telephone Bush with condolences. Still embroiled in the second Chechen war, Putin saw 9/11 as powerful vindication of his warnings about the threat of militant Islam.

Putin decided to share intelligence and aid Washington's campaign against the Taliban regime in Afghanistan, despite opposition from some in the Russian military. According to some reports, Putin only agreed to US bases in Central Asia after Uzbek President Islam Karimov said he would cooperate with the Americans whatever Moscow's position. Still, Moscow was not pleased by the prospect of an indefinite US military presence in the region. After the defeat of the Taliban, Russia declined to send peacekeepers to Afghanistan, in light of its own role in the 1980s war. In August 2003 NATO took over the International Security Assistance Force in Afghanistan—the alliance's first deployment outside Europe.

Putin's visit to the presidential ranch in Crawford, Texas, in November 2001 symbolized the return of the feel-good factor in US–Russian relations, but failed to produce any specific rewards for Moscow. The leaders released a joint statement declaring that 'neither country regards the other as an enemy or threat'. Bush promised to ask Congress to lift the 1974 Jackson–Vanik amendment, which required annual vetting of Russia's emigration policies to maintain normal trade relations with the USA. (But Congress did not budge.) However, the Crawford summit failed to produce a deal to bridge the gap between the two sides on NMD. In December 2001, Secretary of State Colin Powell travelled to Moscow to report that the USA would withdraw from the ABM treaty in six months' time. Putin's response was surprisingly muted: he merely stated that Russian security was not threatened by the development. In return for Putin's acquiescence, in May 2002 Bush signed the Strategic Offensive Weapons Reduction Treaty (SORT) in Moscow, under which each side promised to cut its strategic weapons from 6000 warheads to 1700–2200 over ten years. SORT, unlike START II, did not mandate the destruction of warheads and had no on-site verification procedures.

But it still looked as if a strategic partnership based on mutual security interests might be a realistic goal.

The May 2002 Rome summit saw the creation of a new NATO–Russia Council to give Russia a new voice in the alliance. Despite Moscow's misgivings, NATO embarked on a new round of enlargement. In March 2004 Estonia, Latvia, Lithuania, Bulgaria, Romania, Slovakia, and Slovenia joined the alliance. Five of those countries subsequently entered the EU alongside Poland, Hungary, and the Czech Republic in May 2004. (Bulgaria and Romania joined the EU in January 2007.) Russia's relations with Poland, Estonia, and Latvia remained fractious, but membership in NATO and the EU gave those countries more confidence in their dealings with Moscow.

US business interests were also bullish. Since 1999, the Russian economy had been growing strongly, boosted by the rise in the world oil price. The oligarchs who controlled most of Russia's oil industry were looking for Western partners. In September 2003 the TNK oil company merged with BP, and Mikhail Khodorkovsky's Yukos, Russia's largest oil corporation, seemed to be preparing for a merger with Exxon. Some argued that the oil oligarchs were a new, pro-western elite that would take control of Russia once Putin, a transitional post-Yeltsin figure, had stepped down. Khodorkovsky himself promoted such a scenario, and he became a well-known figure in Washington. The USA saw Russia as a possible source of energy supplies. Russian oil output had recovered since 1998, accounting for half the increase in world oil supply between 1998 and 2004. In this new spirit of cooperation, a joint US–Russian Energy Working Group met in Washington in April 2002, and an energy summit convened in Houston in October 2002.

KEY POINTS

❑ Putin's support for the USA in the wake of 9/11 revived hopes for a strategic partnership between Russia and the United States.

❑ Presidents Bush and Putin managed to strike up a warm personal relationship at their summit meetings in Slovenia and in Crawford, Texas, in 2001.

A reversal of course

The tide of USA–Russia relations turned decisively for the worse in the course of 2003, for three reasons: the US-led war in Iraq, Putin's crackdown on political opposition, and the wave of 'colour revolutions' that brought regime change to three post-Soviet states.

The looming Iraq War was a major challenge for Putin. In November 2002 Russia reluctantly accepted United Nations Resolution 1441 forcing Iraq to accept weapons inspectors. On 5 March 2003 the leaders of France, Germany, and Russia publicly stated they would block UN approval for war against Iraq. The USA went ahead with the invasion anyway, and after the conquest of Baghdad Secretary Rice decided to 'punish France, ignore Germany and forgive Russia'. The fact that the USA went ahead with the invasion despite the warnings from international leaders was taken in Moscow as demonstration that the US administration was a loose cannon and an unreliable ally.

Revelations in 2002 of Iran's secret nuclear enrichment programme led to renewed pressure from the USA for sanctions against Tehran. Moscow agreed that Iran should not acquire nuclear weapons, but opposed sanctions and wanted to complete construction of Iran's Bushehr reactor for commercial reasons. Since 2005 Moscow has been pushing a compromise under which it would supply fuel for Bushehr but reprocess the spent fuel back in Russia.

In 2003 Putin moved against the ambitious oligarch Mikhail Khodorkovsky—the richest man in Russia, with an estimated net worth of $16 billion. Khodorkovsky was arrested in October and sentenced to eight years' imprisonment on charges of tax evasion and fraud. Khodorkovsky's arrest was connected to the upcoming December 2003 State Duma elections. Khodorkovsky was funding parties across the political spectrum, and was possibly planning to challenge Putin for the presidency in the March 2004 election. The pro-Kremlin United Russia Party won a sweeping victory in the Duma election, thanks to the state-controlled mass media and use of 'administrative resources' to steer the election campaign. In September 2004, in the wake of the horrifying siege of a school in Beslan by Islamic terrorists, Putin announced the abolition of direct elections for regional governors. A new law on political parties made it even more difficult for opposition groups to enter parliament. Russia's return to a centralized, authoritarian system of power seemed complete. The US human rights group Freedom House downgraded Russia from 'free' to 'partly free' that same year.

Meanwhile, Putin was moving to extend Kremlin control over the Russian economy. Yukos assets were seized for tax arrears and sold off to state-owned Rosneft. The independent oil company Sibneft was forced to merge with state-owned Gazprom. Putin oversaw the creation of a network of state-owned corporations in energy and engineering and appointed Kremlin officials to chair their boards. Foreign oil companies were forced to give up majority control in the handful of joint ventures that had been allowed to start in the 1990s.

In November 2003 a US-backed opposition movement swept Mikheil Saakashvili to power in Georgia's 'Rose Revolution'. That set off alarm bells in the Kremlin, which perceived a US plot to encircle Russia's borders with pro-western governments. The same month a last-minute US intervention derailed a Russian plan for a settlement between Moldova and the breakaway province of Transnistria. In response, Putin dragged his feet in withdrawing troops from Georgia and Moldova.

In March 2004 veteran diplomat Sergei Lavrov replaced Igor Ivanov as Foreign Minister: he reportedly had testy relations with Secretary Rice. In his May 2004 State of the Union Address, Putin warned western groups not to meddle in Russia's domestic politics. A new law was introduced in November 2005 cracking down on foreign-financed non-governmental organizations. (The US Peace Corps had already been expelled from Russia in 2002.) In an angry speech after the Beslan tragedy in September 2004, Putin publicly referred to western threats against Russia, for the first time since 2001. 'We showed weakness,' Putin said, 'and weak people are beaten.'

Putin's clumsy efforts to influence the Ukrainian presidential election of November 2004 backfired, helping to spark an 'Orange Revolution' that replicated the victory of pro-western forces in Georgia the previous year.

> **❝ KEY QUOTES 14.8:** Foreign jackals
>
> Those who confront us need a weak and ill state. Regrettably, there are those inside the country who feed off foreign embassies like jackals and count on support of foreign funds and governments, and not their own people. If these gentlemen return back to power, they will again cheat people and fill their pockets.
>
> (President Vladimir Putin talking to an election rally, November 2007)

That was followed by a 'Tulip Revolution' in Kyrgyzstan in March 2005, ousting President Askar Akayev. Russia's testy reaction to these developments, and a sharp increase in Russian defence spending, were fodder for those who argued that Russian imperialism was once more on the march. The USA lost its military base in Uzbekistan after criticizing President Islam Karimov for the killing of hundreds of protesters in Andizhon in 2005. In a memo to National Security Adviser Stephen Hadley in July 2006, Defense Secretary Donald Rumsfeld warned that the USA was 'getting run out of Central Asia' by the Russians.

The dramatic interruption of Russian gas supplies to Ukraine in 2006 was a serious blow to Putin's international image. Russia was selling natural gas to Ukraine for $47 per 1000 cubic metres while its European customers were paying $230. Ukraine rebuffed a proposed price hike. Russia's main gas export pipeline crosses Ukraine, so Moscow could not cut deliveries to Ukraine without interrupting supplies to Europe, which gets one-quarter of its gas from Russia. In January 2006 Gazprom closed the pipeline for two days, alarming its western customers. After the Ukrainian shutdown, and as oil prices climbed above $80 a barrel, commentators started talking of Russia as an 'energy superpower'. However, given that the USA imports no oil or gas from Russia, these actions are not of vital importance to US national security. A bipartisan Council of Foreign Relations task force issued a report in 2006 that expressed fears about Russia's backsliding from democracy and its international assertiveness, but still urged the administration to continue engaging with Russia in order to deal with urgent issues such as the threat of nuclear proliferation in Iran and North Korea.

One positive development was the US acceptance of Russia's bid for entry to the WTO in November 2006. The USA had been holding out for Russian concessions on food imports, liberalization of financial services, and improved intellectual property rights. But with 150 countries now members of the WTO, Russia's exclusion was increasingly anomalous. Russia had signed bilateral agreements with nearly all the other member countries: the USA was the main holdout. After the two sides failed to close a deal at the G-8 summit in Petersburg in June 2006, Russia's patience was exhausted. Moscow slapped a ban on US chicken imports, citing sanitary concerns, and passed up a $3 billion option to buy twenty-two Boeing 787 airliners. These Russian actions triggered the shift in the US government's position.

But by the end of 2007, there were few advocates of a conciliatory course towards Russia in the USA. Republican Senator John McCain suggested that Russia should be barred from the G-8 because of its 'diminishing political freedoms' and 'efforts to bully democratic neighbors, such as Georgia'. Referring to President Bush's 2001 comment that he had 'looked into Putin's soul', McCain said, 'I looked into Mr Putin's eyes and I saw three things—a K and a G and a B.'

> **KEY POINTS**
>
> ❑ The US-led war in Iraq led to a sharp deterioration in US–Russian relations.
> ❑ Putin's crackdown on political opposition, symbolized by the arrest of oil magnate Mikhail Khodorkovsky in October 2003, cast a shadow over his acceptability as a trusted partner for the United States.
> ❑ The 'colour revolutions' in Georgia, Ukraine, and Kyrgyzstan were seen by Moscow as part of an American plot to undermine Russian influence in the post-Soviet region.

> **KEY QUOTES 14.9: Coming in from the cold**
>
> The artificial bipolar system is giving way to a more natural multi-centred international system . . . By overthrowing the Soviet system and rejecting its restoration, Russia has laid a basis for forming a state compatible with the rest of Europe.
>
> To use the words of John Le Carre, Russia has 'come in from the cold' after almost a century of isolation and self-isolation.
> (President Dmitry Medvedev in a June 2008 speech in Berlin.)

Two new leaders

2008 saw the election of two new presidents: Dmitry Medvedev and Barak Obama. Both men were aware that US-Russian relations had reached a dangerously low point, and that their countries would benefit from an improved relationship.

Many observers expected Putin to amend the constitution in order to stay on as president for a third term. But Putin stepped aside and nominated his long-time aide Medvedev as presidential candidate of the United Russia party. Medvedev was easily elected in March 2008 and took office in May. Medvedev, 13 years younger than Putin, had worked with Putin in the St Petersburg mayor's office in the early 1990s. He moved to the Kremlin in 1999, rising to the post of chief of staff and then first deputy prime minister. Putin did not leave the political stage, however. He had himself appointed prime minister, inaugurating what was called the 'tandem leadership'. There was much speculation about how much power the new president really enjoyed.

Medvedev, a new and unfamiliar figure, tried to cultivate a progressive, modern image. He was Russia's first post-soviet leader: unlike Putin, he had not served in the KGB—or any other Soviet institution for that matter. Fluent in English, Medvedev was comfortable with the internet, starting his own blog and later a Twitter account.

However, there was no sign of a thaw in US-Russia relations for the remainder of 2008. Moscow responded angrily to NATO's April 2008 Bucharest summit, which seemed to open the door to membership for Ukraine and Georgia. Russia continued to play a somewhat obstructionist role at the United Nations, using its veto or threat of veto to block possible UN intervention in Darfur, Burma, and Zimbabwe. Medvedev actually agreed to impose sanctions against Zimbabwe at the G-8 summit in Japan in July 2008—his first major outing as president. But several days later Russia vetoed the corresponding resolution in the UN Security Council, raising questions about whether Putin or Medvedev was in charge.

In February 2008 Russia had opposed the decision by the USA and most European countries to recognize the independence of Kosovo in the former Yugoslavia, warning that it could be a precedent for Russian recognition of Georgia's breakaway regions. This issue erupted in the Georgian war of August 2008, which became the first major test for Medvedev, just three months after he was inaugurated as president.

The guns of August

Georgian troops attacked the breakaway region of South Ossetia on 7 August 2008. Moscow took the assault as a direct challenge to Russia's credibility as a regional power, since many Ossetians had been given Russian citizenship and Russian peacekeepers patrolled the province's border with Georgia. Russian forces poured into Ossetia and drove out the Georgian troops. Both sides had been preparing for war, though each denied responsibility for starting it.

Prime Minister Putin happened to be at the Olympics opening ceremony in Beijing when the fighting broke out. He immediately returned home and flew straight to North Ossetia. He was shown on TV, talking with troops and refugees, while Medvedev stayed in Moscow. Medvedev managed to regain some credibility with the arrival of a European peace mission in Moscow headed by French President Nicholas Sarkozy. Sarkozy dissuaded the Russians from advancing on Tbilisi and negotiated a cease-fire, which was publicly announced on 12 August with Medvedev at his side.

European opinion tended to blame both sides for the conflict: criticizing Georgian President Mikheil Saakasvili for launching the assault, but also chastising Russia for bombing cities and seizing territory in Georgia beyond Ossetia. Some blamed Moscow for provoking the conflict by encouraging South Ossetian militants to shell Georgian positions. There was also speculation that Russia's true goals were not to protect the lives of its peacekeepers and Ossetian residents, but to prevent Georgia from joining NATO, or even to depose Saakashvili. The USA had been providing extensive economic and military aid to Georgia, so there was puzzlement why Secretary Rice—who had visited Georgia in July—had not been able to deter Saakashvili's brinksmanship.

On 26 August Medvedev shocked the international community by announcing that Russia was recognizing the sovereignty of Abkhazia and South Ossetia. Russia was not able to persuade any of its allies to join them in recognizing the secessionist republics, with the exception of distant Nicaragua. This step dented Medvedev's liberal reputation in the West.

Russia's international image nose-dived in the wake of the Georgian war. On 20 August the Polish government, which had previously been hesitating, signed up to a US plan to install missile batteries on Polish territory, ostensibly to intercept missiles launched from Iran. In a September 2008 speech Secretary Rice condemned a 'Russia increasingly authoritarian at home and aggressive abroad'. Back in May 2008 a civil nuclear agreement had been signed, clearing the way for Russia to import thousands of tons of spent nuclear fuel from the US. But the accord needed Congressional approval, and it was withdrawn from consideration after the Georgian war.

Medvedev tried to clear the air in a speech in Sochi on 31 August 2008 in which he spelt out five principles of Russian foreign policy:

1. the supremacy of international law

2. 'unipolarity is unacceptable'

3. 'Russia does not want isolation'

4. the protection of life and dignity of Russian citizens 'no matter where they live'

5. 'Russia has areas of privileged interests'.

The fifth point was seen as a claim for a Russian sphere of influence in the 'near abroad', and attracted widespread international criticism. During his years as president Putin had never used such a blunt formulation.

At a NATO summit in Brussels in December 2008 France and Germany, wary of provoking Moscow, blocked a US proposal to offer a membership action plan to Georgia and Ukraine. In January 2009 Russia provoked the most severe natural gas crisis with Ukraine yet seen, shutting down supplies for 17 days in order to force Ukraine to pay European-level prices for its gas. This once again demonstrated Europe's energy dependence on Moscow. The election of the pro-Russian Viktor Yanukovich as president of Ukraine in February 2010 meant NATO membership was no longer on the cards for that country.

A new beginning

The inauguration of President Barack Obama in January 2009 offered a chance for a fresh start. Obama was primarily focused on domestic affairs, especially given the ongoing financial crisis. Although Russia was not of major importance for US foreign policy goals, Obama saw an opportunity to score some positive achievements in relations with Moscow and differentiate himself from the outgoing the Bush administration. (There was no scope for easy victories in more important realms, such as relations with China.) Obama saw Russia as a declining power, not likely to constitute a threat to US interests in the foreseeable future, thus saw little risk in reaching out to Medvedev.

Secretary of State Hilary Clinton met with Russian Foreign Minister Sergei Lavrov in Geneva in March 2009 and promised to 'reset' USA–Russia relations. She presented Lavrov with a symbolic 'reset button'. (Unfortunately, due to a mistranslation the Russian word on the button actually said 'overload'.) The main figure shaping Obama's Russia policy was National Security Staff aide Michael McFaul, a Stanford professor who had criticized Russia's democratic backsliding under President Putin. Obama and Medvedev met for the first time in London in April 2009, where they agreed to move ahead with a new nuclear weapons reduction treaty.

President Obama's state visit to Moscow in July 2009 was generally considered a success. He avoided lecturing his hosts on their democratic and diplomatic deficiencies, while praising Russia as a 'great country' and 'great power'. In an address to students, Obama said 'America wants a strong, peaceful, and prosperous Russia'. A new Bilateral Presidential Commission was created with a dozen working groups addressing everything from energy to civil society, but little was subsequently heard of this structure. Critics accused Obama of whitewashing Russia's human rights record, while the administration's strategy was to bet on Medvedev as the best hope for moderate liberalization.

The ambiguities of 'tandemocracy' surfaced during Obama's visit. On the eve of his departure for Moscow, Obama told reporters that Putin has 'one foot in the old ways of doing business and one foot in the new', while praising Medvedev as a forward-looking leader. Most observers saw this as a diplomatic misstep by the US president, since there seemed little to be gained in trying to boost Medvedev at Putin's expense. Obama subsequently praised Putin as someone who 'has been a very strong leader for the Russian people'.

Obama won an important concession on his Moscow trip: Medvedev announced that the USA would be allowed to fly troops and ship supplies by land across Russian territory to Afghanistan, providing an alternative to the longer and more hazardous route across Pakistan. (By 2011 50 per cent of US troops and 20 per cent of US equipment headed for Afghanistan was transiting Russia.) Obama failed to persuade Medvedev to sanction Iran because of its nuclear weapons programme. Medvedev in turn was unable to persuade Obama to abandon the planned missile defence in Poland, with radars located in the Czech Republic. The Polish missile defence plan was eventually shelved in September 2009—not as a sop to the Russians, but ostensibly because of a reassessment of the Iranian missile threat.

The most pressing item on the summit agenda was the extension of the START treaty limiting nuclear weapons, due to expire in December 2009. The new treaty would cut warheads on each side to 1500–1675, while delivery vehicles would be cut to 500–1100, down from the 1600 allowed under the existing agreement. As of January 2009 the USA had 1198 missiles and bombers, capable of delivering 5576 warheads, while Russia had 816 delivery vehicles with 3909 warheads. The new treaty thus represented a halving of the nuclear weapons deployed by the two sides. In contrast to the 2002 SORT treaty, START II would allow for onsite inspection in both countries. Critics noted that the treaty did not mandate the destruction of removed warheads or deal with tactical nuclear weapons. Obama was interested in prolonging the START treaty not so much because he saw the Russian arsenal as a potential threat, but because he wanted to limit proliferation of nuclear weapons to third countries. The collapse of START would send the wrong signal to the rest of the world.

After protracted negotiations over the finer points of warhead storage and telemetry encryption, the New START treaty was signed in April 2010 and sent to Congress. Republicans objected that the treaty might constrain the US NMD programme. After some last minute changes to the preamble, the Senate approved the treaty in December 2010, handing Obama the most substantial foreign policy achievement of his first term. Medvedev's proposals for a joint 'territorial missile defense' with NATO at the Lisbon summit in November 2010 fell on stony ground. Similar proposals had been made several times in the past, but neither side trusted the other sufficiently to engage in the kind of sharing of secrets that such a programme would require.

A cautious partnership

In February 2009 Russia prevailed on President Kurmanbek Bakiev to eject the Americans from their military base in Kyrgyzstan by dangling a promise of $2 billion of investments. The USA relied on the Manas base for the shipment of men and supplies for the war in Afghanistan. Washington offered to raise the annual rent from $17 million to $60 million, with other aid money in the pipeline. In June 2009 Bakiev reversed course and agreed to allow the American base to continue in operation. Washington had outplayed Moscow in that particular round of the 'great game'.

Still, one sign of the new warmth was that in May 2010 US troops marched for the first time in Moscow's Second World War victory parade. On his first official visit to the USA in June 2010 Medvedev toured Silicon Valley, and shared a burger with Obama in a Washington, DC diner. He showed new flexibility with regard to possible sanctions on Iran. Russia's patience with Iran was strained by Teheran's rejection of Moscow's offer to reprocess fuel for Iran's research reactor, and by the US revelation of the uranium enrichment facility which the Iranians had secretly built at Qom. Russia also dropped plans to sell its advanced S300 air defence system to Iran.

In 2011, the Arab Spring caught both Moscow and Washington by surprise. While the USA came to embrace the changes, Russia stayed on the sidelines. Still, in the crucial March 2011 UN Security Council vote authorizing military action in Libya, Russia

> **KEY POINTS**
>
> ❑ President Barack Obama set out to 'reset' relations with Russia, and found a willing partner in new President Dmitry Medvedev.
> ❑ Fruits of the new partnership included the New START nuclear arms reduction treaty and approval for US military transit across Russia to Afghanistan.
> ❑ In the wake of the August 2008 Georgian war the USA backed off from efforts to spread NATO further east.

abstained, along with Brazil, India, and China, and did not use its veto. Putin in contrast criticized the allied intervention as a medieval crusade, and the Russian ambassador to Libya was fired after he spoke out against sanctions on Libya. However, Medvedev himself later backtracked, arguing that the UN resolution merely established a no-fly zone and did not authorize NATO's bombing campaign.

Overall the 'reset' was clearly a success. There were no major confrontations between the two powers. Even incidents such as the arrest of Russian 'sleeper spies' in the USA in June 2010 or the extradition of arms dealer Viktor Bout from Thailand to New York in November 2010 were received fairly calmly. While the two sides showed they could work together on a pragmatic basis, there was still no agreement on long-run principles, from the role of NATO to the quality of Russian democracy.

Conclusion

The past fifteen years have seen the rise and fall of hopes for a breakthrough to partnership in US–Russian relations. The switchbacks in US policy reflect the fact that Russia was in the throes of a major historical transition whose outcome was bound to be uncertain. The USA was slow to recognize the extent of Russia's decline in the 1990s, then slow to realize its rise after 1999. US policy cycled between exaggerated optimism and wary dismissal. Both the Clinton and Bush administrations began with high expectations for a new understanding with Moscow,

and then saw relations driven into a ditch. Strobe Talbott's faith in Russia's democratic transition foundered in the messy realities of post-Soviet Russia. Bush was determined to wage the war on terror according to American priorities, and Putin was not content to be a silent partner. Obama seems to have broken with this pattern. He started off with lower and more realistic expectations, and produced modest but satisfactory results.

One continuity through the whole period has been the tendency to personalize USA–Russia relations.

Clinton's belief that he could understand and manage the mercurial Yeltsin came to dominate Washington's relations with Moscow. A similar dynamic occurred, on a more limited scale, between Bush and Putin, and there are echoes in Obama's reliance on Medvedev.

The fundamental problem is that USA still cannot really decide whether Russia is a potential friend or a future foe, and the same is true for Russia. There are fundamental differences between the strategic perspectives of Moscow and Washington. The United States refuses to grant Medvedev's 'area of privileged interests' in the post-soviet states. Russia in its turn is unwilling to accept a permanent US military presence or support for 'colour revolutions' in their neighbourhood.

Although the USA is smarting from setbacks in Iraq and the lingering recession, it still sees itself as the world's leading power. In contrast, a decade of oil-fueled economic growth has not translated into a more powerful Russian presence on the world stage. On the contrary, Moscow's aggressive energy diplomacy has alienated many of its partners—both European customers and neighbouring transit countries. Moscow would prefer closer economic and political ties with Europe, but the Europeans are wary. Russia cannot decide whether to try to align with China against the USA or to maintain its distance from Beijing lest it be swamped by the Chinese economic juggernaut.

Although Russia says it would prefer to develop multi-lateral relations with Europe and China, in some respects they still get some comfort from the traditional bilateral dealings with Washington. Old habits die hard.

? Questions

1. What were the priorities for US foreign policy during the break-up of the Soviet Union?
2. Would it have served US national interests to launch a Marshall Plan-style aid programme for Russia in 1992?
3. Was it wise for President Bill Clinton to tie US policy so closely to the figure of Boris Yeltsin?
4. What were the main achievements of US policy towards Russia in the 1990s?
5. Was it a good idea for the USA to pursue NATO expansion over Russian objections?
6. How did 9/11 change US–Russian relations?
7. How did personal relations between the national leaders affect US–Russian relations in the Clinton and Bush administrations?
8. What should be the principles shaping US policy towards Russia after the shift to authoritarianism under President Vladimir Putin?
9. What are the areas of common interest and conflicting interests between Russia and the United States?
10. What are the issues of cooperation and conflict between the United States and Russia in the states of the former Soviet Union?

» Further Reading

Baev, P. (2009), *Russian Energy Policy and Military Power, Putin's Quest or Greatness* (New York: Routledge).

Subtle analysis of Russia's strategic options by a Norway-based expert.

Goldgeier, J. and McFaul, M. (2003), *Power and Purpose: US Policy toward Russia after the Cold War* (Washington, DC: Brookings Institution)

An authoritative account of US–Russian relations based on extensive interviews with leading US and Russian officials.

Lucas, E. (2009), *The New Cold War: Putin's Russia and the Threat to the West* (London: Palgrave Macmillan).

Lucas, the former *Economist* Moscow correspondent, stresses Putin's great power aspirations.

Mankoff, J. (2009), *Russian Foreign Policy: The Return of Great Power Politics* (Lanham, MD: Rowman and Littlefield).

A diplomatic history of Russia during the Putin presidency.

Rice, C. (2000), Campaign 2000: Promoting the National Interest, *Foreign Affairs*, Jan–Feb.

A blunt assessment of Russian weakness from candidate George W. Bush's foreign policy adviser.

Simes, D. K. (2007), Losing Russia: The Costs of Renewed Confrontation, *Foreign Affairs*, Nov–Dec.

An argument in favour of continued engagement with Russia despite its turn to authoritarianism.

Talbott, S. (2002), *The Russia Hand* (New York: Random House).

A thorough and occasionally candid description and defence of Clinton's Russia policy, by the man who was primarily responsible for it.

Tsygankov, A. (2006), *Russia's Foreign Policy: Change And Continuity in National Identity* (Lanham, MD: Rowman and Littlefield).

Good introduction, covering military, diplomatic, and identity dimensions of foreign policy.

 For a range of additional resources to support your learning visit the Online Resource Centre that accompanies this book at **www.oxfordtextbooks.co.uk/orc/cox_stokes2e/.**

15 The USA, China, and rising Asia

Michael Cox

Chapter contents

Introduction

At the end of the Second World War the United States faced three historic tasks: one was to create or recreate the conditions that would over time lead to the reconstitution of the world economy after many years of crisis, another was to limit, and if possible defeat, the ambitions of those who after 1945 were pressing to push the world in a radically different direction to that favoured by America, and the third was to incorporate old enemy states while balancing the rising power of others whose interests were diametrically opposed to those of the USA.

Nowhere in the world after the war did the challenge to the United States appear so great as it did in East Asia. Here the legacy of European colonialism, Japanese rule, brutal war, and rising nationalist aspirations combined together to make for an explosive situation—nowhere more critically than in China, where all the tensions within the region converged together to produce major convulsions, culminating in 1949 with communist revolution. Whether communist success in China was the result of superior organization, social discontent, the successful manipulation of nationalist sentiment, or the backing of communist USSR has long been debated by different generations of historians. There has been very little debate, however, about the known consequences of the Chinese revolution. Most obviously, it made the region an epicentre of conflict in an already dangerous Cold War. A year later it then contributed very directly to the Korean War itself. And over the longer term, it compelled the USA to commit itself to the security of the whole region. Europe may have been at the heart

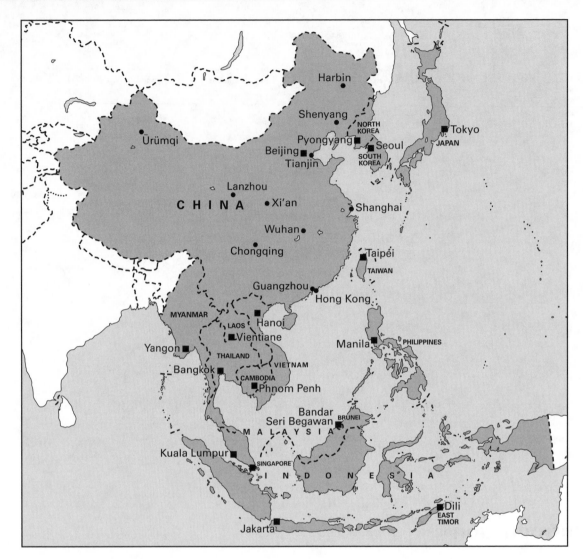

Fig. 15.1 Map of East Asia.

of the Cold War for the United States, but it was in East Asia that it was actually fought out on the ground.

This chapter deals with several issues to do with the US role in Asia, including the role it began to carve out for itself long before the Cold War began. It looks at many different issues but is framed by one very large question: how it was that a region wracked by insurgencies and wars over nearly forty years was transformed from being one of the most disturbed and contested in the second half of the twentieth century, into becoming one of the more stable and prosperous by century's end? This is not how one might have expected things to have turned out. Indeed, even after the Cold War had come to an end in 1989 some

were still predicting that the region was bound for conflict. Yet twenty years on many are now arguing that East Asia has not only become a zone of peace and prosperity, but because it has, it is beginning to have a marked impact on the world more generally. Indeed, more than a few analysts today are now even suggesting that as we move forward into the twenty-first century it will be China and not the United States, the east and not the west, that will hold the key to the international system's future.

In this chapter we will look at the region in its totality and try and asses the impact the United States has had upon it since it achieved total victory over Japan back in 1945. In fact, precisely because it was war against Japan that finally made the United States a serious player in the region, we will look in the first section at the history of the US–Japan relationship. In the next section we go on to look at China, the deeper causes of its hostile relationship with the United States after 1949, and how and why the relationship underwent such a startling change from the 1970s onwards. In the third part we will examine some of the unresolved problems in the region, but most centrally that of a still divided Korea and a nuclear North Korea. Then we will explain why earlier predictions about East Asia being primed for further conflict after the Cold War have turned out to be wrong at worst and misleading at best. Finally, in the last section, we will look at the future role of the United States

and see whether or not its position is likely to remain secure in the region over the longer term. As I will seek to show, although it is easy to be seduced by a crop of contemporary writers predicting that a declining and overstretched America will one day have to withdraw from a region in which China is becoming increasingly influential because of its growing economic power, one has to maintain some semblance of balance. The US position will not remain what it was in the Cold War, to be sure, and China's economic rise will undoubtedly pose a severe test. But in spite of all this, the US is likely to remain a key actor in East Asia, if for no other reason that no other state or regional organization either wants the job or could do it particularly well.

Japan, the United States, and the new Asian order

As an emerging world power in the nineteenth century whose western frontier ended where the Pacific Ocean began, it was almost inevitable that the United States would view the great stretch of shining water to its east as an American lake whose sea-lanes it should control and whose resources it should exploit to the full. At a very early date in its history therefore the United States pursued an expansionist eastward policy that brought it into conflict with Japan by the middle of the nineteenth century and imperial China by the end. Certain in the knowledge that its own brand of muscular Christianity and robust enterprise were superior to anything on offer in Asia itself, Americans, like most 'normal' imperialists, viewed the nations with whom they came into contact with a mixture of contempt—the Chinese according to one American observer were 'cold, snaky, slow, cowardly, treacherous, suspicious, deceitful people'—laced with a large dose of nineteenth-century racism. The peoples of Asia offered little by way of inspiration it seemed, and the best one could do was either convert them to the Christian faith (which might help explain why missionaries later fell foul of most Asian revolutionaries) or conquer them and hope that one day, after years of careful tutelage (as in the cases of Hawaii and the Philippines), they would become as civilized as Americans themselves.

If expansion and the declared policy of maintaining an open door defined the American purpose in East Asia,

it was rising Japan as much as disintegrating China that shaped its long-term thinking. Initially, however, its view of Japan was by no means a hostile one. In fact whereas Americans generally tended to regard other Asians as being either inferior or quaint, they viewed Japan at first with some regard. Indeed, like the Japanese themselves, the United States looked at this modernizing nation from the late nineteenth century onwards as being almost, although not quite completely, Anglo-Saxon in its outlook. Nor was Japan without its uses. Initially a bulwark against imperial Russia (whose powerful navy Japan had defeated in 1904), later a counter to the USSR (after the revolution of 1917), and in possession of an altogether more developed material civilization than that of decadent (and, after the Boxer rebellion of 1900, collapsing) China, the country against which the United States later waged such a devastating war was for a while at least viewed with some respect.

All this was to change, albeit very slowly, as Japan began its own imperial conquest of Asia, beginning with its annexation of Korea in 1910 (about which the United States hardly protested at all), its invasion of Manchuria in 1931 (which again did not provoke much by way of a US response), and its attack on China six years later, through to its conquest of much of the rest of East Asia in 1941 followed shortly thereafter by its attack on the US Pacific fleet at anchor in Pearl Harbor. This 'day of infamy', as President Roosevelt was to call it, not only drew the United States into what turned into a bloody Pacific war with deeply racist overtones, which only concluded with the use of nuclear weapons in August 1945, but led in time to the United States becoming a permanent part of the Asia-Pacific strategic landscape and a major actor in Japan itself. Indeed, for at least seven years after the Second World War the United States effectively governed Japan alone, and did so with a degree of political acumen—made all the more necessary by the onset of the Cold War—that left an indelible and generally positive imprint on the minds of many Japanese.

Critical to the success of the post-war relationship was the making of a series of unspoken but well-understood bargains between the United States and Japan's dominant ruling coalition for over half a century, the Liberal Democratic Party. The first was an acceptance by Japan that Japan would accept its subordinate position within an American-led Pacific order in exchange for an American guarantee of its security. This in turn assumed low military spending by Japan and a declaration that it would never possess, or even seek to acquire, weapons of mass destruction. The second part of the bargain was more specifically economic. This not only allowed Japan easy access to US markets (although Japan only really began its economic recovery because of American Cold War spending), it also placed Japan at the very heart of the East Asian economic region for the next forty years. Finally, underpinning the relationship was a recognition that while Japan might pursue certain external policies of its own, these would never be at the expense of the United States. Japan in effect would be a semi-sovereign state with only a limited capacity to determine its own foreign policy choices.

No relationship remains entirely unchanged, and at times the very unequal 'deal' struck between the winner and loser of the Second World War in the Pacific came under some strain: firstly from the Japanese political left who railed against the United States and therefore against the loss of sovereignty, then increasingly from within the United States itself by those who had become increasingly frustrated by what they claimed were unfair Japanese trade practices, and then by a younger generation in Japan who felt that with the Cold War over by 1991, the country no longer needed such a close and dependent relationship with the US. Marginalized for the most part during the 1990s and the period of the George W. Bush presidency (Japan even sent 1000 military personnel from its own self-defence force to Iraq in 2003) these sentiments

never quite went away, however, and following the election in 2009 of the first non-Liberal Democratic government since 1955, it actually looked for a while as if those now in power in Japan were ready to distance themselves (albeit most carefully) from Washington by becoming more 'proactive' in foreign affairs and 'independent' of the United States. Momentarily alarmed by such rhetoric—one report even talked of it as being a 'watershed' moment (Konichi 2009)—in the end the arguments in favour of maintaining the relationship in its traditional form seemed to outweigh those advanced by those looking for a 'new deal'. In fact, by 2011 there were perhaps more powerful reasons than ever for sticking close to the United States. With China rising to its west, North Korea still an unresolved problem state, and its own economy in anything but robust health, many in Japan felt that in uncertain times working closely with and alongside the United States made more foreign policy sense than seeking any other path. A relationship that had brought nearly forty years of sustained growth in Japan itself, had helped rehabilitate Japan in international society, and had acted as a stimulus for the economic rebirth of the wider East Asian region was not one to be dispensed of lightly.

KEY POINTS

❑ Historically, the United States had interests in East Asia that predated the Cold War; in December 1941 these finally compelled it to respond to what Washington viewed as a Japanese bid for total hegemony in the region.

❑ Defeat by 1945 was followed by an American occupation that integrated a reformed Japan into a US-led Asian Pacific security system; although politically motivated by anti-communism, this system also underwrote a new Asian order that laid the basis for the region's subsequent economic take off.

❑ In spite of the loss of power of the pro-American Liberal Democratic Party in 2009, Japan still looks unlikely to become more independent of the United States. With China fast rising and North Korea still an unresolved issue, there are now more reasons than ever for Japan remaining close to the USA—and the USA remaining close to Japan. The bargain struck between the USA and Japan after the Second World War looks likely to endure for the foreseeable future.

BOX 15.1 Japan: chronology

1945	Japan surrenders.
1947	A new constitution establishes a parliamentary system. Japan renounces war and pledges not to maintain land, sea, or air forces for that purpose.
1951	Japan signs peace treaty with the USA and other nations.
1952	Japan regains its formal independence but the USA retains several islands for military use.
1955	Liberal Democratic Party (LDP) formed. Apart from a brief interlude in the early 1990s, the party governs almost uninterruptedly for the rest of the century.
1956	Japan joins United Nations.
1972	Japanese Prime Minister visits China and normal diplomatic relations are resumed. Japan subsequently closes its embassy in Taiwan.
1989	Emperor Hirohito dies, succeeded by Akihito.
1998	Keizo Obuchi of the LDP becomes prime minister.
2000	Obuchi suffers a stroke and is replaced by Yoshiro Mori. Obuchi dies six weeks later.
2001	A US submarine executes an emergency surfacing manoeuvre off Hawaii and collides with a Japanese training vessel. Nine Japanese are missing after the incident. Junichiro Koizumi becomes new LDP leader and prime minister. Trade dispute with China after Japan imposes import tariffs on Chinese agricultural products. China retaliates with import taxes on Japanese vehicles and other manufactured goods. Koizumi visits Seoul and offers an apology for the suffering South Korea endured under his country's colonial rule.
2002	Koizumi becomes the first Japanese leader to visit North Korea. North Korean leader Kim Jong-il apologizes for abductions of Japanese citizens in 1970s and 1980s. Five Japanese nationals kidnapped by North Korea return home to emotional family reunions.
2003	Government announces decision to install 'purely defensive' US-made missile shield.
2004	Non-combat soldiers arrive in Iraq in the first Japanese deployment in combat zone since the Second World War. Japan launches an application for a permanent seat on the UN Security Council. Dispute with North Korea over the fate of Japanese citizens kidnapped by North Korea during the Cold War. Pyongyang says any imposition of sanctions by Tokyo will be treated as declaration of war.
2005	Relations with Beijing deteriorate amid sometimes violent anti-Japanese protests in Chinese cities, sparked by a Japanese textbook which China says glosses over Japan's Second World War record.
2006	Japan and China fail to reach a breakthrough at talks in Beijing over the issue of who controls oil and gas reserves in disputed areas of the East China Sea. The last contingent of Japanese troops leaves Iraq. Parliament approves the creation of a fully-fledged defence ministry, the first since the Second World War.
2007	Wen Jibao becomes the first Chinese prime minister to address the Japanese parliament. Mr Wen says both sides have succeeded in warming relations.
2009	General Elections in Japan return the Democratic Part of Japan, thus deposing the Liberal Democratic Party of Japan, who have ruled since 1955. The new party leader (Yukio Hatayana) announces he will seek greater independence from the United States.
2010	North Korea officially states that its nuclear programme is more advanced than it had previously admitted.
2011	In February it is announced that China has become the second largest economy in the world, relegating Japan to number 3.

China comes in from the cold

If the foundational building block of America's post-war position in Asia-Pacific was its relationship with a one-time enemy, its greatest challenge was a nation with whom it had been formally allied until the late 1940s.

This challenge was partly ideological, partly strategic, and partly conditioned by American domestic politics following China's entry into the Korean War against US forces on the Korean peninsula in the winter of 1950.

> **KEY QUOTES 15.1:** An alliance upon which the sun never sets?

The United States' long-standing alliance with Japan has been the pillar of US policy in the Pacific for over half a century.

(Calder 2006: 135)

As Japan extends its security profile to become more of a global player, it is doing so wholly within the context of a US–Japanese alliance . . . This should be comforting to other states in the region.

(Cha 2007: 103)

Self-help and power politics are institutions, not essential features of anarchy. Anarchy is what states make of it.

(Wendt 1992: 396)

The earthquake crisis has given relations an important 'human security' element that has often been missing from US–Japan dialogue. Proposals enabling enhanced cultural exchange and working holidays for students are gaining momentum, amplifying the broadening process.

(Dr Kent E Calder, *CNN World*, 23 March 2011)

Indeed, even as late as the 1960s many Americans continued to view China through a distinctly Cold War lens, a perspective reinforced at the time by the sheer turmoil through which China itself was then passing—the so-called Cultural Revolution—and by an increasingly desperate struggle America was waging in Vietnam against a communist enemy supported and armed in part by the Chinese. To complicate matters even more, American conservatives in particular remained closely allied with the Republic of China (Taiwan), whose leaders had every interest in continuing to foster distrust between policy makers in Washington and political leaders in mainland China.

The great strategic shift that initially broke the diplomatic deadlock and subsequently saw the United States open up formal relations with Beijing has been described in great detail by both historians and students of international politics, including some of those who were involved in this most remarkable of diplomatic reversals. It has also given rise to a lively debate as to why it happened. Thus, according to one school of thought, the new deal was the product of Chinese and American recognition that their greatest enemy was less each other and more the USSR. Others have stressed America's effort to decamp as quickly as possible from Vietnam, using China's diplomatic clout as at least one way of covering its retreat. Some have even suggested a longer-term American goal of opening up China and by so doing enticing it back into the Western fold. No doubt all these factors played a role, although what now seems to have been near inevitable looked anything but at the time. Indeed, it is just possible that if Mao

Tse-Tung had not died in 1976, or if the Chinese economy had not been so weakened by his earlier policies (or indeed if the USSR had not acted with such ineptitude in the late 1970s by invading Afghanistan and thus increasing Cold War tensions), the new relationship might have taken much longer to mature or might not have happened at all. But in the end it did, transforming the international scene and drawing China closer to its former 'imperialist' enemy.

The US rapprochement with Beijing, followed in close order by China's implementation of important economic reforms and ready acceptance that its own modernization required an ever closer association with the global economy, set China on a course that over the next twenty-five years would have a major impact on the rest of the world and the United States. For the USA the benefits were of course tremendous. First, by abandoning the path of revolution in Asia, China helped reinforce America's temporarily weakened international position in Asia following its defeat in Vietnam. China also played a significant role in helping contain America's main Soviet rival (some would even argue that by playing the China 'card' the USA accelerated the end of the Cold War itself). Lastly, by helping ease China's move towards the market and away from state control of the economy, the United States opened up a new chapter in the history of world capitalism. Certainly, China's adoption of the market was to have a huge ideological impact. As the well-known American theorist Francis Fukuyama later noted in 1989, the global 'crisis of socialism' in the 1980s occurred for several important reasons, including its own failure to produce efficient economies that could compete under world market conditions. However, it was the effective abandonment of planning in China that did as much as anything else to undermine Marxism as a global political project.

Yet for reasons more to do with ideological stability than economic reality, the Chinese leadership continued to proclaim its own Marxist credentials, all the time arguing that it was not taking China down the once denounced 'capitalist road' but was, rather, building its own form of socialism with 'Chinese characteristics'. Even Chairman Mao was not rejected in his entirety (the official line now was that he had been 70 per cent correct and 30 per cent wrong). Nor of course did China dissolve the Communist Party, which Mao had led to victory back in 1949. Indeed, while communist parties began to collapse in Eastern Europe and the USSR—thus bringing the Cold War to an end in one part of the world—in China at least its position was enhanced following the Tiananmen Square crackdown in June 1989. Very much fearing that what had happened to one part of the old communist camp could very easily happen to another, the leadership in Beijing—even those keenest on economic reform, like Deng Xiaoping—were determined to hold on to power and guarantee stability in China. Assuming (correctly as it turned out) that the United States would in the end do very little or nothing to punish China, following Tiananmen they proceeded to strengthen their own control at home with a powerful patriotic educational campaign, all the time hoping that as the Chinese people began to enjoy the fruits of the reform programme they would exchange material security for freedom, rising livings standards for the right to protest in public against the state. In this the party leadership appeared to have got the balance more or less right, and as the 1990s gave way to a new millennium the position of the Communist Party—now largely legitimized by a steady rise in China's international position and a marked improvement in the economic situation within China itself—seemed to be more secure than it had been for a generation. Drawing upon a mass of foreign capital, a steady supply of cheap Chinese labour, ready access to Western markets, large inflows of investment from the region itself, not to mention a system of very tight political controls, within

twenty years of the Tiananmen Square crisis China now looked to be achieving economically what had taken many countries in Europe two or three generations.

For the United States, and indeed for the West more generally, all of this presented something of an intellectual puzzle and a political conundrum. On the one hand what China was doing clearly did not fit into the normal liberal western model of development whereby economic success was intimately associated with the expansion of political pluralism. On the other hand, China's economic rise was not only transforming China and the region, thus giving both a major stake in the current international order, it was doing all this within a foreign policy framework that found many supporters in the west as well within China itself. The notion or theory of the 'peaceful rise' was first formulated around 2000. It was premised in the first instance on the important and challenging argument that history by definition did not have to repeat itself. Making the strong case that China was not like other rising powers in the past, the theorists of the peaceful rise insisted that China had every interest in working within the pre-existing international order and not against it. This in part was because China had decades of economic development still to undergo. But it was also a function of learning the terrible lessons from what had happened to other states which had sought to challenge the existing international order before. This taught one terrible lesson: namely that far from enhancing their security these other rising powers had, in effect, undermined it by mobilizing an even more powerful coalition against it. It had happened to Napoleon. It had happened to Hitler. And of course it had happened to its still highly distrusted neighbour just across the China sea.

Joining the existing economic system therefore (although all the time guarding against the dangers of western liberal infection) made much more sense than seeking to undermine it. It not only supported China's growth strategy while reassuring its still nervous neighbours that its intentions might be benign, it also seemed to reassure the west and the United States too. Indeed as China rose, and then negotiated the economic crisis of 2008 with much greater skill than the Americans themselves, the United States found itself in the rather unnerving position of becoming increasingly dependent on China buying America's burgeoning debt. Indeed, as China rose it became increasingly clear to Americans—George W. Bush as much as Barack Obama—that the United States would have to treat China less as an object of its own hegemonic foreign policy, and more as a partner with whom it was now bound to consult over a whole host of international issues. Optimists could of course claim—and did—that an increasingly integrated and dynamic Chinese economy was good for the American consumer (cheap imports), good for the American economy, and good for regional economic growth (critically important following the Asian financial crisis of 1998). They could also point to China's willingness to support the USA on a number of big strategic issues such as the war on terror. All this though could not allay some deeper American worries, and there were more than just a few in Washington who wondered where all this might lead one day. One did not have to be an alarmist. Nor was it necessary to assume that all great competition was inevitably going to lead to war. It had not done so during the Cold War when the USSR and the USA had had few economic connections, and it was even less likely to happen now that both countries had so many overlapping economic interests. Yet, as more than one observer was to note, the real issue was not whether China could rise peacefully; but rather what would happen once it had finally achieved its ascent. As the first decade of the twenty-first century drew to an end, few Americans seemed to have a clear answer to this difficult question.

KEY POINTS

❑ The rapprochement between China and the United States in the 1970s not only altered the relationship between Beijing and Washington but transformed world politics while making economic reform in China itself much easier.

❑ China's economic transformation has not been based on a liberal model of development. On the contrary, the model it has used to achieve the success it has, has combined communist political control and western style capitalism.

❑ China's peaceful rise has largely reassured its neighbours and the United States that it remains a *status quo* power. However, as it has risen, there are some (perhaps an increasing number) who predict this will lead to increased regional and global competition.

❝ KEY QUOTES 15.2: The China puzzle

China is a threat, China is a customer, and China is an opportunity. . . . You cannot ignore it.

(Kenichi Ohmae, quoted in Friedman 2005: 117)

China cannot rise peacefully and if it continues its dramatic economic growth over the next few decades, the United States and China are likely to engage in an intense security competition with considerable potential for war.

(Mearsheimer xxxx)

The challenge is going to be how to create a framework where successful models different from the United States' can be incorporated . . . The future institutions are going to have to deal with the fact that China may be rich and non-democratic.

(Donald C. Hellmann, director of the Institute for International Policy at the University of Washington, quoted in Zissis 2007)

China is at a turning point bigger than any since the late 1970s, and that some of the policies that have worked quite successfully for the past 30 years will not work for the next thirty. Continuing with 'peaceful rise' is going to get more difficult.

(Buzan 2010).

BOX 15.2: China: chronology

1949	Communist victory, founding of the People's Republic of China. Nationalists retreat to the island of Taiwan and set up a government there.
1950	China intervenes in the Korean War on the side of North Korea. Tibet becomes part of the People's Republic of China.
1953	Eisenhower ends US naval blockade of Taiwan.
1954	First Taiwan Straits crisis.
1955	US signs mutual defence treaty with Taiwan.
1958	'Great Leap Forward'.
1959	Chinese forces suppress large-scale revolt in Tibet.
1962	Brief conflict with India over disputed Himalayan border.
1964	China's first atomic test.
1969	Differences with USSR culminate in border skirmishes.
1972	US President Richard Nixon visits China. Both countries declare a desire to normalize relations.
1976	Mao dies.
1979	Diplomatic relations established with the USA.
1989	Troops open fire on demonstrators in Tiananmen Square, killing 200. International outrage leads to sanctions.
1992	Russia and China sign declaration restoring friendly ties.
1993	Clinton policy of 'constructive engagement' launched at summit with President Jiang Zemin.
1994	China abolishes the official renminbi (RMB) currency exchange rate and fixes its first floating rate since 1949.
1995	China tests missiles and holds military exercises in the Taiwan Strait, apparently to sway Taiwanese voters against pro-independence presidential candidate Lee Teng-hui. Lee wins by a large margin.
1997	Hong Kong reverts to Chinese control.
1999	NATO bombs the Chinese embassy in Belgrade. Macao reverts to Chinese rule.
2000	US Congress grants permanent normal trade relations.

2001	Diplomatic stand-off over the detention of an American spy plane and crew after a mid-air collision with a Chinese fighter jet. China joins the World Trade Organization.
2003	China and India reach *de facto* agreement over status of Tibet and Sikkim in landmark cross-border trade agreement.
2004	China signs a landmark trade agreement with ten South-East Asian countries; the accord could eventually unite 25 per cent of the world's population in a free-trade zone.
2005	New law on Taiwan calls for use of force should Taipei declare independence from mainland China. China and Russia hold their first joint military exercises. Taiwan's National Party leader Lien Chan visits China for the first meeting between Nationalist and Communist Party leaders since 1949.
2006	China–Africa summit in Beijing results in the signing of business deals worth nearly $2bn and China promises billions of dollars in loans and credits.
2007	Reports say China has carried out a missile test in space, shooting down an old weather satellite. The USA, Japan, and others express concern at China's military build-up.
2008	The US financial crisis generates panic in the west followed by an economic slow down.
2009	Goldman Sachs predicts that China's economy will grow faster than previously predicted.
2010	China and six other South-East Asian countries toasted the inauguration of the biggest free trade area in the world, when the Association of South East Asian Nations, or ASEAN-6, is formally launched. Covering nearly 2 billion people in Brunei, Indonesia, Malaysia, Philippines, Singapore, and Thailand, along with China, the stated aim of ASEAN-6 is to eliminate tariffs on almost all traded goods between its members.
2011	The French finance house BNP Paribas announces that China will become the biggest economy in the world by 2020.

The United States, Korea, and the legacy of the Cold War

If the Chinese leadership revealed a shrewd appreciation of how effectively a formally communist state could take advantage of the global economy without conceding any of its power at home, its neighbour and formal ally North Korea demonstrated an equally shrewd—although to some irrational—understanding of how to survive under conditions where the tide of history was moving against it following the collapse of communism in Europe. Indeed, like South Korea, the North drew some very important lessons from the collapse of one very special communist state in particular, East Germany. However, whereas the leaders in the South drew what seemed at the time the not unreasonable conclusion that the regime in the North was destined to change (its policy then being how to ensure this occurred without causing instability) those in the North concluded that everything had to be done to ensure that the communist state they had built at such cost since 1945 did not change at all.

The method adopted by the regime to ensure its survival in a post-Cold War world was a crude but simple one: to use nuclear brinkmanship and its controversial nuclear programme as a way of extracting concessions from its various opponents—most obviously South Korea—while forcing the wider international community to come to terms with the North. Fearful that its very survival was now in doubt, North Korea—whose nuclear programme had been raising some very real concerns in Washington since the late 1980s—began to act in an increasingly aggressive way, such that by 1993 it was even threatening to withdraw from the Nuclear Non-Proliferation Treaty (NPT). Not surprisingly, this set a series of loud alarm bells ringing in Washington which forced policy makers to look at their very limited options, including the appalling (and impossible) one of conventional war. After much soul searching a decision was arrived at: the so-called Framework Agreement of 1994, a compromise solution that made a series of concessions to the communist regime—including delivery of large amounts of oil and aid—in exchange for a promise that they would remain party to the NPT. Few believed the agreement was perfect. But hardly anybody could see any serious alternative, including a highly nervous South Korea whose leaders by now were desperately keen to maintain some kind of relationship with a regime whose rhetoric they seemed to fear a good deal less than its collapse.

The adoption of what many in the United States regarded as a flawed policy forced upon them by North Korean intransigence on the one hand and a South Korean desire to maintain a détente-style relationship with the North on the other soon came under attack within Washington. The 1994 deal, it was now regularly argued by critics on

the right, was little more than a modern-day form of appeasement whose only consequence would be to preserve a regime already doomed by history by allowing it to play a game of divide and diplomatic rule between the United States and its once steadfast South Korean ally. It also did very little in the opinion of critics to slow down the North's nuclear programme. Thus the Agreement was a failure in nearly every conceivable way. Naturally, no serious policy maker wanted confrontation for its own sake. But there had to be a more robust approach to the North Korean problem, one that weakened this hideous regime rather than strengthening it, that punished it rather than rewarding it for its various transgressions, only one of which was having a highly destabilizing nuclear programme.

It was perhaps only a matter of time before there was a serious policy review, and this finally came in 2001 following the election of a more conservative president, George W. Bush. Initially, North Korea was not a policy priority and little was done. The attack of 9/11, however, followed by President Bush's announcement of an altogether tougher policy towards all 'rogue' regimes, quickly changed all that. Indeed, by early 2002 Bush was already counting North Korea as part of a wider 'axis of evil', stating that the policy of the United States towards it could be nothing less than regime change. Inevitably this provoked a response by the North Koreans, who once more threatened to withdraw from the NPT (which they then did in 2003) while pushing ahead once more with their stalled nuclear programme. Thus began what looked to many observers like a rather dangerous diplomatic game conducted between all the interested parties (going under the official title of the Six-Party talks). It was a game, however, that failed to prevent the North acting in an increasingly aggressive fashion, which was exemplified in 2006 when it conducted its own missile tests and confirmed that it had, at last, exploded a small nuclear device. This provocation had the intended effect of once more forcing its enemies to the negotiating table and in 2007 nuclear inspectors were once again admitted into North Korea while Pyongyang committed itself—yet again—to the NPT. Finally, in November 2007, North and South Korea's prime ministers met for the first time in fifteen years.

The situation, however, remained distinctly fluid, and given the past behaviour of the North Koreans themselves there was no telling what was likely to happen next. The deteriorating economic situation in North Korea, the continuing economic success of its South Korean neighbour, and the total secrecy in which decisions were made at the highest level in North Korea in effect meant that there was no easy way of predicting the regime's actions. It thus came as no great surprise when in March 2010 the North Koreans sank a South Korean ship and eight months later launched a limited, but deadly, barrage against a small South Korean island near the North Korean border. Worse was predicted to follow according to some Korean sources, and as one year gave to another the situation on the peninsula could not have been less certain.

North Korea thus posed many significant challenges for US foreign policy. Indeed, according to many analysts there was no challenge more serious in a region that otherwise was showing enormous economic and political potential now that the Cold War had come to an end. Tragically in North Korea, this last bastion of primitive Stalinism, there seemed to be no indication at all that life was in any way getting better. Indeed, while the rest of Asia, including of course China, was becoming more secure, North Korea behaved as if the world was full of enemies—the most dangerous one being a United States ready to destroy it if given half a chance. From an American perspective this was a most unwelcome distraction; one which if not handled with the utmost care could easily escalate out of control. It might even lead to something the US feared perhaps more than anything else: other non-nuclear powers in the region choosing to go nuclear as a hedge against North Korea. The stakes could not have been higher. There was, however, one compensation to be had: as long North Korea continued to threaten its Asian neighbours while seriously embarrassing its only Asian ally China, nobody was likely to want to see an end to the American presence in the region. While North Korea remained the threat that it did, there would be few players in Asia calling for a US withdrawal.

KEY POINTS

❏ While the end of the Cold War in Europe saw the overcoming of the division of Germany, it did not lead to the same outcome on the Korean peninsula.

❏ North Korea has consciously used nuclear weapons as a bargaining chip in order to ensure the survival of the regime in an increasingly hostile economic and political environment.

❏ US policy has found it difficult to devise a consistent policy towards a highly unpredictable regime like North Korea. But the threat posed by North Korea remains a very powerful argument for a continued American presence in East Asia.

❝ KEY QUOTES 15.3: North Korea and nuclear weapons

What must be avoided is to leave a beleaguered nuclear nation convinced that it is permanently excluded from the international community, its existence threatened, its people suffering horrible deprivation and its hard-liners in total control of military and political policy.

(Carter 2006)

Despite two and a half years of diplomacy, two conspicuous obstacles remain: the commitment or trust problem, and the sequencing of deliverables in any negotiated settlement. Since many North Korean officials probably believe the Bush administration is determined to topple Kim Jong-Il and the Korean Workers' Party, the commitment problem might be insurmountable until Washington undergoes regime change in January 2009.

(Daniel Pinkerton, North Korea's Nuclear Weapons Programme and the Six Party Talk, NTI Issue Brief, James Martin Center for Nonproliferation Studies at the Monterey Institute of International Studies, 2007)

US support for South Korea's defense is unequivocal, and the president has directed his military commanders to coordinate closely with their Republic of Korea counterparts to ensure readiness and to deter future aggression.

(President Obama, 24 May 2010).

US President Barak Obama warned Chinese President Hu Jintao that if China did not increase its pressure on North Korea the US would be forced to redeploy its forces in Asia.

(January 2011)

BOX 15.3:   Korea: chronology

1945   The end of the Second World War leaves Korea divided between communist North and pro-American South.

1948   Anti-communist Syngman Rhee elected President of the Republic of (South) Korea in UN-sanctioned elections and assumes control of the South; in the North, Kim Il-Sung is installed as President of the Democratic Republic of Korea.

1949   US troops depart from South Korea, leaving only a small military advisory force.

1950   North Korean troops cross the border on 25 June, initiating the Korean War. The United Nations provides the United States with a mandate to assist in the defence of the Republic of Korea.

1953   A 27 July armistice brings fighting to a halt and restores the previous border along the 38th parallel. US troops remain stationed in Korea and will contribute to significant military build-up along the demilitarized zone at the border.

1957   The United States begins deployment of nuclear weapons to the Korean peninsula.

1968   North Korean vessels capture the surveillance ship the USS *Pueblo*.

1969   US EC-121 surveillance aircraft shot down over the Sea of Japan.

1972   North and South Korea announce an agreement to seek cooperation and eventual unification. This agreement breaks down in the following year and initiates a decade-long suspension of relations between the two countries.

1976   Two US officers serving with the United Nations Command mission in Korea are killed by North Korean soldiers following an altercation at the DMZ.

1985   North Korea joins the Nuclear Non-Proliferation Treaty (NPT).

1988   The United States places North Korea on the list of state sponsors of terrorism on 20 January following the involvement of North Korean agents in the in-flight destruction of Korean Airlines Flight 858 in November 1987.

1991   The United States withdraws the last of its nuclear weapons from South Korea, prompting an agreement between North and South Korea to denuclearize the peninsula. Both countries join the UN.

1993   The International Atomic Energy Authority (IAEA) refused access to inspect nuclear site; North Korea threatens to withdraw from the NPT.

1994   North Korea announces its withdrawal from the IAEA. Kim Il-Sung dies and is succeeded by his son, Kim Jong-Il. Agreement between North Korea and the United States establishes the Agreed Framework.

1995   Korean Peninsula Energy Development Organization (KEDO) formed—North and South Korea, the United States, and Japan are its founding members.

1996   Talks between North Korea and the United States end with US sanctions and the deployment of US warships to Japan following North Korean declaration that it will conduct missile tests. North Korea announces its abandonment of the 1953 armistice and sends troops into the DMZ.

1998   South Korean President Kim Dae-Jung reveals his Sunshine Policy to seek improved relations and reconciliation with Pyongyang.

1999   USA–North Korea talks produce a suspension of missile testing by North Korea.

2000   Progress towards a normalization of relations continues as sanctions are reduced; North and South Korea agree to 'resolve' the issue of reunification.

2001   President Bush makes statements implying a new, tougher policy towards North Korea, and a repudiation of Kim Dae-Jung's Sunshine Policy, provoking an angry reaction from Pyongyang and cancellation of reconciliation talks in South Korea.

2002   President Bush labels North Korea part of an 'axis of evil' and implies the regime has the desire and intention to support terrorism. USA announces that North Korea admitted to having a nuclear weapons programme, in violation of the 1994 Agreed Framework. Pyongyang denies having made such an admission but admits to possession of a uranium enrichment programme.

2002   Ship carrying North Korean-made Scud missiles bound for Yemen is intercepted by US and Spanish forces but released due to lack of legal authority to seize its cargo.
North and South Korean naval vessels wage a gun battle in the Yellow Sea, the worst skirmish for three years. Thirty North Korean and four South Korean sailors are killed.

2003   North Korea withdraws from the NPT, hints at a resumption of long-range missile testing, and declares it has enough plutonium to start making nuclear bombs. North Korea withdraws from the 1992 agreement to denuclearize the Korean peninsula.

BOX 15.3: (*continued*)

2005 Six-Party talks initially produce an agreement for North Korea to rejoin the NPT and cease all nuclear activity, but then break down.

2006 UN Security Council approves sanctions in response to North Korean missile tests. North Korea detonates what it claims to be a nuclear weapon, and US intelligence officials confirm that the test was in fact of a small nuclear device.

2007 Inspectors readmitted to North Korea; Pyongyang commits to disable three nuclear facilities and declare all its nuclear programmes by year-end. In November, North and South Korea's prime ministers meet for the first time in fifteen years.

2008 In February, widespread food shortages are reported in North Korea.

2009 In May, North Korea conducts its second underground nuclear test.

2010 In March North Korea sinks South Korean vessel. In spring, North Korea announces it will sever all links with South Korea.

In April, former US President Jimmy Carter visits the North Korean capital in an effort to lower tensions.

Asia-Pacific: primed for rivalry?

The continued division of Korea and the many problems it has posed for the United States over several decades points to something more general about East Asia: that the region as a whole appears to contain within it many serious fault lines that are not easily amenable to simple diplomatic solution. Here the contrast with Europe could not be more pronounced, as scholars of international relations have been quick to point out. As they note, whereas Europe after the Second World War managed to create some form of a 'liberal security community', East Asia for a whole host of reasons did not. More worryingly, there was little chance that it would be able to do so now. In fact, according to at least one school of influential American thought, East Asia, far from being primed for peace after the end of Cold War, was becoming ever 'ripe' for new rivalries. As Aaron Friedberg noted in an influential and much quoted article published in 1993, Europe's very bloody past between 1914 and 1945 could easily turn into Asia's future. Uncertainty about the future of North Korea, unresolved tensions between China and Taiwan, Japanese suspicion of China, China's historical dislike of Japan, and the more general legacy of history, taken together meant that the world in general and the United States in particular should remain deeply concerned abut East Asia.

This pessimism (inspired as much by philosophical realism as by a deep knowledge of the region itself) has over the past few years given way to an altogether less bleak assessment by American analysts and policy makers. Few think that Asia-Pacific will be without its fair share of difficulties in the twenty-first century. That said, there is probably now more to look forward to than dread. There are four reasons why.

First, the region has turned into one of the most materially dynamic in the world. Indeed, in global terms, Asian Pacific countries now account for well over 30 percent of world economic production. Nor does there seem much likelihood that they will slip backwards any time soon. On the contrary, the region overall appears to be economically 'blessed', not so much in terms of raw materials but with other, more intangible, but important assets, including a culture of hard work, a system of entrepreneurial values, a plentiful supply of labour, a huge reservoir of capital, and a set of political and economic structures that allow the state to play a critical role in engineering successful economic outcomes. Nor in this lengthy list should one ignore the part played by the United States itself. Indeed, by opening up its market to East Asian goods while providing the region with security on the cheap, the USA has played what some would see as a very important part in generating growth throughout the region.

Secondly, although many states in the region continue to have powerful and emotionally charged memories of past conflicts, in and of themselves these are not enough to generate new conflicts in the present, especially in circumstances where regional trade and investment is rapidly rising. Asia-Pacific certainly carries more than its fair share of historical baggage. The fact remains that economic pressures and material self-interest are increasingly driving countries in the region together rather than apart. The process of East Asian economic integration may have been slow to develop. ASEAN after all was only formed in 1967. Nor has integration been accompanied by the formation of anything like the European Union. However, since regionalism began to take off during the 1990s it has showed no signs of slowing down.

A third reason for greater optimism is Japan itself. Unwilling to apologize unambiguously for past misdeeds, Japan nonetheless has played a most positive role in the region. Indeed, having adopted its famous peace constitution while renouncing force as a means of achieving its goals abroad (Japan still remains one the strongest upholders of the original NPT) it has demonstrated no interest at all in upsetting its suspicious neighbours by acting in anything other than a benign manner. Furthermore, by spreading its not inconsiderable economic largesse in the form of aid and large-scale investment it has gone a very long way to fostering better international relations in the region. Even its old ideological rival China has been a significant beneficiary and by 2003 was home to over 5000 Japanese companies.

Finally, there is China itself. As we have already indicated, much American ink has already been spilt

---

KEY POINTS

❏ As a region East Asia is quite different from Europe and has never formed a genuine 'security community'.
❏ According to one school of thought East Asia is likely to remain a highly disorderly region.
❏ The evidence over the past fifteen years, however, suggests that several factors—including China's economic rise—are leading towards a more stable Asia.

---

worrying about China. Once again, however, there may be more cause for optimism than pessimism. China after all has not only theoretically committed itself to rising peacefully (something we have discussed earlier in this chapter) but has in fact taken several concrete measures to ensure the status quo is not undermined in any serious way. This has not only involved maintaining a good diplomatic relationship with the United States—even as tensions rose in 2010—but constructively engaging with the East Asian region as a whole, first and foremost economically but also in other 'softer' ways such as working responsibly within regional institutions. The strategy seems to be paying off. Indeed, whereas in the 1990s there was deep concern about China in East Asia, this has now given way to a more positive view of its role. As a more recent study has pointed out, what China's neighbours now seem to fear more is not so much a confident China actively cooperating with others from a position of economic strength but a weak and insecure China whose economy can no longer act as the motor of the region.

> **KEY QUOTES 15.4:** Asia-Pacific: bound for conflict?

In the long run it is Asia that seems far more likely to be the cockpit of great power conflict . . . for better or for worse, Europe's past could be Asia's future.

(Friedberg 1993–4)

Most of the structural features . . . [that have been] identified as promoting instability in East Asia actually point in the other direction towards greater regional stability. The balance of

power favours the maintenance of the status quo. Economic interdependence is on the rise. here has been a steady growth of international institutions of all sorts.

(Berger 2000)

Asia's share of the world economy has risen from 18% in 1980 to 27% in 1995 to 34% in 2009.

(East or Famine, *The Economist*, February 27, 2010, p. 77)

Conclusion: the United States—hegemonic still?

As we have shown in this chapter the United States has been a major actor in the Pacific region for a very long time, indeed ever since 1941—a tipping-point year if ever there was one, when in February the famous American publisher Henry Luce announced the onset of an 'American Century', and a few months later Japan launched a do-or-die attack that four years on left the US as the most powerful state in the Pacific region. Powerful though it may have been, however, its position was never entirely secure. Indeed, as new leader of the western world, it was to come under sustained attack throughout most of the Cold War: first when it finally lost out to the Chinese communists in 1949, then in Korea in 1950 when it was sucked into a three-year war, and finally in Vietnam where it committed itself fully to the defence of the 'free world' only to be ejected ignominiously in the 1970s. Meanwhile, in other parts of Asia, insurgencies from Indonesia to the Philippines, Malaya to Laos, constantly threatened to undermine its position. In fact, it was only very late in the day, and then only with the end of the Cold War itself in 1989, that Washington could finally breathe some sigh of relief and conclude that its policies were finally bearing fruit.

Two decades on and the debate about the future of the United States in Asia has taken on a quite different colouration. Now the discussion focuses less on what ideological challenges there are and more on whether or not the United States any longer has a role in a part of the world where China is now increasingly shaping the region's future. Nor is it just a question of China. What looks in Asia to be America's fixation with the Middle East, its more general loss of standing as result of its long war on terror, and, perhaps most important of all, the economic fall out from the financial crisis of 2008 have all raised questions about the leadership role of the US in a region in which it was once the truly 'indispensable nation'.

That such questions are now being asked is perhaps inevitable. However, asking difficult questions is hardly the same thing as always coming up with the same answer concerning America's future decline as a major Asian power. Not only are predictions difficult enough to make at the best of times, in Asia there are still very strong reasons for suggesting that the US will remain a major factor there for some time to come. There are three fairly obvious reasons why.

One relates to the constellation of forces within Asia itself. Many states in the region may resent the US presence, but few, as I have already tried to show, are seriously keen in wanting to see it disappear altogether. China certainly views a continued US role as being critical to East Asia's stability and its own peaceful rise within the region, Japan meanwhile continues to look to Washington for guidance and protection, South Korea remains dependent on the USA for its protection, and a host of other states maintain important bilateral ties with Washington that they have shown little inclination of giving up. Nor are there any serious players or organizations in the region who are willing, or indeed capable, of playing the wider role America plays. Japan of course cannot play such a role because of its history; China is unable to do what America does because it remains wedded to a form of political rule that has too many echoes of Asia's authoritarian past. Indeed, given its communist political character, few in the region can ever bring themselves to completely trust China.

The second reason why the United States will remain firmly embedded in East Asia has to do with something even more fundamental: its own role as a global hegemon and a continuing desire in Washington to manage this vitally important area of the world in a way that conforms to its perception of itself as a 'superpower' while protecting its very real interests in the region itself. The Cold War might have come to an end and the region overall may now have achieved a degree of stability that would have once been seen as unthinkable. But that does not mean the United States has any reason to pack up its bags and go home. Indeed, by remaining precisely where it is, it not only protects its own considerable economic interests—which are growing as the twenty-first century moves forward—but it is also able to shape the policies of other states and thus ensure that they remain more or less within an American sphere of influence.

Finally, the position of the United States is likely to endure because many in Asia-Pacific have fewer doubts about its intentions than they do about their most of their neighbours. Asia-Pacific may be in the process of shedding part of its bloody history, but the legacy of the past lives on in many concrete ways. Thus so long as Taiwan worries about China, China about Japan, Japan about China, and South Korea about its other northern half, there are few in the region willing to contemplate a future without the United States. Many may denounce the United States as being an 'empire' like any other. But even if it is, for the time being at least it is an empire that remains a more or less welcome guest in nearly every capital in most countries in the region. The days when the USA was the sole focus of activity might have gone, but for the foreseeable future it will remain—as one observer has noted—the 'number one' player in the region.[1]

❝ KEY QUOTES 15.5: East Asia and the end of the American Century?

The Pacific Century has not arrived and is not likely any time soon... the American century that Henry Luce first pointed to in 1941 has not yet run its course.

(Foot and Walter 1999)

The rush to proclaim the Asian century and to lump America together with failed imperial giants of the past like Britain in the mid-twentieth century may be rash.

(Joshhua Kurlantzick, January 2011)

?   Questions

1. For how long and why has the United States had interests in East Asia?
2. What impact did the Second World War have on the US position in the region?
3. How did the Chinese revolution of 1949 impact on US foreign policy?
4. How would you characterize the post-war relationship between Japan and the USA?
5. Why were the Korean and Vietnam Wars important for the United States?
6. Why did the United States and China re-establish a diplomatic partnership in the 1970s?
7. What is the connection between nuclear weapons and the end of the Cold War in North Korea?
8. Should the United States fear or welcome China's rise?
9. Is East Asia the prisoner of its past?
10. Can the United States remain hegemonic in East Asia for ever?

»   Further Reading

Acharya, A. (2003–4), Will Asia's Past be Its Future? *International Security*, **28**: 149–64.

Asia, the author contends, is increasingly able to manage its insecurity through shared regional norms, rising economic interdependence, and growing institutional linkages. The 'ripe for rivalry' thesis outlined by Aaron Friedberg in 1993 is thus misconceived.

Bisley, N. (2006), Neither Empire nor Republic: American Power and Regional Order in the Asia-Pacific, *International Politics*, **43**: 219–40.

The regional order of East Asia is not, and is unlikely to be in the foreseeable future, a rules-based or an institution-led order. Rather it is the product of a series of relationships between states, including the most important one that each state in the region has with the United States. The United States, however, is not an imperial overlord nor even a hegemon in the region. Its power is real but it should not be overstated.

Buzan, B. (2003), Security Architecture in Asia: The Interplay of Regional and Global Levels, *The Pacific Review*, **16**: 143–73.

There is a distinct and long-standing regional structure in East Asia that is of at least as great an importance to the global level in shaping the region's security dynamics. The US, however, remains a key player and cannot risk withdrawing from the region. On the other hand, it is not easy to calculate the longer effect of the US being and staying engaged in Asia's security.

Buzan, B. (2010), China in International Society: Is Peaceful Rise Possible? *The Chinese Journal of International Politics*, **3**: 5–36.

Comprehensive examination of China's external relations in the modern era suggesting that while the peaceful rise of China has thus far stood the leadership in good stead, because of changes in China and within the region, the chances of a peaceful rise continuing are likely to diminish.

Christensen, T. J. (1999), China, the US–Japan Alliance and the Security Dilemma in East Asia, *International Security*, **23**: 49–80.

If the security dilemma theory is applied to East Asia the chance for spirals of conflict in the region seems great. Perhaps one factor more than any other makes this outcome less likely: the strength of the US relationship with Japan. US strategy must be to continue to reassure Japan while not triggering concerns in Beijing.

Clark, I. (2011) China and the United States: a succession of hegemonies, *International Affairs*, **87**: 1, 13–28.

Suggests that China's economic rise should not be confused with a hegemonic succession from the United States to China.

Foot, R. and Walter, A. (1999), Whatever Happened to the Pacific Century? *Review of International Studies*, **25**: 245–69.

Argues that predictions suggesting the emergence of a new Pacific Century were based on a flawed political economy whose illusions were exposed by the East Asian economic crisis of 1997–8. The American Century has not yet run its course in East Asia.

Friedberg, A. (1993/4), Ripe for Rivalry: Prospects for Peace in a Multipolar Asia, *International Security*, 18: **3**, 5–33.

Influential realist argument made in the wake of the end of the Cold War suggesting that the future stability of the region was by no means assured.

Hemmer, C. and Katzenstein, P. J. (2002), Why is there no NATO in Asia? Collective Identity, Regionalism and the Origins of Multilateralism, *International Organization*, **56**: 4575–607.

Argues that the failure by the United States to establish genuinely multilateral bodies in Asia such as NATO was the result of an American perception of potential Asian allies—unlike those in Europe—as being alien and in important senses inferior. Absent a collective identity, bilateral rather than multilateral arrangements became the norm.

Ikenberry, G. J. and Tsuchiyama, J. (2002), Between Balance of Power and Community: The Future of Multilateral Security Co-operation in Asia-Pacific, *International Relations of the Asia-Pacific*, **2**: 69–94.

Insists that there is little chance of moving beyond the current ad hoc security system in East Asia which reflects the absence of shared identity within the region itself. The liberal hope of moving beyond this system may not be fulfilled any time soon.

Jianyong Yue (2008), Peaceful Rise of China: Myth or Reality? *International Politics*, **45**: 439–56.

Sceptical look at both the theory and practice of China's peaceful rise.

Kurlantzick, J. (2011), The Asian Century? Not Quite Yet, *Current History*, **110**: 26–31.

Argues that for all its economic successes, Asia remains overall so much poorer than the United States that the region will take decades to catch up, if it catches up at all.

Mastanduno, M. (2000), Models, Markets and Power: Political Economy and the Asia-Pacific, 1989–1999, *Review of International Studies,* **26**: 493–507.

Broad survey of the decade after the Cold War which concludes that while the United States seeks to preserve its dominant position in the region, to do so it will have to act with great diplomatic skill. The US must through its actions seek to avoid the rise of challengers and serious challenges to the US conception of international and regional order.

Renee, J. (2009), Evaluating the 'China Threat': power transition theory, the successor-state image and dangers of historic analogies. *Australian Journal of International Affairs,* **63**: 2, 309–24.

A broad survey of recent literature on China's peaceful rise and why those who predict increased conflict between a rising China and a declining United States are too pessimistic about the region's future.

Ross, R. S. (1999), The Geography of the Peace: East Asia in the Twenty-first Century, *International Security,* **23**: 81–118.

Argues against the notion that a combination of history and geography increase the prospects for regional tension; if anything the geography of East Asia creates the possibility of order by minimizing the likelihood of a power transition and conflict.

Van Ness, P. (2002), Hegemony, Not Anarchy: Why China and Japan are not Balancing US Unipolar Power, *International Relations of the Asia-Pacific,* **2**: 131–50.

What the author terms the 'passive influence of US structural power' continues to shape Chinese and Japanese thinking and makes likely their continued bandwagoning rather than balancing behaviour towards the United States. Indeed, participation in an American-led hegemonic system provides substantial benefits they would be loathe to give up.

 ## Endnote

1. David C. Kang, Dartmouth University, quoted in Zissis (2007).

 For a range of additional resources to support your learning visit the Online Resource Centre that accompanies this book at www.oxfordtextbooks.co.uk/orc/cox_stokes2e/.

16 US foreign policy in Latin America

James Dunkerley

Chapter contents

Introduction

This chapter surveys the historical evolution of US relations with Latin America. The contemporary geopolitical balance of power within the western hemisphere is highly asymmetrical. US policy has usually been determined under various doctrines and was only partly affected by the Cold War, so the post-Cold War period has seen only some changes to the historical pattern. The second section surveys that historical background from the Monroe Doctrine and manifest destiny, which sought to contain European expansion and to justify that of the USA under an ethos of hemispherism. The third section covers the projection of US power beyond its frontiers in the early twentieth century.

Direct intervention in Central America and the Caribbean was common until the depression of the 1930s, when a less unilateral approach was adopted. After 1945 the implementation of policy was often routed through the multilateral institutions set up after the Second World War. However, the Cuban Revolution prompted an aggressively ideological approach. The chapter traces policy towards the left in Central America, where armed conflict prevailed in the 1980s, and that for South America, where the Washington Consensus brought an end to the anti-European aspects of the Monroe Doctrine by promoting globalization. The failure of this freetrade platform to provide sustained

Fig. 16.1 Map of Central and South America.

growth contributed to regional disenchantment and the emergence after 2001 of a political current unsympathetic to Washington's renewed unilateralist tendencies.

Immediately after his inauguration, President George W. Bush declared, 'The best foreign policy starts at home. We've got to have good relations at home.' He meant relations inside the western hemisphere, and particularly with the twenty-one countries of Latin America and the thirteen independent states of the Caribbean. Latin America has sometimes been referred to as the 'backyard' of the United States—an

inferior section of 'home'. This attitude has prompted an uncomfortable coexistence of attitudes in Anglo and Latin America, the former exhibiting a presumption of hegemony (Lowenthal) or the assumption of overwhelming superiority. Latin Americans, by contrast, have often adopted a geographical fatalism in recognition of their proximity to a state of far greater resource and ambition. For no other part of the world has the term 'US empire' been employed for longer or with greater justification. Yet, Latin America, almost by virtue of 'being at home', has also been overlooked and sidelined by US policy makers, except in secondary disputes or as proxy forces for antagonistic extra-hemispheric powers, which is the principal way in which the Cold War affected hemispheric relations.

On 6 September 2001 President Bush had invited Mexican President Fox to a joint session of Congress, declaring that Mexico 'is our most important relationship'. Within a week the attacks of 9/11 meant that this relationship was downgraded for over five years. According to Michael Shifter, 'at least in the short term no other country in the world was as deflated [as Mexico] by the new configuration brought about by September' (Shifter 2002: 52). Latin America as a whole felt the shift nearly as acutely.

Although Bush dutifully attended several of the regular regional summits for heads of states after 9/11, he did not give them priority and he undertook no tour of Latin America until March 2007. By then a third of the governments of the region had been elected on platforms which questioned the US invasion of Iraq, its enthusiasm for free trade, and its approaches to the environment, the International Criminal Court, energy, drugs control, and immigration. Led by the long-term but ailing Cuban leader Fidel Castro and the energetic Venezuelan President Hugo Chávez, the new movement reflected Washington's failure to retain the considerable initial sympathy over 9/11.

This new reality was not substantially reversed under the new Democratic administration of Barack Obama, despite the president's personal and diplomatic success at the April 2009 Organization of American States (OAS) summit at Port of Spain, Trinidad, at which he committed himself to a much more open, consultative style in regional affairs. Indeed, the high expectations of a change in US–Latin American relations in the period up to the 2010 mid-term elections in the US never recovered from Washington's ambivalent stance over a coup in Honduras in June 2009, its clumsy response to the Haitian earthquake of January 2010, the controversial and semi-secret negotiation of new military bases in Colombia, Washington's failure to address the issue of immigration so important to its neighbour Mexico, which was also afflicted by widespread killings by *narcotraficantes* mostly with weaponry freely purchased in the USA, and then the revelation of internal State Department concerns in the Wikileaks scandal, in which about a tenth of the 252,000 leaked cables related to Latin America.

Bush's tour of 2007 to six countries of South and Central America proved less of a failure than some had anticipated in view of the fact that only seven of the regional states had supported the invasion of Iraq (all of them had been in the midst of trade negotiations or, in the case of Colombia, in receipt of annual military aid of $600 million). The tour was less triumphant than the famous visit to South America by Franklin Roosevelt in 1936, when non-intervention and a new-found sense of good neighbourliness were at its peak. On the other hand, Bush's presence never excited the popular venom provoked by Richard Nixon's visit of 1958, when the physical safety of the Vice President was put at risk. Unsurprisingly, given his treatment, Nixon told Donald Rumsfeld in 1971, 'Latin America doesn't matter… People don't give a damn about Latin America now' (Reid 2007: 1). Even during the Cold War, Washington has seen the region as one of limited costs and risks.

Since the Second World War the emergence of global and multilateral institutions has broadened the channels for the development of US policy towards the rest of the hemisphere. This has reduced the image of the unilateralism of the early twentieth century, and it has provided Latin American states with some subordinate voice in hemispheric affairs.

One result of this asymmetry has been the widespread conviction within the region that development policies promoted by Washington and its allies have yielded, at best, very modest results. Although two-thirds of foreign direct investment in Mexico is of US origin and the USA is Mexico's largest trading partner, every year a million Mexicans migrate to the USA. This raises doubts as to the qualities of contemporary globalization and how far the formal bilateral relations between the two states matter in the lives of ordinary Mexicans. Many of these immigrants are returning to territory that was Mexican before 1848, and the issue of national sovereignty and pride remains a key issue in popular culture as well as public policy on both sides of the border.

Brazil, the region's only Portuguese-speaking country and a state of semi-continental proportions, has had no tradition of anti-Americanism. However, since the onset of democratic government in the 1990s, Brazil has increasingly sought to develop a South American bloc of states and to negotiate over Washington's free trade policies on a regional basis rather than the individual bilateral basis preferred by the USA. For the Brazilian foreign ministry there is no such thing as 'Latin America' because Mexico's membership of NAFTA since 1994 has placed that country firmly within the North American economic circuit. At the 2003 World Trade Organization (WTO) summit at Cancún, Mexico, Brazil took the regional lead in contesting the US and European limited versions of free trade, particularly over agricultural production and intellectual property. Brazil, by virtue of its size and regional role, has avoided the need of many states to seek out 'the greatest and most powerful ally' or to accept that 'the USA is our best friend, whether we like it or not'. Yet, even under the Workers' Party governments led by the radical Lula da Silva, Washington has generally found Brasilia to be a reasonable regional partner with which differences over distinct policies have not descended into ideological conflict.

Cuba, along with Puerto Rico, remained a colony of Spain throughout the nineteenth century. Despite frequent US efforts to purchase the prosperous slave-based plantation island up until the Civil War, it was not overtly threatened by the Monroe Doctrine, which was aimed at new European colonies. Although in 1898 Washington invaded Cuba, it did so with the explicit objective of halting the brutal Spanish campaign against the Cuban independence movement. As a result of this and the domestic anti-colonial lobby, it proved impossible to annex the country, which in 1902 acquired the status of an independent republic. However, the Platt Amendment to the US Army Appropriations Act of 1901 restricted Cuba's freedom to trade or form military alliances as well as permitting US intervention should its citizens or their property be threatened. An example of both conditionality and the use of Congress to formulate foreign policy, the Amendment effectively reduced Cuba to informal colonial status until it was withdrawn in 1934 following a revolution in the island.

The Cuban Revolution, which took state power in 1959 and remained in force nearly fifty years later, sealed that country's exceptional status on a number of grounds. It became and long remained the sole communist state in the western hemisphere; for thirty years it

was a highly dependent client of the USSR and so drew the region more tightly into Cold War strategic culture than would otherwise have been the case. Throughout that period Cuba was subject to a US embargo, widespread diplomatic isolation, and exclusion from many regional organizations. The Missile Crisis of October 1962 was a moment of huge international consequence in the nuclear age, and Washington understandably formulated policy towards Cuba with its eyes set on eastern Europe before the rest of the hemisphere. However, within Latin America Cuba increasingly came to stand as a symbol of nationalist resistance, small-state solidarity, and a Spartan critique of the North American consumerist ethos that many Latin American governments had sought and failed to emulate.

From the abortive Bay of Pigs invasion of April 1961 onwards US administrations have both openly called for and covertly planned 'regime change' in Havana (although after the Missile Crisis they pledged not to enforce this unilaterally). In the wake of the collapse of the USSR in the early 1990s and with Castro's severe illness in 2006 such change seemed close at hand, but it did not come about. Nor, indeed, was it broadly supported in a region long suspicious of interventionism. Many Latin Americans who harboured little sympathy for communism recognized the prophecy of Simón Bolívar in 1830 that the United States 'seems destined by providence to plague America with torments in the name of freedom'. Familiar with the core US policy motifs of promoting freedom and democracy, the Latin American response has often been to accept this idealist rhetoric as a constant and to question its practical application in discrete cases on realist grounds. In the case of Cuba, even the pro-US and quite conservative OAS Secretary General José Miguel Insulza felt constrained to advise Condoleezza Rice, 'There is no transition, and it is not your country.'

Jorge Domínguez has argued that the Cold War did not in many respects affect US–Latin American relations: 'The United States had faced military, political and economic competition in the Americas from extra-continental powers before the Cold War, just as it did during the Cold War' (Domínguez in Bulmer-Thomas and Dunkerley 1999: 33). However, he also shows that the Cold War did introduce a strong ideological element that sometimes disturbed Washington's 'normal' interest-based or realist approaches, and this continued to be the case for Cuba even after 1991. So, despite strong evidence that the embargo fortified Castro, the hard-line policy of antagonism was retained. This was in good measure because the vocal and electorally powerful Cuban émigré communities of Florida and New Jersey were able to hold all administrations to account over commitments made from the 1960 election campaign and during the Kennedy administration. Nowhere else—not even in Mexico during the revolution or in Nicaragua under the Sandinistas—has such an unbending policy been sustained for such a time. For this reason it is best seen as exceptional and not representative.

Although Brazil, Cuba, and Mexico may be treated as exceptional in certain key aspects, they have still been subject to the broad conditions of US policy making towards the region described by Lars Schoultz:

> **❝**For nearly two centuries, three interests have determined the content of US policy toward Latin America: the need to protect US security, the desire to accommodate the demands of US domestic politics, and the drive to promote US economic development. Each generation's specific policies have changed with the times and the circumstances, as one year's fear of communist adventurism yields to next year's dismay over human rights violations, as the Big Stick transmutes into Dollar Diplomacy and then Good Neighborliness, as democracy and free trade vie for attention with drug trafficking and immigration . . . (Schoultz 1998: 367) **❞**

Within these parameters we can identify three unique and enduring features. First is the prominence of the doctrinal format, from Monroe, through Theodore Roosevelt's 'Corollary', F. D. Roosevelt's 'Good Neighbour Policy', and John F. Kennedy's 'Alliance for Progress', to a doctrine that seemed almost ashamed of its status—the Washington Consensus.

The second feature is the cultural tension between the two sectors of the hemisphere, and particularly the frequent Anglo-American disparagement of Hispanic Catholic tradition. We shall return in the final section to this theme with respect to the exceptionalist claims about Latin America's present 'threat' to the social and moral fabric of the USA (Box 16.9). We should also note the more prevalent commitment to a modernization theory within US policy circles, non-governmental organizations, and development agencies. This perspective often assumes that the USA's own path of development provides the natural model for the rest of the continent, overlooking significant historical differences. US policy makers frequently misunderstand indigenous cultures or the outlook of poor peasants, who are often key constituents in Latin America but never formed part of the mainstream historiography of the USA.

The third special feature is the degree to which US–Latin American relations have impacted upon the territory and population of the USA itself, from the Louisiana Purchase, through the annexation of half of Mexico's territory in the 1840s, to the mass immigration from the 1990s.

Latin America and the formation of the modern USA

'Latin America' is a term that first appeared in the 1850s and was in regular use before the 1930s. In 1783, when the thirteen colonies had won independence from Great Britain as the United States, Spain controlled a very great part of what would become over the following century the modern, continental USA

Map 16.2 shows how conflicts involving European powers enabled Washington to expand its new 'empire', most notably through the Louisiana Purchase of 1803, when Napoleon, facing defeat at the hands of the ex-slaves of St Domingue (Haiti) turned his attentions back to

European expansion and sold the Spanish-administered mid-section of North America to the USA. Napoleon's subsequent invasions of Portugal (1807) and Spain (1808) removed their monarchies, the first relocating to Brazil, which declared itself an independent empire in 1822, and the second going into exile. As a result, Spain's American colonies began to agitate for self-government.

The Latin American experience of national liberation and decolonization had no precedent other than that of the USA itself from Great Britain. Following the Treaty of Vienna (1814–15), London had sought to restore its ties with Washington and to distance itself from the resurgent absolutism of the European monarchies of the Holy Alliance. As a result, in mid-1823—when Mexico, Central America, and much of South America were free of Spanish rule but unrecognized by the major powers—Foreign Secretary Canning inquired of the Monroe administration whether it would consider a joint statement on policy towards the region. What became known as the Monroe Doctrine was Washington's response to that overture. However, its twin precepts of non-colonization (including the 'non-transferability' of colonies between European powers) and 'two spheres' (the Americas and Europe) proved to be far more consequential than the initial pragmatic rationale for the diplomatic recognition of the ex-Spanish colonies as republics.

Within fifteen years it was plain to the new Latin American states that Washington would not detain its rising and highly mobile population from moving west and south. On the one hand, this involved the dispossession of the traditional lands of the Native American peoples and their relocation to the western territories. On the other, it embodied the idea of manifest destiny, whereby providential powers were invoked to justify expansion into lands held both by indigenous tribes and the successor states to the Spanish empire.

Although fought 160 years ago, the Mexican–American War is still sharply recalled south of the new border established in 1848–53. Mexican national pride was assaulted by a series of defeats inflicted by US troops. The idea that the USA might simply conquer new territory from other republics was anathema to some sections of opinion in New England, whilst many in the slaveholding South felt that Catholic, Spanish-speaking peoples could not be incorporated into the USA without damaging its constitutional balance over the institution of slavery. Today those millions of Mexicans who have migrated to US states west of the Mississippi are moving to lands that were held for far longer by Madrid than they have been by Washington. From one perspective, 'the United States came to us, not we to it'.

If the Mexican War contributed to the origins of the US Civil War, that country also suffered sharply through the collapse of the Union—an experience which served to revive the apparently moribund Monroe Doctrine. With the USA unable to sustain its foreign ambitions in the early 1860s, the European powers returned momentarily to regional affairs, most notably in the effort to administer Mexico under the European Prince Maximilian, sponsored by the French Emperor Louis Napoleon. That tragic adventure presaged the European 'Rush for Africa' over the following decades, but it was already an anachronism in a western hemisphere where the culture of colonialism had been comprehensively repudiated.

Maximilian's nemesis, Benito Juárez, the first indigenous head of an American state, showed some signs of forming with Abraham Lincoln the kind of 'special relationship' sought by Presidents Fox and Bush. However, assassination and the unforgiving course of Mexican political life meant that whilst US Reconstruction was accompanied to the north by self-government in Canada, to the south it coexisted with the long-term dictatorship of Porfirio Díaz (1876–1910). For decades, US talk of democracy in Mexico was rare and empty, and a steep price would be paid for that 'benign neglect' in the revolutionary era that followed. But a pattern was emerging—Washington favoured political stability and economic opportunity in Mexico above all else, including political freedom, for reasons of national security.

With the construction of the trans-continental railroad in 1869, the wars against the Native Americans of the Plains states over the following decades, and the simultaneous intense industrialization, the USA was reaching the limits of a 'home-based' policy towards the rest of the hemisphere. Washington's rising interest in the potential of a Pan-American strategy failed to develop into an enduring hemispheric initiative until the start of the 1890s, when trade and investment had grown to such a level that financial arrangements, particularly currency exchange rates, and the rules of international commerce required agreement on a continental scale.

The 1898 intervention in Cuba occurred, then, at a time when the US frontier had been closed for almost a decade, when Washington was concerned about European economic competition rather than colonial expansion in the rest of the hemisphere, and when overseas opportunities for trade and investment were being avidly sought. Now pledged to a 'two ocean' strategy involving the capacity to operate simultaneously in

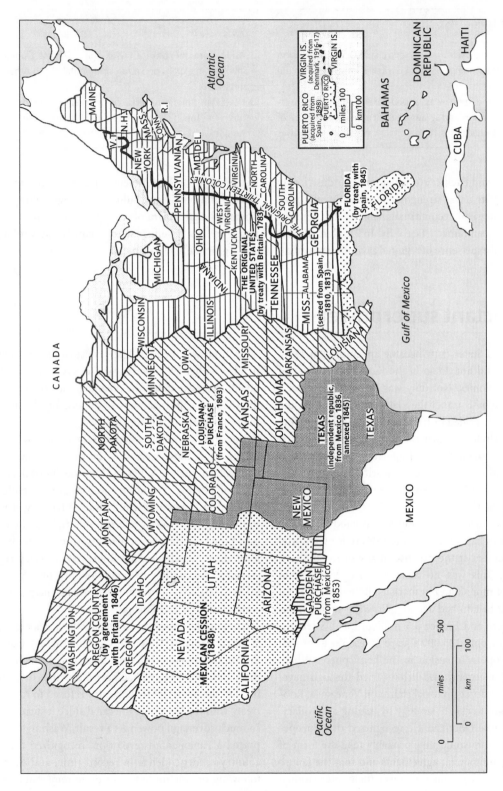

Fig. 16.2 Territorial growth of the United States, 1783–1853.

KEY POINTS

❑ The Monroe Doctrine was not a charter for US expansion but for containing European territorial intervention in the Americas.

❑ 'Manifest destiny' was a popular ideology that justified expansion and assumed the cultural superiority of Anglo-America.

❑ Aside from the Mexican War, the USA was primarily involved in expansion within continental North America until 1898.

❑ US–Latin American relations in the nineteenth century were much stronger in Central America than South America.

---

the Atlantic and Pacific, Washington was industriously building up its naval strength. Extra-continental projection of force had become imaginable by dint of intra-hemispheric supremacy (see Box 16.2). Nonetheless, this first real experience of regional asymmetry brought fast in its wake the problems of conflict management in constitutionally and culturally foreign settings. The unilateral deployment of great power resources proved necessary but insufficient for maintaining prolonged and legitimate leadership.

A reluctant superpower

If the United States truly became an 'empire' in 1898, it certainly did not do so in the European manner of acquiring colonies. Not only was Cuba retained on a protectorate basis under the Platt Amendment but the Supreme Court ruled in 1901 that Puerto Rico 'was foreign to the United States in the domestic sense'. (US citizenship was granted to the population of Puerto Rico in 1917, and the island became a self-governing commonwealth in 1952. Puerto Ricans may travel freely in and out of the USA.)

In 1905 Theodore Roosevelt declared that 'the United States has not the slightest desire for territorial aggrandizement at the expense of any of its southern neighbors'. This was no mere rhetoric: Washington wanted not more land but markets. Between 1870 and 1900 Great Britain had added 4.7 million square miles to its empire and France 3.5 million, but US territories grew by only 125,000 square miles. Yet Roosevelt feared European intrusion in the hemisphere. When, in 1902–3, Germany and Britain tried through naval strength to enforce financial claims on Venezuela, Roosevelt sought to clarify strategy by issuing a 'corollary' to the Monroe Doctrine. He recognized that European intervention would now probably take the form of enforcing commercial agreements and that the failure of Latin American states to meet their international

obligations was the most likely cause of such intrusion. In a December 1904 message to Congress, Roosevelt so qualitatively expanded the meaning and application of the 1823 message that many saw it as a total break with the original Monroe Doctrine.

Roosevelt's 'corollary' retained the notion of the two spheres, but these were now between 'civilized' and 'uncivilized' states. Whereas Monroe had effectively been supporting revolutions, Roosevelt was resolutely opposed to them, and while Monroe had urged non-intervention, Roosevelt reserved that right to the USA, assuming US control over markets, wherever they were located. Above all else, the Roosevelt corollary represented a declaration of conditionality of US policy upon the behaviour of regional states as much as it was a manifesto towards Europe.

The corollary was encouraged by the accelerated and conflictive manner in which Washington had acquired the rights to build an inter-oceanic canal through Panama. Until 1903 Panama had been a province of Colombia, but the Senate of that country refused to ratify the treaty with the USA over the canal since it surrendered so much sovereign power. As a result, Washington supported a Panamanian revolution, recognized the new country's independence in record time, and over the following decade undertook a quite remarkable piece

> **KEY QUOTES 16.1:**   The rights and responsibilities of the mighty: Olney and Roosevelt

Today the United States is practically sovereign on this continent, and its fiat is law upon subjects to which its confines its interposition. Why? It is not because of the pure friendship or good will felt for it. It is not simply by reason of its high character as a civilized state, nor because wisdom and justice and equity are the invariable characteristics of the dealings of the United States. It is because, in addition to all other grounds, its infinite resources combined with its isolated position render it master of the situation and practically invulnerable as against any or all other powers.

(Secretary of State Richard Olney to Thomas Bayard, 18 May 1895)

Chronic wrongdoing, or an impotence which results in a general loosening of the ties of civilized society, may in America, as elsewhere, ultimately require intervention by some civilized nation, and in the western hemisphere the adhesion of the United States to the Monroe Doctrine may force the United States, however reluctantly, in flagrant cases of such wrongdoing or impotence, to the exercise of an international police power.

(President Theodore Roosevelt to Congress, 9 December 1904)

of civil engineering for strategic purposes, allowing two-oceanic naval planning and providing an awesome example of North American industrial vision and capacity.

However, it was precisely in the first three decades of the twentieth century, when the USA secured such manifest superiority over both the local states and its European competitors, that it intervened most often, and to widespread criticism at home and abroad. Roosevelt, always disposed towards belligerence, started this process, but his successors Taft and Wilson failed to replace 'the big stick' with non-violent 'dollar diplomacy' (Taft) and 'peace between equals' (Wilson).

Between 1898 and 1930 US gunboats were sent into Latin American ports more than 6000 times, marines were deployed in Cuba, Mexico, Guatemala, Honduras, Dominican Republic, Nicaragua, Haiti, and Panama, elections were supervised in six states, anti-government rebels actively supported in four countries, loans obligatorily renegotiated in six states, and governments in fourteen countries refused diplomatic recognition (Grandin 2006: 3; Dunkerley in Bulmer-Thomas and Dunkerley 1999: 10). Almost all this activity occurred in Central America and the Caribbean, and most was undertaken under governments which insistently repudiated intervention as their preferred policy.

What happened? Basically, US economic ties with Latin America had widened and deepened to such an extent that it was no longer possible for an administration to determine precisely how it would respond

to circumstances driven by market forces beyond its direct control. US investment overseas had risen from $700 million in 1897 to $3.5 billion in 1914, over half of it in Latin America. With the First World War severely reducing European trade and capital flows, the USA had by the 1920s come to dominate the commercial and financial life of the Caribbean basin. Such economic dominance brought with it political complications, and not all of them were readily negotiable.

In the 1890s criticism of 'the northern colossus' had taken a largely literary or cultural form—in the campaigning journalism of the Cuban martyr José Martí or the essays of the Uruguayan José Enrique Rodó, whose polemic *Ariel* depicted the USA as a vulgar, materialist democracy dominated by the mob and counterposed to the classical tradition. By the 1920s, anti-Americanism was taking a more activist form, with calls for the internationalization of the Panama Canal and widespread support for Augusto César Sandino, who from 1928 led an effective guerrilla campaign against US military occupation of Nicaragua. By 1933 this opposition contributed not only to the withdrawal of the marines but also to a major shift in US policy to the region as a whole.

In Mexico the economic, strategic, and diplomatic issues were of a greater order since US interests in the neighbouring country were the largest in the region and so placed in considerable jeopardy by the revolution (1910–20). After the prolonged and highly profitable US alliance with the pre-revolutionary Díaz regime, the prominent role of US ambassador Henry

Lane Wilson in the assassination of President Madero in 1913 became infamous and set the two countries on a twenty-year course of tense contestation. In 1914 US forces attacked and occupied Veracruz for several months, reviving memories of the 1847 war. Two years later General Pershing invaded the state of Chihuahua in pursuit of the rebel leader Pancho Villa.

In 1917 the new Mexican Constitution reserved to the state all rights over the subsoil, raising doubts over the property rights of US mining and oil companies. However, it was only in 1938 that Mexico finally expropriated all foreign oil companies, and then it promised compensation. Even before the Second World War this nationalist attitude was being extended to manufacturing, the larger Latin American states adopting policies of import-substituting industrialization in order to reduce what would later be termed dependency on the advanced northern economies.

By the time of the 1932 presidential election, a dictatorship in Cuba was enjoying US patronage by default under the Platt Amendment, and this demanded that Washington rethink and eventually repudiate the Roosevelt corollary. The fall in 1933 of the Machado regime in Cuba gave the new administration of F. D. Roosevelt (FDR) a good opportunity to proclaim the Good Neighbour Policy, reversing the Roosevelt corollary, reducing tariffs, and making a virtue out of what many saw as the necessity of isolationism in the Great Depression.

Designed to be high-minded and restore the legitimacy squandered through thirty years of 'gunboat diplomacy', the Good Neighbour Policy did not surrender US national interest. The tariff reductions that revived trade were conditional upon reciprocity from Latin American states. However, the policy did suspend the 'Americanist' vocation to promote freedom abroad. When it was enunciated, of the twenty-one states of the region only Colombia was ruled by a government that had come to power through an open election. Now the policy of non-intervention—or what some would call 'benign neglect'—effectively endorsed the existence of the many dictatorships installed in the wake of the 1929 Crash. In Brazil, Washington's closest ally, party politics was suspended and the authoritarian *Estado Novo* set up by Getúlio Vargas in 1935–7 in emulation of Salazar's Portuguese dictatorship.

The outbreak of the Second World War in Europe in September 1939 found the republics of the western hemisphere less politically invigilated than for fifty years but also tied to the US market to an unprecedented degree. War between European powers posed the long discussed issue of a regional defence treaty that would make the Monroe Doctrine both practical and pluralistic. Although agreements on reciprocal defence were signed in 1940, it was only with the Japanese attack on Pearl Harbor in December 1941 that regional states were obliged to take hard decisions. Very few themselves upheld FDR's four freedoms—of speech

> **KEY QUOTES 16.2:** Burying the big stick: the Clark memo and Good Neighbour Policy

The so-called 'Roosevelt corollary' was to the effect, as generally understood, that in case of financial or other difficulties in weak Latin American countries, the United States should attempt an adjustment lest European Governments should intervene, and intervening should occupy territory—an act which would be contrary to the principles of the Monroe Doctrine . . . it is not believed that this corollary is justified by the terms of the Monroe Doctrine, however much it may be justified by the application of the doctrine of self-preservation . . . So far as Latin America is concerned, the Doctrine is now, and always has been, not an instrument of violence and oppression, but an unbought, freely bestowed, and wholly effective guaranty of their freedom,

independence, and territorial integrity against the imperialistic designs of Europe.

(Undersecretary of State Reuben Clark, to Secretary Frank Kellogg, December 1928)

The essential qualities of a true pan Americanism must be the same as those which constitute a good neighbour, namely, mutual understanding, and, through such understanding, a sympathetic appreciation of the other's point of view . . . the independence of each republic must recognize the independence of every other republic.

(President Roosevelt, speech to Pan American Union, April 1933)

KEY POINTS

❏ The Roosevelt corollary of 1904 made US policy conditional upon the behaviour of Latin American states—a significant shift from the Monroe Doctrine.

❏ The growth of US economic interests in the region not only surpassed its European competition but also complicated a foreign policy based purely on political considerations.

❏ US interventionism in Central America and the Caribbean was extensive in the early twentieth century, although Washington preferred to avoid deployment of military forces.

❏ The Good Neighbour Policy introduced by F. D. Roosevelt in 1933 consolidated prior efforts to reduce direct US intervention but also suspended the promotion of democracy.

and religion, from want and fear—but fewer still could rely on extra-hemispheric alternatives to trade with the USA. Authoritarian Brazil provided troops which engaged with Nazi forces in Italy, but most of Latin America had only to confront the diplomatic and economic consequences of the conflict. All the Caribbean and Central American republics immediately followed Washington in declaring war on the Axis. However, the bi-oceanic nature of the conflict, caution, and ideological sympathies meant that several countries remained neutral until weeks before the end of the war: Chile, Venezuela, Uruguay (February 1945), Argentina, and Paraguay (March 1945).

The prominent anti-fascist profile of the Allied campaign restored a long suspended ideological element to hemispheric politics, and this would feed fiercely into the Cold War era. Yet in the immediate post-war years the region underwent an intense transitional experience whereby the populist Argentine government led by General Perón was targeted as fascistic and intent upon expanding its influence throughout South America. Perón, however, positively flourished on the nationalist backlash against ill-judged accusations, survived, and came to find a sober *modus vivendi* with Washington based on shared anti-communism.

The conflict with Perón presaged policy issues that would dominate US—Latin American relations until the 1990s. How was Washington to distinguish between state-based development policies and 'crypto-communism'? How could it promote liberal capitalism through social reform without undermining anti-communist allies? How were the NATO and traditional hemispheric security needs to be reconciled in the context of ideological challenges from Moscow, Beijing, and the third world movements against imperialism and colonialism?

Cold War coexistence

The Cold War had a partial and uneven effect on US policy towards Latin America. Sometimes ideological aggression and interventionist impulses were given full rein (Guatemala, 1954; Cuba, 1961; Dominican Republic, 1965; Chile, 1970–3; Nicaragua, 1979–90; Grenada, 1983; Panama, 1989), but sometimes a more circumspect policy was applied (Venezuela, 1945–8; Bolivia, 1952–64; Peru, 1968–75; Honduras and Panama, 1972; Mexico, throughout). Washington could tolerate high levels of commerce with the USSR (Argentina) or even extensive arms purchases from it (Peru), provided a fundamental anti-communism was sustained at home. Equally, agrarian reform was encouraged in some countries (Bolivia, Venezuela, Chile, and El Salvador) for its counter-insurgency potential, whereas it was deemed anathema in others (Guatemala, Cuba, Brazil) where it was seen to encourage popular radicalism. On occasion, such as the Falklands War of 1982, even a staunch anti-communist ally would be deserted for an older alliance (although forces within the Reagan cabinet resisted this).

Grandin suggests that one reason for this mixed record was that Washington used the hemisphere as a laboratory for testing the techniques of neo-colonial anti-communism in the third world. Domínguez, on the other hand, uses the destabilization of the Allende government in Chile to question the logic and true usefulness to US national interest of such activity (in Bulmer-Thomas and Dunkerley 1999).

Two factors stand out in this period. First is the regular use by Washington of the new multilateral treaties and organizations. Of particular importance were the regional defence agreement signed at Rio in 1947 and the OAS in 1948. Sometimes described as a 'meeting of pigeons presided over by a cat', the OAS was preferred to the UN for its malleability—it proved unproblematic to suspend Cuba's membership in 1962—but by the 1970s it had become more independent.

As befitted an era of competition between liberal and collectivist development models, the institutions set up at Bretton Woods in 1944, such as the International Monetary Fund (IMF) and related bodies like the World Bank, also became valuable channels for imposing economic discipline and making loans conditional upon fiscal austerity. By the 1980s such policies were no longer enforced in the unilateral manner of the Roosevelt corollary and were accepted as part of a capitalist regime that extended beyond narrow US national interests.

The second distinctive feature of late twentieth-century regional relations has already been noted—the importance of the Cuba revolution. Before 1959 regional anti-communism had either, as Grandin suggests, to experiment or to draw its repertoire of fears, soft-power, and counter-insurgency techniques from extra-hemispheric experiences. Once the rebels took power in Havana, US policy was transformed by a tangible foe occupying state power. Containment was not enough since Cuba initially urged emulation of its example, creating 'two, three Vietnams' in Che Guevara's provocative phrase, which did nothing to persuade Washington that domino theory was neater in theory than practice.

Havana, viewed throughout as a loyal but erratic client of Moscow, preferred supporting guerrilla groups to communist parties, several of which it helped to split. By the 1970s Castro displayed greater pragmatism and urged caution on the Sandinistas after they took power. Often Washington recognized these features but under the Reagan administration (1981–9) its invective was virulent. Moreover, the existence of

---

> **BOX 16.1: The case against Guatemala**
>
> That the domination or control of the political institutions of any American state by the international communist movement, extending to this hemisphere the political system of an extra-continental power, would constitute a threat to the sovereignty and political independence of all the American states, endangering the peace of America, and would call for appropriate action in accordance with existing treaties.
>
> (Draft US resolution on Guatemala, OAS Conference, Caracas, Mar. 1954)

---

a communist regime in the hemisphere sharpened the anti-communism of Latin American conservative forces, which increasingly embraced the ideology of the national security state, militarizing political power and suspending all civil liberties, which sometimes led to the mass murder of citizens by their own states (particularly Chile and Argentina in the 1970s, Guatemala and El Salvador in the 1980s).

The destabilization of the reformist government of Jacobo Arbenz in Guatemala was approved at the highest levels of the Truman and Eisenhower administrations, orchestrated by the CIA, and favoured the interests of the United Fruit Company, whose lands had faced expropriation. Arbenz had been elected president in a fair poll and had adopted a modest programme of reforms. Yet Washington put his close ties to the country's small Communist Party at the heart of a propaganda campaign designed for its deterrent effects elsewhere as well as to destabilize a state that lacked the resources to match its radical rhetoric. The June 1954 overthrow of Arbenz by a band of US-trained rebels was not seriously opposed in the OAS, although it was recognized as Washington's work. That success encouraged a repeat of the combination of diplomatic isolation with covert action by local proxy forces against the Sandinistas in the 1980s.

There was scant criticism of the Guatemalan operation in the USA at the height of the McCarthy era, but when the rebels took power in Cuba five years later the debate over how Washington should respond was sharper. In the 1960 election campaign Kennedy attacked Nixon as weak on the issue, and his new government

---

BOX 16.2: The Cuban Revolution

1952   Batista seizes power and establishes dictatorship.

1953   Castro launches abortive assault on Moncada barracks, Santiago.

1954   Che Guevara observes overthrow of Arbenz government in Guatemala.

1955   Castro and other surviving rebels amnestied, go into Mexican exile.

1956   Rebel yacht *Granma* lands in southern Cuba; guerrilla operations begin.

1957   Second guerrilla column set up under Che Guevara.

1958   Raúl Castro establishes new front in north. Washington imposes arms embargo on Batista government following human rights violations; Batista removed in military coup.

1959   January: rebels take Havana after a general strike brings down military junta; Fidel Castro takes control; agrarian reform starts (May).

1960   May: Cuba establishes diplomatic relations with USSR. June: US oil companies nationalized; further expropriation of foreign-owned property. October: US imposes trade embargo.

1961   January: US breaks diplomatic relations with Cuba. April: abortive counter-revolutionary landing at Bay of Pigs.

1962   October (22–8): Missile Crisis.

---

readily accepted plans for a Guatemalan-style invasion by counter-revolutionaries at the Bay of Pigs in April 1961. That operation was a disaster that helped to radicalize the Castro government, which not unreasonably supposed that it needed a superpower patron if it was to survive for long and so assiduously developed an alliance with a sceptical but enticed Moscow. Within eighteen months this process had led the world to the verge of a stand-off between the world's leading nuclear powers. Kennedy opted for a naval blockade to prevent the USSR from siting missiles within 100 miles of the North American mainland, and Moscow stepped back once promises were secured that Cuba would not be invaded.

Again, criticism was slight since Kennedy's policy upheld the Monroe Doctrine, anti-communism, and regional security. However, by 1962 it was plain that the USA needed more than reactive policies to deal with the influence of Cuba. Military aid rose, counter-insurgency operations were continuously developed and planned—in 1965 the Johnson administration did not hesitate to invade the Dominican Republic—but they were now accompanied by North American calls for agrarian reform, institutional modernization, increased foreign investment, and political liberalization, all under the mantle of an Alliance for Progress.

Very much moulded in the idealistic style of the Kennedy government, the Alliance was driven more by rhetoric than hard cash. Once Kennedy was gone, the policy lost priority, and by the end of the 1960s

Washington had relegated reformist responses to radicalism. Johnson and Nixon welcomed a clutch of right-wing military dictatorships in South America without great concern for their anti-democratic character.

The rapid shift away from encouragement of liberal modernity back towards a threat-driven anti-communist strategy was most marked in the case of Chile. Although President Allende was a socialist and Santiago had diplomatic relations with both Havana and Moscow, the Chilean government was a weak constitutional coalition and did not seek ties with the Soviet bloc like those held by Cuba. Yet beneath a now familiar veil of secrecy, Nixon and Kissinger authorized the CIA to stop Allende's election and then, when that failed, to destabilize his government. The eventual coup of September 1973, in which Allende died, needed no direct US intervention, but the sixteen-year dictatorship of Augusto Pinochet owed much to Washington's support.

Washington's role in destabilizing the Allende government aroused controversy at home, prompting a congressional investigation into US covert operations in the region. In the wake of defeat in Vietnam, this current of criticism helped to reanimate support for the multilateral approach developed by the Carter White House. Carter's deliberate adoption of a 'low profile' included negotiating return of the canal to Panama and criticizing the violation of human rights violations of the dictatorships, which, in a new form of conditionality, lost military aid. This was most telling in Central America.

The radical movements of Central America in the 1980s have been described as 'inevitable revolutions' (LaFeber 1983) because they sprang out of prolonged poverty and political oppression. The movement was most advanced in Nicaragua, where the FSLN (Sandinistas) challenged the sixty-year rule of the Somoza family. When, late in 1978, the FSLN threatened to take power, Washington sought OAS support for multilateral intervention but this was rejected, not least because several dictatorships wanted to avoid a precedent that might be used against them. Carter had to harden his policy, but he came under fierce criticism. Reagan's 1980 election campaign made much of the 'loss' of Central America, and his government subsequently adopted the ideas and services of the Democrat academic Jeane Kirkpatrick, who defended the 'moderate repression' of the Argentine dictatorship (under which at least 15,000 people disappeared) as far more acceptable than the communist alternatives that she saw Carter's policies as encouraging.

Once in office, Reagan sought not just to contain the Sandinistas but to 'make them say Uncle'. At the same time, he provided military aid to El Salvador, where the FMLN guerrillas were strong. These forces were certainly supported by Managua and Havana, but their resilience owed more to popular support, strategic ability, and the unpopularity of the regimes they were fighting. Washington recognized this, held back from close association with the Guatemalan regime, which had a particularly bad record of repression, and forced the Salvadorian government to accept agrarian reform and elections as key counter-insurgency tactics.

Yet Reagan's Central American policy rested on vocal accusations of communist conspiracy. Domestic concern at the renewed threat of covert operations against the government of Nicaragua led to congressional

---

❝ KEY QUOTES 16.3: The Cold War revived in Central America

Human rights is the soul of our foreign policy.

(President Jimmy Carter, 1978)

What did the Carter administration do in Nicaragua? It brought down the Somoza regime... acted repeatedly and at critical junctures to weaken the government of Anastasio Somoza and to strengthen his opponents... hurried efforts to force complex and unfamiliar political practices on societies lacking the requisite political culture, tradition, and social structures not only fail to produce the desired outcomes; if they are undertaken at a time when a traditional regime is under attack, they actually facilitate the job of the insurgents.

(Kirkpatrick 1979)

Many of our citizens don't fully understand the seriousness of the situation, so let me put it bluntly: There is a war in Central America that is being fuelled by the Soviets and the Cubans. They are arming, training and supplying, and encouraging a war to subjugate another nation to communism, and that nation is El Salvador. The Soviets and the Cubans are operating from a base called Nicaragua. And this is the first real Communist aggression on the American mainland.

(Reagan 1983: 1044)

KEY POINTS

- ❏ The Cold War did not have a uniform impact on US–Latin American relations after 1947.
- ❏ Washington retained a pragmatic or 'realist' approach to the region where it did not perceive a serious radical challenge.
- ❏ The Cuban Revolution changed US–Latin American relations, introducing the only communist regime in the western hemisphere.
- ❏ Although Cuba initially sought to encourage other revolutions and was always sympathetic to radical causes, after 1973 it displayed a quite pragmatic policy in the western hemisphere.
- ❏ After the Cuban Revolution US policy alternated between hard-line, military-led approaches (Johnson/Nixon/Reagan) and those that included a significant element of 'soft power' (Kennedy/Carter/Bush Sr./Clinton).

amendments which aimed to avert a repetition of the Chilean experience. However, the CIA and officers of the National Security Council sought to circumvent constitutional restrictions imposed by Congress. They clandestinely raised cash to fund their counter-revolutionary forces based in Honduras and Costa Rica by selling missiles to Iran, then at war with Iraq. When this doubly illegal operation was revealed, a major political scandal—the Iran-Contra Affair—broke out.

The guerrilla wars in Guatemala and El Salvador were eventually settled by UN- and European-brokered peace accords in the 1990s. The Sandinistas were removed from office in 1990, but by the Nicaraguan electorate. The Reagan policy had yielded some success—it had certainly stopped national conflicts combining into a Central American regional war, but it did so at very high costs to its support and legitimacy elsewhere.

The Washington Consensus questioned

In August 1982 Mexico effectively went bankrupt by defaulting on its sovereign debt. Other countries had likewise sought to subsidize national industries and welfare systems by borrowing on the international markets in the wake of the oil crises of the 1970s; they were barely less vulnerable. The governments and the private banks that had lent so generously to them in uncertain times now faced demands from the IMF for stabilization of trading accounts and strictly balanced budgets, which usually meant a substantial reduction in 'public goods' such as health and education—all with the objective of securing growth, and with the alleviation of poverty a strictly secondary issue. Under this 'neo-liberal' agenda, the economies were to be opened up as much as possible to international trade since this would, according to the classical economic theories dominating the multilateral institutions, produce growth, and the results of growth would, sooner or later, 'trickle down' to the benefit of the poor.

In fact, the poor of Latin America grew in number, as did income inequality as a whole. The only tangible benefit of neo-liberalism for the millions under the poverty line was the severe reduction in inflation. Everywhere, the post-war 'boom' was over, and multilateral institutions were enforcing orthodox capitalist policies and management. Almost everywhere public spending was slashed, companies went broke, and employment fell. What failed to follow for over a decade was sustained growth and renewed investment in the public services. Even private foreign investment was cautious, after an upsurge in the late 1990s proved short-lived.

As the larger economies opened up under what became known as the Washington Consensus, they became exposed to the erratic movements of international finance, with the result that Mexico suffered a severe monetary crisis in 1994–5, Brazil in 1998–9, and Argentina in 2001–3. Liberalization had brought its own problems, even if it had lessened the problems of import-substituting industrialization, mixed economies, and unorthodox fiscal policies. What had been sold in the early 1980s as a foolproof 'one-size-fits-all' solution was shown to be very uneven. Even in Chile, where the Pinochet regime introduced an early adjustment programme designed with advice from the University of Chicago, it proved necessary to bale out banks and limit the movement of foreign finance.

Elsewhere, in a very poor country like Bolivia or a medium-sized oil state such as Venezuela, 'stabilization' sparked mass unemployment and enduring social discontent. The most modern form of 'conditionality' had proved to be an insensitive instrument in itself and Washington was not always able to micromanage a controversial 'consensus' founded in its own name. Only in the case of the Mexican crisis of 1994–5 did the Clinton administration act directly to bale out its neighbour—for fear of the consequences for the USA of a second hemispheric debt crisis south of the border.

The free trade policy that stood at the heart of the Washington Consensus attracted much controversy, but one relatively neglected consequence of this endorsement of globalization was its opening of the region to all markets, including those of Europe. In

> **KEY QUOTES 16.4:** The 'drugs war': asymmetry or inequity?

[Bolivian President Evo Morales] is right to complain about American imperialists criminalizing a substance that's been used for centuries in the Andes. If gringos are abusing a product made from coca leaves, that's a problem for America to deal with at home . . . America makes plenty of things that are bad for foreigners' health—fatty Big Macs, sugary Cokes, deadly Marlboros—but we'd never let foreigners tell us what to make and not make. The Saudis can fight alcoholism by forbidding the sale of Jack Daniels, but we'd think they were crazy if they ordered us to eradicate fields of barley in Tennessee.

(John Tierney, *New York Times*, 23 September 2006)

a post-colonial age, this may represent the true termination of the Monroe Doctrine, especially since Washington and the European Union were alike reluctant to allow the opening up of their own more protected markets to competition from the south.

As a result of the recession of the 1980s and the free competition of the 1990s the 'informal economy' of Latin America grew, and nowhere more so than in the illegal production of drugs, overwhelmingly destined for the US market. Drugs policy became a leading policy item from the early 1980s, particularly affecting the Andean countries producing the coca plant used to manufacture cocaine and the Central American and Caribbean countries, used as conduits into the USA. From a Latin American perspective, US drug policy was consistently 'supply led' in that it prioritized eradication at source and interdiction over reducing demand, providing few real economic alternatives to the poor farmers who supplied the mafia with their illicit goods. From the US perspective reduced supply increased the costs and so shrank demand; the imposition of conditionality was reasonable, given the aid that Congress was financing. However, Washington did move in the 1990s to reduce the attention given to government 'certification' of compliance by Latin American states since this plainly wounded pride and was counterproductive. Whether judged by the state of bilateral relations or flows of contraband narcotics from the region, the policy was not a success.

When President Fox visited Washington in September 2001, he did so in search of a solution to the mutual problem of mass and rising immigration to the USA. When President Bush visited Mexico City in March 2007 he had the same issue at the top of his agenda. In the intervening period some five million Mexicans had crossed the border, there being nearly 50 million people of Hispanic descent living in the USA. One in six babies now born in the USA has a Hispanic mother, and the total Hispanic population is projected to be 100 million in 2050.

There is a positive side to this new reality. Hispanic GDP within the USA is now $700 billion—bigger than those of Spain and Mexico—and a significant amount of it is returned to the region in the form of private remittances. However, it is arguable how economically efficient and equitable this is. Moreover, many immigrants are undocumented—both illegal and unable to secure the support of the US welfare system. Within the USA Hispanics are disproportionately poor and overly represented in the armed forces, even if they have avoided the poor health and crime profiles of the African-American population they overtook as the largest minority group early in the twenty-first century.

For some conservative thinkers, such as Harvard Professor Samuel Huntington, this Hispanic diaspora posed a uniquely acute threat to the traditional US 'melting pot' and represented a 'clash of cultures' within the very borders of the USA.

Others expected this fast-developing scenario to provide a beneficial impact on both sides of the border: Hispanic middle-class employees of the State Department would introduce knowledge and sensitivity into bilateral relations, and US politicians would be more responsive to the rising Hispanic electorate. But progress has only been patchy, since those Hispanics who have not grown up in Latin American countries speak the same language but often underestimate the power of nationalist sentiment. Equally, many Hispanics in the USA are not on the electoral

> **KEY QUOTES 16.5: The great fear: Latin America *within* the USA**
>
> Americans, to varying degree, have defined the substance of their identity in terms of race, ethnicity, ideology and culture. Race and ethnicity are now largely eliminated: Americans see their country as a multiethnic, multiracial society. The 'American Creed', as initially formulated by Thomas Jefferson . . . however, was the product of a distinct Anglo-Protestant culture of the founding settlers of America in the 17th and 18th centuries. Key elements of that culture include: the English language; Christianity; religious commitment; English concepts of the rule of law, the responsibility of rulers, and the rights of individuals; and dissenting Protestant values of individualism, the work ethic, and the belief that humans have the ability and the duty to try to create a heaven on earth, a 'city on a hill' . . . In the late 20th century, however, the salience and substance of this culture was challenged by a new wave of migrants from Latin America and Asia, the popularity in intellectual and political circles of the doctrines of multiculturalism and diversity, the spread of Spanish as a second language and the Hispanization trends in American society . . .
>
> (Huntington 2004: pp. xv–xvi)

registers, and their political profile reflects neither a blanket poverty—there is a distinct Hispanic middle class—nor the traditional social sensibilities of a society unused to Catholic values, which, for example, promote with equal energy the right to life and the right to join a trade union.

In the meantime, the new, independently minded governments elected in the first years of the new century showed every sign of moving away from the Washington Consensus, choosing which of its economic instruments they wished to maintain—largely control of inflation—and which they repudiated—largely open access for foreign companies to strategic resources. They had few extra-hemispheric options with which to test Washington, and whilst the Chinese market helped to underpin economic recovery, it did not represent an enduring alternative to the USA. So, even the more radical regimes recognized the continuing continental asymmetry, but they refused to accept the existing political terms—and particularly the presumption of hegemony—through which this had long been expressed.

Despite the considerable enthusiasm in Latin America and amongst US Latinos for the 2008 election campaign of Barak Obama—an enthusiasm not seen since John F. Kennedy's nearly half a century earlier—expectations of a radical improvement in regional relations were soon dashed. Apart from the predictable fact that there was minimal space for the region on Washington's war-led foreign policy agenda, Obama's appointment of Hillary Rodham Clinton as Secretary of State, and the eventual appointment of Professor Arturo Valenzuela as Assistant Secretary of State for the Americas ensured a highly cautious, risk-averse, and low-profile defence of the *status quo*. At the same time, even despite the substantial Republican losses in the 2008 election, some Senators, most notably Jim DeMint (R-S.C.) used the right-wing coup in Honduras in June 2009 as a pretext to hold up Valenzuela's nomination, underscoring the important role of the upper house in foreign relations. Equally, the US pursuit of a Colombian site for alternatives to the military base at Manta, closed by the new radical government in Ecuador, sharpened conflict with Venezuela. More importantly, it showed how far Washington was distanced from Brasilia, which criticized the security agreement, strongly denounced the Honduran coup, and used its temporary position in the UN Security Council to defend Iran's right to develop a nuclear power potential, opposing the US policy of sanctions. In every case, the Obama administration responded with less aggressive rhetoric than had the Bush government, but not in any substantially different manner. After the 2010 US mid-term elections, and the loss of the House of Representatives to the Republicans, the likelihood of a significant new initiative lessened still. Even the long-delayed January 2011 decision to restore US academic visits and financial remittances to Cuba was implemented on a Friday afternoon, when Congress was not sitting and the news agenda was at its lowest ebb. The embargo remained in place as one of the last vestiges of a Cold War now over twenty years passed.

KEY POINTS

❑ The Washington Consensus was a set of orthodox liberal policies designed to stabilize the performance of Latin American economies and open them to international markets after the debt crisis of the early 1980s.

❑ The Consensus was a doctrine supported by the US government but practically implemented by multilateral organizations such as the IMF and World Bank, so it represented an end to the 'hemispherism' of both the Monroe Doctrine and the Roosevelt corollary.

❑ Aside from Central America, the Consensus replaced anti-communism as Washington's prime concern in Latin America.

❑ The economic recession of the 1980s and 1990s, in part prompted by the Consensus, prompted a regional rise in drug production and emigration to the USA, issues that by 2000 had firmly displaced ideology as the key US concerns relating to Latin America.

Conclusion

If in 1803 Thomas Jefferson was seeking to develop the USA into a truly continental power by expanding into lands occupied by Native Americans and Mexicans, in 2003 George W. Bush was concerned to limit the arrival of Latin American people in the assured continental power that the USA had been for over a century. Markets and jobs had replaced land. The colonization feared in the early nineteenth century had not occurred. Large parts of Mexico were annexed after the war in 1846–8, but the Monroe Doctrine was not exploited to extend direct US control and administration of the Latin American republics. When this was sought after 1898 in order to secure and guarantee commercial advantage, it caused a backlash at home and abroad, embarrassed governments formally pledged to the principles of non-intervention and sovereignty, and it yielded insufficient economic advantage to justify the political and diplomatic costs. By 1930 the USA had already outcompeted the European economies and readily dominated the political economy of the hemisphere. FDR's Good Neighbour Policy restored an earlier attachment to non-intervention, and it was only moderated in the Second World War in terms of the need for logistical cooperation. The onset of the Cold War saw a return to a much more ideological and interventionist approach, which was strengthened by the Cuban Revolution. Yet under the Kennedy and Carter administrations, some important variation of approach and style was undertaken. At no time was anti-communist language more virulent than under Reagan, but after the Cold War equally pressing problems of economic failure, drugs, and immigration proved just as difficult to manage.

?   Questions

1. Has US policy towards Latin America been consistent over the nineteenth and twentieth centuries?
2. To what degree has Europe determined the pattern of US–Latin American relations?
3. Is the USA an empire based on neo-colonialism in the western hemisphere?
4. What have been the main consequences of the Monroe Doctrine?
5. To what degree has the Latin American policy of the USA been 'idealist' in the twentieth century?
6. Have Latin American countries consistently been the passive subaltern states of the western hemisphere?
7. To what extent have multilateral organizations affected US–Latin American relations since 1945?
8. Has there been a consistent Latin American anti-Americanism?
9. To what degree is Cuba as 'exceptional' as the USA itself?
10. Has globalization finally ended the era of the Monroe Doctrine?

» Further Reading

Bemis, S. F. (1943), *The Latin American Policy of the United States* (New York: Harcourt Brace).

The standard or 'official' version of regional policy up to the Second World War. Still worth reading for an insight to mainstream attitudes and accounts.

Bulmer-Thomas, V. and Dunkerley, J. (1999), *The United States and Latin America: The New Agenda* (Cambridge, MA: David Rockefeller Center for Latin American Studies/Institute of Latin American Studies, University of London).

A collection of essays covering the historical background, drugs and immigration, and a focus on Cuba as well as the main themes of the relationship in the 1990s.

Carothers, T. (1991), *In the Name of Democracy: US Policy toward Latin America in the Reagan Years* (Berkeley and Los Angeles: University of California Press).

A critical survey that is detailed and well informed.

Grandin, G. (2006), *Empire's Workshop: Latin America, the United States, and the Rise of the New Imperialism* (New York: Metropolitan Books).

A radical reinterpretation of the twentieth-century relationship that argues for a deliberate use of the region by Washington to experiment and develop techniques for wider application.

Joseph, G., Legrand, C., and Salvatore, R. (eds) (1998), *Close Encounters of Empire: Writing the Cultural History of US–Latin American Relations* (Durham, NC: Duke University Press).

A wide-ranging collection of detailed cultural case studies on both hard and soft power.

LaFeber, W. (1983), *Inevitable Revolutions: The United States in Central America* (New York: W. W. Norton).

An historical survey of the origins and development of the social conflict of the 1970s and 1980s that stresses local inequities and is sceptical about Soviet influence.

LaRosa, M. and Mora, F. (eds) (1999), *Neighborly Adversaries: Readings in US–Latin American Relations* (Lanham, MD: Rowman and Littlefield).

A broad selection of excerpts from primary materials, mostly from the twentieth century.

LeoGrande, W. M. (1990), From Reagan to Bush: The Transition in US Policy towards Central America, *Journal of Latin American Studies*, **22/3:** 595–621.

A comprehensive synopsis of how the hard-line Cold War approach to the region was upheld in moderated form.

——(2007), A Poverty of Imagination: George W. Bush's Policy in Latin America, *Journal of Latin American Studies*, **39/2:** 355–386.

A short but comprehensive survey of the policy of George W. Bush Jr. towards Central and South America, laying stress on the resurgence of interventionist elements already in place under Clinton.

Lowenthal, A. (1976), The United States and Latin America: Ending the Hegemonic Presumption, *Foreign Affairs*, **55** (Oct.): 199–213.

A succinct statement about the long-standing 'culture' of US approaches to Latin America and an argument for how policy might be changed.

——(ed.) (1990), *Exporting Democracy: The United States and Latin America* (Baltimore: Johns Hopkins University Press).

A balanced collection that surveys the experience of different countries at the end of the Cold War.

Schoultz, L. (1998), *Beneath the United States: A History of US Policy toward Latin America* (Cambridge, MA: Harvard University Press).

A survey of the entire period since independence based overwhelmingly on primary documentation. Less detailed on the last two decades but a vital source for the earlier years.

Smith, P. (1996), *Talons of the Eagle: Dynamics of US–Latin American Relations* (New York: Oxford University Press).

A useful liberal survey up to the Clinton presidency, aimed at students.

Suárez-Orozco, M. and Páez, M. M. (2002), *Latinos: Remaking America* (Berkeley: David Rockefeller Center for Latin American Studies, Harvard).

The best series of essays covering the Hispanic community from the perspective of the social sciences.

For a range of additional resources to support your learning visit the Online Resource Centre that accompanies this book at **www.oxfordtextbooks.co.uk/orc/cox_stokes2e/.**

17 US foreign policy in Africa

Robert G. Patman

Introduction

Despite historic ties with the continent, US policy toward Africa, in the words of the current US Assistant Secretary of State for African Affairs, has often 'been overlooked as a top priority for the US Government' (Carson 2010a). Throughout the Cold War, Africa was treated as a pawn in the battle between the USA and the Soviet Union, as both sides attempted to limit the influence of the other. Since the end of the Cold War, Africa has been increasingly racked by internal conflict, state failure, famine, poverty, and disease. Despite initial hopes for a USA-led 'New World Order' after the Cold War, in which the international community could work together to tackle such issues, the withdrawal of US troops from Somalia in 1994 marked a period of considerable disengagement from the continent. While limited re-engagement occurred during the second half of the 1990s, it was the events of 9/11 and the fear of state failure in Africa, acting as a breeding ground and safe haven for terrorists, that triggered a fresh American strategic focus on Africa. Emerging Chinese influence in Africa, growing international competition for African resources, and the determination of the Obama administration to promote good governance in Africa has further stimulated and expanded the parameters of American engagement (Obama 2009). Nevertheless, it is proving difficult for the Obama administration to realize the goal of 'a more peaceful, stable, and prosperous Africa' (Carson 2010a).

US policies toward Africa, particularly since the end of the Second World War, exemplify many of the themes

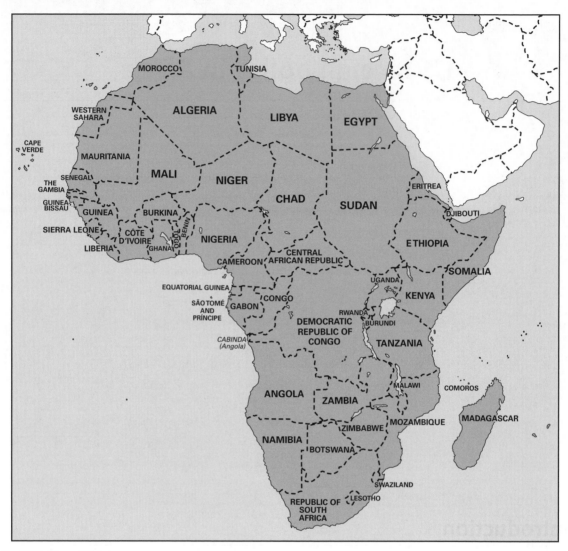

Fig. 17.1 Map of Africa.

already discussed throughout this book. American exceptionalism, the foreign relations of a global hegemon, Cold War dealings with periphery states, the American post-Cold War search for a new foreign policy purpose, the post-9/11 war on terror, and reinvigorating American leadership through partnerships and institutions are all themes which have been played out in the relationship between the USA and Africa. Throughout the Cold War, Africa was an 'active bystander'—on the one hand peripheral to the conflict, and yet on the other a stage on which the USA and the Soviet Union could play out their global struggle while minimizing the risk of nuclear confrontation. In the early post-Cold

War period, President George H. W. Bush's New World Order meant a change in policy toward Africa as the USA went in search of a new mission, yet this quickly changed as humanitarian intervention in the Somali conflict led to the loss of American lives. However, the early twenty-first century has seen another sharp change in policy. The events of 9/11, the recognition that Africa is 'a fundamental part of our interconnected world' (Obama 2009), and China's increasing challenge to the USA's interests in Africa, are all driving a new 'forward looking' American approach to the continent.

This chapter proceeds in four stages. The first part considers US engagement with Africa in historical terms, particularly during the Cold War era of US–Soviet Union superpower rivalry. The second part examines the immediate post-Cold War era, in which a New World Order—a vision in which the USA and the UN could combine to establish freedom and respect for all nations—held out the possibility of positive US involvement in Africa. This section also assesses the post-Somalia period when US policy retreated to a more realist approach that linked America's engagement to perceived strategic or national interests. The last part of the second section outlines the renewal of limited US engagement between 1996 and 2001. The third section considers US Africa policy after 9/11.

Consideration is given to President Bush's efforts to incorporate Africa into Washington's global strategic network as part of the new war on terror, and the fundamentally different approach of the Obama administration, which insists that strong institutions in Africa are the key to resolving both development and security challenges in 'our interconnected world' (Obama 2009). Finally, the concluding section contends that while President Obama's call for political transformation in Africa is an ambitious long-term policy, its sustainability, at least in the near term, will depend on indications that the democratization process is deepening on the continent.

USA–Africa relations: history and the Cold War

Despite deep historic linkages between the USA and Africa, there is general agreement that US Africa policies from the founding of the Republic in 1789 to the present have been marked by indifference at worst, and neglect at best. Africa has very often been treated as marginal in official foreign policy-making circles, compared to the time and resources allocated to other regions considered to be of greater concern (Schraeder 1993: 776).

However, as Box 17.1 makes clear, US engagement with Africa did increase with the onset of the Cold War. The Cold War brought about a fundamental change in American foreign policy. In a policy of 'selective engagement', Washington essentially treated African countries as pawns in a global strategic contest with the Soviet Union (Keller 2006: 3–4). Republican and Democratic administrations alike supported American allies on the African continent and sought to undermine African countries that were friendly towards Moscow. Economic and military assistance was directed to key allies, such as President Mobutu Sese Seko of Zaire, the apartheid regime in South Africa, and Emperor Haile Selassie of Ethiopia, as well as anti-communist rebel organizations, like Jonas Savimbi's UNITA in Angola.

But while US engagement in Africa was largely defined by Cold War competition, developments in Africa did play a part in actually shaping Washington's containment policy, aimed at preventing the spread of communism. Nowhere was this truer than in the Horn of Africa, on the east of the continent, comprising the states of Ethiopia, Djibouti, Eritrea, and Somalia. Having

been displaced in Ethiopia by the Soviet Union, the USA (under President Jimmy Carter) was left as a bystander as Moscow launched a massive military intervention to determine the outcome of the Ethiopian–Somali war of 1977–8 (Patman 1990: 204–54). That experience helped to end the era of superpower détente, a short period in which tensions had eased and exemplified by the signing of the Strategic Arms Limitation treaties (SALT) aimed at reducing nuclear arsenal build-ups.

The new strategic significance of Africa during the Cold War period received some institutional expression in Washington. In 1958, the State Department created a separate Bureau of African Affairs (Schraeder 1994: 16). Then, in 1960, the CIA established its own separate Africa Division within the Deputy Directorate of Operations (DDO), which had responsibility for mounting covert actions throughout the globe. However, the Defense Department was relatively late among the national security bureaucracies in acknowledging the importance of Africa. In 1982, the Office of International Security Affairs (ISA) appointed a Deputy Assistant Secretary of Defense to head the newly created Office of African Affairs (Schraeder 1994: 18). At the same time, a number of other executive agencies became involved in the making of US Africa policy. These included the United States Agency for International Development (USAID), the Departments of Treasury and Commerce, and the US Information Agency (USIA). Sitting on top of this constellation of loosely allied organizations was the president.

BOX 17.1: Presidential leadership

As in other areas of foreign policy, the president has been the dominant influence on US policy towards Africa. At least four variables have affected presidential interest in Africa:

1. *Low level of attention paid to African issues.* Although contacts between the USA and Africa have expanded in both quantity and quality during the post-Second World War period, presidents from Harry Truman to George W. Bush traditionally have been the least interested in, and subsequently have paid the least amount of attention to, Africa, relative to other regions of the world. But the Obama administration has attempted to break this pattern by classifying Africa as a top US foreign policy concern.

2. *American assumption of European responsibility for Africa.* Most presidents (although in varying degrees) traditionally have looked upon Africa as a special area of influence and responsibility of the former European colonial powers. This perception has sometimes manifested itself in relatively slow American responses to some African conflicts, such as Somalia (1988–91), Rwanda (1994), and Sierra Leone

(1999). Again, President Obama has challenged this trend by saying it is high time that Africa took responsibility for shaping its own future.

3. *East–West dimension of the Africa situation.* The Cold War dimension was another element that influenced presidential attention to African issues. The threat posed by the Soviet Union and its allies to US interests in Africa was of concern to presidents from Truman to Bush Sr. Although there were variations in the assessment of the Soviet threat, all presidents during this period sought to limit Soviet influence in Africa.

4. *African-based threats to US national security.* After 9/11, the Bush administration publicly acknowledged that weak or failed states in Africa could provide a sanctuary for terrorist groups, like al-Qaeda, that seek to target the USA. The Obama administration agreed there was a threat but argued such states are not simply African problems—they are global security challenges that affect America, Africa, and the world.

(Adapted from Schraeder 1994: 12–15)

KEY POINTS

❑ Historically the USA has had little interest in Africa, despite the deep historical linkages shared.

❑ During the Cold War US engagement with Africa increased, as the USA attempted to stop the spread of Soviet influence on the African continent, while increasing US influence.

❑ During the Cold War incidents in Africa also helped to shape the USA's policies towards the Soviet Union.

❑ A number of US departments set up divisions focused on Africa during the Cold War.

The USA and Africa in a post-Cold War world

Bush's New World Order and Africa

The end of the Cold War in the late 1980s seemed to offer an extraordinary opportunity for a policy of positive US engagement with Africa. At the beginning of the new era, the George H. W. Bush and Bill Clinton administrations appeared confident about constructing a New World Order. For many observers, the decisive military victory of the US-led coalition in the Persian Gulf War of 1990–1, during which the coalition successfully repelled Iraq's invasion of Kuwait, seemed to affirm the reality of

this new order. Three elements appeared central to Bush's new vision (Sloan 1991: 21–2). First, the conviction that the new order should guarantee security, defend freedom, promote democracy, and enforce the rule of law. Second, the belief that the key diplomatic and political institution for operating and managing the new order was the UN. It should be noted that the UN was the forum in which international opinion against Saddam Hussein's invasion of Kuwait was mobilized. Third, the Bush administration anticipated an active leadership role for the USA, in partnership with the UN, in creating and maintaining this new order. The model of the Persian Gulf crisis was one of strong US leadership, albeit one underpinned by UN-authorized coalition diplomacy.

During the period 1989–92, Africa featured in Washington's vision of a New World Order. In the area of conflict resolution, the USA, Russia, Portugal, Cuba, and South Africa began working together to broker a negotiated settlement to the Angolan civil war (Lawson 2007: 1). At the same time, the USA and Russia worked closely through the UN to bring an end to the civil war in Mozambique and facilitate the independence of Namibia. Political reform was also emphasized. After Mengistu Haile Mariam's exit from Addis Ababa in May 1991, Washington played a crucial role in establishing transitional arrangements in Ethiopia by backing an Ethiopian People's Revolutionary Democratic Front (EPRDF) takeover of the country and endorsing the Eritrean People's Liberation Front (EPLF) proposal for a UN-supervised referendum to decide the issue of Eritrean independence (Dagne 1991: 3). Meanwhile, the USA, Britain, and France each announced that future foreign aid to Africa would be contingent on democratization. Between 1990 and 1992, the USA delivered on this pledge by cutting off assistance to long-time Cold War allies, like Zaire, Liberia, and the Sudan, which resisted political liberalization, and redirecting its resources to countries such as South Africa, Ethiopia, and Mozambique that were actively engaged in the democratization process.

Intervention in Somalia

However, the most visible expression of a new American approach to Africa was the 1992–3 humanitarian intervention in Somalia. In 1992, constant civil war and drought had combined to produce a catastrophic famine killing an estimated 300,000 Somalis. On 3 December 1992, the UN Security Council, in its capacity to decide on matters of international peace and security, recognizing that the situation in Somalia had become 'intolerable', authorized a US-led Unified Task Force (UNITAF) to use 'all necessary means to establish as soon as possible a secure environment for humanitarian relief operations' (UNSCR 794, 3 December 1992).

The intervention was a landmark decision for both the UN and the USA. It was the first time the Security Council had sanctioned a major enforcement action under Chapter VII of the UN Charter, which legally binds all members in a theoretically sovereign state. For the USA, the offer by an outgoing administration of President George H. W. Bush to lead a UN-backed force in Somalia was an abrupt departure from previous American policy. The turnaround followed a 'heated debate'[1] within the US government and President Bush's (belated) recognition in July 1992 that 'something must be done'[2] about Somalia. In any event, the US decision was virtually unprecedented. It was the first time in recent memory that the USA explicitly justified sending its troops to a foreign country, not to safeguard US strategic interests, but to perform a humanitarian mission. At the same time, Bush's decision to intervene in Somalia marked a major change in US policy toward UN peacekeeping. The administration indicated before the humanitarian intervention even began that a sizeable portion of US forces deployed in Somalia would stay on to serve as full members of the UN peacekeeping force that would replace the US-led coalition. Thus, in a clear break from the past, the USA was prepared in principle to allow its forces to operate under UN military command.

The Somali crisis highlighted seven key features of the emerging post-Cold War security environment. First, weak or failed states—that is states with little to no legitimate or functioning government and/or a government with little to no control over its territory—were now the main source of threat and instability in the world; second, these new civil conflicts were typically characterized by the absence or inadequacy of legitimate governance; third, many of the 'new wars' were driven by issues of identity and often involved the mobilization of movements along ethnic, tribal, racial, and religious lines; fourth, civil conflicts such as Somalia served to stimulate calls for higher standards of governance, including the spread of democracy; fifth, the globalized mass media now had the ability—the so-called 'CNN effect', the ability to use their influence through raising awareness—to help internationalize internal conflicts; sixth, the potential for economic and military overspill from intrastate conflicts challenged the old sovereign distinction between domestic and external policy in the field of security; and finally, the capacity of the international community to respond to

> **KEY QUOTES 17.1:** Africa and the US national interest

No other continent has been so consistently ignored by our policy-makers, and yet none but Europe has been so continually connected to important developments in America, from the founding of the Republic in the era of the Atlantic slave trade to the inauguration of training exercises for the new Rapid Development Force.

(Jackson cited in Schraeder 1994)

Africa does not fit into the national security interest.

(George W. Bush cited in Cameron 2002)

The first concern, of course, would be to make sure that Somalia does not become an al-Qaeda safe haven, it doesn't become a place from which terrorists can plot and plan.

(George W. Bush cited in Aljazeera.Net 2006)

I see Africa as a fundamental part of our interconnected world, as partners with America on behalf of the future we want for all of our children. That partnership must be grounded in mutual responsibility and mutual respect.

(Barack Obama, Ghana, 2009)

major security challenges was largely determined by the stance of the USA, the sole superpower.

The retreat to 'the Mogadishu line'

But if Somalia was a paradigm for post-Cold War security, the Bush and Clinton administrations struggled to come to terms with it. The US-led UN operation ran into problems almost immediately and ultimately proved to be a profound disappointment. Nation building was not written into the Unified Task Force's (UNITAF) mandate and instead of striving to stabilize Somalia through political reform, UNITAF concentrated largely on short-term humanitarian needs.

When its successor mission, the United Nations Operation in Somalia (UNOSOM II), became embroiled in major hostilities with the warlord General Aideed's faction, Clinton's handling of the Somali crisis was singled out for fierce criticism by Republicans, like John Bolton and Charles Krauthammer, and conservative Democrats, such as Senator Robert Byrd. They claimed the Clinton administration had abandoned the hard-headed approach of former President George Bush, and taken a multilateralist line that had 'no conceivable connection to the US national interest' (Bolton 1994: 56–66). These observers simply did not believe that the typical failed or failing state was geostrategically important to the USA.

Having warned it would be 'open season' on Americans all over the world if the USA pulled out of Somalia in the wake of the Black Hawk Down episode on

3 October 1993, President Clinton nevertheless proceeded to quickly announce a scheduled withdrawal of US troops by March 1994. That decision effectively ended the US–UN experiment with peace enforcement in Somalia and eventually led to the humiliating withdrawal of all UN troops from the country in March 1995 (Patman 2001: 59).

Reeling from the Somali fiasco, President Clinton sought to quell domestic unease over US participation in future UN operations. In May 1994, the Clinton administration passed Presidential Decision Directive (PDD) 25. This directive said the USA would only participate in UN peacekeeping missions if they were in the US national interest. Moreover, PDD 25 listed seven factors that American officials would review before approving UN operations to be carried out by non-Americans. PDD 25 signalled a clear shift away from Bush's New World Order vision and what Clinton called 'assertive multilateralism' towards a more unilateral, state-centred approach to international security (Lawson 2007: 2).

Thus, in the wake of the unsuccessful US–UN operation in Somalia, there was a determination in Washington not to cross 'the Mogadishu line' and engage in peace operations that had the potential to expand into armed nation-building actions containing the attendant risk of US casualties. The first major test of the new policy would be genocide in Rwanda, which began to unfold as PDD 25 was released. Reluctant to do anything that might draw the USA in, the Clinton administration blocked the idea of an early

---

📢 **MAJOR DEBATES AND THEIR IMPACT 17.1:** The responsibility to protect?

By the early 1990s a wave of brutal internal conflicts was enveloping much of eastern Europe and the developing world. In reaction a challenge to state sovereignty soon arose—the responsibility to protect citizens facing brutal oppression, insurgency, state failure, and genocide was seen by many as giving the right to undertake humanitarian interventions in such countries. International humanitarian law, scholarly opinions, and influential leaders all had a role to play. However, this concept was not without detractors: many in the developing world saw the doctrine of the responsibility to protect as a direct threat to their sovereignty, and for this reason the idea has never been universally accepted. The obligation to protect has been applied in US policies toward Africa in a very on-again off-again fashion. While Somalia was a humanitarian intervention, its consequences led to PDD 25, and in the aftermath the Tutsi population of Rwanda suffered genocide. Many other instances across Africa have shown that the responsibility to protect is a doctrine which is accepted but not often applied by the developed world (see International Commission on Intervention and State Sovereignty 2001).

---

deployment of UN troops in Rwanda in the Security Council (Johnston and Dagne 1997: 191). Requests from General Romeo Dallaire, the commander of UN forces in Rwanda, to oversee the implementation of the Abuja Accords ending the war between the government and the Rwandan Patriot Front, for reinforcements to forestall the prospect of genocide were declined, and when the genocide duly began all UN forces were quickly withdrawn. But while the Clinton administration could use PDD 25 to reject pleas for humanitarian intervention, there was the problem of the obligation to act against genocide under the Geneva Conventions, which govern the laws of war and the treatment of civilians. Consequently, the Clinton administration refused to classify the slaughter in Rwanda as genocide until events had taken their course, and 800,000 people had been killed in the most barbaric circumstances. The only response from the international community to the Rwandan genocide was a very late UN-authorized intervention by France.

US concerns about conflicts in Africa, and the perceived risk of becoming involved when no American national interests were deemed to be stake, had several other consequences. PDD 25 called for regional organizations to take on more of the peacekeeping burden, with UN Security Council endorsement. This move served to reduce US engagement in Africa, where many of the UN peacekeeping missions were deployed. The USA and the UN were already supporting the peacekeeping efforts of the Economic Community of West African States (ECOWAS) in Liberia.

US direct support to the ECOWAS Monitoring Group (ECOMOG) between 1991 and 1996 averaged about $15 million annually. The costs of the operation, around $1 billion, were largely shouldered by Nigeria (Malan 1999).

The period of retreat from Africa also affected US support for democratization on the continent. While the Clinton administration did apply some serious pressure on the autocratic regimes in Sudan and Nigeria to move towards political reform in 1995, there was a tacit recognition in Washington that political liberalization was associated with security problems in several countries in the mid-1990s. These included the Central African Republic, Congo-Brazzaville, Lesotho, and most strikingly Rwanda's neighbour Burundi. In July 1996, the democratic government in Burundi was overthrown in a military coup which returned former president Major Pierre Buyoya to power. But the Clinton administration supported the new military government in the expectation that Buyoya would be able to establish greater security in the country.

Furthermore, US assistance to Africa continued to decline. The decline had begun in the late 1980s with the virtual elimination of Security Assistance and Economic Support Funds to former Cold War allies. In 1995, the US Congress sought to reorganize and substantially trim the existing US foreign assistance programmes. Some members of Congress questioned the logic of assisting Africa in the post-Cold War era. But congressional supporters of African aid opposed the restructuring initiative and managed to limit the severity of the proposed new cuts (Copson 2004).

The renewal of limited US engagement in Africa

A period of renewed but limited US engagement in Africa began in the first year of Clinton's second term of office. It reflected the gradual recognition that in a globalizing world the USA could not afford to strictly condition its involvement in Africa according to PDD 25 criteria. The lessons of Somalia, Rwanda, and Liberia were that the civil wars of the 1990s could be major international security problems; the USA could not be seen to do nothing in the face of such challenges; and the USA could not realistically expect African states to contain instability entirely on their own.

Re-engagement in African security

In its second term, the Clinton administration followed a two-pronged approach to Africa that occupied a middle-ground position somewhere between the narrow confines of PDD 25 and a broader conception of human security that sought to reconcile the security and welfare of the individual (including their economic well-being) with more traditional security concerns. First, the Clinton administration sought to address security threats emanating from Africa, including conflicts between and within states, terrorism, the HIV/AIDS pandemic, trafficking in drugs, and illicit arms. Confronted with the possibility that Burundi would follow Rwanda's descent into civil war, the Clinton administration proposed in October 1996 the establishment of an African Crisis Response Force (ACRF) (Howe 2001: 248–51). It was proposed that ACRF would consist of a standing force of 5000 African troops, trained and equipped by Western countries, which would be capable of rapid deployment for UN-authorized peacekeeping operations. But the plan received a very cool reception from virtually all quarters in Africa. To countries like South Africa and Nigeria, ACRF seemed to be a case of the Clinton administration seeking to exercise power in Africa without accepting responsibility in the process.

Consequently, the ACRF concept was replaced in late 1996 by the African Crisis Response Initiative (ACRI). This new initiative was essentially a bilateral training programme, which was intended to improve the capabilities of African forces participating in peacekeeping. While South Africa and Nigeria showed little interest, other countries, starting with Malawi, Senegal, and Uganda, agreed to accept US training and equipment. However,

critics charged that ACRI-provided equipment was often used against internal and external adversaries rather than in peacekeeping. During the transition from the Clinton to the George W. Bush administration, ACRI evolved into the African Contingency Operations Training and Assistance (ACOTA) programme. The latter focuses on 'training the trainer', delivering programmes to meet the needs of specific recipient countries, and training for peace enforcement as well as peacekeeping. Between 1997 and 2005, the USA spent $121 million to train 10,000 troops from Benin, Botswana, Ethiopia, Ghana, Kenya, Malawi, Mali, Mozambique, and Senegal (Lawson 2007: 4).

Despite these measures, the security threats faced by Africa, and the USA in Africa, worsened. In August 1998, the US embassies in Tanzania and Kenya were bombed by al-Qaeda terrorists, killing 253 people. The al-Qaeda terrorists suspected of involvement were believed to have had links with Somalia and the Sudan (Rothchild 2006: 250). Furthermore, a bloody border dispute between two US allies, Ethiopia and Eritrea, erupted in 1998 and killed more than 70,000 people over the next two years. The civil war in Angola resumed; and a civil war in the Democratic Republic of Congo (DRC) escalated, killing more than one million people and eventually involving seven African countries supporting the government of the DRC or its opponents. Moreover, in 1999, at a time when the Clinton administration endorsed a humanitarian intervention by NATO in Kosovo, Sierra Leone endured a brutal civil war involving rebel groups opposed to a democratically elected government. Eventually, the British, not the USA, intervened militarily to re-establish some semblance of order in Sierra Leone (Keller 2006: 7–14).

Re-engagement in poverty, trade, and health

As Box 17.2 shows, President Clinton's administration was crucial in bringing the AIDS pandemic into the global political arena. However President Clinton's policies in regard to the socio-economic plight of the African continent went beyond this. The Clinton administration sought to accelerate Africa's integration into the global economy. A key political initiative in this area was the Africa Growth and Opportunity Act (AGOA). This was passed in 2000 despite opposition from domestic constituencies in the USA that feared increased textile exports from Africa. AGOA provided $500 million in support of economic development to African countries embracing free market principles, the rule of law, and political pluralism. It also provided preferential access to the US market for African countries deemed eligible. Both Presidents Clinton and Bush designated most African countries as AGOA eligible. As a policy instrument, AGOA was the embodiment of the 'trade not aid' rhetoric of the mid- to late 1990s in which American and African leaders, such as Yoweri Museveni of Uganda, agreed that enhanced access to the American market would prove more effective in facilitating economic growth and development in Africa than decades of foreign assistance.

While the Office of the US Trade Representative hailed the success of AGOA after its implementation, critics charged there was little cause for celebration. The provisions of AGOA included numerous protections for American producers who might be harmed by competition from Africa. At the same time, oil exports have always accounted for the majority of African exports to the USA. Although the USA has a clear interest in increasing its international market share in African oil exports, the oil sector by itself is unlikely to stimulate more broad-based economic growth and development in Africa, especially when non-oil African exporters find it so hard to break into the American market. In other words, critics argue that AGOA served more than anything as a vehicle for the USA to consolidate its own strategic interests around Nigeria and South Africa, two of the bigger economic players in Africa, and, to a lesser degree, mineral-rich countries like Angola, Uganda, and the Sudan (Cheru 2006: 219–22). To a degree, the numbers back up such claims. Records show a remarkable rise in US imports of products from four African nations in particular since the implementation of AGOA, with only slight changes for the remainder of the continent. The total value of imports from Nigeria, Algeria, Angola, and South Africa almost tripled between 2000 and 2006. For Algeria alone imports increased almost sixfold, while Nigerian imports make up well over one-third of all US imports from Africa as of 2006 (source: US Department of Trade and Commerce).

Re-engagement on an official level

Another sign of renewed American interest was the flurry of visits to Africa by high-level officials from Washington. President Clinton spent two weeks in Africa in August 1998, Madeleine Albright, the Secretary of State, visited the continent three times between 1997 and 2000, Richard Holbrooke visited the continent in December 2000 in his capacity as US Ambassador to the UN, and Colin Powell, the Secretary of State for the first George W. Bush administration, paid an official visit to Africa within five months of assuming his new position in January 2001. To some extent, the increased political engagement with Africa reflected the lobbying efforts of the congressional Black Caucus and other African-American groups. Indeed, Clinton took several members of the Caucus with him on his 1998 trip to Africa when he made a major effort to build bridges with the continent (Cameron 2002: 170). He was the first US president to publicly admit that 'the United States has not always done the right thing by Africa', and in a brief visit to Rwanda, Clinton apologized for American inaction during the 1994 massacres, implying that US military power could be deployed to prevent future genocides (Schabas 1999: 6–7). It should be added that the Clinton administration had firmly supported the establishment of a UN tribunal charged with the indictment and prosecution of individuals accused of crimes against humanity and genocide in Rwanda.

Despite the increased US involvement in Africa, there was little sign that President George W. Bush would carry on where the Clinton administration left off. US national interests were central to Clinton's policies in Africa after the Somali fiasco, but he demonstrated, particularly in his second administration, a certain flexibility to balance US needs and objectives with an African environment that had been profoundly changed by the end of the Cold War. But while Bush appointed African-Americans as his main foreign policy advisers, he did not seem to see Africa as a priority for US foreign policy. Initially, President George W. Bush strongly rejected the notion of 'nation building', embraced the traditional view that security was fundamentally determined by the military means of sovereign states, and advocated 'a distinctly American internationalism'. In 2001, the US Congress authorized $1.6 billion in aid to Africa which, as Fraser Cameron points out, was less than Americans spend each day on health care (Cameron 2002: 170).

BOX 17.2: Presidential initiatives on HIV/AIDS

Presidents Bill Clinton, George W. Bush, and Barack Obama have all taken a proactive role in combating HIV/AIDS, a disease which has decimated the African continent. According to a report produced by the National Intelligence Council (NIC) in 2000, sub-Saharan Africa accounted for four-fifths of the 22 million deaths from AIDS since the beginning of the epidemic around 1980. The report added that AIDS was devastating African countries, depriving them of the educated and skilled individuals required to build democratic governments, professional militaries, and free market economies.

The Clinton administration was instrumental in moving the HIV/AIDS pandemic onto the international agenda. AIDS in Africa was the focus of the US presidency of the UN Security Council in January 2000. Vice-President Gore emphasized that 'AIDS is not just a humanitarian crisis. It is a security crisis—because it threatens not just individual citizens, but the very institutions that define and defend the character of a society' (Al Gore in Cameron 2002: 168). Before Clinton left office, he signed the Global AIDS and Tuberculosis Relief Act.

President Bush announced in September 2001 a $200 million contribution to the UN AIDS campaign and committed the USA to an active role in fighting the disease (Cameron 2002: 168–9). Prior to his 2003 visit to Africa, Bush announced the President's Emergency Plan For AIDS Relief (PEPFAR) a commitment of $15 billion over five years to fight this disease. Then, in May 2007, Bush requested a doubling of funding to fight AIDS, with up to an extra $30 billion being invested over the next five years (Office of the US Global AIDS Coordinator 2007). The Obama administration has built on the efforts of the Bush team by pledging in 2009 $63 billion over six years to continue PEPFAR and combating other public health challenges in Africa such as malaria, TB, and polio. According to President Obama, America is 'is called to act by our conscience but also by our common interest' (Obama 2009) in halting the spread of disease in an interconnected world.

KEY POINTS

- ❏ The end of the Cold War gave rise to the opportunity to drastically reassess US policy toward Africa.
- ❏ At the beginning of the 1990s President George H. W. Bush envisioned a New World Order, in which the UN (with strong leadership by the USA) would take a more proactive role, particularly in conflict resolution and peacekeeping.
- ❏ This New World Order came to a dramatic halt after the USA's disastrous intervention in Somalia, and President Clinton's issuing of PDD 25.

- ❏ By President Clinton's second term (1996–2000) the USA began to re-engage with Africa as it became clear that failing states were a threat to international security. During this time a series of training programmes for African troops was undertaken by the USA, and the AGOA Act was implemented in the hope of integrating Africa into the world economy.

The USA and Africa after 9/11

From Bush's war on terror to Obama's democratization push

After the terrorist attacks of 9/11 the Bush administration revised its approach towards Africa and acknowledged that the continent was a major strategic concern for the USA in the war on terror, in which the USA and its allies sought to reduce the ability of terrorist organizations to function and carry out terrorist activities. Previous opposition to nation building was quietly de-emphasized as the Bush administration now recognized that weak or failing states could be a security threat to the USA. Such societies were perceived as potential safe havens for terrorist groups to plan, prepare, and launch attacks against Western targets. The 2002 National Security Strategy (NSS) asserted that 'America is now threatened less by conquering states than we are by falling ones' (Bush 2002: 1–31). Africa was seen as a prime target for terrorist organizations. According to a Pentagon official forty out of forty-eight countries in sub-Saharan Africa were not in control of their borders and could harbour terrorists (Malan 2002). The belief that Africa is susceptible to terrorist penetration also brought a new but narrowly based recognition that poverty and injustice could play a part in this situation.

With respect to the perceived threat of international terrorism in Africa, there were two main Bush policy initiatives: the deployment of the Combined Joint Task Force-Horn of Africa (CJTF-HOA) in December 2002, and the Pan-Sahel Initiative/Trans-Sahel Counter-Terrorism Initiative, which also began in late 2002. CJTF-HOA, staffed by about 1500 US troops in Djibouti, had the mission of 'detecting, disrupting and ultimately defeating transnational terrorist groups operating in the region—denying safe havens, external support and material assistance for transnational terrorism in the region' (US Central Command in Lawson 2007: 7). The Pan-Sahel Initiative (PSI) was a more indirect effort to boost the border defence capabilities of countries to the west of the Horn: Chad, Niger, Mali, and Mauritania.

Beyond this specific counter-terrorism strategy, the 2006 National Security Strategy envisaged, amongst other things, 'focused attention' to anchor states like South Africa, Nigeria, Kenya, and Ethiopia to bolster Africa's resistance to transnational threats. But this approach proved problematic in practice. In December 2006, for example, the Bush administration backed the expansion of an Ethiopian troop presence in stateless Somalia to oust the Islamic Courts Union (ICU) and its militias from the capital, Mogadishu. Instead of buttressing the weak but internationally recognized Transitional Federal Government (TFG), the Ethiopian presence and US air strikes against al Qaeda targets sparked national outrage and enabled Eritrea—a foe of Ethiopia's since their border war of 1998-2000—to arm and co-ordinate an insurgency that quickly spread in 2007 to the relatively peaceful north-east of Somalia and generally boosted the position of al-Qaeda and other foreign Islamist militants in the country (Patman 2007).

Barack Obama had campaigned against George W. Bush's ideas and approach to national security, and his election victory in November 2008 brought a more integrated US approach towards Africa. This shift reflected Obama's personal connection with the continent and also his conviction that in the twenty-first century the world will be shaped by what happens in Africa as well as what happens in Moscow, Beijing, or Washington. In specific terms, the Obama administration jettisoned Bush's war on terror and Islamic terrorism rhetoric, but fully accepted the gravity of the danger presented by failed states in Africa and elsewhere. Obama's 2010 *National Security Strategy* stated that, amongst other things, 'failing states breed conflict and endanger regional and global security' (The White House, 2010, pp. 8–13). And it was the policy response to this challenge that basically differentiated the Africa policy of the Obama administration.

According to President Obama, American policy in Africa is now based on a simple truth: 'Governments that respect, that govern by consent and not coercion, are more prosperous, they are more stable, and more successful than governments that do not' (Obama 2009). In a blunt speech to Ghana's parliament, Obama said democracy is the key to Africa's renaissance: 'That is the ingredient which has been missing in far too many places, for far too long. That's the change that can unlock Africa's potential. And that is a responsibility that can only be met by Africans.' (Obama 2009). In other words, US policy must address the causes of state failure in Africa—authoritarian and unrepresentative government—as well as its symptoms—genocide and terrorism. Ultimately, then, the Obama team believes that if Africa gets the politics right, stability and development will follow. On this view, 'it will be vibrant democracies like Botswana and Ghana which roll back the causes of conflict and advance the frontiers of peace and prosperity' (Obama 2009)

Certainly, the Obama team seems prepared for a higher level of engagement with Africa than previously. Besides the president himself, the administration has a number of players with African experience or expertise. These include Johnnie Carson, the Assistant Secretary of State for Africa, Susan Rice, the Ambassador to the UN and formerly Bill Clinton's Assistant Secretary of State for Africa, and Gayle Smith and Michelle Gavin at the National Security Council (Dowden 2009). At the same time, the Obama administration has actively pursued its diplomatic vision of 'partnership' with Africa. In July 2009 President Obama visited Ghana, in September 2009 Obama hosted a lunch for 26 African heads of state at the UN General Assembly, during 2009 and 2010 Obama met in the US with President Ellen Johnson-Sirleaf of Liberia, President Kikwete of Tanzania, President Khama of Botswana, Prime Minister Morgan Tsvangarai of Zimbabwe, President Goodluck Jonathan of Nigeria, and President Zuma of South Africa. In addition, Secretary of State Hillary Clinton visited Kenya, Angola, South Africa, Democratic Republic of Congo, Nigeria, Liberia, and Cape Verde in August 2009, Vice-President Joe Biden visited Kenya and South Africa in June 2010, the US Ambassador to the UN, Susan Rice, visited Liberia and Rwanda in June 2009, Deputy Secretary of State Jack Lew spent time in Ethiopia and Tanzania in June 2009 and Mali and Nigeria in May 2009, and Under Secretary of State for Democracy and Global Affairs Maria Otero headed the US delegation to the African Union Summit in Addis Ababa in January 2010 (Carson 2010a).

Case study: Sudan's civil war and Obama's peace diplomacy

The Comprehensive Peace Agreement (CPA) encompassed a set of agreements signed by the Sudan People's Liberation (SPLM) and the government of Sudan in January 2005. Pushed largely by the George W. Bush administration, the CPA was intended to end the second North–South civil war in Sudan that had lasted for over two decades and cost about two million lives. It also envisaged the establishment of democratic governance countryside and a timetable by which South Sudan would have a referendum on whether it should be independent or remain united with the North (*Christian Science Monitor* 2011).

But the process of implementing the CPA soon ran into problems. On 11 October 2007, the SPLM withdrew from the government of national unity, accusing the central government led by President Omar al-Bashir of violating the terms of the CPA. The continuing violence in the western region of Darfur, where an estimated 300,000 people died after non-Arabs rebels rose up in 2003 against Sudan's government, helped to fuel suspicions on both sides. While the SPLM agreed to rejoin the government on 13 December 2007, following an agreement for a census—vital for the planned referendum—and the withdrawal of remaining northern Sudanese troops from the south, the CPA still looked fragile when the new Obama administration took office in January 2009.

In an effort to boost the implementation of the CPA, President Obama invested significant 'diplomatic capital' in Sudan. He quickly appointed General Scott Gration as Special Presidential Envoy for Sudan. Gration soon established a reputation as a determined 'hands on' operator who helped applied US pressure on both Khartoum and the south Sudan leadership to finish preparations for the January 2011 referendum (*Reuters* 2011) At times, Gration's methods, which included incentives to Khartoum such as a promise after the referendum to begin work to remove Sudan from the US list of state sponsors of terrorism, caused strains with other Obama administration officials. At the same time, the US added ten new officers to the US Consulate in Juba, including veteran diplomat Princeton Lyman, to help keep the referendum on track. In addition, Vice-President Joe Biden, during a one-week visit to Africa in June 2010, discussed Sudan with President Mubarak, had an extended meeting with Thabo Mbeki, the AU's point person on Sudan, and conferred in Kenya with Salva Kiir, the President of the Government of South Sudan and other Sudanese leaders (Carson 2010b). Moreover, in December 2010, Obama called Salva Kiir by telephone offering strong support for the referendum and frequently mentioned the referendum in conversations with the Presidents of Russia and China, two countries which could wield influence over President al-Bashir's government (Pace 2011).

In January 2011, South Sudan voted overwhelmingly to secede from Sudan and form Africa's newest country.

President Obama hailed the outcome as 'inspiring' and said the US would formally recognize South Sudan's independence in July. Millions of voters, Obama said, had decided 'their own future' and marked 'another step forward in Africa's long journey toward justice and democracy' (*Christian Science Monitor* 2011).

Conflict resolution, aid, and trade

Regarding US support for conflict resolution in Africa, the response of the Bush administration to the Liberian crisis in 2003 and to what it called 'genocide' in Darfur, Sudan, in 2004 could be described as cautious. According to Latitia Lawson, these two cases indicate 'some recovery from the Somalia Syndrome, but also [demonstrate] its continuing influence' (Lawson 2007: 5). In the case of Liberia, the Bush administration came under heavy pressure internationally to intervene as rebel forces began surrounding Monrovia in summer 2003. The Bush administration eventually agreed to send a peacekeeping force but only after President Charles Taylor resigned and left the country. Despite the historical connection between the USA and Liberia, the Bush administration only committed a small number of US peacekeepers and then only briefly. However, it did provide monetary and other forms of support for Nigeria to take a lead peacekeeping role, which reflected the administration's commitment to assisting African states in leading regional peacekeeping endeavours. The crisis in Darfur began in 2003 with a local uprising against what many in the province felt were biased policies and neglect by the government in Khartoum. Consequently 'Arab' *janjaweed* militia forces began methodically evicting 'African' farmers from their land, with widespread reports of killing, raping, and the burning of villages. Within a year, Secretary of State Colin Powell went to Sudan to investigate the situation and declared upon his return that genocide had indeed occurred in Darfur. But as a contracting party to the Geneva Conventions, US action was largely confined to demanding a full UN investigation into Darfur and providing diplomatic and financial support for the African Union to facilitate a negotiated settlement to the conflict (Lawson 2007: 5).

In contrast, the Obama administration appears committed to working with African states and the international community to address conflicts on the continent. President Obama has frankly acknowledged that for many Africans 'conflict is a part of life' and this is 'a millstone around Africa's neck' (Obama 2009). But the administration said America 'must stand up to inhumanity in our midst [in Africa]', and would use diplomacy, technical assistance, and logistical support to do so. These efforts have been evident in a number of hot-spots. The case study above indicates the Obama administration is following a step-by-step approach in Sudan where resolving the north–south conflict is seen as a necessary prelude to tackling the ongoing violent struggle in Darfur. In the DRC, former Congressman Howard Wolpe is spearheading diplomatic actions to bring peace to the Eastern Congo and end the extreme violence against women (Carson 2010b). These concerns were further highlighted when Secretary of State Clinton, following a visit to the DRC in August 2009, announced new funding of $17 million to combat gender and sexual violence in the country (Clinton 2009). Meanwhile, the Obama administration has supported regional initiatives such as the Djibouti peace process to mitigate Somalia's protracted political and humanitarian crisis and provided more than $150 million in humanitarian aid to Somalia in 2009. More recently, some White House officials saw President Obama's pressure on Ivory Coast President Laurent Gbagho to stand down after he refused to concede defeat in an independently monitored election in November 2010 as a model for Obama's growing engagement in Africa. While such involvement could be seen as interference in the internal affairs of African states, President Obama clearly believes he can do something no previous president could do—speak candidly to African leaders without fear of provoking accusations of neo-colonialism or racism (Dowden 2009).

With respect to aid, differences between the two administrations are also evident. The Bush administration launched the Millennium Challenge Account (MCA) initiative in 2003. It called for economic and political reforms in developing countries as a precondition for new additional aid. The USA pledged to increase its core development assistance by 50 per cent over the next three years, resulting in a projected annual increase of $5 billion by 2006 (The White House 2002). While the Millennium initiative represents a step in the direction of recognizing the link between poverty, weak governance, and terrorism, it was slow to actually begin committing funds and to date falls far short of what is required. By the end of 2008, 25 countries were eligible for MCA funding, of which 19 were African, and the MCA had actually signed agreements with eight African countries (Lesotho, Mali, Mozambique, Tanzania, Madagascar, Cape Verde, Benin, and Ghana). These figures suggested the scope of the MCA initiative in Africa is limited by political conditions defined by Washington (Carmody 2005: 97–120).

The Obama administration said it 'can and should do more' to tackle Africa's poverty and relative isolation in the global economy. But any commitment, Obama said, must be greater than annual infusions of foreign aid. It must be based on partnership, not patronage, and help Africa build the capacity on the ground for transformation so that such aid will not be needed in the future (Obama 2009). In 2009, the Obama administration announced a new $3.5 billion food security initiative, Feed the Future, which will assist 12 African countries that are engaged in modernizing their agricultural sectors. This initiative will supply new methods and technologies to African farmers, rather than simply sending American producers or goods to Africa, and is intended to help stimulate 'a Green Revolution in African agriculture' (Carson 2010b) and encourage greater regional integration on the continent. In 2010, the US became the first nation to accredit an ambassador to the new East Africa Community. At the same time, the Obama team built on the aid initiative of the previous administration by concluding MCA compacts with three more African countries, Burkina Faso, Namibia, and Senegal (Millennium Challenge Account 2010).

Furthermore, the Obama administration made it clear that Africa needed more trade and investment. That meant America should do more to open its market to goods and services from Africa, but it also meant that African governments should curb corruption, enforce the rule of law, and deliver results for their people. In the words of Secretary Clinton: 'This is not just good governance—it's also about good business.'(Rice 2009). In particular, the Obama administration wants African countries to maximize the opportunities created by AGOA, a trade preference programme that was intended to boost both the volume and diversity of US

trade with sub-Saharan Africa. Certainly, US–African trade turnover has steadily increased since 2001, the first full year of AGOA implementation. In the last year of the Bush administration in 2008, trade turnover between the US and Africa was $151.8 billion. However, two-way trade actually fell during the first two years of the Obama administration. In 2010, US–African trade turnover stood at $113.2 billion (US Census Bureau 2011). Much of this trade was in energy, textiles, and transportation equipment.

So why has Obama's new partnership with Africa been so disappointing in terms of trade? First, the US economy has severely affected by the worst economic recession since the 1930s and this has impacted on trade relations with Africa. Given this harsh economic environment, there has been little incentive for the Obama team to reduce or dismantle subsidies for US agriculture that distort prices for African farmers. Cotton subsidies, for example, lower the international price, impoverishing cotton-growing countries such as Benin, the Ivory Coast, and Mali (Pace 2011). Second, Obama's approach is ambitious and cannot be expected to generate immediate economic results. The fact that two-thirds of sub-Saharan African nations in 2009 implemented reforms to improve their business environments suggests there may be grounds to anticipate an upturn in US–African trade turnover in late 2011 or 2012. Third, and perhaps most importantly, the African policy of both the Obama administration and the Bush administration has been shaped by internal and external constraints that do not always sit comfortably with American expectations of the continent.

One is America's increasing dependence on African oil. In August 2001, the Assistant Secretary of State for African Affairs, Walter Kansteiner, declared that African oil 'has become a national strategic interest' (Kansteiner in Lawson 2007: 8). African oil currently accounts for 18 per cent of US imported oil and major new American investments are evident in Nigeria, Angola, São Tomé, and Equatorial Africa. Within a decade, African oil is expected to climb to about 25 per cent of US oil imports (Keller 2006: 8). Nigeria is currently the fifth largest crude-oil exporter to the USA; Angola is eighth. Because of the oil imperative, the US imports from Africa have massively and

KEY POINTS

- ❑ After 9/11 the Bush administration revised its policies toward Africa, with the recognition that weak or failing states could be potential safe havens for terrorist organizations.
- ❑ This revision of policy led to two main security initiatives: GJTF-HOA and PSI.
- ❑ Obama campaigned against Bush's approach to national security and his election significantly expanded US policy parameters in Africa.

- ❑ The central focus of the Obama agenda in Africa is the promotion of good governance and democratic institutions.
- ❑ The Obama vision of a US–Africa partnership is potentially complicated by America's growing dependence on African oil and growing Chinese influence on the continent.

consistently exceeded the level of American exports to the continent.

In addition, US diplomacy has been increasingly challenged by China's growing economic (and thus political) engagement of Africa since the turn of the century. China's overall trade with Africa doubled from 2002 to 2003, and then doubled again between 2003 and 2005. This 400 per cent growth in three years comes atop a 700 per cent growth in the decade of the 1990s, and there is no end in sight. China is now Africa's second largest trading partner, behind the USA and ahead of former colonial power Britain. Chinese foreign direct investment in Africa has grown equally dramatically from about $50 million annually between the mid-1990s and 2002, to $100 million in 2003, and $430 million in 2004 (Saunders 2006: 38–54). This budding economic relationship is supported by the China–Africa Cooperation Forum, established by China in 2000 to bring Chinese and African leaders together every three years, much as the France–Africa summit had done throughout the postcolonial period. In stark contrast to the USA's approach to Africa, China maintains a policy of strict non-interference in the internal affairs of its African partners, and seeks mutually beneficial engagement, not good governance. Thus Chinese involvement in Africa threatens to substantially reduce the leverage of the USA and its Western allies, and perhaps undermine the political and economic reform agenda advanced, in particular, by the Obama administration. In 2009, for example, during the 2009 climate summit in Copenhagen the White House was caught off guard when several African countries voted with China and not the US.

Conclusion

While Africa has generally been on the periphery of the USA's foreign policy agenda, the events of 9/11 and the advent of the Obama administration combined to significantly enhance the profile of Africa in American diplomacy. After the attacks on the twin towers, the Bush administration recognized that Africa was part of the battleground for its global war on terror. Amongst other things, the Bush administration established a new military base in Djibouti and bolstered the military capabilities of some state and non-state actors on the African continent. It was a selective form of strategic engagement that included moral concerns, such as poverty relief or resisting the African AIDS pandemic, providing they served US national security interests defined in terms of the global war on terror. Thus, the Bush leadership sought to engage in Africa after 9/11 largely on its own terms. It showed little inclination to acknowledge that in Africa many people faced multiple interlinked threats that included hunger, corruption, lawlessness, disease, and war, as well as terrorism.

Since coming to office in 2009, the Obama administration has gone much further than the Bush administration in the realignment of US Africa policy. Africa is said to be an essential part of an interconnected world and President Obama has called for a new partnership that is based on 'mutual responsibility' (Obama 2009). This approach has elevated Africa as a US foreign policy concern, but also raised the bar in how US policy success is defined in Africa. The Obama administration's call for political transformation in Africa is many ways overdue and sensible, but it has raised hopes that have yet to be fulfilled. On one hand, the Obama agenda in Africa has to compete with other pressing US foreign policy concerns such as winding down the Iraq war, fighting the Taliban in Afghanistan, managing relations with China, and resetting relations with Russia. And even if President Obama can give Africa the attention which it deserves, immense problems on the continent such as intra-state conflicts, widespread poverty, various health pandemics, and the continent's vulnerability to

external pressures will not be quickly resolved by the spread of democracy. On the other hand, despite the difficulties, the Obama strategy in Africa holds some real promise. Given that there are no easy alternative policy options for the White House in Africa, President Obama's focus on political reform on the continent sits comfortably with the values of America's democratic system at home, and a rapidly globalizing world that is challenging the legitimacy of authoritarian regimes in the twenty-first century. Moreover, Obama's personal connection with Africa means he is well placed to deliver the 'tough love' that the continent arguably needs. In 2011, there are expected to be 30 elections across Africa, and this will give the Obama administration a fresh chance to reiterate its central message that partnership with the US requires that these elections be fair, free, and credible.

 CONTROVERSIES 17.1: Trade, pharmaceuticals, and humanitarian interventions

While Presidents Bill Clinton, George W. Bush, and Barack Obama have taken measures to combat HIV/AIDS, and integrate Africa into the world economy, a number of controversies and stumbling blocks remain.

Today drug cocktails are available, which if taken appropriately can transform HIV/AIDS from a virtual death sentence into a chronic disease—in the developed world HIV patients' lifespans have improved exponentially. However, these drugs are still costly; in 2002 the average cost of annual treatment in the USA was $14,000–$34,000 per patient depending on the stage of the disease (CNN.com 2002), which is wholly unaffordable for the majority of regions where HIV/AIDS is most prevalent, particularly the least developing countries. Pharmaceutical companies, many based in the USA, are resistant to significant price reductions in developing countries, given the high cost of research and development. Nevertheless, a loophole in international trade law has allowed an industry of generic anti-retroviral drugs to spring up and developing countries have access to these treatments at far lower prices, around $300 per year. Despite this, for the majority of Africans treatment is still too expensive. Sub-Saharan Africa is more heavily affected by HIV and AIDS than any other region of the world. An estimated 22.5 million people are living with HIV in the region—around two-thirds of the global total. In 2009 around

1.3 million people died from AIDS in sub-Saharan Africa and 1.8 million people became infected with HIV (AVERT 2011).

At the same time US trade policy has been heavily criticized in regard to access and fairness for developing countries. Despite steps forward such as AGOA, protectionist policies remain and developing nations find it impossible to compete and gain access to US markets for many of their primary products. Without a dramatic transformation in US and EU trade policies, and a successful end to the current Doha round of trade negotiations on trade liberalization, developing countries in Africa will have little chance of improving their economic situation through trade.

Finally, the question of humanitarian interventions by the USA in African conflicts has been highly controversial. The cases of Somalia and Rwanda exemplify this. Major debates and their impact 17.1 outlines some of the issues at stake, but a number of questions remain: (1) Should the USA intervene to protect the lives of civilians in other countries when it is not deemed to be in 'the national interest'? (2) Do the USA and the international community have the right to intervene against the wishes of the government of a sovereign state in order to protect the lives of civilians? (3) Should the USA intervene without the authorization of the UN Security Council?

KEY POINTS

❏ While 9/11 led to a change in US Africa policy, the Bush administration largely viewed Africa as a new battle-ground in the global war on terror.

❏ In the post 9/11 period it became evident there was a gulf between the Bush team's national security concerns in Africa and an environment in which many Africans faced multiple interlinked threats.

❏ Despite difficulties, Obama's 'tough love' approach towards Africa—elevating Africa as a foreign policy concern while demanding more democratization there—looks promising and owes a lot to President Obama's family connection with Africa.

? Questions

1. Why was Africa important during the Cold War?

2. How did Africa shape the course of the Cold War? What particular incidents were important in this?

3. How did US policies toward Africa change in the immediate aftermath of the Cold War?

4. What were the implications of the Somali intervention for US policy towards Africa and its foreign policy more generally?

5. How did the USA re-engage with Africa in the mid- to late 1990s? Give specific examples. Do you think it was successful in its efforts?

6. Why did the events of 9/11 change President Bush's attitude toward Africa, and how was this manifested?

7. What were some of the deficiencies in policies under Presidents Clinton and George W. Bush to reduce poverty through the mechanisms of trade and aid?

8. Do you agree with President Obama's view that 'Africa doesn't need strongmen, it needs strong institutions'?

9. What does the outcome of the 2011 referendum in Sudan tell us about the Obama administration's approach to conflict resolution in Africa?

10. Will the Obama administration's focus on good governance in Africa diminish or enhance the Chinese challenge to American interests on the continent?

» Further Reading

Clapham, C. (1996), *Africa and the International System: The Politics of State Survival* (Cambridge: Cambridge University Press).

A solid and thoughtful assessment of the survival challenges facing African states in a radically reshaped international environment.

Davis, J. (ed.) (2007), *Africa and the War on Terrorism* (Aldershot: Ashgate).

A detailed and well-documented portrayal of the war on terror in Africa.

Magyar, K. P. (ed.) (2000), *United States Interests and Policies in Africa: Transition to a New Era* (London: Macmillan).

A useful source for understanding the origins of modern American policy making in relation to Africa.

Morrison, J. S. and Cooke, J. G. (2001), *Africa Policy in the Clinton Years: Critical Choices for the Bush Administration* (Washington, DC: Center for Strategic and International Studies).

This volume focuses on evolving challenges in Africa, examines Clinton's policy toward Africa, and offers some balanced policy recommendations to the new Bush administration.

Rothchild, D. and Keller, E. J. (eds) (2006), *Africa–US Relations: Strategic Encounters* (Boulder, CO: Lynne Rienner Publishers).

An authoritative and multifaceted edited volume of US–African relations in the era defined by both globalization and 9/11.

Schraeder, P. J. (1994), *United States Foreign Policy toward Africa: Incrementalism, Crisis and Change* (Cambridge: Cambridge University Press).

An impressive theoretical and empirical treatment of US policy towards Africa in the Cold War and early post-Cold War period.

Taylor, I. and Williams, P. (2004), *Africa in International Politics: External Involvement on the Continent* (London: Routledge).

A reasonably comprehensive and critical analysis of the policies of the major external actors, including the USA, toward Africa after the Cold War.

 Endnotes

1.   Ambassador Frank G. Wisner, former Under Secretary of State for International Security Affairs, interview with the author, 1 November 1999.

2.   Walter Kansteiner, former Director of African Affairs on the National Security Council staff, interview with the author, 8 November 1999.

 For a range of additional resources to support your learning visit the Online Resource Centre that accompanies this book at www.oxfordtextbooks.co.uk/orc/cox_stokes2e/.

Section 4

Key Issues

18 Global economy

Peter Gowan and Doug Stokes

Chapter contents

Introduction

For a century the United States has had the largest economy in the world and since 1945 it has also possessed the most powerful state, a status enhanced since the collapse of the Soviet bloc. It has thus been in a position to shape the structures of the world economy to a greater degree than any other power. This chapter is designed to introduce you to some of the central debates on how we should understand the efforts of the American state to reshape international economic relations since the 1940s.

We begin by exploring debates on the sources and mechanisms of American policy on the world economy. We then turn to debates about the substance of American efforts to shape the world economy. And we will conclude with a brief assessment of current debates about how successful American efforts in this field have been from the angle of sustaining American economic strength within international capitalism.[1]

The actors and mechanisms of American economic strategy

Despite continual executive efforts to assert institutionalized control over American external economic policy since 1945, the Congress retains an extraordinary degree of power over the conduct of this aspect of American foreign policy. In comparison with other legislatures, the Congress is supremely well equipped for defending specific domestic interests in this field. Its members are acutely sensitive to the business interests of their constituencies and Congress possesses not only constitutional blocking power in this area but also an extraordinary degree of legislative initiative. So groups within it have repeatedly mounted campaigns in this field and especially in trade policy at odds with official opinion in the executive.

All matters pertaining to America's external commercial relations fall squarely within the jurisdiction of Congress. Since the Reciprocal Trade Act of 1934, presidents have repeatedly won negotiating authority from Congress on trade matters, but always only on temporary bases (Pastor 1980). And congressional pressure ensured that from the early 1960s onwards, trade policy was taken out of the hands of the State Department and placed in those of two agencies much more directly sensitive to congressional (and domestic business) influence: the Commerce Department and what is now known as the US Trade Representative (USTR). The latter's role, defined in congressional legislation both as having exclusive responsibility for trade policy advice to the President and as being directly accountable to Congress, ensures congressional leaders a powerful influence over the USTR's work (Low 1993).

Congressional influence is also great in other areas affecting external economic relations. Its role in fiscal policy remains central. And even in the field of monetary policy the US Treasury and the Federal Reserve (the central bank) remain far more accountable to Congress than is the case in most other countries: legislators can in principle rewrite the Federal Reserve's mandate through ordinary legislation, if they wish. Thus, tracking the details of American foreign economic policy since 1945 requires exploring the politics and policies of the US Congress.

The other main institutional actor in the field is, of course, the executive branch, and its roles include attempting both to set the agenda in external economic policy and to maintain the policy initiative against potential opponents in Congress and beyond. Within the executive, external economic policy is handled by a wide array of agencies in addition to Commerce and the USTR: most crucially the US Treasury as well as the White House and the National Security apparatus and its satellite bodies particularly focused on economic aspects of American national strategy.

Battles by the executive to win on foreign economic policy issues in Congress have frequently figured amongst the most dramatic tussles in the American policy-making system. Recent examples of such battles

---

◎ CONTROVERSIES 18.1: Controversies within the United States

- Over the more general strategic emphasis in American trade policies between sectors which consider themselves to be fully competitive in world markets and sectors which feel threatened by foreign competition. The former want the strategic focus of trade policy to be on opening the markets of other countries, rather than on closing American markets to foreign competitors. The latter wish a more protectionist stance on imports. The Clinton administration generally adopted the former approach; the Bush administration was more inclined towards a defensive, protectionist stance, notably in the cases of steel and of agricultural subsidies. The more protectionist constituencies have available to them a large range of policy instruments still on the statute book for penalizing countries for alleged dumping and for other sorts of supposedly unfair trade practices, and these anti-dumping instruments continue to be used, though they are widely viewed among proponents of free trade as rather transparently protectionist weapons.

were the successful efforts of the Clinton administration to win the passing of NAFTA—the North Atlantic Free Trade Agreement—in the early 1990s and to gain acceptance of China's entry into the World Trade Organization (WTO).

Conventional accounts of US external economic policy making then explore how various domestic groups and influences seek to capture the levers of decision-making power within the executive and Congress (Verdier 1994). Both pluralist and public choice theorists stress the predominant role of market-based groups with narrowly focused, intensely held preferences, pitted against broader groups with diffuse interests. Others give weight to the interests of election candidates and elected officials seeking funding and other kinds of electoral support through appealing to groups concerned about external economic policy. What Thomas Ferguson has called the 'investment theory of American politics' suggests that both domestic and external economic (and political) policy is strongly influenced by the specific sectors and even companies which have produced large, early funding for the victorious presidential candidate: Ferguson himself stresses those who contribute large funds before the start of the primary races. More generally, this perspective views US foreign economic policy as driven by conflicts between different US business sectors. A consequence of this approach is to read different administrations as favouring specific and rather narrow sectors, such as Wall Street, the military industrial sector, the pharmaceutical industry, or information and communication technology (ICT) companies (Cox and Skidmore-Hess 1999). Yet others give weight to broad trends in public opinion concerning economic ideologies and doctrines, such as free trade or mercantilism (Goldstein 1988). What all such theories have in common is a stress on the centrality of electoral politics and a suggestion of the predominant role of its interaction with various domestic business interests.

Others who stress policy capture by special interest groups offer a more elitist perspective, outside the purely electoral arena. Bichler and Nitzan, for example, argue that those business groups which can offer the highest rates of return tend to gain policy dominance.

From this angle they see a conflict over the last fifteen years in external economic (and political) policy between what they call the Technodollar–Merger Dollar coalition, broadly reflected in the Clinton administration, and the Petro-dollar–Weapon Dollar coalition, represented by the Bush administration since 2001 (Bichler, Rowley, and Nitzan 1989). A similar stress on elitist links between business groups and groups within the American state apparatus has been advanced by others like Robert Wade, who has written about the role of what he calls a Wall Street–Treasury–IMF complex in the foreign economic policies of the Clinton administration (Wade and Veneroso 1998). These kinds of analysis are in some ways reminiscent of earlier debates of the 1960s and 1970s over the extent to which American state policy had been captured by a 'power elite' combining state managers and the managers of powerful business organizations (Wright-Mills 1959).

All these approaches yield fruitful insights on nuances and conflicts within US external economic policy. The electoral and institutional dimensions of the politics of external economic policy are certainly inescapable realities. But so too are the elitist dimensions of the policy-making system. Yet much of the work on these elitist dimensions is either devoted to stressing elite divisions or inclined towards a rather managerial conception of elites as leaders of big powerful organizations.

The work of Gabriel Kolko, drawing upon the Marxist tradition, has combined a stress on the class divisions within American society with an emphasis on the centrality of the leaders of the American business class in the formulation of American foreign economic policy. He thereby stresses a number of features of the American policy-making system which have been downplayed by other authors. In the first place, he emphasizes the centrality of the power of this business class in American politics since the days of McKinley at the end of the nineteenth century: business funds politics at all levels and business interests predominate in the mass media. Secondly, he stresses the informal mechanisms through which the American business class throws up and establishes its own leaderships in the field of strategy and policy. Thirdly he stresses the zones of consensus within the business class on fundamentals of domestic and international policy despite differences on tactics and style. Fourthly, he stresses the way in which the leaders of the American business class seek to treat politics and economics as an integrated field, rather than as two separate spheres with autonomous logics. And finally Kolko stresses the mechanisms through which strategic conceptions for American foreign economic policy amongst the leaders of the American business class are translated into state policy in Washington (Kolko 1976: chs 7 and 8).

The dominance of the interests of the American business class in American society and politics is expressed in the set of core values embodying the organizing principles of the American state and American capitalism. These principles have remained remarkably unchanged within the American business class despite the inflections produced by the New Deal: what Philip Bobbitt has called the principle of the 'market state' in which individuals determine their own future in the marketplace and the state's role is largely confined to organizing and policing the market (as well as, often, underwriting it) rather than making large social policy commitments to citizens (Bobbitt 2002); in which the needs of business should come first in the fashioning of state policy since a thriving capitalism is the key to people's welfare; and for which American capitalism needs a secure and friendly environment through the preservation and enlargement of a capitalist world outside the United States sympathetic to the distinctive values of American capitalism.

As such, the self-understanding of the policy elite since 1945 has been that their task is to do more than to champion American interests within the world economy: it is to shape that world economy itself as a more or less integrated, America-centred order. It is this standpoint which has marked out the role of these elites and which has given rise to distinctive labels for their approach to policy making since 1945. One such label has been that they are 'globalists'. Another is that they have had a 'hegemonic' agenda, rather than a narrowly and immediately America-first agenda. Whichever label is used, American foreign economic policy making since 1945 has thus been marked by a dialectic between two poles or what we might call a 'dual logic': one pole has been that of immediate, focused interests within American society, articulated within the

Congress; the other has been that of American strategic elites, preoccupied with shaping and sustaining an American-centred world economic order. The outputs of the American foreign economic policy-making system have been the result of the often conflictual interaction of these two poles.

This dialectic has also provided Washington's policy elites with their central policy-making dilemma in handling foreign economic strategy. The drive for preponderant American global power to reshape the world in an American-friendly way will, if successful, enable the American state to impose its will on others for direct and immediate American interests in economic as well as other fields. And this will, in turn, generate resistance and hostility elsewhere to American power. Yet building a world order in which other centres can flourish under American tutelage may require the United States to sacrifice its own direct interests in favour of the interests of other centres. Paul Nitze expressed this dilemma clearly in the late 1950s: 'The most difficult problem facing the formulators of United States foreign policy is that of relating and bringing into some measure of convergence policies appropriate to the coalition of free nations, the alliance system, and the United States as an individual nation' (Nitze 1959).

The central task of America's policy elites since 1945 has been to find ways of managing this contradiction. While Congress may be the sounding board for those demanding the defence of immediate American interests first, America's strategic elites must find ways of mediating between such nationalist pressures and the requirements of the American-centred world order as a whole: they must be American globalists, putting first the needs of a global economic order, fashioned to suit American long-term interests. This mission may, on occasion, require action which breeds strong hostility amongst America's subaltern allies, raising charges of American empire; but it may also, on occasion, require reshaping domestic American arrangements and sacrificing some immediate American interests for the sake of the longer-term gains that can be harvested from an American-friendly global economic and political order.

Against this background, in the second part of this chapter we will explore debates about how the American state has actually defined and pursued its goals in the world economy.

KEY POINTS

Sources of American foreign economic policy

❏ Pluralists and public choice analysts, who view public policy as the outcome of decentralized group politics involving coalition building and conflict linked to electoral politics, see this arena, centred on Congress, as the key source of foreign economic policy.

❏ Elitists, who view state and business elites as the shapers of public policy, downplay the role of broad electoral influences and view policy as being shaped in and around the executive.

❏ Writers in the Marxist tradition, like Kolko, have argued that both the American state and American society have been shaped as a distinctive type of capitalist social system with distinctive values and institutions which shape approaches to foreign economic policy. And business-

funded mechanisms for debating foreign economic strategy have helped overcome both institutional fragmentation and group conflicts of interest, thus providing continuity and a large measure of consensus on fundamental, strategic issues. This third approach enables us to integrate the insights of both the pluralists and the elitists.

The big strategic dilemma

❏ Since 1945 America has had the power to shape and reshape the world economy.

❏ This power presented the leaders of the American business class and state with a central strategic dilemma: how to fashion a global order that would both favour American economic interests and gain sustained support from other centres of the world economy.

Perspectives on American economic strategy since 1945

We approach the debates about the substance of American external economic policy since 1945 by classifying varying perspectives on this question in three alternative images. The first such image is that of America as the promoter of a cooperative, multilateral order in international economics. This implies that the United States is not predominantly seeking either its own immediate advantage or its own one-sided long-term strength *vis-à-vis* other economic centres. Instead it is promoting change in the collective interests of world prosperity. We will call this the 'multilateral' image of American economic strategy.[2]

The second image is that of an American economic nationalism: a drive to both protect important American domestic business interests and rather aggressively champion key American business interests abroad, in particular through opening other markets to American operators and through structuring international markets to favour American businesses over their competitors.

Both these first two images assume that American external economic strategy is focused rather exclusively on economics as opposed to international politics, although supporters of both images would concede that international power politics has been present as an

external constraint on economic strategy. But the third image is what we will call that of an American empire. This implies that American external economic policy has been part of a larger project of constructing and sustaining an American-centred international political order embracing more than economics and within which the purely economic aspects must be understood. It also implies that American policy in the economic field is driven neither by multilateralism nor by economic nationalism but by the goal of maintaining and expanding a zone of both politics and economics covering the main centres of capitalism and under effective American leadership. Proponents of this image would view instances of American multilateralism and American economic nationalism as being merely aspects of a larger American project.

Each of these three images includes scholars working within different normative and analytical perspectives. Thus those who view American external economic policy as having been broadly multilateral include many liberal economists, but also others who reject liberal— or neoclassical—economics. Those who view American economic strategy as having been marked by nationalist mercantilism may themselves be normative liberals or indeed mercantilists or Marxists. And those with an American world empire image stretch from neo-con-servative theorists on the right to Marxists of various kinds on the left. We will briefly explore each of these images before suggesting some conclusions of our own.

The multilateral image

The image of American external economic policy as being predominantly multilateral since 1945 rests above all on two simple but powerful indicators: levels of pro-tectionism in the field of goods and services, and levels of America's international economic integration, in par-ticular the growth of the share of imports as a percent-age of gross domestic product (GDP). On both these indicators, American policy since 1945 would seem to have broadly favoured economic multilateralism: both tariff and non-tariff barriers, historically high in the United States throughout the nineteenth and first half of the twentieth century in the industrial field, have, in aggregate, been dramatically reduced since 1945 and the American economy has become progressively more integrated into the world economy, its trade rising rap-idly as a percentage of GDP, notably in the last quarter of a century.

A third indicator supporting the multilateral image is the discourse of American administrations and of the broader American policy-making community in the post-war period. This has been couched overwhelming-ly in the language of international liberalism and mul-tilateralism. And even where Washington has adopted policies contradicting liberalism, as in the case of the Nixon administration in the early 1970s or, for that matter, the Reagan administration in the 1980s, it has justified its backsliding always on the grounds that it has been driven to protectionism by the economic national-ism of others, notably the Japanese government.

The case for this multilateral image would seem to be especially strong for the quarter of a century after 1945, paradoxically because Washington did not, at that time, use its enormous power resources to force open the markets of the rest of the capitalist world in a wrenching way, as a strategy of economic national-ism would have suggested, given American business's economic ascendancy at that time. Instead, Washing-ton scaled back its earlier plans for a radically open

post-war world economy and placed the economic revival of both western Europe and Japan first.

At the same time the United States' goal for the world economy was not in doubt: a liberal, open world econ-omy as envisaged in the Bretton Woods agreements and in the early discussions of an International Trade Organization.

Those adhering to this multilateral image of Ameri-can post-war economic strategy acknowledge a turn away from multilateralism on the part of the Nixon administration, notably with the closing of the Gold Window in 1971 and with the linked imposition of a 15 per cent import surcharge. These steps were followed by others, indicating a mounting turn in a protectionist direction on trade matters through the 1970s and 1980s. Yet these shifts can be, and often are, explained not as a strategic shift amongst economic policy elites in the USA but rather as a consequence of the effectiveness of rent-seeking special interest politics within the Amer-ican Congress. At the same time, the claim was often made that the revival of European and Japanese indus-try posed such a radical competitive challenge to Amer-ican business that Washington was no longer willing or able to play the role of a multilateralist, liberal hegemon, paying the costs of leading the world economy in a more open direction. Thus the argument was made that the American shift was more from that of playing the role of hegemonic stabilizer of the international economy than a shift from a commitment to multilateralism as such.

The other side of this story is Washington's long campaign for a further and more radical opening of the world economy, through the battle for the Uru-guay Round and through the campaign to end capital controls and thus free the international movement of private finance. The triumph of these two campaigns is often viewed as the triumph of a new, more radical opening of the world economy in a liberal direction, often known as 'economic globalization'. Many com-mentators view the long boom which began in 1994 and continued until 2001, followed by a shallow recession in 2002 and renewed growth up to 2007, as the fruits of this continuing commitment to liberal multilateralism. They point to the faster rise in productivity indicators in the USA during the second half of the 1990s. They have also viewed 'economic globalization' as broadly benefi-cial on a world scale (Wolf 2004).

MAJOR DEBATES AND THEIR IMPACT 18.1: US foreign economic policy

The 1940s

- Over the Bretton Woods project for international monetary arrangements, especially the roles of the International Monetary Fund and restrictions on the movements of private finance.
- Over the Truman administration's plan for an International Trade Organization.

The late 1960s and early 1970s

- Over the future of the dollar and of the Bretton Woods monetary system.

The 1980s

- Over the high dollar and rising US trade deficits in the first half of the 1980s.

- Over whether the US government should adopt a sectorally targeted industrial policy in the early 1980s.
- Over more aggressive trade policy action against industrial competitors like Japan and the Asian Tigers, and over European agricultural protectionism.

The 1990s

- Over strategic trade theory as a guide to foreign economic policy.
- Over the North American Free Trade Agreement (NAFTA).
- Over the World Trade Organization.

Since 2000

- Over outsourcing jobs to China and to other emerging market economies.

CONTROVERSIES 18.2: Controversies between the USA and other countries

- All the issues listed above have generated controversy between the United States and other governments. Particularly prominent have been battles in the WTO's current Doha Round over American subsidies for domestic agriculture. This issue, along with similar hostility to EU agricultural subsidies, has been at the centre of the deadlock over the Doha Round.
- A major international controversy over current American foreign economic policy has concerned how the large US current account deficit and rising US foreign debt should be dealt with. While American opinion has generally favoured a solution through the foreign exchange markets lowering the exchange rate of the dollar, other governments have favoured domestic US measures to tackle the

very low (or negative) levels of US household and government saving.
- Another set of arguments between American official opinion and some governments abroad as well as left-oriented political movements abroad concerns both the free movement of private finance and the unregulated nature of activities by many financial operators, notably 'hedge funds'—operators seeking to exploit price differences in markets for financial gain—mainly centred in the USA. The activities of such hedge funds were a major issue in disputes concerning the East Asian crisis of 1997–8 and they continue to cause controversy, notably between the German government and Washington.

The final and perhaps most decisive argument for the multilateral image of American foreign economic policy is the extraordinary degree of acceptance on the part of other governments of the American-led projects for the Uruguay Round and the WTO as well as for the liberalization of private finance and many other aspects of characteristically American conceptions of capitalism. If there is continuing hostility to aspects of this programme in parts of the global south, its widespread acceptance within the OECD countries suggests that

the multilateral image fits better than the mercantilist one, at least as regards the main thrusts of American policy towards the advanced capitalist core over the last fifteen years.

The mercantilist image

A large group of students of American foreign economic policy view it as having a much more strongly national-mercantilist edge, which cannot be dismissed as the work of scattered special interest lobbies managing to use their political influence to blunt a mainly multilateral thrust. Those who stress this mercantilist bent are themselves diverse, ranging from liberal international economists to conservatives and Marxists.

A number of writers on the history of American international economic policy in the century and a half before 1945 have stressed the centrality of mercantilism in traditional American foreign economic policy, most especially in the field of industrial trade. As Paul Bairoch has put it, the USA and most particularly the industrial North-East became, in the nineteenth century, the 'mother country and bastion of modern protectionism' (Bairoch 1993). Even in 1925 in the middle of inter-war trade liberalization, US tariffs on industrial goods were 37 per cent of total import value. As Rune Skarstein puts it, 'No other country in history has accomplished a more protectionist policy during industrialisation than the United States' (Skarstein 2005). And if the rhetoric shifted under Cordell Hull in the 1930s,[3] American wartime planning for the post-war economic order was rather aggressively focused upon opening up the European empires, especially the British, to American capital and upon reorganizing the world economy under American, rather than European, dominance. Evidence of American restraint on opening the trade regimes of other countries in the post-war decades overlooks the centrality of foreign direct investment (FDI) rather than exports in American expansion and the way in which, by ensuring that West Germany was entirely open to American FDI, American capital could deeply penetrate European markets in the 1960s and thereafter.

There is an increasingly influential trend amongst historians of America's twentieth-century foreign policy to stress the centrality of Washington's drive to open other markets to American capitals. Associated with the work of William Appleman Williams and his followers, this school has stressed the economic expansionist dynamic in American foreign policy and the drive for what Williams called an 'Open Door world'.[4] On this reading, the language of liberal free trade has supplied a legitimizing discourse for a strategy devoted to opening the markets of others to American capital.

This theme has also been expressed at times by figures on the right of the political spectrum like Samuel Huntington, who argued that in the post-war period America used its military power as a bargaining lever, offering to protect governments with it provided that they 'permit access to their territory by a variety of US governmental and non-governmental organizations pursuing goals which those organizations considered important.... The "Pax Americana," as I. F. Stone put it, "is the 'internationalism' of Standard Oil, Chase Manhattan, and the Pentagon"' (Huntington 1973: 344). David Rothkopf argued similarly that 'If a country depended on the United States for security protection, it dealt with the United States on trade and commercial matters' (Rothkopf 1998: 1).

Proponents of the mercantilist image also argue that the liberal characteristics of the international trade regime which emerged in the 1950s and 1960s were a reflection not of a strategic commitment to multilateralism on the part of American leaders but instead of their confidence in the competitive ascendancy of American industry. Thus when that ascendancy faced evident challenges in the 1970s, American economic strategy turned against liberal principles.

At the top of the charge list over this mercantilist turn would come Washington's abandonment of the gold-linked international monetary regime from the time when the Nixon administration closed the Gold Window in August 1972.

A cardinal principle for an open international economy since the mid-nineteenth century was that business operators should have a stable unit of account for calculating the profitability of their international ventures and for giving monetary security and predictability to their international operations. The Bretton Woods system fulfilled this function, with the dollar as the key unit of account, at a fixed, though in principle adjustable, exchange rate to gold. This system required the American Treasury to adjust American macroeconomic policy to ensure the stability of the dollar against gold. Yet by breaking the link with gold, Washington refused to allow American national economic policy to be constrained in this way, thus subordinating the stability of international monetary relations to purely American national interests. Since that time the dollar has swung wildly up and down against the other main currencies and the world has lacked a stable international monetary unit and indeed any universal and homogeneous international monetary system (Williamson and Milner 1991).[5] This move was a staggering blow to the efficient functioning of the international capitalist economy, often creating dramatic swings in the macroeconomic conditions facing other countries, swings which have frequently plunged one country or another into financial crises. At the same time, businesses engaged in international operations across currency zones have faced extremely volatile and risky conditions, surviving through transfer pricing, paying the costs of hedging, and abandoning trade wherever possible in favour of transplant operations in other centres. But Washington was able to maintain the dollar as the main global vehicle currency, partly as a result of the continued centrality of the American market but also in large part because of the American state's political hegemony as the protector of the main centres of the capitalist world. Such security dependence on the USA also encouraged the Saudis both to keep the international oil trade denominated in dollars and to recycle the resulting petro-revenues through the American banking system as dollars (Spiro 1999). And the whole system was powerfully supported by the dollar zone's London satellite, acting as an offshore financial market.

The success of this dramatic American strategic manoeuvre to make the fiat dollar the world's vehicle currency ensured that the American national economy could remain central to the global capitalist economy. It enabled the USA to run progressively larger current account deficits and thus keep its market open as a vital revenue source for capitals around the world. It enabled the USA to let its foreign debt rise to ever larger heights without strain and to fund the American state's overseas operations without difficulty. Dollar dominance has ensured that imports, debts, and overseas military-political operations could all be paid for with greenback paper produced by the American state. The regime has also allowed the US Treasury and Federal Reserve the unique privilege among states of being able to gear its domestic macroeconomic management exclusively to domestic conditions within the USA without a significant external constraint.

While many promoters of the multilateral image of American external economic policy view the scrapping of capital controls and the emergence of free movement of both finance and financial services as an indicator of deepening international economic liberalism, some liberal theorists strongly disagree. Jagdish Bhagwati, for example, a passionate advocate of liberal free trade, considers that the liberal argument applies to trade in goods but does not necessarily apply to financial services or require untrammelled free movement of private finance (Bhagwati 2001). Instead the large, fast, and unpredictable flows of funds in and out of small economies, particularly in the south, have been viewed by many as extremely dangerous and indeed as a potential source of vulnerability for the entire international economic system. Yet both the free movement of finance and freedom for financial services to extend their reach internationally has been enormously profitable for the American financial sector, while financial crises in the south as well as the East Asian crises of 1997 have been widely viewed as offering opportunities for the US Treasury to pursue policies restructuring crisis-ridden economies to the advantage of American capitals (Wade and Veneroso 1998). The free movement of finance has also been an essential prop both to the preservation of the fiat dollar and to the capacity of the American national economy to sustain chronic current account deficits with the rest of the world.

Supporters of the mercantilist image are able to provide powerful evidence of a sharp and deep turn in American trade policy from the 1970s to the mid-1990s towards aggressive forms of industrial mercantilism which took extreme forms in some high-tech sectors.[6] Jagdish Bhagwati dubbed this turn a move towards 'aggressive unilateralism' in American trade policy (Bhagwati and Patrick 1990). It was also in the late 1980s and early 1990s that for the first time in the post-war period, influential voices at the level of American policy elites mounted an open and vigorous attack on liberal principles in international economics, arguing that these principles were flawed since they rested on factual premises which were false: above all the foundational assumption that firms face constant or decreasing returns to scale (Lawrence and Schultze 1990). Given that in most industrial sectors, not least high-tech sectors, firms face increasing returns to scale, the logic of maximizing efficiency must push them towards gaining monopoly power over markets. In such circumstances states should rationally opt for so-called 'strategic trade theory' in which their task is to assist their companies in key sectors to gain maximum international market power: in other words, the USA should adopt a mercantilist strategy in key, high-tech sectors. Leading proponents of this view were subsequently brought into senior positions in the Clinton administration.[7] And that administration also established a new National Economic Council with the explicit goal of ensuring American economic security, widely viewed as, in fact, a vehicle for assertive economic nationalism on the part of the Clinton team.

Proponents of the mercantilist image view much of the substance of the Uruguay Round as having strong mercantilist accents, not least in such fields as intellectual property rights and the field of services, while at the same time American (and European) policy makers have continued to maintain heavily protected agricultural sectors despite their promises to dismantle these protections when the Uruguay Round was signed.

While it is true that the penchant for what Bhagwati called 'aggressive unilateralism' has dramatically declined since the WTO came into existence, some see it as continuing in a somewhat different guise, through the drive by both the Clinton administration and its Bush successor for so-called free trade agreements (FTAs).[8] Bhagwati has argued strenuously that these should be viewed as new forms of protectionist preferential trade arrangements which threaten to undermine the liberal multilateral system. Meanwhile the end of confrontation with Japan in high-tech sectors like ICT can be viewed not as the result of a change of strategy by Washington but rather as the result of a recognition that the USA had won the battle for leadership in ICT against the Japanese challenge.

The world empire image

Though not new, the image of American external economic strategy as integrally linked to a world empire project has emerged strongly over the last decade, particularly since the arrival in office of the Bush administration

in 2001. As in the case of the other two images we find proponents of this view amongst very diverse schools of thought from neo-conservatives close to the Bush administration itself to realists, liberals, and various kinds of Marxists on the left. We will take as the distinguishing feature of proponents of this image a series of shared ideas. First, that external economic policy is internally linked to the projection of American military-political power outwards. It is this link between political expansionism and economic strategy which requires the concept of 'empire' as a political term. Second, in marked contrast with earlier European empires, this American empire stretches out over the other core centres of industrial activity with a telos of stretching across the main centres of Eurasia, rather than concentrating on what World System Theorists have called the periphery and semi-periphery. Thirdly this empire involves restructuring politics and culture as much as economics. And finally the proponents of this empire image do not necessarily believe either that empire is a project for the benefit of all American citizens or that it is disadvantageous to all social groups outside the United States but within the empire zone. Yet it is, at the same time, an American empire not only in its geographical origins but in the interests which it serves and the goals which it pursues.[9] Authors as diverse as Andrew Bacevich, Christopher Layne, and neo-conservatives have then argued that the American drive to expand its sphere of influence into Eurasia after 1945 was not merely a negative, reactive response to Soviet threats but a positive, empire-construction project. The distinctive feature of the political side of this project was that Washington effectively took over the security functions of other main capitalist centres, turning them into members of an American-managed security zone, most directly in the cases of Germany and Japan, and in a more attenuated way for, say, France and Britain. What had been a central, crucial attribute of such states in the pre-1945 world—defence of their realm and of their external sphere of influence—was effectively transferred to the United States. In the jargon of American grand strategy this American takeover of its allies' security is known as 'primacy'—a concept of direct security management of allies rather than a looser posture of 'offshore balancing' of the sort practised by Britain towards the continent of Europe in the nineteenth century. And it also forms the essential background, in American strategic thought, for the construction of an integrated capitalist world economy.

The American commitment to supplying security for its core capitalist allies has extended beyond protecting them from major powers outside the security zone (like the Soviet Union during the Cold War or China today) and protecting them from each other to guaranteeing their sources of supply of strategic materials from the south, above all oil, and where possible also protecting their markets and investments in the south. Thus, insofar as the United States could deliver on such commitments, the only rational grounds for any other core capitalism to break out of the security zone would be to make an anti-American challenge for regional dominance and their own sphere of influence.

Nevertheless, this American approach to organizing world order has entailed significant costs to its subaltern allies, since they have been required to forgo substantial independent economic linkages with states outside the zone. Particularly wrenching in the early post-war years was Washington's insistence that the other core centres cut their economic links with the Soviet bloc and China. This requirement has continued to cause tensions between the United States and its core allies in the post-Cold War period, whether over German energy dependence on Russia, South Korean dependence on the Chinese market, or efforts by allies to build independent links with oil states such as Iran.

If states outside the security zone have faced exclusion to a greater or lesser degree from access to major markets and from legal protections for their international economic activities, states within the zone have been supplied with economic rules largely, though by no means entirely, protected in international law and managed through inclusive international institutions. This regime has been legitimized by liberal international economic theory, with its stress on multilateral free trade. Indeed, neo-conservative supporters of this image justify it precisely on the grounds that within the borders of the empire, the American record has been an overwhelmingly benign one in the field of economic relations. At the same time, the largest businesses within the zone find, in American military-political power, a welcome protector of their markets and investments.

Proponents of the American empire image on the left have a less benign view of the role of the American state in structuring market and state institutions both within the security zone and outside it. They generally view this role as one of transforming the internal regimes of other states in the direction of Philip Bobbitt's notion of a 'market state': a brand of capitalism very much along the lines favoured by the American business class in which the lives of citizens are decided by their ability to cope with unfettered market imperatives. Yet this can also be a source of strength for a strategy of global empire since these very values of the American business class should win strong support from the wealthiest and most powerful social groups within the other states of the global empire—the business classes of those states.

As the protector of all the main centres of capitalism and of an open, integrated international market, the American state can claim special privileges to enable it to preserve the zone effectively. One such special privilege is certainly the fiat dollar system, despite its dysfunctionality as a monetary system. Others may include a self-assigned right to ensure American dominance in what Washington considers to be strategic economic sectors, as in the case of ICT and the confrontation over it with Japan. And the consequences of the political empire dimension for American bargaining capacity over the rules of the world economic order are immense. Students of international economic diplomacy have long recognized the important role of military-political capacities in international economic bargaining (Odell 2000; Meunier 2005). Thus a perspective on American external economic policy which recognizes the existence of an American imperial political dimension in relations with other main economic centres will stress the special capacity which this dimension gives Washington to shape procedures and outcomes in the world economy. And it also suggests that narrowly economic frameworks for analysing American external economic policy, whether liberal-multilateral or mercantilist-nationalist, may miss central aspects of that policy and also central preoccupations of the framers of that policy. We now turn to examine the global financial crisis of 2008 and its implications for the US in the global economy.

The global financial crisis

Before we can examine the crisis we need to examine the conditions of possibility that allowed the crisis to erupt. The story starts with the Glass–Steagal Act of 1933 that was enacted in response to the global depression of the early 1930s and was designed to inoculate 'high-street' commercial banks (which primarily took care of loans and deposits from ordinary savers) from the complex forms of derivates investment (a financial instrument that lays claims to future values based upon the asset it is linked to) commonly undertaken by investment banks. Simply put, the idea was to protect ordinary savers and depositors from the kinds of high-risk 'casino' type activity that many of the large investment banks undertook.

The repeal of the Glass–Steagal Act in 1999 under the presidency of Bill Clinton effectively merged both commercial and investment banking, and meant that the so-called 'real' economy of ordinary savers and small businesses was increasingly bound up with high stakes, complex derivatives, and securities trading as banks took on both investment and commercial operations. This also meant that ordinary savers were exposed, via the actions of the now merged banks, to complex and high-risk forms of derivates trading. Banks increasingly 'securitized' credit whereby they would lend money and then sell on the debt to other financial institutions. This in turn created a very dangerous form of incentivization for these financial institutions. First, banks were less concerned with the capacity for the debtor to pay than the process of securitization itself (as this was where they made their money). Banks thus were far less careful about the credit worthiness of their debtors. Second, the debt ratings agencies, whose job was to rate these trades and risk accordingly, were actually employed by the very institutions whose debt they were rating. This created a toxic structural logic for financial institutions to endlessly extend credit with little to no oversight as to the quality of the underlying assets that their securitized revenues streams were linked to. Rather inevitably, the crisis began when it was apparent that these assets could not be paid off. With hundreds of billions of dollars worth of securitized debt obligations linked to these underlying assets, and the 'slicing and dicing' of

bad debt into the heart of the financial system, a panic was triggered which led to a 'credit crunch', with financial institutions withholding what had prior to the crisis been very easy credit from other banks and businesses. In effect, the repeal of the Glass–Steagal Act effectively destroyed the firewall between high-risk, high finance, and the ordinary economy, and incorporated into the heart of the global economy a multiple debt-based game of pass the parcel (only most of the parcels were in fact empty).

Why did the systemic shocks in the US economy take on such a global scale? First and most obviously, the US economy continues to remain central to global markets. Even today, the US economy soaks up approximately 25 per cent of the world's exports. A systemic locking of credit in US markets would thus have a massive knock-on effect on the global economy: when the US economy sneezes, the global economy catches a cold. Second, given global economic interdependence, systemic shocks can rapidly spread beyond the initial shock zone. For example, in 2008 the non-regulated over-the-counter (OTC) derivatives market accounted for a staggering $615 trillion in trades (to give a sense of perspective US GDP in 2008 was around 15 trillion dollars). More importantly, these trades were not confined to the domestic US market, with numerous non-US financial institutions, especially in the Eurozone, being exposed to these toxic assets.

The response to the crisis was extraodinary, with many of the tottering US banks taken over and administered by the federal government as these institutions were seen as simply 'too big to fail'. The largest intervention was the 2008 rescuing of the insurer AIG, with a massive $180 billion bailout. The crisis also saw an aggressive interest rate cut by the US federal reserve to ease interest payments on loans as well as to weaken the dollar *vis-a-vis* other currencies and thus stimulate US exports to address the still glaring US balance of payments deficit. In dealing with the fallout, the most significant legislation to emerge from the crisis has been the Dodd–Frank Bill passed under the Obama administration in 2010. The bill has sought to end the 'too big to fail' problem with caps on the amount of debt banks can have on their books as well as the setting up of a

Consumer Protection Agency. Perhaps most importantly, the bill also sought to regulate the derivatives markets through increasing transparency and reducing bilateral credit risk. Traders are now encouraged to trade derivatives on registered exchanges (unlike the non-regulated OTC) and second trades need to be cleared through registered central counterparties. Lastly, the Frank–Dodd Bill also imposes a margin and capital requirement on derivatives. Although still at an early stage, there are already indications that the Frank–Dodd bill will not be able to fully address the causes of the financial crisis. For example, whilst derivative trading was central to the financial collapse, these trades will be excluded from regulatory oversight until 2015 and even then a substantial proportion will be excluded from regulatory oversight.

Conclusions on the debate about the three images

Debate between proponents of the three different images of American foreign economic policy rests not only on disputes about empirical evidence but on differing concepts and theories, not least in the field of economics itself. Many of those favouring a multilateral image of American external economic policy identify the economics of capitalism very closely with the idea of market exchanges. Within this perspective, the United States has fairly consistently championed the spreading and deepening of such exchanges both within and across national economies and this trend has evidently accelerated since the collapse of the Soviet bloc.

At the same time champions of the mercantilist image can draw strength from strategic trade theory. which gives much more weight to the industrial dynamics of capitalism and to the consequences for capitalist competition of pervasive increasing returns to scale. When such trends are present, companies are driven to strive for market power so that they can defeat their rivals through maximizing their returns to scale. In such a world, the national economy with the biggest domestic market can hope to generate the most powerful companies capable of competing effectively on a global level. And that national economy has been, and will remain

for some time, the United States. In such circumstances, an American insistence on an international level playing field for interfirm competition would actually favour those companies with the largest home base— American companies.

Proponents of the American global empire image tend to follow Joseph Schumpeter's insistence that 'the social process is really one, indivisible whole' (Schumpeter 1934: 3), and thus view capitalism not as a purely economic system but as a whole social system in which arrangements in the economic field are profoundly conditioned by social and political context. In such a system financial elites are as much concerned about their security and well-being as about more technical economic matters and may be ready to accept an American leadership of a distinctive kind of security-zone empire in exchange for being provided with a politically safe environment for prospering. Within such a perspective American external economic strategy should be seen as being only one aspect of a more holistic strategy for maintaining and managing the entire capitalist order within its zone.

It is this last image which we favour as the most fruitful one for exploring the many different aspects of American external economic strategy which are otherwise so seemingly contradictory. But this empire image in turn raises questions about the new challenges faced by the United States as a result of the Soviet bloc collapse, the turn by Russia and China towards capitalism, and the global financial crisis that impacts upon US global economic leadership. In respect to Russia and China, the political and indeed economic configuration of the American empire was structured in large measure through the Cold War exclusion of these states. Thus American external economic and political strategy since the start of the 1990s should be seen in the context of US efforts to reconstruct an American empire zone on a global scale—a task by no means completed. The financial crisis of 2008 has also impacted upon US global economic leadership not least through the repudiation of many of the tenets of the so-called neo-liberal 'Washington Consensus' as well as a decisive shift of global economic fortunes in China's favour as a result of the crisis.

Conclusion

Within the scope of this chapter, we cannot hope to draw a detailed balance sheet of the success of US strategy in international economics, far less risk confident predictions on the future. But we can, at least, briefly address some of the main current debates about the strength of American capitalism in the world economy.

America's macroeconomic performance

Official figures for American GDP show that since 1994 the American economy has grown at a significantly faster rate than during the previous fifteen-year period and has also grown substantially faster than the other main advanced capitalist centres, the Eurozone and Japan. Growth declined sharply in 2001 and remained low in 2002 but recovered strongly if not quite to the growth rates of over 4 per cent a year from the start of 1997 to 1999. The global financial crisis has affected US growth, but the US economy continues to remain vibrant with a \$14.3 trillion GDP in 2009, which is more than that of the entire Eurozone area (\$12.5 trillion). Thus, according to these figures, the relative weight of the US economy in the total output of the advanced capitalist countries has increased substantially. If we look at the US share in total output of the G-7 countries, we find that it has risen from 46.6 per cent of the total in the period 1989–95 to 49.6 per cent during the period 2000 to 2004, and this continues to be the case after the financial crisis.[10]

But there are problems with all these claims. In the first place, GDP figures for growth exclude patterns of indebtedness. US growth has been strongly driven by high levels of household consumption, yet much of this has been funded by rising indebtedness, in both the household and government sectors. In the long term this pattern of growth is not sustainable and is likely to entail a phase of stagnation or much slower growth in the future.

A second set of criticisms refer to the technical inadequacy both of GDP statistics in general and of the methodologies used in the United States for calculating GDP and productivity trends. GDP statistics rest on national accounting systems which count as production all market-based activity except personal consumption. Thus, police and defence agencies, all kinds of financial services, and the retail and wholesale sectors all fall within the sphere of 'production' in the calculation of GDP. This accounting system thus casts American growth in a particularly favourable light since so much of this growth has been in financial services and the retail sector.

The basis for this kind of accounting lies in neo-classical economics, which uses a subjectivist way of measuring value and thus argues that all exchanges which people enter into are subjectively valuable to them and should be judged to be socially necessary and productive. But both classical economists and Marxists, using an objective concept of value, define production much more narrowly, arguing that it should be confined to the output of use values. Using this approach, American growth since the mid-1990s would appear much less impressive (Sheikh and Tomak 1994).

To these criticisms we should add criticisms of the specifically American accounting rules adopted in the USA since the mid-1990s. At this time, the USA decided to treat all military investment and production as productive, while other OECD countries have generally treated as productive only military investments which have at least potentially a dual use—such as military hospitals. This shift may add as much as 0.5 per cent annually to US GDP growth figures since the mid-1990s. The USA also calculates output in its financial services in a way which makes US GDP growth about 1 per cent greater per annum than the EU, which calculates its financial services output more conservatively (Giles 2006). And finally, since 1995 the US Bureau of Economic Analysis, which calculates US GDP, has used a controversial technical device known as the Hedonic Price Index for calculating the value of output in the ICT sector. This technique, not used in other countries, has been implemented in such a way as to greatly enlarge the calculated value of output in this field, which has been a key growth sector in the USA since 1995. Thus there are grounds for suggesting that the US boom since the mid-1990s has been much less impressive than its GDP statistics imply.

Similar problems beset official American claims about labour productivity—taken by most economists to be a key indicator of the underlying strength of a national economy. Reputable American research bodies like the Conference Board have claimed that from

1995 through to about 2003, US productivity grew significantly more rapidly than that of other advanced countries (McGuckin and Van Ark 2005). They claim that since 1995 output per hour grew 1 per cent per year faster in the USA than in EU Europe and also exceeded Japan's growth in output per hour, by a somewhat smaller margin.

Yet these claims have also been challenged. The main areas of US productivity growth have been financial services and the retail sector (including firms such as Wal Mart). For those who use a narrow definition of production, productivity gains in these sectors do not have great significance. Furthermore, the method used to calculate productivity gains, again using hedonic indicators for ICT, is challenged by many for it involves making assumptions about increased productivity in sectors using more powerful computers, which are open to challenge.

Linked to these debates are others about American capitalism's underlying international competitiveness. Here the focus has been on the USA's current account deficits and its mounting international indebtedness. Critics of America's economic performance see these trends both as signs of underlying weakness and as harbingers of long-term structural problems. Their opponents are inclined to argue that the current account deficit derives from currency misalignments and can be corrected by a fall in the dollar against East Asian currencies. They will thus often tend to blame the deficits on manipulation of exchange rates by East Asian central banks, especially by China, as Tim Geithner did in 2009 in one of his first speeches as Obama's treasury secretary.

The argument that the deficit and foreign debt is the result of currency misalignments focused on East Asia lacks credibility since less than half of the US trade deficit derives from East Asian export surpluses with the USA. Furthermore, the notion that there is a tight correlation between trade patterns and currency values, though true in the Bretton Woods era, is open to challenge today, in the age of free movement of private finance. An alternative reading would suggest that the deficit and foreign debt are driven by the collapse of saving in the United States. On this reading, the solution should lie in a domestic austerity drive in the USA, cutting US budget deficits and constraining households to save more—a policy mix that would entail a large recession in the USA and a reduction in American living standards.

But behind these debates lies a deeper set of issues concerning America's overall position in the world economy, issues which raise questions about the units of analysis that we use for discussing such matters. The activities of the American business class are no longer largely confined within the frontiers of the American national economy and within the field of exports from that base. They derive a large share of their profits from activities around the world, centred on their ability to establish operations in other countries. An increasingly large segment of these activities is in the financial field and in the various asset markets around the world. And the sustainability of these international activities depends upon the jurisdictions of other states being open to American operators, an ultimately political matter. Insofar as the American state has the political capacity to shape market rules to further the operations of American capitals in such markets, there is every reason to believe that an American capitalism centred on financial operations can continue to flourish, even in the face of the financial collapse.

Secondly, both the American current account deficit and American foreign debt must be viewed in the context of the continued dominance of the dollar and the linked centrality of US asset markets. In this light the deficits, however large, can be funded in dollars. If the dollar ceased to be the dominant currency, this would change and the US national economy would be in serious deficit and debt difficulties. But the dollar's ascendancy is not seriously under threat at the present time. One key reason lies in the fact that American asset markets remain by far the largest and most liquid in the world. This is especially true of the huge Treasury bond market, a safe haven for the reserves of the rest of the world's central banks, but it applies also to other US asset markets, from agency bonds, through stocks and shares, to other types of securities. Demand for US debt continued to remain strong even after the financial crisis, with China and Japan, the largest holders of US debt, continuing to purchase US bonds. China alone held $906 billion in US debt in 2010. Moreover, there is no integrated market for euro-denominated government bonds in Europe—arrangements in this field remain fragmented along national lines and as such

there is currently no market of equal liquidity (and thus attractiveness) for foreign buyers.

None of this means that the state elites of the rest of the capitalist world consider the fiat dollar to be a satisfactory world currency: with the wild swings of the dollar against other main currencies it is in many ways a dysfunctional system. Yet paradoxically this same system, in combination with free movement of short-term private finance, creates great opportunities for financial arbitrage and speculation, offering extraordinarily high returns to the richest segment of the world's population insofar as they gain access to the top American investment banks and the hedge funds linked to them.

And the sheer size of the American economy as a product market makes it an important magnet for capitalisms in the rest of the world, particularly if their growth strategy centres on exports. This encourages other centres, particularly the East and South-East Asians, to accept the American-centred international economic regimes and to cooperate with American economic policy managers.

The dollar will not cease to be the dominant currency unless it is replaced by a positive alternative and such an alternative does not exist at the present time. It would have to be created by political decisions, above all by decisions to create an East Asian currency zone that would link up with the euro, uniting Eurasia as a stable, independent monetary zone. Such a set of moves, conceivable if China's currency became fully convertible and became the key currency in East Asia, would mark a serious threat to the dollar and thus to the sustainability of US deficits and foreign debt.

Thus, the ascendancy of American capitalism within the world economy is not simply the result of the industrial dynamism of the domestic American economy. It is also crucially related to the political ascendancy of the United States over the capitalist world and its ability to use its political power to shape the regimes of the world economy and to block political decisions in other centres that would disfavour key sectors of American business strength. In the wake of the Soviet bloc collapse, the American state was extraordinarily successful in using its political influence to reshape market rules internationally to favour the ascendancy of American business. Thus the ascendancy of American capitalism within the world economy is as much a question about

American success in constructing a global empire in the post-Soviet world as it is a question about economics.

And in this context, the effects of the Soviet bloc collapse and the turn by China and Russia towards capitalism and integration have been ambivalent in their effects. The political cohesiveness of the post-war capitalist core under American security protection in the Cold War has weakened. And China, as well as, to a lesser extent, Russia, seem likely to acquire substantial influence over both economic trends and the rules of the world economy while rejecting a role of geopolitical subordination to the United States. At the same time, the scale of the Chinese market as it deepens and grows offers scale economies that could dwarf those currently enjoyed with the American market. Thus, for those who adopt an American empire perspective on American external economic policy and for those who stress the centrality of economies of scale in international competition, the political and economic challenges to American global ascendancy in the twenty-first century may seem formidable.

> **KEY POINTS**
>
> ❑ The appropriateness and reliability of the indicators of American economic revival since the mid-1990s.
> ❑ The significance for American economic ascendancy of its current account deficits and its mounting foreign debt.
> ❑ The continued grounds for arguing that the USA is likely to maintain its economic ascendancy over the next two decades.
> ❑ Challenges on the horizon.

? Questions

1. Research American political debates and press opinion on any free trade agreement between the United States and another country in order to establish why the America government has promoted this agreement and why some powerful groups in Congress have opposed the agreement. Who do you think was right and why?

2. What sectors of the American civilian economy, if any, should be protected from foreign takeover and why?

3. In what ways does America's enormous military-political strength and reach make a major contribution to enabling the United States to shape the rules of the world economy?

4. During the 1980s and much of the 1990s successive American administrations perceived a serious industrial threat from Japan and imposed managed trade and managed production on some high-tech and medium-tech Japanese industrial sectors. Were they right about the threat and in the actions they took against Japan during this period?

5. Do you view America's chronic current account deficits as beneficial for the world economy or an irresponsible exploitation of American power in world affairs?

6. Does the readiness of American corporations to outsource jobs abroad and to relocate production in countries with cheap labour enhance or undermine the welfare of ordinary Americans? What, if anything, could be done to stop such moves?

7. What have been the main driving forces of protectionist political pressures in the United States since the 1980s?

8. To what extent do you think there is a broad, bipartisan elite consensus on the main lines of American external economic strategy at the present time?

9. What do you consider to have been the major disagreements on foreign economic policy between the Bush administration and the Democratic Party in Congress since 2001?

10. Some authors have stressed the importance for American external economic policy of special interest coalitions such as a 'military-industrial complex' or a 'Wall Street–Treasury complex'. Do you consider that such authors are right about the power of such coalitions?

11. Do you think those authors who talk about competitive threats to the American economy and about the need for strong external action against such competitive threats from other economies are right?

» Further Reading

On the sources of US foreign economic policy

Bhagwati, J. N. (2001), *The Wind of the Hundred Days: How Washington Mismanaged Globalization* (Cambridge, MA: MIT Press).

Cox, R. W. and Skidmore-Hess, D. (1999), *US Politics and the Global Economy: Corporate Power, Conservative Shift* (Boulder, CO: Lynne Rienner).

Dam, K. W. (2004), *The Rules of the Global Game: A New Look at US International Economic Policymaking* (Chicago: University of Chicago Press).

Foreign Affairs (1994), *Competitiveness: An International Economics Reader* (New York: Foreign Affairs).

Goldstein, J. (1988), Ideas, Institutions and American Trade Policy, *International Organisation*, 42/1 (Winter): 178–218.

Kolko, G. (1976), *Main Currents in Modern American History* (New York: Harper & Row), chs 7 and 8.

Lawrence, R. Z. and Schultze, C. L. (eds) (1990), *An American Trade Strategy: Options for the 1990s* (Washington, DC: Brookings Institution).

Verdier, D. (1994), *Democracy and International Trade* (Princeton: Princeton University Press).

On debates over what US economic strategy should be

On the politics of international economics

Gilpin, R. (1987), *The Political Economy of International Relations* (Princeton: Princeton University Press).

Meunier, S. (2005), *Trading Voices: The European Union in International Commercial Negotiations* (Princeton: Princeton University Press), ch. 2.

Odell, J. S. (2000), *Negotiating the World Economy* (Ithaca, NY: Cornell University Press).

Endnotes

1. Our focus in this chapter is on American policy for international economics. It therefore does not discuss American 'economic state-craft'—the ways in which the American state uses its economic and political resources to influence other states for political purposes, but altering their economic environment. On this important field of American external economic policy see Baldwin (1985).

2. Neo-Gramscian theorists would call this image a hegemonic one in Gramsci's sense of hegemony as leadership of others rather than a corporatist form of dominance. On Gramsci and hegemony see Cox (1996).

3. Hull's influence on the international policy of the Roosevelt administration was, in fact, small. See, for instance, Hathaway (1984).

4. See Williams (1970, 1972). Other American historians who have been linked with Williams's perspective include Walter LaFeber and Lloyd C. Gardner. On the school's influence, Michael Hogan writes that it 'constitutes perhaps the most creative contribution to our field in the last century and the only contribution to frame a grand, master narrative for American diplomatic history' (Hogan 2004: 13).

5. John Williamson has aptly called the monetary arrangements since 1971 a 'non-system' (Williamson and Milner 1991: 387).

6. See Major debates and their impact 18.1.

7. Notably, Laura D. Tyson, who became chair of Clinton's Council of Economic Advisers from 1993 to 1995 and director of the National Economic Council between 1995 and 1996.

8. FTAs are bilateral agreements giving preferential trade treatment outside multilateral frameworks such as those of the WTO. The economic case for this 'bilateralist' strategy was made in the 1990s by Rudiger Dornbusch. See his contribution in Lawrence and Schultze (1990).

9. Thus we exclude from this group those like Negri and Hardt who argue that the empire is not distinctively American in our sense. See Negri and Hardt (2000).

10. International Monetary Fund, accessed 17/01/2011 http://www.imf.org/external/pubs/ft/weo/2010/01/weodata/index.aspx.

19 Global terrorism

Paul Rogers

Chapter contents

Introduction: the 9/11 attacks

At 8.46 am on 11 September 2001, American Airlines Flight 11, a Boeing 767, crashed into the North Tower of the World Trade Center in New York. The immediate belief was that this was a horrifying accident, not least because there had been a similar incident in 1945 when a military aircraft crashed into the Empire State Building. However, sixteen minutes after the North Tower was struck, United Airlines Flight 175, also a Boeing 767, struck the South Tower. This was followed at 9.37 am by American Airlines Flight 77, a Boeing 757, crashing into the Department of Defense headquarters, the Pentagon, in Washington. Just under half an hour later, United Airlines Flight 93, also a Boeing 757, crashed into a field in Pennsylvania, after passengers had attempted

to take over the plane from hijackers. Both of the World Trade Center towers collapsed and the toll in New York, Washington and Pennsylvania was 2973 people killed and 24 missing presumed dead.

Within minutes of the North Tower being struck, live television coverage was available throughout the United States and the rest of the world, and tens of millions of Americans saw the towers collapse. The impact has been compared with the Japanese attack on Pearl Harbour in December 1941, but many would argue that it was substantially greater (see Box 19.1). The administration of President George W Bush responded to the atrocity with great vigour, starting what was termed the 'global war on terror'. All four planes had been taken

---

BOX 19.1: 9/11 and Pearl Harbor

The shock of the 9/11 atrocities to the people of the United States was so great that many commentators compared them to the only other surprise attack of any magnitude—the Japanese attack on the US naval base at Pearl Harbor in Hawaii on 7 December 1941. That attack left over 2400 people dead and more than 1000 injured, and brought the United States into the Second World War, but it had less immediate impact in at least four respects.

- The attacker was another country with which there was already a state of tension—risk of a war against Japan already existed.
- The attack was directed against a major naval base in distant Hawaii and, however much of a surprise, could be understood as a traditional, if particularly shocking, act of war against military targets.

- The greatest impact of 9/11 was the destruction of the twin towers in down-town New York and the killing of nearly 3000 civilians.
- The 9/11 attacks were witnessed live on television by tens of millions of Americans, whereas Pearly Harbour had a less visceral impact, given the virtually non-existent TV systems at that time.

Television coverage gave 9/11 an immediacy that was particularly shocking, as so many Americans witnessed the collapse of the two towers as they happened, knowing that thousands of people were being killed. In all of these respects, the impact of 9/11 was much greater than that of Pearl Harbor and, given the nature of the Bush administration, a war was inevitable even if it was to be against an enemy that was far more amorphous and dispersed than was Imperial Japan.

---

over by people associated with the radical Islamist group al-Qaeda, and the Bush administration made clear its intention to bring those behind the attacks to justice. This would clearly involve punishing the Taliban regime in Afghanistan if it did not cooperate, since it was harbouring the leaders of al-Qaeda.

Although the Bush administration was confident in its determination to destroy the al-Qaeda movement, early progress in the war on terror, including the termination of the Taliban regime, was not matched by the subsequent developments—close to ten years after the 9/11 attacks the United States remained mired in a protracted conflict in Afghanistan and the al-Qaeda movement was still active and seen in many countries as a persistent threat, in spite of the death of Osama Bin Laden. In Iraq the war had cost the lives of over 120,000 civilians and had left a deeply unstable and conflict-ridden country. The war

on terror had by this time become deeply controversial across the world and was even losing support in the United States itself. More generally, the 9/11 attacks and the robust American response were raising questions over the nature of terrorism in the early twenty-first century and whether the approach of the Bush administration had been either effective or even appropriate.

This chapter begins by discussing definitions of terrorism and then examines US experience of terrorism prior to 9/11 as well as the political environment in Washington at the time of the attacks. It then analyses the response of the Bush administration in Afghanistan and Iraq as well as the nature and aims of the al-Qaeda organisation. After making an assessment of the conduct of the war on terror in the first nine years, it concludes by discussing the options available to the United States in what came to be called the 'Long War against Islamofascism'.

Terrorism and the background to 9/11

Defining terrorism

A commonly used definition of terrorism is:

❝the threat of violence and the use of fear to coerce, persuade, and gain public attention. (National Advisory Committee 1976)❞

A more widely used definition, and one that is regarded as being particularly helpful, is that of Wardlaw (1982):

❝Political terrorism is the use, or threat of use, of violence by an individual or group, whether acting for or in opposition to established authority, when such action is designed to create extreme anxiety and/or fear-inducing effects in a target group larger than the immediate victims with the purpose of coercing that group into acceding to the political demands of the perpetrators. **"**

This definition is particularly helpful several respects. Firstly, it specifically focuses on 'political terrorism' as distinct from criminal use of terror, as in enforcing protection rackets. Referring to political terrorism does not mean that such terrorists cannot be considered criminals. Indeed, many analysts argue that doing so reduces their significance as actors fighting for a political cause.

Secondly, it specifically refers to state terrorism as well as sub-state terrorism, a distinction that is largely lacking in most post-9/11 studies on terrorism where almost the entire emphasis is on sub-state terrorism. This is important because the overwhelming majority of the victims of terrorism, certainly in recent decades, have been the victims of terror instituted by their own governments. Such terror has involved the deaths and detention of many millions of people in almost all regions of the world. It includes major terror campaigns in Stalin's Soviet Union, Nazi Germany, and post-war China, and the actions of many governments across Africa, Latin America, and Asia. It also includes the use of terror in many late colonial conflicts by the colonial powers. Almost all of this is lost in current terrorism studies where the emphasis may extend to state-sponsorship of sub-state groups, but rarely acknowledges the activities of states, including some democracies.

Finally, Wardlaw's definition is useful because it places emphasis on a key aspect of terrorism, the determination to cause fear in a wider community than those immediately targeted. This, too, applies to state terrorism, where detention without trial, torture, disappearances, and death squads have been employed and are still being employed in many countries. While the concern of this chapter is specifically with the American experience of sub-state terrorism, especially since the 9/11 attacks, it is necessary to remember this wider context, especially as there is a persistent tendency to apply the terms 'terror' and 'terrorist' in a pejorative sense, referring to legitimate political movements and individuals who cannot easily be described as terrorists.

The American experience before 9/11

Western European countries experienced paramilitary violence in the 1970s and 1980s from politically motivated groups, and there were sustained paramilitary actions in Northern Ireland, from the Provisional IRA and loyalist groups, and in Spain from the Basque Separatists, ETA. Across the Middle East, prior to 9/11, there were numerous paramilitary groups, many of them associated with the Palestinian cause. Elsewhere in the world, the Liberation Tigers of Tamil Elam (LTTE) in Sri Lanka used political violence repeatedly, although they would claim it was in response to government violence against the Tamil community. Many other countries have experienced terrorist activity, although the great majority of those killed, injured, or traumatized have been victims of state terrorism rather than of the activities of sub-state actors.

Prior to 9/11, the American experience of terrorism was relatively small, at least in terms of the conventional understanding of the term. At a time of political unrest in Europe in the 1960s and early 1970s, there were small-scale equivalents in the United States, including the left-wing Weathermen and the Symbionese Liberation Army, the latter famous for the kidnapping of the heiress Patty Hearst in February 1974. In parallel with these were the right-wing Minutemen, and it was from the political right that the worst individual act of terrorism came with the bombing of the Alfred P Murrah Federal Government building in Oklahoma City on 19 April 1995, killing 168 people and injuring more than 500 (Anderson and Sloan 2002). Although less serious than the Oklahoma bombing in terms of casualties, the first attack on the World Trade Center, on 26 February 1993, was potentially catastrophic. The intention was to collapse the tower over the Vista Hotel, which connected the two towers, and then into the South Tower, completely destroying all three buildings. In the attack, six people were killed and over a thousand were injured, although most of these involved relatively minor instances of smoke inhalation. While some of those responsible had already left the country, a number of others were detained and later imprisoned for long terms.

The Oklahoma and 1993 World Trade Center bombings are generally considered to be the main examples of terrorist action in the United States prior to 2001, although many people would argue strongly that there had been highly significant examples of systematic terrorism directed against minorities. These included many incidents involving First Nation (native American) groups during the mid and late 1800s, some involving massacres on a considerable scale. The argument from a First Nation perspective was that these should be properly described as acts of terrorism as they were intended to use large-scale fear for direct political purposes. Similarly, the innumerable examples of beatings, torture, and lynching of Black Americans, especially in Southern states well into the mid-twentieth century, have been described as systematic terrorism—the deliberate use of violence to instil fear into a wider community, ensuring their compliance with their allotted and subservient position in society.

More problematic in terms of foreign relations and controversial with regard to perceptions of terrorism was the widespread support among Irish Americans for the activities of the Provisional IRA in Northern Ireland and Britain, especially in the 1970s and 1980s. Even more controversial has been the question of US government support for paramilitary groups and what has been described as state terrorism in Latin America (George 1991). The arguments revolve around direct or indirect support for anti-leftist paramilitary groups in countries such as Nicaragua, El Salvador, and Guatemala, as well as for autocratic regimes such as that of General Augusto Pinochet in Chile, the main period being the 1970s and 1980s. Frequent claims were made of the training of military and paramilitary personnel at sites such as the School of the Americas, with training including the use of torture and other forms of terror. The counter argument was that support for such groups did not extend to terrorism and was, in any case, necessary in the context of the intense Cold War competition with the Soviet Union.

US foreign policy and the Bush administration

The election of George W. Bush to the White House resulted in an administration that developed its foreign and security policy in a particular direction. This was largely due to the influence of a group of neoconserva-

tive opinion formers, backed by a wider circle of politicians and advisers from an assertive realist background. Following the collapse of the Soviet Union at the end of the Cold War, the post-Cold War world was seen as a vindication of free market liberal democracy, and many in the Bush administration were convinced of the possibility of envisaging a New American Century for the twenty-first century. In such a global environment the United States would play a world-wide civilizing role, ensuring an era of peace and security for humankind.

One particular concern was that what was seen as an excessive involvement in multilateral initiatives and negotiations could limit freedom of action, to the detriment both of the United States and its role in ensuring the New American Century. As a consequence, a number of early moves by the Bush administration signalled a desire to avoid such limits. It was clear that a Comprehensive Test Ban Treaty would not be ratified by the United States, there would be a withdrawal from the Anti-Ballistic Missile Treaty, there were grave doubts about aspects of the planned International Criminal Court and proposals to control arms transfers between states, and the United States would be highly unlikely to support negotiations to prevent the weaponization of space. Of particular concern to a number of western European states was the decision of the Bush administration to withdraw from the Kyoto climate change protocols, but there was also concern that the administration might not back the complex negotiations under way in Geneva to strengthen the 1972 Biological and Toxin Weapons Convention.

From the perspective of the Bush administration, however, all of these policy changes fitted in with the

---

KEY POINTS

- ❏ Terrorism is most commonly conducted by states against their own populations.
- ❏ Prior to the 9/11 attacks, the United States had relatively limited exposure to terrorism.
- ❏ Some US activities in support of Irish republican groups and of paramilitary groups in Latin America were controversial.
- ❏ As the sole superpower, the United States political system was particularly shocked by the 9/11 attacks.

idea that the United States, as the sole superpower, had the right and duty to determine the world's future. Furthermore, it had a historic responsibility to promote its political and social ideals in a manner that was confidently expected to make the world a better place. By the late summer of 2001, the mood in Washington was one of ebullience as it appeared that the administration really could further the idea of a New American Century with little prospect of any serious opposition. It was in this mood that the United States was to respond to the 9/11 attacks, and it was perhaps inevitable that the response would be very robust, given the sudden perception of vulnerability at a time when the future looked so bright.

The war on terror I

9/11 and the start of the war

Prior to the 9/11 attacks, the United States had already experienced a number of paramilitary attacks on facilities in the Middle East and North Africa. These included the killing of a number of US soldiers in Riyadh in Saudi Arabia in the mid-1990s, and the much more substantial attack on the Khobar Towers accommodation block at the US Air Force's King Abdul Aziz Air Base at Dhahran in eastern Saudi Arabia on 25 June 1996. In that attack, 19 US service personnel were killed and 500 people injured. The bombing was claimed to have been down to internal Saudi paramilitaries, possibly linked to the al-Qaeda movement, but some investigators pointed to a possible connection with Iran.

Even more costly than the Khobar Towers attack were the bombings of the US embassies in Nairobi and Dar es Salaam on 7 August 1998. The Dar es Salaam attack killed ten Tanzanians, with one American employee wounded, but the Nairobi attack was far more devastating as it caused the collapse of an office building alongside the Embassy. The huge blast killed twelve US citizens and wounded six more, but the cost in lives for Kenyans was even higher than the Oklahoma bombing a year earlier, with 279 Kenyans killed and around 5000 injured. Even so, neither the Khobar Towers nor the Embassy bombings were sufficient to prepare Americans for the impact of the 9/11 attacks.

The immediate response of the Bush administration to the 9/11 atrocities was to demand that the Taliban regime in Afghanistan cease harbouring the leadership of the al-Qaeda movement or risk the use of US military force to do so, implying the termination of the regime if it did not comply. In the wake of the attacks the United States had strong support from people and governments in western Europe, with the French newspaper *Le Monde* famously using the headline 'We Are All Americans Now', the day after the attack. Support in much of the rest of the world was far more muted. It ranged from a degree of satisfaction, especially among many people in the Arab world, that the United States was on the receiving end of a violent attack, to a much more nuanced concern that a resultant worldwide war on terror might be deeply counterproductive (see Box 19.2).

In the absence of the required response from the Taliban regime in Kabul, the United States then moved rapidly to destroy the regime and the al-Qaeda militias in Afghanistan. Although the al-Qaeda movement might have hoped for a full-scale US military occupation of Afghanistan, in order to lure it into a protracted guerrilla war, a rather different route to regime termination was taken, involving three elements. The main one was the decision to re-arm and re-supply the Northern Alliance forces, at that time the losing parties in the Afghan civil war. Supplies came largely from former Soviet states, although funded by the United States. Secondly, the United States used extensive air power, both to destroy specific targets of value to the Taliban and also to use area impact munitions to kill Taliban units when they could be caught in any sizeable concentrations. Finally, the United States made extensive use of Special Forces, partly for target acquisition but also for direct support of Northern Alliance forces. US conventional military units were deployed in due course, principally troops from the Marine Corps in the south east of the country, especially around Kandahar.

BOX 19.2 9/11 and the majority world

One of the most astute analysts of the immediate aftermath of the 9/11 attacks from a perspective away from the North Atlantic community was the academic and activist Walden Bello, a former academic at the University of California and later a Professor at the University of the Philippines and also Director of the influential Focus on the Global South non-government organization in Bangkok. In a remarkably prescient analysis written barely two weeks after the 9/11 attacks, Bello pointed to the risk of an endless war if the United States concentrated almost exclusively on a military response. He was forthright in condemning the attacks themselves but counselled against a response that ignored the widespread view of the United States across much of the majority world, pointing to the massive use of force in Vietnam and the bitter mood of opposition to US policies in the Middle East, not least in terms of US support for Israel and for elitist and autocratic regimes in countries such as Saudi Arabia and Egypt.

According to Bello, a quite different response was required:

"The only response that will readily contribute to global security and peace is for Washington to address not the symptoms but the roots of terrorism. It is for the United States to re-examine and substantially change its policies in the Middle East and the Third World, supporting for a change arrangements that will not stand in the way of the achievement of equity, justice and genuine national sovereignty for currently marginalized people. Any other way leads to endless war.' (Bello 2001)"

Some indication of the radically different responses to the 9/11 attacks is that such a view would be roundly condemned in most political circles in Washington, just as it struck a loud chord with many opinion formers in the world away from the countries of the North Atlantic community.

The Afghan War initially appeared to be a conspicuous success, with the Taliban regime terminated by the end of November 2001, little more than six weeks after the start of the war, but this was somewhat misleading. In many cases, most notably in Kabul, the Taliban militia simply melted away, with their armaments intact, to towns and villages in Afghanistan and western Pakistan. Very few of the al-Qaeda militia were killed or detained, with most of the training camps found to be deserted when US troops eventually entered them. There were some instances when US troops came under intensive attack, especially in the Tora Bora mountains, but for the most part both the Taliban and al-Qaeda militias simply dispersed.

Even so, many hundreds were detained and there was an immediate controversy over the Bush administration's decision to detain large numbers of suspected terrorists at a camp established at the Guantanamo Bay military base in Cuba. This was out of the area of the US judiciary but was not subject to the Cuban judiciary. As a result, the detainees were fully under the control of the Pentagon and were widely seen outside the United States as being illegally detained. This was strongly disputed by the administration in Washington and there was initially little opposition within the United States to the establishment of the Guantanamo detention centre.

The State of the Union and West Point speeches

The first six months of 2002 can be said to have marked the high point of the success of the war on terror and are particularly significant for the manner in which the early achievements in Afghanistan led on to a significant expansion of the war aims, an expansion that was expressed in two key addresses by President Bush, the 2002 State of the Union address in January and the Graduation Address at the West Point Military Academy five months later. The State of the Union address was delivered to both Houses of Congress in the manner of a victory speech, with numerous rounds of applause. While signalling the extent of the victory in Afghanistan it went much further in extending the concept of the war on terror well beyond retaliatory action against the al-Qaeda movement in two specific ways.

The first of these was to make it clear that the enemy in the war on terror was not just limited to the al-Qaeda movement but to other Islamic radical organizations such as Hezbollah, Hamas, and Islamic Jihad. President Bush cited US operations in Bosnia, Somalia, and the Philippines, and placed particular emphasis on the need to destroy training camps wherever they might be, 'in remote jungles and deserts, and hides in the centres of large cities' (Bush 2002). He made it clear that it was essential for all legitimate states to control such movements and went on to emphasize that if some governments chose not to act, then the United States would do so.

The second extension announced in the Address was even more significant. The global war on terror was to go well beyond the issue of sub-state terror groups to include a number of rogue states that were defined as working against US security interests, both by their support for terrorist organizations and by their determination to develop weapons of mass destruction. Using the key phrase an 'axis of evil', President Bush expanded the war to include such states as Iraq, Iran, and North Korea, and made it clear that these states would not be allowed to threaten the United States. Either they gave up their activities in relation to terrorism and the pursuit of weapons of mass destruction or they would face regime termination.

This major extension of the war was generally popular in the United States in early 2002, and there was specific support for possible action against the Saddam Hussein regime in Iraq. At the same time, it gave rise to considerable unease in other countries that had otherwise been sympathetic to the American predicament after 9/11. This was reflected in the cautious response of some western European governments to the speech, but much more so in terms of adverse public opinion, even in countries such as Britain where the Prime Minister, Tony Blair, was fulsome in his support for the Bush administration.

Four months after the State of the Union address, President Bush's speech at the West Point Military Academy went even further, making it clear that the United States had the right to take pre-emptive action against an enemy that might be a future threat to US security. This clearly included military action against states, with key members of the axis of evil such as Iraq and Iran being obvious candidates for enforced regime change if there were not internal transformations. In the intervening period between the two addresses there were many indications that the Saddam Hussein regime in Iraq would be the first candidate for pre-emptive military action.

The Iraq War

In March 2003, following discussions and a relatively weak resolution at the United Nations, a coalition of states led by the United States began a military campaign to terminate the Saddam Hussein regime. Within three weeks this had been achieved and there was an expectation that Iraq would make a rapid transition to a stable pro-western country, with the coalition forces welcomed as liberators. This proved to be a gross misreading of the situation on many counts. The first was that weapons of mass destruction were not found, despite this being the primary stated motive in going to war. Secondly, little evidence emerged of any relationship between the Saddam Hussein regime and the al-Qaeda movement. This was hardly surprising given that Iraq had had a largely secular regime under Saddam Hussein, a form of governance anathema to the al-Qaeda movement.

In the immediate aftermath of the termination of the regime, there was extensive public disorder, widespread looting, and rampant criminality as the coalition forces proved hopelessly inadequate to maintain control. Furthermore, the intentions of the US-appointed Coalition Provisional Authority (CPA), answerable to the Pentagon and not the State Department, failed almost from the start. A plan to establish a free market economy with a flat-rate tax and wholesale privatization of state assets was made almost impossible to achieve by the decision to terminate the employment of public service officials who had been members of the Ba'ath Party of the old regime. Such membership was a pre-requisite for most posts and did not necessarily imply strong support for Saddam Hussein, and the loss of a huge cohort of technocrats, managers, and administrators meant that much of the state apparatus ceased to function. A further mistake was the wholesale dismissal of the Iraq Army, throwing several hundred thousand trained soldiers onto the streets, where many could join an evolving insurgency.

That insurgency developed rapidly within four months of the start of the war, one of most notable examples being the bombing of the UN headquarters in Baghdad. The killing of Uday and Qusay Hussein in July 2003 and the capture of Saddam Hussein himself five months later had no discernible effect on the insurgency, which continued to develop over the next three years. By early 2007, the United States military had lost nearly 3500 people killed and over 25,000 injured, with many of those injured being maimed for life. Countering a largely urban insurgency by determined paramilitary groups proved very difficult, and there was a marked tendency for US forces to use their immense firepower advantages, often resulting in considerable collateral damage and civilian casualties. The assault on the city of Fallujah in November 2004 was a notable example of this and had an effect well beyond Iraq (see Box 19.3). Although Iraqi civilian casualties were difficult to measure with any accuracy, at least 100,000 were killed in the first four years; at times in the fourth year of the war, the monthly civilian casualties in Iraq were as great as the entire loss of life in the 9/11 attacks.

BOX 19.3 Case study: Fallujah—whose terrorism?

In November 2004, with the war in Iraq barely eighteen months old, the US Army and Marine Corps launched a combined assault on the city of Fallujah, west of Baghdad, believing it to be the epicentre of the insurgency that was proving so difficult to counter. To the Bush administration, the Fallujah assault was an entirely necessary part of countering the terrorism that lay at the heart of the insurgency. As a result, considerable access was given to TV channels to record the assault, from the American perspective, as it progressed. To Muslims across the Arab world, the assault on Fallujah, which killed thousands of people, was nothing less than terrorism, and was widely compared to the 9/11 attacks. There was therefore a complete discontinuity in how the events were seen, and exploring this throws some light on the vexed question of why the war on terror has lasted so long.

A year after the termination of the Saddam Hussein regime, the insurgency in Iraq was developing rapidly, with American forces already losing scores of soldiers and hundreds wounded every month. The city of Fallujah was in the heart of central Iraq and was very largely populated by Sunni Muslims, many of whom had supported the previous regime of Saddam Hussein and were bitterly opposed to what was widely seen as a US occupation of their city and country, not a liberation from an oppressive regime. In April 2004, Fallujah was not under the control of the US forces, but a major attempt was made to change that in the wake of a particularly violent incident. On 31 March, five US Marines were killed when their armoured personnel carrier was blown up and on the same day four American private security contractors were seized by insurgents and killed. Their bodies were then mutilated and burnt before being hung from the girders of a bridge in front of a large angry crowd.

The subsequent attempt by the US Marine Corps to gain control of the city was partly in reaction to this atrocity, but US military units frequently found themselves engaged in bitter fights in an enclosed urban environment. On one occasion, a group of Marines was ambushed in the city by insurgents, suffered injuries, took refuge in nearby buildings and was only rescued by a heavily armed and armoured convoy after many hours of fighting. While Marine Corps representatives spoke proudly of the Marines' code of leaving no one behind, tensions in the city were exacerbated by an intensive reprisal raid on the area of the fighting by US AC-130 gunships several hours later. This destroyed several city blocks.

Six months later the city was considered to be such a centre of insurgency that a much larger assault and occupation was thought likely to cause the insurgency irreversible damage. As a result, a large force of around 15,000 troops and Marines was assembled for an all-out assault on the city. Over a protracted operation lasting more than two weeks Fallujah was indeed brought under control. The full extent of Iraqi casualties remains unknown but appears to have been several thousand people killed. About half of the 39,000 houses in Fallujah were either destroyed or badly damaged during the conflict, as well as most of the schools and other public buildings.

What was particularly notable about Fallujah was the remarkably contrasting images of the conflict as seen on US and Middle Eastern television channels. In the United States there was copious coverage of the artillery, tanks, and other weapons used in the assault. Particularly graphic images were broadcast of tracer bullets arcing over the river and into the city. Other images showed mosques and other buildings being hit as US troops systematically moved through the densely packed streets. All of them demonstrated the power of the US military and they were generally well-received by many Americans as proof of the progress of the war. Here was a clear example of US forces taking the war to the enemy

BOX 19.3 Case study: Fallujah—whose terrorism?—continued

and taking control of the heartland of the insurgency—a city in which atrocities had been carried out against Americans earlier in the year. Throughout the assault, the administration repeatedly described the insurgents as terrorists. For the United States, Fallujah was a major success in the war in Iraq, and since this was seen as part of the wider war on terror, then the Fallujah attack could be seen as a battle won in that difficult war.

Even as the images of US military success were being broadcast, regional stations such as Al-Jazeera were showing graphic and uncensored images from within the city, with corpses and body parts strewn across the streets, and with women and children critically wounded and waiting in understaffed and under-equipped medical centres. The scene for Arab and Muslim audiences was almost a mirror-image of the view from Washington. Fallujah was known as 'the city of mosques' and the American attack was seen as a direct assault by 'crusader' forces on what was almost a holy city. Furthermore, both the US TV footage of the firepower directed into the city, and the regional coverage from within the city, strongly reinforced this view. In particular, the US TV images of the heavy firepower being used to great effect may have gone down well in the United States but had the directly opposite effect in the Middle East. Whatever the value of the taking of Fallujah to the US military, its propaganda value for the insurgents and, indeed, the wider al-Qaeda movement, was very much greater.

Moreover, Fallujah did not turn out to be in any sense a turning point for the United States in Iraq. In the months that followed, the city was garrisoned by US and Iraqi government troops and was subjected to very high levels of security. These included a cordon around the entire city, with all vehicles subject to search and all adult males searched with particular diligence. In spite of this, improvised explosive devices were being manufactured in the city and used against American forces within months of the original attack.

Across Iraq as a whole, the insurgency gathered pace in the following months. Indeed at the very time that the US forces were engaged in the assault on Fallujah, the insurgency moved north to the city of Mosul. Such was the intensity of the sudden outbreak of fighting that the United States had to move in 2400 troops to reinforce the units there. Not only did the November 2004 assault on Fallujah fail to stem the insurgency, it almost certainly increased antagonism to the United States in Iraq and beyond, a result directly counterproductive to the original aim of the operation. What remains most significant, though, is the opposing views of the same events. For many Americans it was a reassuring demonstration of military capabilities in a bitter war against uncompromising terrorists but for millions of people across the region it was proof of the ruthlessness of a foreign invader.

The Iraq War was primarily against insurgents who were Iraqis, but there were also paramilitary elements drawn in from other states, with some of them connected to the al-Qaeda movement. Partly on this basis, the Bush administration persistently represented the Iraq War as an essential part of the overall war on terror, seeking to establish it within the United States as part of the justified response to the original 9/11 attacks. Even so, support for the war decreased markedly during 2006, leading to the loss of control of Congress by the Republican Party. Furthermore, even as this was happening, developments in Afghanistan and in the capabilities of the al-Qaeda movement were such that more general aspects of the war on terror were becoming pertinent to any assessment of its progress.

KEY POINTS

❑ The immediate US reaction after 9/11 was to terminate the Taliban regime in Afghanistan and disperse the al-Qaeda movement.

❑ The war on terror was extended in 2002 to include an axis of evil of rogue states such as Iraq, Iran, and North Korea.

❑ The Saddam Hussein regime was terminated early in 2003.

❑ An insurgency developed rapidly, against the expectations of the Bush administration.

The war on terror II

Afghanistan

When the US-led coalition successfully terminated the Taliban regime in Afghanistan, the Bush administration was confident that the al-Qaeda network had been substantially disrupted and that Afghanistan would make a rapid transition to a stable pro-western state, increasing US influence in Central Asia. At the time, however, some of the most experienced analysts, especially senior UN personnel, expressed the need for very substantial aid for Afghanistan, in addition to the immediate deployment of a peacekeeping force of around 30,000 troops to ensure stability. Given that the country had experienced decades of war, it was considered wholly unrealistic to think that it could achieve a peaceful transition without substantial external help. There was also a particular concern, largely ignored by the Bush administration, that the Taliban militias had disappeared from sight rather than had been defeated, and that they and their al-Qaeda associates had substantial scope for redeveloping their capabilities given that the frontier districts of Pakistan, such as North and South Waziristan, were areas where there was little or no central Pakistani government control.

In spite of these warnings, the United States was already pre-occupied with preparing for regime termination in Iraq, and European states were very slow in providing aid or security assistance for the country. As a result, Taliban and other militias began to regain influence and control, especially in the south and south-east of Afghanistan so that within five years of regime termination a serious insurgency was developing. Insurgents were aided by a substantial increase in opium poppy cultivation, with record harvests being declared in 2006. Moreover, far more of the raw opium was now being refined into heroin and morphine within the country rather than exported in its raw form. This greatly increased the illicit finances coming into the country. During the period 2002–2007, NATO's International Security Assistance Force (ISAF) was eventually increased to around 30,000 troops, together with many thousands more US combat troops not under NATO command. While much of northern and western Afghanistan made slow progress, large areas of the south and east of the country were mired in conflict between coalition forces and a resurgent Taliban.

The Taliban capabilities were greatly aided by the lack of Pakistani government control of frontier districts. With the Taliban and other militias drawing largely from ethnic Pashtuns, and with the Pashtun community stretching well into Pakistan, the result was that the border districts were secure areas in which paramilitary groups were relatively safe from attack, and could train recruits and move supplies into Afghanistan. Furthermore, although the al-Qaeda movement was substantially dispersed, it too could treat areas of western Pakistan as safe havens. Given a strong mood of anti-Americanism across much of Pakistani society, it was not initially feasible for US forces to extend the war against the Taliban or al-Qaeda elements to Pakistan, although by 2010 the extensive use of armed drones was doing just this, while proving highly unpopular in Pakistan.

By early 2009, numbers of coalition troops in Afghanistan had been increased steadily and when Barack Obama took office in January 2009 he accepted the need for a further surge in troop numbers even while he committed the United States to a progressive withdrawal of most US troops from Iraq. By early 2011 US forces in Afghanistan exceeded 100,000, with a further 40,000 troops from other coalition states. The Obama administration saw the troop surge as a means of enabling an eventual withdrawal from Afghanistan following negotiations with Taliban and other armed opposition groups conducted from a position of strength. It was far from clear that this would be possible, with some evidence suggesting that the surge in foreign troop numbers was actually having the effect of increasing armed opposition to what was seen as a foreign occupation. What was more immediately significant, however, was that the Obama administration was implementing a different policy to that of its predecessor. Under President Bush, the Afghan policy was one of comprehensively defeating the Taliban movement. For the Obama administration there was a singular lack of conviction that this was possible, and the purpose of the troop surge in 2010 was primarily to negotiate withdrawal from a position of military strength. This would hopefully involve a substantial element of withdrawal before the President sought re-election in 2012.

The Al-Qaeda movement

In the 1980s there was vigorous opposition to the Soviet occupation of Afghanistan, coming mainly from radical Islamic paramilitaries known as the *mujahidin*. Aided by the Inter-Services Intelligence agency in Pakistan and strongly supported by the CIA, the *mujahidin* were eventually successful and the Soviet armed forces withdrew in some disarray. The Afghan defeat was one of the reasons for the collapse of the Soviet system, although some Islamic radicals believed that it was almost entirely due to the resistance.

One significant member of the *mujahidin* was a young Saudi of Yemeni extraction, Osama Bin Laden. His main role was in logistics and he had considerable wealth inherited from his father, who had run the leading construction company in Saudi Arabia, although he also had support from the CIA. Osama bin Laden and others, especially the Egyptian intellectual Ayman Zawahiri, regarded the Soviet withdrawal from Afghanistan as a great achievement, but were subsequently rebuffed by the Saudi authorities when they offered their expertise to help safeguard the Kingdom of the Two Holy Places (Mecca and Medina) when the Saddam Hussein regime occupied Kuwait in 1990.

After the 1991 Iraq War, bin Laden and others were bitterly opposed to the continuing US military presence in Saudi Arabia, regarding it as an utter affront to Islam that such 'crusader' forces could be entrenched in the heart of the Islamic world. Their opposition resulted in bin Laden's exile to Sudan during the 1990s and later to Afghanistan, where the radical Taliban regime enabled him and his associates to develop training camps and build a radical paramilitary movement known as al-Qaeda ('the base'). While the al-Qaeda movement tends to be regarded as a nihilistic terrorist organization that cannot be considered in any way a political entity, this is a basic misreading of a movement that is an unusual combination of fundamentalist religious belief with very clear-cut political aims that stretch from a few decades through to a century or more.

Al-Qaeda is therefore best seen as a revolutionary movement with a religious belief rather than a specific political ideology at its root. In the short term it seeks the expulsion of all 'crusader' (i.e. western) forces from the Islamic world, commencing with Saudi Arabia, and the termination of what it sees as elitist, corrupt, unrepresentative, and pro-western regimes in countries across the Islamic world, especially Saudi Arabia and Egypt. The movement also supports some separatist groups such as those in southern Thailand and Islamic radicals in Kashmir and Chechnya. It is bitterly anti-Zionist and supports the Palestinian cause, even though most Palestinians do not want to be associated with the movement. All of these aims are regarded as achievable over a timescale measured in several decades, with the removal of uniformed US military forces in Saudi Arabia already having been achieved. In the long term, the movement seeks to establish a radical Islamist Caliphate, centred on the Middle East, but this is an aim that may take 50 to 100 years.

Four aspects of the movement are particularly important. One is that it works on an entirely different timescale to that of western political systems. They may look four to five years ahead whereas al-Qaeda measures its progress in decades. Secondly, and related to this, the al-Qaeda leadership does not envisage its long-term aims being achieved in its lifetime. This therefore has an eschatological dimension that is quite different from most revolutionary movements in the last three centuries, where the revolutionaries have depended on support generated substantially through the prospect of short-term success.

A third feature of the movement concerns its dispersal since the 9/11 attacks and the remarkable manner in which this has been combined with a maintenance of support. Regime termination in Afghanistan and the killing or detention of significant elements of the leadership might have been expected to have hugely weakened the movement, but this has not proved to be the case. It has transformed itself into a very loose connection of groups, with some modest degree of centralization, primarily in western Pakistan. It has been

---

BOX 19.4   Television and terrorism

One of the reasons for the very robust response of the Bush administration to the 9/11 attacks was that there was tremendous support from across the United States, partly because of the manner in which the atrocity had been witnessed live on television by many tens of millions of Americans (see Box 19.1). In the months that followed, television footage of the war in Afghanistan on US TV networks showed little of the civilian casualties of the war, but this was not the case for audiences across the Middle East and the majority world. In Afghanistan and even more so in Iraq, a new generation of 24-hour satellite TV news channels was covering the wars not from an American perspective but from the position of civilians who were on the receiving end of US firepower. Two of the most significant channels were Al-Arabiya, based in Dubai, and, even more so, Al-Jazeera, based in Qatar.

Al-Jazeera, in particular, developed a reputation for technical competence and professionalism, but took a much more robust approach to broadcasting images of casualties, showing dead and injured people in a far more graphic manner than was common among western networks. A few months into the Iraq War, Al Jazeera was getting audiences for its prime-time bulletins of some tens of millions of people across the Middle East. Moreover, it acquired a reputation for authenticity because it also screened debates about major Arab themes, some of them covering thorny questions such as corruption, with implied criticisms of some of the elites controlling countries such as Egypt and Jordan. This later proved particularly significant in relation to its coverage of political change in Tunisia and Egypt in early 2011, with Al-Jazeera English extending the organization's reach to new constituencies across the world.

---

hugely aided by the coverage of the wars in Afghanistan and Iraq, especially the reporting of large numbers of civilian casualties on satellite TV news channels such as Al-Jazeera (see Box 19.4). Such reporting has combined with overtly propagandistic videos, DVDs, and internet communications to produce a sense of Islam under attack that has powerfully aided support for the movement.

The value of Iraq

Finally, the greatest single advantage to the al-Qaeda movement was the seven-year US-led war in Iraq. This benefited the movement in two quite different ways. The first is that it could be readily represented as a 'crusader' occupation of a key Arab/Islamic state and, as such, an affront to Islam as a whole. This may be the direct opposite to a view still common in the United States that the Iraq War was a war of liberation of the Iraqi people from a dangerous and brutal dictatorship. The second benefit was for Iraq to become what might be described as a jihadist combat training zone, steadily producing an accumulation of young paramilitaries who travelled to Iraq from across the Middle East and North Africa, and gained combat experience in the cities and towns of central Iraq.

The proportion of foreign paramilitaries in Iraq may have been small, perhaps barely a tenth of the insurgents, but as they moved in and through Iraq they made up a growing cohort. Moreover, their experience was more significant than that of an earlier generation of paramilitaries in Afghanistan in the 1980s. They were opposing a Soviet occupation primarily by young conscripts in a largely rural environment. Jihadist paramilitaries in Iraq gained combat experience against professional and exceptionally well-equipped US forces in a largely urban environment. Given that the wider al-Qaeda movement is concerned with terminating regimes across the Middle East over a period of several decades, such an evolving cohort of paramilitaries may well turn out to be one of the most disturbing aspects of the Iraq War.

The status of Al-Qaeda in 2010

Two decades after it first evolved, and a decade after the 9/11 attacks, the al-Qaeda movement was still developing and was attracting substantial support from across the Middle East and beyond. In terms of its direct capabilities and leaving aside the substantial involvements in Afghanistan and Iraq, by late 2010 the movement could be said to have been far more active in the nine years following the 9/11 attacks than in a similar period before. This alone is enough to suggest that the conduct of the US-led war on terror had not achieved its anticipated aims.

Over the period 2002–10, the al-Qaeda movement or its loose affiliates carried out attacks in many countries. They included major incidents in London, Madrid, and Bali, and many other attacks against western or Israeli targets, or against local elites. Examples included a number of attacks on US interests in Pakistan, two double bombings against Jewish and British targets in Istanbul, the bombing of the Marriott Hotel and the Australian Embassy in Djakarta, a synagogue in Tunisia and four western-orientated targets in Casablanca. Israeli interests were attacked at the Paradise Hotel in Kikambala, Kenya, the attempt to shoot down an Israeli tourist jet, also in Kenya, and the bombing of the Taba Hilton and a camp site in Sinai, both popular with Israeli tourists. In addition to other attacks in Sinai, there was an attempt to damage an American warship in Aqaba Harbour in Jordan, the bombing of three western hotels in the Jordanian capital of Amman, and several attacks in Saudi Arabia, including an attempt to disrupt oil exports by bombing the Abqaiq oil processing plant. Many other planned attacks in London, Paris, Rome, Singapore, and elsewhere were disrupted, but the overall situation, nine years after 9/11, was of a movement that was not in retreat and of a United States military predicament in Afghanistan that did not lend itself to easy solutions unless there were major changes in policy.

The Arab Spring and the death of Bin Laden

While al-Qaeda remained a potent if dispersed movement at the end of 2010, two major developments in the early months of 2011 had the potential to damage the movement. The first was the development of the Arab Spring, a series of mass public protests against autocratic regimes across the Middle East. Beginning in Tunisia in January, protests spread rapidly to Egypt, where the previously stable and repressive Mubarak regime collapsed within three weeks. Protests spread across the region and were met with a mixture of reform and repression. In Morocco and Jordan there were significant political responses to public demands for reform, and in Yemen the Saleh regime looked particularly vulnerable. Elsewhere, however, there was considerable repression in Bahrain and especially Syria. In Libya there was western intervention under a UN Security Council mandate in pursuit of humanitarian protection, but there were also clear signs of a desire by the leaderships in the United States, France, and Britain to see the termination of the Gaddafi regime.

For the al-Qaeda movement, which had long sought the overthrow of autocratic regimes across the region and their replacement by Islamist rule, the Arab Spring presented a major challenge. The role of radical Islam in the public protests was minimal and instead the opposition to autocracy and the desire for emancipation and democracy was coming from multiple sources, with a strong secular element. As such, the al-Qaeda movement was effectively being sidelined, a circumstance that represented the greatest threat to its viability for at least a decade. Even so, the movement remained viable and much would depend on the further progress of the Arab Spring in the early 2010s. If it led on to genuine reform in countries right across the regime, then there was every chance that al-Qaeda would sink into obscurity, at least in the Middle East if not South Asia. If, on the other hand, the Arab Spring failed to evolve and there was substantial repression and rigidity, then the al-Qaeda movement would have a remarkable opportunity to provide an enduring focus for dissent.

The second issue facing the movement was the killing of Osama Bin Laden by a US Navy SEAL team on 1 May 2011. Bin Laden was killed in a compound in the Pakistani military garrison town of Abbottabad, to the north of the capital Islamabad and adjacent to one of Pakistan's main military academies. The location made it plausible that elements within Pakistani military intelligence were colluding in ensuring Bin Laden's security, a concern that heightened the problems the United States had in its relationship with Pakistan. The death of bin Laden was hugely welcomed in the US, and was widely seen as constituting an element of closure in the ten-year war on terror, but in a wider perspective, the reality was that Bin Laden was primarily a figurehead for the movement rather than a serious leader. By 2011, al-Qaeda had long since evolved into a highly dispersed entity with many loose affiliates across the world, including active groups in Yemen, Somalia, and across North Africa as well as individuals who were active within diasporas in western Europe and North America. While it was weaker than in the early 2000s, it retained a potency that suggested that Bin Laden's death would do little to bring closure to the western conflict with the movement.

KEY POINTS

❑ Afghanistan did not make the transition to a peaceful society and the Taliban re-emerged.

❑ The al-Qaeda movement was more active in the six years following 9/11 than before.

❑ The al-Qaeda movement operates on a timescale measured in decades.

❑ Iraq became a useful combat training zone for Islamist paramilitaries.

❑ The death of Osama Bin Laden and the prospect of regional reform following the Arab Spring of early 2011 represented the biggest threats to the viability of the movement in at least a decade.

Conclusion: rethinking the war on terror

In the first decade of the war on terror the United States and its coalition partners terminated two regimes, in Afghanistan and Iraq, took action in Yemen, Pakistan, and Somalia, and engaged with intelligence and security agencies across the world. While the United States did not experience another major paramilitary attack on its own territory, there were several attempts that were prevented, including intended bombings in Los Angeles and New York, and the hi-jacking of aircraft. At the same time, the al-Qaeda movement engaged in many actions against western interests, including attacks on US facilities such as diplomatic missions and US-owned hotels.

During the first decade, well over 100,000 people were detained without trial for varying periods, with some detained for over seven years, not least at Guantanamo Bay in Cuba. At any one time for much of that period, around 20,000 people were in detention, mainly in Iraq and Afghanistan. At least 120,000 civilians were killed in Iraq and Afghanistan, probably many more. A confrontation with Iran was possible. Across the Middle East and much of the majority world, there was a measurable increase in anti-American attitudes and the coalition of states supporting the United States in Iraq was reduced to a handful. US military casualties were high, with close to 4000 killed and well over 30,000 injured. Because of improvements in body armour and battlefield medicine,

many of the injured who survived had grievous wounds, frequently likely to have lifetime effects.

While US troop numbers decreased markedly in Iraq in 2009–10, the country remained mired in insecurity, with at least 4000 civilians killed in each year. Meanwhile, in Afghanistan and Pakistan prospects for a transition to a more peaceful polity seemed remote, indicating the need for a fundamental reassessment of security policy. Even so, long-term changes in the conduct of the war on terror are constrained by two factors. One is that the al-Qaeda movement is working on a very long timescale, certainly measured in decades rather than years. The other is that while US domestic politics may be subject to short-term change, the enduring significance of the Persian Gulf for the security of oil supplies means that any total US withdrawal from the region as a whole would be seen by many as a foreign and security policy disaster at least as great as the defeat in the Vietnam War (see Box 19.5).

At the same time, the al-Qaeda movement, and like-minded groups, could lose support as a result of major changes in US and coalition policies. This would include progressive withdrawal of military forces from Afghanistan, successful support for an enduring and just settlement of the Israeli/Palestinian conflict, support for political and social emancipation in Saudi Arabia, Egypt, Pakistan, and some other Islamic states,

BOX 19.5 Terrorism and oil security

The war on terror has been substantially complicated by the strategic importance of the Persian Gulf region as the location of most of the world's remaining proved oil reserves. While the argument that the United States occupied Iraq in 2003 is at best tenuous and at worst no more than a conspiracy theory, there certainly has been a long-term US concern with Persian Gulf security, not least with the establishment of the Joint Rapid Deployment Task Force in 1979 and its expansion into US Central Command five years later. From a US perspective, ensuring Persian Gulf security is a necessary part of the US defence posture for two reasons. One is the sheer concentration of reserves (see table), with 60 per cent of world oil reserves located in five countries in the Gulf region—Saudi Arabia, Iran, Iraq, Kuwait, and the United Arab Emirates—and a further 21.5 per cent in Venezuela, Russia, and Kazakhstan. The other is the increasing dependence of both the United States and China on imported oil as they run down their small remaining domestic reserves. In 2000, the United States imported about 58% of its oil requirements and this is expected to grow to 74% by 2020. China's import dependency is increasing even faster—it was self-sufficient in 1993 but needed to import half its requirements by 2010.

World oil reserves 2010

Country	Billion barrels	Percentage of world total
Saudi Arabia	264.6	19.8
Venezuela*	172.3	12.9
Iran	137.6	10.3
Iraq	115.0	8.6
Kuwait	101.5	7.6
United Arab Emirates	97.8	7.3
Russia	74.7	5.6
Libya	44.3	3.3
Kazakhstan	39.8	3.0
Nigeria	37.2	2.8
Canada**	33.2	2.5
United States	28.4	2.1
Qatar	26.6	2.0
China	14.8	1.1

Source: BP Statistical Review of World Energy, June 2010. *The Venezuela total includes substantial heavy oil deposits that are difficult and expensive to extract. **Canada also has large reserves of low-grade tar sands.

and a policy of counter-terrorism rooted primarily in policing and criminal investigation rather than vigorous pursuit of military solutions.

While the Obama administration has decreased the US military involvement in Iraq and advocates political change in the region, there is little prospect of an Israeli/Palestinian settlement or of an early withdrawal from Afghanistan, and those significant policy changes that did follow President Obama's election in 2008 may not be sustained. There thus remains the real prospect of a prolonged conflict measured in decades rather than years. Much will depend on the potential for political, social, and economic reform across the Middle East following the emergence of the Arab Spring. This represents the most serious challenge to the al-Qaeda movement and it is salutary that such a challenge should come not from the United States and its western coalition partners but from within the Arab world.

? Questions

1. What were the main examples of terrorism in the United States before the 9/11 attacks?
2. Why did the Bush administration extend the war on terror to include an 'axis of evil'?
3. What are the aims of the al-Qaeda movement?
4. Why was the termination of the Saddam Hussein regime and the subsequent occupation of Iraq of value to the al-Qaeda movement?
5. What were the different perceptions of the US attack on Fallujah in November 2004?
6. Why is the strategic significance of the Persian Gulf oil reserves relevant to the conduct of the war on terror?

» Further Reading

Allen, C. (2006), *God's Terrorists, The Wahhabi Cult and the Hidden Roots of Modern Jihad* (London: Abacus).

Places the development of the al-Qaeda movement in a broad historical perspective.

Anderson, S. K. and Sloan, S. (2002), *Historical Dictionary of Terrorism* (Latham and London: The Scarecrow Press).

An impressive and comprehensive survey with a good discussion of definitions of terrorism.

Bergen, P. (2010), *The Longest War: The Enduring Conflict between America and al-Qaida* (New York: Simon and Schuster).

A perceptive overview of the war against al-Qaeda.

Burke, J. (2007), *Al-Qaeda, the True Story of Radical Islam* (Isleworth: Penguin Books).

This remains the best account of the origins and development of the movement.

Horgan, J. (2005), *The Psychology of Terrorism* (London and New York: Routledge).

A wide-ranging study of the motivations and behavioural traits relevant to political violence.

Jackson, R., Murphy, E., and Poynting, S. (eds) (2010), *Contemporary State Terrorism: Theory and Cases* (Abingdon: Routledge).

A robust analysis of state involvement in political violence.

Jackson, R., Breen Smyth, M., Gunning, J., and Jarvis, L. (2011), *Terrorism: A Critical Introduction* (Basingstoke: Palgrave-Macmillan).

A wide-ranging analysis of terrorism in its different forms.

Lawrence, B. (ed.) (2005), *Messages to the World: The Statements of Osama Bin Laden* (London and New York: Verso).

A translation of Osama Bin Laden's main speeches and writings, with a succinct introduction to the al-Qaeda movement by Bruce Lawrence.

Rashid, A. (2010), *Taliban* (London: I B Tauris).

An updated edition of a standard text.

Rogers, P. (2010), *Losing Control: Global Security in the 21st Century* (London: Pluto Press).

Analyses the significance of paramilitary actions and asymmetric warfare in international security.

 For a range of additional resources to support your learning visit the Online Resource Centre that accompanies this book at **www.oxfordtextbooks.co.uk/orc/cox_stokes2e/**.

20 Global environment

Robyn Eckersley

Chapter contents

Introduction

This chapter critically explores the evolution of US foreign policy on environmental issues over four decades, from the Nixon administration to the Obama administration. It shows that while the USA was widely regarded as an environmental leader during the Cold War period, it has increasingly become an environmental laggard in the post-Cold War period. This has occurred at the same time as international environmental problems have moved from the periphery towards the centre of international politics. The decline in US leadership is attributed to the USA's new status as the sole superpower, the more challenging character of the new generation of global environmental problems that emerged in the late 1980s, the structure of the US economy and

political system, and key features of US grand strategy, which include the ways in which US foreign policy elites frame and prioritize security threats and risks.

During most of the period of the Cold War, the environment was widely regarded as a matter of 'low politics' for state foreign policy makers as well as international relations scholars (Smith 1993). When the Cold War came to an end, however, some observers looked forward to the possibility that the new world order would not only be more peaceful but also more ecologically sustainable. Lester Brown, in the 1991 *State of the World Report,* went so far as to suggest that 'the battle to save the planet will replace the battle over ideology as the organizing theme of the new world order'

(Brown 1991: 3). The signs did appear promising. The increasing prominence of trans-boundary and global environmental problems in the 1980s, the proliferation of environmental non-government organizations (NGOs), and the publication of *Our Common Future* by the World Commission on Environment and Development (the Brundtland Report) (World Commission on Environment and Development 1987) helped generate the momentum for the spectacular 1992 Earth Summit held in Rio de Janeiro—the largest ever gathering of heads of state at the time. The emergence of local and transnational environmental networks behind the Iron Curtain had played a role in the transformations that led to the collapse of the Soviet Union while the leader of the world's emerging sole superpower, US President George H. W. Bush Sr., declared himself 'the environmental president' when he came to office in 1989. Yet despite the unprecedented rise in international environmental concern in the 1980s, the environment proved not to be a central foreign policy priority for George Bush Sr., or indeed any previous or subsequent US president (as distinct from vice-president). Indeed, the neo-liberal New World Order that Bush championed after the demise of the Soviet Union has become less, rather than more, hospitable to environmental concerns.

Yet as the Cold War period recedes, both foreign policy makers and international relations scholars are increasingly recognizing that environmental problems can no longer be quarantined from, or relegated as secondary to, security and economic concerns. Growing rates of species extinction, land degradation, deforestation, natural resource depletion, pollution, and, above all, the multiple risks to life-support systems and human communities from human-induced climate change are now being reframed as sources of potentially catastrophic risk that pose major 'threats' to human health, economic stability, and physical security while also challenging traditional strategies of territorial defence. In the wake of four, increasingly serious, assessment reports by the Intergovernmental Panel on Climate Change (IPCC), the problem of climate change has gradually moved from the periphery towards the centre state of international politics and foreign policy concerns. The much publicized, and appropriately titled, *Stern Review on the Economic Costs of Climate Change* (Stern 2007), released in October 2006, argued that the economic costs of mitigating global warming are minuscule when set against the longer-term economic costs of failing to take action. In April 2007, the UN Security Council held its first meeting to discuss the international security implications of climate change.

This chapter provides a historical survey and critical evaluation of the United States' shifting response to international environmental problems. It begins with the administration of President Richard Nixon, which is the period when international environmental problems first rose to international prominence, and tracks the USA's involvement in major international environmental summits and environmental treaties up to and including the administration of Barack Obama (to the end of 2010). It will be shown that the USA was regarded as a leader in both domestic and foreign environmental policy making in the 1970s and to some extent in the 1980s, but by 1992 it had lost this international leadership mantle and by the mid-2000s it was widely regarded as a laggard, especially in relation to the world's most significant global environmental challenge—climate change.

The central puzzle raised by this history is: why has US leadership tended to wane at a time when global and trans-boundary environmental problems have become more rather than less serious and threatening to both US and global security? In order to address this question, the chapter seeks to locate the evolution of US foreign environmental policy in the context of the evolution of domestic environmental policy, on the one hand, and the evolution of US grand strategy in response to key geopolitical developments, on the other hand. It will be shown that both of these developments have shaped the negotiating context for US foreign environmental policy making, but that US grand strategy is emerging as an increasingly significant barrier to US environmental leadership in the post-Cold War period in the context of more demanding global environmental challenges. Finally, the chapter offers a critical analysis of theories of foreign policy making and argues that critical constructivist interpretations provide a more satisfying account of the decline in US international leadership in the environmental policy domain than the materialist and rationalist explanations offered by realists, traditional Marxists, and neo-liberal institutionalists.

Environmental multilateralism and the USA

The late 1960s are typically singled out as the birth of the modern environmental movement as a widespread and persistent social movement. The long period of economic boom and population growth following the end of the Second World War produced a range of mass-produced goods but also a mass of ubiquitous ecological problems, an increasing number of which crossed state boundaries. Although most political leaders rejected the doomsday scenarios generated by the limits-to-growth advocates of the early 1970s, a steady stream of studies of global environmental trends has continued to underscore the increasing gravity of the global ecological crisis, culminating in the biggest global environmental challenge of all—human-induced climate change.[1] In response to these broad developments, the post-Second World War period also witnessed a spectacular increase in environmental lawmaking at the national and international levels. Yet the spectacular rise in environmental multilateralism, punctuated by three major earth summits—in Stockholm in 1972, in Rio de Janeiro in 1992, and Johannesburg in 2002—has also brought into relief a range of tensions between developed and developing countries over environment and development priorities, the meaning of sustainable development, environmental justice, and environmental security, and the assignment of environmental international responsibilities and burdens. Throughout this period, the world has looked to the USA for environmental leadership as the world's richest country, with the largest per capita ecological footprint. However, for a complex range of reasons, the US response to global environmental problems has been uneven, and since the early 1990s the USA has been less inclined to assume a leadership role.

From environmental leader to environmental laggard

In the early 1970s, the USA stood out as a world leader in domestic environmental law and policy (much of which has since been emulated by other states), and under the presidency of Richard Nixon the USA pursued a relatively proactive role at the 1972 Stockholm Conference on the Human Environment. Indeed, Richard Nixon (along with Lyndon Johnson) has received the strongest rating in a survey of the environmental records of the ten presidents from Truman to Clinton (Soden and Steel 1999: 347–9). Yet Soden and Steel (1999: 347–8) suggest that even the greenest presidents were 'merely caught in the tide of congressional efforts, public support, and environmental realities that demanded a federal response to a growing number of programs'. They conclude that the credit for US domestic and international environmental leadership in the 1970s must go to the environmental movement (which generated a major momentum for environmental concern in American society), to their lobbyists, and to Congress, which displayed mostly bipartisan support for environmental initiatives during this period.

As the following brief history shows, although the US president is chief diplomat and chief executive officer, US foreign environmental policy decisions have been largely shaped by domestic environmental politics, and the president is merely one, albeit one very significant, player in a complicated set of political processes in the deeply fragmented US political system. While there has never been a 'substantial "environmental president"' (Soden and Steel 1999: 349) there have certainly been some substantial and unapologetic anti-environmental presidents, most notably Ronald Reagan and George Bush Jr. No president has yet exploited the full capacity of their constitutional or leadership powers to promote, as distinct from obstruct or compromise, environmental goals.

The Nixon years: setting the pace

President Richard Nixon was not known for his environmental sympathies but he nonetheless presided over one of the most innovative periods of environmental policy making and lawmaking in US history, which included the enactment of the National Environmental Policy Act (NEPA) in 1969 that established the Council on Environmental Quality (CEQ) within the White House, and the Environmental Protection Agency (EPA), set up in 1970. The 1960s had seen the spectacular growth of environmental organizations and public environmental awareness in the USA, culminating in the first nationwide 'Earth Day' in 1970. Nixon had assumed office in 1968 on a tide of rising environmental concern and he signed a range of new environmental treaties relating to fisheries and the protection of Antarctic seals, which was consistent with a history of longstanding US leadership in the protection of marine resources and marine mammals. He also signed a treaty designed to protect the seabed from nuclear testing.

However, it was the 1972 Stockholm Conference where the USA sought to develop a green reputation. During the period 1968–72 the Nixon administration was facing a major crisis over its intervention in Vietnam, including international criticism for the 'ecocide' resulting from the use of Agent Orange by the US military, along with international criticism for its atomic testing. Against this broader background, both Nixon and his advisers saw Stockholm as a significant opportunity to reassert moral leadership, gain electoral advantage, and divert attention from 'that war'. Preparations for the conference were dominated by the executive, particularly the State Department and the CEQ, with very little involvement by US environment or business organizations. Hopgood attributes this lack of involvement to the relative insulation of the State Department and CEQ from domestic social pressures, and also the relative lack of international focus of US environmental organizations at that time (Hopgood 1998: 87). However, Stockholm acted as a major catalyst for the development of both domestic and international environmental NGOs, which have played an increasingly significant role in subsequent international environmental negotiations.

The USA's two most prominent initiatives at Stockholm were support for the establishment of the United Nations Environment Program (UNEP) to coordinate environmental matters within the UN, and a pledge to contribute 40 per cent of a $100 million voluntary fund to support UNEP. The USA also used the occasion to promote the development of a convention on ocean dumping, the establishment of a World Heritage Trust, and a ten-year moratorium on whaling. These were relatively ambitious initiatives when judged by the standards of the day. Yet they also provide a good illustration of the limited scope of environmental policy making at the international level (Hopgood 1998: 79).

For example, the USA rejected calls for additional funding to developing countries to assist them with meeting their environmental commitments.

Nixon pursued fewer environmental initiatives in his second term of office, which coincided with the energy crisis of 1973–4 and the Watergate scandal, which led to his resignation. Nixon's successor, President Gerald Ford, was largely preoccupied with the political fallout from Watergate (including his pardoning of Nixon) and an economy suffering from stagflation. Although Ford had once worked as a park ranger at Yellowstone national park, he took very few domestic or international environmental initiatives during his brief tenure, and his international efforts largely involved follow-up work arising from previous administrations. This period saw the signing of the two conventions dealing with ocean pollution, the ratification of the Convention on Trade in Endangered Species of Wild Fauna and Flora (CITIES) in 1974, and the signing of a treaty on the conservation of polar bears (Long, Cabral, and Vandivort 1999: 207).

The Carter years: the well-intended but under-achieving president

President Jimmy Carter is widely regarded as the first US president to adopt a global environmental perspective, evidenced by his commissioning in May 1977 of the *Global 2000 Report to the President* (Council on Environmental Quality and Department of State 1980), which was released in 1981. Through this report, Carter sought a comprehensive overview of global environmental trends on population, resources, and the environment. Although Carter's international environmental concerns may have been more sincere and noble than those of Nixon, his international environmental record turned out to be more modest. Confronted with an ongoing energy crisis and an ailing economy at home, and the Iranian hostage crisis abroad, the Carter administration was unable to play any concerted leadership role in addressing the alarming global environmental trends that were revealed in the *Global 2000 Report to the President*. Nonetheless, he began the difficult process of addressing the USA's growing dependence on imported energy. He introduced the Public Utilities Regulatory Policy Act, which included energy conservation measures, appointed a White

House Task Force on National Energy Policy, placed the Department of Energy in the presidential cabinet, and introduced a major energy bill (which failed to pass Congress) and a bill establishing a Synthetic Fuels Corporation, which passed Congress (Long, Cabral, and Vandivort 1999: 208). Two further major domestic environmental initiatives were the Superfund Act (later signed off by Reagan), to regulate the clean up of toxic waste sites, and the protection of vast areas of Alaskan wilderness.

On the international front, Carter extended the application of the NEPA to US government activities abroad (Executive Order 12114 in January 1979) and he banned the export of toxic waste to other countries in 1981 (Executive Order 12264). He initiated negotiations with Canada on acid rain and signed the Convention on Long Range Transboundary Air Pollution 1979. Shortly before leaving office, he ensured US participation in the World Climate Conference 1979, which contributed to the growing international research effort on climate change. However, Carter's most significant environmental legacy was his preparedness to question America's dependence on imported oil and his efforts to promote energy conservation and a renewable energy industry in America. Yet he also saw Persian Gulf Oil as vital to US interests and created a new military command structure in the region, which eventually became the United States Central Command.

The Reagan years: winding back the clock

Ronald Reagan's first official act in coming to office was to dismantle the solar panels that Carter had installed on the roof of the White House (Hartmann 2003)—an act that set the environmental tone of his presidency. As the first US president with an explicit anti-environmental agenda, Reagan embarked upon a comprehensive effort to reduce, and where possible eliminate, many of the environmental regulations that had been enacted over the previous decade. His Economic Recovery Act 1981 sought to reduce taxation and wind back spending on social and environmental programmes, including Carter's tax incentives for renewable energy, and to make way for the efficiency of the market. Reagan also devolved environmental responsibilities to the states and local governments, and screened all senior appointments to environmental agencies to ensure their conformity

with his anti-environmental agenda (Vig 2006: 105). Although his attempt to abolish the CEQ failed to gain congressional approval, he succeeded in sidelining the agency by cutting its staff and ignoring its advice (Vig 2006: 105). Reagan's budget cuts also made it impossible for federal environmental agencies, such as the EPA and the Department of the Interior, to implement their mandates. However, Reagan's anti-environmental campaign slowed down considerably in his second term as a result of growing public opposition. Indeed, Reagan's efforts to demonize environmentalists provoked a surge in the funding and membership of US environmental organizations (Dryzek et al. 2003: 34).

Although Reagan's anti-environmental agenda was mainly directed towards US domestic policy he made it clear that he would not sign any international environmental treaties that would compromise US economic competitiveness (Long, Cabral, and Vandivort 1999: 211). Reagan reversed Carter's 1981 executive order banning the export of toxic waste to other countries, declined to sign the 1989 Basel Convention which regulated the trans-boundary movement of hazardous waste, and stalled the acid rain negotiations with Canada. His administration rejected the United Nations Convention on the Law of the Sea (UNCLOS III) on the grounds that the USA should not be made to share its technological capabilities regarding seabed mining and offshore fishing with other nations. Reagan also ceased funding US population projects and withdrew from UNESCO, although his attempt to end US contributions to UNEP was successfully resisted by Congress (Hopgood 1998: 125–6). However, Reagan did support a number of international environmental initiatives, such as the Convention on the Conservation of Antarctic Marine Living Resources 1982 and the International Tropical Timber Agreement 1985.

Yet it is no small irony that the most significant foreign environmental policy development that occurred during Reagan's second term—US ozone diplomacy—also stands out as the most significant example of US environmental leadership and multilateral engagement in the twentieth century. Scientists had discovered the link between the release of chlorofluorcarbons (CFCs) and the thinning of the earth's ozone layer in the early 1970s, and the USA had phased out non-essential CFC aerosols as early as 1978 under its Clean Air Act. The

USA also played a leading role in pushing for a complete phase-out of ozone-depleting substances (compared to the weaker proposal for a 30 per cent cut proposed by the European Union (EU)) in the negotiations leading to the 1985 Vienna Convention for the Protection of the Ozone Layer. The discovery of the so-called Antarctic ozone hole in 1985 had prompted a concerted push for a phase-out by the US EPA. Moreover, in response to EU resistance, the US State Department mounted a major international consensus-building campaign to persuade other countries to agree to a worldwide phase-out of ozone-depleting substances, including ongoing periodic assessment of the list of ozone-depleting substances (Sitaraman 2001: 123–4). This campaign required all US embassies to explain the US negotiating position, beginning with like-minded countries and then extending to reluctant countries (Benedick 1991: 55–67). Domestically, the State Department worked closely with all branches of the US government, the major environmental and science agencies, and the CFC producers.

Although US CFC producers initially formed a united front against EPA regulatory proposals for a unilateral phase-out, they shifted their stance to support the international harmonization of regulations following the signing of the Vienna Convention in 1985 (which supported the principle of protecting the ozone layer, but without specific commitments). Key producers such as DuPont and Allied Chemical had invested in new production facilities for CFC substitutes and the US negotiators supported the industry's commercial interests in the negotiations for the Montreal Protocol 1987, which introduced a mandatory phase-out regime (DeSombre 2000: 93–4; Bang et al. 2007). The establishment of a multilateral fund has assisted developing countries with the financial and technical resources required to meet the costs of compliance with the regime.[2]

Many analysts of US ozone diplomacy have argued that the USA's international leadership role can be understood as an attempt by the USA to internationalize its domestic environmental regulation. According to Elizabeth DeSombre (2000) this situation arises when there is a set of domestic environmental regulations in place and an agreement between US environmentalists and US industry that international regulation would be both environmentally and economically advantageous.

On this analysis, the Reagan administration's ozone diplomacy is consistent with its position that it would not support any international environmental treaty that would compromise US economic competitiveness.

Bush the elder: the failed 'environmental president'

In the wake of public criticism of Reagan's anti-environmentalism, the resurgence of the US environment movement during the 1980s, and growing international concern over global warming, George Bush Sr. chose to badge himself 'the environmental president' in the 1988 presidential race. Once elected, Bush surprised his critics by appointing key environmental advocates to head the EPA and CEQ, and he supported the further strengthening of the Clean Air Act in 1991, which included more stringent reductions in sulphur dioxide emissions. These amendments also pioneered the system of tradable pollution permits in sulphur dioxide and prepared the ground for the negotiation of an acid rain treaty with Canada in 1994 to reduce sulphur dioxide emissions by 50 per cent by 1994. Bush also agreed to amendments strengthening the ozone treaty in 1992.

Yet despite this promising start, and the significant opportunity for environmental leadership presented by the 1992 Earth Summit, George Bush Sr. failed to live up to his promise to be America's environmental president. Having served for eight years as Reagan's vice-president, which included actively supporting his campaign of environmental deregulation, Bush reverted to type in negotiations over the two biggest international environmental challenges confronting his administration: climate change and biodiversity protection. Indeed, President Bush negotiated his presence at the 1992 Earth Summit on the condition that the United Nations Framework Convention on Climate Change (UNFCCC) include no specific targets or timetables for greenhouse gas (GHG) emissions reductions on the grounds that this would place an intolerable burden on the US economy. Bush also declined to sign the Convention on Biological Diversity (CBD), bowing to pressure from the US biotechnology and pharmaceutical industries, which argued that the provision requiring royalties to be paid to developing countries for the use of their native genetic diversity did not provide adequate patent and copyright protection for US industry.

President Bush also attracted international condemnation for his oft-quoted declaration at the summit that 'America's lifestyle is not up for negotiation'.

The Bush administrations' early initiatives on domestic environmental policy were overshadowed by a reassertion of his conservative economic ideology in the last eighteen months of his presidency, when he installed Vice-President Dan Quayle as head of the Council on Competitiveness to respond to industry complaints of excessive regulation, including environmental regulation (Vig 2006: 107).

The Clinton years: unfulfilled promises

Bush's failure as an environmental president served as a key target in Bill Clinton's presidential campaign in 1992. Clinton, and his green Vice-President Al Gore, received strong endorsement from the US environment movement, and their Democratic campaign included a wide range of environmental promises, including signing the CBD, committing to quantitative targets to reduce US carbon dioxide emissions (i.e. to return to 1990 emissions levels by 2000), raising the corporate average fuel economy (CAFE) standard for motor vehicles, and promoting renewable energy research and development (Paarlberg 1999; Vig 2006: 108). The Clinton–Gore team also emphasized the economic advantages that would flow from an increased investment in more environmentally friendly technologies as an antidote to the traditional discourse of 'environment versus the economy' that had characterized the Reagan and Bush administrations. On winning office, Clinton abolished the Council on Competitiveness, appointed a

number of well-known environmental professionals to key executive positions, and established an Office for Environmental Policy to ensure the integration of environmental policies in all departments (Vig 2006: 108). This push for integration also extended to foreign policy. Vice-President Al Gore was a key advocate of enlarging the USA's security framework to include environmental concerns (see Key quotes 20.1) and Secretary of State Warren Christopher announced in 1997 that the Clinton administration would 'put environmental issues where they belong: in the mainstream of American foreign policy' (Christopher 1998: 412). Indeed, Long, Cabral, and Vandivort (1999: 218) assert that Clinton had 'assembled one of the most environmentally friendly (greenest) administrations in American history'.

Despite this initial enthusiasm, the Clinton administration faced a number of significant obstacles in promoting a new environmental agenda. The 1992 presidential race had taken place in the context of a declining economy, declining public interest in environmental issues, and falling funding and membership of environmental organizations. Even before the 1994 congressional elections, which gave control of both houses to the Republicans, Clinton suffered a major congressional defeat over his proposal to introduce a broad-based tax on fuels, which was his major initiative for fulfilling his commitment to reduce US carbon dioxide emissions to 1990 levels by 2000. The initiative was eventually replaced with a much more modest tax on gasoline. Moreover, his Climate Change Action Plan, which relied on voluntary measures, bore little relationship to his climate pledge.

❝ KEY QUOTES 20.1: Letter from Vice-President Al Gore

We have moved beyond Cold War definitions of the United States' strategic interests. Our foreign policy must now address a broad range of threats including damage to the world's environment—that transcend countries and continents and require international cooperation to solve.

Environmental problems such as global climate change, ozone depletion, ocean and air pollution, and resource degradation—compounded by an expanding world population—

respect no border and threaten the health, prosperity, and jobs of all Americans. All the missiles and artillery in our arsenal will not be able to protect our people from rising sea levels, poisoned air, or foods laced with pesticides. Our efforts to promote democracy, free trade, and stability in the world will fall short unless people have a livable environment.

(Letter from Vice-President Albert Gore Jr. attached to US Department of State 1998)

Although Clinton signed the CBD in 1993 (subject to certain reservations), he failed to secure ratification from a highly partisan Senate, despite gaining the approval of representatives from the US biotechnology and pharmaceuticals industry as a result of the reservations based on side agreements with industry (Paarlberg 1999: 239). A similar fate befell the USA's signing of the Kyoto Protocol in 1997. Prior to the negotiations at Kyoto, the Republican-dominated Senate—sensitive to the concerns of coal-producing states in the USA—had unanimously passed the Byrd–Hagel resolution making any support by the Senate conditional on developing states also taking action within the same time period. This was followed by a $13 million advertising campaign by the US fossil fuel industry in the lead-up to the Kyoto meeting that warned Americans of the economic costs of implementing the mooted Protocol (Oberthur and Ott 1999: 72). The US delegates at Kyoto were initially constrained by a limited mandate: to accept only a zero growth emissions reduction target, and only if developing countries also accepted emissions reductions targets in the same time period. However, last-minute intervention by Al Gore to break a deadlock in the negotiations resulted in the USA agreeing to cut emissions by 7 per cent by 2008–12 from 1990 levels without developing country participation. Although this diplomatic shift by the USA was hailed as a major breakthrough in the international climate negotiations, it was clear that the Clinton–Gore administration would be unable to win Senate ratification. Indeed, Clinton avoided such a confrontation with the Senate by not submitting the Protocol for approval, despite the fact that the USA had successfully negotiated a range of so-called flexibility mechanisms under the Kyoto Protocol (such as carbon trading, joint implementation, and the clean development mechanism) that would make it easier for the USA to reach its target.

In the negotiations for the Cartagena Protocol on Biosafety 2000, under the CBD, the USA led the so-called Miami group of nations that opposed trade restrictions on the trans-boundary movement of genetically modified organisms. Moreover, Clinton's negotiation of the North American Free Trade Agreement with Canada and Mexico attracted strong criticism from US environmental organizations for setting off a 'race to the bottom' in environmental regulation and enforcement,

which he sought to allay through the inclusion of new environmental provisions and side agreements. A concerted campaign by US environmental organizations against the environmental limitations of the General Agreement on Tariffs and Trade also prompted the USA to play a role in ensuring the inclusion of the objectives of sustainable development and environmental protection in the 1994 Marrakesh Agreement establishing the World Trade Organization.

In the end, the Clinton administration failed to make any significant progress on climate change, failed to secure the ratification of the Kyoto Protocol or CBD, and declined to sign the Cartagena Biosafety Protocol. This may be attributed largely to a well-organized industry opposition and a hostile Congress, which gave considerable airing to the views of global-warming sceptics (McCright and Dunlap 2003: 361), but also to Clinton's pragmatic disposition, which included a readiness to compromise environmental goals, and an overriding concern to maintain the competitiveness of the US economy. Nonetheless, the Clinton administration did seek to grapple with the challenge of policy integration by promoting the discourses of ecological modernization and introducing environmental security as a component of US foreign policy and defence planning (The White House 1996). However, critics such as Barnett (2001: 84) have pointed to the Clinton administration's mostly narrow framing of environmental problems as direct or indirect 'threats' to US interests, as if environmental problems were a danger emanating from outside the USA. Such a framing obscured the USA's own complicity in, and responsibility for, the production of environmental problems.

Bush Jr.: the fossil fuel president

The election of George Bush Jr. to the White House in 2001 following his narrow victory over Al Gore in the 2000 presidential race saw the return of a strong pro-business agenda and a corresponding roll-back and revision of many domestic environmental regulations that was reminiscent of the Reagan years (Vig 2006: 115–17). However, whereas the Reagan administration had led the world in the negotiations to protect the ozone layer, the Bush administration attracted widespread international criticism for its rejection of environmental multilateralism in general, and its repudiation of the Kyoto Protocol in particular (despite the fact that US public opinion was in favour of ratification in early 2001).[3]

The Bush administration's major reasons for repudiating Kyoto have been that the 7 per cent emission reduction target negotiated by the Clinton–Gore administration would harm the US economy, and that the Protocol is flawed because it does not require major developing country emitters to commit to mandatory emissions reduction targets in the same time period. Although the USA has continued to play a major role in climate change research, the Bush administration remained deeply sceptical of the science of climate change.

The Bush administration also sought to undermine the Kyoto Protocol by developing 'environmental coalitions of the willing', in the form of voluntary partnerships for clean technology development that cut across the developed/developing country divide. The most significant of these partnerships is the Asia Pacific Partnership on Clean Development and Climate 2006, which provides a non-binding framework for cooperation to promote the diffusion of new 'clean' technologies[4] (Christoff and Eckersley 2007). The partnership is based on market-friendly procedural norms of equality of commercial opportunity rather than the UNFCCC's principles of equity and common but differentiated responsibility (McGee and Taplin 2006: 188).

The Bush administration rejected prescriptive domestic legislation such as mandatory emissions reductions targets (including a national carbon trading scheme), carbon taxes, or mandatory renewable energy targets. Instead, through its Climate Change initiative, it sought to reduce the GHG emissions intensity of the US economy by 18 per cent by 2012, largely through voluntary measures and technology development (The White House 2002). However, GHG intensity reflects the amount of GHG produced per unit of GDP, not aggregate emissions, and by the Bush administration's own admission the GHG intensity of the US economy has been in long-term decline and the 18 per cent target is only slightly above forecasts based on a business-as-usual scenario (Depledge 2005: 23).

More significantly, the Bush administration's climate change strategy was overshadowed by its National Energy Strategy, which was based on recommendations from an Energy Task Force chaired by Vice-President Cheney. Drafted in secrecy by representatives from the fossil fuel and related industries, the report of the Task Force (concluded in May 2001) sought to step up the supply of energy (primarily, but not exclusively, fossil fuels) rather than reduce demand. Many of the report's recommendations were incorporated into the Energy Policy Act, which passed Congress in 2005. The Act provided greater subsidies to the oil and gas industries to encourage exploration and drilling, the streamlining of environmental regulations to accelerate increased energy production, the opening up of the Alaskan National Wildlife Refuge to exploration and drilling, and low-interest loans and research grants for the development of nuclear power plants (The White House 2006). Although President Bush acknowledged America's vulnerability arising from its addiction to oil in his 2006 and 2007 State of the Union Addresses (Bush 2006, 2007) his response was primarily technology driven and concerned to secure supply rather than reduce demand in order to maintain a cheap energy supply for America.

Vice-President Cheney's energy strategy proved to be the single most important initiative shaping the Bush administration's domestic and international climate change policy. The USA's dependence on externally sourced oil rose to 56 per cent in 2006, almost half of which came from the Middle East.

The Bush administration also turned its back on other environmental agreements and follow-up work arising from the 1992 Earth Summit. It declined to press for ratification of the CBD and declined to sign or ratify the Cartagena Protocol on Biosafety 2000. President Bush also declined to attend the World Summit on Sustainable Development in Johannesburg in 2002 and his administration did not pursue any integrated sustainability planning at the national level. Throughout this period the US environmental movement has had negligible influence on the executive and legislative branch of government, prompting two environmentalists to proclaim the 'death of environmentalism' in the USA in a widely circulated critique that argued the movement had lost its way in focusing on technical fixes at the expense of developing a broad vision that is commensurate with the magnitude of the crisis of climate change (Schellenberger and Nordhaus 2004).

CONTROVERSIES 20.1:   The multiple risks of the USA's oil addiction

President Jimmy Carter was the first US president to demonstrate serious concern about the risks of US dependency on imported oil. In his famous 'crisis of confidence speech' televised to the nation on 15 July 1979 during the second energy crisis he declared that 'In little more than two decades we've gone from a position of energy independence to one in which almost half the oil we use comes from foreign countries, at prices that are going through the roof.' (Carter 1979) In response to soaring inflation and gasoline queues he announced a range of measures, including import quotas, significant investment in developing domestic sources of energy (including renewables and coal), and domestic energy conservation.

Between 1979 and 2010, the risks associated with America's dependence on imported oil have increased. Alongside the problem of rising oil prices from any future disruption of supply are the risks of climate change from the burning of fossil fuels, the predicted onset of peak oil, and the deteriorating security situation stemming from the US military presence in the oil-rich Persian Gulf. This confluence of risks has prompted calls for a new US energy strategy based on aggressive demand management and the promotion of renewables and low-carbon energy alternatives.

However, the Bush–Cheney energy strategy continued US dependence on oil. Although President Bush acknowledged America's vulnerability arising from its addiction to oil in his 2006 and 2007 State of the Union Addresses (Bush 2006, 2007) his administration provided major tax breaks to the US oil industry and avoided aggressive demand management or a major switch to renewables. On the foreign policy front, the Bush administration strongly resisted efforts at the Johannesburg Summit in 2002 to seek agreement on an international renewable energy target and it has continued to use oil as a strategic resource in pursuing its general foreign policy objectives. Although the Bush administration denied that oil was a motivation behind the US invasion of Iraq in 2003, gaining access to Iraq's oil fields for foreign multinationals has nonetheless emerged as the only significant pay-off from the war. However, US presence in the region has fanned anti-Americanism and Islamic fundamentalism.

In a provocative essay on the Greening of Geopolitics, *New York Times* journalist Thomas Friedman argued that since

9/11, the USA has been financing both sides of the war on terrorism. As he puts it: 'We were financing the US military with our tax dollars; and we were financing a transformation of Islam, in favour of its most intolerant strand, with our gasoline purchases.' (Friedman 2007) According to Friedman, the next president will have to rally America with a new green patriotism: 'green' must become 'the new red, white and blue' because it is the only agenda that can simultaneously address the challenges of 'jobs, temperature and terrorism'.

The massive oil explosion from BP's Deepwater Horizon rig in the Gulf of Mexico on 20 April 2010 provided a basis for both President Obama and the Congressional supporters of climate action to highlight the dangers of the US's excessive dependence on oil. While the disaster prompted President Obama to impose a six-month moratorium on deepwater drilling it failed to galvanize support for a cap-and-trade bill. President Obama has supported the end of fossil fuel subsidies and taken significant measures to increase the uptake of renewable energy, but he has not been prepared to stake his Presidency on climate change.

However, recognition that the US's dependence on oil may undermine the US's security and economic interests is gradually gaining traction among security analysts (Busby 2008). As the largest consumer of energy in the US, the Department of Defense has emerged as one of the key innovators in new low-carbon technologies. In *Powering America's Defence: Energy and the Risks to National Security* the CNA's (formerly the Center for Naval Analysis) Military Advisory Board (MAB) highlighted the multiple risks, including climate change, that were inextricably tied to the US's energy posture. The MAB's key findings were that excessive dependence on oil weakens international leverage, undermines economic stability, and increases US vulnerability, and that 'inefficient use and overreliance on oil burdens the military, undermines combat effectiveness, and exacts a huge price tag—in dollars and lives' (CNA 2009, vii). An earlier report on *National Security and the Threat of Climate Change* (CNA 2007) had found climate change to be a 'threat multiplier' to existing security risks, especially in the most volatile regions of the world.

In all, the Bush administration's foreign policy was overwhelmingly preoccupied with the war on terror. While the USA remains the largest financial contributor to the IPCC and UNFCCC it rejected a precautionary approach on climate change and biosafety while pursuing an aggressive policy of prevention and pre-emption in addressing terrorist threats, including military intervention in the territories of states that harbour terrorists. By 2006, the costs to the USA of the Iraq War had exceeded the anticipated costs of conforming to the stiff Kyoto targets negotiated by the Clinton–Gore administration (Sunstein 2007).

Obama: the thwarted president

The election of Barack Obama marked an important shift in domestic environmental and energy policy and international climate diplomacy. The Obama administration declared climate change to be one of its key priorities and it has made significant budget allocations for the advancement of renewable energy, and the inclusion of clean energy provisions and environmental infrastructure expenditure in the so-called green economic stimulus package in response to the financial crisis (The White House 2011). Unlike his predecessor, President Obama welcomed the Supreme Court ruling that allows the EPA to regulate GHGs as a pollutant under the Clean Air Act following an 'endangerment finding'. President Obama has also supported the repeal of fossil fuel subsidies and given his approval to the EPA to allow California and other states to enact stringent regulations on tailpipe emissions and measures to increase the fuel efficiency of cars and light trucks.

Nonetheless, President Obama had initially indicated his preference for Congress to enact national cap-and-trade legislation rather than rely on EPA regulations. Although a cap-and-trade scheme narrowly passed the House of Representatives on 26 June 2009 (the Waxman–Markey bill [HR 254] by 219 votes for, 212 against), in July 2010 the Democratic leadership in the Senate abandoned its efforts to push through a cap-and trade bill after failing to build sufficient Senate support. The heavy Democratic losses in the mid-term Congressional elections in November 2010 gave the Republicans control of the House of Representatives (242–193) and narrowed the Democrat's majority in the Senate to 53. A majority (128 or 53 per cent) of the 242 Republicans in the House of Representatives publicly question the science of climate change (Johnson 2010). This conservative swing, which reflects high unemployment following the global financial crisis (GFC) and an aggressive campaign against action on climate change by the Tea Party movement, has significantly diminished the prospects of any significant climate or energy bill passing the 112th Congress. Indeed, the Tea Party movement has helped to make the denial

of human-induced climate change a litmus test of US conservatism and 'true Republicanism'.

On the international front, the international climate negotiations have been the Obama administration's overriding foreign environmental policy preoccupation. Although President Obama has made no effort to revive and sell domestically the Clinton administration's Kyoto commitments, he has committed to long-term targets through the G-8 decision in July 2009 to support a halving of global emissions by 2050, which requires an 80 per cent reduction in emissions from developed countries during the same time period to allow for growth on the part of developing countries. The Obama administration has also continued the second Bush administration's major economies initiative, which was renamed and launched in March 2009 as the Major Economies Forum on Energy and Climate. The Forum, made up of seventeen economies responsible for around 75 per cent of global emissions, launched a Global Partnership for low-carbon and climate-friendly technologies in July 2009 (MEF 2009).

At the fifteenth conference of the parties (COP15) in Copenhagen in December 2009, the Obama administration pledged to reduce the US's emissions by 17 per cent by 2020 from a 2005 baseline, which amounts to a cut of around 3 to 4 per cent, rather than stabilization, from a 1990 baseline. This pledge was in step with the targets embodied in the Congressional bills in 2009, but falls well below the minus 25 to 40 per cent range recommended by the IPCC for developed countries. This stands in stark contrast to the EU's emissions reduction target for 2020, which is to reduce emissions by 20 per cent by 2020 from a 1990 baseline, rising to 30 per cent if other developed countries make comparable commitments.

The problem for the Obama administration is that even its modest Copenhagen target will be difficult to reach following the mid-term Congressional elections. International political attention has therefore turned to the EPA's existing regulatory powers, and to regional cap-and-trade schemes in the north-east, mid-west and the west (especially in California), which provide the Obama administration with its best chance of moving the US towards its Copenhagen pledge—if the EPA's regulations can survive litigation (see Major debates and their impact 20.1).

MAJOR DEBATES AND THEIR IMPACT 20.1: The EPA's authority to regulate GHG emissions

Although George Bush Jr. had promised to regulate carbon dioxide as a pollutant under the Clean Air Act during his presidential campaign, he reversed this position shortly after coming to office in 2001. He also made it clear that he would not order the federal EPA to regulate GHG emissions under the Clean Air Act and that his administration would pursue a voluntary approach to mitigation based on technological innovation. The Bush administration's refusal to adopt a more prescriptive approach to reducing GHG emissions attracted widespread criticism from the Kyoto parties as well as from environmentalists, scientists, and many 'progressive' states and municipal governments within the USA.

However, on 2 April 2007 in the landmark case of *Massachusetts v. Environmental Protection Agency*, 548 US (2007) the US Supreme Court ruled by a majority of five to four that the EPA has the authority and the obligation to regulate GHG emissions as pollutants under the Clean Air Act if it found that such emissions endangered public health and welfare. The ruling overturned a decision of the US Court of Appeals of the District of Columbia Circuit in September 2005.

The case had been brought by twelve states (mostly Pacific and north-east coast states) led by Massachusetts, and a coalition of municipal governments and environmental and public health organizations, claiming that the EPA had abdicated its responsibilities under the Clean Air Act in choosing not to regulate GHGs as pollutants. The case was defended by the EPA, a variety of automobile industry associations, and ten US states, most of which are significantly dependent on the oil, coal, or motor vehicle production industries.

The Administrator of the EPA had claimed in 2003 that it lacked authority to regulate GHG emissions, and that even if it did have the requisite legal power it had discretion to decide whether or not to regulate. Among the list of reasons given for declining to act were scientific uncertainty and the fact that regulating GHG emissions might interfere with the president's foreign environmental policy. The EPA believed that regulation 'might impair the President's ability to negotiate with "key developing nations" to reduce emissions'. However,

Justice Stevens, who presented the majority opinion of the Court, rejected the argument and ruled that the EPA's decision should be determined on the basis of the requirements of the Clean Air Act and not the executive's foreign policy. The president's broad executive authority was held not to 'extend to the refusal to execute domestic laws' (Supreme Court of the United States 2007).

In December 2009, the EPA assessed the scientific evidence on climate change and promulgated an 'endangerment finding' for GHG emissions in response to the Supreme Court's ruling. In April 2010 it promulgated new regulations to reduce GHG emissions from cars and light trucks. Under the Clean Air Act, the implementation of new vehicle standards also triggers an obligation to review standards for new stationary sources of pollution and for major modifications of existing sources. The EPA has 'tailored' this obligation so that it is confined to power plants and refineries, which are two of the largest industrial sources, responsible for nearly 40 per cent of US emissions.

The regulations for new facilities came into effect in January 2011, and those for the modification of existing facilities are expected in May 2011. Instead of a cap-and-trade scheme the EPA regulations impose performance standards under the Clean Air Act, which require new and modified power plants and refineries to install best available technology. The regulations will be primarily implemented by state authorities. The regulations for stationary sources have drawn significant opposition from the fossil fuel industry, states dependent on fossil fuel, most Republicans, and some Democrats.

In 1970, in the heyday of US environmentalism, Congress saw fit to confer considerable discretion on the EPA to identify and regulate pollutants. Forty years later, there have been various attempts in Congress to constrain the EPA's regulatory power through attempts to disapprove the regulations under the Congressional Review Act or amend the Clean Air Act (McCarthy and Parker 2010). Thirteen states have launched legal proceedings challenging the regulations, and the state of Texas has refused to change its permitting programme (Nelson 2010).

Another problem for the Obama administration is that the UNFCCC imposes an obligation on developed countries to take the lead in combatting climate change according to the burden-sharing principles of 'common but differentiated responsibilities and capabilities'

(Article 3(1)). This obligation arises from their greater historical and per capita emissions, and their superior economic and technological capacity compared to developing countries. The UNFCCC also acknowledges the special vulnerability of developing countries to climate change, and recognizes that their emissions will need to grow to meet their unmet development needs. Although China has overtaken the USA as the world's largest aggregate emitter, the USA is nonetheless responsible for the largest share of cumulative emissions since the industrial revolution (around 30 per cent), it is in the top league of per capita emitters (around four to five times larger than China), and has the largest economy and the largest financial, technological, and administrative capacity of any single state, which has been derived in part from its fossil fuel exploitation. China and the G-77 have argued that US leadership must be demonstrated before developing countries can be expected to take on international mitigation commitments.

Whereas President Bush had effectively rejected the climate regime's burden-sharing principles of common but differentiated responsibilities, President Obama has rhetorically embraced them but sought to re-interpret them in ways that accommodate domestic political concerns and pressures, on the one hand, and the US's position *vis-à-vis* rising powers in the developing world, on the other. The Obama administration has repeatedly drawn attention to the new 'post-Kyoto environment' and China's rapid emissions growth trajectory as a backdrop for a recalibrated understanding of differentiated responsibilities that requires commitments from the major emerging emitters in the developing world in the same commitment period, rather than at some future unspecified time *after* the USA has demonstrated leadership (Obama 2009).

While the EU has been widely recognized as the climate leader, since COP15 at Copenhagen in 2009 the EU's 'normative power' has been increasingly sidelined by the 'emissions power' of the USA and China in reshaping the negotiations. The Copenhagen Accord, which was initially drafted by the USA and the so-called Basic Group (China, India, Brazil, and South Africa), introduced a flexible 'pledge and review' approach that departs significantly from the Kyoto architecture. The Accord requires both developed and developing countries to register their pledges for mitigation action by 31 January 2010 but none of these pledges are legally binding. Tensions have emerged between the USA and China over the degree to which developing country pledges should be considered an international commitment, as distinct from merely a domestic measure,

and whether they should be 'reportable, measurable and verifiable'. Nonetheless the political pledges were formally endorsed at COP16 at Cancún in 2010 and they provide the basis for ongoing negotiations for a treaty on long-term cooperative action. The future of the Kyoto Protocol, which is due to expire at the end of 2012 if a second commitment period is not negotiated, is increasingly uncertain. Whereas China and the G-77 insist on the continuation of the Kyoto Protocol, the USA (with the support of Canada and Japan, and the sympathy of Russia and Australia) regard it as a dead letter.

Despite the Obama administration's declared commitment to fight climate change, it has been a much lower priority than economic recovery following the global financial crisis or the administration's proposed changes to health care. In the face of continued climate skepticism in Congress, high unemployment, entrenched dependence on fossil fuel, a long legacy of inaction or weak action on climate change by previous administrations, and fear of a 'rising China', the Obama administration has failed to convert its rhetoric of climate leadership by the USA into reality.

Key trends and puzzles in US foreign environmental policy

Table 20.1 provides a summary of the USA's involvement in the major international environmental treaties negotiated since the 1970s (excluding treaties on occupational health and safety and amendments to protocols), showing the date of the USA's signature and subsequent ratification, accession, or acceptance where relevant. One striking trend emerges from this history, which is depicted in the bar graph in Figure 20.1. If we take the 1992 Earth Summit as marking the beginning of the post-Cold War period then the USA has ratified or acceded to twelve of the fifteen environmental treaties it signed in the period 1970–1991 but has ratified only six of the twelve treaties it has signed in the period 1992–2010 (and three of these ratifications were protocols dealing with three different air pollutants under the same Convention on Long-Range Transboundary Air Pollution).[5] The average ratification rate has dropped from 80 per cent in the period 1970–1991 to 50 per cent in the period 1992–2010, or 33 per cent if we bundle the three Protocols on Air Pollution into one effective

Table 20.1 History of USA's signature and ratification of major international environmental treaties: 1970–2010

Name of treaty	Date of signature	Date of ratification or acceptance
1. Convention on Wetlands of International Importance especially as Waterfowl Habitat (Ramsar) 1971	2 February 1971	18 December 1986
2. Treaty on the Prohibition of the Emplacement of Nuclear Weapons and other Weapons of Mass Destruction on the Sea-bed and Ocean Floor and in the Subsoil Thereof 1971	11 February 1971	18 May 1972
3. Convention on the International Trade in Endangered Species 1972	3 March 1973	14 January 1974
4. London Convention on Ocean Dumping 1972	29 December 1972	30 August 1975
5. United Nations Convention on the Law of the Sea 1972	Not signed	
6. World Heritage Convention 1972	16 November 1972	7 December 1973
7. Convention on the Conservation of Migratory Species or Wild Animals 1979	Not signed	
8. Geneva Convention on Long-Range Transboundary Air Pollution 1979	13 November 1979	30 November 1981
9. Convention on the Conservation of Antarctic Marine Living Resources 1980	20 May 1980	2 February 1982
10. Protocol to the 1970 Convention on Long-Range Transboundary Air Pollution on Long-Term Financing of the Co-operative Programme for Monitoring and Evaluation of the Long-Range Transmission of Air Pollutants in Europe 1984	28 September 1984	29 October 1984
11. Vienna Convention for the Protection of the Ozone Layer 1985	22 March 1985	27 August 1986
12. Montreal Protocol on Substances that Deplete the Ozone Layer 1987	16 September 1987	21 April 1988
13. Protocol to the 1970 Convention on Long-Range Transboundary Air Pollution Concerning the Control of Emissions of Nitrogen Oxides or their Transboundary Fluxes 1988	1 November 1988	13 July 1989
14. Basel Convention on Control of the Transboundary Movement of Hazardous Waste and their Disposal 1989	22 March 1990	Not ratified
15. Convention on Environmental Impact Assessment in a Transboundary Context 1991	26 February 1991	Not ratified
16. Protocol on Strategic Environmental Assessment to the Convention on Environmental Impact Assessment in a Transboundary Context 1991	Not signed	
17. Madrid Protocol on Environmental Protection to the Antarctic Treaty 1991	17 October 1991	1 November 1996

Table 20.1 (*continued*)

18. Protocol to the 1970 Convention on Long-Range Transboundary Air Pollution concerning the Control of Emissions of Volatile Organic Compounds or their Transboundary Fluxes 1991	19 November 1991	Not ratified
19. United Nations Framework Convention on Climate Change 1992	12 July 1992	15 October 1992
20. Convention on Biological Diversity 1992	4 June 1993	Not ratified
21. United Nations Convention to Combat Desertification 1994	14 October 1994	17 November 2000
22. International Tropical Timber Agreement 1994 (replacing the 1983 Agreement)	27 December 1988	14 November 1996
23. Comprehensive Test Ban Treaty 1996	24 September 1996	Not ratified
24. Protocol to the 1972 London Convention on Ocean Dumping 1996	31 March 1998	Not ratified
25. Kyoto Protocol 1997	12 November 1998	Not ratified
26. Protocol to the 1979 Convention on Long-Range Transboundary Air Pollution on Heavy Metals 1998	24 June 1998	10 January 2001.
27. Protocol to the 1979 Convention on Long-Range Transboundary Air Pollution on Persistent Organic Pollutants 1998	24 June 1998	22 November 2004
28. Rotterdam Convention on Pesticides and Industrial Chemicals 1998	11 September 1998	Not ratified
29. Protocol to the 1979 Convention on Long-Range Transboundary Air Pollution to abate Acidification, Eutrophication and Ground-level Ozone 1999	1 December 1999	22 November 2004
30. Cartagena Protocol on Biosafety 2000	Not signed	
31. Stockholm Convention on Persistent Organic Pollutants 2001	23 May 2001	Not ratified

Sources: United Nations Environment Program (2005a) and the United Nations Treaty Collection, available at http://treaties.un.org/pages/ParticipationStatus.aspx.

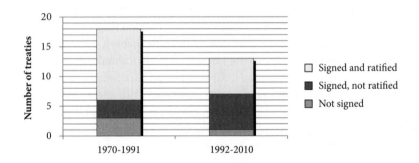

Fig. 20.1 International environmental treaties ratified by the USA, 1970–2010.

KEY POINTS

❑ A Republican-controlled Congress is considerably more hostile to environmental treaty obligations than a Democrat-controlled Congress.

❑ US international environmental leadership has waned significantly in the post-Cold War period.

❑ The USA has actively opposed the Kyoto Protocol, which seeks to address the most significant global environmental problem facing the international community since the rise of modern environmentalism.

❑ The USA has been increasingly influential in shaping the architecture of the post-Kyoto treaty towards a flexible, 'pledge and review' approach. However, the USA's Copenhagen pledge falls well below scientific recommendations.

Protocol. Another noteworthy feature of this history is that a Republican-controlled Congress is considerably more hostile to environmental treaty obligations than a Congress controlled by the Democrats. Indeed, fifteen of the seventeen environmental treaty ratifications since 1970 were by a Democrat-controlled Congress.[6]

The foregoing history of US environmental foreign policy making since the 1970s raises two interesting puzzles. First, why has US leadership tended to wane as global and trans-boundary environmental problems have become more, rather than less, serious and threatening to the global economy and global security? Second, why has the USA devoted so many resources and adopted a risk-averse posture to tackling terrorism yet rejected a precautionary approach to climate change?

Explaining US foreign environment policy

Before exploring possible explanations for these puzzles, we can draw together a number of key insights that have emerged from the history of US environmental foreign policy making since the 1970s.

First, it is clear that a single-minded focus on the environmental sympathies or antipathies of successive US presidents or their senior staff in the White House is not sufficient to explain shifts in US foreign environmental policy making. It is also necessary to examine the composition of other agencies in the executive branch (the EPA, the State Department) and other branches of government, most notably Congress. Despite the president's significant executive power and foreign policy prerogatives, it is Congress that passes laws, levies taxation, and controls spending. Moreover, the ratification of treaties rests with the Senate. As we have seen, a pale green president (even with a dark green vice-president) faced with a hostile Congress can do very little (e.g. the Clinton and Obama administrations), while a dark green Congress together with a strong environmental movement and growing public environmental concern can do a great deal to prod an indifferent president (Richard Nixon) to support international environmental initiatives.

Second, different environmental problems (biodiversity loss, ozone depletion, marine mammal protection, climate change) vary considerably in their complexity, gravity, incidence, and lead time; in the degree of certainty of scientific understanding associated with the problem and the causal factors that contribute to it; in their relationship to American culture and values; and in the scale of change that is required to address the problem, including the associated costs of abatement. Accordingly, different environmental problems present different challenges and opportunities for the USA at home and abroad, and help to explain the relative influence of different interest groups. As we shall see, the international environmental challenges of the post-Cold War period have proved to be much more confronting across most of these dimensions than the challenges raised during the Cold War period.

Third, the history of USA engagement in environmental treaty making since the 1970s has shown that the USA will not enter into an international environmental treaty if it is incompatible with domestic regulations, or if existing domestic regulations cannot easily be changed without a significant backlash from political elites and key interest groups. While the USA has never been an importer of 'foreign environmental policy' ideas from abroad it has often sought to export its environmental regulations (DeSombre 2000).

Fourth, and flowing on from the previous point, USA interest groups tend to have less direct influence on foreign policy than domestic policy, but their influence on domestic environmental initiatives can have significant indirect effects on foreign policy (as demonstrated by the previous insight). Business interest groups have had much more influence on domestic and foreign environmental policy than domestic environmental NGOs (Falkner 2001) when the potential economic costs of international cooperation are high (the Kyoto Protocol, Cartagena Protocol), while environmental NGOs have had relatively more influence when the costs are low (e.g. the whaling moratorium, Montreal Protocol).

Finally, US foreign environmental policy cannot be examined in isolation from broader developments in US foreign policy. As we have seen, President Nixon's leadership at the 1972 Stockholm Conference cannot be understood in isolation from the political fallout from the Vietnam War, while President George Bush Jr.'s international response to climate change cannot be understood in isolation from his preoccupation with the war on terror and the pivotal role played by the national energy strategy in the USA's national security strategy. President Obama's response to climate change has been profoundly shaped by its domestic and international response to the global financial crisis.

Yet none of the foregoing insights explain why US leadership has tended to wane as global and trans-boundary environmental problems have become more, rather than less, serious and threatening to both US and global security. That the end of the Cold War served as a key turning point in the waning of US international environmental leadership is significant in one respect, yet merely coincidental in another. The 'significant respect' is that the end of the Cold War changed the geopolitical context in which international environmental negotiations were to take place. The disintegration of the Soviet Union had removed a major incentive for US cooperation with its allies and others within its sphere of influence. As the sole superpower in the post-Cold War world, the USA has chosen to take full advantage of its greater range of exit options than any other state to avoid entanglement in the increasingly demanding and ever-growing international processes of multilateralism. The USA's increasing inclination to act unilaterally, via coalitions of the willing, rather than multilaterally, has affected environmental diplomacy, as it has many other policy domains. Indeed, even when the USA has sought to play a proactive environmental role, it still prefers to act through informal partnerships where it can control the process.

However, added to the changed geopolitical context is the fact that the end of the Cold War happened to coincide with the emergence of a new and more complex set of global environmental problems that have challenged what might be called 'core' US national interests. Most of the US environmental initiatives during the 1970s and 1980s (such as the establishment of the United Nations Environment Program, or protecting natural heritage, whales, oceans, or the ozone layer) were relatively uncomplicated issues, and they bore little relationship to, or otherwise did not directly threaten, US security interests or economic competitiveness. The same cannot be said for the environmental problems confronting world leaders at the 1992 Earth Summit. For the USA in particular, the mitigation of climate change, the management of intellectual property over biodiversity, or the regulation of the trans-boundary movement of genetically modified organisms posed direct challenges to the USA's security, energy, and/or economic interests. Indeed, the more general insight emerging from this foreign environmental policy history after the end of the Cold War is that international environmental problems have increasingly challenged US grand strategy, and that key elements of US grand strategy have increasingly constrained the ability of the USA to adopt a proactive response to key international environmental problems.

US grand strategy and the environment

US grand strategy represents an overriding prioritization of US foreign policy objectives and goals, backed up with particular strategies, preferred modes of engagement (multilateral, bilateral, unilateral), and preferred policy tools. As we have seen, US foreign environmental policy has never played a role in shaping US grand strategy (despite the promotion of the discourse of environmental security by President Clinton) and it has generally been accorded low priority in the pecking order of foreign policy objectives and goals. As Robert Falkner has noted, 'unlike trade and monetary policy, environmental policy has never been central to the US effort to create international order' (Falkner 2005: 586). But while environmental policy has had little impact on US grand strategy prior to the end of the Cold War, US grand strategy has increasingly set significant limits on US foreign environmental policy after the Cold War. Indeed, this provides one important key to the puzzle raised above: why has the USA not responded to the security and environmental threats of climate change by reducing the USA's dependence on petroleum? The other keys are the energy-intensive structure of the US economy, the US preference for economic neoliberalism and therefore minimal regulation, and the fragmented character of the US political system, which favours the status quo.

US foreign environmental policy during the period 1970–2010 has been shaped and constrained by significant continuities and changes in US grand strategy. Throughout both the Cold War and post-Cold War periods, US grand strategy has remained committed to securing the military and economic supremacy of the USA, promoting a stable world capitalist system, and promoting the spread of liberal democracy. While the last of these foreign policy goals is generally conducive to environmental social learning, the others stand in a more problematic relationship.

First, to the extent to which the growth of an unreconstructed world capitalist system based on neoliberal economic ideology remains a central pillar of US grand strategy, then we are unlikely to see the USA emerge as a leader in promoting the meta-environmental strategy of sustainable development endorsed at the 1992 Earth Summit. This strategy requires all policy makers and economic actors to move beyond issue-by-issue environmental problem solving by integrating environmental considerations into all areas of policy making and decision making, including foreign policy. However, the appealing rhetoric of policy integration papers over a set of deep-seated debates over whether a rapidly growing world capitalist system of the kind promoted by the USA is capable of delivering ecological sustainability and intra- and intergenerational equity of the kind defended in the Brundtland Report. Critics point out that while capitalism can deliver improved efficiency of resource and energy use through technological innovations that decrease the amount of environmental degradation produced per unit of GDP, this will not necessarily translate into a decrease in environmental degradation in absolute terms. Indeed, in the absence of overarching sustainability parameters at the national and international levels, the environmental productivity gains of technologically driven ecological modernization invariably serve to fuel more consumption and growth.

While the 'embedded liberalism' of the post-Second World War era might have been compatible with integrated sustainability planning, the neo-liberal economic ideology promoted by the USA since the 1980s, and especially since the end of the Cold War, is deeply resistant to the kind of 'thick regulation' demanded by proponents of ecological sustainability or 'strong ecological modernization' (Christoff 1996; Eckersley 2004). The recession triggered by the sub-prime mortgage crisis, a product of international financial deregulation promoted by the USA, considerably impaired the ability of the Obama administration to address climate change. The high-consumption lifestyles of Americans have also remained largely non-negotiable during the period 1970–2010, despite the growth of the green consumer movement. As we have seen, the US presidents' enthusiasm for integrated environmental policy planning has never been high and President Clinton's modest efforts to promote policy integration have been dismantled. In contrast, the European Union emerged in the 1990s as the green leader not only in environmental diplomacy but also in domestic efforts at policy integration through the adoption of sustainable development in the Treaty of the European Union (Article 6).

Second, both the US economy and US hegemony developed on the basis of a cheap and abundant supply of fossil fuels. US style capitalism is thus highly 'carboniferous' (Paterson 2009: 148). The US has the world's largest coal reserves (around 22 per cent) and coal is extracted from twenty-six states, which means that fifty-two Senators come from states in which coal contributes to the state economy and employment (Fisher 2006: 480). Likewise, cheap and abundant oil has been central 'to the vigor and growth of the American economy and to the preservation of a distinctly *American* way of life' (Klare 2004: pp. xiii–xiv). Oil has also fuelled the USA's vast military apparatus. Even more significantly, oil has also been used as a strategic resource by the USA during the Cold War in pursuing its strategy of containment and in the overall management of its Western leadership (Bromley 1991, 2005). As Keohane puts it, 'In a material sense, oil was at the centre of the redistributive system of the American hegemony' (1984: 140). These links between US energy policy and foreign policy are entrenched and long standing and may be traced to the end of the Second World War, when President Roosevelt offered the Saudi regime military support in return for reliable access to the Saudis' vast oil reserves. US dependence on Middle Eastern oil grew during the Cold War period at the same time as US oil capital shifted 'from a powerful interest in US foreign policy-making into a key arm of US power' (Bromley 1991: 123). The net effect of these developments is that oil (along with the US oil industry) became integrated into the structural components of US hegemony. Indeed, Ran Goel (2004: 478) has characterized the international political economy of oil as a US-led order based on a bargain between the US executive and US oil industry to manipulate the international oil market and secure supply. This special arrangement (or 'petro-military-industrial-complex', after Boal et al. 2005) has seen the executive working to overcome obstacles to US investment and the oil industry providing the investment capital and technologies to extract and transport the oil (Klare 2004: 62). This strategic use of oil has remained central to US grand strategy in the post-Cold War period, despite the predicted onset of peak oil and scientific warnings that the world must move rapidly towards a low-carbon economy. The US oil majors and allied industries have been key players in obstructing domestic efforts to reduce US dependence on oil (Newell and Paterson 1998). They have formed the backbone of US opposition to the Kyoto Protocol and domestic cap-and-trade bills, run orchestrated political campaigns to disparage the science of climate change, and served as key participants in the Cheney Energy Taskforce. Most of the US oil majors have negligible investment in non-carbon forms of energy compared to their European counterparts (Goel 2004: 476; Kolk and Levy 2001).

Notwithstanding these continuities in US grand strategy, there have also been some significant shifts that have impinged upon foreign environmental policy. The terrorist attacks on the World Trade Center and Pentagon on 11 September 2001 have profoundly reshaped the USA's threat perceptions and national security strategy. The second Bush administration singled out terrorism and the acquisition of weapons of mass destruction (WMD) by so-called rogue states or terrorists as the most significant security threats facing the USA. While the search for WMD was the official reason for the USA's invasion of Iraq in 2003, the invasion has also paved the way for the restructuring of Iraq's oil industry, which had been nationalized during the OPEC oil crisis and has been operating well below full production (Boal et al. 2005: 13). This is consistent with the US's long-standing supply-driven foreign petroleum policy, which has severely limited the scope for US leadership in low-carbon energy alternatives.

In all, the USA's ongoing commitment to economic neo-liberalism (including financial deregulation), its dependence on oil to maintain its economic competitiveness and military supremacy, its use of oil as a strategic commodity to maintain hegemony, and its preoccupation with the war on terror and the global financial crisis have together significantly constrained the ability of the USA to play a proactive role in responding to the most serious environmental problem of the new millennium.

Making sense of environmental foreign policy

The foregoing analysis concerning the relationship between domestic and US foreign environmental policy, and US grand strategy highlights the necessity of a multilevelled analysis that incorporates the international system, the state, society, and key individuals in the political elite in order to explain US foreign policy (Barkdull and Harris 2002). Yet the choice of level or levels of analysis does not determine the epistemology, or the explanatory priority accorded to power, interests, and/or ideas/norms. The importance of US security and economic interests in shaping foreign environmental policy might appear at first blush to play into the hands of rationalist and/or materialist explanations of foreign policy, such as realism, neo-liberal institutionalism, and traditional Marxism. Yet these accounts ultimately remain crude and unsatisfactory for several reasons.

First, security and economic constraints do not explain the particular menu of policy choices, or the particular policy responses, selected by the US executive in response to different domestic or international pressures. Realist and traditional Marxist accounts, in particular, attribute minimal autonomy to the state on the assumption that its decisions are essentially a reflection of systemic imperatives that derive from the anarchic structure of the state system or from particular configurations of economic power. Yet there is no single, obvious path to US military or economic supremacy, and it cannot be assumed that different foreign policy elites would produce the same strategies in response to similar challenges. Indeed, most scholars who have undertaken a detailed examination of US foreign environmental policy making have shown that the domestic institutional landscape plays a much more significant role in explaining these environmental policy choices than international influences (Hopgood 1998; DeSombre 2000, 2005; Falkner 2005). This research challenges the assumption that states are unitary, rational actors, by pointing to internal divisions within states and their societies. According to Hopgood (1998: 222), the central actors in American foreign policy are state officials, and it is the intrastate struggles within the executive branch of government that are ultimately determinative of policy choices.

Second, materialist and rationalist explanations do not offer sufficiently fine-grained tools to explain the waxing and waning of US environmental leadership. They are better at explaining the absence rather than the presence of environmental leadership. For example, materialists and rationalists can provide plausible accounts of why the USA will not enter into an international environmental treaty if it is incompatible with domestic regulations, the interests of key industry groups, or core security interests. But they cannot explain why the USA would bother to take a leadership role in relation to environmental issues that do not impinge upon security or economic interests. Why, for example, has the USA gone to such great lengths (employing persuasion, economic sanctions, and bribery) to support an international moratorium on whaling if not for a strong normative commitment to the preservation of whales within American society?

Neo-liberal institutionalism, which provides the dominant interest-based analysis of environmental regime formation, predicts whether a state will be a leader, a bystander, or a laggard on the basis of relative ecological vulnerability and relative abatement costs (Sprinz and Vaahtoranta 1994). So, for example, if abatement costs are high and vulnerability is low, then states are likely to be laggards, whereas if abatement costs are low and vulnerability is high then they are likely to be leaders. Yet prediction becomes difficult when both abatement costs and vulnerability are high, as in the case of climate change. More importantly, these predictions assume that states are rational, unitary actors, and that their cost–benefit analyses and strategic calculations can be uncritically transposed from one jurisdiction to another in response to similar external challenges.

Third, since rationalist explanations take the security and economic interests of states as given, they are unable to account for historical and geographical variability in the social construction of these interests. Indeed, the significant differences in foreign environmental policy between the USA and the EU since the end of the Cold War directs attention to the idiosyncratic ways in which US foreign policy elites have constructed their security, economic, and environmental agendas—some of which defy standard realist or rationalist analysis. If climate change is a source of catastrophic risk, why has this not been incorporated into US security policy? If states are rational actors, why has the USA not sought to reduce its dependence on imported petroleum by developing an aggressive domestic demand-management strategy? While there are important differences in the imminence of risks of terrorism compared to climate change, the longer-term risks of climate change are more pervasive, serious, and certain than the short-term risks of terrorism.

Foreign policy making is a purposive activity that involves the formulation and pursuit of objectives, goals, and strategies by particular decision makers. Understanding this activity requires locating decision makers in their historical context or 'operating environment', understanding their traditions and cultures, causal ideas, and principled beliefs and how they have interpreted their operating environment by selecting and endowing some phenomenon with significance while screening out others. In the case of the USA, there has been plenty of 'screening out' in the case of the science of

KEY POINTS

- ❑ US foreign environmental policy cannot be examined in isolation from domestic environmental policy, on the one hand, and broader developments in US foreign policy, on the other hand.
- ❑ The USA has never been an importer of 'foreign environmental policy' ideas from abroad but it has often sought to 'export' its domestic environmental regulations.

- ❑ The key international environmental problems of the post-Cold War period have increasingly challenged US grand strategy, while US grand strategy has increasingly constrained the ability of the USA to adopt a proactive response to these problems, especially climate change.

global warming. While US scientists have played a major role in the IPCC they have had very little influence on US domestic or foreign policy, until recently. In contrast, the findings and warnings of the IPCC have been much more influential in Europe and climate change scepticism has been much less pronounced among political leaders, the media, and the public (McCright and Dunlap 2003; Boykoff and Boykoff 2004). The social construction of new security risks and new ecological risks by political elites in the USA since the end of the Cold War has remained firmly rooted in the traditional 'high' versus 'low' politics distinction, which rests on particular understandings of the 'core' and 'peripheral' business of the US state. In contrast, the EU has displayed a more risk-averse posture in the post-Cold War period, particularly in response to the potential risks of not only

climate change but also genetically modified organisms (GMOs) (Falkner 2007). In the case of GMOs, whereas the USA has pushed for regulatory harmonization to promote trade liberalization in what it regards as a benign technology, in the EU NGOs have played a major role in framing the problem as a matter of both sovereign and consumer choice; the right to know and to choose safe food based on the precautionary principle, and resistance to corporate control over the agri-food chain (Levidow 2007: 133).

From a critical constructivist standpoint, the economic, energy, and security interests of the USA are not pre-given and they are always open to redefinition by social agents, including foreign policy elites. As it happens, an increasing number of Americans within both the state and civil society are beginning to rethink the meaning of these interests.

Conclusion

If there is one major lesson to be learned from the foregoing history of US foreign environmental policy making it is that a considerable confluence of domestic political forces is needed to produce US international environmental leadership. Strong leadership requires widespread acceptance of the need for an integrated energy, economic, and environmental strategy for sustainable development that guides both domestic and foreign policy making. Ideally, this would require a green president surrounded by a forceful and environmentally sympathetic cabinet, an environmentally sympathetic Congress, a well-funded scientific community, a vigorous environmental movement, and an

environmentally proactive business community that cooperates with the environment movement because it sees market advantage in being an environmental pace setter. The existing US political system and political culture is unlikely ever to produce this perfect alignment of political and economic forces for environmental change, but if it comes to pass then US international environmental leadership could be formidable. However, if some kind of rough alignment of at least some of these forces is not produced within the next decade (particularly in Congress), then the outcome for the world's climate could be unthinkable.

? Questions

1. How relevant are the environmental sympathies of the President in accounting for US international environmental leadership?
2. What role has Congress played in US foreign environmental policy making?
3. Why was the USA an international environmental leader in the 1970s?
4. Why did the USA play a leadership role in the Montreal Protocol given the anti-environmental sympathies of the Reagan administration?
5. Why was the end of the Cold War a turning point in US foreign environmental policy making?
6. What was the relationship between US grand strategy and foreign environmental policy before the end of the Cold War? In what ways did this relationship change in the post-Cold War period?
7. Why did President George Bush Jr. repudiate the Kyoto Protocol in 2001?
8. What is the relationship between energy security and environmental security?
9. What theories of foreign policy can best explain the shifts in US foreign environmental policy making from the 1970s?
10. Why has the Obama administration failed to move the USA from a climate change laggard to a leader?

» Further Reading

Bromley, S. (1991), *American Hegemony and World Oil* (Cambridge: Cambridge University Press).

A detailed analysis of US hegemony in the domain of oil politics based on a 'conjunctural' model of world politics that combines the geopolitical economy of the world oil industry and the global power of the USA in the system of states.

Harris, P. G. (ed.) (2000), *Climate Change and American Foreign Policy* (New York: St Martin's Press).

This edited collection explores the role of the USA in the climate change negotiations prior to the election of George Bush Jr.

Harris, P. G. (ed.) (2001), *The Environment, International Relations, and US Foreign Policy* (Washington, DC: Georgetown University Press).

This edited collection covers a range of case studies of US environmental policy making.

Hopgood, S. (1998), *American Environmental Foreign Policy and the Power of the State* (New York: Oxford University Press).

A detailed examination of US foreign environmental policy from the Stockholm Summit to the Rio Summit that rejects realist, pluralist, and Marxist accounts, and highlights the core role played by senior members of the US executive in shaping foreign policy.

Klare, M. (2004), *Blood and Oil* (New York: Metropolitan Books).

This book provides a detailed analysis of America's growing petroleum dependence and the ways this has shaped national energy and security strategies and led to the increasing use of the US military to secure supply.

Paterson, M. (2009), Post-hegemonic climate change? *British Journal of Politics and International Relations* **11**(1), 140–58.

This article explains the differences between US and EU climate policy and diplomacy in terms of different strategies of accumulation, characterized as 'carboniferous capitalism' versus 'ecological modernisation'.

Soden, D. (ed.) (1999), *The Environmental Presidency* (Albany, NY: State University of New York Press).

This edited collection provides a detailed examination of the role of the US president in environmental and natural resource policy, focusing on the different facets of the president's constitutional and leadership powers.

Vig, N. and Kraft, M. (eds) (2006), *Environmental Policy: New Directions for the Twenty-First Century* (Washington, DC: Congressional Quarterly).

A comprehensive edited collection on all facets of US environmental policy making in the domestic and international context.

 Endnotes

I am grateful for the research assistance provided by Aron D'Souza and Gerry Nagtzaam.

1. These include the Brundtland Report (WCED 1987), the United Nations Environment Program's *Millennium Ecosystem Assessment* (UNEP 2005b), the regular State of the World Reports prepared by the Washington-based Worldwatch Institute (e.g. 2007), the UK Stern Report (Stern 2007), and the reports of the Intergovernmental Panel on Climate Change (e.g. IPCC 2007).

2. Major amendments to the Montreal Protocol have since been made (in 1990, 1992, 1997, and 1999) which have expanded the list of ozone-depleting substances covered by the regime.

3. According to Michael Lisowski (2002: 114), an ABC News poll released on 17 April 2001 revealed that 61 per cent of Americans supported ratification of the Kyoto Protocol.

4. The six original partners are the USA, Australia, Japan, China, South Korea, and India. Canada joined the partnership in 2007.

5. Only one new environmental treaty of significance has been negotiated since 2004, which is the Nagoya Protocol on Access to Genetic Resources and the Fair and Equitable Sharing of Benefits Arising from their Utilization to the Convention on Biological Diversity, accepted in Nagoya, Japan on 29 October 2010. However, this is not open for signature until 2 February 2011.

6. The only two environmental treaties ratified by a Republican-controlled Senate during this period were the Protocol to the 1970 Convention on Long-Range Transboundary Air Pollution on Heavy Metals (Aarhus 24 June 1998), which the USA signed in 24 June 1998 and ratified on 10 January 2001, and the Protocol to the 1970 Convention on Long-Range Transboundary Air Pollution to abate Acidification, Eutrophication and Ground-level Ozone (Gothenburg, 30 November 1999), which the USA signed on 1 December 1999 and ratified on 22 November 2004.

 For a range of additional resources to support your learning visit the Online Resource Centre that accompanies this book at www.oxfordtextbooks.co.uk/orc/cox_stokes2e/.

Section 5

Futures and Scenarios

21 American foreign policy after 9/11

Caroline Kennedy-Pipe

Chapter contents

Introduction

In his book *The Landscape of History* the distinguished Cold War historian John Lewis Gaddis (Gaddis 2002) makes an arresting suggestion: 'If you think of the past as a landscape,' he tells us, 'then history is the way we represent it, and it's that act of representation that lifts us above the familiar to let us experience vicariously what we can't experience directly: a wider view' (Gaddis 2002: 5).

That wider view is what this chapter as a whole seeks to place upon contemporary American foreign policy. By seeing the past and the present of American foreign policy as a 'landscape', in Gaddis's sense, one might be able to suggest certain features of a particular landscape, prominent now, which were also apparent long before 9/11. We might then be able to reflect upon whether the consequences of those features might be similar. In other words, however much the foreign policy of George W. Bush and his neo-conservative agenda might strike us as having led the USA down entirely new avenues in terms of the conduct of American foreign policy—the alleged emphasis upon securing oil resources, for example, or the desire to remove dictators and 'spread democracy'—as this chapter will suggest, these tendencies are as much a part of certain traditions within US foreign policy as they are in some ways a departure from it.

Thus, this chapter will try to give an outline account of US foreign policy after the 9/11 attacks with a view to looking at continuities as well as the disjunctions of Washington's engagement with the world. The terrorist attacks unquestionably altered the shape and thrust of US foreign policy in the short to medium term and have raised many questions, not just about the direction of US foreign policy but also about the shape of the international system itself. The question, however, is the extent to which they have, can, or should change the direction of US foreign policy in the longer term, and so this chapter will try to assess the extent to which US foreign policy after 9/11 manifests familiar tendencies as well as unfamiliar ones.

The background

The period between the mid-1990s and the early twenty-first century was certainly not one that was shy of challenges for the USA. The early euphoria of the immediate post-Cold War world wore off rather rapidly and there was little left of the first President Bush's much vaunted New World Order, which he had announced in the aftermath of the Gulf War of 1990–1 in a speech to Congress (Nye 1992). Nonetheless, the Clinton administration had sought to position itself as central to a wide range of mulilateral and bilateral relationships, to be, as Secretary of State Madeleine Albright termed it, 'the indispensable nation' (Albright 2004). Thus the USA was throughout the decade after the Soviet Union collapsed heavily involved in the Middle East, in negotiations over world trade and the replacement of the General Agreement on Tariffs and Trade (GATT) with the World Trade Organization (WTO), in trying to support newly established democracies in eastern and central Europe and Latin America, and in building free trade areas throughout the Americas. It had also become somewhat reluctantly but centrally involved in the conflicts in the former Yugoslavia with the bombing campaign that eventually led to the Dayton Agreement of 1995, and then in the controversial NATO (but US-#and British-led, some might say British-inspired) intervention in Kosovo in 1999 Milosovic (Halbestam 2003; Holbrooke 1999).

Despite the turmoil of the international system and the resurgence of genocide in both Africa and Europe, however, the American presidential election of 2000 was chiefly and somewhat predictably about domestic politics. Foreign policy played little part in the tussle over the White House. The Republican candidate, George W. Bush, son of the forty-first president, was in fact critical of President Clinton's 'overambitious' foreign policy (as he saw it) and the supposed tendency to interventionism. He pressed a range of relatively familiar criticisms of Clinton's policies although he had little knowledge or background in foreign policy. This 'ignorance' was a fact in which he almost seemed to glory and he chose to run in the election as a 'compassionate conservative', focusing on a domestic agenda and issues guaranteed to appeal to his core supporters on the Christian right—such as opposition to abortion, stem cell research, and marriage between gay couples.

The people who actually did advise the Bush campaign formed the nucleus of the team that became the key foreign policy makers of his administration in 2001. His campaign director of foreign policy was Condoleezza Rice, who became National Security Adviser in the first Bush administration and then Secretary of State in the second. His second campaign adviser, Paul Wolfowitz, later became Deputy Secretary of State and one of the chief architects of the Iraq War. Perhaps most important of all, Bush's running mate, Dick Cheney, had huge experience of foreign policy, having served in Congress and as White House chief of staff (under President Ford) and having been Defense Secretary under Bush's father. As James Mann has argued, this was an important choice as 'the selection of Cheney was of surpassing importance for the future direction of foreign policy' (Mann 2004: 252).

Many of these individuals were part of a network of policy intellectuals and activists generally referred to as neo-conservatives. Perle, Wolfowitz, and Cheney especially had ties to this group (Mann 2004). Neo-conservatism is a very broad intellectual movement in American public life and can be traced back to reactions to both communism and liberalism in American life and, in foreign policy terms, to a radical critique of the 'realism' of Henry Kissinger, Richard Nixon's National Security Adviser and Secretary of State (see Kissinger 1982, 1994; Isacson 1996).

The neo-conservatives resisted realist claims. As one of the major architects of neo-conservatism, Irving Kristol, said, realism had no purchase on the future because it was simply a defence of the status quo. But, to his mind, modern politics is necessarily ideological since it is, fundamentally, a battle over 'who owns the future' (Stelzer 2005) and changing the shape of global politics.

9/11 put the neo-conservative agenda in pole position as far as foreign policy was concerned. It was only halfway through Bush's second term that that alliance really stared to unravel and the neo-conservatives began to lose their dominance in a wealth of acrimony about the failure in Iraq.

Perhaps the most important figure to play a role in Bush's foreign policy who was not part of the Bush inner circle was in fact Colin Powell. As the chairman of the Joint Chiefs of Staff during the 1990–1 Gulf War, as a highly decorated black American, and as a figure who in many respects stood above politics in the eyes of many Americans, Powell's active endorsement of the Bush candidacy was an enormous boost. His reward was to be appointed Secretary of State.

The most surprising appointment was in fact that of Donald Rumsfeld as Secretary of Defense. He had been Secretary of Defense before, under President Gerald Ford some twenty-five years previously, but had not been part of the circle around the previous President Bush. However, he had experience, ability, and was perceived as 'tough', somebody who the military couldn't overawe, and it was that factor that seemed to clinch his appointment.

The Bush foreign policy team, then, was set. What of the world they would confront? Initially, it looked as though relatively traditional foreign policy issues would be the order of the day. The first major visitor to Washington with serious foreign policy concerns was the South Korean President Kim Dae Jung, and

---

KEY POINTS

❏ After the collapse of the USSR in 1991 the United States proclaimed a New World Order.
❏ The USA did seem to be the indispensable nation and throughout the 1990s was engaged in a range of activities which included negotiations over world trade, the promotion of democracy in central and eastern Europe, and discussions over the Middle East peace process.
❏ Throughout the 1990s, the USA displayed a continuing preoccupation with dictators and dictatorships.

Kim found a distinct toughening of the US stance in relation to North Korea. This coldness was in keeping with a paper that Condoleezza Rice had published in the influential periodical *Foreign Affairs* just before the election (Rice 2000). Entitled 'Promoting the National Interest', the article was a fine example of the latest version of what some might call 'national security realism'. There was in that early discussion of policy towards North Korea a hint of the views and debates that were to characterize US foreign policy after 9/11. This was the predilection of Powell and the State Department for negotiation and multilateralism versus an emergent and powerful unilateralist view. It was this latter position which was supported by Cheney, Rumsfeld, and Wolfowitz at the Pentagon. We might also note a very public commitment by George Bush to modernize the military capabilities of the United States and his stress on the importance of diversifying US oil supplies.

Aside from Korea, the early months of the Bush administration's foreign policy were concerned with relations with China, now dubbed a 'strategic competitor', and with Russia, no longer a superpower but still a major player in Eurasia and one with an increasingly authoritarian domestic agenda. Washington's relations with its European allies were also something of a priority, especially as sharp differences had emerged over environmental questions, particularly the US refusal to ratify the Kyoto Protocol. Indeed, it appeared to be business in the US world as usual—how to balance friends and foes with the protection of US interests. And then came the events of 9/11.

Framing 9/11 and its aftermath

It is now a commonplace to claim that 9/11 changed everything in world politics. John Lewis Gaddis invoked a powerful emphasis on the 'newness' and radically transformative character of that autumn day in his meditations on the US experience of the 9/11 attacks. He has written thus:

> It's as if we were all irradiated, on that morning of September 11 2001, in such a way as to shift our psychological makeup—the DNA in our minds—with consequences that will not become clear for years to come. (Gaddis 2004: 4–5)

Whether this is true in general or not—and we will come back to this question at the end of the chapter—it was certainly true at least in the short to medium term in the context of American foreign policy and US cultural politics. The impact of 9/11 on America itself is certainly hard to overstate. Both in intellectual circles and in many arenas 9/11 became central to what one might call the 'cultural shape' of the USA in the early twenty-first century. Films like *United 93* and *World Trade Center* sought specifically to grapple with the events of 9/11. Peter Jackson's *Lord of the Rings* trilogy owed a good deal to 9/11. So for example in the final film, the King, Aragorn, gives a speech to his own troops before they engage in battle with the forces of the enemy. He uses the evocative phrase 'Stand, Men of the West'. Presumably his forces are to counter, in a war

they did not seek, an enemy seeking to undermine and destroy the values of the west.

In particular, the assumptions that have gone to make up the key organizing principle of US foreign policy in the immediate aftermath of 9/11—the so-called 'war on terror' later redefined by the Bush administration as 'the long war'—are incomprehensible without the context of the terrorist attacks of 9/11. How a few men could hijack American planes and launch surprise attacks on US soil against probably the world's greatest military power was quite simply, for many citizens, astounding. No wonder that comparisons with the Japanese attack on Pearl Harbor in 1941 proved compelling. One example of this was the development of what amounts to a preventive war strategy as articulated in the National Security Strategy of 2002. This strategy had at its core the right of the USA to eliminate any challenge (real or perceived) to US security. Alongside this articulation of American determination came a vibrant propaganda campaign which claimed that Saddam Hussein was himself a clear and present danger to the security of the United States and perhaps even involved in the events of 9/11 (Chomsky 2003). Saddam, for so long a thorn in the side of the USA after the First Gulf War, was obviously at some point going to be a target for US vengeance, something the neo-conservatives had long sought.

Significant change was also apparent in respect to traditional assumptions about the relationship between law and national security. This was marked most obviously by the creation of the Department of Homeland Security, the establishment of the highly controversial internment centre at the Guantánamo Bay military base in Cuba, and the activities of the CIA in operating so-called 'black sites' in which suspected enemies of the USA would be held outside of normal legal jurisdiction. (Here we might note that 'black sites' had operated under the Clinton regime but the scale of these operations intensified after 9/11.) Most obviously in the months and years that followed 9/11, the use of war seemingly made a comeback as the tool of choice for those in the White House.

So, on the evening of 9/11, President Bush declared that 'night fell on a different world' (Fawn and Buckley

---

BOX 21.1   The war on terror

The phrase 'war on terrorism' is not one that was dreamt up by George Bush. It was used as far back as the nineteenth century to refer to attempts by anarchists to attack and assassinate political leaders. Indeed many anarchists used the term 'terrorist' to describe their actions. After the terrorist attacks of 9/11, George W. Bush resurrected the term and argued that the war on terror would begin with al-Qaeda but not end with al-Qaeda. It has been used not just to justify the use of war in Afghanistan and Iraq but also to underpin a series of controversial activities, including extraordinary rendition and torture (see Box 21.3).

KEY POINTS

❑ Whatever we think of the claim that 9/11 irrevocably transformed global politics we cannot doubt that for many Americans it was a cataclysmic event.

❑ Bush responded to the events of 9/11 with the war on terror and a New National Security Strategy, which was enunciated in 2002.

❑ The war on terror challenged many accepted legal norms, such as the prohibition on torture. It also led to the controversial practise of extraordinary rendition.

2003). As this chapter goes on to argue, yes, 9/11 was a defining moment for the USA and did herald shifts in US behaviour, especially allowing the neo-conservatives to put into policy their specific world view, but as we go on to note there were also constants in the shape of debates about the foreign policy and the place of the USA in global politics.

I shall suggest that there were three overarching framings for US foreign policy after 9/11: the ideological shape of US politics and the agents/individuals who interpreted that ideology, the impact of previous US policy/decisions taken both during the years of Cold War and after, and the new assumptions about the utility of the use of force/war and specifically the idea that the USA could 'go it alone'. It is on this issue of the utility of war that I argue that the USA has antagonized long-standing allies and foes, Muslim sentiment, and some of its own citizens. The war in Iraq, although not perhaps a Vietnam, has diminished the Bush presidency and the reputation of the United States. But before we come to the war in Iraq, let me take each of the three categories in turn.

The triumph of ideology: the neo-conservatives in the ascendent

Perhaps the most obvious way in which 9/11 changed US foreign policy, and which has been much commented upon, was the extent to which it created an opportunity for the most overtly ideological elements of the Bush administration to take the initiative: that is to say to allow the neo-conservatives to influence policy (see Box 21.2).

President Bush has emphasized that this period of world history is as much, if not more, a struggle about values as it is about interests. As Bush himself argued in the autumn of 2001, 'We wage a war to save civilization itself. We did not seek it, but we must fight it and we will prevail.' Current American leaders therefore see this struggle with radical Islam as in part a cultural or civilizational conflict; a war for a certain type of 'civilization' even if it is not a war actually against moderate Islam. Politicians such as Bush make clear for public consumption that al-Qaeda does not actually represent Islamic 'civilization'.

These complex ideological dimensions of the struggle between certain parts of Islam and what extremists claim are the perils of modernity played into the hands of those who thought, as the neo-conservatives did (and do), that

'all politics is a battle over who owns the future'. It also fed into a view which was widely believed about the 'real' nature of the geopolitical conflicts that faced the USA at the opening of the twenty-first century: to wit that they were fundamentally civilizational, or cultural (and even religious), in character. Amongst the most widely cited (semi-)academic books of the last ten years that sought to emphasize this feature of international politics was Samuel Huntington's controversial *The Clash of Civilizations and the Remaking of World Order* (Huntington 2002). Huntington's thesis is now well known. It is perhaps worth pointing out though just how widely taken up his ideas were. It is perhaps now usual to speak of the inevitable 'clash' of civilizations as a motor of conflict in twenty-first-century world politics, and there are echoes of this language in the academic, journalistic, and political commentary of, for example, the collapse and bloody wars of the former Yugoslavia or the possible emergence of a Chinese 'threat' to American primacy.

Yet in some of the language that has been routinely used in the war on terror there are clear ideological claims made by the United States about the battle with

---

BOX 21.2 The neo-conservatives

The neo-conservatives were originally liberals but liberal thinkers who had become disillusioned with the so-called New Left culture of the 1960s. These liberals began to take up increasingly conservative positions based on the thinking of Irving Kristol. They were critical of the failures of liberalism both in domestic and foreign policy. Specifically in foreign policy they were dismayed by the degree of anti-Americanism they perceived in critiques of the Vietnam War and the trend towards the downgrading of defence and military issues. More recently neo-conservative thinkers were critical of Clinton and what they saw as a lack of idealism and patriotism in foreign policy as well as, crucially, a lack of moral purpose to the conduct of policy abroad. Neo-conservatives wanted Saddam Hussein removed after the first Gulf War.

KEY POINTS

❑ It became common after the events of 9/11 to depict global politics as a battle of civilizations or a competition of competing world views.
❑ The USA became preoccupied after 9/11 with Islamic fundamentalism, its causes, and its ambitions.
❑ It is important to consider how and why ideas and beliefs matter in international relations.

---

the terrorists. The term of preference for the 'Islamic fundamentalism' of Osama bin Laden and his peers, for example, seems increasingly to be 'Islamofascism', a deliberate harking back to an earlier period of ideological struggle in the turbulent years of the 1930s. President Bush himself has also used terms such as 'Islamic caliphate' or 'militant jihadism', themselves evocative of earlier struggles with non-Christian forces. References to the struggle against communism during the years of Cold War as similar to the current battles with al-Qaeda are also frequently made, especially in the United States.

This is understandable. It is clear that bin Laden and his allies entertain notions of representing a specific type of world view based on a certain reading of fundamentalist Islam. Some—for example Bernard Lewis—have therefore seen these undeniable ideological rigidities and apparent certainties that have characterized world politics after 9/11 as a trend that is new

and distinct. One aspect of this that has perhaps been most commented on—and for some years now—is the apparent resurgence of religious sentiment in world and domestic politics (Thomas 2005).

In fact religious conflict was a powerful feature of the shape of politics throughout the twentieth century, as Michael Burleigh's work has recently shown (Burleigh 2004, 2006). His term 'political religions' is certainly one useful way through which the current ideological struggles that dominate world politics can be seen. In this respect, the Bush administration itself is a conspicuously religious one, with both Bush himself and many of his closest advisers avowedly and militantly 'born again' Christians. The tendency to see political situations, especially conflict, through explicitly religions lenses was present from the start. President Bush's initial reaction to 9/11 was to speak in terms of a 'crusade' and while that was quickly altered to avoid embarrassing Islamic and Arab allies, it revealed a certain mindset. Therefore the attacks of 9/11 seemed to allow for a resurgence of neo-conservative thinking about the world in which democratic (and Christian) forces are pitted against anti-democratic and Islamic forces at both state and sub-state levels. The terrorists had to be countered, defied, and defeated by the USA or another 9/11 might occur.

Blowback: US foreign policy against itself?

But the point is that the attacks of 9/11 did not simply come out of nowhere. Clinton himself knew of the attacks on the USS Cole in Aden in October 2000 and the earlier bombing of the World Trade Center by radical forces in 1993. There had for many years been

those scheming to take a certain type of 'revenge' on the USA. In this respect some of Osama bin Laden's appeal to Muslims worldwide must lie in his skilful use of the very real grievances such as the question of Palestine and the humiliations many of his audience have or feel, just as communism as an ideology genuinely appealed to the many who were, or felt themselves to be, at odds with a rich and perhaps decadent west. But for the purposes of this chapter, we come to the debates about the nature of US foreign policy over the last few decades and its ability to create antagonisms that can and have returned to haunt the USA both at home and abroad.

Bernard Henri Levy wrote, shortly after 9/11, that there is a tendency in the west to ignore the voices throughout the developing world antagonized by a succession of American policies over a considerable period. As he has written:

> "There are other kamikazes ready to say to the nations of the world, You ignored us while we were alive: now we are dead: you didn't want to know about our deaths as long as they happened in our own countries; now we throw them at your feet, into the same fire that is consuming you. (Levy, quoted in Chan 2004: 57)"

To repeat: the attacks of 9/11 did not come out of nowhere. The hijacking of aircraft and the deliberate destruction by those terrorists intent on suicide can and perhaps must be seen as part and parcel of longer-term patterns of resistance to established US power. Here contemporary global politics remains deeply affected by the origins and development of the Cold War and by the choices made by earlier generations of 'agents', especially—if not exclusively—the United States. The rise of a variant of militant Islam itself, al-Qaeda for example, can be traced to the emergence of groups like the Muslim Brotherhood in Egypt, groups who were profoundly affected by the revolutionary changes of the inter-war period and by the emergence of the Cold War. Events, as the old saying has it, have consequences. The Iranian Revolution of 1979 was in many respects independent of the Cold War, but the revolutionary methods of the Bolsheviks had been studied to great effect by some of the Iranians, and the passions roused by the

> **KEY POINTS**
>
> ❑ The events of 9/11 were preceded by a number of terrorist attacks against US personnel and assets both abroad and at home.
>
> ❑ Some elements of al-Qaeda emerged out of the Soviet War in Afghanistan, most notably Osama bin Laden, a Saudi, was radicalized by his experiences of Soviet–US rivalry in the country.
>
> ❑ Blowback is the notion that the USA is now suffering the consequences of its actions, especially its covert actions during the period of Cold War.

events that followed it (such as the Iraq/Iran War and the growth of groups like Hamas and Hezbollah) were all framed by the overarching structures of the Cold War and the decisions taken by those in Washington to contest the ideological battles with Moscow on every front, especially those of the Middle East.

Most obviously of all, al-Qaeda itself, and the leadership of Osama bin Laden in particular, was forged in the reaction to the Soviet invasion of Afghanistan in late 1979, and the passions that were subsequently inflamed throughout the Muslim world were themselves an offshoot of the Cold War obsession with spheres of influence (Keppel 2005; Rashid 2001). The *mujahidin* in Afghanistan—including bin Laden and al-Qaeda— were supported by the Pakistani intelligence service (ISI) for largely Islamic reasons, but also supported by the USA and the Central Intelligence Agency (CIA) for geopolitical ones—not least because they were considerable thorns in the side of the Soviet Army. The logic of the Cold War therefore had, in some respects, more than a hand in the creation of al-Qaeda, an irony of history perhaps best summed up in Chalmers Johnson's now infamous term for it: 'blowback' (Johnson 2002). The key question for those in the White House was how to react to this 'blowback'. Their choice was that of war.

The centrality of military power—and 'imperial overstretch'?

One of the areas in the contemporary context that has received most comment is the extent to which the post-9/11 world has given a hefty new impetus to

those who have always believed in the central utility of force/war in global politics (Gray 2005). Much of the legacy of the 'nuclear era' had been premised on the idea of the 'declining' utility of force. Nuclear deterrence was considered to render major war unthinkable. Certainly within the European Union, militaries lost much of their resonance and even within the United States, despite victory in the first Gulf War, there seemed little enthusiasm for the deployment of troops abroad. None of this meant that wars did not happen, or that states gave up their right to use force in defence of their own interest, but certainly war seemed to be on the wane.

Perhaps the general assumptions governing this were best laid out in the late 1970s by Robert Keohane and Joseph Nye. In their now classic study *Power and Interdependence* they asserted, as one of the three central characteristics of the now dawning age of interdependence, the 'declining utility of military force' (Keohane and Nye 2000).

In the immediate aftermath of 9/11, this trajectory seemed to shift, almost overnight. For many, what 9/11 seemed to demonstrate was not the declining utility of force, but actually its huge importance. The Bush administration followed up the events of 9/11 not only with the invasion of Afghanistan but also, as we noted earlier, with the new National Security Strategy, which made it perfectly clear that the United States now saw pre-emptive war as a legitimate form of defence and also expanded and redefined the general assumptions on which defences of pre-emption had rested in the past. The war in Iraq was initially justified, in 2003, by the removal of the dictator but soon morphed into a different set of justifications for the Bush administra-

> ### KEY POINTS
>
> ❏ Although many analysts believed that war had a declining utility in international relations, the war on terror proved them wrong.
> ❏ The emphasis of the Bush administration on war as an instrument of policy proved problematic for many allies of the USA.
> ❏ The war in Iraq, although initially popular with the American public, has increasingly become regarded as the new Vietnam.

tion. Not the least of these were the supposed linkages between Iraq and the production of weapons of mass destruction (WMD), and Iraq and the encouragement of terrorism. There was also a determined effort to reject multilateralism and a determination to 'go it alone' in terms of shaping regional politics. This has had a series of consequences, not the least of which was a rejection of the authority of the United Nations but also a widening gap with its European allies (apart from Britain) and an increasingly difficult period for the USA in the Middle East. Franco-American relations became characterized by a barrage of diplomatic wrangling and insults. Most notably a number of American journalists and indeed politicians characterized the French nation as a bunch of 'cheese eating surrender monkeys'. (This memorable phrase was actually taken from the American hit cartoon *The Simpsons*.) But beneath this Euro-Atlantic difference of opinion lay the critical issue of the American determination to be unfettered in its choice of war.

The shape of America's wars

If ideology, the unintended consequences of previous US policy, and the increasing belief in the utility of military power set the parameters of post-9/11 US foreign policy, what were the key decisions and consequences?

The first major decision after the 9/11 attacks was, of course, what to actually do in response. After all, this was like the Japanese attack on Pearl Harbor in 1941, taken as a horrific crime against the USA itself. Very swiftly it became clear that al-Qaeda was responsible for the attacks (Wright 2006), but al-Qaeda itself, unlike Japan,

was not a state, but rather a transnational or subnational movement. However, it did have very close ties with the government of a state—the Taliban in Afghanistan, which had sheltered the leadership, provided training and basing facilities for the terrorists, and was openly and ideologically sympathetic. The decision was taken, therefore, to request the Taliban to surrender the leaders of al-Qaeda and, if they did not do so, to launch an invasion to remove the Taliban and eliminate al-Qaeda's infrastructure in Afghanistan. George W. Bush, in his recently published memoirs, describes how the radical mullahs in Afghanistan offered sanctuary to Osama bin Laden, the leader of al-Qaeda. The Taliban refused the US request and so, on 7 October 2001, the USA and the UK initiated military operations against this primitive regime.

To begin with these operations were largely air assaults, the fighting on the ground being largely the work of the anti-Taliban factions within Afghanistan itself, principally the Northern Alliance. There were strong indications that al-Qaeda's leadership expected some response along these lines, as shortly before the 9/11 attacks they had successfully assassinated the Alliance's legendary battlefield commander, Ahmed Shah Massoud, the so-called 'lion of the Panshir' and the greatest of the guerrilla *mujahidin* who had fought against Soviet troops throughout the 1980s. In the last few months of 2001, the US delivered 767 tonnes of supplies and 70 million dollars to equip and fund some 50,000 militiaman to fight Taliban forces.

From 2002, however, US and British troops were present on the ground (special forces had been deployed earlier). While the invasion was largely successful in the short term—the Taliban were removed from power and al-Qaeda's infrastructure in Afghanistan was destroyed—the invasion did not succeed in capturing or killing the senior al-Qaeda leadership, who escaped, probably into the wild borderland between Pakistan and Afghanistan, after the battle of Tora Bora at the end of 2001. Moreover, the decision to invade Iraq (of which more in a moment) took forces and resources away from Afghanistan at a crucial time and allowed the Taliban to regroup.

In general, the reaction of the international community to the invasion of Afghanistan was muted. Most states understood that the USA was bound to respond to the 9/11 attacks and the Taliban regime had few if any friends in any event. The USA's NATO allies in particular rallied round, with even the sometimes critical French declaring, famously and in light of what we discussed earlier ironically, that after 9/11 'we are all Americans now'. So 9/11, or so it had seemed, united much of the world in support of the USA, and the invasion of Afghanistan was widely viewed as a reasonable, just, and proportionate response to the appalling acts of savagery perpetrated by the terrorists. After the 9/11

attacks, any fetters upon US power were not only seen as problematic in themselves but they could be painted as being dangerous to the USA 'in a time of war' (Hansen 2002).

This tendency in US foreign policy was visible in President Bush's 2002 State of the Union Address to Congress, perhaps the signature statement of the US intention to wage a 'war on terror'. One phrase in particular from that address became notorious. It is worth quoting the passage:

> “Iraq continues to flaunt its hostility toward America and to support terror. The Iraqi regime has plotted to develop anthrax, and nerve gas, and nuclear weapons for over a decade. This is a regime that has already used poison gas to murder thousands of its own citizens—leaving the bodies of mothers huddled over their dead children. This is a regime that agreed to international inspections—then kicked out the inspectors. This is a regime that has something to hide from the civilized world.
>
> States like these, and their terrorist allies, constitute an axis of evil, arming to threaten the peace of the world.' (www.whitehouse.gov/news/releases/2002/01/20020129-11.html)”

By expressly linking the 'axis of evil' to the global jihad of al-Qaeda and its affiliates, President Bush was greatly expanding the administration's original mission and, arguably, running together problems that were perhaps

---

BOX 21.3 Extraordinary rendition and black sites

Legal rendition has been used by the United States for over two decades as a means of dealing with foreign suspects/defendants. Extraordinary rendition is a different and highly controversial process that became common after 9/11 and forms a central part of the war on terror. Suspects/alleged terrorists are placed in US custody but then are taken to a third-party state without ever coming before the US judiciary. Commonly suspects are taken to Egypt, Jordan, Uzbekistan, or certain states in central and eastern Europe. Critics of the process allege that the movement of suspects to such sites allows the CIA to avoid US legislation that prohibits torture and allows CIA operatives to gain evidence/confessions through the physical and mental abuse of suspects over a prolonged period. These are the so-called 'black sites'.

best kept separate. Most significantly of all, perhaps, it seemed to flag up to many the increasing stridency of US intentions and the increasing unwillingness of the administration to act within the parameters that their predecessors had been prepared to accept.

A corollary of the above, which also seems to flag up a similar trajectory, was the additional policies the USA put in place after 9/11 and the Afghan invasion. The creation of the special detaining centre at Guantánamo Bay, the passing of the Patriot Act, the increasing reports on the use of torture, and the practice of extraordinary rendition all pointed towards a USA that was increasingly going its own way, independent of what even its allies might think (Kennedy-Pipe and Rengger 2006).

All of this came to a head, however, in what was certainly the most controversial decision in post-9/11 policy, the decision to invade Iraq.

> **KEY POINTS**
>
> ❑ After the terrorist attacks of 9/11 parallels were immediately drawn with the shock Japanese attack on Pearl Harbor in Hawaii in December 1941.
>
> ❑ It was apparent that the USA would seek to destroy the terrorist groups which had perpetrated the attacks. Afghanistan and its Taliban rulers were chosen as the target because of their links to al-Qaeda.
>
> ❑ The Bush administration made the military response the central one, enabled by a surge of patriotism and a resolve to support America that was apparent in the immediate months after 9/11.
>
> ❑ Unilateralism characterized the Bush administration. This is the approach by which the USA avoids any permanent alliance with foreign powers and argues against entanglement with international institutions such as the International Criminal Court (ICC) or the UN. It seeks to avoid prohibitions upon the making of US policy.

Iraq: a new Vietnam?

It is now clear that this decision was one with deep roots in the administration. According to the veteran journalist Bob Woodward, Bush asked Rumsfeld about the status of the military plans for an invasion of Iraq very soon after 9/11 itself (Woodward 2004). Part of the frustration was that the USA had been for more than a decade involved in an undeclared war with Saddam in attempting to enforce the two designated no-fly zones put in place after the end of the first Gulf War. The problem, of course, was that while other states accepted the need of Washington to strike back after 9/11, and while the Taliban had few allies, an attack on Iraq, which was unconnected to 9/11 and did have some allies, was bound to be much more difficult diplomatically.

So, indeed, it proved. In the months running up to the invasion in March 2003, the US found that its policy was opposed by many of the powers that had supported it over Afghanistan. Of its major allies only Britain, Australia, and Spain remained firmly committed and in each of those countries there was substantial political and popular opposition to an invasion of Iraq. Part of the problem was simply that despite many attempts, no

link between Iraq and al-Qaeda could be established and, indeed, there was in fact a good deal of evidence of hostility to Saddam from the al-Qaeda leadership (Saddam was, after all, a notorious and very public secularist). That led to a focus on what might be termed the 'axis of evil' rationale for intervention, i.e. the prevention of the spread of WMD. The difficulty here was that the evidence for Iraq's possession of WMD was at best sketchy, and both the International Atomic Energy Agency (IAEA) and the inspectors who had been seeking to verify Iraq's destruction of its previous programmes were saying they needed more time to make a proper assessment.

This, of course, bogged down the USA in the UN timetable. The USA had successfully obtained a first UN resolution criticizing Iraq and had, largely at the insistence of the British, gone back to the UN for a second resolution explicitly authorizing the use of force if Iraq continued to be in 'material breach' of its obligations under the 1991 ceasefire agreement. It very quickly became clear, however, that this would be effectively vetoed by the Russians, the Chinese, and the French. Thus the resolution was never put to the vote.

For many in the USA this confirmed their fears about the restrictions being imposed on US power by the 'multilateralism' of the international system. It was doubtless this in part which fed into Rumsfeld's dismissive comment about 'old Europe' and 'new Europe' (many of the newly emerging eastern and central European states supported Washington in its ambitions). His point was that old Europe was failing to take up its responsibilities for maintaining peace (Kagan 2003).

The official rationale for the Iraq invasion was set out by Secretary of State Powell, in his now famous set-piece presentation to the UN Security Council on 5 February 2003:

❝Given Saddam Hussein's history of aggression . . . given what we know of his terrorist associations and given his determination to exact revenge on those who oppose him, should we take the risk that he will not some day use these weapons at a time and the place and in the manner of his choosing at a time when the world is in a much weaker position to respond? The United States will not and cannot run that risk to the American people. Leaving Saddam Hussein in possession of weapons of mass destruction for a few more months or years is not an option, not in a post-September 11th world.**❞**

We might note the extent to which the statement presents not only an unquestioned attempt to link Saddam to al-Qaeda but also an emphasis that, even in the absence of such a link, indeed even in the absence of clear evidence of Saddam possessing WMD, it is not possible to leave Saddam with possible WMD 'in a post

> **KEY POINTS**
>
> ❏ The decision to wage war against Saddam and Iraq proved controversial with long-standing US allies.
> ❏ The ground invasion of Iraq was actually a success with Baghdad falling rapidly to US troops.
> ❏ Debate still continues as to the actual motivations for the US invasion. Was it about revenge on Saddam, WMD, oil, or an attempt to reshape Middle Eastern politics?

September 11th world'. This is the point at which 9/11 had clearly shaped the priorities of US foreign policy.

The invasion itself began on 20 March 2003, preceded by an attempted so-called 'decapitation' strike against senior military and political figures (including Saddam himself) that was only partially successful. The initial campaign, however, was relatively swift. Unlike previous campaigns (for example the Gulf War of 1990–1 and the Afghan campaign in 2001) there was not a long period of aerial bombardment followed by a ground campaign. Rather there was a combination of both together. The ground campaign lasted just over three weeks and the Iraqi military crumbled quickly, outgunned by allied firepower, skill, and equipment. Baghdad fell in April 2003 and President Bush declared (unwisely, as it turned out) 'mission accomplished' on board the aircraft carrier *Abraham Lincoln* on 1 May 2003.

After Iraq: continuity and disjunction in US foreign policy

The problem, however, was not the military campaign itself; the problem which very rapidly became apparent was that there was less than coherent planning for the post-war scenario. The result of a series of bungled decisions taken in the immediate aftermath of the victory—the decision to disband the Iraqi army, the reluctance to stamp early on local looting, and a host of many others—helped to turn a chaotic and patchwork post-conflict Iraq into a hotbed of dissent and

insurgency. This was aside from the anger and emotion at the civilian casualties inflicted by the invading forces. This in turn inflamed Muslim sentiment across the world against the USA and its allies, sucked in Muslims from outside Iraq, and acted as a recruiting sergeant for al-Qaeda, which was, to all intents and purposes, one of the chief beneficiaries of the post-war shambles. The terrorist group established a presence in Iraq for the first time.

The immediate post-Iraq setting for US foreign policy was, however, very bullish. Those in charge in Washington felt that they had achieved a good deal and were keen to continue further with this trajectory. In the presidential election the following year—unlike in 2000, as we saw—foreign policy and the record of the administration in the post-9/11 climate was the major campaign issue and the incumbent beat his Democratic Party challenger (Senator John Kerry) convincingly.

After the election, however, problems began to multiply for the Bush administration. The situation in Iraq went from bad to worse and popular support for the occupation in the USA began to ebb away. The situation in Iraq went from bad to worse and popular support for the occupation in the USA began to ebb away and the resurgence of comparisons between Iraq and the Vietnam quagmire began.

In 2006, the Republican Party suffered its biggest defeat in a mid-term election for over a decade—and primarily because of the Iraq issue, although the debacle over Hurricane Katrina and the inadequate presidential response appears not to have helped Bush's popularity.

There seemed to be a recognition on the part of some that the 'perceived' unilateralism of the first Bush term had hurt US interests and there began a concerted effort to change the diplomatic 'mood music'. Attempts were made to come to terms with the new French leader, Sarkozy, who seems at least on an initial showing to be more persuaded by President Bush than his predecessor, even remarking that, like all families, amongst allies there will be arguments, but France remains within the family. More telling were the repeated attempts by Bush to persuade the UN to play an enlarged role in post-war Iraq. In August 2007 Resolution 1770 was adopted by the UN Security Council, and this paved the way for a wider political role for the UN within Iraq. Although cynics argued that Bush was simply using the UN to pick up the pieces of a failed strategy, more optimistically it reflected the fact that the Bush administration recognized the complexities of the aftermath of war and the futility of even a superpower attempting alone to shape a complex and dangerous regional problem.

Obama: a new direction?

The election of Barak Obama in 2008 seemed to herald a revision of some of the worst excesses of the 'war on terror'. Obama promised a different vision of foreign policy associated with an emphasis not just on war but on diplomacy and development. However, whilst Obama and those around him have proved more thoughtful in the rhetoric they have employed over the struggle with al-Qaeda, shifting policy on the ground has proved more problematic.

As has so often been noted, Obama is the first non-white President of the United States. Much has been made of his family roots in Africa and Arabic name. Some commentators have extrapolated from this exotic background that this would mean a reversal of the 'warrior state' that had grown up under his predecessor. In his pronouncements on foreign affairs, Obama seemed clear that there would be revisions in the war on terror. Torture would be unthinkable, Guantánamo closed, and troops withdrawn from the Iraq. If the war

in Afghanistan was to be continued Obama would want resources shifted out of the Iraq theatre. Obama had anyway opposed that war and in a debate on 31 January 2008 in California he went further than simply opposing the war in Iraq he wanted to 'end the mind-set that got us into that war in the first place'.

The use of torture and Guantánamo were, Obama argued, stains on the reputation of the United States. He made promises that when he was President 'special facilities' or black sites would be closed. More importantly Obama signalled an end to the unilateralism of the Bush years and made clear that the United States could not achieve its objectives alone. What has become known as the Obama Doctrine is a form of realism that is not afraid to assume the burdens of leadership, but one with practical limits.

Obama has also made a clear link between diplomacy and development. His often stated view is that the breeding ground for the root causes of terrorism is that of global poverty. His spokesmen and-women, including his Special Assistant, Samantha Power, who wrote an award-winning book on genocide, have made the idea of 'dignity' key to the way in which individuals and groups must be set free from hunger and insecurity.

The greatest running sore for the Obama administration has unquestionably been the continued war in Afghanistan. Originally after the events of 9/11, as we saw above, the US worked with the Northern Alliance in a bid to depose the Taliban government, which was widely perceived as a positive venture to destroy an unsavoury regime that had for many years oppressed the peoples of Afghanistan and provided sanctuary for international terrorism. However, by 2005 the war was proving problematic on a number of counts and by the time that Obama was elected there was a widespread view that the US was if not losing the war in Afghanistan then certainly not winning it. The Taliban and associated insurgent groups had proved resilient and clever in countering NATO forces. Michael O'Hanlon has argued in an excellent article in *Foreign Affairs* that by the end of 2009 the Taliban had become a 'smarter insurgent' force. Rather than engaging in large-scale assaults on NATO forces the targets were changed to smaller, more vulnerable, NATO enclaves. Smaller-scale attacks could and did prove lethal, with the widespread use of roadside bombs and IEDs followed-up by attacks using small arms. The Taliban eschewed attacks on civilians and concentrated attention on 'foreign' troops and Afghan security personnel, with 2009 proving an especially a bloody year for NATO forces.

Under Obama there is a degree of fatigue at the ongoing and seemingly inconclusive war. With 100,000 troops deployed, fewer than half of Americans now support the war. It is not just a concern about popular opinion at home, which presidents are notoriously sensitive about given the way in which the war in Vietnam damaged the body politic in the 1960s and 1970s, allies are also proving far from durable as casualties and costs mount. While it is true that the International Security Assistance Force (ISAF) involves some forty countries, many have already left or will do so imminently, for example the Netherlands and Canada, leaving the Americans to carry out the brunt of the fighting.

The Obama response to the Taliban resurgence, after much debate, was an approach put together by General Stanley McChrystal. The strategy was to implement a limited degree of state building, which placed the onus on Afghan forces to eventually control territory in the south and the east of the country. Building institutions that provide order means that the Taliban cannot retake power and thus denies al-Qaeda sanctuary.

McChrystal also emphasized the limiting of civilian casualties in a bid to win over more of the civilian population. In July 2010, in show of presidential power, General McChrystal was sacked by Obama for having breached military accountability to the civilian authority. McChrystal's mistake was to offer contentious and contemptuous comments about senior political figures such as the Vice President Joe Biden and by extension the President himself to journalists from *Rolling Stone* magazine. McChrystal was replaced with the man widely credited with having 'won' in Iraq, General David Petraus.

This was widely seen at the time as a master stroke in that Petraeus, a Republican who may harbour his own political ambitions, was now yoked to the President's own agenda. Of course it could also be that Petreus will enhance his already formidable reputation if the second 'surge' succeeds. More worryingly, however, it has also made Obama's Afghan policy dependent on Petraes. If he were to resign citing differences over Obama's strategy it could rebound on Obama in the 2012 presidential election, whether or not Petreus is himself a candidate.

The public doubts about the mission of US forces in Afghanistan seem to be shared by the President himself. Bob Woodward, the eminent journalist and essayist, has had access to both President Bush and his successor, and his published tale of the Obama administration thus far is one of persistent concern over the war effort and its endgame. While Obama has always pledged that Afghanistan is the right war (as opposed to the wrong war waged by President Bush in Iraq) he has promised that by the summer of 2011 America will start bringing its troops home. In August 2011 he argued that 'open-ended war serves neither our interests nor the Afghan people.'

While the war in Afghanistan remains a central preoccupation for the administration, with Obama announcing that as from the summer of 2011 there will be a phased withdrawal of foreign troops, it is far from being the only serious foreign policy headache for the administration. In a perhaps conscious echo of debates from the 1970s, commentators have begun to talk about a new 'arc of crisis', running from North Africa, through the Middle East and into Iran. The 'Arab Spring' and US withdrawal from Iraq have added to this perception. Also geo-politically notable is the seemingly continuous rise of China as a major world power, plus the rise of the other BRIC countries (e.g. Brazil and India), all of which portend a rather less favourable international system for the US and its allies.

Four problems are profoundly interwoven. The first is the continued and, at least according to some, growing instability in Pakistan. This threatens to tip a US ally into being a problem for US policy on a major scale (what if the Pakistani bomb were to fall into the hands of a regime sympathetic to al-Qaeda) but has already created major problems of a lesser sort. There are now more drone attacks being carried out by US forces in the tribal areas of Pakistan than in Afghanistan, a fact that is greatly resented in Pakistan at all levels, yet the Pakistani state and military seem unable (or unwilling) to restrain al-Qaeda or the Taliban. On top of this there is, of course, the ongoing standoff with Iran about its nuclear policy. There seems to be no sign of this being any closer to resolution than when Obama came into office and is perhaps, over the longer term, the most damaging persistent problem in the region, aside of course from the still-central Israeli–Palestinian dispute, itself still held hostage by the issues of Israeli settlements.

All these issues were thrown into further ambiguity with the so-called Arab Spring, in early 2011, which has seen revolution and rebellion ripple across the Middle East and North Africa. Perhaps most troublesome of all in this context has been the political implosion of Libya, which many Americans fear may yet lead to an influx of young radical forces into Afghanistan and which has in any event launched perhaps a new wave of 'liberal interventionism', albeit not one led by the US. The Obama administration's caution in this regard is one of the most telling things about Obama's new direction. Nonetheless, 2011 has opened with yet further western military intervention in the Middle East, albeit this time backed with a UN resolution and supported at least in part by local actors (for example the Arab league). But it is very hard to see how this will turn out. The possibilities for miscalculation and error remain enormous.

Obama's 'new direction', while real and important in its own right, should not blind us to the ongoing realities of the US position in the world; it certainly does not do that to Obama himself. His campaign rhetoric to one side, his whole career to date shows a man very much in charge of himself, but aware of the difficulties of always controlling the general agenda. He is after all a great admirer of the protestant theologian Rheinhold Niebuhr. Recalling Niebuhr from his days at Harvard as having a lasting influence, Obama gleaned that, 'There's serious evil in the world, and hardship and pain. And we should be humble and modest in our belief we can eliminate those things. I take away … the sense we have to make these efforts knowing they are hard, and not swinging from naïve idealism to bitter realism.' He then called Niebuhr his 'favourite philosopher' (Allen, 2008).

This suggests that while Obama certainly marks a change from the neo-conservative agenda prevalent in the previous administration, he will not lack the capacity to enforce America's will if he believes it necessary to do so. The assassination of Osama bin Laden by US special forces in 2011 indicates that the President, whatever he may say, recognizes that to end the war on terror its chief protagonists could not be left alive. The killing of bin Laden enables the President to close a decade-long chapter that began on 9/11.

> **KEY POINTS**
>
> ❑ The lack of post-war planning for Iraq led to a situation in which many critics claim that the US was mired in a civil war, with US and British troops suffering increasing casualties—hence the idea of Iraq as a Vietnam.
> ❑ The Obama administration has signalled the withdrawal of troops from Afghanistan beginning in the summer of 2011.
> ❑ Barack Obama has signalled an end to unilateralism in the conduct of foreign policy and stressed the importance of allies such as France.
> ❑ Barack Obama and Hiliary Clinton have stressed poverty and individual degradation as motors of terrorism.

? Questions

1. To what extent did the events of 9/11 alter US foreign policy?
2. What influence did neo-conservatism have on the making of US foreign policy?
3. What were the motivations for the US attack on the Taleban?
4. Why was the war in Iraq an error for the USA?
5. Are the attacks on Pearl Harbor and 9/11 comparable?
6. Is the enduring success of the presidency of George W. Bush the promotion of an anti-tyranny agenda?
7. What constituted the 'axis of evil'?
8. How has President Obama reshaped policy over the war in Afghanistan?
9. Has the use of extraordinary rendition and torture injured the image of the United States?
10. Can President Obama redeem the reputation of the United States in the Muslim world?
11. Has the Vietnam Syndrome been buried?

» Further Reading

Bush, G. W. (2010), *Decision Points* (New York: Random House).

An account of the former President and his thoughts on the war on terror and the war in Iraq.

Ikenberry, G. J. (2001), *After Victory: Institution, Strategic Restraint and the Rebuilding of Order after Major Wars* (Princeton: Princeton University Press).

An analysis of how major states respond to victory after war. It explores the US response to the end of Cold War and its options at the beginning of the twenty-first century.

Kagan, R. (2003), *Paradise & Power* (New York: Knopf).

Looks at the ideological divide between the European powers and the United States. It explores the transatlantic relationship and provides a lively and concise account of recent troubled times in diplomatic circles.

Ricks, T. E. (2006), *Fiasco: The American Military Adventure in Iraq* (New York: Penguin).

An account of the war in Iraq up until the middle of 2006. It is a searing indictment of bad strategic judgements and spares few of the political and military elites.

Woodward, B. (2004), *Plan of Attack* (New York: Simon & Schuster).

Looks at how those around President Bush actively sought to pave the road to war with Iraq.

It demonstrates the increasing enthusiasm for the removal of the Iraqi dictator and the decision to wage war unilaterally.

Woodward, B. (2010), *Obama's Wars, The Inside Story* (New York: Simon & Schuster).

Looks at how President Obama inherited the mantle of war and wrestled with doctrine in Afghanistan.

Endnote

Some of the ideas in this chapter were first explored in Kennedy-Pipe and Rengger (2006).

 For a range of additional resources to support your learning visit the Online Resource Centre that accompanies this book at www.oxfordtextbooks.co.uk/orc/cox_stokes2e/.

22 The future of US foreign policy

Anatol Lieven

Chapter contents

Introduction

This chapter analyses and portrays possible futures for US foreign policy in terms of the interests and ideology of the US elites (and to a lesser extent the population at large), the structures of US political life, the real or perceived national interests of the US, and future developments on the world stage, especially concerning the rise of China and the instability of the Muslim world.

On this basis, it suggests that there will not be a fundamental change in US global strategy whichever party comes to power, since both share the same basic view of US goals internationally, and the same class interests domestically, and are subject to the same domestic and international constraints. This has already been demonstrated by the failure of the Obama administration

seriously to change the course of US foreign and security policy, despite all the hopes for change invested in Obama when he came to power.

However, US administrations may differ quite considerably when it comes to the adoption of more or less reckless tactics in pursuit of their policies. This chapter argues that as a result of the extremely costly war in Iraq and Afghanistan, US foreign policy will probably follow the line of the Obama administration (and even the Bush administration's second term) in becoming more cautious when it comes to radical actions and major interventions, but will not necessarily become wiser. Interventionism will be replaced by drift, until some major global crisis occurs to upset the entire present international order.

The analysis of possible futures of US foreign policy set out in this chapter will be based on a combination of elements from two different traditions in international relations analysis: the realist tradition, which focuses above all on state interests and the relative power of states, and what in German is called the *Primat der Innenpolitik*, the predominant influence of domestic policy on foreign policy. Domestic policy in this sense is defined not just as domestic political agendas and ambitions, but the constitutional, political, economic, social, and ideological structures of the domestic political order.

Realism dictates that many US 'vital national interests' must at present be regarded as givens, even though historians of the future may see them as not really in the interest of the great majority of Americans. This is because they are defined as vital, unchangeable interests by the great majority of the US political classes, the security establishment, and the media. I argue here that the leaderships of the Republican and Democratic parties are to a great extent drawn from the same US establishment, share the same basic class interests, are subject to the same domestic pressures on key issues, and are shaped by the same nationalist and imperialist ideology, in somewhat different forms.

This being so, it is likely that future US foreign policy will share the same basic contours whether the Republicans or Democrats form the administration at the time. In addition—from a realist perspective—all US administrations will face certain irreducible constraints and imperatives stemming from US external interests, the international balance of power, and the extent of US power or the lack of it. The severe limits on the freedom of action of US administrations in the face of domestic and international constraints has been demonstrated by the inability of the Obama administration to bring serious change to most areas of policy, or to bring about results when policies were changed. On the other hand, Obama's partially successful 'reset' of relations with Russia demonstrates that US policy is not set in stone, and does retain a certain flexibility in some areas of secondary importance.

US power, to be assessed accurately, has to be judged not in absolute terms—total US military spending, the numbers of US aircraft carriers and warplanes, the size of the US economy and so on—but in terms of the US power that can actually be mobilized domestically behind a given objective, and applied locally, to a particular place or issues, relative to the power that other states can bring to bear on the same place or issue.

Viewed in these terms, US foreign policy for the foreseeable future will be chiefly defined by two desires: the desire of the US political elites, and a large part of US public opinion in general, for the US to play a hegemonic role on the world stage, and their equally profound desire, as individuals, not personally to pay or fight to maintain this role. This unwillingness has been increased still further since 2008 by the depression gripping the US economy. The US is in fact facing its own version of the experience of previous empires entering on their period of decadence: led by the elites, the population starts evading both military service and taxes. The difference is that in the case of the US this behaviour is perfectly legal, as in the case of tax cuts—but it is no less damaging to US power.

This creates a severe mismatch between American ambitions and the American power actually to achieve them. The problems stemming from this mismatch are likely to be made considerably worse by two additional factors. The first is the rise of China as a global rival to US power, with Russia, Iran and even India also competing in different ways in their own regions. The second factor is sharpening geopolitical competition over access to vital and increasingly scarce natural resources. At present this refers above all to oil, but if the economic rise of China and India continue, and concerns about oil and global warming continue to fuel the diversion of grain to ethanol production, within a generation the world may also be facing shortages of grain and other vital products.

In these circumstances, it would seem obvious for the US to seek to redraw its priorities (or at least choose between them) and reduce its commitments in certain parts of the world that are not in fact central to US vital interests—the strategy pursued by Britain in the generation before 1914. However, this is not easy for any empire, and for reasons that this essay will explore, it is especially difficult for the United States.

Belief in America's mission to lead the world towards freedom, democracy, and progress stems from an American nationalism whose roots stretch back almost 500 years, to the Protestant Reformation in England and Scotland. And for reasons which will be explored in this essay, the US political system has become so cumbersome, so snarled by powerful and even in-domitable interest groups, that it may no longer even be capable of making clear decisions that offend any significant domestic lobby. The US might then come to resemble France under Louis XV and Louis XVI—a country whose immense latent strengths simply could not be mobilized behind an effective foreign policy, without revolutionary domestic change.

The ideological roots of US foreign policy

The great majority of Americans do not believe that they have or should have an empire. At the same time, how-ever, a sense of America's mission to bring democracy, freedom, and progress to the rest of the world is deeply rooted in American culture, and deeply entwined with American civic nationalism. It is connected to a wide-spread sense of the innate goodness of America's actions on the world stage, and of the US military in particular. This in turn goes to strengthen an intense nationalist pride in American power.

This is a key link between the ideological bases of American civic nationalism (based on general belief in the values of what has been called 'the American Creed') and American imperialism. Insofar as they can use this rhetoric in support of their plans, the imperialists have a tremendous means of seduction as far as many Americans are concerned. This is America's version of the missions of the great civilizational empires of the past: of the duties of Rome and imperial China—as seen by their rulers, elites, and intellectuals—to spread their civilizations to the barbarians beyond their borders, of the Spanish to Christianise the New World, of the *missions civilisatrices* of the nineteenth century European empires, of the Soviet Union to bring the light of Com-munism to the rest of humanity.

In the words of Russell Nye,

> ❝All nations . . . have long agreed that they are chosen peo-ples; the idea of special destiny is as old as nationalism itself. However, no nation in modern history has been quite so consistently dominated as the United States by the belief that it has a particular mission in the world. (Nye 1966, quoted in Cobb 1998: 4)❞

So powerful is this form of nationalism, and so continu-ously reinforced by the media, popular culture in general, much of the school system, many of the churches, and the rhetoric of politicians, that it survived what should have been the searing lessons of Vietnam, and will probably survive what ought to be the equally searing lessons of Iraq. It played a key part in the rhetoric of the Bush ad-ministration in the 'war on terror'. This ideological na-tionalism also, however, profoundly influences most of the leadership and established intelligentsia of the Dem-ocratic Party, including those who call themselves liberal internationalists. Lines written by C. Vann Woodward during the Vietnam War are no less valid today:

> ❝The characteristic American adjustment to the current foreign and domestic enigmas that confound our national myths has not been to abandon the myths but to reaffirm them. Solutions are sought along traditional lines. . .What-ever the differences and enmities that divide advocates and opponents (and they are admittedly formidable), both sides seem predominantly unshaken in their adher-ence to one or another or all of the common national myths. (Woodward 1968: 218)❞

Louis Hartz wrote of the American Creed's 'compul-sive nationalism' and the 'fixed, dogmatic liberalism of a liberal way of life' (Hartz 1955: 9, 15, 175, 225–37). One result of this ideological conformity is to make it much more difficult for most Americans to imagine America as a country among others, or an international commu-nity that includes America as a member rather than a hegemon.[1] It thereby contributes to the shortage of true internationalists in the US, and indeed to an absence of real debate on key underlying principles of foreign policy.

In the areas of foreign relations and security, a capacity for really open debate on underlying principles has also been discouraged by the close links between govern-ment, particular university departments, think tanks, and journalists working in this field. Paradoxically, the

American system of political appointments, whereby a President chooses some 4000 officials from outside the civil service, has worked if anything to limit the advice coming to government. Rather than opening the bureaucracy, it has tended to bureaucratize those sections of academia with a role in the foreign policy debate.

Because they are divided into two political tribes, these parabureaucrats retain a capacity to criticize specific policies of particular administrations. With very few exceptions, however, like most bureaucrats they lack completely an ability to distance themselves from the supporting myths of the state system which supports them.

As a result of this complex of factors, in the view of Andrew Bacevich, the basic American consensus on foreign policy 'is so deep-seated that its terms have become all but self-evident, its premises asserted rather than demonstrated'. As a result, much of the public and media debate on international issues within the US is no more than 'political theatre' (Bacevich 2002: 9, 33).

The effects of this ideology and this conformism are twofold. Overall, it is extremely difficult within the US establishment to question whether the US actually needs to remain the sole global superpower, with all the immense costs and risks that this involves. In specific regions and on specific issues, it makes it much more difficult to propose reasonable compromises with local great powers because this can always be presented as 'appeasement' and 'betraying American values'. As the example of Colonel Bacevich and others show, it is of course possible to put forward these ideas in the US—but the general result is to be excluded from the establishment, and to a great extent from the mainstream media.

Key contemporary challenges for US foreign policy

Relations with China

The United States obviously possesses tremendous latent strength, as both the world's largest economy and the world's greatest military power by far. However, China's economic growth is rapidly eroding America's lead. This has been most strikingly the case since the economic crisis of 2008–09, which for some time at least has plunged the US economy into near-stagnation, while China's double-digit growth has been barely affected.

To judge by this Chinese achievement, and the previous East Asian examples of Japan, Taiwan, and South Korea—and barring the collapse of Communist rule or an international war—present Chinese growth rates may well continue for another two decades or more. If so, and unless US growth can recover to levels not seen for many years, the Chinese economy will surpass that of the US by 2030. This would be a development of truly epochal significance, reversing the global economic trend not only of the past 100 but of the past 400 years. Adapting and reacting to China's rise will be the biggest challenge facing US statesmen in the first half of the twenty-first century and perhaps beyond.

KEY POINTS

❑ The US public debate on foreign policy takes place within a framework of exceptionally strong civic nationalist myths about America's uniquely good institutions and mission. These myths limit how far Americans can think frankly and deeply about their country and its international role.

❑ This includes a commitment to military spending vastly in excess of any potential rival, and a military presence in a number of key areas of the world.

❑ American world "leadership" is seen as necessary and desirable by the vast majority of the foreign policy establishment, the leading elements of both political parties, and the media.

Managing such a shift in the balance of power requires immense reserves of caution and restraint in both countries concerned. Unfortunately, on the Chinese side the aggressive language and economic pressure used against Japan after a clash between a Chinese trawler and Japanese coastguards near the disputed Senkaku (Diaoyu) islands in September 2010 strongly suggests that as Chinese power grows, so will Chinese assertiveness, at least when it comes to Chinese territorial claims (though not necessarily in the Middle East and elsewhere). Particularly striking has been the extent of militant nationalism in the mass of the Chinese educated population, revealed through the internet and the blogosphere.

On the US side, the rise of the Tea Party movement among the Republicans suggests that if the economic decline of the US white middle classes over the past generation continues, it is likely to lead to more and more irrational politics on their part. This will not necessarily lead to more aggressive external policies, for the US conservative masses also harbour deep isolationist sentiments. At the same time, they are passionately nationalistic and are highly unlikely to react well to the increasing eclipse of the US by China, and especially by a China whose economic policies can be portrayed as directly responsible for their own economic woes.

It should of course be recognized that in terms of pure military power, even a China which has passed the US economically is unlikely to be able to project anything like the same degree of global might. For example, as of 2011 China is only beginning to develop aircraft carrier capacity, and as past Soviet experience shows, this is something which it takes a very long time to develop from scratch. In China's own region, however, US military power is likely to become more and more eclipsed. A particular threat to the US presence is China's development of ballistic anti-ship missiles, which could potentially make it impossible for US aircraft carriers to operate within effective striking distance of China's coast. That would render US security guarantees to Taiwan meaningless.

On the other hand, the US does possess other strategic assets in the region which may even be strengthened by China's rise. These are the US alliances with Japan and South Korea, and security relationships with South East Asian states. The rise of China, and what seems to be an increasingly aggressive Chinese nationalism (including territorial claims to disputed islands and their surrounding seas) may well drive these countries closer to the US, guaranteeing Washington military bases and therefore a set of unsinkable aircraft carriers in the region.

Moreover, while the US navy and air force's capacity to inflict catastrophic damage on infrastructure targets is irrelevant to the fight against terrorist and guerrilla enemies, it is a very important latent means of pressure on organized states, as was shown by the Kosovo air campaign of 1989. In contemplating any military confrontation with the US, the Chinese leadership would have to be influenced, for example, by the tens of billions of dollars they had spent on the Three Gorges Dam—and the consciousness that it could all be knocked to pieces by American missiles.

US military power

Apart from the changing military balance with China, elsewhere in the world the problem for the US then is not its absolute strength, but the twin questions of how to bring that strength to bear on particular issues and, even more importantly, how to persuade the American political classes and population actually to mobilize that strength for foreign policy goals.

The US military itself is profoundly ambiguous about the use of military power. A mixture of colossal military spending (dwarfing that of the State Department), the role of that spending in what is in effect an unadmitted US strategy of supporting industrial and technological development, and the instinctive deference to the military on the part of politicians and the population combine to give the military immense power within the state. This power, and the successful record of retired US generals in running for political office, means that the Democratic Party in particular has to be very careful indeed not to anger the military and allow itself to be portrayed by the Republicans as hostile to the military and weak on security.

The power of the US military within the state was demonstrated by its ability to dictate Afghan policy to the Obama administration after 2008. However, the US military should not be seen as aggressive and warmongering in the style of pre-1914 European militaries.

They are of course absolutely committed to US global power and when already involved in wars like Iraq and Afghanistan, the US military are naturally determined to win them, or perhaps more accurately not to be seen to lose them. But the attack on Iraq was the work of civilian officials, not the uniformed military, much of which was highly skeptical about the operation.

The uniformed military and US intelligence played a major part in blocking a US attack on Iran during the last year of the Bush administration, fearing the massive, unpredictable, and open-ending conflict that might result. Above all, the senior ranks of the military deeply fear any new prolonged ground conflict, seeing that this would impose crushing burdens on their budgets and recruitment. Some are even beginning to return to Eisenhower's recognition that the true underlying strength of a country lies more in its economy and fiscal stability than in its military. Finally, the military are well aware that in almost no circumstances will the US public agree to a reintroduction of conscription. The spectre of Vietnam is something of which the US generals are well aware.

The contrast between a desire for imperial glory and an unwillingness to pay or fight for empire is not new in western history. The British and French empires were conquered very much on the cheap, often largely by native auxiliaries recruited and paid for by the colonies themselves. The outrageous cost (by previous imperial standards) of the Boer War brought about a major revulsion of public feeling in Britain.

Until the First World War, the British always rejected conscription. Concern about the deaths of British conscript soldiers in colonial wars was one reason for the speed with which British empire was wound up in the 1950s. The French did have conscription, but this was restricted to service in metropolitan France, and was legitimized to the French public as necessary to fight in Europe, in the defence of France herself. Hence the creation of the Foreign Legion, explicitly for imperial campaigns.

The suggestion that the US lacks the military power to conduct a successful strategy of world hegemony may seem absurd in the face of US military spending that as of 2007 probably exceeds the rest of the planet put together, based on a US economy which remains by some distance the largest on earth. However, military and geopolitical power and influence are not abstract things. In the end, all true power is local, and relative: that is to say, it is power that can actually be brought to bear on a particular place or a particular issue, relative to the power that can be brought to bear on the same place and issue by another power or powers.

Moreover, in concentrating on US military spending, on US high technology, and on the number of US aircraft carriers, warplanes, and tanks, military analysts have too often forgotten an older, but still extremely important, measure of military strength: the number of 'bayonets' an army possesses, in other words, the number of its fighting infantry. This too is an old dilemma for western empires, as Kipling noted in his poem 'Frontier Arithmetic'.

As the wars in Iraq and Afghanistan demonstrate, while conquering a territory may well require comparatively few troops, holding it afterwards, protecting a client government in the face of local revolt, and ensuring basic local stability require very large numbers indeed—numbers which probably cannot be generated in the long term, or for multiple such operations, without a resort to conscription. In April 2007, a senior retired General, Barry McCaffrey, warned publicly that the US military was now so overstretched that if faced with a successful North Korean invasion of South Korea it could have to resort to an early use of nuclear weapons (Robberson 2007).

As of 2011, conscription is categorically rejected by both political parties, the overwhelming majority of US politicians, and the US public, and indeed the US military itself, which has no desire to replace well-trained and motivated professionals by demoralized conscripts. It is just conceivable that conscription might be agreed to in the public hysteria following a massive new terrorist attack on the US or the large-scale disruption of oil

> **KEY QUOTE 22.1**

The [US] military is grossly under-resourced. It's a flippin' disaster… Their equipment is shot. It's coming apart. We are in a position of enormous strategic peril. What happens if the other shoe drops [in Iran or North Korea]?

General (retd) Barry McCaffrey

supplies to the US, but if so, in the long run anxieties and protests about conscript losses would probably restrain and even end future imperial operations, not enable them.

The number of casualties suffered by the US military in Iraq and Afghanistan is not high by historical standards, although one should be careful to note that as of the start of 2011, not only had 5876 US servicemen been killed, but more than 35,000 had been wounded. Recent advances in medical technology mean that many of these wounded who in previous wars would have died can now be saved. They are, however, in many cases disabled, and have to retire from the military. Moreover, extensive disabilities have as great or even greater effects on morale and recruitment as do deaths in action.

As several leading generals and military experts have warned, over time, this level of casualties is incompatible with the maintenance of a volunteer army. This is all the more so since unlike in the nineteenth century, even ordinary soldiers have to be able to master quite complicated military technologies. They also of course have to be able to understand not just orders but manuals in English. This fact, as much as political considerations, renders highly questionable the strategy advocated by Max Boot and others, of recruiting increasing numbers of soldiers from the impoverished masses of Mexico and Central America in return both for pay and US citizenship for themselves and their families.

These constraints make it almost impossible to imagine the US being able to generate the forces that would be able to defeat and occupy Iran or Pakistan, for example—which in turn places obvious limits on the degree of pressure and influence Washington can exert over those countries. In the past, empires have sought to circumvent such constraints by eschewing outright conquest in favour of punitive expeditions, intended not to replace or rule over another state, or even necessarily to replace a government, but rather to inflict sufficient damage to force the government, country, or people concerned to bow to the will of the imperial power on specific issues; at the milder end of this range of options is the strategy known as 'gunboat diplomacy'.

Gunboat diplomacy was the strategy that the British Empire generally adopted towards Afghanistan and the Pashtun tribes of the Afghan frontier after the crushing British defeat of 1842. On a larger scale,

this punitive strategy was essentially the military approach of the British and other western imperial powers towards China in the nineteenth century; since, unlike the Russians and Japanese, they did not believe that it was possible for them actually to incorporate large parts of China into their empires. Some aspects of the western military campaigns in China were 'punitive' in the sense of extracting financial compensation. Others, like the infamous destruction of the Summer Palace near Peking in 1860, were directly and crudely punitive in terms of deliberate destruction and vandalism.

This strategy has indeed sometimes been adopted by the US in recent decades, including the bombardment of Libyan government buildings and military positions in 1988, and the Clinton administration's repeated attacks on Iraq in the 1990s (Peters 2006). US economic sanctions against various countries, a strategy beloved of the US Congress in particular, can also be seen as a non-military version of the punitive approach.

However, as these examples demonstrate, there are many problems with the punitive approach to the exertion of US power. In the case of Libya, the US attack did not deter—and may have provoked—the Lockerbie terrorist attack. Sanctions did have an effect, but took a generation to work. They have not worked at all in the cases of Cuba, Syria, or as yet Iran; partly, it has been argued, because by reducing international economic contacts and the usual workings of the market, they actually strengthen the power of ruling elites which control access to key economic resources and goods. In the case of Iraq, a mixture of US economic sanctions and intermittent bombardment had no effect in either taming or bringing down the Ba'athist regime, and their failure helped lead in the end to US invasion, with severe consequences for US power in terms of fiscal health, military prestige, and popularity in the Muslim world.

The rise of international terrorism as a threat has greatly increased interest in punitive strategies, but has also made them much more problematical. Punitive action always brought with it the risk that rather than coercing the state concerned, it would lead to its collapse. This indeed was the eventual result, in 1911, of seventy years of humiliation of the Manchu Dynasty in China by western powers. Collapse may be followed either by the appearance of a new, even more hostile, regime or by anarchy; either may be seen to necessitate the direct intervention and rule of the imperial power.

The US political order and foreign policy

The difficulty the US has in mobilizing its wealth for foreign policy goals is shown most glaringly in the area of foreign aid. During the Cold War, both Democratic and Republican administrations saw aid as an absolutely critical part of US strategy in the struggle against Communism. Since the end of that conflict, spending on aid has declined precipitously, and even 9/11 has led to no really significant improvement, even in most of the Muslim world.[2] In 2011, the Republicans in Congress tried to impose deep cuts in the foreign aid budget as part of their programme of reducing the deficit and diminishing 'big government'.

The foreign aid that the Obama administration was seeking was only $56 billion—around one-ninth of America's military budget. The prestige of foreign aid within the US system has worsened in recent years because of the massive shift of resources and influence from the State Department (including USAID) to the Pentagon. This reflects not only administration but Congressional priorities. Congress will not pay much any longer to build up countries like Pakistan which may emerge as economic competitors of the US in particular fields, as South Korea and Taiwan did during the Cold War. They will pay for the military, not only because of security paranoia or the allure of military 'pork' for their own states, but because more broadly the US military budget serves as something that according to its free market ideology, the US does not have: a massive, and in some areas extremely successful, programme of state-subsidized industrial development, heavily slanted towards high technology.

The militarization of the structures of US foreign policy does not necessarily mean a more bellicose stance—on the contrary, the US Army and Marine Corps have emerged as forces for relative moderation and caution in Washington. It does, however, naturally mean that more and more of America's significant diplomatic contacts with key states will be military to military, and that less aid will be for development and more is likely to be security related, or at best humanitarian

aid administered by the US military, as after the Asian tsunami and the Pakistan earthquake.

As a result, the US is not merely failing to project influence and goodwill, but is being heavily outspent by rival powers in certain parts of the world. Thus Chinese aid to the Philippines (a former US colony) in 2006 was four times that of the United States. Even after the rise in Russian gas prices at the start of 2006, Russian annual energy subsidies to Ukraine exceed many times over US aid to that country. In several parts of Latin America, a strategic combination of the oil wealth of Hugo Chavez's regime in Venezuela and the numerous, highly trained medical and engineering cadres of Communist Cuba are greatly overshadowing limited US aid to the region; indeed, Cuba did more to help Pakistan after its 2005 earthquake than did the US. As Colonel Larry Wilkerson, former chief of staff of the State Department, remarked in 2007, 'People are beginning to like Cuban public diplomacy and despise ours.'[3]

The severe limits on foreign assistance have been especially striking on America's own continent. In Central America and the Caribbean, economic stagnation and the transfer of the cocaine trade from Colombia (a malign but inevitable consequence of the US 'war on drugs' in the region) has led to a degree of organized criminal violence in Mexico, Guatamela, and elsewhere that is crippling these states. As of 2011 the US seems both impotent and curiously indifferent in the face of this emerging threat, which prior to the First World War would have been seen as *the* priority of US foreign and security policy. Meanwhile, the rapid economic growth of Brazil may create an alternative pole of political and economic influence for the countries of Latin America, although so far this has not raised great concern in Washington.

The inability to generate increased foreign aid reflects the unwillingness of US taxpayers to provide the funds, but also profound structural problems in the US political system, which make it extremely difficult to carry out any radical change of policy—even one supported by a majority of the population and the establishment—if this is opposed by even one really powerful lobby or interest group. From this point of view, the inability to raise spending on foreign aid, the inability to end the utterly counter-productive forty-year-old embargo against Cuba, the pursuit of pointless and dangerous anti-Russian agendas, and unconditional support for Israel all find their echoes in certain domestic failures, for example the inability to reform America's horribly costly and inefficient private health system or to introduce restrictions on gun sales, despite the existence of large national majorities in favour of these reforms.

The power of small but determined lobbies is favoured by a number of factors: broad church political parties with little central party leadership or direction, Senators who are enabled by this and by the constitution to act as virtually autonomous political princes in Washington politics, the need for larger and larger sums in order to fight elections, above all for television advertising, presidential elections which increasingly hinge on a small number of evenly divided states, making the votes of every lobby count.

Perhaps the single most important factor of all is the apathy of the wider public, which makes it extremely difficult to mobilize large numbers of people behind any broad programme of reform. If this is impossible when it comes to gun controls—even after a series of horrors like the massacre at Virginia Technical University in April 2007—how much more difficult it would seem to get masses of Americans to demand radical shifts in policies towards foreign countries of which most know nothing. As a result, US foreign policy will for the foreseeable future be run by a mixture of an unrepresentative security elite deeply attached to its own agendas and interests (a pattern very familiar in the history of many states in the past) and particular lobby groups with no concern for the wider national interest at all. It is not just difficult radically to change course with such a system, it is often difficult to steer any rational and coherent course at all.

Future foreign policies

On the basis of the above, we can predict with reasonable confidence that for a long time to come the basic contours of US foreign policy will remain the same, under both Republican and Democratic administrations. An unkind summary of the most likely course of US foreign policy is that in the wake of the debacle in Iraq, it will become more cautious without necessarily becoming any wiser.

For US foreign policy to change radically would require a revolutionary shift in the US domestic political and economic systems, the international balance of power, or most likely both simultaneously. In a few generations, such a revolutionary change is extremely probable, as the impact of global warming undermines many of the basic structures of international order. Long

---

KEY POINTS

❏ The United States seems set for a prolonged period of economic stagnation, which will undermine American power and influence in the world.

❏ This decline is being made worse by the dysfunction of the U.S political system and America's inability to generate funds for international aid even to vital allies.

❏ Barring severe domestic upheaval in China, that country will overtake the United States in terms of real GDP sometime in the 2020s. Since Chinese power projection capacity will remain limited, this is unlikely to lead to China

challenging the US in the wider world, but it will definitely lead to greater Chinese assertiveness in its own region.

❏ The United States civilian establishment has very little idea of how to respond to this challenge. Higher military spending is very difficult in present circumstances, and military alliances against China risky and not necessarily desired by China's neighbours.

❏ Even in the event of major terrorist attacks on the United States, new wars of invasion and occupation are highly unlikely. Punitive strikes however may only increase terrorism.

before that, it also seems probable that a really severe global economic recession will destroy many of the assumptions on which American power and the international system are now based. When this will happen is, however, impossible to predict with any certainty. The recession which began in 2008 has done severe damage, especially to US economic power *vis-à-vis* China, but it has not so far crippled US power.

The rest of this chapter will therefore deal only with US policy over the next generation, not the next century. It will be based on the assumption that during that period, the world situation will continue to develop roughly along existing lines, or at least within the parameters of presently recognized alternatives, for example either that China will continue to grow in wealth and power until it becomes a serious global rival to the US or that it will suffer a severe setback from some combination of political and economic factors.

The most important features of US foreign policy are likely to remain the following:

The Middle East

At some point in the future the US will cease to be dependent on oil because environmental concerns have finally begun seriously to bite, because competition with China has forced prices up to uneconomical levels, or simply because the oil itself has run out. Until this comes to pass, however, the US establishment will see vital US interests as lying in a maintenance of the open flow of oil from the Persian Gulf, at reasonable prices.

The price, and not the oil itself, is the reason for this interest. The great majority of imported US oil comes from Canada, Latin America, and Africa, but Gulf supplies are essential to world supplies and therefore to the world market price. The only alternative to dependence on the world market would be a strategy of controlling the oil at source through outright conquest and military occupation, or some form of locked-in relationship of patronage and defence with a local government.

Such a strategy may have partly underlain the decision to invade Iraq. It was discussed by the Nixon administration with regard to the Saudi oilfields during the first oil shock of 1973, and this possibility has been raised again in neo-conservative circles in recent years. Contingency plans to this effect certainly exist in the Pentagon. Leaving aside the question of the security of Gulf supplies, it is possible that in the decades to come, geopolitical rivalry with China will lead the US (and maybe China too) to intervene militarily in some troubled oil producer to ensure that supplies continue to flow to the US. Nigeria has occasionally been mentioned as a future candidate in this regard.

However, the miserable example of the US occupation of Iraq, and what is likely to be the ongoing conflict in Afghanistan, will for a considerable time to come act as a deterrent to further military occupations. More likely is continued strong military and political commitment to key oil producers, led of course by Saudi Arabia.

Just as there is no sign that the US will seriously reduce its dependence on oil in the near to medium term, so the bipartisan US political elite seems locked into support for Israel, to the exclusion of any real possibility of a genuine peace settlement with the Palestinians, the Arab world, and Iran. If the twin triumphs of the disappearance of the enemy Soviet superpower and the defeat of Iraq at the start of the 1990s could not persuade most Israelis that it was safe to make peace, then nothing will.

 CONTROVERSIES 22.1

In March 2006 Professors John Mearsheimer (University of Chicago) and Stephen Walt (Harvard) published an essay in the London Review of Books entitled 'The Israel Lobby', strongly criticizing the role of that lobby in shaping US policy towards the Middle East and suppressing free debate of the issue in the US. Although their essay was unexceptionable by European standards, and certainly not anti-semitic, the authors were subjected to a storm of criticism in the US. However, in a sign that the atmosphere of debate may be very gradually changing, leading journals like *Foreign Policy* did actually invite them to debate their work, rather than—as would have generally been the case in the past—either ignoring it or printing only their critics.

And if the shock of 9/11 could not persuade the present US elites that it was necessary to put real pressure on Israel for the sake of better relations with the Muslim world, then nothing will. To break the grip of the Israel lobby on the US political system would take a tremendous political upheaval, involving either a fundamental transformation of one of the two US political parties, or the replacement of one of them by a new party. This will happen one day—but most probably not for a considerable time.

Partly in consequence, we can equally confidently predict that the US will not achieve most of its key objectives in the Greater Middle East, whether in terms of eliminating Islamist extremism as a serious threat, bringing about the acceptance of Israel by the Muslim states, or bringing acceptance of US hegemony by Iran, Syria, and other states. On the contrary, the overthrow of pro-US regimes by street protests in Tunisia and Egypt suggests that the US will have more and more difficulty in keeping allies in the Middle East, and that fear of Israel more than US domination will be what maintains the sham of 'peace' between Israel and the Arabs.

This does not of course mean that—in the short to medium term at least—the US will suffer any really shattering defeats, such as outright military catastrophe or another massive attack on the US itself. These scenarios are possible at some time in the future, but it may be a long time, unless the US itself precipitates a disaster by another military attack on a major state. Apart from anything else, fear of Islamist revolution and a new oil shock is likely to restrain China from active involvement in backing anti-US and anti-Israel states in the region. This means that unlike during the Cold War, such states will have no outside superpower backing.

More likely seems to be a kind of long-term US holding action, in which the US will suffer a constant drain on its manpower, resources, and international prestige, without coming under the kind of pressure that will force it from the region altogether or draw it into a general regional war. Disastrous scenarios—like a US war with Iran or intervention in Pakistan—do, however, exist, and will be examined briefly at the end of this section.

For the further future, one critical question for US strategy in the Middle East is whether the US remains the only international superpower with major influence in the region, as it has been since the collapse of the Soviet Union (or even, by some estimates, since Egypt changed geopolitical sides under Anwar Sadat more than thirty years ago.

China is obviously the most likely contender for such a role, driven by a thirst for oil, but India suffers the same thirst, and Russia retains a certain residual strength (especially through relations with Iran and Syria). Moscow seems to be working cautiously towards the possible of an international gas cartel on the model of OPEC, although its ability actually to achieve this will depend on the spread of liquid natural gas technology and a very considerable reduction in its cost as compared to the cost of fixed pipelines.

The Far East

If China does adopt this role, it will also have a severe impact on wider relations with the US. By twenty years from now, these will in any case be largely shaped by competition for increasingly scarce resources, including not only oil and liquid natural gas but grain and paper. As Chinese power grows, it is now clear that the spirit of 'China's Peaceful Rise' (as the official slogan has it) is likely to be progressively abandoned, and China will become increasingly assertive in pursuit of its interests in the Far East and possibly beyond. This will risk clashes with US allies in the region, including possibly India.

Rivalry with China, and pressure from within the US (especially on the Democratic Party) for tougher protectionist measures against Chinese imports, must be set against the strong impulse in the US for good relations with China, the roots of which have been explored earlier in this chapter. Given the very great interdependence of the US and Chinese economies, and US fears of Chinese power, this impulse is likely to survive both of these countervailing factors, and the constant irritant of Taiwan.

In the case of North Korea, the Bush administration between 2001 and 2007 conducted what amounted to a 180 degree turn towards attempts at compromise with Pyongyang. The key reasons for this were not only that due to the Iraq War the US military was badly overstretched, but even more importantly that the US could in any case not conduct any successful policy *vis-à-vis*

North Korea without the help of China. But Chinese pressure on North Korea has not been forthcoming, and in consequence US policy under both Bush and Obama has been paralysed.

Given the fact that militarily China seems set to grow stronger and stronger—and the possibility of a deeply provoked China backing North Korean aggression—it seems for the foreseeable future extremely unlikely that the US would sanction a Taiwanese declaration of outright independence, or that Taiwan would make such a declaration without US sanction.

However, if US economic relations with China were to suffer really serious disruption, then latent hostilities could quickly rise to the surface. As has often been remarked, the present structure of US–Chinese economic relations creates a kind of 'Mexican stand-off', whereby neither side can seriously hurt the other without doing terrible damage to itself. If China seriously provokes the US, then US protectionism will smash China's export economy. On the other hand, if the US seriously provokes China, then China will cease to support the dollar and the US consumer boom, bringing the domestic US economy down in ruins.

The problem for the US is that this equation is not stable, and whatever changes in China over time the outcome may be unfavourable for the US. If China continues to grow as at present, then sooner or later China will produce a group of middle-class consumers so large and prosperous that its economy will no longer depend on exports to the US. At that point, Beijing will be able to use its ownership of US bonds and support for the dollar as a massive lever of influence.

If, on the other hand, China's economic growth comes to a halt as a result of some combination of domestic economic and political shock, then equally China will no longer be able to support US finances in the same way, quite possibly leading to a deep US recession and a radical reduction in the US population's willingness to pay the costs of global hegemony. Fortunately, key officials on both sides have so far recognized the need to preserve stable relations—a striking contrast with the rhetorical bluster and immoderate ambition that characterizes US policy towards Russia and the lands of the former Soviet Union.

Russia and the former Soviet Union

So deep-rooted is hostility to Russia in much of the US establishment that it is difficult to foresee any formal and public change of course in US strategy, for example a deal with Moscow on abandoning further NATO expansion in return for greater Russian support in the Middle East. This hostility is multi-faceted, and often does not present itself, or even see itself as hostility.

The first source is of course the legacy of the Cold War, reflected not only in attitudes but also in a range of institutions with built-in antagonism to Russia and instinctive support for Russia's enemies. These include semi-official media outlets like Radio Liberty/Radio Free Europe, and democracy promotion/propaganda outfits like Freedom House and the National Endowment for Democracy. Created to serve the struggle against the Soviet Union and its global Communist agenda, these institutions have to a considerable extent simply continued this attitude since the end of the Cold War. This legacy naturally strongly affects older security figures like Vice President Dick Cheney, whose entire being was shaped by the Cold War, but it has been passed down to younger generations. In any dispute involving Russia, no matter how distant, and no matter its relationship to real US interests, their natural tendency is to take the other side.

Deliberate hostility to Russia, especially in the US Congress, is also encouraged by the role of east European and Baltic ethnic lobbies in shaping the attitudes and behaviour of Senators and Congressmen drawn from these ethnic groups, or in whose constituencies these ethnic groups are strongly represented. The disproportionate influence of ethnic and other lobbies, due to the structure of the US political system and the apathy of the US public, has already been noted.

These factors have created a mood towards Russia in the leaderships of both major parties that has been very different from the mood regarding China. This is to be seen in the push in 2006 for an offer of a NATO membership action plan to Ukraine, in the face of vehement Russian opposition and private threats of drastic retaliation, despite the fact that US military officials warned in private that the US would not even be able to defend Ukraine against any future Russian aggression or internal revolution, and despite the fact that according to opinion polls a large majority of the Ukrainian population did not even want to be part of NATO. This plan was eventually suspended, not because of opposition within the US establishment, but because of events on the ground in Ukraine, the collapse of the pro-Western 'Orange Coalition', the return to power as prime minister of the pro-Russian Viktor Yanukovych, and not least the defeat of Georgia by Russia in the war over South Ossetia initiated by Georgia in August 2008—apparently in the hope of US military support, which was not forthcoming.

Initially, the Russia–Georgia war led to an outburst of hostile rhetoric from Washington. With time, however, it seems to have had a sobering effect. The Obama administration devoted considerable effort to a 'reset' of relations with Moscow, based on the shelving both of NATO enlargement and of plans for missile defence systems in eastern Europe. At the end of 2010, the US and Russia signed a new START (Strategic Arms Reduction Treaty) on limits on nuclear arms, which had been strongly desired by Moscow. In response, Moscow has become considerably more helpful to the US over Iran's nuclear programme—although without producing any concessions on the Iranian side—and as of 2011 has not sought to exploit US difficulties in the Middle East. Russia's good will is also increasingly important when it comes to supply routes to US and NATO forces in Afghanistan through the former Soviet Union, since as of 2011 Pakistan's internal unrest was making the route through Pakistan more and more unreliable.

The Obama administration has therefore adopted a realist policy of scaling back US ambitions and commitments in one area so as to be able to concentrate forces and resources on more important challenges. However, with the exception of START—which was passed with the support of a number of Republican senators—this new relationship with Russia has not been formalized by treaty. As a result, the possibility exists that a future Republican administration will resume policies that would be seen in Russia as hostile, leading to a fresh breakdown in relations. This is especially true of missile defence, to which the Republicans have an almost religious adherence.

In consequence, Russia's commitment to better relations with the US will also remain limited and provisional. This may be the most the US political system can achieve, since any kind of 'grand bargain' with Russia (on the analogy of Nixon's and Kissinger's reconciliation with China) would be massively unpopular in the US political classes. The problem about such a future—as already noted with regard to US strategy towards Iran, Taiwan, and North Korea—is that the absence of a formal agreement with the rival power makes the relationship vulnerable to shifts in perception or actions by third parties.

Europe and the transatlantic relationship

Relations with Russia constitute one area of US foreign policy where the traditional transatlantic relationship with Europe continues to matter in Washington—not surprisingly, since the entire structure of transatlantic relations during the Cold War was built around the alliance against Moscow. In other areas, the real importance of relations with Europe does not necessarily correspond to the importance they are given in the language of the US media and the US political class.

In fact, economic relations and the issue of global warming aside, there is a certain degree of conscious or unconscious play-acting about certain aspects of the present—and probably future—relationship, which stem more from domestic political and even psychological needs than from objective international reality. On the European side, a mixture of factors stemming from the Second World War and Cold War continue to combine to produce a sense of dependence on the US: memories of the self-inflicted horrors of Europe's modern history, residual (or in the case of the east Europeans, actual) fear of Russia, and acute consciousness of Europe's weakness and division. As long as the US does not do something quite exceptionally wild, like invading Iraq, sullen European adherence can usually be taken for granted.

However, this does not add up to a willingness to make serious sacrifices for the sake of US strategy. With the partial exception of Britain, the military contributions of America's European allies in Iraq and Afghanistan have been so pathetic that one might wonder why the US even bothered to go to the diplomatic effort of asking for them. Then again, however, it is equally true that the US in recent years has never made a serious change of any important policy in order to win European support.

Rather, in the geopolitical and security fields (as opposed to the equally vital but at present largely separate ones of trade, international finance, and the environment), this relationship operates on both sides at the level of psychological comfort. The Europeans need America to reassure them that they have not been left alone in the wild wood of international geopolitics, from which most instinctively shrink (except for the British establishment, for its own post-colonial reasons).

The Americans (with the exception of the neo-conservatives and the ultra-nationalists of the Cheney–Rumsfeld type) need the Europeans to reassure them that they are still 'leaders of the Free World'. This is especially true in the 'liberal internationalist' school in the Democratic party intellectual establishment, which in the run-up to the 2008 elections is doing its best to convince the American political classes (and perhaps most of all themselves) that the old centrality of the democratic west to US strategy is essentially sound and that it can be extended to strategy in the Middle East—and indeed to the whole world, through the idea of a global 'alliance of democracies'. In truth, Europe is practically almost worthless to the US in the critical area of the Muslim world.

For a long time to come, therefore, US–European relations will be characterized by a version of an old Soviet joke: the Americans will pretend to listen to the Europeans, and the Europeans will pretend to work for the Americans. The transatlantic alliance will not collapse completely, but neither will it amount to anything much in real geopolitical terms. If as seems likely Afghanistan remains permanently unsettled, then sooner or later most European forces will be withdrawn, and NATO will have lost its last *raison d'etre* other than hostility to Russia and job creation for otherwise unemployable military bureaucrats and staff officers.

KEY POINTS

- There will be in the United States a continued bipartisan determination to remain the world's dominant power, although most probably stripped of the extreme unilateralism and anti-diplomacy of the Bush administration.
- The U.S. will rely above all on military structures (including at least one multilateral one, NATO) as the chief vehicles for US global power and influence.
- Leaders of both the Democrats and the Republicans will engage in continued rhetoric concerning America's role as the leader of the free world and America's right and duty to spread democracy and freedom.
- In practice, however, Washington will remain cautious about actually putting this into practice, except in the case of real or perceived enemies.
- Whether Democrats or Republicans are in power, there will be a continued effort to manage the relationship with China along basically non-confrontational lines. This, however, is likely to come under increasing strain from protectionist impulses in the US, from rivalry over access to natural resources, and from popular nationalist impulses within both China and the US.
- There will be widespread underlying emotional hostility towards Russia in the US establishment, and a desire to diminish Russian influence. In practice, however, this strategy is likely to be severely limited by the already mentioned constraints on America's own power, both military and economic.
- There will be repeated attempts to validate US global leadership through gaining the formal support of western Europeans for US strategies, irrespective of the very limited real help that Europe can or will give to the US on most issues.
- Indifference to Latin America will continue, increased by growing Democratic hostility to open trade and by growing hostility in US society to illegal immigration.
- There will be growing rivalry over access to key international commodities. This will increasingly overshadow US relations with China, but over time could also lead to increased tension with India and even Europe.
- Because of US dependence on imported oil and commitment to Israel, for a long time to come the Greater Middle East will be the most important and dangerous subject of US foreign policy. The erosion of US economic power and economic assistance will diminish US influence in certain areas, and the US will find it more and more difficult to control internal changes in Muslim countries.
- Due to economic stagnation, the cost of change, the influence of energy companies, and prejudice against science on the American Right, no significant action will be taken to limit greenhouse gas emissions.

Catastrophic scenarios

Most of the scenarios set out in this chapter have envisaged drift, overstretch, and relatively slow decline rather than disaster. However, in many areas of the international scene the potential for disaster does exist, and if in every individual case the odds are against this happening, if you add all of these possibilities together, then the chances of the US avoiding all of them begin to seem much less promising. Yet, as noted, it seems impossible for the US establishment as presently configured to take the radical action that would be necessary to extricate the US from any one of these potentially disastrous entanglements.

The potential disasters can be broken down into three main groups: actions by the US itself, actions by third parties, with the US drawn in, and global economic crisis, crippling US power and leading to the triumph of radical chauvinist and anti-American forces in key countries of the world. Of these, the greatest danger may come from what could be called the 1914 scenario: a situation in which the US has committed itself rhetorically to some local state (Georgia, Taiwan, and above all Israel) which then carries out some highly provocative action, leading to a regional war in which the US is forced to intervene on its behalf, just as Russia came to Serbia's help against Austria in July–August 1914.

The chief specific possibilities are the following:

- An Israeli or US attack on Iran, leading to a drastic intensification of attacks on US troops in Afghanistan, a withdrawal of European and British forces from both countries, and a radical growth in the extent and effectiveness of anti-US terrorism.

- Another major terrorist attack against the continental United States, leading to a savage and indiscriminate US response that further radicalizes much of the Muslim world and drastically increases anti-western terrorism. In the case of a US ground attack on Taleban and al-Qaeda bases in Pakistan, this could provoke the mutiny of the Pakistani army, the collapse of the state, and the entanglement of the US in a conflict so severe that it could in itself bring US global hegemony to an end.

- The internal collapse of a major Muslim state (once again, such as Pakistan), leading to US intervention and another disastrous war of occupation.

- The collapse of the Israeli–Egyptian peace treaty and a new war between Israel and some or all of its neighbours, leading to Islamist revolution across the region.

- A much deeper global economic crisis than the one experienced after 2008, leading to a collapse of the US–Chinese economic relationship and a surge in mutual hostility.

- A Taiwanese declaration of independence or a clash between China and a neighbour over rival territorial claims in which the US helped China's enemy, leading to a military conflict between the US and China. This conflict would be limited to sea and air operations, but from a US point of view even if the US prevailed it would have a disastrous effect on the US economy. In the worst-case scenario China would destroy or drive off US naval forces and occupy Taiwan, bringing US global hegemony to an end.

Conclusion

Any of the above scenarios would be capable of severely shaking, and even possibly shattering, the existing global order and bringing US global power to an early end. Assuming that none of them take place, then what we are likely to see instead will be a slower decline in US power. Afghanistan on top of Iraq will emphasize the limitations of US military power, and more states will

therefore feel able to defy the US without fearing US invasion. The Middle East will remain deeply troubled and a constant drain on US resources and attention, but without an abrupt collapse of US power.

The rise of China will mean that more and more states in the developing world will look to China, rather than the US, as their key partner. Russia will consolidate its predominance—although not outright control—in the area of the former Soviet Union, without the US being able to do much about i. Europe, crippled by internal divisions, will make mostly impotent noises from the sidelines, neither really challenging nor really supporting US strategies.

If this is the future, then the US may be able to handle the gradual decline of US hegemony and the rise of China without disastrous convulsions. The US will never formally abandon its hegemonic ambitions, but over time will be drawn more and more to treat China and even other leading regional powers on a footing of equality. Increasing disasters as a result of global warming will make many of the seemingly vital problems of today seem less and less important, and will push major states towards closer co-operation.

This is the benign version of the decline of US hegemony and the future of US foreign policy. It must be said, however, that history offers few encouraging examples when it comes to the decline of empires. Most such experiences have been bloody and disastrous in the extreme. This is true even if one takes the west European empires of Britain, France, Belgium, and Holland, ruled by west European democracies and with self-assigned civilizing missions not dissimilar to that of the United States.

The end of all these empires involved terrible wars and convulsions, and only took place at all because the countries concerned had previously been crippled by two world wars which exhausted the will of their metropolitan populations to pay or fight for empire, and undermined the entire claim of Europe to civilizational and racial superiority.

The US may do better, given its own anti-imperialist traditions, the even greater unwillingness of its population to fight, and the fact that with rare exceptions it is not trying to maintain a territorial empire in which it rules directly over other people. However, Israel—perceived by the Muslim world as identical to the US—fulfils that bitterly unpopular and dangerous role on America's behalf as far as a large proportion of the world's population is concerned. Moreover, while most Americans may not believe that they possess an empire, belief in America's pre-ordained right to lead humanity is so deeply rooted in the culture of the establishment and most of the population as easily to match the popular imperialism of Europe in the past. Drifting along, in the style of the Democrats, may not be as openly reckless as steaming full speed ahead, in the style of the Bush administration. But given the number of icebergs about, it is still extremely dangerous.

? Questions

1. What are the principal ideological forces shaping US foreign policy?
2. What are the chief domestic political forces and structures shaping US foreign policy?
3. Why is the belief in America's mission to lead the world towards freedom so strong?
4. What are the positive and negative consequences of this belief for US policy and America's role in the world?
5. What are America's chief strengths and weaknesses when it comes to projecting power and influence?
6. Why is US international aid so low compared to America's previous record during the Cold War?
7. What is the role of domestic ethnic lobbies in shaping US foreign policy?
8. How great a challenge does China pose to US global leadership?
9. What are the different possible future courses of US foreign policy with regard to China?
10. What role does Europe play in the US foreign policy mentality?
11. What are some possible future disasters that could accelerate the decline of US power?

» Further Reading

Bacevich, A. J. (2004), *American Empire: The Realities and Consequences of US Diplomacy* (Harvard University Press: Cambridge, Mass).

Cohen, W.I. (210), *America's Response to China: A History of Sino-American Relations* (5th edn, Columbia University Press: New York).

Holmes, S. (2007), *The Matador's Cape: America's Reckless Response to Terror* (Cambridge: Cambridge University Press)

Hunt, M. H. (1987), *Ideology and US Foreign Policy* (Yale University Press: New Haven CT).

Ikenberry, J. G. (2004), *American Foreign Policy*: Theoretical Essays (Longman: New York).

Lieven, A. (2012), *America Right or Wrong: An Anatomy of American Nationalism* (HarperCollins and Oxford University Press, New York)

Lipset, S (1976), *American Exceptionalism: A Double-edged Sword* (W.W. Norton: New York)

Marshall, W. (ed.) (2006), *With All Our Might: A Progressive Strategy for Defeating Jihadism and Defending Liberty* (Rowman and Littlefield).

Mead, W.R. (2002), *Special Providence: American Foreign Policy and how it Changed the World* (Routledge: New York)

Mearsheimer, J and Walt, S.M. (2008), *The Israel Lobby and US Foreign Policy* (Farar, Straus and Giroux: New York)

Perle, R. and Frum, D. (2004), *An End to Evil: How to Win the War on Terror* (Ballantine Books: New York).

Smith, T. and Leone, R. C. (1995), *America's Mission* (Princeton University Press: Princeton NJ).

Walt, S. M. (2005), *Taming American Power: The Global Response to US Primacy* (W.W. Norton: New York).

Yahuda, Michael (2011), *The International Politics of the Asia-Pacific* (3rd edn, Routledge: New York).

Zakheim, Dov S. (2011), *A Vulcan's Tale: How the Bush Administration Mismanaged the Reconstruction of Afghanistan* (Washington DC: Brookings Institution).

 ## Endnotes

1. For the historical background to this belief, see Tuveson (1968) and Hughes (2003: 19–41). For fictional versions of America as liberating and/or modernizing redeemer, see Mark Twain, *A Connecticut Yankee in King Arthur's Court* (1889) and the original TV series of *Star Trek*. Cf also McDougall (1997: 81), Smith (1979: 21–45).

2. For a discussion of this theme, see Lieven and Hulsman (2006).

3. Speech at the New America Foundation, Washington DC, 18 April 2007.

 For a range of additional resources to support your learning visit the Online Resource Centre that accompanies this book at **www.oxfordtextbooks.co.uk/orc/cox_stokes2e/**.

23 US decline or primacy? A debate

Christopher Layne, William Wohlforth, and Stephen G. Brooks

Chapter contents

Editors' introduction

This chapter is composed of two distinct and separate contributions to a single and very important debate: is US power in decline and if so, what is the best grand strategy that the US needs to pursue? The editors of this volume asked the leading experts in these fields, Christopher Layne, William Wohlforth, and Steven Brooks, to give us a state of the art summary.

For Layne, a combination of the US's high relative debt levels coupled with the rise of new 'great powers', most notably China, means that the US's position at the top of the global food chain is now in dire jeopardy. As a result, he argues that the US is now in inexorable decline and the pursuit of global primacy in the post-Cold War period has merely hastened this process of decline. Primacy, Layne argues, engenders balancing by other great powers as well as erodes America's 'soft power' global consensual leadership. The key question to emerge from this analysis is if we accept the fact of US decline, what would be a sensible strategy to pursue? In answer, Layne forcefully advocates US 'offshore balancing' whereby the US reduces its global military reach and uses regional proxies to pursue its national security interests.

In contrast, Wohlforth and Brooks argue that the United States not only remains the sole superpower, but faces comparatively weak systemic constraints on the global exercise of its power. A US grand strategy of primacy may confront many problems, they contend, but counterbalancing by other great powers is not among them. They argue that analysts overestimate the speed of China's path to matching US power (if we take Chinese per capita GDP—rather than aggregate GDP—China currently ranks below even former war-torn countries like Bosnia). And China, in their view, continues to face the kinds of systemic constraints many commentators wrongly think confront Washington. Moreover, they argue that the US has much greater potential to extract itself from 'overstretch' as the US can strategically withdraw from global hotspots without the threat of subsequent great power war (as previous global hegemons did) or systemic constraints on the withdrawal process itself. In short, the pace of American decline on the world stage is widely exaggerated: unipolarity is a long way from ending.

These two individual contributions thus speak to a broader debate on contemporary US power, its longevity and viable US grand strategies as we move further into the twenty-first century.

US Decline

Christopher Layne

Introduction

Before the Great Recession's foreshocks in autumn 2007, most American security studies scholars and policy makers dismissed the idea that the US was experiencing relative decline. On the contrary, it was widely believed that American unipolarity—and perforce hegemony—would be enduring features of international politics far into the future. Judging from some important recently published books, many of them still believe in the long-term durability of American hegemony—the Great Recession notwithstanding (Brooks and Wohlforth 2008; Zakaria 2008, Norrlof 2010). American policy makers also cling to their belief in the durability of US hegemony. In September 2010, for example, Secretary of State Hillary Clinton proclaimed a 'new American moment' that would lay the 'foundations for lasting American leadership for decades to come.'[1] Even those who have acknowledged that US hegemony will end—sometime in the distant future—contend that the post-Second World War Pax Americana will endure even if American primacy does not (Brooks and Wohlforth 2008; Ikenberry 2000, 2011).

In the Great Recession's aftermath, it is apparent that much has changed since 2007. Predictions of continuing unipolarity have been superseded by intimations of American decline and geopolitical transformation. The Great Recession has had a two-fold impact. First, it has raised doubts about the economic and financial underpinnings of US primacy. Second, just as the Great Recession has focused attention on American decline, China's breathtakingly rapid rise to great power status has confirmed the erosion of American geopolitical dominance. Of course, this is not the first time that the US has been gripped by fear of decline. In the 1980s Paul Kennedy's *The Rise and Fall of the Great Powers* triggered an intense—but brief—debate about whether

America's power was in relative decline (Kennedy 1987).

In arguing that the United States was experiencing the relative decline of its economic power, Kennedy was not alone. Other prominent scholars making this case included Robert Gilpin, David Calleo, James Chace, and Samuel P. Huntington (Gilpin 1987; Calleo 1982, Chace 1981; Huntington 1988). *The Rise and Fall of the Great Powers* resonated because it dovetailed with popular fears that the US—enervated by the costs of the Cold War—was being surpassed economically by West Germany and—especially—Japan. While Kennedy's thesis struck a chord with the public, the US foreign policy elite lashed out at the notion that the US was declining. Indeed, one of the leading establishment scholars, Harvard Professor Joseph S. Nye, Jr., went so far as to label Kennedy and the others as 'declinists'—a subtle use of the English language that implied that they were advocates of US decline rather than dispassionate analysts of what they regarded as worrisome trends in the United States' great power trajectory (Nye 1990).

Counterfactual questions—'What would have happened if?'—are difficult to answer. Nevertheless, it is useful to ask where the US might be today if the warnings of the 'declinists' been heeded. After all, they did not claim that the US would suffer a precipitous, catastrophic collapse. Rather they argued that the United States would be afflicted by a kind of slow, termite-like decline as fundamental structural weaknesses in the American economy—too much consumption and not enough savings, persistent trade and current account deficits, chronic federal budget deficits and a mounting national debt, and de-industrialization—gradually weakened the foundations of the United States' economic power. Over time, they said, the United States' goals of geopolitical dominance and economic prosperity would collide. Robert Gilpin's 1987 description

of America's economic and grand strategic dilemmas could just as easily describe the United States after the Great Recession.

Had the warnings of the so-called declinists been taken more seriously in the late 1980s, perhaps the United States would have taken corrective economic and fiscal steps two decades ago that would ameliorated the crisis in which it now finds itself. However, just as the debate about US decline was heating up it ended abruptly when, in short order the United States' main geopolitical and economic rivals—the Soviet Union and Japan, respectively—experienced calamitous misfortune. The Soviet Union unravelled and in the early 1990s Japan's economic bubble burst—plunging it into a cycle of deflation and low growth from which, two decades later, it has yet to recover. Seemingly overnight the only two threats to the United States' military and economic supremacy were removed from the international chessboard. The 1990s subsequently witnessed a euphoric American triumphalism that wiped away any thoughts of US decline. On the contrary, the 'unipolar moment' and the 'end of history'—along with the emergence of the so-called Washington consensus—seemed to confirm that both America's power and its ideology were unchallengeable in the post-Cold War world.

The Soviet Union's implosion transformed the bipolar Cold War international system into a unipolar system in which the United States—as senior US officials never tired of pointing out—was the 'sole remaining superpower'. Unipolarity objectively described the post-Cold War distribution of power in the international system. At the same time, preserving the United States' hegemonic role in a unipolar world has been the overriding grand strategic objective of every post-Cold War administration from George H. W. Bush's to Barack Obama's. With the notion of American decline apparently put to rest by the Cold War's end, a new debate

---

> **KEY QUOTES 23.1: US dilemmas in the 1980s**

With a decreased rate of economic growth and a low rate of national savings, the United States was living and defending commitments far beyond its means. In order to bring its commitments and power back into balance once again, the United States would one day have to cut back further on its overseas commitments, reduce the American standard of living, or decrease domestic productive investment even more than it already had. In the meantime, American hegemony was threatened by a potentially devastating fiscal crisis.

(Gilpin 1987: 347–48).

emerged. This was about unipolarity's implications, and it focused on two key questions: how long would unipolarity last and is the maintenance of hegemony a wise grand strategy for the United States?

In the immediate aftermath of the Cold War, a few scholars—notably Christopher Layne and Kenneth Waltz—argued that unipolarity would be a short-lived transitional phase from bipolarity to multipolarity (Layne 1993; Waltz 1994). Unipolarity, they argued, would spur the emergence of new great powers to act as counterweights to US hegemony. These unipolar pessimists also questioned the wisdom making the preservation of US dominance in a unipolar world the overriding goal of the United States' post-Cold War grand strategy. Pointing to a long historical record, they argued that failure is the fate of hegemons. The hegemonic bids of the Habsburgs (under Charles V and Philip II), France (under Louis XIV and Napoleon), and Germany (under Wilhelm II and Adolph Hitler) were all defeated by the resistance of countervailing alliances and by the consequences of their own strategic over-extension. In a unipolar world, they argued, the US would not be immune from this pattern of counter-hegemonic balancing. However, from the Soviet Union's collapse until the Great Recession, unipolar pessimism was a distinctly minority view among security studies scholars and US policy makers.

- Heretofore, the conventional wisdom has been that unipolarity and US hegemony will last for a very long time. Unipolar optimists have maintained that the US would buck the historical trend of hegemonic failure

> **KEY POINTS**
>
> ❑ The Great Recession has focused attention on the question of American decline.
> ❑ The Great Recession has dramatized China's great power rise.
> ❑ The Great Recession has called into question arguments about 'unipolar stability'.

for two reasons. First, they said, the magnitude of US power precludes other states from balancing against its hegemony. In a word, the military and economic power gap between the US and its nearest rivals is insurmountable—so wide that no state can hope to close it (Wohlforth 1999, 2002). Second, they argued that because US hegemony is 'benevolent' there is no reason why other states would want to balance against the United States. The argument for US benevolence has three prongs. One is that other states have strong incentives to align with American power because they derive important security and economic benefits from US hegemony (Brooks and Wohlforth 2002, 2008). The second prong is that by practising self-restraint, demonstrating sensitivity for others' interests, and acting through multilateral institutions, the United States can allay others' fears that it will use its hegemonic power for self-aggrandizing purposes (Walt 2005; Mastanduno 1997). The third prong is that the United States' 'soft power'—the attractiveness of its ideology and culture—draws others into its orbit (Nye 2002).

From the unipolar moment to the unipolar exit

Some twenty years after the Cold War's end, it now is evident that both the 1980s declinists and the unipolar pessimists were right after all. The Unipolar Era has ended and the Unipolar Exit has begun. The Great Recession has underscored the reality of US decline, and only 'denialists' now can bury their heads in the sand and maintain otherwise. To be sure, the Great Recession itself is not the *cause* either of American decline or the shift in global power, both of which are the culmination of decades-long processes driven by the big, impersonal

forces of history. However, it is fair to say the Great Recession has both accelerated the causal forces driving these trends and magnified their impact.

There are two specific drivers of American decline, one external and one domestic. The external driver of US decline is the emergence of new great powers in world politics and in the unprecedented shift in the centre of global economic power from the Euro-Atlantic area to Asia. In this respect, US relative decline and the end of unipolarity are linked inextricably: the rise of new great powers—especially China—is in itself the most tangible evidence of the erosion of the United States' power. Simply put, China's rise signals unipolarity's end. Domestically, the drivers of change are the relative—and in some ways absolute—decline in America's economic power, the looming fiscal crisis confronting the US, and increasing doubts about the dollar's long-term hold on reserve currency status.

Unipolarity's end also means the era of the post-Second World War *Pax Americana is over*. When the Second World War ended, the United States was incontestably the most powerful actor in the international system. Indeed, 1945 was the United States' first unipolar moment. The United States used its commanding, hegemonic position to construct the postwar international order—the *Pax Americana*—which has endured for more than six decades. During the Cold War, the *Pax Americana* reflected the fact that outside the Soviet sphere, the US was the hegemonic power in the three regions of the world it cared most about: Western Europe, East Asia, and the Persian Gulf. The *Pax Americana* rested on the foundational pillars of US military dominance and economic leadership, and was buttressed by two supporting pillars: America's ideological appeal ('soft power') and the framework of international institutions that the US built after 1945.

Following the Cold War's end, the United States used its second unipolar moment to consolidate the *Pax Americana* by expanding the scope of its geopolitical

---

KEY POINTS

❑ External and domestic factors are the drivers of American decline.

❑ The military, economic, ideational, and institutional foundations of the present international order—the *Pax Americana*—are being eroded.

---

and ideological ambitions. In the Great Recession's aftermath, however, the economic foundation of the *Pax Americana* has crumbled and its ideational and institutional pillars have been weakened. Although the US remains preeminent militarily, the rise of new great powers like China, coupled with US fiscal and economic constraints, means that over the next decade or two the United States' military dominance will be challenged. The entire fabric of world order that the United States established after 1945—the *Pax Americana*—rested on the foundation of US military and economic preponderance. Remove the foundation and the structure crumbles. The decline of American power means the end of US dominance in world politics and the beginning of the transition to a new constellation of world power. Without the 'hard' power (military and economic) on which it was built, the *Pax Americana* is doomed to wither in the early twenty-first century. Indeed, it already is withering.

The external driver of American decline: the rise of new great powers

American decline is part of a broader trend in international politics: the shift of economic power away from the Euro-Atlantic core to rising great and regional powers (what economists sometimes refer to as the 'emerging market' nations). Among the former are China, India, and Russia. The latter category includes Indonesia, Turkey, South Korea, Brazil, and South Africa. In a May 2011 report, the World Bank predicted that six countries—China, India, Brazil, Russia, Indonesia, and South Korea—will account for one-half of the world's economic growth between 2011 and 2025. In some respects, of course, the emergence of new great powers is less about rise than restoration. As Figure 23.1 indicates, in 1700 China and India were the world's two largest economies. From their perspective, they are merely regaining what they view as their natural, or rightful, place in the hierarchy of great powers. Pricewaterhouse Coopers has forecast that by 2050, India and China—in that order—once again will be the world's two top economies. In the early twenty-first century, however, China is exhibit A for the shift in the world's centre of geopolitical gravity.

Historical Share of Global GDP

Fig. 23.1 Historical share of global GDP.

Source: Deloitte: http://www.deloitte.com/view/en_BA/ba/industries/consumer-business/article/b58eb44d3f0fb110VgnVC-M100000ba42f00aRCRD.htm; Kalish: *China and India: the Reality Behind the Hype*. Adapted from data from Maddison: *The World Economy Historical Statistics,* OECD 2003.

The strongest evidence of that unipolarity is ending is the ascent of new great powers. The two most important indicators of whether new great powers are rising are relative growth rates and shares of world GDP (Gilpin 1981; Kennedy 1987). The evidence that the international system is rapidly becoming multipolar—and that, consequently, America's relative power is declining—is now difficult to deny. China illustrates how, since the Cold War's end, potential great powers have been positioning themselves to challenge the US.

To spur its economic growth, over the past fifteen years China has accommodated the US and integrated itself in the American-led world order. But Beijing's long-term goal is to become wealthy enough to acquire the military capabilities it needs to compete with the US for regional hegemony in East Asia. China has taken a low profile and avoided direct conflict with the US. In fact, China's self-described 'peaceful rise' has followed the script written by Deng Xiaoping: 'Lie

low. Hide your capabilities. Bide your time.' The Great Recession, however, has caused a dramatic shift in Beijing's perceptions of the international balance of power. China now sees the US in decline while simultaneously viewing itself as having risen to great power status. Chinese newly gained self-confidence was evident in its foreign policy muscle-flexing in 2010.

Objective indicators confirm the reality of China's rise—and the United States' corresponding relative decline. In 2010, China displaced the United States as the world's leading manufacturing nation—a crown the US had held for a century. As Figure 23.2 demonstrates, the International Monetary Fund (IMF) forecasts that China's share of world GDP (15 per cent) will draw nearly even with the US (18 per cent) by 2014. This is especially impressive given that China's share of world GDP was only 2 per cent in 1980, and as recently as 1995 was only 6 per cent. Moreover, China is on course to overtake the US as the world's largest economy. While analysts disagree on the date when this will happen, as Figure 23.3 indicates the most recent projections by leading economic forecasters have advanced the date dramatically over what was being estimated just a few years ago. For example, in 2003 Goldman Sachs predicted that China would surpass the US as the world's largest economy in 2041. In 2008, Goldman Sachs advanced the date to 2028. However, the most recent forecasts now indicate China will pass the US much sooner than 2028. The Economist Intelligence Unit (2009) predicts China will become the world's largest economy in 2021, Pricewaterhouse Coopers (2009) says 2020, and the *Economist* (2010) says 2019. More strikingly, according to a 2011 IMF study, in terms of purchasing power parity (PPP), China will overhaul the United States in 2016. In fact, also using PPP, some economists have calculated that China *already* is the world's largest economy.[2] What could be clearer proof of US relative decline than the fact that China—if indeed it has not already done so—soon will wrest from the United States the title of world's largest economy?

That China is poised to displace the US as the world's largest economy has more than economic significance. It has geopolitical significance. The pattern of great power rise is well established. First, China's claims of 'peaceful rise' notwithstanding, the emergence of new great powers in the international system invariably has been destabilizing geopolitically. The near-simultaneous emergence of the United States, Germany, and Japan as great powers in the later nineteenth and early twentieth centuries triggered two world wars (Layne 1993). Second, as they become wealthier, their political ambitions increase and emerging great powers convert their newfound economic muscle into the military clout they need to attain their growing geopolitical ambitions (Zakaria 1998). Already, China is engaged in an impressive military build-up. While it has not yet caught up to the United States' sophisticated military technology, it clearly is narrowing the US advantage. Third, rising powers invariably seek to dominate the regions in which they are situated (Mearsheimer 2001). This means China and the US are on a collision course in East Asia—the region where the United States has been the incumbent hegemon since 1945, and which an increasingly powerful and assertive China sees as its

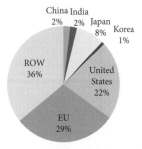

World GDP 1980

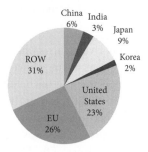

World GDP 1995

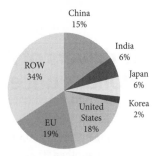

World GDP 2014 (Est.)

Fig. 23.2 World GDP (as a percentage of total) in terms of PPP. *Source*: **IMF**

own backyard. Fourth, as they rise, new great powers acquire economic and political interests abroad, and they seek to acquire the power projection capabilities to defend those interests (Zakaria 1998). Reflecting its deepening interest in protecting its lines of communication to its overseas markets and sources of raw materials, China's naval ambitions could trigger a Sino–American naval rivalry.

The bottom line is that China's great power emergence matters. For nearly two decades after the Soviet Union's demise, the United States faced no challenges

Fig. 23.3 When will China's GDP surpass the United States?

from peer competitor rivals. This is what, in geopolitical terms, unipolarity was all about. China's rise, however, means that the unipolar era of uncontested US dominance in international politics is over. That the US now confronts a *risen* China—a China that in the near term is poised to actually surpass the US as the leading great power—is powerful evidence of the United States' relative decline.

> **KEY POINTS**
>
> ❏ China and India are not rising to great power status— they are being *restored* to it.
> ❏ China has displaced the US as the world's number one manufacturing power.
> ❏ China will pass the US in aggregate GDP—the key metric of relative power—by the end of this decade.

Domestic drivers of American decline: debt, deficits, and the dollar's uncertain future

China's rise is one powerful indicator of America's relative decline. The United States' mounting economic and fiscal problems are another. There are two closely interconnected aspects of the United States' domestic difficulties that merit special attention: the spiralling US national debt and deepening doubts about the dollar's future role as the international economy's reserve currency. Between now and 2025, the looming debt and dollar crises almost certain will compel the US to retrench strategically and begin scaling back its overseas military commitments.

The causes of the looming US fiscal crisis are manifold and complex. Perhaps the best way to understand the gathering fiscal storm is to recall the observation of the late political scientist Arnold Wolfers. Modern great powers, he said, must be both national security states and welfare states. More colloquially, the state must provide both guns and butter. That is, the state must mobilize the resources necessary to defend the its external interests while simultaneously managing the economy to ensure prosperity for its citizens and also providing needed social services (education, health care, pensions). Since the Second World War, the United States has largely been able to avoid making difficult 'guns or butter' decisions precisely because of its hegemonic role in the international economy. The dollar's role as the international system's reserve currency allows the US to live beyond its means in ways that other nations cannot. As long as others believe that the US will repay its debts, and that uncontrollable inflation will not dilute the dollar's value, the United States can finance its external ambitions ('guns') and domestic social and economic programmes ('butter') by borrowing money from foreigners. This is what the

US vs. China current account balance (BoP, current US$)

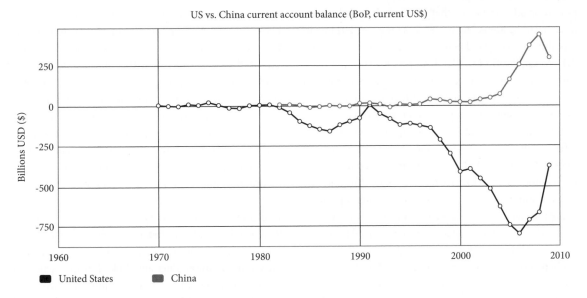

Fig. 23.4 US vs. China current account balance (BOP, current US $).

Source: IMF (Chart by World Bank), Balance of payments statistics yearbook and data files

United States has had to do since the 1980s because it has run a chronic current account deficit. That is, the US owes the world more than it makes from its various economic and financial transactions with the rest of the world. Moreover, the majority of US government debt is owed to foreign, not domestic, investors, and China is the largest single holder of US government debt.

Following the Great Recession, it has become increasingly apparent that unless dramatic measures to rein-in spending are implemented, by the end of this decade there will be serious questions about the United States' ability to repay its debts and control inflation The causes of mounting US indebtedness are many. More immediate causes can be attributed to the Great Recession, which caused the Obama administration and the Federal Reserve to inject a massive amount of dollars into the economy—in the form of stimulus spending, bail-outs, and 'quantitative easing'—to avert a replay of the Great Depression of the 1930s. Longer-term causes can be attributed to the mounting costs of entitlement programmes like Medicare, social security, and Medicaid—costs which will escalate because of the ageing of the 'baby boomer' generation. Another factor is the cost of the wars in Iraq and Afghanistan, which have been financed by

borrowing (mostly from abroad) rather than raising taxes to pay for them. These wars have been expensive. Joseph Stiglitz, the Nobel Laureate in economics, and his co-author, Linda Bilmess, have calculated that the ultimate direct and indirect costs of the Iraq war will amount to $3 trillion (Stiglitz and Bilmess 2008). Although no similar study has as yet been done of the cost of the Afghanistan war, it is certain to be substantial.

Because of the combined costs of Federal government expenditures—on stimulus, defence, Iraq and Afghanistan, and entitlements—the US, as the Congressional budget office has warned, is looking at deficits of $1 trillion or more until at least the end of this decade (Congressional Budget Office 2009). As the Congressional Budget Office warned in 2009, 'Even if the recovery occurs as projected and the stimulus bill is allowed to expire, the country will face the highest debt/GDP ratio in 50 years, an increasingly urgent and unsustainable and urgent fiscal problem (Congressional Budget Office, 2009: 13).' In a subsequent 2010 report, the Congressional Budget Office noted that if the US stays on its current fiscal trajectory, the ratio of US government debt to GDP will be 100 per cent by 2020 (Congressional Budget Office, 2010). Economists regard a 100 per cent debt-to-GDP ratio as critical indicator that a state will default on its financial obligations. In an even less sanguine 2011 analysis, the IMF forecast that the US will hit the 100 per cent debt-to-GDP ratio in 2016. If these estimates are these correct, over the next decade the growing US national debt—and the budget deficits that fuel it—could imperil the dollar by undermining foreign investors' confidence in the United States' ability to repay its debts and keep inflation in check. This is important because, for the foreseeable future, the US will depend on capital inflows from abroad both to finance its deficit spending and private consumption, and to maintain the dollar's position as the international economic system's reserve currency.

The dollar's reserve currency role is central to America's geopolitical preeminence and if it loses that status US hegemony will be literally unaffordable. The dollar's reserve currency status has, in effect, been a very special kind of 'credit card'—special because when the bills come due the United States can print money and/or borrow from abroad to pay them—that has permitted the US to live beyond its means by borrowing money from foreigners to pay for its military dominance, its costly domestic programmes (including entitlements), and excessive private consumption. Without the use of the credit card provided by the dollar's reserve currency status, the US would have had to pay for its extravagant external and internal ambitions by raising taxes and

interest rates, and by consuming less and saving more, or by tightening its belt and reducing its military and domestic expenditures. In other words, the US would have had to learn to live within its means. And that would entail forgoing its geopolitical primacy. As a leading expert on international economic affairs observed just before the meltdown began, the dollar's vulnerability 'presents potentially significant and underappreciated restraints upon contemporary American political and military predominance' (Kirshner 2008).

Although doubts about the dollar's long-term health predated the Great Recession, the events of 2007–09 have amplified them in two key respects (Helleiner 2008; Kirshner 2008). First, the other big players in the international economy are now either military rivals like China or ambiguous 'allies' like Europe, which has its own ambitions and no longer requires US protection from the now-vanished Soviet threat. Second, the dollar faces an uncertain future because of concerns that its value will diminish over time. Indeed, China, which has vast holdings of American assets (more than $2 trillion) is worried that America's fiscal incontinence will leave Beijing holding the bag with huge amounts of depreciated dollars. China's vote of no confidence in the dollar's future is reflected in its calls to create a new reserve currency to replace the dollar, the gradual 'internationalization' of the renminbi, and in the lectures China's leaders

 CONTROVERSIES 23.1: American deficit

American budget and trade deficits have not been a serious problem heretofore because US creditors have believed that the United States is able to repay its debts. There are signs that this confidence gradually may be eroding. For example, in March 2010 Moody's indicated that over the next decade linked concerns about the United States' sovereign debt and the risk of future inflation could result in the downgrading of the credit rating of US government bonds (Jolly and Rampell 2010). Standard and Poor's issued a similar warning in April 2011. Even before the Great Recession, key central banks were signalling their lack of long-term confidence in the dollar's soundness by diversifying their currency holdings. There were rumblings, too, that OPEC was thinking about pricing oil in euros, and that the dollar could be supplanted by the euro as the international economy's reserve currency. (These

suggestions have quieted down in the wake of the sovereign debt crisis in the Eurozone periphery.) In the wake of the Great Repression, doubts about the dollar's future have grown. If, whether for economic or, conceivably, *geopolitical* reasons, others are no longer willing to finance American indebtedness, Washington's choices will be stark: significant dollar devaluation to increase US exports (which will cause inflation and lower living standards) or raising interest rates sharply to attract foreign capital inflows (which will shrink domestic investment and worsen America's long-term economic problems). Moreover, given the de-industrialization of the US economy over the past three decades, it is questionable whether, even with a dramatically depreciated dollar, the United States could export enough to make a major dent in its foreign debt (Gilpin 1987: 33).

have delivered to Washington telling the United States to get its fiscal house in order. Alarm bells about the dollar's uncertain status now are ringing. In April 2011, Standard and Poor's warned that in the coming years there is a one in three chance that the United States' triple A credit rating could be reduced if Washington fails to solve the fiscal crisis, and in a May 2011 report the World Bank declared that the dollar probably will lose its status as the primary reserve currency by 2025.

In coming years, the US will be pressured to defend the dollar by preventing runaway inflation and reassuring foreign investors (i.e. China) that it can pay its debts. This will require some combination of budget cuts, tax increases, and interest-rate hikes. Because exclusive reliance on the last two options could choke-off growth, there will be strong pressure to slash the federal budget in order to hold down taxes and interest rates. It will be almost impossible to make meaningful cuts in federal spending without deep reductions in defence expenditures (and entitlements) because, as Figure 23.5 shows, that is where the money is.

With US defence spending currently at such high absolute levels, domestic political pressure to make steep cuts in defence spending is almost certain to increase. As the Cornell international political economist Jonathan Kirshner puts it, the absolute size of US defence expenditure 'is more likely to be decisive in the future when the US is under pressure to make real choices about taxes and spending. When borrowing becomes more difficult, and adjustment more difficult to postpone, choices must be made between raising taxes, cutting non-defense spending, and cutting defense spending' (Kirshner 2008: 431). In spring 2011, the Obama administration proposed to cut US defence spending by $400 million over eleven years. But that is a drop in the bucket, and cuts of a much larger magnitude almost certainly will be required.[3] If this analysis is correct, during the next ten to fifteen years the United States will be compelled to scale back

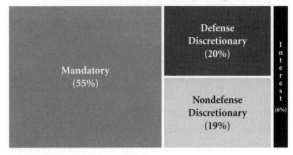

Fig. 23.5 2010 total spending.
Source: CBO

its overseas military commitments. This will have two consequences. First, as the US spends less on defence, China (and other new great powers) will be able to close the military power gap with the United States. Second, as fiscal constraints lessen US military capabilities, the United States' ability to act as a regional stabilizer and guardian of the global commons will be vitiated. In this respect, America's fiscal crisis and the dollar's uncertain future—and the likely geopolitical consequences they will cause—are compelling evidence of American decline.

- The U.S. Faces A Severe Long-Term Fiscal Crisis
- The U.S. is the World's Largest Debtor
- The U.S. Runs Chronic Balance of Payments and Balance of Trade Deficits
- The Dollar's Role as the International System's Reserve Currency is the Foundation of U.S. Hegemony
- It is Widely Predicted That the Dollar Will Lose its International Reserve Currency Status Sometime Next Decade
- Fiscal and Economic Problems Will Force the U.S. to Retrench Strategically

The end of the *Pax Americana*

US decline—which will cause the unwinding of the *Pax Americana*—has profound implications for the future of international politics. Hegemonic stability theory holds that an open international economic system requires a single hegemonic power that performs critical military and economic tasks (Gilpin 1975; Kindelberger 1973; Posen 2003). Militarily, the hegemon is responsible for stabilizing key regions and for guarding the global commons. Economically, the hegemon provides public goods by opening its domestic market to other states, supplying liquidity for the global economy, and providing a reserve currency. As US power continues to decline over the next ten to fifteen years, the United States will be progressively unable to discharge these hegemonic tasks.

The US still wields preponderant military power. However, as discussed above, in the next ten to fifteen years the looming fiscal crisis is almost certain to compel Washington to retrench strategically. As the United States' military power diminishes, its ability to command the commons and act as a hegemonic stabilizer will be compromised. The end of the United States' role as a military hegemon is still over the horizon. It is now apparent that the US no longer is an economic hegemon—as the Great Recession dramatized. An economic hegemon is supposed to solve global economic crises, not cause them, but it was the freezing-up of the US financial system triggered by the sub-prime mortgage crisis that plunged the world into economic crisis. The hegemon is supposed to be the lender of last resort in the international economy. The US, however, has become the borrower of first resort—the world's largest debtor. When the global economy falters, the economic hegemon is supposed to take responsibility for kick-starting recovery by buying other nations' goods. From the Second World War's end until the Great Recession, the international economy had looked to the US as the locomotive of global economic growth. As the world's largest market since 1945, America's willingness to consume foreign goods has been the firewall against global economic downturns. But this is not what happened during the Great Recession, however. The US economy proved too infirm to lead the global economy back to health. In a dramatic reversal of fortune, others—notably a rising China—had to step up to the plate to do so. The United States' inability to galvanize global recovery suggests that in key respects it is no longer capable of acting as an economic hegemon. Indeed, President Barak Obama said as much during the April 2009 G-20 meeting in London, where he acknowledged that the US is no longer able to be the world's consumer of last resort, and that the world needs to look to China (and India and other emerging market states) to be the motors of global recovery. Two other examples illustrate the US loss of economic hegemony: Washington's failure to achieve global economic re-balancing by compelling China to revalue the renminbi and the failure to win the 'austerity versus stimulus' debate with Europe.

- Militarily the U.S. Continues to Guard the Global Commons and Act as a Regional Stabilizer
- U.S. Military Power is Eroding and Its Long-Term Ability to Continue Its Hegemonic Role is Problematic
- The U.S. Already Has Lost its Role at the World's Economic Hegemon

Conclusion: after the *Pax Americana*, whither US foreign policy?

Because of the United States' decline, America's unipolar moment is ending. The Unipolar Exit into which we have entered presages major changes in international politics. Under the *Pax Americana* the world has enjoyed a long era of great power peace and international prosperity. This holiday from history, however, is coming to an end and international politics is headed back to the future. With the end of American primacy, the *real* the post-American world will be one of de-globalization, rising nationalism and neomercantilism, geopolitical instability, and great power competition.

When historians look to pinpoint the end of US hegemony, they probably will identify two moments. The first is the period between August and December 2008. The Beijing Olympics (which was staged deliberately as China's great power coming-out party) and the Russian invasion of Georgia in August 2008 announced the impending return of multipolarity. The reality of

> **KEY QUOTES 23.2: The rise of China—a return to multipolarity**
>
> | | |
> |---|---|
> | Coming at a moment when Chinese prestige is growing and the US is facing enormous difficulties, Mr Obama's trip has symbolised the advent of a more multi-polar world where | US leadership has to co-exist with several rising powers, most notably China. |
> | | (Dyer and Luce 2009) |

US relative economic decline and the beginning of the end of the post-1945 liberal era of international politics became evident when the full force of the Great Recession hit in fall 2008. The second pivotal moment was President Obama's November 2009 trip to China, which provided both substantive and symbolic evidence of US decline and the dramatic shift in the relative power relationship between the US and China.

In the wake of Obama's trip, China both has taken an assertive stance toward the United States on a number of crucial issues on the bilateral agenda and simultaneously flexed its geopolitical muscles in East and South East Asia. Beijing's perceptions of the balance of power have shifted: it sees China as ascendant and the US in decline. The lesson of the events that transpired between August 2008 and November 2009 is simple: history and multipolarity are staging a come-back. In coming years the world looks to become a much more turbulent—and dangerous—place geopolitically than it was during the era of the *Pax Americana*. Adjusting to the new reality of the Unipolar Exit—coming to grips with its own decline and the emerging multipolarity—will be the United States' central foreign policy preoccupation during the next ten to fifteen years.

- The Curtain is Falling on the *Pax Americana*
- The Key Challenge For the U.S. Over the Next Twenty Years is Coming to Terms with Its Decline and Adjusting to a Multipolar World

US Primacy

The big picture: a one-superpower world[4]

William Wohlforth and Stephen G. Brooks

Introduction

As recently as the middle of the last decade, pundits considered the term 'unipolar' to be too modest to capture the extraordinary position of power that the United States appeared to occupy. Only 'empire' would do. But in the eyes of the foreign policy commentariat, the United States fell from global empire to hapless Gulliver in a historical eyeblink. As the decade closed, the US National Intelligence Council's *Global Trends 2025* report (Directorate of National Intelligence 2008) added an authoritative voice the to growing chorus of decline (e.g. Layne 2006; Rachman 2011; Zakaria 2008; Khanna 2009). It was the report's 'assumptions of a multipolar future, and therefore dramatic changes in the international system' that most clearly differentiated it from its predecessor—*Mapping the Global Future*, released only four years earlier (Directorate of National Intelligence 2004). Those who had long heralded the end of a one-superpower world were quick to claim vindication (e.g. Layne 2011).

The United States' post-2008 setbacks have rightly punctured the 'empire' bubble of the early-to-mid 2000s, but the rapidity and scale of the perceptual pendulum's swing towards expectations of multipolarity's arrival should give us pause. In the absence of major war or state collapse, the scales of global power move slowly. And there is a powerful human tendency to overreact to salient trends, allowing expectations of a changed tomorrow to affect assessments of today's reality. Did the 2008 financial crisis and ensuing recession, coupled with the continuing rise of China, India, and other emerging powers really radically transform the power landscape in a scant five years? Or are analysts merely thinking about what might someday happen as if it were already happening today?

This essay offers three correctives to the currently popular narrative concerning global power trends. First, the scale and rapidity of the power shift are routinely and radically overstated. We still live in a one-superpower world; multipolarity is not just around the corner. Second, analysts misunderstand the causes and nature of the United States' 'imperial overstretch', leading them to overestimate its severity and underestimate its reversibility. While the United States' fiscal problems will generate pressure to reduce expenditures, equating these constraints to those faced by overstretched great powers of the past is profoundly misleading. Third, the core dynamics that have characterized great-power politics since the advent of unipolarity two decades ago remain robustly in place. Key features of the international system that constrained leading states of the past do not work against the United States to anything like the same degree. Yet, rising second-tier powers, notably China, continue to strongly face those constraints. The result is a very different picture of the United States' place in the world, with important implications for US foreign policy, which we address in the concluding section.

American decline and the return of multipolarity? Not so fast

The problem with the current multipolarity talk is simple: Comprehensive, aggregate capabilities—the kind of capabilities powers need to create and sustain global orders—remain concentrated in the United States to a historically unprecedented degree. Scholars from Morgenthau to Gilpin and Waltz have long recognized that what matters when thinking about the big questions of grand strategy and systemic change is a state's share of aggregated power capabilities: raw economic heft, technological prowess, military and naval power, innovation, organizational-institutional competence, size and location, the lot. As seductive as it is to single out one index—so much easier to measure!—it's misleading because each element interacts with others to support a state's capacity to act on the international stage.

If you read carefully the heralds of multipolarity, you will notice a near myopic focus on aggregate GDP. Yet by that measure, India would have surpassed Britain in the mid-nineteenth century—obviously not a good measure of their relative capabilities. Forecasting precisely when China's aggregate GDP will surpass America's is a highly uncertain game. But what we can be certain of is that matching US aggregate GDP will not make China America's peer in overall capabilities.

Indeed, there are strong reasons to suspect that analysts overestimate the speed of China's path to matching US power. Their focus on aggregate GDP growth obscures three important general features of the systemic setting and the US–China power transition. First, the only way a unipolar system can end rapidly is if the unipole collapses or loses a hegemonic war. Barring these unlikely events, the system changes as the result of the cumulative effect of differential rates of growth in overall capabilities, a prolonged process. The last polarity shift from bi- to unipolarity occurred extremely rapidly with the implosion of the Soviet Union. That experience may underlie contemporary expectations that multipolarity is around the corner. But even the most extreme declinists do not believe that the United States' grasp on superpowerdom is as fragile as Moscow's was in the mid 1980s.

Second, as impressive as China's rise has been over the past three decades, we should not forget that it has ascended from an extremely impoverished base and it still remains a developing country on the basis of the

CONTROVERSIES 23.2: The difficulties of forecasting a return to multipolarity

As scholars who have studied power assessment and forecasts over the years, we are well aware that neither economists nor political scientists nor country experts possess crystal balls that tell them when a state's overall capacity will cross a certain threshold. We do not pretend to be able to perform such magic. We cannot rule out the possibility that the myriad social, economic, technological, and institutional factors that underlie China's power will all line up favourably so as to propel it *and* that the similarly complex set of factors underlying US power will all conspire against it. We cannot rule out the possibility that, in addition, Beijing will make all the right decisions and Washington all the wrong ones. Nor can we rule out the possibility that the other major states in Asia and globally will seek to facilitate China's rise and hasten America's decline. And were that concatenation to occur, yes, we might see a very consequential shift in aggregate power relations in a comparatively short time. Although many things are possible, in social science we work with probabilities, and the balance of what we know about economic growth, technological change, diplomatic relationships, institutional and political stability, and adaptability suggests that a rapid end of a single superpower world is extremely unlikely.

standard measures (China's GDP per capita is currently on a par with that of Ecuador). Because of its huge population, it has a large economy. And because its economy is large, analysts began to think of it as the 'key challenger' to American primacy long before it entered the top league in technological capacity (both generally and in the military realm specifically). Previous challengers have not been thought of as such until their overall technological and military capacities had approached or even surpassed those of the dominant state. Although China's economic rise is swift, its rise in other capabilities is more gradual. The lag between when China will match the US in economic size and match the United States' technological and military capacity is thus likely to be much longer than in previous historical cases in which the rising challenger was technologically close or equal to the dominant state.

Third, China's growth trajectory is likely to flatten out with time—China would be defying all recent history if it continues to be able to grow in the 9–10 per cent range even as it becomes rich. In the most comprehensive analysis to date of when fast-growing economies slow down, Eichengreen, Park, and Shin maintain that 'Periods of high growth in late-developing economies do not last forever…. International experience suggests that rapid-growing catch-up economies slow down significantly, in the sense that the growth rate downshifts by at least 2 percentage points, when their per capita income reach around $17,000 US in year-2005 constant international prices, a level that China should achieve

on or soon after 2015…[On average], at that point the growth rate slowed from 5.6 to 1.2 per cent per annum.' They note further that while China's economic openness augurs favourably for it being able to maintain rapid economic growth, a series of other factors point in the opposite direction: 'higher old-age dependency ratios make growth slowdowns more likely, and China will have a higher old-age dependency ratio in the not-too-distant future. Higher and more volatile inflation rates also make slowdowns more likely, and there are reasons to worry about China on this score. Most provocatively, slowdowns are more likely and occur at lower per capita incomes in countries that maintain undervalued exchange rates and have low consumption shares of GDP.' (Eichengreen, Park, and Shin 2011).

None of these points is directly disputed by scholars of international relations, who generally agree that comprehensive capabilities are what matters, and that they tend to change slowly. Why then does there seem to be such heated discussion about the impending end of American primacy? One answer is the many meanings analysts attach to the term 'unipolarity', which for some even seems to be a synonym for global empire or hegemony.[5] When unipolarity comes to be defined as the United States' ability to defend Georgia from Russia, as Chris Layne comes close to doing in a recent essay (Layne 2011), we know the term's usefulness is in trouble. In our past writings, we went to great pains to define and use this term in ways consistent with its origins in polarity theory (Brooks and Wohlforth 2008: 11–13). It is not about influence or outcomes, e.g. whether the

> **❝ KEY QUOTES 23.3:** A one superpower world
>
> There is only one superpower, and there are no other plausible candidates on the horizon for that status for at least a couple of decades.
>
> (Buzan 2004: 65)

KEY POINTS

- ❑ Aggregate capability, not just economic size, is the key to power, and on that metric the US lead remains robust.
- ❑ Aggregate capabilities shift slowly, and China has a long way to go.
- ❑ China's growth trajectory is likely to flatten out with time.

United States can defend this or that former imperial province of Moscow, but about whether the system 'contains one state whose share of capabilities places it in a class by itself compared to all other states' (Brooks and Wohlforth 2008: 13). Barry Buzan most aptly describes the current system as a '1 + X world,' with 1 superpower and X number of great powers.

Although we use the more conventional terminology of unipolarity, 'our analysis does not hinge on the particular term used to describe the current system' (Brooks and Wohlforth 2008: 12). What matters for students of US foreign policy is how a world with one superpower operates; and while China is rising it is not and will not soon be a superpower.

It's not your grandfather's imperial overstretch

The US military is stretched thin in two wars, and its government budget is awash in red ink. These pressures will constrain Washington for years to come. For scholars such as Layne, this is an obvious case of what historian Paul Kennedy called 'imperial overstretch'. Kennedy (1987) used the term to describe the fate of past leading states whose 'global interests and obligations' became 'far too large for the country to be able to defend them all simultaneously'. By using this term, Layne and others imply that the fiscal constraints and military stresses of recent years are necessitated by the United States' structural position in the international system. In this view, the United States is stuck in a structural trap with a vicious feedback loop: its position as the leading state in a unipolar system demands ever more resources, which then serves to undermine America's place in it. It sounds like a theoretically derived, structurally determined argument for the rapid end of American primacy. The problem is that it is wrong for two reasons.

First, unipolarity did not emerge because the United States took on some new, expensive commitment. Rather unipolarity emerged because the Soviet challenger collapsed—at a time when the United States was already the strongest power. Today the costs and

dangers of the Cold War have faded into history, but they need to be kept in mind in order to assess the current US position accurately. The United States has significantly reduced defence expenditure from the Cold War norm. During the peak Cold War years 7–12 per cent of US GDP went to defence. Today the figure is 4–5 per cent. Risks are lower as well. Cold war crises—Berlin, Cuba, the nuclear alert during the Yom Kippur War of 1973, the 1982 Able Archer exercise that spooked the Soviets into a war scare—all raised the spectre of a global thermonuclear war. Today, despite many new security challenges, American decision makers do not confront or court risks of this magnitude. This is not to say the American grand strategy in the unipolar era is without costs and risks. There have been interventions that have imposed heavy economic costs and the tragic human cost of some 7000 killed in action and tens of thousands of wounded. But the human and economic toll of US Cold War grand strategy, and, indeed, the grand strategic commitments of most powers in bi- and multipolar systems of the past, was much higher.

Second, and even more important, neither the US invasion of Iraq, nor its 'nation-building' effort in Afghanistan, nor indeed its ballooning deficit are necessitated by its structural position as the leading superpower. These constraints emerge mainly from wars of choice, domestic entitlements, decisions regarding taxes, and the financial crisis and great recession of 2008–10. All serious matters, to be sure, but not the kind of 'imperial overstretch' Paul Kennedy analysed. In all those cases, overstretch emerged from commitments to contain great power counterbalancing or hegemonic rivalry. These states had to frame policy in the shadow of a potential major war with peer rival great powers, which meant that devoting a large share of their GDP to defence and extracting more resources from their societies for security policy could be plausibly be seen as an existential necessity. Solving the problem of imperial overstretch through retrenchment was extremely hard for such powers, for cutting back on various commitments seemed to risk geopolitical catastrophe. Unipolarity spares the US that kind of trade-off. Because its international position does not hinge on the specific policies that got it into its current military and fiscal constraints, it has much greater potential to extract itself from 'overstretch' with its position intact than did the historical leading states examined by Kennedy, Gilpin (1981) and others. Will this be easy to do? No. It is simply easier than if the US faced the kind of strategic situations confronted by the overstretched powers analysed by Gilpin and Kennedy.

One way to see this is to look at the balance of power realists' own analysis. To their credit, Layne and many fellow realists—notably John Mearsheimer and Stephen Walt (2002, 2003)—opposed the US decision to invade Iraq (Coalition for a Realistic Foreign Policy 2002). Reading their writings in the lead-up to the invasion, two salient facts emerge. First, balance of power theory is not part of their reasoning for counselling the US against the invasion. They predicted that an invasion would have high costs, but counterbalancing by other great powers was not among them. And they proved to be right. The costs of invading Iraq turned out to be high because of the challenges intrinsic to nation building and counterinsurgency, not because of systemic constraints identified in balance of power realism (or any other systemic constraints, for that matter). Second, their main argument was precisely that the invasion was not necessary for the United States' security and global position. They urged Washington to adopt other policies—containment and deterrence—that would serve US interests at a much lower cost. At no point did they suggest that invading Iraq was a necessary condition of maintaining the US position of global primacy.[6]

Bad choices can lead to bad outcomes. The United States chose to pursue major military undertakings simultaneously in two tough countries even as it sharply cut taxes, expanded domestic entitlements, and made some regrettable decisions about its financial system. The consequences of these choices are serious but their origins are not systemic. After all, balanced power is no guarantee against bad choices—think of the Vietnam War, the savings and loan debacle,[7] and the very fiscal crises that sparked Kennedy's and Gilpin's concerns in the first place. Having a peer competitor not only did not induce prudence in Washington, it clearly fed into a whole series of costly and dangerous interventions in the third world. Invading Iraq and pursuing a more than decade-long nation building effort in Afghanistan are choices—arguably poor ones—but not a requirement of the United States' position.

Ultimately, Charles Glaser (2011) is right to conclude that 'the overreach claim is more of an observation about the past than a well-supported prediction about the future.... None of the basic arguments about unipolarity explain why [poor choices] are unavoidable.' America may well exhaust itself, but its position of primacy means that the margin of error is actually much greater: it will require a longer series of bad choices to reach true overstretch than if the external environment did powerfully constrain the US.

KEY POINTS

❑ America's fiscal travails are in significant part the result of domestic not foreign policy.

❑ Thanks to unipolarity, the US is far better positioned than leading states of the past to extricate itself from foreign policy challenges.

Still unipolar politics as usual

Many events are obviously not going America's way. Scholars frequently read these difficulties as evidence of their claim that the international system tightly constrains the United States. Many realists, in particular, argue that great power balancing either is already occurring (and thus that America's current foreign difficulties are partly due to the effects of counterbalancing) or is in the process of re-emerging (and thus that American foreign policy will only become harder to manage in the future). These assessments are wrong: balancing is not occurring and is not set to do so anytime soon.

A little history may help put this debate in perspective. After the Soviet Union collapsed in 1991, balance of power realists claimed that the resulting unipolarity would be but an evanescent 'moment' because great powers would balance against the United States, thereby recreating a multipolar system (Layne 1995; Waltz 1993). Towards the end of the decade, with great-power balancing nowhere in sight, one of us (Wohlforth 1999) analysed the dynamics of unipolarity, arguing that the concentration of power in the United States made balancing strategies infeasible for other major powers. Subsequent studies (Brooks and Wohlforth 2002, 2005; Wohlforth 2002) built upon this analysis and provided the basis for the examination in our 2008 book, *World out of Balance*, in which we presented the most fulsome analysis showing why balance of power theory does

not apply to a unipolar system. We tested the argument empirically, delineating the observable implications we would expect to find in the historical record if our argument were valid as well as those we would expect to find if balance of power realism had any purchase in the current era. The results showed not only that balancing was not happening, but also clearly illuminated a crucial reason *why* it wasn't happening: the concentration of power in the United States as well as the geography of unipolarity made it just too expensive and hard for would-be balancers like China and Russia.

The balance of power realists' response has been, essentially, just wait, balancing and multipolarity are coming, this time for real (e.g. Layne 2011). Space constraints forbid a full discussion of the evidence here. Readers may consult our analysis and evaluate for themselves the evidence we present for why our argument is valid. The main point is that we have presented a falsifiable argument and tested it, while balance of power realists, thus far, have generally responded by simply reiterating their argument and asserting that balancing will occur eventually. For further discussion see Campbell Craig's comments in Key quotes 23.4.

Indeed, amidst all the talk of balancing and 'soft balancing', analysts have missed the main story of the past fifteen years: systemic constraints on other major powers, not the United States. China began and ended

---

❝ KEY QUOTES 23.4: Military balancing and realist arguments

The absence of traditional military balancing against the US since the end of the Cold War, a fact of international life that almost no one now denies, poses a major problem for balance-of-power Realists, who argue that major powers are destined to build up their own military forces, and/or create formal military alliances, in order to balance against a dominant state. Prominent structural realists have predicted such balancing behaviour since the early 1990s, but it hasn't happened yet. . . . [B]alance-of power Realists must show why major powers have not shown any indication of balancing so far over two decades, indisputably a long time in the context of modern international history . . . . Otherwise, [they] are forced simply to assert that a new polar system will

emerge, someday, simply because that is how international politics operates. This, as any student of social science knows, is an unfalsifiable argument. Nations simply are not trying to match the US in military capabilities or to form formal military alliances as they constantly did with respect to far less preponderant states over the past 300 years. Conventional Realists need to account for this: they need to show how balance-of-power theory can explain this absence. Responses that amount simply to a plea to 'just wait', or to describe behaviour as 'balancing' that never would have been called that before, do not fulfil this demand.

Craig (2010)

the 2000s with a single reliable ally: North Korea. In comparison, in the post-2001 period, nine eastern European countries joined NATO, and Japan and Australia buttressed their alliances with the United States and participated in US-led military operations in Iraq and Afghanistan. Moreover, India jettisoned its foundational principle of non-alignment to cooperate with the United States on a range of military activities. By one calculation, of the thirty-nine states that surround the rising regional powers of Russia and China, all but five have engaged in activities that more closely link them to the United States since 2001 (Selden 2010).

Consider also international institutions and globalization. Because most other powers lack the material capacity to help redefine rules and provide public goods, international rules and norms constrain them far more than Washington. And the global economy constrains smaller powers far more than the US: while other powers are constrained by America's outsized role in the global economy from using economic statecraft (e.g. sanctions) against the US, Washington

uses them with impunity against others (albeit not always effectively).

In short, notwithstanding important new developments in international affairs, the United States continues to operate in a permissive systemic environment, while other states, notably China, do not. This hardly means that the US is omnipotent or that China is ineffectual; it simply means that they face very different systemic pressures.

> **KEY POINTS**
>
> ❏ For 20 years, balance of power realists have predicted that great-power counterbalancing would soon occur, and bring about multipolarity.
> ❏ Predicted great power-balancing has not occurred and there is little evidence that it is about to.
> ❏ The United States continues to operate in a permissive systemic environment.

Conclusion: why it matters

To understand the significance of the permissive systemic environment facing the United States, one needs to go beyond today's headlines. Analysts typically reckon US power as the ability to get others to *do* something they otherwise would not have done. They are certainly right that the US often lacks power of this kind, for example it can't get the Chinese to help much regarding Iran, it has been unsuccessful in getting North Korea to relinquish its nuclear weapons, and it struggles to get the Pakistanis to combat al-Qaeda and the Taliban more effectively. But we also to need to keep in mind another way of conceptualizing power: power is also the ability to get others to *not* do something they otherwise would have done. Unipolarity conveys a lot of such 'blocking power' on the US, but we almost never see it. Just because this kind of power cannot be seen does not mean that it is unimportant.

And when the United States does seek to translate its power capabilities into favourable foreign policy outcomes, the international system does not push back

against it the way it did against leading powers in the past, and the way it still does against other powers today. As they ponder potential security policies, US decision makers do not confront the prospect that other great powers will construct a counterbalance through alliances or internal efforts. They need not fear escalating 'soft balancing' measures on the part of other powers that would rein the US in and eventually morph into conventional hard balancing. They do not need to worry that other states are in a strong position to use America's links to the global economy strategically to force it to toe their line. They do not need to be apprehensive that failure to cooperate in a given international institution might spoil their government's general reputation for cooperation and thus deny it all the benefits it gets from the institutional order. And they need not worry that if they break some international rule or norm America's overall legitimacy will necessarily be strongly reduced and its leadership role will come crashing down.

In different combinations, various of these four constraints powerfully shaped the security policies of great powers in the bi- and multipolar systems of the past, and many continue to shape the policies of other powers in the unipolar one of today. Systemic international relations theory, developed by hundreds of scholars over five decades, is not a naked emperor. These theories are often powerful tools for explaining the contours of state behaviour. They just do not apply to the contemporary United States. One way to escape the pervasive 'presentism' of debates about US foreign policy and get a sense of the importance of these constraints is to perform two mental tasks that American international relations scholars often seem reluctant to undertake: think historically and think cross-nationally

Our book, *World out of Balance*, provides short case studies of previous leading powers with international positions roughly comparable to the United States' today, except that they were in multi- and bipolar international systems: Britain at its nineteenth century peak and the United States in the latter Cold War. These cases remind readers what it's like to run a great power's foreign policy in the face of systemic constraints like counterbalancing. As noted, the peak Cold War years found the United States devoting a major proportion of its economy to defence. Increases in US military capabilities were predictably and reliably countered—one way or another—by a Soviet superpower with the means and the motive to check America. And during the latter Cold War, US policy makers considering any major undertaking in most of the world's regions had to reckon the probability that the Soviet Union's formidable military machine might lend its weight to the other side of the scale. Today, by contrast, defence expenditure as a percentage of the economy is roughly half the peak Cold War norm, and increases in US capabilities are not counterbalanced

(the combined share of the other major powers' GDP devoted to defence has shrunk since the 1990s). Does this mean the US can do whatever it wants? No. But when the US contemplates an action—e.g. the surge in Afghanistan—it doesn't have to consider what will happen if other major powers put their military power at the disposal of US adversaries.

The bottom line is that as challenging as the world may seem, it would be a whole lot more challenging if the United States had to tackle all the foreign policy problems it faces while also confronting tight systemic constraints. Of course, the US can manage its systemic opportunity wisely or unwisely; the choices Washington makes matter greatly. Because it faces a permissive systemic environment, the United States can potentially avail itself of policy options to better advance its interests that would not otherwise exist. Most notably, the US is now in a favourable position to pursue a policy we call 'systemic activism'—altering the institutions that govern the international system (see Brooks and Wohlforth 2008: 214–18, 2009). And yet, having more foreign policy choices could also enable poor decisions. If the United States truly faced counterbalancing and now had a global rival that was providing military assistance to the Taliban as the United States aided the *mujahedin* against the Soviet Union in the early 1980s, then Washington would face a very different calculus about whether to continue its expensive nation-building exercise there. Those who wish for the United States to end its costly commitment to Afghanistan might well wish that it did, in fact, face tight systemic constraints. Regardless, the underlying point is simple: the world is clearly a different place for the United States due to the permissive systemic environment that it faces and in all likelihood will continue to face far into the future. Properly understanding of the consequences of American primacy thus remains imperative

» **Further Reading**

Directorate of National Intelligence (2008), *Global Trends 2025: A Transformed World* (Washington: US Government Printing Office), online at http://www.dni.gov/nic/NIC_2025_project.html.

Nye, J. S. (2011), *The Future of Power* (New York: Public Affair).

Endnotes

1. Glenn Kessler, 'Clinton Declares 'New Moment' in US Foreign Policy Speech, *Washington Post*, September 9, 2010, http://www.washingtonpost.com/wp-dyn/content/article/2010/09/08/AR2010090807133.html.

2. Arvin Subbramanian, 'How We Undervalue China,' *Washington Post*, May 1, 2011, p. A23. On the Peterson Institute for International Economics website, Subbramanian explains his methodology in 'Is China Already Number One? New GDP Estimates,' http://www.iie.com/realtime/?p=1935.

3. Over an eleven-year period, the Obama proposal would result in annual cuts averaging about $37 billion. The US spent nearly $550 billion on defence in FY 2011, so the proposed Obama cuts would be well under 10 per cent of that amount.

4. This essay builds upon the analysis in Brooks and Wohlforth (2011).

5. See, for example, Huntington (1999) and Mearsheimer (2001a).

6. The same applies to Afghanistan; see Mearsheimer (2001b) and Posen (2001/2002).

7. In the late 1980s some 750 US savings and loan institutions—akin to building societies in the UK—failed, partly owing to unsound real estate lending. This contributed to major losses in the financial sector and possibly to the deep 1990-91 recession.

 For a range of additional resources to support your learning visit the Online Resource Centre that accompanies this book at www.oxfordtextbooks.co.uk/orc/cox_stokes2e/.

References

Chapter 1

Brooks, S. and Wohlforth W. (2008), *World Out of Balance: International Relations and the Challenge of American Primacy* (Princeton: Princeton University Press).

Bush, G. W. (2002), *The National Security Strategy of the United States* (Washington, DC: The White House).

Chomsky, N. (2004), *Hegemony or Survival: America's Quest for Global Dominance* (New York: Henry Holt and Co.).

Clinton, W. J. (1995), *A National Security Strategy of Engagement and Enlargement* (Washington, DC: The White House).

Dueck, C. (2006), *Reluctant Crusaders: Power, Culture, and Change in American Grand Strategy* (Princeton: Princeton University Press).

Grieco, J. (1997) 'Realist International Theory and the Study of World Politics', in M. Doyle and G. J. Ikenberry (eds), *New Thinking in International Relations Theory* (Boulder, CO: Westview Press), 163–201.

Hartz, L. (1991), *The Liberal Tradition in America* (San Diego: Harcourt Brace).

Ikenberry, G. J. (2000), 'America's Liberal Grand Strategy: Democracy and National Security in the Post-War Era', in M. Cox, G. J. Ikenberry, and T. Inoguchi (eds), *American Democracy Promotion: Impulses, Strategies, and Impacts* (Oxford: Oxford University Press), 103–26.

——(2002), 'Democracy, Institutions, and American Restraint', in G. J. Ikenberry (ed.), *America Unrivaled: The Future of the Balance of Power* (Ithaca: Cornell University Press), 213–38.

Jervis, R. (1978), 'Cooperation Under the Security Dilemma', *World Politics*, 30: 167–214.

Kennan, G. (1984), *American Diplomacy, Expanded Edition* (Chicago: University of Chicago Press).

Kolko, G. (1969), *The Roots of American Foreign Policy: An Analysis of Power and Purpose* (Boston: Beacon Press).

Layne, C. (1994), 'Kant or Cant? The Myth of the Democratic Peace', *International Security*, 19: 5–49.

——(2006), *The Peace of Illusions: American Grand Strategy from 1940 to the Present* (Ithaca: Cornell University Press).

Lynn-Jones, S. (1995), 'Offense–Defense Theory and its Critics', *Security Studies*, 4: 660–91.

Mearsheimer, J. (2001), *The Tragedy of Great Power Politics* (New York: W. W. Norton).

Pape, R. (2005), 'Soft Balancing against the United States', *International Security*, 30: 7–45.

Rose, G. (1998), 'Neoclassical Realism and Theories of Foreign Policy', *World Politics*, 51: 144–72.

Rosenau, J. (1971), *The Scientific Study of Foreign Policy* (New York: The Free Press).

Russett, B. (1993), *Grasping the Democratic Peace: Principles for a Post-cold War World* (Princeton, NJ: Princeton University Press).

Schmidt, B. and Williams, M. (2008), 'The Bush Doctrine and the Iraq War: Neoconservatives Versus Realists', *Security Studies*, 17: 191–220.

Schwarz, B. and Layne, C. (2002), 'A New Grand Strategy', *The Atlantic Monthly*, January: 36–42.

Smith, T. (1994), *America's Mission: The United States and the Worldwide Struggle for Democracy in the Twentieth Century* (Princeton: Princeton University Press).

Snyder, J. (1991), *Myth of Empire: Domestic Politics and International Ambition* (Ithaca, NY: Cornell University Press).

Walt, S. (2002), 'The Enduring Relevance of the Realist Tradition', in I. Katznelson and H. V. Milner (eds), *Political Science: The State of the Discipline* (New York: W. W. Norton), 199–230.

Waltz, K. (1979), *Theory of International Politics* (New York: Random House).

——(1996), 'International Politics is Not Foreign Policy', *Security Studies*, 6: 54–57.

Wendt, A. (1992), 'Anarchy is What States Make of It: the Social Construction of Power Politics', *International Organization*, 46: 391–425.

Williams, W. (1972), *The Tragedy of American Diplomacy* (London: W. W. Norton).

Zakaria, F. (1992), 'Realism and Domestic Politics: A Review Essay', *International Security*, 17: 177–98.

Chapter 2

Deudney, D. (1995), 'The Philadelphian System: Sovereignty, Arms Control, and Balance of Power in the American States Union, ca.1787–1861', *International Organization*, 49/2 (Spring): 191–228.

——(2007), *Bounding Power: Republican Security Theory from the Polis to the Global Village* (Princeton: Princeton University Press).

Hartz, L. (1991), *The Liberal Tradition in America: An Interpretation of American Political Thought since the Revolution*, 2nd Harvest/HBJ edn (San Diego: Harcourt Brace Jovanovich).

Hendrickson, D. C. (2003), *Peace Pact: The Lost World of the American Founding* (Lawrence, KS: University Press of Kansas).

Huntington, S. P. (2004), *Who Are We? The Challenges to America's National Identity* (New York: Simon & Schuster).

Johnson, C. (2004), *The Sorrows of Empire: Militarism, Secrecy, and the End of the Republic* (New York: Henry Holt).

Katzenstein, P. and Keohane, R. O. (2007), *Anti-Americanism in World Politics* (Ithaca, NY: Cornell University Press).

Kinzer, S. (2006), *Overthrow: America's Century of Regime Change from Hawaii to Iraq* (New York: Times Books).

Kramer, P. A. (2006), 'Race-Making and Colonial Violence in the US Empire: The Philippine–American War as Race War', *Diplomatic History*, 30/2: 169–210.

LaFeber, W. (1963), *The New Empire: An Interpretation of American Expansion, 1860–1898* (Ithaca, NY: Cornell University Press).

Lieven, A. (2004), *America Right or Wrong: An Anatomy of American Nationalism* (New York: Oxford University Press).

Lipset, S. M. (1996), *American Exceptionalism: A Double-Edged Sword* (New York: W. W. Norton).

Mead, W. R. (2001), *Special Providence: American Foreign Policy and How it Changed the World* (New York: Routledge).

Morone, J. A. (2003), *Hellfire Nation: The Politics of Sin in American History* (New Haven: Yale University Press).

Tocqueville, A. de (1988), *Democracy in America*, trans. G. Lawrence, 1st Perennial Library edn. (New York: Harper & Row).

Chapter 3

Adams, B. (1902), *The New Empire* (London: Macmillan).

Ferguson, N. (2004), *Colossus: The Price of America's Empire* (New York: Penguin Press).

Gardner, L. (1984), *Safe for Democracy: The Anglo-American Response to Revolution, 1913–1923* (New York: Oxford University Press).

——et al. (1976), *Creation of the American Empire*, 2 vols. (Chicago: Rand McNally College Publishing Co.).

Jefferson, T. (1903), *The Writings of Thomas Jefferson*, ed. A. A. Lipscomb, 20 vols. (Washington, DC: US Government Printing Office).

Johnson, C. (2004), *The Sorrows of Empire: Militarism, Secrecy, and the End of the Republic* (New York: Metropolitan Books).

Record, J. (2006), *The Specter of Munich: Reconsidering the Lessons of Appeasing Hitler* (Dulles, VA: Potomac Books).

Sherwin, M. (1975), *A World Destroyed* (New York: Alfred K. Knopf).

Stimson, H. L. and Bundy, M. (1949), *On Active Service in Peace and War* (New York: Scribner's).

Tocqueville, A. de (1948), *Democracy in America*, 2 vols. (New York: Alfred A. Knopf).

Van Alstyne, R. (1960), *The Rising American Empire* (Chicago: Quadrangle Books).

Chapter 4

Ambrose, S. and Brinkley, D. (1997), *Rise to Globalism: American Foreign Policy since 1938*, 8th edn. (Harmondsworth: Penguin).

Barnet, R. (1972), *Intervention and Revolution: The United States in the Third World* (New York: New American Library).

Campbell, D. (1998), *Writing Security: United States Foreign Policy and the Politics of Identity* (Manchester: Manchester University Press).

Carew, A. (1987), *Labour under the Marshall Plan: The Politics of Productivity and the Marketing of Management Science* (Manchester: Manchester University Press).

Colás, A. and Saull, R. G. (eds) (2006), *The War on Terrorism and the American 'Empire' after the Cold War* (London: Routledge).

Cox, M. (1984), 'Western Capitalism and the Cold War System', in M. Shaw (ed.), *War, State and Society* (London: Macmillan).

Cox, R. (1987), *Production, Power, and World Order: Social Forces in the Making of History* (New York: Columbia University Press).

Crockatt, R. (1995), *The Fifty Years War: The United States in World Politics, 1941–1991* (London: Routledge).

Cumings, B. (1981/1990), *The Origins of the Korean War*, 2 vols. (Princeton: Princeton University Press).

Department of State Bulletin Volume 51 (1964), August 24 (Washington, DC: Office of Public Communication).

Feis, H. (1967), *Churchill, Roosevelt, Stalin: The War They Waged and the Peace They Sought* (Princeton: Princeton University Press; 1st pub. 1957).

——(1970), *From Trust to Terror: The Onset of the Cold War, 1945–1950* (London: Blond).

Foreign Relations of the United States 1950 (1976), (Washington: Government Printing Office).

Gaddis, J. L. (1987), *The Long Peace: Enquiries into the History of the Cold War* (New York: Oxford University Press).

——(1997), *We Now Know: Rethinking Cold War History* (Oxford: Clarendon Press).

Halliday, F. (1986), *The Making of the Second Cold War* (London: Verso).

——(1994), *Rethinking International Relations* (Basingstoke: Macmillan).

Horowitz, D. (1967), *From Yalta to Vietnam: American Foreign Policy in the Cold War* (Harmondsworth: Penguin).

——(1969), *Imperialism and Revolution* (London: Allen Lane).

Kennan, G. (1947), 'The Sources of Soviet Conduct', *Foreign Affairs*, 25/4 (July): 566–82.

——(1984), *American Diplomacy* (Chicago: University of Chicago Press).

Kissinger, H. (1961), *The Necessity for Choice: Prospects of American Foreign Policy* (New York: Harper and Brothers).

——(1994), *Diplomacy* (New York: Simon & Schuster).

Kolko, G. (1969), *The Roots of American Foreign Policy: An Analysis of Power and Purpose* (Boston: Beacon Press).

——and Kolko, J. (1972), *The Limits of Power: The World and United States Foreign Policy* (New York: Harper and Row).

LaFeber, W. (1989), *The American Age: US Foreign Policy at Home and Abroad—1750 to the Present* (New York: W. W. Norton).

Lebow, R. N. (1994), 'The Long Peace, the End of the Cold War, and the Failure of Realism', *International Organization*, 48/2: 249–77.

Leffler, M. (1994), *The Specter of Communism: The United States and the Origins of the Cold War, 1917–1953* (New York: Hill & Wang).

——and Painter, D. (eds) (1994), *Origins of the Cold War: An International History* (London: Routledge).

Lippman, W. (1947), *The Cold War: A Study in US Foreign Policy* (London: Hamilton).

Lundestad, G. (1998), '*Empire' by Invitation: The United States and European Integration, 1945–1997* (Oxford: Oxford University Press).

Mearsheimer, J. (2001), *The Tragedy of Great Power Politics* (New York: W. W. Norton).

Morgenthau, H. (1951), *In Defense of the National Interest* (New York: Alfred A. Knopf).

——(1969), *A New Foreign Policy for the United States* (New York: Frederick A. Praeger).

Paterson, T. (1988), *Meeting the Communist Threat: Truman to Reagan* (New York: Oxford University Press).

Prados, J. (2004), '40th Anniversary of the Gulf of Tonkin Incident', *National Security Archive* (August), online at www.gwu.edu/~nsarchiv/NSAEBB/NSAEBB132/essay.htm.

Public Papers of the Presidents of the United States: Harry S. Truman, 1947 (1963) (Washington, DC: Government Printing Office).

Risse-Kappen, T. (1994), 'Did "Peace through Strength" End the Cold War?', *International Organization*, 16/1: 162–88.

Rupert, M. (1995), *Producing Hegemony: The Politics of Mass Production and American Global Power* (Cambridge: Cambridge University Press).

Saull, R. G. (2001), *Rethinking Theory and History in the Cold War* (London: Frank Cass).

——(2007), *The Cold War and After* (London: Pluto Press).

Schlesinger, A. Jr. (1967), 'Origins of the Cold War', *Foreign Affairs*, 46: 22–52.

Sheehan, N. (1971), *The 'Pentagon Papers': As Published by the New York Times* (London: Routledge Kegan Paul).

Waltz, K. (1979), *Theory of International Politics* (Reading, Mass.: Addison-Wesley).

Weinberger, C. (1990), *Fighting for Peace: Seven Critical Years in the Pentagon* (New York: Michael Joseph).

Young, M. (1991), *The Vietnam Wars, 1945–1990* (New York: HarperCollins).

Chapter 5

9/11 Commission Report (2004), *The 9/11 Commission Report: Final Report of the National Commission on the Terrorist Attacks upon the United States* (New York: W. W. Norton).

Albright. M. (2003), *Madam Secretary: A Memoir* (London: Macmillan).

Asmus, R. (2002), *Opening NATO's Door: How the Alliance Remade Itself for a New Era* (New York: Columbia University Press).

Bacevich, A. J. (1996), 'The Impact of the New Populism', *Orbis*, 40: 31–43.

Berger, S. R. (1998), 'Challenges Approaching the Twenty-First Century', in R. L. Hutchings (ed.), *At the End of the American Century: America's Role in the Post-Cold War World* (Washington, DC: Woodrow Wilson Center Press).

Bert, W. (1997), *The Reluctant Superpower: United States Policy in Bosnia, 1991–95* (Basingstoke: Macmillan).

Beschloss, M. R. and Talbott, S. (1993), *At the Highest Levels: The Inside Story of the End of the Cold War* (Boston: Little, Brown).

Branch, T. (2009), *The Clinton Tapes: Wrestling with History in the White House* (London and New York: Simon and Schuster).

Brinkley, D. (1997), 'Democratic Enlargement: The Clinton Doctrine', *Foreign Policy*, 106: 111–27.

Brown, S. (1994), *The Faces of Power* (New York: Columbia University Press).

Bush, G. and Scowcroft, B. (1998), *A World Transformed* (New York: Alfred A. Knopf).

Chollet, D. and Goldgeier, J. (2008), *America Between the Wars: From 11/9 to 9/11* (New York: PublicAffairs).

Chomsky, N. (1994), *World Orders, Old and New* (London: Pluto Press).

Christopher, W. (1995), 'America's Leadership, America's Opportunity', *Foreign Policy*, 98: 6–28.

Clark, I. (2001), *The Post-Cold War Order: The Spoils of Peace* (Oxford: Oxford University Press).

Crabb, C. V., Sarieddine, L. S., and Antizzo, G. J. (2001), *Charting a New Diplomatic Course: Alternative Approaches to America's Post-Cold War Foreign Policy* (Baton Rouge, LA: Louisiana State University Press).

Daalder, I. H. (1996), 'Knowing When to Say No: the Development of US Policy for Peacekeeping', in W. Durch (ed.), *UN Peacekeeping, American Policy, and the Uncivil Wars of the 1990s* (New York: St Martin's Press).

DiPrizio, R. C. (2002), *Armed Humanitarians: US Interventions from Northern Iraq to Kosovo* (Baltimore: Johns Hopkins University Press).

Doyle, M. W. (1995), 'On the Democratic Peace', *International Security*, 19: 164–84.

Dumbrell, J. W. (2009), *Clinton's Foreign Policy: Between the Bushes* (London and New York, Routledge).

Fisher, L. (1995), *Presidential War Power* (Lawrence, KS: University Press of Kansas).

Freedman, L. and Karsh, E. (1994), *The Gulf Conflict, 1990–91: Diplomacy and War in the New World Order* (London: Faber and Faber).

Fukuyama, F. (1989), 'The End of History', *National Interest*, 16: 61–84.

Haney, P. J. and Vanderbush, W. (1999), 'The Role of Interest Groups in US Foreign Policy: The Case of the Cuban American National Foundation', *International Studies Quarterly*, 43: 341–61.

Hendrickson, R. C. (2002), *The Clinton Wars: The Constitution, Congress, and War Powers* (Nashville: Vanderbilt University Press).

Hoffman, S. (2002), 'Clash of Globalizations', *Foreign Affairs*, 81: 76–91.

Hurst, S. (1999), *The Foreign Policy of the Bush Administration: In Search of a New World Order* (London: Cassell).

Jentleson, B. W. (1992), 'The Pretty Prudent Public: Post-Vietnam American Opinion on the Use of Military Force', *International Studies Quarterly*, 36: 49–74.

Kiger, P. J. (1997), *Squeeze Play: The United States, Cuba and the Helms Burton Act* (Washington, DC: Center for Public Integrity).

Kolb, C. (1994), *White House Daze* (New York: Free Press).

Krauthammer, C. (1991), 'The Unipolar Moment', *Foreign Affairs*, 70: 23–33.

Kull, S. (1995–6), 'What the Public Knows that Washington Doesn't', *Foreign Policy*, 101: 102–15.

Lake, A. (1994), 'Confronting Backlash States', *Foreign Affairs*, 73: 45–55.

Maechling, C. (1990), 'Washington's Illegal Invasion', *Foreign Policy*, 79: 113–31.

Marsden, L. (2005), *Lessons from Russia: Clinton and US Democracy Promotion* (Aldershot: Ashgate).

McCormick, J. M. (2005), *American Foreign Policy and Process* (Belmont, CA: Thomson Wadsworth).

McHenry, D. F. (1994), 'Post-Cold War Foreign Policy: Toward Shared Responsibility', in D. Yankelovich and I. M. Destler (eds), *Beyond the Beltway: Engaging the Public in US Foreign Policy* (New York: W. W. Norton).

McNamara, R. S. (1989), *Out of the Cold* (New York: Pantheon).

Mearsheimer, J. J. (2011), 'Imperial by Design', *The National Interest*, 111: 16–34.

Melanson, R. A. (1996), *American Foreign Policy since the Vietnam War: The Search for Consensus from Nixon to Clinton* (Armonk, NY: M. E. Sharpe).

Nye, J. S. (1991), *Bound to Lead: The Changing Nature of American Power* (New York: Basic Books).

——(2004), *Soft Power: The means to Success in World Politics* (New York: Public Affairs).

Ornstein, N. J. (1994), 'Congress in the Post-Cold War World', in D. Yankelovich and I. M. Destler (eds), *Beyond the Beltway: Engaging the Public in US Foreign Policy* (New York: W. W. Norton).

Paarlberg, R. L. (1995), *Leadership Abroad Begins at Home: US Foreign Economic Policy after the Cold War* (Washington, DC: Brookings Institution).

Polsby, N. (1990), contribution to 'IGS Panel Assesses the Bush Administration', *Public Affairs*, Sept.

Public Papers of the Presidents of the United States: George Bush, 1992–3, book II (1993) (Washington, DC: US Government Printing Office).

Rielly, J. E. (1995), *American Public Opinion and US Foreign Policy, 1995* (Chicago: Chicago Council on Foreign Relations).

Ritter, S. (2005), *Iraq Confidential: The Untold Story of the Intelligence Conspiracy to Undermine the United Nations and Overthrow Saddam Hussein* (London: I. B. Tauris).

Rosner, J. D. (1995–6), 'The Know-Nothings Know Something', *Foreign Policy*, 101: 116–29.

Ross, D. (2004), *The Missing Peace: The Inside Story of the Fight for Middle East Peace* (New York: Farrar, Straus and Giroux).

Russett, B. (1993), *Grasping the Democratic Peace* (Princeton: Princeton University Press).

Steel, R. (1995), 'The Domestic Core of Foreign Policy', *Atlantic Monthly*, June: 85–92.

Talbott, S. (2003), *The Russia Hand: A Memoir of Presidential Diplomacy* (New York: Random House).

Tucker, R. W. and Hendrickson, D. C. (1992), *The Imperial Temptation* (New York: Council on Foreign Relations).

Walt, S. (2000), 'Two Cheers for Clinton's Foreign Policy', *Foreign Affairs*, 79: 63–79.

Zegart, A. B. (2007), *Spying Blind: The CIA, the FBI and the Origins of 9/11* (Princeton: Princeton University Press).

Zelikow, P. D. and Rice, C. (1995), *Germany United and Europe Transformed: A Study in Statecraft* (Cambridge, MA: Harvard University Press).

Chapter 6

Anholt, S. (2009), 'The $2 Trillion Man', *Foreign Policy*, December. See also 'Briefing Barack Obama's first year', *The Economist*, January 16, 2010, 29.

Arquila, J. and Ronfeldt, D. (1999), *The Emergence of Noopolitik: Toward an American Information Strategy* (Santa Monica: RAND).

Atkinson, C. (2009), 'Does Soft Power Matter?' *Foreign Policy Analysis*, 6, No 1 (January), 3. See also Spilimbergo, A. (2009), 'Democracy and Foreign Education', *American Economic Review*, 99, 1 (March), 528–43.

Berger, J. (2010), 'U.S. Commander Describes Marja Battle as First Salvo in Campaign', *New York Times*, February 22.

Gamel, K. (2008), 'Afghanistan Need More Than Military Force, Petraeus Says', *Atlanta Journal-Constitution*, September 15.

Gelb, L. (2009), *Power Rules: How Common Sense Can Rescue American Foreign Policy* (New York: HarperCollins), 69.

Ikenberry, G. J. (2006), *Liberal Order and Imperial Ambition* (Cambridge: Polity).

Lundestad, G. (1998), *Empire by Integration: The United States and European Integration, 1945–1997* (New York: Oxford University Press), 155.

Pells, R. (1997), *Not Like Us* (New York: Basic Books), xxii.

Chapter 7

Amnesty International (2007), 'War on Terror', http://www.amnestyusa.org/waronterror/index.do.

Andrew, C. (1996), *For the President's Eyes Only: Secret Intelligence and the American Presidency from Washington to Bush* (London: HarperCollins).

Arnold, T. C. (2006), 'Executive Power, the War on Terrorism, and the Idea of Rights', *Politics & Policy*, 34/4: 670–88.

Brzezinski, M. (2005), *Fortress America: On the Front Lines of Homeland Security* (New York: Bantam).

Burns, J. M. (1973), *Presidential Government: The Crucible of Leadership* (Boston MA: Houghton Mifflin).

Bush, G. W. (2002), 'President Bush, President Havel Discuss Iraq, NATO', Press Conference by President Bush and President Havel of Czech Republic, 20 November, http://www.whitehouse.gov/news/releases/2002/11/20021120-1.html.

Corwin, E. S. (1957), *The President: Office and Powers 1787–1957* (New York: New York University Press).

Dombey, D. (2010), 'Tribal Warfare', *Financial Times*, 11 March.

Fisher, L. (2003), 'Deciding on War Against Iraq: Institutional Failures', *Political Science Quarterly*, 118/3: 389–410.

——(2007), 'Invoking Inherent Powers: A Primer', *Presidential Studies Quarterly*, 37/1: 1–22.

Franck, T. M. and Weisband, E. (1979), *Foreign Policy by Congress* (New York: Oxford University Press).

Gordon, M. R. (2007) *Cobra II: The Inside Story of the Invasion and Occupation of Iraq* (New York: Vintage).

Grimmett, R. F. (2010), 'War Powers Resolution: Presidential Compliance', Congressional Research Service, *Report for Congress*, 23 September, http://www.fas.org/sgp/crs/natsec/RL33532.pdf.

Hamdan v. Rumsfeld (2006), 126 S.Ct 2749.

Hargrove, E. C. (1974), *The Power of the Modern Presidency* (New York: Knopf).

Hart, J. (1995), *The Presidential Branch: From Washington to Clinton*, 2nd edn (Chatham NJ: Chatham House).

Hendrickson, R. C. (2010), 'War Powers in the Obama Administration', *Contemporary Security Policy*, 31/2: 204–24.

Hetherington, M. J. and Nelson, M. (2003), 'Anatomy of a Rally Effect: George W. Bush and the War on Terrorism', *PS: Political Science and Politics*, 36/1: 37–42.

Hinckley, B. (1994), *Less Than Meets the Eye: Foreign Policy Making and the Myth of the Assertive Congress* (Chicago: University of Chicago Press).

Hook, S. W. (2010), *U.S. Foreign Policy: The Paradox of World Power*, 3rd edn (Washington DC: CQ Press).

Inderfurth, K. F. and Johnson, L. (eds) (2004), *Fateful Decisions: Inside the National Security Council* (New York: Oxford University Press).

Jeffreys-Jones, R. (1998), *The CIA and American Democracy*, 2nd edn (New Haven CT: Yale University Press).

Johnson, L. (1991), *America's Secret Power: The CIA in a Democratic Society* (New York: Oxford University Press).

——(2004), 'The Contemporary Presidency: Presidents, Lawmakers, and Spies: Intelligence Accountability in the United States', *Presidential Studies Quarterly*, 34/4: 828–37.

Kernell, S. (2007), *Going Public: New Strategies of Presidential Leadership*, 4th edn (Washington DC: CQ Press).

Koh, H. H. (1988), 'Why the President (Almost) Always Wins in Foreign Affairs: Lessons of the Iran-Contra Affair', *Yale Law Journal*, 97/7: 1255–342.

Kupchan, C. A. (2010), 'Enemies Into Friends: How the United States Can Court its Adversaries', *Foreign Affairs*, March/April 89/2: 120–34.

Lindsay, J. M. (1994), *Congress and the Politics of U.S. Foreign Policy* (Baltimore: John Hopkins University Press).

Mueller, J. E. (1973), *War, Presidents, and Public Opinion* (New York: John Wiley).

——(2005), 'The Iraq Syndrome', *Foreign Affairs*, 84/6: 44–54.

Nathan, J. A. and Oliver, J. K. (1987), *Foreign Policy Making and the American Political System* 2nd edn (Boston: Little, Brown).

Ornstein, N and Mann, T. (eds) (2000), *The Permanent Campaign and Its Future* (Washington DC: AEI Press).

Pious, R. M. (1979), *The American Presidency* (New York: Basic Books).

Ricks, T. E. (2006), *Fiasco: The American Military Adventure in Iraq* (New York: Penguin).

Ripley, R. E., Lindsay, J. M., and Farrell, T.(1993), *Congress Resurgent: Foreign and Defense Policy on Capitol Hill* (Ann Arbor MI: University of Michigan Press).

Schlesinger, A. M., Jr. (1974), *The Imperial Presidency* (London: Andre Deutsch).

Skelley, E. M. (2006), *The Crisis of American Foreign Policy: The Effects of a Divided America* (Lanham, MD: Rowman & Littlefield).

Spanier, J. (1981), 'Introduction: Congress and the Presidency: The Weakest Link in the Policy Process', in J. Spanier and J. Nogee (eds), *Congress, the presidency and foreign policy* (New York: Pergamon), ix–xxxii.

Sundquist, J. L. (1981), *The Decline and Resurgence of Congress* (Washington DC: Brookings).

The Prize Cases (1862), 67 U.S. 635.

Traub, J. (2010), 'The Two Obamas', *Foreign Policy*, 6 August, http://www.foreignpolicy.com/articles/2010/08/06/the_two_obamas.

United States v. Curtiss-Wright Export Corp. (1936), 299 U.S. 304.

Wiarda, H. J. (2009), *Divided America on the World Stage: Broken Government and Foreign Policy* (Dulles, VA: Potomac Books).

Woodward, B. (2010), *Obama's Wars* (New York: Simon & Schuster).

Yoo, J. (2005), *The Powers of War and Peace* (Chicago: University of Chicago Press).

Zegart, A. and Quinn, J. (2010), 'Congressional Intelligence Oversight: The Electoral Disconnection', *Intelligence and National Security*, 25/6: 744–66.

Chapter 8

BBC (2002), 'Afghan Bombing "Most Accurate Ever" ', BBC News, 10 April, www.news.bbc.co.uk/1/hi/world/south_asia/1921614.stm.

Deutch, J. (2005), 'A Nuclear Posture for Today', *Foreign Affairs*, January–February: 49–60.

Gordon, M. R. and Trainor, B. E. (2007), *Cobra II: The Inside Story of the Invasion and Occupation of Iraq* (New York: Vintage).

McNamara, R. S. (2005), 'Apocalypse Soon', *Foreign Policy*, May–June: 29–35.

Olson, L. (2010), 'Growth in US Defense Spending Since 2001,' The Center for Arms Control and Non-Proliferation, March 11. Online at http://armscontrolcenter.org/policy/securityspending/articles/fy11_growth_since_2001/.

Powell, C. (1992–3), 'US Forces: The Challenge Ahead', *Foreign Affairs*, Winter: 32–45.

Rice, C. (2000), 'Promoting the National Interest', *Foreign Affairs*, January–February: 45–62.

Risen, J. (2006), *State of War: The Secret History of the CIA and the Bush Administration* (New York: Free Press).

Woodward, B. (2004), *Plan of Attack: The Definitive Account of the Decision to Invade Iraq* (New York: Simon & Schuster).

——(2006), *State of Denial: Bush at War*, Part III (New York: Simon & Schuster).

Chapter 9

Agnew, J. (1987), *The United States in the World-Economy* (Cambridge: Cambridge University Press).

Bensel, R. (1984), *Sectionalism and American Political Development, 1880–1980* (Madison: University of Wisconsin Press).

Burnham, W. D. (1970), *Critical Elections and the Mainsprings of American Politics* (New York: W. W. Norton).

Key, V. O. (1964), *Politics, Parties, and Pressure Groups* (New York: Thomas Y. Crowell).

Kupchan, C. A. and Trubowitz, P. L. (2011), 'The Illusion of Liberal Internationalism's Revival,' *International Security*, 35 (Summer): 95–109.

Markusen, A. (1987), *Regions: The Economics and Politics of Territory* (Totowa, NJ: Rowman & Littlefield).

Narizny, K. (2007), *The Political Economy of Grand Strategy* (Ithaca, NY: Cornell University Press).

Schattschneider, E. E. (1960), *The Semisovereign People: A Realist's View of Democracy in America* (New York: Holt, Rinehart and Winston).

Silverstone, S. A. (2004), *Divided Union: The Politics of War in the Early American Republic* (Ithaca, NY: Cornell University Press).

Trubowitz, P. (1998), *Defining the National Interest: Conflict and Change in American Foreign Policy* (Chicago: University of Chicago Press).

——and Mellow, N. (2005), 'Going Bipartisan: Politics by Other Means', *Political Science Quarterly*, 120 (Fall): 433–54.

——and Mellow, N. (2011), 'Foreign Policy, Bipartisanship, and the Paradox of post-September 11 America,' *International Politics*, 48 (March): 164–87.

Chapter 10

Aldrich, J.H., Sullivan, J. L., and Borgida, E. (1989), 'Foreign Affairs and Issue Voting: Do Presidential Candidates 'Waltz before a blind Audience?', *American Political Science Review*, 83: 123–41.

Almond, G. (1950), *The American People and Foreign Policy* (New York: Harcourt, Brace).

Althaus, S. L. (2003), 'When News Norms Collide, Follow the Lead: New Evidence for Press Independence', *Political Communication*, 20(3), 381–414.

Baum, M. (2003), *Soft News Goes to War: Public Opinion and American Foreign Policy in the New Media Age* (Princeton: Princeton University Press).

——and Groeling, T. J. (2010), *War Stories: the causes and consequences of public views of war* (Princeton and Oxford: Princeton University Press).

Bennett, W. L. (1990), 'Toward a Theory of Press–State relations in the United States', *Journal of Communication*, 40/2: 103–25.

——, Lawrence, R. G., and Livingston, S. (2006), 'None Dare Call it Torture: Indexing and the Limits of Press Independence in the Abu Ghraib Scandal', *Journal of Communication*, 56/3: 467–85.

Cohen, B. (1973), *The Public's Impact on Foreign Policy* (Boston: Little, Brown).

Domke, D. (2004), *God Willing? Political Fundamentalism in the White House, The War on Terror and the Echoing Press* (London: Pluto Press).

Entman, R. (1991), 'Framing US Coverage of International News: Contrasts in Narratives of the KAL and Iran Air Incidents', *Journal of Communication*, 41/4: 6–27.

——(2000), 'Declarations of Independence' in B. L. Nacos, R. Y. Shapiro, and I. Isernia (eds), *Decision-making in a Glass House: Mass Media, Public Opinion and American and European Foreign Policy in the 21st Century* (London: Rowman and Littlefield), 11–26.

——(2004), *Projections of Power: framing news, public opinion and US Foreign Policy* (Chicago and London: University of Chicago Press).

Gilboa, E. (1998), 'Media Diplomacy: conceptual divergence and application', *Press/Politics*, 3/3: 56–75.

Gowing, N. (1994), 'Real-time Coverage of Armed Conflicts and Diplomatic Crises: Does it Pressure or Distort Foreign Policy Decisions?', Working Paper (Harvard: Joan Shorenstein Barone Center).

Hallin, D. (1986), *The Uncensored War* (Berkeley: University of California Press).

Herman, E. and Chomsky, N. (1988), *Manufacturing Consent: the political economy of the mass media* (New York: Pantheon).

Herring, E. and Robinson, P. (2003), Special Section, 'Forum on Chomsky', *Review of International Studies*, 29(4) pp 551–620.

Hoge, J. (1994), 'Media Pervasiveness', *Foreign Affairs*, 73:136–44.

Holsti, O. R. (1992), 'Public Opinion and Foreign Policy: Challenges to the Almond-Lippman Consensus', *International Studies Quarterly*, 36/4: 439–66.

Iyengar, S. and Kinder, D. R. (1987), *News That Matters: Television and American Public Opinion* (Chicago: University of Chicago Press).

——and Simon, A. (1994), 'News Coverage of the Gulf Crisis and Public Opinion: a study of agenda-setting, priming and framing', in W. L. Bennett and D. P. L. Paletz (eds), *Taken by Storm: the media, public opinion and US foreign policy in the Gulf War* (Chicago: University of Chicago Press).

Kennan, G. F. (1993), 'Somalia, Through a Glass Darkly,' *News York Times*, 30 September.

Lang, K. and Lang, G. (2004), 'Noam Chomsky and the Manufacture of Consent for US Foreign Policy', *Political Communication*, 21(1): 93–101.

Lawrence, R. (2000), *The Politics of Force* (Berkeley: University of California Press).

Lippman, W. (1922), *Public Opinion* (New York: Free Press paperbacks; Simon and Schuster).

——(1955), *Essays in the Public Philosophy*, (Boston: Little, Brown).

Livingston, S. (1997) 'Clarifying the CNN effect: An Examination of Media Effects According to Type of Military Intervention', Research paper R-18 June (Cambridge, MA: The Joan Shorenstein Barone Center on the Press, Politics and Public Policy at Harvard University).

——and Bennett, W. L. (2003) 'Gatekeeping, Indexing and Live-Event News: Is Technology Altering the Construction of News?' *Political Communication*, 20/4: 363–80.

Mandelbaum, M. (1994), 'The Reluctance to Intervene', *Foreign Policy*, 95: 3–8.

McCombs, M. E. and Shaw, D. L. (1972), 'The Agenda-Setting Function of the Press', *Public Opinion Quarterly*, 36: 176–87.

Milbank, D. and Deane, C. (2003), 'Hussein Link to 9/11 Lingers in Many Minds', *Washington Post*, September 6, Page A01.

Mueller, J. E. (1973), *War, Presidents and Public Opinion* (New York: John Wiley and Sons).

Nixon, R. (1978), *The Memoirs* (New York: Grosset and Dunlap).

Nye, J. (1990), *Bound to Lead: The Changing Nature of American Power* (New York: Public Affairs).

——(1999), 'Redefining the National Interest', *Foreign Affairs*, 78(4): 22–35.

Robinson, P. (2002), *The CNN Effect: the myth of news, foreign policy and intervention* (London and New York: Routledge).

——Goddard, P., Parry, C., Murray, C., and Taylor, M. P. (2010) *Pockets of Resistance: British news media, war and theory in the 2003 invasion of Iraq* (Manchester and New York: Manchester University Press).

Taylor, P. M. (2006), 'Strategic Communications and the Relationship Between Government 'Information' Activities in the Post 9/11 World', *Journal of Information Warfare*, 5/3: 1–25.

Wittkopf, E. R. (1990), *Faces on Internationalism: Public Opinion and American Foreign Policy* (Durham, NC: Duke University Press).

Wolfsfeld, G. (1997), *The Media and Political Conflict* (Cambridge: Cambridge University Press).

Woodward, B. (2004). *Plan of Attack* (London and New York: Pocket Books).

Chapter 11

Agathangelou, A. and Ling, L. (2004), 'Power, Borders, Security, Wealth: Lessons of Violence and Desire from September 11', *International Studies Quarterly*, 48/3: 517–38.

Allison, G. and Zelikow, P. (1999), *Essence of Decision: Explaining the Cuban Missile Crisis*, 2nd edn (New York: Longman).

Anderson, B. (1991), *Imagined Communities: Reflections on the Origins and Spread of Nationalism* (London: Verso).

Aspin, L. (1992), 'An Approach to Sizing American Conventional Forces for the Post-Soviet Era', 24 January, memorandum.

Barkawi, T. (2004), 'On the Pedagogy of "Small Wars"', *International Affairs*, 80/1: 19–37.

Barthes, R. (1973), *Mythologies*, translated by Annette Lavers (St Albans: Paladin).

BBC News (2000), 'US Rebrands Its Rogues Gallery', 19 June, online at http://www.news.bbc.co.uk/1/hi/world/middle_east/797950.stm (accessed 13 July 2007).

Bennis, P. (2003), *Before and After: U.S. Foreign Policy and the September 11th Crisis* (Moreton-in-Marsh, Gloucestershire: Arris Publishing).

Blum, W. (2003), *Killing Hope: US Military and CIA Interventions since World War II* (London: Zed Books).

Boot, M. (2002), 'The Case for American Empire: The Most Realistic Response to Terrorism is for America to Embrace its Imperial Role,' *The Weekly Standard*, 15 October, online at http://www.weeklystandard.com/content-public-articles-000-000-000-318qpvmc.asp (accessed 13 July 2007).

Bush, G. H. W. (1990a), Remarks at the Aspen Institute Symposium in Aspen Colorado,' 2 August, repr. in Public Papers of the Presidents of the United States: George Bush, 1990, book II (Washington, DC: Government Printing Office), 1092.

——(1990b), 'Address before a Joint Session of the Congress on the Persian Gulf Crisis and the Federal Budget Deficit', 11 September, in *Public Papers of the Presidents, George Bush, 1990*, Book II (Washington, DC: Government Printing Office), 1219.

Bush, G. W. (2001a), 'Remarks following a meeting with the National Security Team', 12 September, online at http://www.presidency.ucsb.edu/ws/index.php?pid=58058&st=&st1=#axzz1QqSXP6Zd (accessed 1 July 2011).

——(2001b), 'Remarks on Arrival at the White House and an Exchange with Reporters', 16 September, online at http://www.presidency.ucsb.edu/ws/index.php?pid=63346&st=&st1=#axzz1QqSXP6Zd (accessed 1 July 2011).

——(2001c), 'Address Before a Joint Session of the Congress on the United States Response to the Terrorist Attacks of September 11', 20 September, online at http://www.presidency.ucsb.edu/ws/index.php?pid=64731&st=&st1=#axzz1QqSXP6Zd (accessed 1 July 2011).

——(2001d), 'The President's News Conference With President Vladimir Putin of Russia in Shanghai', 21 October, online at http://www.presidency.ucsb.edu/ws/index.php?pid=73441&st=&st1=#axzz1QqSXP6Zd (accessed 1 July 2011).

——(2001e), 'Remarks to the United Nations General Assembly in New York City', 10 November, online at http://www.presidency.ucsb.edu/ws/index.php?pid=58802&st=&st1=#axzz1QqSXP6Zd (accessed 1 July 2011).

——(2002a), 'Address Before a Joint Session of the Congress on the State of the Union', 29 January, online at http://www.presidency.ucsb.edu/ws/index.php?pid=29644#axzz1QqSXP6Zd (accessed 1 July 2011).

——(2002b), 'Remarks to the Troops at Elmendorf Air Force Base in Anchorage, Alaska', February 16, online at http://www.presidency.ucsb.edu/ws/index.php?pid=73257&st=&st1=#axzz1QqSXP6Zd (accessed 1 July 2011).

——(2002c), 'Remarks to the People of Lithuania in Vilnius', 23 November, online at http://www.presidency.ucsb.edu/ws/index.php?pid=64476&st=&st1=#axzz1QqSXP6Zd (accessed 1 July 2011).

——(2003), 'Address to the Nation on Iraq', 19 March, online at http://www.presidency.ucsb.edu/ws/index.php?pid=63368&st=&st1=#axzz1QqSXP6Zd (accessed 1 July 2011).

——(2004), 'Remarks in a Discussion on Education in Springfield, Ohio', 27 September, online at http://www.presidency.ucsb.edu/ws/index.php?pid=63415&st=&st1=#axzz1QqSXP6Zd (accessed 1 July 2011).

——(2005a), 'Remarks to the American Legislative Exchange Council in Grapevine, Texas', 3 August, online at http://www.presidency.ucsb.edu/ws/index.php?pid=73865&st=&st1=#axzz1QqSXP6Zd (accessed 1 July 2011).

——(2005b), 'Remarks on the War on Terror in Tobyhanna, Pennsylvania,' 11 November, online at http://www.presidency.ucsb.edu/ws/index.php?pid=64753&st=&st1=#axzz1QqSXP6Zd (accessed 1 July 2011).

——(2006a), 'Remarks on the War on Terror and a Question-and-Answer Session in Manhattan, Kansas', 23 January, online at http://www.presidency.ucsb.edu/ws/index.php?pid=65144&st=&st1=#axzz1QqSXP6Zd (accessed 1 July 2011).

——(2006b), 'Remarks at the American Legion National Convention in Salt Lake City', 31 August, online at http://www.presidency.ucsb.edu/ws/index.php?pid=749&st=&st1=#axzz1QqSXP6Zd (accessed 1 July 2011).

Carter, J. (1980), 'Address to the Nation on Afghanistan', 4 January, online at http://www.millercenter.virginia.edu/scripps/digitalarchive/speeches/spe_1980_0104_carter (accessed 13 July 2007).

Carver, T. (2002), 'Discourse Analysis and the 'Linguistic Turn'', *European Political Science*, 2/1, online at http://www.essex.ac.uk/ecpr/publications/eps/onlineissues/autumn-2002/research/carver.htm (accessed 13 July 2007).

Chomsky, N. (1991), 'The U.S. and the Gulf Crisis', in H. Bresheeth and N. Yuval-Davis (eds), *The Gulf War and the New World Order* (London: Zed Books), 13–29.

——(2003), *Understanding Power: The Indispensable Chomsky* (New York: Vintage).

Clinton, W. J. (1993), 'Address to the Nation on Somalia', 7 October, *Weekly Compilation of Presidential Documents*, online at http://frwebgate4.access.gpo.gov/cgi-bin/waisgate.cgi?WAISdocID=30452724457+0+0+0&WAISaction=retrieve (accessed 13 July 2007).

——(1999), 'Remarks by the President to the Veterans of Foreign Wars on Kosovo', 13 May, *Weekly Compilation of Presidential Documents*, online at http://frwebgate3.access.gpo.gov/cgi-bin/waisgate.cgi?WAISdocID=3047394619+3+0+0&WAISaction=retrieve (accessed 13 July 2007).

Cohn, C. (1987) 'Sex and Death in the Rational World of Defense Intellectuals', *Signs* 12/4: 687–718.

Collins, J. and Glover, R. (2002), *Collateral Language: A User's Guide to America's New War* (New York: New York University Press).

Cox, M. (1984), 'Western Capitalism and the Cold War System,' in M. Shaw (ed.), *War, State and Society* (New York: St Martin's Press), 136–93.

Dean, R. D. (2001), *Imperial Brotherhood: Gender and the Making of Cold War Foreign Policy* (Amherst: University of Massachusetts Press).

Doty, R. L. (1993), 'Foreign Policy as Social Construction: A Postpositivist Analysis of U.S. Counterinsurgency Policy in the Philippines', *International Studies Quarterly*, 37/3: 297–320.

——(1996), *Imperial Encounters: The Politics of Representation in North–South Relations* (Minneapolis: University of Minnesota Press).

Eisenhower, D. D. (1961), 'Farewell to the Nation', 17 January, reprinted in S. Melman, *Pentagon Capitalism: The Political Economy of War* (New York: McGraw-Hill), 235–39.

Enloe, C. (1996), 'Margins, Silences and Bottom Rungs: How to Overcome the Underestimation of Power in the Study of International Relations', in S. Smith, K. Booth and M. Zalewski (eds) *International Theory: Positivism and Beyond* (Cambridge: Cambridge University Press), 186–202.

Entman, R. M. (2004), *Projections of Power: Framing News, Public Opinion, and U.S. Foreign Policy* (Chicago: University of Chicago Press).

Farmanfarmaian, A. (1992), 'Sexuality in the Gulf War: Did You Measure Up?' *Genders*, 13: 1–29.

Gaddis, J. L. (1982), *Strategies of Containment: A Critical Appraisal of Postwar American National Security Strategy* (Oxford: Oxford University Press).

Griffin, P. (2007), 'Sexing the Economy in a Neo-liberal World: Neo-liberal Discourse and the (Re)production of Heteronormative Heterosexuality', *British Journal of Politics and International Relations*, 9/2: 220–38.

Hall, S. (1997a), 'Introduction', in S. Hall (ed.), *Representation: Cultural Representations and Signifying Practices* (London: SAGE Publications), 1–11.

——(1997b), 'The Work of Representation', in S. Hall (ed.), *Representation: Cultural Representations and Signifying Practices* (London: Sage Publications), 13–64.

Hallin, D. (1989), *The 'Uncensored War': The Media and Vietnam* (Berkeley, CA: University of California Press).

Hardt, M. and Negri, A. (2000), *Empire* (Cambridge, MA: Harvard University Press).

Hearn, J. (2004), 'From Hegemonic Masculinity to the Hegemony of Men', *Feminist Theory*, 5/1: 49–72.

Herman, E. S. and Chomsky, N. (1988), *Manufacturing Consent: The Political Economy of the Mass Media* (New York: Pantheon Books).

Herz, J. (1951), *Political Realism and Political Idealism: A Study in Theories and Realities* (Chicago: University of Chicago Press).

Hooper, C. (2001), *Manly States: Masculinities, International Relations and Gender Politics* (New York: Columbia University Press).

Ignatieff, M. (2003), *Empire Lite: Nation Building in Bosnia, Kosovo, Afghanistan* (London: Vintage).

Jackson, R. (2005), *Writing the War on Terrorism: Language, Politics and Counter-Terrorism* (Manchester: Manchester University Press).

Jeffords, S. (1986), 'The New Vietnam Films: Is the Movie Over?', *Journal of Popular Film and Television*, 13/3: 186–95.

Kennedy, J. F. (1961), 'Radio and Television Report to the American People on the Berlin Crisis', 25 July, online at http://www.jfklibrary.org/Historical+Resources/Archives/Reference+Desk/Speeches/JFK/003POF03BerlinCrisis07251961.htm (accessed 13 July 2007).

——(1962), 'Arms Quarantine of Cuba: the Soviet Military Build-up', Television and Radio address, 22 October, *Vital Speeches of the Day*, XXIX(3), 15 November, 66–68.

Kimmel, M. (2003), 'Globalization and its Mal(e)contents: The Gendered Moral and Political Economy of Terrorism', *International Sociology*, 18/3: 603–20.

Klare, M. (1996), *Rogue States and Nuclear Outlaws: America's Search for a New Foreign Policy* (New York: Hill & Wang).

Kline, S. (2004), 'The Culture War Gone Global: "Family Values" and the Shape of US Foreign Policy', *International Relations*, 18/4: 453–66.

Kolko, G. (1988), *Confronting the Third World: United States Foreign Policy 1945–1980* (New York: Pantheon).

Laffey, M. and Weldes, J. (2004), 'Methodological Reflections on Discourse Analysis', *Qualitative Methods*, 2/1: 28–30.

Layne, C. and Thayer, B. A. (2007), *American Empire: A Debate* (New York and London: Routledge).

Mallaby, S. (2002), 'The Reluctant Imperialist: Terrorism, Failed States, and the Case for American Empire', *Foreign Affairs*, 81/2: 2–7.

Mayer, J. (2007), 'Whatever it takes', *The New Yorker*, 19 February, online at http://newyorker.com/printables/fact/070219fa_fact_mayer (accessed 13 July 2007).

Milliken, J. (1999), 'The Study of Discourse in International Relations: A Critique of Research and Methods', *European Journal of International Relations*, 5/2: 225–54.

Morgenthau, H. J. (1993), *Politics among Nations: The Struggle for Power and Peace*, brief edition, revised by K. W. Thompson (New York: McGraw-Hill).

Msnbc.com (2010), 'Last Full U.S. Combat Brigade Leaves Iraq,' 19 August, online at http://www.msnbc.msn.com/id/38744453/ns/world_news-mideast/n_africa/(accessed 28 January 2011).

National Highway Traffic Safety Administration (2011), 'National Statistics,' online at http://www-fars.nhtsa.dot.gov/Main/index.aspx (accessed 28 March 2011).

Nayak, M. (2006), 'Orientalism and "Saving" U.S. State Identity after 9/11', *International Feminist Journal of Politics*, 8/1: 42–61.

Niva, S. (1998), 'Tough and Tender: New World Order Masculinity and the Gulf War,' in M. Zalewski and J. Parpart (eds), *The 'Man' Question in International Relations* (Boulder, CO: Westview Press).

Obama, B. (2009), 'Address at Cairo University in Cairo, Egypt', 4 June, online at http://www.presidency.ucsb.edu/ws/index.php?pid=86221&st=obama&st1=cairo (accessed 19 January 2011).

Peterson, V. S. (2003), *A Critical Rewriting of the Global Political Economy: Integrating Reproductive, Productive and Virtual Economies* (London: Routledge).

——and Runyan, A. S. (1999) *Global Gender Issues* (Boulder, CO: Westview Press).

Project for the New American Century (no date), online at http://www.newamericancentury.org/ (accessed 30 July 2007).

Purvis, T. and Hunt, A. (1993), 'Discourse, ideology, discourse, ideology, discourse, ideology…', *British Journal of Sociology*, 44/3: 473–99.

Record, J. (2007), 'The Use and Abuse of History: Munich, Vietnam and Iraq', *Survival*, 49/1: 163–80.

Rice, C. (2000), 'Campaign 2000: Promoting the National Interest', *Foreign Affairs*, 79/1, online at http://www.foreignaffairs.org/20000101faessay5/condoleezza-rice/campaign-2000-promoting-the-national-interest.html (accessed 13 July 2007).

Robb, D. L. (2004), *Operation Hollywood: How the Pentagon Shapes and Censors the Movies* (Amherst, NY: Prometheus Books).

Rogin, M. (1987), *Ronald Reagan, the Movie and Other Episodes in Political Demonology* (Berkeley: University of California Press).

Rotberg, R. I. (2002), 'The New Nature of Nation-State Failure,' *Washington Quarterly*, 25/3: 85–96.

Said, E. W. (1991), 'Thoughts on a War: Ignorant Armies Clash By Night', in P. Bennis and M. Moushabeck (eds), *Beyond the Storm: A Gulf Crisis Reader* (New York: Olive Branch Press), 1–6.

Scott, J. C. (1987), *Weapons of the Weak: Everyday Forms of Peasant Resistance* (New Haven: Yale University Press).

Shapiro, M. J. (1986), 'Metaphor in the Philosophy of the Social Sciences', *Cultural Critique*, 2: 191–214.

Sharp, J. (2000), *Condensing the Cold War: Reader's Digest and American Identity* (Minneapolis: University of Minnesota Press).

Shepherd, L. J. (2006), 'Veiled References: Constructions of Gender in the Bush Administration Discourse on the Attacks on Afghanistan post-9/11', *International Feminist Journal of Politics*, 8/1: 19–41.

Smeeta, M. and Shirazi, F. (2010), 'Hybrid Identities: American Muslim Women Speak,' *Gender, Place & Culture*, 17/2: 191–209.

Smith, A. D. (1991), 'The Nation: Invented, Imagined, Reconstructed?', *Millennium*, 20/3: 353–68.

Stokes, D. (2005), 'The Heart of Empire? Theorising US Empire in an Era of Transnational Capitalism', *Third World Quarterly*, 26/2: 217–36.

Stuckey, M.E. (1991), *The President as Interpreter-In-Chief* (Chatham, NJ: Chatham House Publishers).

Terry, J. J. (2005), *U.S. Foreign Policy in the Middle East: The Role of Lobbies and Special Interest Groups* (Ann Arbor, MI: Pluto Press).

The American Presidency Project (n.d.), online at http://www.presidency.ucsb.edu/ (accessed 1 July 2011).

The Independent (2007), 'How Brown Distances Himself from Blair' 12 July, 7.

The White House (2010) *National Security Strategy*, online at http://www.whitehouse.gov/sites/default/files/rss_viewer/national_security_strategy.pdf (accessed 19 January 2011).

Truman, H. S. (1947), 'Address to a Joint Session of Congress', 12 March, online at http://www.hbci.com/~tgort/truman.htm (accessed 13 July 2007).

——(1950), 'Radio and television report to the American people on the situation in Korea', 1 September, *Public Papers of the Presidents, Harry S. Truman, 1950* (Washington, DC: Government Printing Office, 1965), 609–610.

Valantin, J. (2005), *Hollywood, the Pentagon and Washington: The Movies and National Security from World War II to the Present Day* (London: Anthem Press).

Weldes, J. (1999a), *Constructing National Interests: The United States and the Cuban Missile Crisis* (Minneapolis: University of Minnesota Press).

——(1999b), 'Going Cultural: *Star Trek*, State Action and Popular Culture', *Millennium*, 28/1: 117–134.

——Laffey, M., Gusterson, H., and Duvall, R. (1999), 'Introduction: Constructing Insecurity', in J. Weldes, M. Laffey, H. Gusterson, and R. Duvall (eds), *Cultures of Insecurity: States, Communities, and the Production of Danger* (Minneapolis: University of Minnesota Press), 1–33.

Williams, W. A. (2004), *The Tragedy of American Diplomacy*, new edited edition (New York: W. W. Norton).

Zalewski, M. (2000), *Feminism after Postmodernism: Theorising through Practice* (London: Routledge).

Chapter 12

Bacevich, A. J. (2005), 'The Realist Persuasion', *Boston Globe*, 6 November, online at www.boston.com/news/globe/ideas/articles/2005/11/06/the_realist_persuasion/?page=full.

Bard, M. G. (1994), 'The Influence of Ethnic Interest Groups on American Middle East Policy', in E. R. Wittkopf (ed.), *The Domestic Sources of American Foreign Policy: Insights and Evidence* (New York: St Martin's Press).

Brown, L. C. (1984), *International Politics and the Middle East: Old Rules, Dangerous Game* (Princeton: Princeton University Press).

Bush, G. H. W. (1990), 'Toward a New World Order', The President Addresses a Joint Session of Congress, 11 September, online at http://se2.isn.ch/serviceengine/FileContent?serviceID=23&fileid=02FE0D5C-D6BD-7295-48EB-F1D4393A71A7&lng=en.

Bush, G. W. (2002a), 'The President's State of the Union Address', 29 January, online at www.whitehouse.gov/news/releases/2002/01/20020129-11.html.

——(2002b), *The National Security Strategy of the United States of America*, online at www.whitehouse.gov/nsc/nss.html.

——(2003), 'Remarks by the President of the United States at the 20th Anniversary of the National Endowment for Democracy', United States Chamber of Commerce, Washington, DC, 6 November.

Cox, R. (1986), 'Social Forces, States and World Orders: Beyond International Relations Theory', in R. O. Keohane (ed.), *NeoRealism and its Critics* (New York: Columbia University Press).

Dershowitz, A. (2006), 'Debunking the Newest—and Oldest—Jewish Conspiracy: A Reply to the Mearsheimer–Walt "Working Paper"', online at www.ksg.harvard.edu/research/working_papers/facultyresponses.htm.

Dodge, T. (2005), *Inventing Iraq: The Failure of Nation Building and a History Denied* (New York: Columbia University Press).

——(2006), 'Iraq: The Contradictions of Exogenous State Building in Historical Perspective', *Third World Quarterly*, 27/1: 187–200.

——(2007), 'The Causes of US Failure in Iraq', *Survival*, 49/1: 85–106.

Gaddis, J. L. (1987), *The Long Peace: Inquiries into the History of the Cold War* (Oxford: Oxford University Press).

——(2002), 'A Grand Strategy of Transformation', *Foreign Policy*, November–December, online at www.foreignpolicy.com/issue_novdec_2002/gaddis.html.

Gates, R. (2011), 'Speech at United States Military Academy, West Point, New York', 25 February, online at http://www.defense.gov/speeches/speech.aspx?speechid=1539.

Halliday, F. (1994), *Rethinking International Relations* (Basingstoke: Macmillan).

——(2005), *The Middle East in International Relations; power, politics and ideology,* (Cambridge: Cambridge University Press).

Harvey, D. (2003), *The New Imperialism* (Oxford: Oxford University Press).

Hudson, M. (2005), 'The United States and the Middle East', in L. Fawcett (ed.), *International Relations of the Middle East* (Oxford: Oxford University Press), 283–305.

Ignatius, D. (2009), 'Testing Obama's Doctrine; Lofty Ideals and Afghan Reality', *Washington Post*, 8 October, online at http://www.washingtonpost.com/wp-dyn/content/article/2009/10/07/AR2009100703044_pf.html.

Khalidi, R. (2004), *Resurrecting Empire: Western Footprints and America's Perilous Path in the Middle East* (London: I. B. Tauris).

Little, D. (2002), *American Orientalism: The United States and the Middle East since 1945* (London: I. B. Tauris).

Lizza, R. (2011), The Consequentialist: How the Arab Spring remade Obama's foreign policy', *The New Yorker*, 2 May, online at http://www.newyorker.com/reporting/2011/05/02/110502fa_fact_lizza?printable=true#ixzz1KWzFQym6

Lynch, M. (2011), 'America and Egypt after the uprisings', *Survival*, 35(2), April–May.

Mamdani, M. (2004), *Good Muslim, Bad Muslim: America, the Roots of the Cold War and the Roots of Terror* (New York: Three Leaves Press).

Massing, M. (2006), 'The Storm over the Israel Lobby', *New York Review of Books*, 53/10: 1–5.

Mearsheimer, J. (2005), 'Hans Morgenthau and the Iraq War: Realism versus Neo-conservatism', online at www.opendemocracy.net/debates/article.jsp?id=3&debateId=77&articleId=2522.

——and Walt, S. (2006), 'The Israeli Lobby', *London Review of Books*, 28/6, 23 March, online at www.lrb.co.uk/v28/n06/mear01_.html.

——and Walt, S. (2007), *The Israel Lobby and US Foreign Policy* (New York: Farrar, Straus and Giroux).

Morgenthau, H. J. (1985), *Politics among Nations: The Struggle for Power and Peace* (New York: Alfred A. Knopf).

Obama, B. (2009a), 'Remarks on a new beginning', Cairo University, Cairo, 4 June, online at http://www.whitehouse.gov/the-press-office/remarks-president-cairo-university-6-04-09.

——(2009b), 'Remarks by the President to the United Nations General Assembly', United Nations Headquarters, New York, 23 September, online at http://www.whitehouse.gov/the-press-office/remarks-president-united-nations-general-assembly.

——(2009c), 'Remarks by the President at the Acceptance of the Nobel Peace Prize', Oslo City Hall, Oslo, Norway, 10 December, online at http://www.whitehouse.gov/the-press-office/remarks-president-acceptance-nobel-peace-prize.

——(2011a), 'Remarks by the President on the situation in Egypt', The White House, Washington DC, 1 February, online at http://www.whitehouse.gov/the-press-office/2011/02/01/remarks-president-situation-egypt.

——(2011b), 'Remarks by the President in Address to the Nation on Libya', National Defense University, Washington, DC, 28 March, online at http://www.whitehouse.gov/the-press-office/2011/03/28/remarks-president-address-nation-libya.

Packer, G. (2005), *Assassins' Gate: America in Iraq* (New York: Farrar, Straus and Giroux).

Ruggie, J. G. (1998), *Constructing the World Polity: Essays on International Institutionalization* (London: Routledge).

Shlaim, A. (1995), *War and Peace in the Middle East: A Concise History* (Harmondsworth: Penguin).

Wendt, A. (1999), *Social Theory of International Politics* (Cambridge: Cambridge University Press).

Westad, O. A. (2005), *The Global Cold War: Third World Interventions and the Making of our Times* (Cambridge: Cambridge University Press).

Wilson, W. (1918), 'Fourteen Point Speech', 8 January, online at http://net.lib.byu.edu/~rdh7/wwi/1918/14points.html.

Chapter 13

Albright, M. K. (1998), Statement to the North Atlantic Council, Brussels, 8 December.

Allen, D. and Smith, M. (1983), 'Europe, the United States and the Middle East: A Case Study in Comparative Policy-Making', *Journal of Common Market Studies*, 22/2 (December): 125–46.

——and Smith, M. (1989), 'Western Europe in the Atlantic System of the 1980s: Towards a New Identity?', in S. Gill (ed.), *Atlantic Relations: Beyond the Reagan Era* (Brighton: Harvester/Wheatsheaf).

Andrews, D. (ed.) (2005), *The Atlantic Alliance under Stress: US–European Relations after Iraq* (Cambridge: Cambridge University Press).

Baker, J. A., III (1989), Address to the Berlin Press Club, 12 December.

Bush, G. W. (2005), Speech in Concert Noble, Brussels, 21 February.

Calleo, D. (1970), *The Atlantic Fantasy: The US, NATO and Europe* (Baltimore: Johns Hopkins University Press).

——(1987), *Beyond American Hegemony: The Future of the Western Alliance* (New York: Basic Books).

Cleveland, H. van B. (1966), *The Atlantic Idea and its European Rivals* (New York: McGraw-Hill for the Council on Foreign Relations).

Cooper, R. (1968), *The Economics of Interdependence: Economic Policy in the Atlantic Community* (New York: McGraw-Hill for the Council on Foreign Relations).

Cromwell, W. (1978), 'Europe and the "Structure of Peace"', *Orbis*, 22/1: 11–36.

DePorte, A. (1986), *Europe between the Superpowers: The Enduring Balance*, 2nd edn (New Haven: Yale University Press).

de Vasconcelos, A. and Zaborowski, M. (eds) (2009), *The Obama Moment: European and American Perspectives* (Paris: European Union Institute for Security Studies).

Duke, S. (2009) 'Providing for European-Level Diplomacy after Lisbon: The Case of the European External Action Service', *The Hague Journal of Diplomacy*, 4/2, 211–33.

Eagleburger, L. (1984), Speech to the National Newspaper Association, Washington, DC, 7 March.

Fursdon, E. (1980), *The European Defence Community: A History* (London: Macmillan).

Gompert, D. and Larrabee, S. (1997), *America and Europe: A Partnership for a New Era* (Cambridge: Cambridge University Press).

Gordon, P. (2010) 'The United States and Europe: An Agenda for Engagement'. Remarks at the Center for Transatlantic Relations, Paul H. Nitze School of Advanced International Studies, Johns Hopkins University, Washington DC, 18 October.

Gordon, P. and Shapiro, J. (2004), *Allies at War: America, Europe, and the Crisis over Iraq* (New York: McGraw-Hill).

Grosser, A. (1982), *The Western Alliance: European–American Relations since 1945* (New York: Vintage Books).

Heller, F. and Gillingham, J. (eds) (1996), *The United States and the Integration of Europe: Legacies of the Postwar Era* (New York: St Martin's Press).

Hocking, B. and Smith, M. (1997), *Beyond Foreign Economic Policy: The United States, the Single European Market and the Changing World Economy* (London: Pinter/Cassell).

Hoffmann, S. (1978), *Primacy or World Order: American Foreign Policy since the Cold War* (New York: McGraw-Hill).

Hogan, M. (1987), *The Marshall Plan: America, Britain, and the Reconstruction of Western Europe, 1947–1952* (Cambridge: Cambridge University Press).

Howorth, J. (2000), *European Integration and Defence: The Ultimate Challenge?* (Paris: WEU Institute for Security Studies).

——(2005), 'From Security to Defence: The Evolution of the CFSP', in C. Hill and M. Smith (eds), *International Relations and the European Union* (Oxford: Oxford University Press).

——(2007) *Security and Defence Policy in the European Union* (Basingstoke: Palgrave/Macmillan).

Joffe, J. (1987), *The Limited Partnership: Europe, the United States, and the Burdens of Alliance* (Cambridge, MA: Ballinger).

Joint Study (2010) *The Lisbon Treaty: A Second Look at the Institutional Innovations* (Brussels: Centre for European Policy Studies/Egmont Institute/European Policy Centre).

Kagan, R. (2003), *Of Paradise and Power: America and Europe in the New World Order* (New York: Knopf).

Krause, L. (1968), *European Economic Integration and the United States* (Washington, DC: Brookings Institution).

Lindberg, T. (ed.) (2005), *Beyond Paradise and Power: Europe, America and the Future of a Troubled Partnership* (London: Routledge).

Lindstrom, G. (ed.) (2003), *Shift or Rift? Assessing EU–US Relations after Iraq* (Paris: EU Institute for Security Studies).

Lundestad, G. (1998), *'Empire' by Integration: The United States and European Integration, 1945–1997* (Oxford: Oxford University Press).

McGuire, S. and Smith, M. (2008), *The European Union and the United States: Competition and Convergence in the World Arena* (Basingstoke: Palgrave/Macmillan).

Marshall, G. C. (1947), Address at the Commencement Exercises of Harvard University, Cambridge, MA, 5 June.

Milward, A. (1984), *The Reconstruction of Western Europe, 1945–1951* (London: Methuen).

Peterson, J. (1996), *Europe and America in the 1990s: Prospects for Partnership*, 2nd edn (London: Routledge).

——and Pollack, M. (eds) (2003), *Europe, America, Bush: Transatlantic Relations in the Twenty-First Century* (London: Routledge).

Philippart, E. and Winand, P. (eds) (2001), *Ever-Closer Partnership: Policy-Making in US–EU Relations* (Brussels: PIE/Peter Lang).

Pollack, M. (2003), 'Unilateral America: Multilateral Europe?', in M. Pollack and J. Peterson (eds), *Europe, America, Bush: Transatlantic Relations in the Twenty-First Century* (London: Routledge).

——and Shaffer, G. (eds) (2001), *Transatlantic Governance in the Global Economy* (Lanham, MD: Rowman and Littlefield).

Rees, G. W. (2006), *Transatlantic Counter-Terrorism Cooperation: The New Imperative* (London: Routledge).

Rosecrance, R. (ed.) (1976), *America as an Ordinary Country: US Foreign Policy and the Future* (Ithaca, NY: Cornell University Press).

Rumsfeld, D. H. (2003), Briefing at the Foreign Press Center, Washington, DC, 22 January.

Sloan, S. (2005), *NATO, the European Union, and the Atlantic Community: The Transatlantic Bargain Challenged*, 2nd edn (Lanham, MD: Rowman and Littlefield).

Smith, M. (2000), 'The United States and Western Europe: Empire, Alliance and Interdependence', in A. McGrew (ed.), *The United States in the Twentieth Century: Empire* (London: Hodder and Stoughton).

——(2004), 'Between Two Worlds? The European Union, the United States and World Order', *International Politics*, 41/1: 96–117.

——(2007), 'The European Union and International Order: European and Global Dimensions', *European Foreign Affairs Review*, 12/4: 437–56.

——(2011), 'European Responses to US Diplomacy: 'Special Relationships' Transatlantic Governance and World Order', *The Hague Journal of Diplomacy*, forthcoming.

——and Woolcock, S. (1993), *The United States and the European Community in a Transformed World* (London: Pinter for the Royal Institute of International Affairs).

——and Woolcock, S. (1994), 'Learning to Cooperate: The Clinton Administration and the European Union', *International Affairs*, 70/3: 459–76.

Steffenson, B. (2005), *Managing EU–US Relations: Actors, Institutions and the New Transatlantic Agenda* (Manchester: Manchester University Press).

Treverton, G. (1985), *Making the Alliance Work: The United States and Western Europe* (London: Macmillan).

——(ed.) (1992), *The Shape of the New Europe* (New York: Council on Foreign Relations).

Webber, M. (2007) *Inclusion, Exclusion and the Governance of European Security* (Manchester: Manchester University Press).

Winand, P. (1993), *Eisenhower, Kennedy and the United States of Europe* (London: Macmillan).

Zaborowski, M. (ed.) (2006), *Friends Again? EU–US Relations after the Crisis* (Paris: EU Institute for Security Studies).

Zielonka, J. (2006), *Europe as Empire* (Oxford: Oxford University Press).

Chapter 15

Berger, T. (2000), 'Set for Stability? Prospects for Conflict and Cooperation in East Asia', *Review of International Studies*, 26/3: 405–28.

Buzan, B. (2010) 'China in International Society: Is 'Peaceful Rise' Possible?', *Chinese Journal of International Politics*, 3(1): 5–36.

Calder, K. E. (2006), 'China and Japan's Simmering Rivalry', *Foreign Affairs*, March–April: 129–39.

Carter, J. (2006), 'Solving the Korean Stalemate, One Step at a Time', *New York Times*, 11 October.

Cha, V. D. (2007), 'Winning Asia; Washington's Untold Success Story', *Foreign Affairs*, November–December: 98–113.

Foot, R. and Walter, A. (1999), 'Whatever Happened to the Pacific Century?', *Review of International Studies*, 25/5: 245–69.

Friedberg, A. L. (1993–4), 'Ripe for Rivalry: Prospects for Peace in Multipolar Asia', *International Security*, 18/3: 5–33.

Friedman, T. L. (2005), *The World is Flat: A Brief History of the Globalized World in the Twenty-First Century* (London: Allen Lane).

Konichi, W. S. (2009), *Japan's Historic 2009 Elections: Implications for US Interests* (Washington: Congressional Research Service), September 8.

Mearsheimer, J. (2005), 'Clash of The Titans', *Foreign Policy*, 146, January–February: 46–49.

Zissis, C. (2007), 'Crafting a US Policy on Asia', Council on Foreign Relations Backgrounder, 10 April, online at www.cfr.org/publication/13022/crafting_a_us_policy_on_asia.html#2.

Chapter 16

Bulmer-Thomas, V. and Dunkerley, J. (1999), *The United States and Latin America: The New Agenda* (Cambridge, MA: David Rockefeller Center for Latin American Studies/Institute of Latin American Studies, University of London).

Grandin, G. (2006), *Empire's Workshop: Latin America, the United States, and the Rise of the New Imperialism* (New York: Metropolitan Books).

Huntington, S. (2004), *Who Are We?* (New York: Simon & Schuster).

Kirkpatrick, J. (1979), 'Dictatorships and Double Standards', *Commentary*, 68 (November): 34–45.

LaFeber, W. (1983), *Inevitable Revolutions: The United States in Central America* (New York: W. W. Norton).

Reagan, R. (1983), *Public Papers of the Presidents of the United States: Ronald Reagan* (Washington, DC: US Government Printing Office).

Reid, M. (2007), *Forgotten Continent: The Battle for Latin America's Soul* (New Haven: Yale University Press).

Schoultz, L. (1998), *Beneath the United States: A History of US Policy toward Latin America* (Cambridge, MA: Harvard University Press).

Shifter, M. (2002), 'A Shaken Agenda: Bush and Latin America', *Current History*, February.

Chapter 17

Aljazeera.Net (2006), 'Somalia Unrest Worries Bush', 8 June, online at http://english.Aljazeera.net/English/archive/archive?Achiveld+23427 (accessed 13 April 2007).

AVERT (2011), 'HIV and AIDS in Africa: AVERTing HIV and AIDS', online at http://www.avert.org/hiv-aids-africa.htm.

Bolton, J. R. (1994), 'Wrong Turn in Somalia', *Foreign Affairs,* 73/1: 56–66.

Bush, G. W. (2002), *The National Security of the United States of America*, online at www.whitehouse.gov.nsc.nss.pdf (accessed 16 February 2007).

Cameron, F. (2002), *US Foreign Policy after the Cold War: Global Hegemon or Reluctant Sheriff?* (London: Routledge).

Carmody, P. (2005), 'Transforming Globalization and Security: Africa and America Post-9/11', *Africa Today*, 52/1: 97–120.

Carson, J. (2010a) 'U.S. Priorities of sub-Saharan Africa', Washington, DC, 14 June, online at http://www.state.gov/p/af/rls/rm/2010/143144.htm (accessed 10 December 2010).

——(2010b) 'U.S.–Africa Policy Under the Obama Administration' Harvard University Africa Focus Program, 5 April, online at http://www.state.gov/p/af/rls/rm/2010/139462.htm (accessed 8 December 2010).

Cheru, F. (2006), 'Aid and Trade Policies: Shifting the Debate', in D. Rothchild and E. J. Keller (eds), *Africa–US Relations: Strategic Encounters* (Boulder, Colo.: Lynne Rienner Publishers), 217–44.

Christian Science Monitor (2011), 'Sudan after the referendum: a test case for Africa', February 9, online at http://www.csmonitor.com/Commentary/the-monitors-view/2011/0209/Sudan-after-the-referendum-a-test-case-for-Africa (accessed 10 February 2011).

Clinton, H. (2009), 'What I Saw in Goma' people.com, 21 August, online at http://www.state.gov/secretary/rm/2009a/08/128317.htm (accessed 8 December 2010).

CNN.com (2002), 'Study Explores High Cost of HIV/AIDS Care in US', 10 July, online at http://archives.cnn.com/2002/HEALTH/conditions/07/10/aids.costs/(accessed 27 July 2007).

Copson, R. (2004), 'Africa: US Foreign Assistance Issues', *CRS Issue Brief for Congress*, 9 December.

Dagne, T. S. (1991), 'Ethiopia: New Thinking in US Policy', *CRS Report for Congress*, 91–489F.

Dowden, R. (2009) 'Obama's direct line to the heart of Africa' *The Times*, 10 July, online at http://www.timesonline.co.uk/tol/comment/columnists/guest_contributors/article6676860.ece (accessed 14 January 2011).

Howe, H. M. (2001), *Ambiguous Order* (Boulder, CO: Lynne Rienner).

International Commission on Intervention and State Sovereignty (2001), *The Responsibility to Protect* (Ottawa: International Development Research Centre), online at www.iciss.ca/pdf/Commission-Report.pdf (accessed 27 July 2007).

Johnston, H. and Dagne, T. (1997), 'Congress and the Somalia Crisis', in Walter Clarke and Jeffrey Herbst (eds), *Learning from Somalia: The Lessons of Armed Humanitarian Intervention* (Boulder, CO: Westview).

Keller, E. J. (2006), 'Africa and the United States: Meeting the Challenges of Globalization', in D. Rothchild and E. J. Keller (eds), *Africa–US Relations: Strategic Encounters* (Boulder, CO: Lynne Rienner Publishers).

Lawson, L. (2007), 'US Africa Policy since the Cold War', *Strategic Insights*, 6/1, online at http://www.ccc.nps.navy.mil/si/2007/Jan/lawsonJan07.pdf (accessed 22 March 2007).

Malan, M. (1999), 'Leaner and Meaner? The Future of Peacekeeping in Africa', *African Security Review*, 8/4, online at www.iss.co.za/pubs/ASR/8No4/Malan.html (accessed 1 June 2007).

——(2002), 'The Post 9/11 Security Agenda and Peacekeeping in Africa', *African Security Review*, 11/3, online at www.iss.co.za/pubs/ASR/11No3/Malan.html (accessed 1 June 2007).

Millennium Challenge Account (2010), US Aid to Africa, online at http://www.gov/pages/about (accessed 8 December 2010).

Obama, B. (2009) 'Remarks by the President to the Ghanaian Parliament', Accra, 11 July, online at http://www.america.gov/st/texttrans-english/2009/July/20090711110050abretnuh0.1079783.html (accessed 2 December 2010).

Office of the US Global AIDS Coordinator (2007), *The United States President's Emergency Plan for AIDS Relief*, online at www.pepfar.gov/press/87565.htm#ogac (accessed 6 July 2007).

Pace, J. (2011) 'Obama to Increase Engagement With Africa in 2011' CNSNEWS.COM, 3 January, online at http://www.cnsnews.com/news/article/obama-increase-engagement-africa-2011 (accessed 15 January 2011).

Patman, R. G. (1990), *The Soviet Union in the Horn of Africa: The Diplomacy of Intervention and Disengagement* (Cambridge: Cambridge University Press).

——(2001), 'Beyond "the Mogadishu Line": Some Australian Lessons for Managing Intra-State Conflicts', *Small Wars & Insurgencies*, 12/1: 59–75.

——(2007), 'Somalis Test Bush's Anti-Terror Strategy', *Dominion Post*, 22 June.

Reuters (2011), 'US to move its Sudan envoy to new diplomatic post', February 10, online at http://af.reuters.com/article/topNews/idAFJOE71A03P20110211 (accessed 11 February 2011).

Rice, X. (2009) 'Hillary Clinton kicks off seven-nation African tour in Kenya', guardian.co.uk, 5 August, online at http://www.guardian.co.uk/world/2009/aug/05/hillary-clinton-kenya-africa/print (accessed 21 January 2011).

Rothchild, D. (2006), 'Trends in US–Africa Relations: Implications for the Future', in D. Rothchild and E. J. Keller (eds), *Africa–US Relations: Strategic Encounters* (Boulder, CO: Lynne Rienner Publishers).

Saunders, P. C. (2006), 'China's Global Activism: Strategy, Drivers, and Tools', *Institute for National Strategic Studies*, Occasional Paper 4: 38–54.

Schabas, W. (1999), 'The Genocide Convention at Fifty', Special Report, United States Institute of Peace.

Schraeder, P. J. (1993), 'Reviewing the Study of US Policy towards Africa from Intellectual 'Backwater' to Theory Construction', *Third World Quarterly*, 14/4: 775–86.

——(1994), *United States Foreign Policy toward Africa: Incrementalism, Crisis and Change* (Cambridge: Cambridge University Press).

Sloan, S. R. (1991), 'The US Role in a New World Order: Prospects for George Bush's Global Vision', *CRS Report for Congress*, 91–294 RCO.

The White House (2002), 'President Proposes $5 Billion Plan to Help Developing Nations', White House News Release, online at www.whitehouse.gov/news/release/2002/03/20020314-7.html.

The White House (2010), National Security Strategy, pp. 8-13, online at http://www.whitehouse.gov/sites/default/files/rss_viewer/national_security_strategy.pdf (accessed 17 November 2010).

UNAIDS (2006), *2006 Report on the Global AIDS Pandemic*, online at www.unaids.org/en/HIV_data/2006GlobalReport/default.asp (accessed 27 July 2007).

United Nations Security Council Resolution 794, 3 December 1992.

US Census Bureau (2011), *Foreign Trade Statistics, U.S. Trade Balance with Africa*, online at http://www.census.gov/foreign-trade/balance/c0013.html (accessed 14 February 2011)

Chapter 18

Bairoch, P. (1993), *Economics and World History: Myths and Paradoxes* (New York: Harvester Wheatsheaf).

Baldwin, D. A. (1985), *Economic Statecraft* (Princeton: Princeton University Press).

Bhagwati, J. N. (2001), *Wind of the Hundred Days: How Washington Mismanaged Globalization* (Cambridge, MA: MIT Press).

——and Patrick, H. T. (eds) (1990), *Aggressive Unilateralism: America's 301 Trade Policy and the World Trading System* (Ann Arbor: University of Michigan Press).

Bichler, S., Rowley, R., and Nitzan, J. (1989), 'The Armadollar–Petrodollar Coalition: Demise or New Order?', Working Paper 11/89 (Montreal: Department of Economics, McGill University), 1–63.

Bobbitt, P. (2002), *The Shield of Achilles: War, Peace and the Course of History* (New York: Knopf).

Cox, R. (1996), 'Gramsci, Hegemony and International Relations: An Essay in Method', in R. Cox with T. J. Sinclair (eds), *Approaches to World Order* (Cambridge: Cambridge University Press).

——and Skidmore-Hess, D. (1999), *US Politics and the Global Economy: Corporate Power, Conservative Shift* (Boulder, CO: Lynne Rienner).

Giles, C. (2006), 'A Productivity Prescription: How the US has Pulled Away from Europe and Japan', *Financial Times*, 25 January: 19.

Goldstein, J. (1988), 'Ideas, Institutions and American Trade Policy', *International Organisation*, 42/1 (Winter): 178–218.

Hathaway, R. (1984), '1933–1945: Economic Diplomacy in a Time of Crisis', in W. H. Becker and S. Wells, Jr. (eds), *Economics and World Power: An Assessment of American Diplomacy since 1789* (New York: Columbia University Press).

Hogan, M. (2004), 'The "Next Big Thing": The Future of Diplomatic History in a Global Age', *Diplomatic History*, 28/1 (January): 1–21.

Huntington, S. P. (1973), 'Transnational Organisations in World Politics', *World Politics*, 25/3: 333–68.

Kolko, G. (1976), *Main Currents in Modern American History* (New York: Harper and Row).

Lawrence, R. Z. and Schultze, C. L. (eds) (1990), *An American Trade Strategy: Options for the 1990s* (Washington, DC: Brookings Institution).

Low, P. (1993), *Trading Free: The GATT and US Trade Policy* (New York: The 20th Century Fund Press).

McGuckin, R. H., III and Van Ark, B. (2005), *Performance 2005: Productivity, Employment and Income in the World's Economies, Report R-1364-05 RR, May* (New York: The Conference Board).

Meunier, S. (2005), *Trading Voices: The European Union in International Commercial Negotiations* (Princeton: Princeton University Press).

Negri, A. and Hardt, M. (2000), *Empire* (Cambridge, MA: Harvard University Press).

Nitze, P. H. (1959), 'Coalition Policy and the Concept of World Order', in A. Wolfers, *Alliance Policy in the Cold War* (Baltimore: Johns Hopkins University Press).

Odell, J. S. (2000), *Negotiating the World Economy* (Ithaca, NY: Cornell University Press).

Pastor, R. A. (1980), *Congress and the Politics of US Foreign Economic Policy* (Berkeley and Los Angeles: University of California Press).

Rothkopf, D. J. (1998), 'Beyond Manic Mercantilism' in J. Shinn (ed), *US Commercial Diplomacy* (New York: Council on Foreign Relations).

Schumpeter, J. A. (1934), *The Theory of Economic Development* (New York: Knopf).

Sheikh, A. and Tomak, E. A. (1994), *Measuring the Wealth of Nations: The Political Economy of National Accounts* (Cambridge: Cambridge University Press).

Skarstein, R. (2005), 'Economic Development by Means of Free Trade?', in G. Chaloupek, A. Heisse, G. Matzner-Holzer, and W. Roth (eds), *Sisyphus als Optimist* (Hamburg: VSA Verlag).

Spiro, D. E. (1999), *The Hidden Hand of American Hegemony: Petrodollar Recycling and International Markets* (Ithaca, NY: Cornell University Press).

Verdier, D. (1994), *Democracy and International Trade* (Princeton: Princeton University Press).

Wade, R. and Veneroso, F. (1998), 'The Asian Crisis: The High Debt Model Versus the Wall Street–Treasury–IMF Complex', *New Left Review*, 1/228 (March–April): 3–22.

Williams, W. A. (1970), *The Roots of the Modern American Empire* (London: Anthony Blond).

——(1972), *The Tragedy of American Diplomacy* (New York: Dell Publishing).

Williamson, J. and Milner, C. (1991), *The World Economy* (New York: Harvester Wheatsheaf).

Wolf, M. (2004), *Why Globalisation Works* (New Haven: Yale University Press).

Wright-Mills, C. (1959), *The Power Elite* (Oxford: Oxford University Press).

Chapter 19

Anderson, S. K. and Sloan, S. (2002), *Historical Dictionary of Terrorism* (Latham and London: The Scarecrow Press).

Bello, W. (2001), *Endless War?* Manila: Focus on the Global South, online at www.focusweb.org/publications/2001/endless_war.html.

Bush, G. W. (2002), *State of the Union Address* (Washington, DC: US Government Printing Office).

George, A. L. (ed.) (1991), *Western State Terrorism* (Cambridge: Polity).

National Advisory Committee on Criminal Justice Standards and Goals (1976), *Report of the Task Force on Disorders and Terrorism* (Washington, DC: US Government Printing Office).

Wardlaw, G. (1982), *Political Terrorism: Theory, Tactics and Countermeasures* (Cambridge, MA: Cambridge University Press).

Chapter 20

Bang, G., Bretteville Froyn, C., Hovi, J., and Menz, F. C. (2007), 'The United States and International Climate Cooperation: International "Pull" versus Domestic "Push"' *Energy Policy*, 35/2: 1282–91.

Barkdull, J. and Harris, P. (2002), 'Environmental Change and Foreign Policy: A Survey of Theory', *Global Environmental Politics*, 2/2: 63–91.

Barnett, J. (2001), 'Environmental Security and US Foreign Policy: A Critical Examination', in P. G. Harris, *The Environment, International Relations, and US Foreign Policy* (Washington, DC: Georgetown University Press).

Benedick, R. (1991), *Ozone Diplomacy: New Directions in Safeguarding the Planet* (Cambridge, MA: Harvard University Press).

Boal, I., Clark, T. J., Matthews, J., and Watts, M. (2005), 'Blood for Oil?', *London Review of Books*, 27/8 (21 Apr.), review, online at http://bnarchives.yorku.ca/168/02/050421_Boal_et_al_Blood_for_oil_(print).htm.

Boykoff, M. and Boykoff, J. M. (2004), 'Balance as Bias: Global Warming and the US Prestige Press', *Global Environmental Change*, 14: 125–36.

Bromley, S. (1991), *American Hegemony and World Oil* (Cambridge: Cambridge University Press).

——(2005), 'The United States and the Control of World Oil', *Government and Opposition*, 40/2: 225–55.

Brown, L. (1991), *State of the World 1991* (Washington, DC: WRI).

Busby, J. (2008), 'Who Cares About the Weather?: Climate Change and US National Security', *Security Studies*, 17/3: 468–504.

Bush, G. (2006), 'State of the Union Address' (The White House), online at www.whitehouse.gov/stateoftheunion/2006/(accessed 19 April 2007).

——(2007), 'State of the Union Address' (The White House). online at www.whitehouse.gov/stateoftheunion/2007/index. html (accessed 19 April 2007).

Carter, J. (1979), 'The Crisis of Confidence Speech', PBS American Experience, online at www.pbs.org/wgbh/amex/carter/filmmore/ps_crisis.html.

Christoff, P. (1996), 'Ecological Modernisation, Ecological Modernities', *Environmental Politics*, 5/3: 476–500.

——and Eckersley, R. (2007),'Kyoto and the Asia Pacific Partnership on Clean Development and Climate' in T. Bonyhady and P. Christoff (eds) *Climate Law in Australia* (Sydney: Federation Press), 32–45.

Christopher, W. (1998), *In the Stream of History: Shaping Foreign Policy for a New Era* (Stanford, CA: Stanford University Press).

CNA Corporation (2007), *National Security and the Threat of Climate Change* (Alexandria, VA: CNA Corporation).

CNA Corporation (2009), *Powering America's Defense: Energy and the Risks to National Security* (Alexandria, VA: CNA Corporation).

Council on Environmental Quality and Department of State (1980), *The Global 2000 Report to President of the US: Entering the 21st Century the US President* (New York: Pergamon Press).

Depledge, J. (2005), 'Against the Grain: The United States and the Global Climate Change Regime', *Global Change, Peace and Security*, 17/1: 11–27.

DeSombre, E. (2000), *The Domestic Sources of International Environmental Policy: Industry, Environmentalists and US Power* (Cambridge, MA: MIT Press).

——(2005), 'Understanding United States Unilateralism: Domestic Sources of US International Environmental Policy', in R. Axelrod, D. Downie, and N. Vig (eds), *The Global Environment: Institutions, Law and Policy* (Washington, DC: Congressional Quarterly Press).

Dryzek, J., Downes, D., Hunold, C., and Schlosberg, D. (2003), *Green States and Social Movements: Environmentalism in the United States, United Kingdom, Germany and Norway* (Oxford: Oxford University Press).

Eckersley, R. (2004), *The Green State: Rethinking Democracy and Sovereignty* (Cambridge, MA: MIT Press).

Falkner, R. (2001), 'Business Conflict and US International Environmental Policy: Ozone, Climate and Biodiversity', in P. G. Harris, *The Environment, International Relations, and US Foreign Policy* (Washington, DC: Georgetown University Press).

——(2005), 'American Hegemony and the Global Environment', *International Studies Review*, 7: 585–99.

——(2007), 'International Cooperation against the Hegemon: The Cartagena Protocol on Biosafety', in R. Falkner (ed.), *The International Politics of Genetically Modified Food* (London: Palgrave).

Fisher, D. R. (2006), 'Bringing the Material Back in: Understanding the US Position on Climate Change', *Sociological Forum*, 21/3: 467–94.

Friedman, T. (2007), 'The Power of Green', New York Times Magazine, 15 April, online at www.nytimes.com/2007/04/15/magazine/15green.t.html?ex=1334289600&;en=77253fdf8f321a95&ei=5088&partner=rssnyt&emc=rss.

Goel, R. (2004), 'A Bargain Born of Paradox: The Oil Industry's Role in American Domestic and Foreign Policy', *New Political Economy*, 9/4: 467–91.

Hartmann, T. (2003), 'Creating a World in Balance, Instead of an Empire of Oil', *Garlic and Grass: A Grassroots Journal of America's Political Soul*, 4 (June), online at www.garlicandgrass.org/index04.cfm (accessed 4 April 2007).

Hopgood, S. (1998), *American Environmental Foreign Policy and the Power of the State* (New York: Oxford University Press).

Intergovernmental Panel on Climate Change (2007), *Climate Change 2007: Impacts. Adaptation and Vulnerability: Summary for Policy Makers* (Geneva: IPCC Secretariat), www.ipcc.ch/SPM13apr07.pdf (accessed 19 April 2007).

Johnson, B. (2010), The Climate Zombie Caucus of the 112th Congress. *ThinkProgress Wonk Room Climate Editor*, Updated 23 November 2010 with elections of Ann Buerkle and Blake Fahrenthold, online at http://wonkroom.thinkprogress.org/climate-zombie-caucus/.

Keohane, R. (1984), *After Hegemony* (Princeton: Princeton University Press).

Klare, M. (2004), *Blood and Oil: The Dangers and Consequences of America's Growing Petroleum Dependency* (New York: Metropolitan Books).

Kolk, A. and Levy, D. (2001), 'Winds of Change: Corporate Strategy, Climate Change and Oil Multinationals', *European Management Journal*, 19/5: 501–9.

Levidow, L. (2007), 'The Transatlantic Agbiotech Conflict as a Problem and Opportunity for EU Regulatory Policies', in R. Falkner (ed.), *The International Politics of Genetically Modified Food* (London: Palgrave).

Lisowski, M. (2002), 'Playing the Two-Level Game: US President Bush's Decision to Repudiate the Kyoto Protocol', *Environmental Politics*, 11/4: 101–19.

Long, C., Cabral, M., and Vandivort, B. (1999), 'The Chief Environmental Diplomat: An Evolving Arena of Foreign Policy', in D. Soden (ed.), *The Environmental Presidency* (Albany, NY: State University of New York Press).

McCarthy, J. E. and Parker, L. (2010), 'EPA Regulation of Greenhouse Gases: Congressional Responses and Options', CRS Report for Congress (Washington, DC: Congressional Research Service).

McCright, A. M. and Dunlap, R. (2003), 'Defeating Kyoto: The Conservative Movement's Impact on US Climate Change Policy', *Social Problems*, 50/3: 348–73.

McGee, J. and Taplin, R. (2006), 'The Asia-Pacific Partnership on Clean Development and Climate: A Complement or Competitor to the Kyoto Protocol?', *Global Change, Peace and Security*, 18/3: 173–92.

MEF (2009), Major Economies Forum on Energy and Climate, online at http://www.majoreconomiesforum.org/.

Nelson, G. (2010), 'Report: All States but Texas on Track to Issue Greenhouse Gas Permits', Greenwire, 28 October, online at http://www.nytimes.com/gwire/2010/10/28/28greenwire-report-all-states-but-texas-on-track-to-issue-94346.html.

Newell, P. and Paterson, M. (1998), 'A Climate for Business: Global Warming, the State and Capital', *Review of International Political Economy*, 5/4: 679–703.

Obama, B. (2009), 'Obama in Copenhagen Speech: Full Text', *Huffington Post* (posted 18 December 2009), online at http://www.huffingtonpost.com/2009/12/18/obama-in-copenhagen-speec_n_396836.html.

Oberthur, S. and Ott, H. (1999), *The Kyoto Protocol: International Climate Policy for the 21st Century* (Berlin: Springer-Verlag).

Paarlberg, R. (1999), 'Lapsed Leadership: US International Environmental Policy since Rio', in N. Vig and R. Axelrod (eds), *The Global Environment: Institutions, Law and Policy* (Washington, DC: Congressional Quarterly).

Paterson, M. (2009), 'Post-hegemonic Climate Change?', *British Journal of Politics and International Relations*, 11/1: 140–158.

Schellenberger, M. and Nordhaus, T. (2004), *The Death of Environmentalism: Global Warming Politics in a Post-Environmental World*, online at www.thebreakthrough.org/images/Death_of_Environmentalism.pdf (accessed 19 April 2007).

Sitaraman, S. (2001), 'The Evolution of the Ozone Regime: Local, National, and International Influences', in P. G. Harris, *The Environment, International Relations, and US Foreign Policy* (Washington, DC: Georgetown University Press).

Smith, S. (1993), 'The Environment on the Periphery of International Relations', *Environmental Politics*, 2/4: 28–45.

Soden, D. and Steel, B. (1999), 'Evaluating the Environmental Presidency', in D. Soden (ed.), *The Environmental Presidency* (Albany, NY: State University of New York Press).

Sprinz, D. and Vaahtoranta, T. (1994), 'The Interest-Based Explanation of International Environmental Policy', *International Organization*, 48/1: 77–105.

Stern, N. (2007), *The Economics of Climate Change: The Stern Review* (Cambridge: Cambridge University Press).

Sunstein, C. (2007), 'On the Divergent American Reactions to Terrorism and Climate Change', *Columbia Law Review*, 107: 503–58.

Supreme Court of the United States, *Massachusetts et al. v. Environmental Protection Agency et al.* 548 US (2007); No. 5 1120, decided 2 April 2007, online at www.supremecourtus.gov/opinions/06pdf/05-1120.pdf.

The White House (1996), *National Security Strategy of Engagement and Enlargement*, February (Washington, DC: White House), online at www.dtic.mil/doctrine/jel/research_pubs/nss.pdf (accessed 19 April 2007).

——(2002), *Global Climate Change Policy Book* (Washington, DC), online at http://whitehouse.gov/news/releases/2002/02/climatechange.html (accessed 19 April 2007).

——(2006), *A Realistic, Growth-Oriented Approach to Global Climate Change: A Synopsis*, online at http://whitehouse.gov/infocus/environment/index-cont.html (accessed 19 April 2007).

——(2011), *Blueprint for a Secure Energy Future* (Washington, DC: The White House), March 30, online at www.whitehouse.gov/sites/default/files/blueprint_secure_energy_future.pdf.

United Nations Environment Program (2005a), *Register of International Treaties and Other Agreements in the Field of the Environment*, online at www.unep.org/law/PDF/register_Int_treaties_contents.pdf (accessed 24 August 2007).

——(2005b), *Millennium Ecosystem Assessment Synthesis Reports* (UNEP), online at www.maweb.org/en/Synthesis.aspx (accessed 19 April 2007).

Vig, N. (2006), 'Presidential Leadership and the Environment', in N. Vig and M. Kraft (eds), *Environmental Policy: New Directions for the Twenty-First Century* (Washington, DC: Congressional Quarterly).

World Commission on Environment and Development (1987), *Our Common Future: The Report of the World Commission on Environment and Development* (Oxford: Oxford University Press).

Chapter 21

Albright, M. (2004), *Madame Secretary: A Memoir* (London: Pan).

Allen, P. (2008), 'The Obama Niebuhr connection', *The Star*, 14 June, online at http://www.thestar.com/News/USElection/article/443383 (accessed 4 January 2012).

Burleigh, M. (2004), *Earthly Powers* (New York: HarperCollins).

——(2006), *Sacred Causes* (New York: HarperCollins).

Chan, S. (2004), *Out of Evil* (London: Hurst).

Chomsky, N. (2003), *Hegemony or Survival: America's Quest for Global Dominance* (London: Penguin).

Fawn, R. and Buckley, M. (eds) (2003), *Global Responses to Terrorism: 9/11, Afghanistan and beyond* (London: Routledge).

Gaddis, J. L. (2002), *The Landscape of History: How Historians Map the Past* (Oxford: Oxford University Press).

——(2004), *Surprise, Security and the American Experience* (New Haven: Yale University Press).

Gray, C. S. (2005), *Another Bloody Century: Future Warfare* (London: Weidenfeld & Nicolson).

Halbestam, D. (2003), *War in a Time of Peace* (London: Bloomsbury).

Hansen, V. D. (2002), *An Autumn of War* (New York: Anchor Books).

Holbrooke, R. (1999), *To End a War* (New York: Modern Library).

Huntington, S. P. (2002), *The Clash of Civilizations and the Remaking of World Order* (New York: Free Press).

Isacson, W. (1996), *Kissinger* (New York: Touchstone).

Johnson, C. (2002), *Blowback* (New York: Time Warner).

Kagan, R. (2003), *Paradise & Power: America and Europe in the New World Order* (New York: Knopf).

Kennedy-Pipe, C. and Rengger, N. (2006), 'Apocalypse Now? Continuities and Disjunctions in World Politics after 9/11', *International Affairs*, 82/3: 539–53.

Keohane, R. and Nye, J. (2000), *Power and Interdependence*, 3rd edn. revised and expanded, World Politics in Transition (Boston: Little, Brown).

Keppel, G. (2005), *The Roots of Radical Islam* (Paris: Saqi Books).

Kissinger, H. (1982), *Years of Upheaval* (Boston: Little, Brown).

——(1994), *Diplomacy* (New York: Simon & Schuster).

Mann, J. (2004), *The Rise of the Vulcans* (London: Penguin).

Nye, J. S., Jr. (1992), 'What New World Order', *Foreign Affairs*, Spring: 83–96.

Rashid, A. (2001), *Taliban* (New Haven: Yale University Press).

Rice, C. (2000), 'Campaign 2000: Promoting the National Interest in Foreign Affairs', January–February, 79/1, online at www.foreignaffairs.

Stelzer, I. (2005), *NeoConservatism* (London: Atlantic Books).

Thomas, S. (2005), *The Global Resurgence of Religion and the Transformation of International Relations* (London: Palgrave).

Woodward, B. (2004), *Plan of Attack* (New York: Simon & Schuster).

Wright, L. (2006), *The Looming Tower: Al Qaeda and the Road to 9/11* (New York: Knopf).

Chapter 22

Bacevich, A. J. (2002), *American Empire: The Realities and Consequences of US Diplomacy* (Cambridge, MA: Harvard University Press).

Cobb, W. J., Jr. (1998), *The American Foundation Myth in Vietnam: Reigning Paradigms and Raining Bombs* (New York: University Press of America).

Hartz, L. (1955), *The Liberal Tradition in America* (New York: Harcourt Brace Jovanovich).

Hughes, R. (2003), Myths America Lives By (Urbana, IL: University of Illinois Press).

Lieven, A. and Hulsman, J. (2006), *Ethical Realism: A Vision for America's Role in the World* (London: Pantheon).

McDougall, W. A. (1997), *Promised Land, Crusader State: The American Encounter with the World since 1776* (Boston: Houghton Mifflin).

Nye, R. (1966), *This Almost Chosen People: Essays in the History of American Ideas* (East Lansing, MI: Michigan State University Press).

Peters, R. (2006), *Never Quit the Fight* (Mechanicsburg, PA: Stackpole Books).

Robberson, T. (2007), 'US in Strategic Peril, US General Warns', *Dallas Morning News*, 4 December.

Smith, T. L. (1979), 'Righteousness and Hope: Christian Holiness and the Millennial Vision in America, 1880–1900', *American Quarterly*, 31/1 (Spring): 21–45.

Woodward, C. V. (1968), *The Burden of Southern History* (Baton Rouge, LA: Louisiana State University Press).

Chapter 23

Decline

Brooks, S. G. and Wohlforth, W. C. (2002), 'American Primacy in Perspective,' *Foreign Affairs*, 81/4: 20–33.

——and Wohlforth, W. C. (2008), *World Out of Balance: International Relations and the Challenge of American Primacy* (Princeton: Princeton University Press).

Calleo, D. (1982), *The Imperious Economy* (Cambridge, MA: Harvard University Press).

Chace, J. (1981), *Solvency: The Price of Survival* (New York: Random House).

Congressional Budget Office (2009), 'A Preliminary Analysis of the President's Budget and an Update of the CBO's Budget and Economic Outlook,' (Washington, DC: Government Printing Office).

Congressional Budget Office (2010), 'The Budget and Economic Outlook, Fiscal Years 2010 to 2020' (Washington, D.C.: Government Printing Office).

Dyer, G. and Luce E., (2009), 'Obama Calls for Stronger Renimbi,' *Financial Times*, 18 November.

Gilpin, R. (1975), *U.S. Power and the Multinational Corporation: The Political Economy of Foreign Direct Investment* (New York: Basic Books).

——(1981), *War and Change in World Politics* (Cambridge: Cambridge University Press).

——(1987), *The Political Economy of International Relations* (Princeton: Princeton University Press).

Helleiner, E. (2008), 'Political Determinants of International Currencies: What Future for the U.S. Dollar? *Review of International Political Economy*, 15/3: 370–71.

Huntington, S.P. (1988), 'Coping With the Lippmann Gap,' *Foreign Affairs—America and the World 1987*, 66/3: 453–77.

Ikenberry, G. J. (2000), *After Victory* (Princeton: Princeton University Press).

——(2011), *Liberal Leviathan: The Origins, Crisis, and Transformation of the American World Order* (Princeton: Princeton University Press).

Jolly, D. and Rampell, C. (2010), 'Moody's Says US Debt Could Test Triple-A Rating,' *Financial Times*, March 15.

Kennedy, P. (1987), *The Rise and Fall of the Great Powers: Economic Change and Military Conflict, 1500 to 2000* (New York: Random House).

Kindelberger, C. P. (1973), *The World in Depression, 1929–1939* (Berkeley: University of California Press).

Kirshner, J. (2008), 'Dollar Primacy and American Power: What's at Stake? *Review of International Political Economy*, 15/3: 418.

Layne, C. (1993), 'The Unipolar Illusion: Why New Great Powers Will Rise,' *International Security*, 17/4: 5–51.

Mastanduno, M. (1997), 'Preserving the Unipolar Moment: Realist Theories and U.S. Grand Strategy After the Cold War,' *International Security*, 21/4: 49–88.

Mearsheimer, J. J. (2001), *The Tragedy of Great Power Politics* (New York: W. W. Norton).

Norrlof, C. (2010), *America's Global Advantage: U.S. Hegemony and International Cooperation* (Cambridge: Cambridge University Press).

Nye, J. S., Jr. (1990), *Bound to Lead: The Changing Nature of American Power* (New York: Basic Books).

——(2002), *The Paradox of American Power: Why the World's Only Superpower Can't Go It Alone* (New York: Oxford University Press).

Posen, B. R. (2003), 'Command of the Commons: The Military Foundation of U.S. Hegemony,' *International Security*, 28/1: 5–46.

Stiglitz, J. and Bilmiss, L. (2008), *The Three Trillion Dollar War: The True Cost of the Iraq Conflict* (New York: W.W. Norton).

Walt, S. (2005), *Taming American Power: The Global Response to U.S. Primacy* (New York: W. W. Norton).

Waltz, K. N. (1994), 'The Emerging Structure of International Politics,' *International Security*, 18/2: 44–79.

Wohlforth, W. C. (1999), 'The Stability of a Unipolar World,' *International Security*, 24/1: 5–41.

——(2002), 'U.S. Strategy in a Unipolar World,' in G. J. Ikenberry (ed,), *America Unrivaled: The Future of the Balance of Power* (Ithaca, NY: Cornell University Press), 98–120.

Zakaria, F. (1998), *From Wealth to Power: The Unusual Origins of America's World Role* (Princeton: Princeton University Press).

——(2008), *The Post-American World* (New York: W. W. Norton)

Primacy

Brooks, S. G. and Wohlforth, W. C. (2002), 'American Primacy in Perspective', *Foreign Affairs*, 81(4): 20–33.

——and Wohlforth, W. C. (2005), 'Hard Times for Soft Balancing' *International Security*, 30(1): 72–108.

——and Wohlforth, W. C. (2008), *World Out of Balance: International Relations and the Challenge of American Primacy* (Princeton: Princeton University Press).

——and Wohlforth, W. C. (2009), 'Reshaping the World Order: How Washington Should Reform International Institutions', *Foreign Affairs*, 88(2): 49–63.

——and Wohlforth, W. C. (2011), 'Assessing the Balance', *Cambridge Review of International Affairs*, 24(2).

Buzan, B. (2004), *The United States and the Great Powers: World Politics in the 21st Century* (Cambridge: Polity Press).

Coalition for a Realistic Foreign Policy (2002), 'War With Iraq is not in America's Interest', *New York Times*, September 26.

Craig, C. (2010), 'Rebuttal of John Glenn's "The flawed logic of a MAD man"' *Review of International Studies*, online on CJO 2011 doi:10.1017/S0260210510001464.

Directorate of National Intelligence (2004), *Mapping the Global Future* (Washington: US Government Printing Office).

——(2008), *Global Trends 2025: A Transformed World* (Washington: US Government Printing Office).

Eichengreen, B., Donghyun P., and Kwanho S. (2011), 'When Fast Growing Economies Slow Down: International Evidence and Implications for China', National Bureau of Economic Research Working Paper 1619 (Cambridge, MA: National Bureau of Economic Research).

Gilpin, R. (1981), *War and Change in World Politics* (Cambridge: Cambridge University Press).

Glaser, C. (2011), 'Why Unipolartiy Doesn't Matter (Much)', *Cambridge Review of International Affairs*, 24(2).

Huntington, S. (1999), 'The Lonely Superpower', *Foreign Affairs*, 78: 35–49.

Kennedy, P. (1987), 'The (Relative) Decline of America', *Atlantic Monthly*, August.

Khanna, P. (2009) *The Second World: How Emerging Powers Are Redefining Global Competition in the Twenty-First Century* (New York: Penguin).

Layne, C. (1995), 'The Unipolar Illusion: Why New Great Powers Will Rise', in *The Perils of Anarchy: Contemporary Realism and International Security*, M. E. Brown, S. M. Lynn-Jones, and S. E. Miller (eds) (Cambridge, MA: MIT Press), 130–76.

——(2006), 'The Unipolar Illusion Revisited: The Coming End of the United States' Unipolar Moment,' *International Security*, 31(2), 7–41.

——(2011), 'The Unipolar Exit: Beyond *Pax Americana*,' *Cambridge Review of International Affairs*, 24(2).

Mearsheimer, J. (2001a), *The Tragedy of Great Power Politics* (New York: W. W. Norton).

——(2001b), 'Guns Won't Win the Afghan War,' *New York Times*, November 4.

Mearsheimer, J. and Walt, S. (2002), 'Realists Are Not Alone in Opposing War With Iraq', *Chronicle of Higher Education*, November 15, 50–59.

——and Walt, S. (2003), 'An Unnecessary War', *Foreign Policy*, January–February, 50–60.

Posen, B. R (2001/2002), 'The Struggle Against Terrorism: Grand Strategy, Strategy and Tactics', *International Security*, 26(3), 39–55.

Rachman, G. (2011), 'Think Again: American Decline. This Time it's for Real', *Foreign Policy*, January/February.

Selden, Z. (2010), 'Soft Bandwagoning and the Endurance of American Hegemony', paper presented at the 2010 Annual Meeting of the American Political Science Association, September.

Waltz, K. (1993), 'The Emerging Structure of International Politics', *International Security*, 18, 44–79.

Wohlforth, W. C. (1999), 'The Stability of a Unipolar World', *International Security*, 21(1), 5–41.

——(2002), 'U.S. Strategy in a Unipolar World', in G. J. Ikenberry (ed.), *America Unrivaled: The Future of the Balance of Power* (Ithaca, NY: Cornell University Press).

Zakaria, F. (2008), *The Post-American World* (New York: Norton).

Index

A

Abbottabad
  killing of Osama Bin Laden in 347
Abkhazia
  Russia recognizes sovereignty of 254
Able Archer exercise (1982) 424
abolitionism 29
abortion 29, 378
Abqaiq oil processing plant
  bombing of 347
Abraham Lincoln, USS
  President Bush aboard 387
absolute objectivity 181
abstractions
  political process of representation 184
Abu Ghraib 102, 174, 190
  images from on internet 176
  treatment of Iraqi prisoners at 160–1
Abuja Accords 303
Accuracy in Media (AIM) 171
acid rain
  negotiations with Canada on 355–6
Adams, President John [1735–1826] 44
Adams, President John Quincey
    [1767–1848] 46
'adversarial partnership' rhetoric 222
advertising revenue
  media reliance on 171
aerosols 355
Afghanistan 6, 142, 190, 198, 208, 336,
    343, 385–6, 390, 397
  additional troops sent to 5, 97–8, 140
  al-Qaeda 339
  communists seize power in (1978) 199
  controversy over 160
  cost of war in 417
  criticism of war in 176
  death of eight CIA employees in 125
  effect of war on future foreign
    policy 392
  ending of Taliban regime in 344
  European military contribution to
    operations in 404
  as 'failed state' 184
  future involvement with 401
  increase in opium production 140
  increasing troops in 126
  International Security Assistance
    Force 250
  intervention in (2001) 75, 123
  military deployment in 136

missile attacks on 83, 93
most high-tech war ever 140
opium poppy cultivation 344
poor decision-making on 425
President Obama's policy on 388
prospects for peace 348
removal of Taliban from 216
riots following Florida pastor burning
    Koran 105
roadside bombs and IEDs 389
Russia declines to send
    peacekeepers to 250
Russian cooperation on 255
Russian goodwill needed on 404
Russian withdrawal from 241
Soviet army trapped in 207
Soviet invasion (1979) 199, 207, 383–4
Soviet occupation of 345
Taliban 339
television coverage of war in 346
US campaign to overthrow
    Taliban in 35
US casualties 398
US–EU cooperation on 231
Vietnam Syndrome and 163
war in 2, 140, 340, 344–5
women 185
Africa
  border controls 307
  China's interests in 298
  conflict resolution 309–11
  Defense Department acknowledges
    importance of 299
  demands for independence from 50
  democratization 301
  engagement at official level 305
  failed states 307
  fear of state failure in 297
  foreign aid 310
  foreign policy on 297–313
  historic links with 299–300
  HIV/AIDS 304, 306
  increase in trade with 310
  increase of US diplomacy in 311
  market access 305
  movement of people from 29
  oil 310, 401
  peacekeeping 304
  perceived as prime target for terrorist
    organizations 307
  post-9/11 relations with 306–8

post-Cold War policy towards 300–6
poverty 304–5
public health issues 306
pursuit of 'partnership' with 308
relations with China 311
renewal of limited engagement
    in 304–5
'trade not aid' rhetoric 305
US assumption of European
    responsibility for 300
US national interest and 302
US relations with 3
violence against women 309
Africa Division
  CIA 299
Africa Growth and Opportunity Act
    (AGOA) (2000) 304–5, 310, 312
African Contingency Operations
    Training and Assistance (ACOTA)
    programme 304
African Crisis Response Force (ACRF)
  establishment of 304
African Crisis Response Initiative
    (ACRI) 304
African Union 309
African-Americans
  civil rights 29
  military service 30
Africans 29
  immigration of 28
agenda setting 169–70
Agent Orange
  US accused of 'ecocide' for using 354
aggression 9, 188
  connotations with totalitarianism 188
'aggressive unilateralism' 325
agrarian reform
  Latin America 287
agricultural land
  availability and cheapness of 26
agricultural polity
  decentralized 27
agriculture 147–8
  modernising African 310
  protectionism in 326
  subsidies 318
Aideed, Mohamed Farrah
    [1934–96] 88, 302
AIG
  rescue of 328
air pollution 363

O